LAYARD OF NINEVEH

Layard of Nineveh

GORDON WATERFIELD

FREDERICK A. PRAEGER, *Publishers*

New York · Washington

BOOKS THAT MATTER
Published in the United States of America in 1968
by Frederick A. Praeger, Inc., Publishers
111 Fourth Avenue, New York, N.Y. 10003

© 1963 in London, England, by Gordon Waterfield

Library of Congress Catalog Card Number: 68–16722

Printed in Great Britain

Contents

Contents

PART IV

DIPLOMACY: SPAIN 1869–1877

PART V

DIPLOMACY: TURKEY 1877–1884

PART VI

RETIREMENT 1884–1894

vi

Illustrations

Illustrations

Illustrations

Illustrations

Introduction

The drawing-room of a villa looking out over Florence used to be hung with pictures of distinguished and bearded Victorians who had been friends of my Great-Aunt Janet Ross, but only one picture aroused my interest as a small boy—that of a clean-shaven man in Albanian dress gazing pensively out of a cave with a string of beads in his right hand. He was called 'Mr. Bull' because he had dug up stone Assyrian bulls from Nineveh and I liked him because there were exciting stories about hunting lion, having adventures, and getting into 'hot-water'.[1]

Henry Layard was a phenomenon even in the Victorian age of rough and energetic characters. His parents were not wealthy enough to send him to a public school or university and at the age of sixteen he went into a solicitor's office in London but he became so bored that in 1839, at the age of twenty-two, he decided to ride on horseback across the Ottoman Empire and Persia to find employment in Ceylon where he had relatives. On the way he became intrigued by the mounds of Nineveh and Nimrud and the Assyrian sculptures with their cuneiform inscriptions in various parts of Mesopotamia and Persia. He lived many months very happily with the Bakhtiari tribes and remained with them when they were attacked by a Persian army, events which he described in his book *Early Adventures*. For various reasons he decided not to continue the journey to Ceylon (as his companion, Edward Mitford did), and returned to Constantinople in July 1842 on his way back to London after three years of wandering. The knowledge Layard had acquired was valuable to the British Ambassador, Sir Stratford Canning, and he remained with him until 1845 when Canning lent him about one hundred and sixty pounds to make a report on Nimrud. Layard's excavations there, described in his first book *Nineveh and Its Remains*, made him world famous and was followed by a second expedition to Mosul, 1849 to 1851, and his *Nineveh and Babylon*.

Layard returned to England aged thirty-five without any knowledge of home politics but such was his fame that he was, strangely enough, made Under-Secretary for Foreign Affairs in

Introduction

1852 in the short-lived Whig Government of Lord John Russell. His discovery of Nineveh both made and marred his political career. During the Crimean War he saw England as another Nineveh, brought low by mismanagement and pride, and himself as another Jonah prophesying doom to the oligarchy of Whig aristocrats who were angered at his radical views. Emily Eden, for instance, said that she could forgive Layard for discovering Nineveh but not Nineveh for discovering Layard. He enraged Gladstone by being anti-Russian and pro-Turk and alienated his radical friends by becoming a disciple of the Tory Disraeli, who described Layard as a genius. He did not become Foreign Minister as his friends expected, nor lead a revolution as others thought he might. But he did many things brilliantly which gives him a right to a place among the great Victorians.

Soon after Sir Henry Layard's death in 1894, Sir Henry Reeve wrote: 'The man who writes the life must be one who understands archaeology, politics, diplomacy, literature, and art, and it is not easy to find one.' Biographers are not intimidated by such arguments and it is seldom considered necessary to be a specialist in all the appropriate subjects, yet no biography was written. Layard went out of fashion for various reasons. The bitter political enemies he had made during his life remained to denigrate him after his death. At the beginning of this century there was an Anglo-Russian honeymoon so that Layard was unpopular because of his violent attacks against Russia as a menace to the British Empire and to the world. The generations after his death were brought up on stories of 'Abdul the Damned' and of the Armenian massacres, so that they disliked Layard who had been pro-Turk and sympathised with the Sultan. Today there is a reassessment of Abdul Hamid, concentrating more on the reforms he carried out than on the massacres. The Turks are now popular in the West and Russia is once more regarded as a danger.

After three years as Ambassador in Constantinople during the critical period from 1877 to 1881, when he did as much as anyone to prevent the Russians from occupying the city, Layard described the events in a *Memoir* of half a million words which has not been published. 'I look on what happened during the time I was at Constantinople', he wrote, 'as the end of the

Introduction

Turkish rule in Europe and ultimately elsewhere. My own reputation requires that I should leave a record for those who come after me.' His widow wanted the *Memoir* published but the Foreign Office did not agree to release the material until many years later. A Foreign Office official wrote to Lady Layard in 1900:

> Sir Henry Layard's great services to his country have been to a great extent undervalued owing to party passions, and also because Sir Henry's force of character and outspoken frankness raised up against him many bitter enemies. . . . The present generation has been too closely connected with a period in which the map of Europe has been recast, and during which the passions of men were roused to a pitch almost of frenzy, to form a dispassionate judgement upon man, who played at that time so prominent a part upon the political stage.[2]

The great battles between Disraeli and Gladstone over the Eastern Question are now part of history. The Ottoman Empire has disappeared and the Eastern Question has taken another form, but Russia still has the same ambitions and what Layard has to say is of value.

Political animosity also affected Layard's archaeological reputation. Sir Wallis Budge of the British Museum was a protégé of Gladstone, who was one of Layard's bitterest critics. The hostility which existed between the elderly Layard and Budge, both determined characters, was accentuated as a result of an unfortunate law case. Layard supported his old friend Hormuzd Rassam who won a libel action against Budge. 'Regrettably, Budge did all he could to revenge himself during the rest of his long life-time', writes Dr. R. D. Barnett of the British Museum, 'by devoting himself to blotting out every record of Rassam's considerable discoveries and to toning down Layard's greatness—a kind of *damnatio memoriae*, which Roman Emperors used to decree towards those of their predecessors whom they did not like.'[3] Wallis Budge was a man of strong prejudices and a powerful influence in the British Museum. A story that Layard was a careless and ignorant pioneer archaeologist gained ground. This was repeated by Stanley Lane-Poole, nephew of R. S. Poole of the British Museum, in his obituary of Layard in *The*

Introduction

Athenaeum :—'He could hardly claim to be a scholar at all, and his want of the true archaeologist's feeling was sufficiently shown by his presenting to his friends neatly cut tablets containing fragments of cuneiform inscriptions, which, of course, left serious lacunae in priceless historical documents.' This is all nonsense, for Layard knew enough about cuneiform to cut out only from the standard inscriptions which were endlessly repeated and he had to reduce the weight in order to be able to get these heavy monuments on to rafts to float down the Tigris to Basra. L. W. King, who worked under Budge in the British Museum, perpetuated this story in his account of Layard in the *Dictionary of National Biography*. He also ridiculed, as does Sir Wallis Budge in his publications, the fact that Layard's famous book *Nineveh and Its Remains* was about Nimrud. But it was Major Rawlinson, later Sir Henry Cheswicke Rawlinson, who at first insisted that Nimrud was Nineveh. As he was the authority on cuneiform Layard accepted his theory, but Rawlinson changed his mind after Layard had published his book.

Layard's reputation as an archaeologist is being re-established. The more his work is studied the more remarkable is seen to be his achievement, left as he was single-handed, short of funds, having to do his own drawings, copy cuneiform, keep records, invent methods of excavating and keep the wild tribes under control. Dr. C. J. Gadd of the British Museum has written : 'In particular I could wish that a further revelation of what we owe to the assiduity of Layard, alike with the pencil and the pen, exercised often when he was obliged to do everything unaided and subject to every impediment, might check some of the detraction which it has become an unworthy commonplace to bestow upon that remarkable pioneer. . . . The history of the great days of Assyrian discovery in the middle of the nineteenth century is dominated by the figure of Austen Henry Layard, a man so all-pervading that it is difficult to observe the bounds of relevancy in writing of him.'[4] Dr. Barnett is now continuing the work of identifying and uniting the scattered fragments of Assyrian antiquities 'so that the full importance of Layard's discoveries can be appreciated and the full value of the information be extracted'.[5] Professor M. E. L. Mallowan, who for long directed excavations at Nimrud and elsewhere in Mesopotamia and

Introduction

Dr. Barnett have written appreciations of Layard which are at the end of this book. 'He was possessed', writes Professor Mallowan, 'of a visionary genius; it was he who foresaw the desirability of making a series of controlled expeditions at sites widespread throughout Mesopotamia, and with an unerring eye probed ancient mounds which have subsequently become famous, or else remain a potential mine of discovery for archaeologists in time to come. . . . Layard must take his stand among the immortals.'

*   *   *

The main sources for the biography are the three hundred and forty volumes of Layard Papers in the Manuscript Room of the British Museum; letters in the possession of the Layard and Guest families and of Sir John Murray; Layard's own publications and thirteen volumes of the diary of his wife, Enid Guest, from 1869 to 1894. In the years after Sir Henry Layard's death his widow devotedly collected all the letters of interest. Wherever he went Layard set up his own intelligence service by writing and receiving large numbers of letters, from various parts of the Ottoman Empire, from the Crimea during the war, from India during the Mutiny, from Italy about paintings, and from various parts of Spain. During the five years he was Under-Secretary for Foreign Affairs, 1861 to 1866, he kept many official documents; he also kept copies of the despatches written and received while he was Minister in Spain, from 1869 to 1877, and while he was Ambassador in Turkey, from 1877 to 1881. He put together nearly a million words about these two periods in his unpublished *Memoir*.

In order to deal with the many thousands of letters in the Layard Papers, I was fortunate to have the able assistance of Mrs. St. George Saunders. The letters show that a vast number of friends regarded him as entertaining, highly intelligent, and likely to succeed in politics, as he had succeeded in archaeology. Layard was especially helpful and loyal to those who needed help, and he was on especially good terms with intelligent women such as Harriet Grote, Elizabeth Eastlake, Lucie Duff Gordon, Janet Ross, and Sara Austen. The Layard Papers have been drawn on by specialists writing on Assyrian archaeology,

5

Introduction

on the Eastern Question, on Italian painting, and on banking, but much of the material used in this biography has not been previously published and his life has not been dealt with as a whole. It would have been possible to write a volume on each of the above subjects in view of the interest and range of the letters, and it has not been easy to reduce his varied life to one volume.

While the letters to Layard show that he was an attractive character and an amusing companion, this is not the general impression given by many of his own letters. After enjoying the published letters of his friend Charles Dickens, Layard wrote to Miss Hogarth: 'In a man's letters—especially when they extend over a long life—the writer's true character must come out.' Private letters however can be misleading unless one knows the character of the recipient and the relationship in which the correspondents stand to each other; in this case they can be even more misleading since the emotional Layard often wrote letters to relieve his spleen and frustrations, but when he had time to think and to calm down, as when writing his books, he showed that he had humour and charm. Part of the reason for his failure to achieve his high ambitions in politics was that he had to react immediately to attacks in the House of Commons and was often too angry to think clearly. Sir Henry Bulwer, brother of Lord Lytton the novelist, took a rather malicious pleasure in studying Layard and giving him advice: 'I know no one who means more honestly than you, or is more likely to be right if he takes time to get information and reflect. But I know no one more prone to start off immediately on the wings of the wind in the wrong direction. An impulse seizes you and off you go. This fault has made you bitter enemies; . . . but always remember what Melbourne said: "I wish I was as cocksure of any *one* thing, as Tom Macaulay is *cocksure* of *everything*". . . . But there is such a fund of energy, good nature and talent, that anyone who appreciates such quality and is acquainted with you, must like you.' Henry Bruce (Lord Aberdare) referred to his sense of humour 'which gave a peculiar charm and zest to his daily intercourse'. In the introduction to Layard's *Early Adventures* he wrote: 'I am happy to think that materials unusually ample exist for a biography extending over the whole of his active life. When this biography has been written, I do not fear the verdict of his

Introduction

countrymen. The admiration once felt for his marvellous Travels and Discoveries will revive, and the impress of his striking personality once more will rise before us.'

*   *   *

I am especially indebted to the late Miss Julia Du Cane, niece of Lady Layard, for letting me have family letters, photographs and paintings, and to Miss Phyllis Layard, great-niece of Sir Henry, for letters and drawings. Viscount Wimborne and the Earl of Bessborough kindly let me quote from the unpublished parts of Lady Charlotte Schreiber's diaries and from other papers belonging to the Guest family. My thanks are due to Dr. C. J. Gadd, Professor M. E. L. Mallowan and Dr. R. D. Barnett who have been most helpful in giving advice on Layard's work as an Assyriologist, and to the Director-General of the Iraq Antiquities Department who helped me to visit Nimrud, Nineveh, Bavian, and Sheikh Adi at a time when it was not easy to obtain permission to visit the north of Iraq. The kind hospitality of Sir Bernard and Lady Burrows enabled me to stay in the old British Embassy in Istanbul during the time that Sir Bernard was Ambassador in Turkey. Mr. Edward Hodgkin, who at first intended to write this biography, generously lent me his notes. My wife has helped with research and advice. I am grateful to Sir John Murray and Mr. John Grey Murray for giving me access to private papers in their possession and to Miss Jane Boulenger for her work in preparing the book for publication.

G.W.

London, 1963.

PART ONE

Travel

1817–1845

1

Disraeli and the
Arabian Nights

Austen Henry Layard was descended from a distinguished family
of Huguenots* who fled from the persecutions in France and
settled in East Kent; Queen Elizabeth gave permission to these
French Protestants to hold their special services in the crypt of
Canterbury Cathedral which they still do today. From his Huguenot forebears he inherited characteristics which made him
aggressively on the defensive, an intrepid fighter on behalf of
minorities and single-minded in his championship of what he
considered to be right. His hot temper may have come to him
from his grandfather, who was Dean of Bristol and the centre of
much controversy; but he had an amiable and friendly side to
him which probably came from his gentle father, Henry Peter
John Layard, and his mother, Marianne, who encouraged him
to be interested in literature and the fine arts.

The Dean of Bristol was anxious to get his daughters well
settled and Charlotte married the Earl of Lindsey, giving birth
in 1814 to Lady Charlotte Bertie†; but he did not trouble much

---

* 'My family, as the name denotes, is of French origin', states Henry
Layard in his *Autobiography*. 'It claims to be of a very ancient stock and
to have descended, like many others, in a somewhat mythical way from
Raymond of Toulouse.' Layard's great grandfather married the daughter
of Colonel Louis Chevalleau de Boisragon by a Mademoiselle de Ram-
bouillet, a member, like himself, 'of an ancient and noble French
family and a Huguenot refugee'. He died in 1803 leaving three sons,
two of whom became generals in the English army and the third
entered the Church to become Prebendary of Worcester, one of the
Chaplains-in-Ordinary of King George III and Dean of Bristol.

† The Earl of Lindsey was the great grandson of the Hon. Charles
Bertie of Uffington, near Stamford, and became Earl of Lindsey in
1809 when he married Charlotte, daughter of the Very Reverend
Charles P. Layard, Dean of Bristol. A few years after the death of the

about the education of his sons. Henry Peter John was his second son, born on 15 July 1783, and farmed out at an early age to a Mr. Christian in Ramsgate, together with a younger brother Charles. When they were old enough they sailed to seek their fortune in Ceylon; Charles remained to make a fortune, but his elder brother after some years developed such bad asthma that he had to return to Ramsgate. Soon after the battle of Waterloo he married in the Church of St. Lawrence, Marianne, the attractive daughter of Nathaniel Austen, a banker.

Marianne was born in 1789, the year of the French Revolution; she was well read and used to pay visits to the eccentric scholar Richard Warburton Lytton* in his charming old house at St. Lawrence, where some of her happiest days were spent: 'He kindly took an interest in me and I can even now feel grateful when I look back upon these associations and reflect upon the influence they had upon my later life.' Marianne and Peter Layard had very little money and decided to try living abroad. With the defeat of Napoleon, it was possible for the English to travel once more on the Continent and they went to France. Their first son, Henry, was born in an hotel on the Left Bank in Paris on 5 March 1817 when Marianne was twenty-eight. On their return to Ramsgate in July he was baptised Henry Austen. Later three other boys were born—Frederick, Arthur, and Edgar.

Peter and Marianne went in search of a climate where his asthma would be less severe, trying Bath, Moulins, Switzerland, and Pisa; Florence was found to be the best and pleasantest place in which to live. They rented a floor of the Rucellai Palace

Earl of Lindsey in 1818 his widow married her first cousin, the Reverend Peter William Pegus and had a daughter, Mary Antoinette. Henry Layard was therefore first cousin to Lady Charlotte and to her half-sister, Mary Pegus.

* Richard Warburton Lytton could not afford to live at Knebworth and moved to St. Lawrence, near Ramsgate. His daughter married Colonel Bulwer and gave birth to Edward George Earle Bulwer-Lytton, the novelist and friend of Benjamin Disraeli, who was created Baron Lytton of Knebworth. His son, Edward Robert Lytton, poet and diplomatist, became Viceroy of India in 1876 and was created Earl of Lytton and Viscount Knebworth. The novelist's elder brother was Henry Bulwer, author and diplomat, who became Baron Dalling and Bulwer.

and lived there happily and fairly economically, considering that Peter Layard entertained generously having become accustomed to the hospitable habits of Ceylon; poets, painters, writers, antiquaries and travellers were always welcome to a meal. Henry was for a short time at a school in Putney, the Lycée at Moulins in France and a small school at Florence, but most of his real education was at home, reading the Elizabethan poets and playwrights, history, and Walter Scott's novels. His favourite book was *The Arabian Nights* and he used to spend hours on the floor under a great gilded table in the Rucellai Palace 'poring over this enchanting volume'.* His father was a connoisseur of Italian painting. 'He took pleasure', states Layard in his *Auto-biography*, 'in pointing out to me the beauties of the works of the great Masters and in teaching me how to distinguish them by their peculiar style or "manner".' By the age of eight Henry knew most of the principal buildings and pictures, acting as a guide to visitors. He was very fond of an altar-piece by Filippo Lippi which hung over his bed and was distressed when he damaged it with a shoe thrown at his brother Frederick, who shared the bedroom.† Seymour Kirkup, the painter and student of Dante, enjoyed having Henry in his studio on the Ponte Vecchio, told him stories about the history of Florence and let him look at his remarkable library on magic. Henry took lessons in drawing and wanted to take up painting as a profession, but his father thought he should find a more profitable way of earning his living. Byron's friend, Trelawny, used to come to the Layards' house and tell romantic stories about his adventures. There was plenty to feed Henry's imagination. Benjamin Disraeli was one

---

* 'My admiration for the *Arabian Nights*', wrote Layard in his *Autobiography*, 'has never left me. I can read them even now [1885] with almost as much delight as I read them when a boy. They have had no little influence upon my life and career; for to them I attribute that love of travel and adventure which took me to the East, and led me to the discovery of the ruins of Nineveh. They give the truest, the most lively, and the most interesting picture of manners and customs which still existed amongst Turks, Persians, and Arabs when I first mixed with them, but which are now fast passing away before European civilisation and encroachments.'

† The picture is in the National Gallery, London, and for some years the mark of the shoe was still visible.

of the fantastic figures who intrigued him; he came to stay with the Layards at Moulins in 1826, dressed extravagantly with his black hair in curls. Disraeli was then twenty-two and had become seriously ill through overwork and anxiety about unsuccessful stock exchange speculations. Marianne Layard's brother, Benjamin Austen, a successful London solicitor, and his wife Sara were close friends of the Disraeli family and had agreed to take Benjamin Disraeli on a European tour; one of their stopping places was with the Layards at Moulins. Sara was a competent business woman and a close friend who had helped Disraeli publish three volumes of his first novel *Vivian Grey* in 1826, copying it out herself and sending it anonymously to Colburn the publisher. 'You appear', Disraeli wrote to her, 'to be the only person in the world, except myself, who has any energy; what would I give to have you always at my right hand!'

Walter Savage Landor, living an eccentric life on the Fiesole hill-side, was another important influence. He took an interest in Henry, taught him the beauty of the Greek language and impressed on him the importance of Greek in order to speak and write good English.* The Layards, who were respectable Tories, would not receive the free-thinking Landor in their house; all the same, Henry was encouraged to read *Imaginary Conversations*, long passages of which he learned by heart: 'They produced one effect which my father little contemplated. I imbibed from them those radical and democratic opinions, which I sturdily professed even when a boy.'

The family was very happy in Florence but in 1829, when Henry was twelve and Frederick was ten, it was considered that they both needed a more formal education. Henry described himself as 'very idle, self-willed, and troublesome'. Benjamin and Sara, who had no children of their own, offered to pay for their nephews' education if the family would come to England. Sorrowfully they returned to Ramsgate and Henry was sent by his uncle to a school at Richmond where he was very unhappy. He had been brought up with friends of his father and mother and was not clever at dealing with his own contemporaries. The account he gives of his school days in his *Autobiography* shows

---

* Landor later wrote an ode to Layard which is to be found among his poetical works.

that he resented any interference with his views and that he must have been a good target for bullies. It was not easy for him; whereas at the Lycée at Moulins he had been maltreated for being English and a Protestant, he was roughly handled at Richmond as a 'foreigner' because he could speak French and Italian. When he quoted Landor's radical views he was punished by the headmaster, the Rev. James Bewsher, for 'preaching sedition and revolution' which Henry described as 'an undue and tyrannical interference' with his political opinions. In France he had been handicapped by the fact that there was still resentment against the English after the defeat of Napoleon and he considered that he was something of a martyr for his religion. A popular amusement in the Lycée was to make a cross with white chalk upon the dirty floor and then to endeavour to force him to kiss it: 'When I resisted with all my might, I was held down by main force and beaten on the head and elsewhere with wooden shoes, or *sabots*. . . . They never succeeded in doing more than rubbing my nose on the sacred symbol.' When he refused to kneel to the Host, which was being borne in procession through the town, his school-fellows dragged him to the fast-flowing river Allier and would have thrown him in if a Frenchman had not saved him. Henry believed from an early age that the only way to deal with opposition was to fight back and he went on fighting throughout his life. His treatment at school recalled to him the sufferings of his Huguenot ancestors; he felt at times that he was a member of a persecuted minority, which made him aggressive and unsure of himself in spite of an underlying confidence in his own powers. If he had been settled from an early age in school in England, as his uncle had wished, he might have learned better how to come to terms with his contemporaries, acquiring ease of manner and *savoir faire*. On the other hand, his education abroad with his parents and their friends had developed his powers of observation, his curiosity, his artistic taste, and his passion for independence. Mr. Bewsher was impressed by his taste for literature and art and by his essays which showed more general knowledge than the other boys; the headmaster also praised him for a translation into Latin verse of a Greek tragedy by Aeschylus and one by Euripides. As his parents could not afford to send him to a college or university

Henry considered that the tutors did not take as much trouble over his studies of the classics as they might otherwise have done. 'Had I been properly taught', he wrote later, 'and had I received a university training, I might have become a fair scholar, as I was extremely fond of such works of the great writers of antiquity as I was able to master, and I had some aptitude for acquiring languages.'

Henry also felt uncertain of himself perhaps because at this period he saw little of his mother and father, to whom he was devoted; they escaped to Florence as often as they could. With his brother Frederick he spent some of the holidays in London with the Austens at their house in Guilford Street. Sara was accomplished, handsome and intelligent, collecting round her a *salon* of many of the authors and painters of the day. Benjamin Disraeli, whom she admired as a literary genius, was her great favourite; when, in 1829, he went on a tour of the Mediterranean, she was able to devote more time to her nephews who were then at school at Richmond and became very fond of them. They were, she told Disraeli, 'really so clever and very amusing and so tractable that I positively felt sorry when they went away again'. He had been able to go abroad because Benjamin Austen had finally agreed to advance the money for the expedition. 'You are my sheet-anchor and the most valuable of friends', Disraeli wrote.

Henry was always eager to hear about Disraeli's adventures in the East described in vivid letters which Disraeli advised the Austens to keep 'for if I become half as famous as I intend to be, you may sell them for ten guineas apiece'. Inspired by Byron, Disraeli had planned to volunteer for war service, but in his case it was with the Turkish forces who were suppressing a rebellion in Albania—the rebellion was over before he was ready; instead he went to Janina to congratulate Reshid Pasha, the Grand Vizier, who was in command of the Turkish army. 'For a week', Disraeli wrote to Austen, 'I was in a scene equal to anything in the *Arabian Nights*. Such processions, such dresses, such cortèges of horsemen, such caravans of camels!' Henry's father had given Disraeli a letter to his friend James Clay, who was then in Malta; Disraeli was most grateful for he thought Clay was a wonderful character.

Ch. 1 Disraeli and the Arabian Nights

'To govern men', Disraeli wrote to Austen, 'you must excel them in their accomplishments or despise them. . . . Clay does one, I do the other, and we are both equally popular.' Clay considered that Disraeli was one of those people who 'ought never to travel without a nurse'. Henry first heard about the beauty of Constantinople in the letters from Disraeli : 'All here is very much like life in a pantomime or Eastern tale of enchantment, which I think very high praise.' Disraeli had as much influence as the *Arabian Nights* in inspiring Henry with dreams that one day he himself would go to the East but as a schoolboy at Richmond there seemed little chance of realising them. Henry longed to go to a public school and university, as his companions were planning to do, but he knew that his father could not afford it and his uncle had arranged that he should be articled as a clerk in his office in Gray's Inn.

On 24 January 1834, when Henry was nearly seventeen, a solemn document of enrolment was drawn up, signed by Benjamin Austen, Henry Peter John Layard, and by Henry. There was jealousy among the many Austen and Layard relations, for Benjamin Austen was regarded as the richest member of the family, and it was thought that the document meant that young Henry was to be Austen's heir. Henry thought so himself, especially as his uncle had insisted that he should take Austen as his first name rather than Henry, though he was never called Austen by his family or friends.

For the next few years Henry led a miserable life. As there was very little money he had to go without food to buy the books he took back to his cold London lodgings, where he read a great deal and played a flute to keep himself cheerful. Visits were paid to his father and mother at Ramsgate and very occasionally they would come to London to stay in a cheap hotel when his father would write to ask him not to bring his flute. When preparing to take a boat for Ramsgate* to spend Christmas of 1833 with his parents, Henry had proposed bringing a chicken, but Peter Layard was worried about the expense, finding living in England a great deal more costly than in Italy. 'You must

---

* The cheapest way to travel was by boat. It was not until 1846 that the South-Eastern Railway line was extended from Ashford to Canterbury and a year later it was taken as far as Ramsgate.

remember I am a very poor man just now', he replied. The
writing is that of a very ill man and he must have known that
he had not long to live if he stayed in England, but he was
anxious to be near his children and he was eager that Henry
should make a success of life: 'Look up to your uncle and aunt
as your best friends'; he also wanted Henry to find time to call
on his cousin, Lady Charlotte Bertie: 'It would be a great pity
not to keep up her acquaintance.' Advice which he often repeated
was 'Read Blackstone', but all law books were 'repugnant' to
Henry, and Benjamin Austen was shocked by his saying that he
could not concentrate as he was thinking of Petrarch, Boccaccio,
and of the hills around Florence. Henry also read everything
that Disraeli published, *Contarini Fleming* with its pictures of
oriental life; *The Wondrous Tales of Alroy*, describing how
a prince of the House of Judah was to restore the Jews to
their native land and establish once more an independent
nation, and *The Rise of Iskander*. 'I looked upon him', said
Layard, 'as a great traveller in Eastern lands, which had a
mysterious attraction for me, and with which my earliest
dreams were associated.' Henry used to see him in the Austens'
house:

> He excited my wonder—perhaps my admiration—by his extra-
> ordinary and foppish dress. He wore waistcoats of the most gorgeous
> colours and the most fantastic patterns, with much gold embroidery,
> velvet pantaloons, and shoes adorned with red rosettes. I thought
> him conceited and unkind because he would not answer the
> questions about his Eastern travels which I had the impertinence
> to put to him, and because I thought he treated me with contempt.

Disraeli had become more conceited even than before, having
been taken up by Society—Edward Bulwer-Lytton, Count
d'Orsay, Lady Blessington, and the leaders of fashion. Disraeli
said he was as popular with the Dandies as he was hated
by the second-rate men. Sara and Benjamin Austen were hurt
because he was so much taken up with Mayfair parties that he
seldom came to see them, unless he wanted a loan. Disraeli was
spending large sums of money and was harassed by creditors.
'My life has not been a happy one', he wrote in his diary on
1 September 1833. 'Nature has given me an awful ambition and

18

fiery passions.' In December, he asked Austen in desperation for
the loan of the large sum of twelve hundred pounds. Austen had
had great difficulty in recovering earlier advances and was
seriously worried at the strange stories Disraeli told him about
his complicated financial deals and intrigues. 'I am sorry to say,
my dear Disraeli, that you have tried me too often and more so
to add that I have felt for some time past that your recollections
of it [friendship] ceased with the necessity. . . . I have long
looked on with fear and trembling.' Benjamin Disraeli wrote
six large pages by return of post on the theme that to ask for a
loan was the greatest favour that one man could ask of another
and was a high example of friendship: 'I really thought you
would have done anything for me and that's the truth. . . .
Once I thought that the day might arrive when you wd look
back to your assistance with pleasure, perhaps with pride.' But
Austen for the moment had had enough. He had not been impressed when Disraeli had announced at a dinner-party that he
intended to be Prime Minister! At that time Disraeli had decided
to achieve literary fame as the successor to Byron, and was
writing a long poem called 'The Revolutionary Epic' which, he
told Austen, would realise fourteen hundred pounds—enough
to cover the proposed loan. Austen could not maintain his confidence in Disraeli and yet he was fascinated by this eccentric,
clever, and confident young man who set about achieving his
ambitions in such extraordinary ways; but Sara remained a
constant admirer. She was doing research on Napoleon and the
Empress Josephine for his new poem. 'Are you sure that a creole
is dark?' Disraeli asked her. When the author said that he was
coming to the Austens for dinner the next day, 16 January 1834,
to read 'The Revolutionary Epic', Sara was delighted, while
Austen was curious to know whether it would be good enough
surety for the twelve hundred pounds. Henry Layard was
among the party assembled to listen to the poem, which
Disraeli read in a bombastic way. When he left, Samuel
Warren, well known as a mimic, improvised a mock-heroic
poem which he recited in the Disraeli manner to their greater
entertainment. 'There was', wrote Henry Layard of Disraeli,
'something irresistibly comic in the young man dressed in the
fantastic, coxcombical costume that he then affected—his black

hair pomatumed and elaborately curled, and his person redolent with perfume—announcing himself as the Homer or Dante of the Age!'*

There were others, however, who appreciated Disraeli's flamboyance. Henry's twenty-one-year-old cousin, Lady Charlotte Bertie, for instance, met him in a box at the opera and found him a stimulating companion:

> He is wild, enthusiastic & very poetical. The brilliance of my companion infected me, & we ran on about poetry & Venice & Bagdad & Damascus, & my eye lit up & my cheek burned; in the pauses of the beautiful music (*Tancred*) my words flowed almost as rapidly as his. He tells me . . . nothing could compensate to him for an obscure youth, not even glorious old age. . . . With all his enthusiasms & contradictions he pleased me & we were very good friends I think.†

She expressed surprise that he wanted to get into Parliament. Disraeli had been contesting the seat at High Wycombe and in June 1832 he had told Benjamin Austen: 'I start on the high Radical interest. . . . Toryism is worn out and I cannot condescend to be a Whig.' He made a brilliant speech from the portico of the Red Lion, but the Government had spent a great

* Layard in *The Quarterly Review*, January 1889, on *Lord Beaconsfield's Letters, 1830 to 1852*. He was seventy years old when he wrote the account of the scene he had witnessed when he was seventeen. He considered, however, that the conception of the epic had 'grandeur and originality'. The first idea for it had come to Disraeli on 'the windy plain of Troy' and there was a passage in the preface of the published work which Layard was to appreciate later when he was Ambassador at Constantinople:

> Standing upon Asia, and gazing upon Europe, with the broad Hellespont alone between us, and the shadow of night descending on the mountains, those mighty continents appeared to be, as it were, the rival principles of government that, at present, contend for the mastery of the world.

† *Lady Charlotte Schreiber's Journals*, edited by Montague J. Guest, (John Lane). Dr. B. R. Jerman in *The Young Disraeli* (Oxford University Press, 1960), considers that Disraeli was thinking of proposing to Lady Charlotte Bertie, believing her to be very wealthy. There was correspondence between his sister, Sarah, and Mrs. Austen, who did not consider that Lady Charlotte had anything like as much money as Disraeli thought.

deal of money and Colonel Grey, son of the Prime Minister, was elected with twenty-three votes against Disraeli's twelve and that was the total number of voters. Disraeli stood a second time on the passing of the Reform Bill in November 1832, but by then he had lost the support of the Radicals and had not yet been accepted by the Tories; he claimed then to be 'the preacher of a new creed and the founder of a new party' which made him distrusted.

Peter Layard had moved to Aylesbury, near High Wycombe, and in the early summer of 1834 he told Henry that he would not feel properly settled in until he had his pictures; Frederick was showing an aptitude for drawing, was interested in the family's genealogical tree and had been drawing the family arms. In October Disraeli called on Peter and Marianne Layard during an electioneering tour and wrote to Austen that he was grieved and astonished to find both very ill—'Layard in bed & really dangerously ill & your sister a terrible sufferer.' Henry rushed down to Aylesbury but found that there was no hope of saving his father, who died of congestion of the lungs at the age of fifty-one. He was deeply distressed at the loss and at his mother's unhappiness.

At the age of seventeen he had become the man of the family, which entailed greater dependence on his uncle in order to earn a living. 'Do not forget my last words to you—read Blackstone' ran through his head, but he could not bring himself to concentrate on law and had a nervous breakdown. It was decided that he should have a holiday in France and Italy with William Brockedon, the artist, a friend of the Austens.

When Henry returned from abroad the Austens were moving house. They had gone up in the world and were buying No. 6 Montague Place, near Montague House, which was then the British Museum. There had been more trouble between Austen and Benjamin Disraeli, who kept on promising to repay money which was badly needed to cover expenses for the new house. 'You really exhaust my patience & put me to serious inconvenience', wrote Austen. 'These constant disappointments annoy me exceedingly. You deal too much in mysteries & you know I am a plain matter-of-fact man.'

2

'*We rode alone*'

Benjamin Austen was also disappointed in his nephew who
seemed to be an impractical dreamer like Disraeli and he entirely
disapproved of Henry's radical views and of the 'revolutionary'
friends he had made in London among exiled Poles and in Italy
among the Carbonari; nor did he like the debating society Henry
had joined in London, nor his friendship with the elderly Henry
Crabb Robinson, the radical friend of Lamb, Coleridge, and
Wordsworth. Henry said of his uncle that to accuse a man of
being radical was 'to believe him capable of committing almost
any crime'. Henry gained the impression that he was no longer
welcome at the Austens' house and so he kept to himself. He
spent part of the summer and autumn of 1837 in northern Italy
with the Cavour family, to whom he had been introduced by
Brockedon. In Italian country-houses he met 'handsome and
accomplished women' with some of whom he fell in love; he
attended meetings of the Carbonari who were planning to overthrow the Austrian and Papal authorities, and was initiated into
some of their secrets. He bitterly regretted having to leave 'this
idle and too fascinating life' to return to work in Gray's Inn. *

Henry was refreshed by his holiday but he was in an unhappy
state of mind. He was full of ambition to achieve fame but he
did not know how to set about it. Like Disraeli, 'Nature had
given him an awful ambition and fiery passions'. The only
solution, it seemed to him, was for his uncle to take him into

* Layard wrote of his first visit abroad with Brockedon in a diary
entitled *A Journey to the Alps*. He wrote later of the young Piedmontese
and Liberal refugees from other parts of Italy who took shelter in the
north: 'To their indomitable courage and perseverance and to their
readiness to sacrifice even life to their country, Italy owes her freedom
and regeneration. I little thought that it was under the lead of the young
men whose acquaintance I had made at Turin that this great work
was to be accomplished' (*Autobiography*).

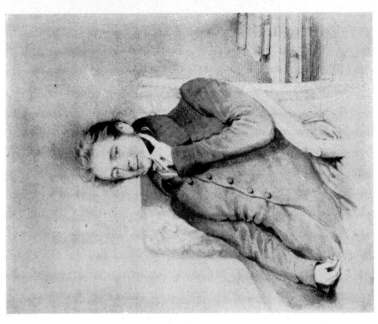

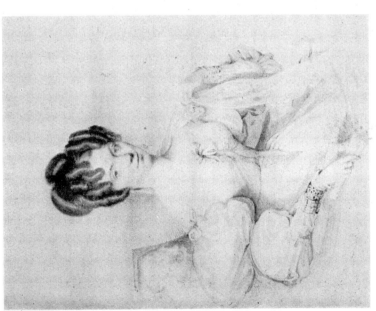

Sara and Benjamin Austen (1828) by Daniel Maclise

Henry Layard by William Brockedon

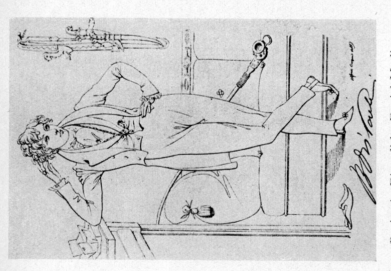

Benjamin Disraeli by Daniel Maclise

partnership, even though he hated law. His upbringing had taught him to resent authority, and he could not bring himself to accommodate himself to his uncle's wishes. Once his interest was aroused he was capable of great industry and had surprising powers of concentration, but his uncle had not as yet had an opportunity of observing this. Benjamin Austen was puzzled; he realised that Henry had ability and ambition, but could not understand why he should not work hard at law to achieve what he wanted. Although he did not consider Crabb Robinson a suitable friend, he decided to consult him for he seemed the only person who had any influence over Henry.* Crabb Robinson was asked to dinner at 6 Montague Place in December 1837, and he noted afterwards in his diary that the Austens had 'a genteel establishment' but he deplored their Tory connections:

> Mrs. Austen is a handsome woman of some pretensions—she talks well and is up to the points of the day. But their connections are thoroughly *wrong*. They are very intimate with young D'Israeli, but seem only to smile and not to grieve at his ridiculous display.† They are evidently attached to young Layard and they think themselves obliged to me for my notice of him. . . . She is apprehensive that he is wayward and unsettled and fears he may offend his uncle by not settling himself to business.

He felt obliged to agree with Austen that Henry was not, at the age of twenty-one, old enough or sufficiently experienced to be made a partner in the firm, which Henry insisted was his right. Robinson remarked that Henry wanted to pluck the fruit before he had sown the seed: 'He feels himself no one in society, forgetting that a young man of 21 ought not to be anything in society.' Layard agreed with the remark made by Disraeli to his

* 'His uncle accused me of misleading him', wrote Crabb Robinson in 1852 when Henry Layard was being lionised in London because of his Assyrian discoveries. 'I believe that I did set his mind in motion, and excited in him tastes and a curiosity which now will not be a matter of reproach, seeing that the issue has already been so remarkable.' *Reminiscences and Correspondence* (vol. iii, p. 399). The other quotations are from the manuscript diary of Henry Crabb Robinson in Dr. Williams' Library in Gordon Square, London.

† This was his maiden speech in the House of Commons after he had been elected for Maidstone in 1837. He was hooted and shouted down.

cousin, Lady Charlotte—that nothing could compensate him for an obscure youth, not even glorious old age. Henry bitterly resented the fact that his uncle and aunt were eager to help the foppish young Disraeli, but were not willing, he considered, to help or encourage their own nephew. He became so harassed with anxiety for his future that he found it quite impossible to do any work at all.

In the long vacation of the next year, 1838, Henry travelled again, visiting Finland, Denmark, and Russia. In his journal he set down facts and figures about Russian trade and was impressed by the government cotton factory at Alexandrovsky; but the Poles he met recounted terrible stories about living conditions in Russia. In London he had many Polish friends who had fled the Russians in 1830 and who always expected a revolution to break out, supported by one of the great Powers, which would restore Poland's freedom.

Henry had already shown by his diaries that he was very interested in collecting facts and when he returned to London he supplied information for John Murray's *Handbook for Denmark*, published in 1839, and he checked through all the proofs. He also arranged with Smith, Elder, the publishers, to bring out a history of the Russian Campaign of 1814 in France by General Danilefsky, who was private secretary to the Czar Alexander. Danilefsky had been kind to Layard and had offered to arrange for him to accompany the trading caravan which went across the steppes of Turkestan to the Chinese frontier. Layard hated law all the more that he was unable to take advantage of such an exciting opportunity. Layard returned to family life which was, said Marianne, 'full of undercurrents'. He was devoted to his family, but at the same time very sensitive to tensions. His mother was very highly strung and did not get on well with her brother and sister-in-law. Other brothers, who were ambitious for their children, criticised Henry for expecting to be a partner with his uncle without knowing much about law. There were also emotional scenes at Montague Place about Louisa Rickett, who lived with her elder sister, Sara Austen. There had been a quarrel a few years earlier because Louisa had wanted to marry Ben Lindo, nephew to Mrs. Isaac Disraeli, and Sara had put difficulties in the way; when Louisa had wanted to marry a

Mr. Linton there had been the same opposition. Henry was very fond of his Aunt Louisa and Sara believed that he was encouraging her to marry Mr. Linton, so that relations were strained.

Fortunately there arrived in England Henry's uncle, Charles Layard, who had accompanied Peter Layard to Ceylon and now held high office in the civil service. When Austen told him about his trouble with Henry, Charles suggested that he should go to Ceylon to practise as a barrister and introduced him to Edward Mitford, an adventurous man of thirty-two who had been in business in Morocco and was preparing to go to Ceylon to grow coffee, with the idea that they should travel together. The normal route would have been by sea to Alexandria, up the Nile to Cairo, across by road to Suez and thence by ship to Ceylon—a journey of only some months. If the young men had followed that route Layard would never have seen Nimrud and Nineveh and it is unlikely that he would have won fame. It was his good fortune that Mitford, to avoid sea-sickness, had decided to make his way overland, across the Ottoman Empire in Europe to Constantinople, through Asia Minor, Syria, Jerusalem, Bagdad, Kermanshah in Persia, across the great Seistan Desert to Kandahar, and through India to Ceylon. Henry miraculously recovered from his depression at the thought of this grand idea of visiting the East and of realising 'the dreams which had haunted me from my childhood'.

Mitford at first was uncertain as to whether young Layard would be able to stand up to such a journey which would at times be dangerous; Britain had recently broken off diplomatic relations with Persia and travel there would be especially hazardous. Henry was only twenty-two, knew no oriental language and had never been astride a horse. The journey would take many months, possibly a year, and there was no proof that he was able or prepared to undergo great hardship. Henry, however, had no misgivings. His enthusiasm for the adventure swept away all objections from his family who regarded the scheme as insane, and even friendly Crabb Robinson described it as 'a wild goose-chase'. At the same time he realised that it was useless to try to stop Henry once his mind was made up; the latter brought Mitford to one of Crabb Robinson's fashionable breakfasts and

Robinson was relieved to find that he looked a man of character and intelligence.

Henry surprised his relatives by the earnestness with which he prepared for the journey. He quickly passed his examinations in law, took lessons in trigonometry, consulted with members of the Royal Geographical Society and with Sir Charles Fellows, famous for his discoveries of the remains of ancient Greek cities in Asia Minor.* He went to see his favourite author, Baillie Fraser, who had travelled much in Kurdistan and Persia; he consulted Sir John McNeill, who had been British Minister in Teheran until relations had been broken off. Smith, Elder were sufficiently interested in the journey to advance the travellers two hundred pounds for the manuscript of the journal they were to keep and Mitford undertook to send it to London within six months of reaching Ceylon. Marianne Layard managed, with difficulty, to give her son three hundred pounds for expenses and paid a similar amount to Charles Layard for Henry's use when he arrived in Ceylon. By July 1839 preparations were complete and Henry Layard left England regretting, he said, only the separation from his mother. He was now twenty-two, independent and delighted to be no longer exposed 'to the vexatious interference and control' which he had so much resented.

Mitford and Layard travelled by horse-bus and Rhine steamer to Coblenz, Heidelberg and Munich where Layard was excited to see the wonderful collections of pictures in the galleries there. They travelled on in a light carriage from one post-house to another as far as Venice which was then approached by gondola from Mestre. Layard fell in love with Venice on this first visit and spent two days seeing the principal monuments and galleries; he was interested to meet there Mr. George Dennis, who had been making a tour of the ancient sites and cemeteries of Etruria, for he had as a boy been interested in the Etruscan collection in Florence. Mr. Dennis was on the way to London to find a publisher for his work on the Etruscans and Layard gave him a letter to John Murray who later published Dennis's classic work *The Cities and Cemeteries of Etruria*.

* Sir Charles Fellows published articles on his travels in the 1830's and *Travels and Researches in Asia Minor* (Murray, 1852).

The two travellers continued by carriage and steamer to Trieste, Fiume, and through Croatia to Dalmatia where they bought saddles. 'Tell my Uncle Ben', Layard wrote to his mother, 'that I made my debut on horseback better than he expected; the first day we rode 16 hours, the second 14, and the third 26 without stopping, except for half-an-hour or so to rest & to change'. Both young men were delighted by the adventure and with the Dalmatians who carried long guns, pistols, and knives or *yataghans* for they were constantly fighting either the Austrians or their Mohammedan neighbours of the Ottoman Empire.

They arrived at Cattaro in the ancient Republic of Ragusa and sent forward a messenger to Prince Danielo, the bishop who ruled Montenegro, asking permission to visit him at his capital of Cettigne. It was now the end of August and Layard wrote a letter to Louisa Rickett as he sat under a tree: 'We have drunk our coffee and finished our rice, cooked by our hands, & I now divide our hour's rest between you & a Turkish pipe, for I have become a most inveterate smoker.' He told her that he had bought the dress of a Montenegrin girl of rank who, with many others, had been killed in an Albanian attack; 'the man, who stripped the poor girl of her finery', had offered the dress for much less than its value and Layard said that he was sending it to Mary Thomson, a young friend at Ramsgate: 'The things are nearly new & rich & original.' There is no hint in the letter that Mary might be disturbed by this macabre present.

Prince Danielo sent word that the travellers were welcome and guides escorted them by tracks over precipitous mountains to the strange world of Cettigne. Layard told his mother that they were hospitably looked after and were lodged in what seemed like a comfortable English house, but there were two differences; firstly, it was filled with armed men 'intruding with the greatest coolness into our room, where they place themselves on the bed smoking their pipes with the utmost indifference; there are two in the room while I write, quietly watching our movements'; secondly, looking into the bedroom was a circle of forty-five gory Turkish heads stuck on poles, trophies from a battle of the previous week. An account was given of the smell and the blood still hanging on their pale cheeks, crude details to include in a letter to his mother who was highly nervous by temperament and very anxious about her son's well-being in the wilder parts of Europe.

Prince Danielo was twenty-seven years of age, over seven feet tall, dressed in black silk robes and wore the high round cap of the Greek Orthodox Church; fond of learning, a skilful horseman, a poet, and devout, he was at the same time a champion killer of Turks. He was very proud of his large billiard-table, which had been carried up from Cattaro along the mountain paths, and insisted on playing a game with his guests but they were interrupted by the noise of firing as a war-party returned from a raid on Turkish territory near Scutari, and a cloth containing several heads was triumphantly placed at the feet of the prince. Henry expressed his disgust and reminded his host of all that he had been saying about civilising his people. The bishop agreed that these were barbarous customs, but argued that they were absolutely necessary in order to maintain a war-like spirit; there was nothing he dreaded more than a long peace, for that would lead them to forget their martial valour and end in their being conquered. The Montenegrins were, indeed, dreaded by both Turks and Christians for their ferocious acts of cruelty and for generations they had successfully resisted attempts by both the Austrian and Turkish Governments to subdue them. The prince revealed that he received a monetary subsidy from the Czar of Russia and had been to St. Petersburg to thank him, though he also insisted that his people were entirely free and owed allegiance to none.

From Cettigne the travellers continued their journey to the Turkish territory of Scutari in Albania, their Montenegrin guides having to leave them at the frontier. In his letters home Layard expressed his excitement at seeing the mixture of races—Turks, Albanians, Greeks, and others in their gay and varied costumes. The Englishmen excited some curiosity, for there were few European travellers to that part of the Ottoman Empire. In order to make use of the post-houses along the route to Constantinople, they obtained an order from the Turkish Governor, through the Austrian Consul. At each of the post-houses, which were about eighteen miles apart, travellers could obtain fresh horses, a system which had continued ever since the days of the Roman Empire. They rode on through forests, over

28

mountains, and along precipitous paths, through Monastir and Adrianople, sleeping in their cloaks in the open or spending a few hours on their carpets in a *khan* or inn. They reached Constantinople on 20 September 1839, having been two and a half months on their journey.

'With this place I am much delighted', Henry wrote to his Aunt Louisa. 'It even exceeds any description I have seen. The imagination could not picture a site more beautiful as that occupied by Constantinople. In the hands of any other European Power it would have been the strongest city in the world; in the hands of the Turks it has become the most picturesque.'

Sara Austen, who was more devoted to Henry than he realised, had been much upset at his departure from England, and was extremely hurt that he wrote interesting letters about his travels to her sister Louisa and only letters of complaint to his Uncle Benjamin and herself. Henry was still resentful that his uncle had not made him a partner in the firm. He wrote Austen a self-justifying letter in which he argued paradoxically that he would never have been prepared to accept the position of heir to his uncle, which would have entailed living at ease in England 'while his brothers were compelled to work for their bread and leave their native land'. Austen knew that Henry was exceptionally sensitive and that when rebuffed he had a habit of denying that he wanted what in fact he most desired.

The letters from home contained urgent advice to the travellers not to proceed through Asia Minor to Syria, as the English newspapers were full of reports of the unsettled nature of the country. It was thought that the Egyptian armies of Mohamed Ali, the Viceroy of Egypt who had rebelled against the Sultan, might still advance on Constantinople, especially as only three months earlier the Egyptians had completely routed a large Turkish army at the Battle of Nissib (13 June 1839). The old Sultan, Mohamed II, had died before he had heard the news of the battle and his son Abdul Mejid, who was only sixteen years of age, had become Sultan. With a weak Sultan and the French Government supporting Mohamed Ali of Egypt, there was danger of the war involving the European Powers.

Layard and Mitford, however, were intent on continuing without delay. They engaged a young Greek named Giorgio to act as their servant, cook and interpreter, and they obtained permission to travel as far as the Syrian border; through Syria and Palestine they would have to make what arrangements they could with the Egyptian authorities. As they were about to leave Constantinople Henry fell seriously ill with malaria and nearly died. Dr. Zohrab, an Armenian who had studied medicine at Edinburgh University, marked a large circle on Henry's stomach and ordered it to be filled with leeches. This treatment made him worse and Dr. Millingen was called in, but the bleeding was continued. The study of malaria was still in its early stages and the copious bleeding almost certainly did more harm than good, * but he had a strong constitution and recovered in time to catch up with Mitford who had gone to Mudania in Asia Minor where they met at the beginning of October.

They were now starting on a very much more difficult stage of their journey and it was fortunate that they got on together as well as they did, for they differed in temperament, in interests, and in politics. Layard was impulsive, rash, radical in his political opinions, and a free-thinker; Mitford was experienced, careful, devout Church of England, and a strong Tory; but they found everything of such absorbing interest as they travelled that they had little time, or indeed inclination, to quarrel. Mitford's interest was mainly in birds and animals while Layard visited as many Assyrian, Greek, Roman, and Christian ruins as he could find. Layard mapped their route most carefully, keeping a 'road-book' ruled into equal spaces, each representing half an hour's journey, about one and a half miles. He plotted the course with a compass and his notes were sufficiently detailed to enable him to send a good map of their route to the Royal Geographical

* Dr. Millingen had attended Byron before his death and in 1890 Layard's wife, Enid, had a curious conversation in Venice with Countess Pisani, Dr. Millingen's daughter. She said that her father had been very unhappy in his old age and she believed that he considered that he was responsible for Byron's death. She told Lady Layard: 'He had been called in as consulting doctor and had counselled bleeding and not recognised the illness to be pernicious fever. I once said to him: "I suppose Lord Byron died of brain fever", to which my father said: "I fear it was pernicious fever, but I did not think so at the time and I persuaded him to be bled to which he was greatly opposed."' (*Enid Layard's Diary*, British Museum, No. 46163, 25 October 1890.)

Society. They were travelling through an area of Asia Minor which was even richer in the remains of Greek temples than it is today, and Layard was delighted by the beauty of the marble columns 'of the purest Ionic order and of exquisite loveliness'. In many of the early Christian churches in Anatolia they could still see the remains of early Byzantine paintings. 'It was curious', Henry wrote to his mother, 'to see in these places, deserted for centuries, the figures of saints & martyrs resembling those which exist in the paintings of Giotto and Masaccio.'

Crossing the great range of the Taurus which separates the table-land of Anatolia from the coast, they reached the Mediterranean at Selefkeh (Cilician Seleucia), looking across to the northern tip of Cyprus. They rode along the coast to Tarsus through exquisite scenery rich in Greek remains. 'I was accompanied', wrote Layard, 'by one no less curious and enthusiastic than myself. We were both equally careless of comfort and unmindful of danger. We rode alone; our arms were our only protection; a valise behind our saddle was our wardrobe and we tended our own horses, except when relieved from the duty by the hospitable inhabitants of a Turcoman village or an Arab tent. Thus, unembarrassed by needless luxuries and uninfluenced by the opinions and prejudices of others, we mixed amongst the people.'

Mitford also was pleased not to be embarrassed by needless luxuries and described how well they lived on dried fish-roes, carob beans, and unleavened bread: 'On one occasion I lived for four or five days on the small dry figs, which are strung like necklaces and sold in the bazaars, and yet my health did not suffer; there is no doubt in our ordinary life at home most people eat too much; hence the multiplicity of diseases and our consequent slavery to doctors.' Mitford did not always feel so philosophical: 'Of all the imaginable wretched and miserable undertakings which experience has realised or imagination pictured, nothing can equal in discomfort a winter journey . . . combining rain, or rather water *en masse*, mud up to the girths, intense cold, nothing to eat, no shelter at night. . . .' Like Layard he was impressed by the hospitality of the Turks but he did not consider that their friendliness was due to the liberality of travellers; 'the exact contrary is the case, for nothing

is more demoralising than ill-judged liberality'. He said that it
cost them about four shillings a day for board and lodging for
three men and three horses, 'and the people were always
content'. They both considered that Sir Charles Fellows had
'saved their lives' by introducing them to the 'Levinge bed'.
They each had one and it kept off insects from above and below,
consisting 'of a pair of sheets sewn together with Muslin con-
tinuations, to hang above the head, expanded by a cane hoop'.

They obtained permission to cross into Syria and in November,
1839, reached Adana which was full of Egyptian troops. Here
they lodged with Dr. Nani, who received them very cordially as
did other Italians in the Egyptian service; these were mostly
young men forced to leave Italy for political reasons. When
Mohamed Ali's Egyptian armies had invaded Arabia, the Italians
had visited various areas unexplored at that time by Europeans.
Layard was fascinated to hear that several of them had even
reached Mecca and Medina, but disappointed in the little they
could tell him; their background knowledge of history and geography, he considered, was so slight that they failed to take any
advantage of their unique opportunities. Layard himself was
always most assiduous in finding out all he could about an area
he was visiting, but he never felt that he knew enough; twenty
years later he was still worrying that he had not prepared sufficiently for his travels: 'Half the usefulness of my journeys has
been thrown away.'

They travelled through Iskanderoun (Alexandretta), Antioch,
and Suedia, to Aleppo where Layard had another attack of
malaria. When he recovered they struck south along the coast
to Beirut whence Layard sent a report on their journey to the
Royal Geographical Society. Their Greek servant, Giorgio, decided
to return to Constantinople and they continued their ride to
Saida (Sidon), where they were entertained by the remarkable
Colonel Sève, better known as Suleiman Pasha, who was Chief
of Staff to Ibrahim Pasha, Commander of the Egyptian forces.
He was a typical French officer of Napoleon's Grande Armée, of
which he was intensely proud, and after an excellent dinner
they retired to drink and smoke in Sève's *Cabinet Napoléon* the
walls of which were covered with pictures of the Emperor and his
family, and the spoils of the Battle of Nissib were surmounted

by Napoleon's bust. Sève criticised England's policy of restricting the authority of Mohamed Ali Pasha and restoring Syria to 'the corrupt and effete' rule of the Sultan. If the Powers did not interfere, the Egyptian armies, he considered, would have no difficulty in seizing Asia Minor and Constantinople.

Layard and Mitford visited Acre, where the fortifications were being strengthened under Colonel Sève's orders, Mount Carmel, Nazareth, and Nablus, reaching the outskirts of Jerusalem on 10 February 1840:

> After winding until midday through the mournful and deserted country, we came suddenly in sight of the Dome of the Mosque of Omar, and the cupolas of the Church and Convent of the Holy Sepulchre. . . . Our joy at having accomplished so much of our long and perilous journey, and at seeing at last the City before us after so many disappointments, was scarcely less than that of the pilgrim crusaders when, for the first time, the Holy City burst upon their view.

They had, indeed, travelled across Europe as the crusader knights had done, on horse-back, and had followed the same old Roman routes. In eight hundred years there had been little improvement in the means of communication.

The main topic of conversation in Jerusalem was Russian intrigue. The Russian Consul in the city claimed that he pro-tected the Orthodox Greeks and also the Jews, most of whom came from Poland and other parts of Eastern Europe. Russia was said to be scheming to obtain possession of the Sacred Places, including the Holy Sepulchre, and this had angered the French who laid claim to them. It was the beginning of the quarrel which led to the Crimean War. There had been bloodshed between the Latin and the Greek Orthodox communities within the Church of the Holy Sepulchre itself; the previous Easter several lives had been lost and the Egyptian authorities, said Layard, 'had driven out the pious combatants at the point of the bayonet'. He visited the Holy Sepulchre on a Saint's Day and found Egyptian officers and a guard seated in the portico of the church smoking their pipes, ready to take action to preserve order.

The Egyptians, however, had not yet established their authority over the area of Petra, Moab, and Jerash, east of the

Dead Sea, which Layard was eager to explore; they were strongly opposed to his venturing into that area, as was Mr. Young the British Vice-Consul. The latter insisted that the only way of travelling through the country was to pay influential sheikhs large sums of money as protection; neither Layard nor Mitford could afford to do this. The difficulties and dangers seemed to the more sensible Mitford so great that he decided not to go. When Layard eventually obtained the necessary authority from the Egyptians and insisted on going alone, the two travellers came near to quarrelling. Mitford had been asked by Layard's family to look after him and to try to curb his impulsiveness and over-confidence. Mitford was also anxious to get to Ceylon and considered that Layard's journey was an unnecessary delay, nor did he wish Layard to come to any harm. He had not expected at first that this short, stocky, bearded youth of twenty-two would acquire such a single-minded passion to visit antiquities, even at the risk of his life. Layard had read of the Jewish civilisation in the Dead Sea area in his Bible, and of the Roman, Crusader, and Nabataean civilisations in Gibbon, Laborde, and Burckhardt; he wanted to see the remains of these wonderful cities for himself. He knew very well that there were difficulties and had written to the Royal Geographical Society from Beirut that the tribes of the Dead Sea area were at war and travellers had to buy their way through; three Frenchmen had had to pay large sums of money to the Chief of Akaba, but even so had been unable to accomplish their journey: 'I trust that an Englishman can succeed better.' Burckhardt had written in high praise of the Beduin and Disraeli in *Contarini Fleming* had referred to 'this singular people, who combined primitive simplicity of habits with the refined feelings of civilisation'. Layard believed in his own capacity to overcome difficulties, but he admitted afterwards that he had been wrong not to heed the warnings: 'I had romantic ideas about beduin hospitality and believed that if I trusted to it, and placed myself unreservedly in the power of beduin tribes, trusting to their respect for their guests, I should incur no danger.'

Layard was about to entrust himself to the mercy of hostile tribes without funds to buy his way out and without knowledge of Arabic, for he had been dependent upon Mitford to act as interpreter. Eventually he found an Arab who came from the desert east of the Dead Sea who knew some Italian and was too young to realise what dangers he was going to suffer; he was called Antonio because he had been brought up in Jerusalem by Italian Roman Catholic monks. It was not many days before Antonio realised that he had been very unwise to undertake a mission with a master who was obstinately rash. Layard considered him a coward: 'He was persuaded that every Arab we saw, far and near, was a robber.' Most of them were.

The first adventure occurred after entering the narrow gorge into Petra. Layard arrived by camel with two guides, Musa and Awad, furnished by the Sheikh of the Jehalin tribe to whom the Egyptian Pasha of Jerusalem had sent letters. As soon as the party had entered the precincts of this hidden Nabataean city and Layard had spread his carpet to rest, swarms of Arabs surrounded them demanding money for permission to visit the tombs and temples cut into the high cliffs. There was a furious outcry when payment was refused and it seemed as if the party of four would be overwhelmed—'men and women issued from the rock-cut tombs like rabbits from a warren'. The tribesmen of the Wadi Musa were armed with swords and spears and had recently been at war with the Jehalin tribe.

> A violent altercation ensued, which nearly led to bloodshed, as swords were drawn on both sides. An attempt was made to seize my effects, and I was told that I should not be allowed to leave the place until I had paid the sum demanded of me. As I still absolutely refused to do so, one, more bold and insolent than the rest, advanced towards me with his drawn sword, which he flourished in my face. I raised my gun, determined to sell my life dearly if there was an intention to murder me. Another Arab suddenly possessed himself of Musa's gun, which he had imprudently laid on the ground whilst unloading the camels.

Fortunately the Sheikh of the tribe arrived and Layard did not have occasion to fire, for otherwise he and his companions would probably have been killed.

Layard was watched closely but not molested as he explored the strange rock architecture, which he considered 'debased and wanting in both elegance and grandeur. It is of a bad period and of a corrupt style'* but he found the situation most impressive :

> The gigantic flights of steps cut in the rocks leading to the tombs ;
> the absence of all vegetation to relieve the monotony of the brown,
> barren soil; the mountains rising abruptly on all sides ; the silence
> and solitude scarcely disturbed by the wild tribes lurking among
> the fragments of pediments, fallen cornices and architraves which
> encumber the narrow valley, render the ruins of Petra unlike those
> of any other ancient city in the world.

The party went northwards through the mountains towards
Kerak to the east of the southerly tip of the Dead Sea. Before
reaching the fortress they were attacked in the mountains
of Moab by large numbers of the Aranat tribe, who robbed
Layard of all he had; they would have killed him if he had not
managed to seize the Sheikh of the tribe and hold him as hostage
threatening him with his gun. Arrived at Kerak, Layard delivered
the Governor of Jerusalem's letter to Sheikh Ahmed, the son of
the chief of the fortress, who was away. Layard gives an exciting
account of a hostile assembly of the tribe being won over by the
oratory of the handsome Sheikh Ahmed. Finally Layard's clothes,
medical stores, and other valuables were restored. Layard had
admired the young Sheikh's bravery and courtesy in helping a
stranger and an infidel; but he was soon to realise that Sheikh
Ahmed's object was to retain the valuables for himself and to
make as much money as possible out of his visitor. When the
Sheikh was finally convinced that Layard was either too poor or
too obstinate to be a worth-while proposition, he 'sold' his guest
to a wealthy and powerful Beduin Chief who was visiting Kerak.
The Chief was told that the Englishman wished to visit ruins
and would pay large sums of money for the privilege. The
Beduin Chief, Sheikh Suleiman-Ibn-Fais of the Beni Sakhr tribe,

---

* It is not surprising that Layard should have preferred the Greek
remains he had already seen in Ionia and elsewhere farther north.
There was still controversy in the 1840's among travellers and Bible
students as to the correct site of the true Petra, the ancient capital
of Arabia Petraea. The Crusaders had referred to Kerak as Petra
and when Burckhardt rediscovered the strange city in the Wadi Musa
he aroused controversy with his assertion that it was the ancient capital.
He referred to it in his *Travels in Nubia* published in 1819 and
developed the argument in *Travels in Syria* (1822); his arguments
were endorsed by the Editor, Colonel Leake.

was quite eager to take Layard over in return for a payment of one thousand piastres (£10) and a beautiful robe of Damascus silk he was wearing, which Ahmed coveted. Layard knew nothing of this when he sat down to a feast with the two men, who were celebrating the agreement; he was overjoyed to learn that Sheikh Suleiman's tribe was at that time encamped near the great ruins of Ammon (Amman) which he was determined to visit. Layard was impressed by Sheikh Suleiman who was 'a tall, handsome man of dignified appearance, with regular features, bright, restless eyes, and a long bushy black beard, such as is rarely seen among Arabs'. In his girdle he carried a pair of silver-mounted pistols of English manufacture.

Sheikh Suleiman left with his guest, but very soon lost his good manners when he found that Layard continued to argue that he had no money. He could not believe that an Englishman would embark on such a perilous journey without sufficient funds to buy protection from the tribes, which was the accepted custom; he was overcome with fury when Layard refused even to repay the 'purchase' price paid to Sheikh Ahmed. Instead of taking the direct route to Ammon, Sheikh Suleiman took Layard backwards and forwards through little valleys, arguing with him about money at each stopping-place. This journeying became more boring to the Beduin Chief than to Layard, who discovered many interesting remains of ancient buildings and reservoirs for water which he carefully noted. Eventually the Beduin Chief gave up and conducted Layard to his main encampment. He stopped arguing about money and became once more a charming host, entertaining Layard very hospitably as his guest; 'he sought', said Layard, 'to justify the good opinion which I endeavoured to make him understand that I had formed of him.' The Sheikh showed off his suit of chain armour, which had been handed down from one generation to another, perhaps from the time of the Crusaders, and was still worn in battle. Layard remarked later that in his intercourse with Beduins he had many opportunities of noting 'this double character in the Arab. The same man who, at one moment, would be grasping, deceitful, treacherous, and cruel, would show himself at another, generous, faithful, trustworthy, and humane.'

He was left free to continue his journey to Ammon. There it

was peaceful, for it was then uninhabited except for a few Beni Sakhr tribesmen looking after their sheep and camels, and he was much more impressed by the architecture than he had been by Petra. He made a rough plan showing the sites of the buildings, which were 'very extensive, of great interest, and very picturesque', but most of them have now been destroyed or engulfed by the new buildings of the capital of Jordan. Today Layard would scarcely recognise it, except for the great theatre carved partly out of the cliff which rises majestically in front of the Philadelphia Hotel. This city was originally the biblical Rabbath-beni-Ammon, the capital of the Ammonites, which was incorporated into the Kingdom of Israel until laid waste by the Assyrians under Tiglath-pileser. (Proof of the Bible story was later to be found by Layard in his excavations.) Rebuilt by Ptolemy Philadelphus and called Philadelphia, it was the remains of these buildings that Layard visited.

He was equally impressed by Gerasa (or Jerash): 'I was enchanted by the beauty of the scene, and surprised at the extent and magnificence of the remains. On all sides I saw long avenues of graceful columns leading to temples, theatres, baths, and public edifices constructed of marble, to which time had given a bright pinkish-yellow tint'; there were two hundred and fifty columns still standing. When he found that plague had broken out in the area he decided to leave for Damascus but was told that the city was surrounded by a *cordon sanitaire* and that there were long quarantine delays. Owing to storms and heavy rain, Layard and Antonio had to sleep in crowded huts with Arabs, some of whom probably had plague. They went on as quickly as possible to Tiberias, where help was obtained from a friendly Polish Jew, enabling Antonio to return to Jerusalem and Layard to go to Damascus. He managed to avoid the quarantine and looked like a mendicant Arab when he arrived at the house of Mr. Wherry, the British Consul, who revived him with cups of tea. Mitford had grown tired of waiting in Damascus and had returned to stay with the Barker family in Aleppo. There Layard joined him after further adventures, visiting Baalbeck and crossing the Lebanon mountains through deep snow.

They prepared for their long journey to Mosul and Bagdad, purchasing a couple of horses and cutting down their luggage to

Sir Stratford Canning (Viscount Stratford de Redcliffe) by George Richmond

Henry Layard in Constantinople by Mina K. Kellogg

a minimum. It consisted of a change of clothes, four blue shirts each, maps, sketch-books, and a few necessaries weighing altogether about fifteen pounds. These were packed in saddle-bags made to fit over the cantle of the saddles. 'Looking forward as a general rule to sleep in our clothes', wrote Mitford, 'all our bedding consisted of a coverlet or quilt which was double and strapped with a surcingle over the saddle, making a comfortable seat, and a cloak fastened on behind; we each slung a double-barrelled gun and a pair of pistols, with necessary ammunition; and thus equipped we set off to traverse some off the most unfrequented roads of Turkish Arabia.' They left Aleppo on 18 March 1840, and were lost on their first day in heavy rain, but found refuge in a cave with a family of Yezidis, known as 'devil-worshippers', a people with whom Layard became very friendly on his subsequent travels. Mosul was reached at the beginning of April.

3

'Mystery hangs over Assyria'

Across the Tigris from Mosul, like a line of low hills, lay the great mounds, four miles in circuit, all that remained of what was believed to have been the great city of Nineveh. These man-made mounds, which every now and again yielded up ancient stone monuments, fired Layard's imagination more than the beautiful Greek and Roman buildings they had visited. Perhaps it was after all fortunate that he had not had a classical education, otherwise he might have remained spell-bound by the glamour of Greece, as were so many of his contemporaries.* He had,

---

* Dr. Seton Lloyd, who worked for many years as an archaeologist in the area where Layard pioneered, wrote: 'By his prompt appreciation of the obscure qualities which are the country's central distinction, Layard places himself in a class apart among European travellers.' *Foundations in the Dust* (OUP, 1947).

indeed, been delighted by the beauty of the antiquities of ancient Greece in Asia Minor and Syria, 'the graceful column rising above the foliage of the myrtle, ilex, and oleander', but he preferred 'the stern, shapeless mound rising like a hill from the scorched plain, the fragments of pottery, and the stupendous mass of brick-work occasionally laid bare by the winter rains'. He gives in *Nineveh and Its Remains* a personal and moving account of the impact on a traveller such as himself.

> He has left the land where nature is still lovely, where, in his mind's eye, he can rebuild the temple or the theatre, half doubting whether they would have made a more grateful impression upon the senses than the ruin before him. He is now at a loss to give any form to the rude heaps upon which he is gazing. Those of whose works they are the remains, unlike the Roman or the Greek, have left no visible traces of their civilisation, or of their arts: their influence has long since passed away. The more he conjectures, the more vague the results appear. The scene around is worthy of the ruin he is contemplating; desolation meets desolation: a feeling of awe succeeds to wonder; for there is nothing to relieve the mind, to lead to hope, or to tell of what has gone by.
>
> These huge mounds of Assyria made a deeper impression upon me, gave rise to more serious thoughts and more earnest reflection, than the temples of Baalbek and the theatres of Ionia. . . . A deep mystery hangs over Assyria, Babylonia, and Chaldaea. With these names are linked great nations and great cities dimly shadowed forth in history; mighty ruins in the midst of deserts, defying, by their very desolation and lack of definite form, the description of the traveller; the remnants of the mighty races still roving over the land; the fulfilling and fulfilment of prophecies; the plains to which the Jew and the Gentile alike look as the cradle of their race. After a journey in Syria the thoughts naturally turn eastward; and without treading on the remains of Nineveh and Babylon our pilgrimage is incomplete.

At the time of Layard's first visit to Mosul there were scarcely any records of the great Assyrian Empire, whose former power and luxury were described in stories recounted by Greek and Roman authors and in the Old Testament. 'It is indeed one of the most remarkable facts in history', wrote Layard, 'that the records of an empire, so renowned for its power and civilisation, should have been entirely lost; and that the site of a city as eminent for its extent as its splendour, should for ages have been a matter of doubt.' Layard had read what he could find on Assyria, including the works of Claudius James Rich who had been for many years Political Resident of the East India Company at Bagdad, and had visited the mounds near Mosul in 1820. Rich had great knowledge and collected fragments of sculpture and tablets with cuneiform writing from Nineveh and Babylon. He died of cholera at Shiraz at the age of thirty-four and never returned to Nineveh as he had intended. His small collection was placed in the British Museum, 'a case scarcely three feet square enclosed all that remained, not only of the great city of Nineveh, but of Babylon itself!' It was, however, the writings of this remarkable young man which aroused interest in Assyria in the nineteenth century.[1]

Layard was so anxious to see as much as he could of the mounds of Nineveh that he insisted on staying for over a fortnight. Mitford watched for birds while Layard explored and was fortunate to meet in Mosul the well known French traveller, M. Texier, just returned from visiting the ancient monuments of the Achaemenid era in Persia of which he had made careful drawings. As Layard studied them he wondered whether similar monuments might not possibly be concealed beneath Nineveh. Texier and Layard spent several days examining the mounds and Layard obtained information from him which proved most useful to him on his travels.

Mr. Christian Rassam, the British Vice-Consul, was also very helpful to Layard. He was a Chaldean who had accompanied Colonel Chesney as interpreter with the Euphrates Expedition. Mr. Ainsworth, who had also been with the expedition, was staying with him at Mosul.* They had planned to explore the ruins of al Hatra in the Mesopotamian desert; Layard and Mitford were invited to accompany them. The only information

* Three years previously Colonel Chesney had led the famous expedition to transport materials from the Mediterranean overland to the Euphrates for the assembly of two iron ships; these were to ply on the Euphrates and Tigris to encourage trade between India, the Persian Gulf, and the interior of Mesopotamia, a subject in which Layard became extremely interested.

on the area which they had was a paper written by Dr. John Ross, the surgeon attached to the Political Resident in Bagdad.(2)

The party left Mosul on 18 April. Layard had been delirious for some hours from another attack of malaria but he soon recovered in the fine air of the desert. They stopped the first night at the village of Hammam Ali, where there are warm sulphur springs. Layard was always to remember this visit for he had his first view of Nimrud:

> As the sun went down, I saw for the first time the great conical mound of Nimrud rising against the clear evening sky. It was on the opposite side of the river and not very distant, and the impression that it made upon me was one never to be forgotten. After my visit to Kuyunjik and Nebbi Yunis, opposite Mosul, and the distant view of Nimrud, my thoughts ran constantly upon the possibility of thoroughly exploring with the spade those great ruins.

They spent the next night by the Tigris, lighting a huge fire to keep away lions which were then still found in the jungle parts by the rivers. The next day they stopped to explore the extensive Assyrian ruins of Kalah Shergat, spending the day taking measurements and drawing plans. There was a tradition among the Arabs that strange figures carved in black stone lay among the ruins but they searched for these in vain. A *cawass* who had been sent with them by the Turkish Governor of Mosul was so frightened by the solitude of this ancient place that he decided to return to Mosul but was caught and killed by marauding Arabs. After leaving Kalah Shergat the expedition lost its way in mist and rain, but suddenly a slight breeze sprang up and Layard was delighted to have his first view of al Hatra as the morning mist lifted like a curtain:

> Not far from us rose a vast and magnificent pile of buildings, and a long line of walls of stone masonry with equidistant towers. Around them were scattered flocks of sheep and innumerable camels, and on all sides we could see the black tents of the Beduin, rising upon the green sward, and marked by the spears tufted with ostrich feathers which were planted in the ground before them. This picturesque and striking scene thus suddenly disclosed to us filled me with wonder and delight. It was so fairy-like and unexpected that I could scarcely believe my senses, and fancied myself in a dream. We had reached the object of our adventurous journey.

The dangers were, however, not yet over. Rassam, who knew
Beduin customs, urged them to gallop so that they might enter
the encampment and claim the hospitality of the Sheikh of the
tribe before their approach was noticed. This they succeeded in
doing. Even so, the Sheikh had great difficulty in preventing his
tribesmen from attacking the party.

When Layard and Ainsworth began to take measurements and
make drawings the tribesmen, who were watching closely,
believed that they were seeking the place where the gold was
buried. Some said that the foreigners would bring an European
army which would take possession of the country and of the
treasure which the Beduin considered belonged to them. This
preoccupation with treasure was to cause Layard a great deal of
trouble in all his travels. The Sheikh himself acted as escort to the
party at the outset of their four-day return journey to Mosul and
in the afternoon he handed them over to members of the Jebour
tribe to escort them back to Mosul.

The easiest and most comfortable way of travelling to Bagdad
was to float down the Tigris. A raft was hired, twelve feet long
and eight feet wide, supported by fifty inflated sheep-skins, a
method of travel which had been used for thousands of years;
an arch of bamboos covered with felt was erected over two
wooden beds as protection against the sun. They embarked on
29 April 1840 for the three hundred mile journey by river.
The Tigris was flowing fast, swollen with the melting snow from
the mountains of Armenia; a single boatman, who never seemed
to sleep, guided the raft through the currents. About twenty
miles downstream from Mosul they could see the ruins of Nimrud
on their left; then the water suddenly broke into foaming whirl-
pools and the boatman prayed aloud as they approached a cataract
formed by an artificial barrier built across the stream. Once over
the danger the boatman explained that there had been a great
dam there in ancient times used as a causeway by Nimrod, the
mighty hunter, to cross from the city of Nimrud to the baths of
Hammam Ali on the other side of the Tigris. Layard was fascinated: 'He was telling me of the histories and fate of the Kings
of a primitive race, still the favourite theme of the inhabitants
of the plains of Shinar, when the last glow of twilight faded
away and I fell asleep as we glided on to Bagdad. My curiosity

had been greatly excited, and from that time I formed the design of thoroughly examining, whenever it might be in my power, these singular ruins.' As they travelled down the river, Layard was ever on the look-out for ancient mounds and remains of buildings and would try to discover their names from the boatman, while Mitford was delighted with the variety of birds and small animals which lived along the banks: 'We travelled three nights in this manner, yet fortunately escaped without serious accident, although often awoke in alarm by the roaring of a rapid, into which we had been drawn by the current: or the thundering fall of the sandbanks as they were undermined by the stream and fell into the water. The effect . . . is very impressive in the silence of the night, and occurring as it does at short intervals, resembles successive claps of thunder.' Sometimes the sheep-skins, which supported them, lost so much air that the raft would heel over dangerously and the Arab boatman had to let himself over the side to re-inflate them. On the morning of the fourth day they came to Tekrit, the birthplace of Saladin, and disembarked in a beautiful grove of palm trees round the village. Here were orange, lemon, and pomegranate trees in the full bloom of spring. A gentle breeze carried a delicious scent of blossom and innumerable turtle-doves were cooing in the trees: 'The creaking of the water-wheels worked by oxen, and the cries of the Arabs on the banks added life and animation to the scene. I thought that I had never seen anything so truly beautiful, and all my Arabian Nights dreams were almost more than realised.'

Nearing Bagdad they changed into their best clothes to face the English and European society, for they had heard that Colonel Taylor, the Agent of the East India Company, maintained even greater state than the Queen's Ambassador at Constantinople. Unfortunately Layard, having put on his only suit, slipped while stepping back on to the raft and plunged into the Tigris. He trusted that his character, 'as an adventurous traveller with small means' would be sufficient excuse for his forlorn appearance. The British Residency on the banks of the Tigris was even more impressive than they had expected. They entered through a vaulted passage-way, passed sepoy sentinels, *cawasses*, and attendants in resplendent uniforms, and came into a spacious court-yard round which were balconies or terraces. They were hospitably received by Colonel Taylor, who was a 'small, slight, and wizened man, considerably past middle-age, with a bright and intellectual countenance'. Before his appointment as 'Resident in Turkish Arabia', he had distinguished himself by his profound knowledge of Eastern languages and his general learning. This charming man, who was to help Layard greatly in his researches, invited them to be his guests in Bagdad and placed at their disposal a small house in a garden near the Residency; at meal-times members of the English community and travellers were made welcome with the Taylor family. Layard and Mitford found it agreeable company. In the mornings they used to ride at daybreak with the Residency party who would leave by one of the Bagdad gates and explore the palm groves along the Tigris. The English women wore European riding costume but when they went into the streets and bazaars they dressed as orientals. 'Their faces', said Layard, 'were completely concealed by the thick horse-hair veil worn by Arab women of the city, from whom they were only to be distinguished by their European shoes.' It was many years after his first visit before they wore European clothes in public and the first one to appear, 'wearing the capacious and ugly straw bonnet of the period, was hooted and assailed with cries of: "Yah! Mother of the dirt basket!"'

A few years before Layard and Mitford arrived in Bagdad, Daoud Pasha, the last of the semi-independent Governors of the Province, had been removed under a new system of reform introduced by Sultan Mahmud. Daoud had been ruthless and cruel, even impaling evil-doers on stakes at the end of the bridge of boats as a warning to all, but at least he was a good administrator, kept order, and took an interest in the prosperity of the province. With the reforms a certain Ali Pasha had been sent from Constantinople as Governor, with other officials who had no interest in the province and whose only concern was to make as much money as they could. Colonel Taylor took Layard, Mitford and two other travellers to be presented:

We were mounted on Arab horses with splendid trappings embroidered with gold, sent by the Pasha. The head dragoman of

the Embassy, an Armenian, in flowing silk robes and ample turban
of cashmere shawl, accompanied us. We were preceded by several
cawasses on horseback in picturesque costume, carrying silver-
headed maces, and by runners with staves of the same metal. A
guard of sepoys and a number of attendants on foot completed the
procession.

They were received by the Pasha in the *serai*, 'a chamber quite
worthy of Haroun el Rashid in his prime'. The Pasha was 'dis-
gustingly obese', overcome by the heat, and ill-dressed. 'When
one saw', said Layard, 'the kind of men to whom the government
and welfare of the Sultan's subjects were confided, the condition
of his Empire, the signs of poverty, misery, and decay which
surrounded one on all sides, could scarcely be a matter for
surprise.'

Layard, however, was impressed by the city's wonderful
position with the great navigable rivers of the Euphrates and Tigris
almost uniting the Mediterranean with the Persian Gulf and
the Indian Ocean. He believed that in the course of time it
would again be rendered 'as rich and populous as it was when it
formed the most important portion of the Babylonian, Assyrian,
and Persian Empires, and of the dominion of the Caliphs'. But
a great change would have to take place before the terrible
effects of misgovernment could be repaired. 'I trust that it may
be the destiny of England to bring about that change, of such
vast importance and of such incalculable benefit to peace, commerce, and civilisation.'

The two travellers stayed for a couple of months in Bagdad
learning Persian in readiness for the next stage in their journey
to India and Ceylon. Layard spent many hours each day in
Colonel Taylor's library studying his valuable collection of
Arabic and Persian manuscripts. He learned with great interest
of Major Rawlinson's work the previous year in Bagdad trying
to decipher cuneiform and discover the language of the
Babylonians, making use of the inscriptions he had copied at
Bisutun near Kermanshah; these were trilingual and as important for deciphering cuneiform as the Rosetta Stone had been
for deciphering Egyptian hieroglyphs. He had had to abandon
temporarily his cuneiform researches on being appointed British
Agent in Kandahar, where he was later to be besieged by the

Afghans.* Layard decided he would visit Bisutun when he reached Kermanshah; he wanted himself to try to find the key to this ancient language and in the library he studied the ancient Pehlevi and Zend writings. Colonel Taylor helped him, impressed by the eagerness with which he studied. Layard had a passion for acquiring information which he had not revealed when studying law. Dr. John Ross gave information about the ruins of al Hatra, about the Beduin tribes of the Mesopotamian plains, and of the Kurds in the hills beyond. Information about India was given by the Nawab Ekbal ed Dowleh, a former ruler of Oudh who had been exiled by the East India Company; as a Moslem of the Shia sect he had settled in Bagdad to be near the Shia shrines of Ali, Hassan, and Hussein at Kerbela and Kathimain; tales of Persian intrigue were told by the three sons of Fathi Ali Shah (the former Shah of Persia) who had been banished because their cousin, Mohamed Shah, the reigning sovereign, believed that they had plotted against him. The rivers were explored with Captain Lynch, Captain Felix Jones, and other officers of the Indian Navy who were carrying out valuable surveys in the steamers brought by the Chesney expedition. Layard visited all the ancient ruins including Ctesiphon and Babylon:

> I shall never forget the effect produced upon me by the long lines and vast masses of mounds, which mark the site of ancient Babylon, as they appeared in the distance one morning as the day broke behind them. The desolation, the solitude, those shapeless heaps, all that remain of a great and renowned city, are well calculated to impress and excite the imagination. As when I first beheld the mounds of Nineveh, a longing came over me to learn what was hidden within them, and a kind of presentiment that I should one day seek to clear up the mystery. . . . I visited all the principal ruins, including the Birs Nimrud, believed by the old travellers to be the ruins of the Tower of Babel itself, and the vast mound which they had identified with the palace and hanging gardens of Semiramis. At that time no remains of antiquity were

* Major Rawlinson had been recalled from Bagdad to India at the end of 1839. The Russians were intriguing with Dost Mohamed of Afghanistan and the British marched into Afghanistan in the spring of 1839 capturing Kandahar and Kabul.

to be found above ground, except a rude sculpture in black basalt representing a lion standing over a prostrate man.

In May 1840 Layard wrote to his Aunt Sara that they were preparing to leave Bagdad and were looking for a caravan to join, as the road was not considered safe for lone horsemen. The Governor of Bagdad was preparing to repel a Persian army which was advancing into Mesopotamia, and the countryside was in a state of unrest. 'We now put on the dress of the country and abandon as far as possible our character of Europeans', Henry told his aunt. He had been advised that in Persian dress they would attract less attention and that the Shias considered the European dress as indecent. Layard had grown a beard; he wore a long, flowing robe held at the waist by a shawl, loose trousers and a tall, black lamb-skin hat; on horseback he stuffed his robes into the full trousers and passed as a Persian provided he kept his mouth shut. It is not certain that Mitford agreed to put on Persian dress, although Layard, when he wrote to his aunt, was expecting him to; but Mitford had strong views on the matter: 'I always wore an English dress, as any disguise would have exposed me to danger and detention; disguise should never be resorted to but in cases of extreme emergency, and quitted as soon as its purpose has been answered.' Their journey by caravan was not 'an emergency' and they could not conceal the fact that they were not Moslems. There were about seventy persons and fifty-five animals led by two old Turks on very small donkeys whose duty it was to find the way during the early part of the night when there was no moon. Layard wrote to his mother:

> Our caravan is chiefly composed of poor pilgrims and their wives. One or two, however, boast the title of *Mirza*, a writer (equivalent to our ancient term 'clerk'), and consider themselves considerably above the common herd. They are attended by their hookah-bearer, a man whose sole employment, day and night, is to light the hookah and present it to his master. This he does on horseback with great dexterity, carrying the pipe with all its fragile appendages at arm's length, when at full gallop. As these good priests and pilgrims are returning with a bellyful of religion, and the Persians are notoriously more fanatic than the Turks and Arabs, we are looked at with no little contempt.

Whenever the caravan stopped the Englishmen had to spread their carpets away from the 'True-Believers'; the water brought from the village was jealously guarded lest 'the infidels' should defile the pots by drinking from them and a mullah from Meshed cursed them in a loud voice as they rode through the night. Some of the pilgrims became so insolent that Layard and Mitford had to defend themselves against them with the butt-ends of their rifles. The Englishmen's difficulties increased when they crossed the Turco-Persian frontier as relations between Britain and Persia were still strained and there were many rumours of a possible war. Layard's mother had written to say that young Edgar was a very keen lepidopterist and hoped that his brother would be able to send him some unusual insects during his travels, 'You must tell Edgar', Layard wrote at the end of the journey, 'that I found it utterly impossible to collect insects for him, altho' I often think of his wishes on the subject.'

The two Englishmen arrived in Kermanshah after about ten days of travel. The day after their arrival Layard took Mitford to see the wonderful sculptures at Taki-Bostan. Here they found M. Flandin, who was attached to the French Mission at Teheran and was making drawings of the sculptures.

Layard wrote an enthusiastic letter to his mother about the sculptures of Tak-i-Bostan and of Bisutun.* He wanted to spend many days exploring, but the travellers were told that in order to obtain permission to pursue their journey they would have to see the Shah or his Vizier, who were with the Persian army. Layard was also very anxious to visit the great Seistan Desert, a hundred miles across, part of it in Persia and part in Afghanistan. He was interested because it was the birthplace of the ancient

* The drawings of these beautiful monuments were published by MM. Flandin and Coste in *Voyage en Perse* (Paris, 1851). The two Frenchmen had arrived in Persia in April 1840 and were part of the Mission of Ambassador M. de Sercey sent by King Louis Philippe to Mohamed Shah. Flandin and Coste had been entrusted with the task of copying as much as possible of the trilingual cuneiform inscription on the high rock of Bisutun, some of which had already been copied by Major Rawlinson at considerable risk to himself. The French savants, such as Burnouf and Julius Mohl, were extremely anxious to have these copies but Flandin and Coste were unable to make them since they were deterred by the difficulty of the ascent.

Bisutun, showing the famous tablet with the trilingual cuneiform inscriptions high up on the smooth cliff-face. (Drawing by MM. Flandin and Coste

51

Tak-i-Bostan

Zoroastrian religion and there were reports of great ruined cities near Lake Furrah and the Helmond river. At that time it was practically unexplored, except for an expedition sent from India by Sir John Malcolm consisting of Captain W. P. Grant and Lieutenant Henry Pottinger; the latter had published an account in 1816 but Captain Grant, with Lieutenant Fotheringham, had been murdered in 1810 by the Feili Lurs of Pusht-i-Kuh, and his account was not published until 1829. A year after Layard's visit to Hamadan the traveller, Dr. Forbes, was murdered while travelling in the Seistan.

Layard and Mitford caught up with the Persian army at Kangobar near Hamadan and they waited at the roadside to see the Shah and his army pass by. First came the ladies of the harem enveloped in thick veils, some riding horses and others carried in closed litters. Mohamed Shah then followed riding a magnificent white Turcoman horse adorned with gold and silver ornaments, accompanied by his son and Vizier, the Haji Mirza Agasi; then came the Ministers, the Shah's household and a great retinue of officers and notables. Four elephants, fantastically painted with all the colours of the rainbow and adorned in richly embroidered trappings, had been sent out from Hamadan to meet the Shah. 'The country and villages they pass through', Layard wrote, 'are left a desert, the crops destroyed and the trees uprooted.' After several days waiting for an audience the Englishmen were eventually received by the Vizier, who was notorious for his misgovernment and for his hatred of Christians; he refused to let them go to the Seistan Desert through Yezd or Kerman. Layard was so anxious to go that he even went to the length of arguing that when Captain Grant and Lieutenant Fotheringham had been murdered, the British Government had demanded no redress because they were simple travellers, and that he and Mitford were in the same position. The Vizier finally gave in to Layard's persistence on condition that they signed a declaration that they had taken the route contrary to his advice, and that the Persian Government was in no way responsible for their safety. Layard with his usual impetuosity 'willingly consented' but Mitford declined, considering that it would be a mad idea to go under such conditions; the Persians obviously thought them spies and would kill them once they were in open country. The Vizier had, in fact, been told that the Englishmen were on a mission to explore a new route by which an English army could invade Persia from Afghanistan. After yet another meeting the Vizier finally allowed them to journey anywhere in the Shah's territory, but withdrew the permission he had previously given to Layard to travel through the Seistan. Mitford, who had had enough of the Persians—'the vilest race that ever were called into a nation'—wanted to leave and accepted the Vizier's offer to travel to India via Meshed and Herat. Layard, however, was not to be deflected. He intended to see some ruins in the Bakhtiari mountains described by Rawlinson, and he believed that, if he waited until the spring, he would be able to make his way to India through the Seistan.

The two men thus reached the parting of their ways. It is difficult to tell how much of Layard's decision was due to an obstinate refusal to be thwarted by authority or how eager he was to return to the Mosul area—he certainly tried to induce the French architect Coste, who was with Flandin, to come with him to make drawings at al Hatra and Nineveh. What he had seen of Assyrian and ancient Persian remains had certainly excited his imagination, and there are indications that he was uncertain as to whether he intended to continue the journey to Ceylon. Mitford was distressed at the prospect of parting. He had seen how necessary it was to curb Layard's impetuosity; he was also anxious for Layard's health, since malaria at times made him delirious for many hours and was followed by complete exhaustion. He argued that it was much safer for the two of them to travel together, but Layard was obdurate.

Mitford and Layard had been together for over a year and estimated that they had not spent more than about four shillings a day between them since they had left England—but this did not include sums of money of which Layard had been robbed in the mountains of Moab and in Hamadan where his purse had been stolen. Of the three hundred pounds placed with Messrs. Coutts for Layard's journey, over two hundred pounds was still in the bank, but he had no means of drawing a bill in Hamadan and was without funds. He was saved embarrassment by the arrival of Baron de Bode of the Russian Embassy in Teheran, who helped both Layard and Mitford to obtain permission from the Shah to travel and advanced Layard ten pounds against a bill on Coutts' Bank. Mitford was now ready to leave and on 20 August 1840 they parted company. Layard said that Mitford had proved 'an excellent fellow-traveller, never complaining, ready to meet any difficulties or any hardships, and making the best of everything'.

Adventures with the Bakhtiari

After Mitford's departure Layard tried to cross the Bakhtiari mountains southwards into the rich plains fed by the Disful and Karun rivers, but he met hostile tribesmen, had another bout of malaria and decided to make his way eastwards to Isfahan. There he was befriended by a Frenchman, M. Boré, who was in charge of several Roman Catholic schools financed by the French Government; he also made friends with Mr. Edward Burgess, an English merchant of Tabriz who was visiting Isfahan. Layard asked for an audience with the Governor, Manuchar Khan, who had quarrelled with Rawlinson three years earlier and was to play a sinister part in Layard's life during the next few months. He was a Georgian, born of Christian parents, who had been purchased as a slave when a boy, castrated, and brought up as a Moslem. Because of his ability and ruthlessness he had risen high in the service of the Shah and had been appointed to govern the great province of Isfahan. This included the wild and independent Bakhtiari and Lur tribes, often in rebellion, and the unruly Arabs of the plains between the Luristan mountains and the Euphrates river. Manuchar Khan was hated and feared for his cruelty. 'He was known', said Layard, 'for the ingenuity with which he invented new forms of punishment and torture to strike terror into evil-doers' but he maintained order 'with a kind of rough justice.'

Layard was accompanied by Edward Burgess at his first audience. He found Manuchar Khan sitting on a chair by a large open window in a beautifully ornamented room. Those who had business with him advanced with repeated bows and then stood humbly before him as if awe-struck by his presence; the sleeves of their robes were closely buttoned and their hands were joined in front in the usual attitude of respect which can be seen in ancient eastern sculptures. In the pond of fresh water in the centre of the large court were bundles of long switches cut from the pomegranate tree, ready for use in the bastinado; in one corner was a pole with two loops of cord to raise the feet of the victims who would writhe on the floor and scream for mercy. Manuchar Khan had the usual characteristics of the eunuch; he was beardless, had a smooth colourless face with sagging cheeks, a wearied and listless appearance, and a weak, shrill, feminine voice. He was short, stout, and flabby with ungainly limbs; his tunic was of the finest cashmere and he carried a jewel-handled dagger in the shawl folded round his waist.

Manuchar Khan received Layard and Burgess courteously, said a few civil things about the English nation, which he distinguished from the English Government, and invited them to take their places on a carpet spread near him. After seeing the Shah's firman he gave Layard permission to visit the Bakhtiari country, but refused to allow him to travel through Yezd or Kerman to the Seistan, arguing that the British occupation of Afghanistan had caused great unrest in central Asia and on the Persian eastern and southern frontiers. It was reported that Aga Khan, who was venerated in southern Persia, was raising an insurrection against the Shah, supported by the British Government. Owing to the danger of trouble to the east of Persia, the Shah had decided to bring back his army from the contemplated

invasion of Bagdad. Layard realised that it was useless to argue
further about visiting the Seistan, but he welcomed being
allowed to travel into the Bakhtiari mountains with one of the
chiefs, Shefia Khan, who was then in Isfahan. He went to find
Shefia Khan to obtain his permission to travel with him; the
latter was about to return to the mountain stronghold of Kala
Tul, the headquarters of Mohamed Taki Khan, the powerful
chief of the Chehar Lang tribe of the Bakhtiari. Shefia Khan was
friendly but said that he must take Layard to Ali Naghi Khan.

> Ali Naghi Khan was the second brother of Mohamed Taki Khan,
> who at that time exercised authority over the greater part of the
> Bakhtiari mountains. He was on his way to Teheran, to be kept as
> hostage for the good conduct of the chief, whose loyalty was
> suspected, and who had recently been in open rebellion against the
> Shah. . . .
> He was a short, thick-set man, of about forty years of age, not
> ill-looking, and with an intelligent, though somewhat false,
> countenance. Shefia Khan, kneeling down by his side, whispered
> to him the object of my visit. As soon as he learnt that I was an
> Englishman, he begged me to sit on the felt rug by his side, bade
> me welcome in very cordial terms, * and offered me a cup of iced
> Shiraz wine and sweetmeats, which I could not refuse. We soon
> became boon companions over the bottle.

While Layard waited for the Bakhtiari to leave for the mountains his friends in Isfahan continued to urge that it was folly to
trust himself to so treacherous and cruel a tribe, but he looked
forward to the expedition with enthusiasm. He was especially
anxious to investigate a report by Major Rawlinson† to the
Royal Geographical Society that the famous and ancient city of
Susan or Susa, 'Shushan the Palace' of the Bible, was on the
banks of the Karun river in the Bakhtiari mountains. Rawlinson
was considered to be the authority on the area and this statement
had aroused considerable controversy among experts in London,

* The English were popular because they were at enmity with the
Persians.
† 'Notes on a March from Zohab at the foot of the Zagros along the
Mountains of Khuzistan (Susiana) and from thence through the Pro-
vince of Luristan to Kirmanshah in the year 1836', by Major Rawlinson
of the Bombay Army serving in Persia. R.G.S. *Journal*, vol. ix.

for it had long been considered that the Susa near Disful on the Kerkhah river, many miles to the west, was the true site. Rawlinson had not himself visited the site, and Layard was determined to go there.

Layard thought very little about the journey to Ceylon and hardly mentioned it in his letters from Isfahan to Montague Place where his mother was staying with the Austens. He told her that his expedition westwards into the Bakhtiari mountains would enable him to visit a country which had been almost inaccessible to Europeans: 'There are many ruins of great interest in it and I hope to make some very important discoveries'; he would then visit Persepolis, Shapur, and the southern province of Persia and he thought of reaching Kandahar by the following winter: 'Should I find Major Rawlinson in the latter city I may probably spend the winter there, as I should be glad of his assistance in acquiring the eastern languages.' Marianne Layard had already been most upset by her son's letters about his adventures in Moab in an area where there had been plague. Crabb Robinson had visited the Austens and had been shocked that Layard should have written 'a most unfeeling letter to his mother' about his life being threatened by an Arabian chief and of his touching bodies infected by plague, 'all either false, or exaggerations or most unfeeling and thoughtless disclosures'. Marianne Layard then received letters from Isfahan giving terrible stories of Persian barbarities; a man had had his teeth pulled out and hammered into his head, wrote Layard, another was shod with his own teeth and left to die with his head forced into a bag of hay; the Governor of Shiraz had built a tower of tribesmen who had rebelled, covering each successive layer of living men with mortar. His mother wrote that she would be only too relieved when she heard that he had quitted Persia, as he was 'among a set of savages without faith, justice, or mercy'. Benjamin Austen could find no explanation in any of Layard's letters as to why he had parted company with Mitford and now intended to travel back westwards instead of eastwards towards Ceylon to earn his living. Unsatisfactory as these letters might be they were the last news they received of him for the next six months.

*   *   *

Ch. 4   *Adventures with the Bakhtiari*

The caravan finally assembled and started on 23 September 1840. The tribesmen looked ferocious but seemed friendly; as they journeyed two wives of one of the Bakhtiari chiefs talked to Layard who was now fluent enough in Persian to converse. One had a daughter of five years old with large black eyes and long, silken lashes, who insisted on riding with him on his saddle. When the caravan halted they sat together on a carpet and she played with his watch. 'She was', said Layard, 'adorned with all the trinkets that her mother had been able to save from the pawn-brokers of Isfahan; her little feet were dyed with henna, and her wrists and ankles encircled with numerous gold and silver bangles. Her name was Bibi Mah—Lady Moon.'

They travelled over high mountain passes by such steep and rough tracks that the horses were badly lamed. 'I could trace the line of route by the blood from our horses' feet', he told his mother. After twelve days they arrived at the castle of Kala Tul. To the north lay the mountains over which they had come, while to the west were the rich valleys fed by several rivers, the great Syrian desert stretching to the mountains of Lebanon and to the Mediterranean, a thousand miles away. Crowds were there to welcome their friends and relations in the caravan, for no news had come of them in their absence, and the Bakhtiari always distrusted the Persian authorities. Mohamed Taki Khan, the Chief of the Chehar Lang, was away and his three brothers escorted Layard to a large guest-room where were a number of visitors. He spread his carpet and possessions in a corner and settled down. Among the visitors were two holy men, reputed to be doctors, who had been brought to attend Mohamed Taki Khan's eldest son suffering from high fever. Soon after his arrival Layard was asked by the Chief's principal wife, Khatun-jan Khanum, to visit her ten-year-old son, Hussein Kuli. Layard was taken to a large hut constructed from boughs of trees, the floor of which was spread with the finest carpets. The mother was unveiled and watching over her son, her young women attendants with her. She was a tall, dark, graceful woman, still young and singularly handsome; her hair fell in tresses down her back, and a purple silk kerchief bound her forehead. She came forward to welcome Layard to Kala Tul in the name of her husband and he was captivated by her sweet and kindly

59

expression. She entreated him with tears to save her son; the boy was in a very weak state from intermittent fever of which Layard had had plenty of experience. He gave her quinine but the Moslem doctors would not allow it to be taken and insisted on continuing their own primitive treatment.

As nothing could be done to help the boy, and as Mohamed Taki Khan had not yet returned, Layard decided to set out to explore Susa: 'On the first day I reached an encampment in the plain of Mal-Emir', he told his mother. 'In a rocky ridge forming the western boundary to the plain I found four tablets sculptured in the rock with several colossal human figures, accompanied by several long inscriptions in the most complicated of the cuneiform character, a great part of which was unfortunately effaced. I believe these sculptures, from their appearance and accompanied as they are by this character, to be of the most remote antiquity.' He made a drawing of the figures and copied thirty-six lines of cuneiform, but he was hampered by a crowd of tribesmen who were angry that he would not reveal the hiding place of treasure, and he had to return on another occasion to check his copy[1]. The figures were at the entrance to a cave known as Shikefti-Salman, 'much larger than life, sculptured in the rock . . . in high relief and skilfully executed'. He had considered returning to Kala Tul since the tribesmen were so hostile, but having found the Assyrian sculptures he was determined to go on, hoping that he would discover that Rawlinson had been right in asserting that ancient Susa was in the neighbourhood. 'The following day', he told his mother, 'I quitted the encampment for Susan [Susa]. A high range of mountains separate Susan from Mal-Emir. On crossing them I was attacked in a narrow gorge. Unfortunately I had been prevailed upon to leave my arms at the castle, and had only a small dagger. I defended myself, however, as well as I could, but was soon forced to submit, and to deliver up my watch and the little money I had in my possession.' They also took his compass, which meant that he could not make observations required for mapping. After a difficult journey he crossed the Karun river and delivered a letter he had brought from Kala Tul to the Chief of Susa. Layard was the first European they had seen and he spent two anxious days as they were extremely suspicious: 'The most ridiculous causes were assigned for my arrival. Some asserted that I had come to spy the country previous to an attack projected by the King of England; whilst others asserted that my object was the acquisition of a treasure which my forefathers, who had once occupied the land, had deposited there, and the site of which had been written in our books.' Rawlinson had correctly stated that there was a *mesjid*, or temple, at Susan and the ruins of a bridge. When Layard asked to be taken to see them they were utterly at a loss to understand how he could know about them and their suspicions were increased. At first they refused to send a guide with him but finally agreed.

I had not proceeded far when several armed men joined us. I perceived that their matchlocks were lighted. They were no doubt ready to fight for their share of the treasures which they were convinced I was about to discover. Being unarmed, I was unable to resist any violence that might be offered to me. I deemed it therefore best to assume an indifferent and unconcerned air, as if I entertained no suspicion of my unwelcome companions. After crossing numerous swampy rice-fields we came to the Karun, and continued along its banks until we reached a narrow gorge in the mountains, through which the river issues into the valley of Susan. About a mile within this gorge, in a small open space, I found the ruins of what was called the *mesjid*, or temple. There was nothing above ground to show that an edifice of any importance had ever stood there—no columns nor dressed stones, not even a mound, only some rough masonry, apparently the foundations of a building of the Sassanian period. These remains were, however, known to the Lurs as the Mesjid-i-Suleiman, the temple of Solomon.* At a short distance beyond them were the ruins of a bridge, of which four massive buttresses still resisted the force of the torrent. . . . I could trace on both banks an ancient paved causeway, a continuation, no doubt, of the road that I had seen in the valley of Susan . . . possibly the remains of one of the great highways which in the time of Darius led from the plains of Susiana to the highlands of Persia and to Persepolis. I traced it subsequently in many places between Mal-Emir and Shuster.

---

* On 26 May 1908, oil was struck at Mesjid-i-Suleiman, which became known in the oil world in the shortened form of MIS, and it was the beginning of great developments which transformed wild tribesmen into skilled mechanics.

Layard subsequently paid another visit to Susan on the Karun river to make sure that he had not missed anything, but he found no trace of cuneiform writing or any ancient mounds to confirm Rawlinson's story that this was the site of the famous city. He was disappointed that there had been little to find of the Assyrian and Babylonian periods. In the notes on his journey, which were later published by the Royal Geographical Society, he stated that the description given by Rawlinson of the ruins of Manjanik was also 'far from correct'. There were the remains of what must have been quite a large city but there were no mounds of any consequence and the buildings had probably been of the Sassanian period: 'I have experienced', he wrote, 'the difficulty of obtaining correct information as to things and places from the Persians, and I am not surprised that Major Rawlinson should have been misled by their exaggerated accounts.*

It is not known what were Rawlinson's reactions when he read that account for he did not require a lesson in the unreliability of Persian information but, like Layard, he was impulsive; although he thought he had checked and counter-checked the information, he had been unwise to publish details without paying a visit himself to both Manjanik and Susan. Professor Long, who had published papers to prove that the famous city of Susa was near Disful, made use of Layard's first-hand report to discredit Rawlinson and referred to the 'worthlessness of his evidence' in saying that the correct site was on the Karun river.

*   *   *

Layard returned to the castle of Tul after his first expedition. He reported the loss of his watch and compass, and a horseman was immediately despatched to the Chief of the Mal-Emir tribes with a message that his nose and ears would be cut off if the property were not immediately given up. The watch and compass were returned.

Layard found the Chief's son very gravely ill and Mohamed Taki Khan had been sent for in haste as it was believed that the

* *Journal* of the Royal Geographical Society, vol. xii, 1842, p. 102. 'Ancient Sites among the Bakhtiari Mountains' extracted from a communication by A. H. Layard, Esq., dated 31 December 1840.[2]

boy was dying. Layard waited anxiously with the assembled Bakhtiari for his arrival, wondering whether or not he would be well received. The Chief of the Chehar Lang rode into the crowd on a beautiful Arab stallion; he was about fifty years old, rather corpulent but with a commanding presence, his face disfigured by the blow of a mace which had broken his nose. Layard presented his firman from the Shah and his letter from Manuchar Khan, the Governor of Isfahan. The Chief threw them contemptuously on the ground saying that the Shah's firman had no authority among them; he added, however, that he had heard good reports of Layard from his brother Shefia Khan, who had escorted him to Tul, and that he was welcome. He then went into the women's quarters to see his wife and son. It was not long before the Englishman was summoned. The Chief was crouched on the ground sobbing and the women wailing; the two Moslem physicians had said that they could do no more and that the boy would die. Layard was begged to do what he could. This time he was allowed to administer medicine—quinine and Dr. Dover's Powder.

It was a classic situation. If the child recovered Layard would earn the gratitude of the father and mother; if the boy died he would probably be accused by the Moslem doctors of having poisoned him and might well have been put to death. He remained at the boy's bedside watching anxiously. Towards midnight Hussein Kuli broke into a violent sweat and began to recover. From then on Layard was counted as a member of the Chief's family. Khatun-jan Khanum was, he said, one of the kindest women he ever knew; she treated him with the affection of a mother, nursed him when he was delirious with fever, and took charge of his valuables when he went in search of Assyrian sculptures. Her young sister, Khanumi, was the most beautiful woman in all the tribe: 'Her features were of exquisite delicacy, her eyes large, black and almond-shaped, her hair of the darkest hue; she was intelligent and lively.' Mohamed Taki Khan often said that if Layard would become a Moslem and settle with them he should have her as a wife.

Layard found the women very attractive. They wore, he said, loose trousers of chintz or of red silk or velvet, frequently embroidered with gold. Their breasts and bodies down to the waists were exposed, except when receiving strangers, when they would also hide their faces and necks: 'What women may leave uncovered and what they must keep carefully concealed not to offend modesty, is a question of habit and fashion. I have seen Arab girls on the banks of the rivers of Mesopotamia raise their one solitary blue shirt and bring it over their heads to hide their faces from a European.' He was very interested in the custom of *sigha* which enabled a man 'to marry for a period, however short—even for twenty-four hours—and which makes the contract for the time legal'. He told Sara Austen that he did not think that he would ever be idle enough to marry, but he wished he could, like the Persians, take a partner for a week or any other reasonable period. As he was treated as a member of the Chief's family, hospitality might have included even the beautiful Khanumi herself.

*   *   *

Layard gives a delightful picture of life with Mohamed Taki Khan and his family in his *Early Adventures*: Lord Curzon described it as 'one of the most romantic narratives of adventure ever penned'. Rawlinson, Layard, and Baron de Bode were among the first to make a real study of this part of the country and to write about the Bakhtiari who have played so important a part in the history of Persia. 'The Bakhtiari', Layard told Benjamin Austen, 'are without doubt the descendants of the Parthians and have occupied their mountains free and unconquered for centuries'; he described the many things that the Chief had done to try to settle his people and to keep them from plundering caravans and murdering travellers. 'He has built castles and founded villages and encouraged, as far as it lay in his power, a steady cultivation of the rich valleys of his mountains.'

Layard spent several weeks hunting lion, exploring ruins, and talking with Mohamed Taki Khan about developing trade between the rich hinterland controlled by the Bakhtiari and the Persian Gulf and India. Layard was delighted to find the Chief well aware of the advantages of such trade.

This happy picture of Layard and the Chief planning the

development of the country, a subject which interested Layard as much as ancient ruins, was soon to be shattered. There was a great deal of unrest in Persia and the exiled Persian princes, whom Layard had met in Bagdad, were intriguing against the Shah, and had offered various inducements to Mohamed Taki Khan to join with them. The Chief received a letter from one of his brothers, held hostage in Teheran, revealing that the Governor of Isfahan was aware that Mohamed Taki Khan had received these communications and had informed the Shah. At the same time orders came from the Persian Government in Teheran that he was to pay the equivalent of five thousand pounds in tax and that Manuchar Khan was being sent with an army to collect the money. The Chief could not decide what to do and called on his brother, Shefia Khan, and on Layard to advise him. Shefia Khan recommended that every effort should be made to placate the Persian Government in order to prevent an invasion of the mountains, and it was agreed that Shefia Khan should visit the tribes and collect as much tribute as possible. Layard was to visit the British military authorities in the island of Karak (Kharg) in the Persian Gulf to find out if they intended to invade Persia. The British had occupied the island in 1838 in order to threaten the Shah's southern provinces and force him to withdraw his troops from the siege of Herat in Afghanistan; the manoeuvre had been successful but the British troops had remained, and aroused much discussion and rumour. Mohamed Taki Khan must have suspected Layard of being a British political agent and hoped that the Bakhtiari might become independent if there were war between England and Persia. The Shah wished to break the power of Mohamed Taki Khan and the Chehar Lang before the British or the Persian exiles in Bagdad and other dissidents exploited the situation. Layard realised how useful the Bakhtiari would be to an invading British force and how important he himself would be to them. It was estimated that Mohamed Taki Khan could muster twelve thousand foot soldiers and three thousand horsemen, the best troops in Persia. Mohamed Taki Khan told Layard that he did not want to take up the cause of the exiled Persian princes until he knew whether there was a chance of the British going to war against Persia.

Layard left the castle of Tul on horseback on 8 December

1840, and ten days later reached Karak, where he found Colonel Hennell, Resident of the East India Company, with a small military force and a squadron of the East India Company's navy. Layard was informed that differences between Britain and Persia were likely to be settled in the near future and that on no account should he encourage the Bakhtiari Chief to think that any British support would be forthcoming. Whilst in Karak Layard received letters from his family written four months previously which had been sent on from Bombay. His Aunt Louisa said that she found it difficult to write, so strong was her feeling that he would be dead before the letter reached him; she said she would start a letter, put it back in her desk and set off for a walk 'or do anything I could to shake off the impression which haunted me'. Henry Layard was now twenty-four, self-centred, full of romantic ideas, and like a Bakhtiari in his passion for independence. It would have been wiser to have told his family less about the Bakhtiari and more about his plans for earning a living or, at least, to have shown that he understood their anxiety. His letters continued to encourage his uncle and aunt to think that he had no intention of proceeding to Ceylon, but was going to wander about until he had spent all the money that his mother had given to him. He wrote to his Uncle Benjamin:

> The little confidence that is to be placed in the greater part of mankind has made me sick of the civilised and semi-civilised world and I live happier under a black Bakhtiari tent with liberty of speech and action and nobody to depend upon, no-one to flatter, certain that I shall have dinner tomorrow—for there is always bread and water—and without need of that source of all evil, money . . . I trust the period I may spend in seeing men and manners; visiting countries almost unknown at this time but once the seat of civilisation and from whence the sciences, the arts, philosophy, and all that tends to enlarge men's minds, flowed into Europe, may not be considered as time ill-spent.

He argued, though not very clearly, that he could do all this without expense. He would have enough funds to reach Bombay and would make no further calls upon his mother; his three hundred pounds was still untouched, he said, and in the hands of his Uncle Charles in Ceylon. Layard did not then know that the bill on Coutts's, which he had given to Baron de Bode, had been refused in London because the bank had not received adequate instructions (the fifteen pounds that he borrowed in Karak from the British Resident against a similar bill was to suffer the same fate); nor did he know that his Uncle Charles was on the verge of bankruptcy. He may have heard rumours that all was not well, for in one letter to Austen he remarked that he trusted that his uncle's family in Ceylon was such as he had been led to expect it was. If so, he might spend many happy days there 'but I fear the course to be pursued in order to get on in India and Ceylon would little agree with my feelings; I have never and shall never bend to any man and if my advancement in life depends upon flattery and hypocrisy I shall most probably remain where I am'. Layard left Karak at the end of the year, 1840, and his family heard nothing further from him for another nine months.

*   *   *

At the castle of Tul, Layard was greeted joyfully by Khatun-jan Khanum and the other women; some had thought he would remain with his countrymen once he had reached the island of Karak. Mohamed Taki Khan and the other chieftains, with most of their retainers and horsemen, had gone to the plain of Mal-Emir to meet Manuchar Khan, Governor of Isfahan, who was crossing the mountains with a large army. He was determined to reduce the power of Mohamed Taki Khan and to collect arrears of taxes from the Bakhtiari tribes and from the rich townsmen of Shuster and Disful in the plains to the west of the mountains; with him was the chieftain's brother, Ali Naghi Khan, as hostage.

While Layard had been travelling from Karak to Kala Tul, which had taken him many days, Mohamed Taki Khan had been undecided whether to prevent the Persian army from crossing the mountains with their artillery, which he could easily have done, or whether to wait to greet Manuchar Khan in a friendly manner on the plain of Mal-Emir. He waited—a decision which he was soon to regret.

Khatun-jan Khanum was worried lest harm might befall her

husband and she thought there was a danger of Kala Tul being attacked by Bakhtiari who were at emnity with him, since so few able-bodied tribesmen remained. There was rumour that a raiding party had been seen a few miles away and she was sending a small force under one of her relations to reconnoitre. Layard accompanied them and at dawn the next day they saw in the distance a company of horsemen. The Bakhtiari hid in a ravine and made preparations to attack, eager for booty. Layard thought he saw an European amongst the party and prevailed upon his companions to let him reconnoitre. It shows the influence that Layard had acquired and in what trust he was held that they agreed to let him go. Layard went out alone and when he was near to the European addressed him in French. 'He was not a little surprised to be addressed in that language by a Bakhtiari for whom, on account of my dress, he at first mistook me. I found him to be the Baron de Bode, the Secretary of the Russian Embassy, whose acquaintance I had made in the Shah's camp at Hamadan. He was accompanied by an escort of irregular horse, which had been furnished him by the Persian authorities, and had a train of servants and baggage mules. He informed me that he was on his way to join the Matamet [Manuchar Khan].'

Layard returned to Kala Tul and then left to join Mohamed Taki Khan with the Chief's two elder sons whom Khatun-jan had committed to his care. Layard and Hussein Kuli had become very good friends: 'He was one of those beautiful boys who are constantly seen in Persia, and especially among the mountain tribes, and was intelligent, high-spirited, brave, and dauntless— inheriting all the qualities of his father.' The boys would have been safer at home, but Mohamed Taki Khan wished to do full honours to the Governor of Isfahan in the hope that he would appease him. When he was told that there would be no help from the British, as they were likely to make peace with the Persians, the Chief believed at first that he had taken the right decision. They waited in the plain while Ali Naghi Khan guided the Persian army through the mountain passes; the Bakhtiari tribesmen in the mountains had even been told to help the Persian artillerymen to get their guns through the difficult places.

When Layard had previously seen the plain of Mal-Emir he

had been alone and it had been a deserted enclave in the mountains. There were now about eight thousand wild and savage-looking men, firing off guns, careering about on fine horses, performing war dances, and shouting war cries. Baron de Bode, who accompanied Manuchar Khan, was astonished at the sight when he first saw the assembly of Bakhtiari in the plain: 'I never witnessed a greater display of beautiful Arab-blooded horses than on the plains of Mal-Emir at the camp of the Bakhtiari Chief.' [3] Layard described the meeting between Mohamed Taki Khan and Manuchar Khan, who is given his abbreviated title, Matamet:

> Accompanied by his two little sons, and by a large retinue of horsemen mounted upon the finest Arab horses, he went to meet the Matamet. The road by which the Eunuch entered the plain was lined by several thousand men, armed with matchlocks, which they discharged incessantly, whilst clouds of Bakhtiari and Arab horsemen engaged in mimic fight—pursuing each other, bringing up their horses on their haunches at full speed, firing their guns or pistols as they turned back in their saddles, and performing various other feats for which their ancestors in Parthian times were renowned.
>
> The Matamet appeared surrounded by his officers and guards and followed by a motley crowd of horsemen. Before him walked the *farrashes* dealing blows right and left with their long sticks upon all within reach, on pretence of clearing a way for the great man. They were preceded by *lûtis,* or buffoons, with oboes and drums, and by a number of dervishes invoking Allah and the Prophet with loud cries.

Mohamed Taki Khan sent his two sons in advance to welcome his guest; they were lifted from their horses to be kissed by Manuchar Khan. The Chief followed them and dismounted to show respect to the Shah's representative. Layard followed and was at once recognised by Manuchar Khan, who expressed surprise at seeing him still with the Bakhtiari. The Persian army pitched their tents in the plain about two or three miles from the Bakhtiari camp.

Once the Bakhtiari chiefs had seen that the Persian army was not large or well-disciplined and could be easily overcome, they advised Mohamed Taki Khan to carry out a surprise night-time attack. He was at first in favour of the plan, but Ali Naghi

Khan, the hostage, argued that an attack would only lead to the ruin of the Bakhtiari, since the Shah would take revenge. He said that when Manuchar Khan found he could not break the power of the Chief by force or through treachery, he would tire of life in the mountains; if he could be given a sufficiently large sum of money he would move on to Shuster. Mohamed Taki Khan finally yielded to his brother's cautious advice; unfortunately the unity that existed amongst the various Bakhtiari tribes did not endure. Manuchar Khan paid a visit to the castle of Tul and then moved to Shuster; from there he set to work to suborn or subjugate the petty chieftains. In the plains he was able to display the strength and quality of his artillery which helped to win over waverers.*

Mohamed Taki Khan was no match for Manuchar Khan in cunning and it became clear to those waiting to see which side to take that the Chief was steadily losing the initiative. Manuchar Khan having observed his deep affection for his eldest son, demanded that Hussein Kuli, and the son of Ali Naghi Khan, be handed over as hostages; at the same time he took a solemn oath that he would abandon his expedition and return with his army to Isfahan when the boys were handed over. Ali Naghi Khan, the hostage, brought this message to the castle of Tul and again persuaded his brother to follow a policy of appeasement. There was a tragic scene at the castle when Khatun-jan Khanum refused to part with Hussein Kuli and denounced Ali Naghi Khan as a traitor who had given evil advice and betrayed the Bakhtiari.

When Hussein Kuli was placed on his horse, ready to leave the castle, she dragged him off again, and, clinging to him refused to let him go. He was at last taken by force from her by the attendants. When she found that her efforts to retain him were of no avail, she consented to his departure on condition that I accompanied him to Shuster and watched over his safety, as she believed that my presence would prevent the Matamet from threatening the boy with cruelty. I consented to do so to satisfy her, but with little hope of being able to protect him.

* The Persian artillery was better trained than other elements of the army. Baillie Fraser and Baron de Bode considered that European troops could not have handled their heavy field-pieces in difficult ground so well.

Mohamed Taki Khan was sitting by the gate sobbing like a woman and beating his naked breast; Khatun-jan and the other women followed the horsemen on foot wailing and crying aloud, then they cut off their long tresses and trampled them in the dust. Khatun-jan kissed her son and returned to the castle. Hussein Kuli was much moved at the parting but he showed no fear. He was mounted on his father's favourite mare and was dressed as a Bakhtiari chief; round his waist was a leather belt, which held a long pistol, a jewel-handled dagger, and his powder flask. Across his saddle-bow was a small gun of Khorassan damascene work which his father had had made for him; his silver-mounted sword hung on one side of his saddle-girths and an inlaid iron mace on the other; he was 'the very picture of a young warrior'. His cousin, the son of Ali Naghi Khan, was about sixteen, studious, unarmed, and with a copy of the Koran suspended round his neck. The boys' tutor and a small body of horsemen accompanied them. On the afternoon of the fifth day they reached Shuster. They found Manuchar Khan in a stronghold built on a rock overhanging the river Kerkhah. Layard accompanied the two boys and gives an account of the scene in his *Early Adventures*:

> He received us at once. He could not conceal the smile of satisfaction and triumph which passed over his bloated and repulsive features when the children stood before him. I saw at once that he had no intention of keeping the oath he had taken to renounce the expedition against Mohamed Taki Khan now that he had secured his son as a hostage. . . . He addressed Hussein Kuli sternly in his thin, shrill voice:
>
> "Why have you not brought your father with you? Is he not coming to Shuster to see me?"
>
> "No", replied the boy with an undaunted air, his hand resting on his gun.
>
> "What if I were to send soldiers to fetch him?"
>
> "Let them go to Kala Tul. They will all come back naked like this", putting his forefinger into his mouth and then withdrawing it and holding it up—a significant gesture employed by the Bakhtiari to denote that they have stripped a man to his skin. The Matamet could not help laughing and admiring the boy's courage and calm intrepidity. But addressing him in a menacing tone:

"Has not your father got much gold?"

"I know nothing of such things as I am a child."

"You know, however, the place where he conceals it, and if you do not tell me where it is willingly, I shall have to make you."

"It is not likely that my father should have shown me the spot where he hides his money. If I knew I should not tell you, and if I were compelled to do so, he would not let you have it."

Layard was astonished at the courage and self-possession of the ten-year-old Hussein Kuli and disgusted by the treachery of Manuchar Khan. Some of the Persian officers who had been present were ashamed at the Governor's behaviour and afterwards did their best to show friendliness to the children. Layard realised that it was essential to warn Mohamed Taki Khan that he was in danger and he left immediately before an order might be given to detain him. He rode hard, stopping at night in Bakhtiari tents where he had to tell the story of what happened in great detail. One old woman threw her arms round his neck saying: "Hussein Kuli will not bring shame upon his tribe." Mohamed Taki Khan was proud to hear of his son's behaviour, but he realised at last that Manuchar Khan intended to try to depose him. Khatun-jan attacked her husband for having trusted a cruel and treacherous eunuch, who held no oath sacred. Almost immediately a message came from Manuchar Khan to say that, unless Mohamed Taki Khan surrendered himself, the hostages would be put to death. The Bakhtiari Chief was in a tragic position and for some time could not make up his mind what to do. As a result of bribes and threats from Manuchar Khan, the Bakhtiari tribes were in disarray, confused in their loyalties, and fighting among themselves. Further north was the large Haft Lang Bakhtiari tribe ruled over by the powerful Jaffer Kuli Khan, who lived in an extraordinary mountain fortress which was said to be impregnable where Mohamed Taki Khan might have been safe if he could have trusted him. Negotiations continued between Mohamed Taki Khan and the Georgian Manuchar Khan without result. Layard realised that the Bakhtiari Chief was held back from taking action because Hussein Kuli was a hostage and so he rode back to Shuster to try to arrange his escape. There were many there who were prepared to help. The plan was to dress Hussein Kuli as a girl and there was no

reason why it should not have succeeded but at the last moment
the boy's tutor lost his nerve and refused to let Hussein Kuli
leave the house.

Learning that Mohamed Taki Khan had left Kala Tul, Layard
joined a number of Bakhtiari who intended to find him. It was
believed that the Chief had taken refuge in the marshes near
the Persian Gulf with the Cha'b tribe under the powerful and
friendly Sheikh Thamer. Layard and the Bakhtiari tried to escape
unnoticed by leaving Shuster singly and by different gates but
they were seen and, in the chase that followed, Layard was
separated from his companions and had to go on alone. He was
soon lost but was relieved when he came upon 'a strange and
forbidding company of dervishes'. The country was so unsettled
as a result of the Persian invasion that he decided that it was
safer to remain with the dervishes who were entertaining
companions.

> One or two were what the Persians call 'luti', young men with
> well-dyed curls, long garments, and conical cloth caps embroidered
> in many colours—debauched and dissolute fellows, who, under the
> guise of poverty and affecting abstinence and piety, were given to
> every manner of vice. Others were half-naked savages, with long
> hair hanging down their backs, and with the skin of gazelles on
> their shoulders—barefooted, dirty, and covered with vermin. They
> carried heavy iron maces, and seemed more disposed to exact than
> to ask for charity. One of the party was a hideous negro, with
> enormous projecting lips and of most ferocious mien. He wore
> nothing but a lion's skin, and carried a huge hatchet in his hand.

Layard lent his horse to one of them who was ill and travelled
with the dervishes on foot for several days. 'Although they were
a reckless and debauched set, they treated me with kindness,
shared the little food they had with me, and entertained me by
their proceedings. I learnt something from them of dervish life
and consequently of Eastern manners and habits little known to
Europeans.' It was unfortunate that the dervishes were on their
way to Shuster and that Layard felt obliged to remain with them.
The Georgian, however, had left with his army in pursuit of
Mohamed Taki Khan and no one in Shuster bothered to detain
Layard. He stayed in the house of a man of religion, Seyyid
Abou'l-Hassan whom he had met at Kala Tul. He also became

friendly with many of the merchants who were interested in his
ideas of developing trade with India making use of the rivers
leading to the Persian Gulf. Layard decided that he would make
another attempt to find Mohamed Taki Khan and at the same
time explore the area where the Euphrates and Tigris joined
and formed the Shatt el Arab before flowing into the Persian
Gulf. He believed that it would be possible for large boats to sail
up from the Persian Gulf through Basra as far as Shuster, which
would be a great advantage to trade. Equipped with line and
lead he took passage on a small boat leaving Shuster for Ahwaz
and spent the night in a crowded boat surreptitiously sounding
the depth of the water. He was satisfied that one of the Euphrates
steamers could navigate the river.

After a series of adventures Layard arrived at Kareiba, a large
village on the banks of the Jerrahi river. It was still a considerable
distance from Fellahia, Sheikh Thamer's headquarters, where
Layard expected to find Mohamed Taki Khan. Soon after his
arrival a message came from Sheikh Thamer ordering all the
villagers to leave immediately with their property for Fellahia,
as the Persians were advancing. The whole village was thrown
into commotion; rafts were made of the thick reeds which
covered many square miles of the area, and these were loaded
with household goods, animals, and families. By evening all had
started on their journey downstream; the Sheikh of the village
was the last to go and Layard expected to be invited to accompany
him, but he was refused, as he was an infidel Christian. Night
approached in the deserted village full of ravenous pariah dogs.
When the moon rose Layard could see well enough to build a
raft, though he had difficulty in beating off the dogs. Finally he
got aboard and floated down to Fellahia, where he was well
received by Sheikh Thamer. After some difficulty Layard managed to find Mohamed Taki Khan and Khatun-jan. They had
not thought that Layard would undergo so many hardships to
find them, and greeted him with great joy. Mohamed Taki
Khan hated the heat and monotony of the reedy swamps;
pointing towards the snowy peaks of Mungasht, he said:
"*Inshallah!* We shall drink snow up there together before the
summer is over." Khatun-jan called Layard to her tent and
handed him some of the things he had left behind at Kala Tul,

which she had looked after even in her flight. She wept bitterly:
"The Khan now repents that he did not take my advice and
refuse to give up Hussein Kuli, for he loved that boy better than
his life, and he will never be happy again now that he has lost
him."

Manuchar Khan had relentlessly pursued Mohamed Taki
Khan and was only a few miles away with his army, but it was
not easy to enter the swamp area against the Cha'b tribe. He
was in communication with Sheikh Thamer and sent various
distinguished envoys who were all prepared to swear oaths that
Mohamed Taki Khan would be safe if he submitted; if he did
not submit his son and nephew would be killed. It was stated
that the Chief's brother, Shefia Khan, had been captured and
would be put to death. Soon afterwards Shefia Khan arrived in
Fellahia with a mission led by the Persian Commander-in-Chief,
Suleiman Khan. Shefia Khan argued that on this occasion at
least, Manuchar Khan would keep his word. Despite the arguments against acceptance put forward vehemently by other
Bakhtiari chiefs, by Khatun-jan and by Sheikh Thamer,
Mohamed Taki Khan decided that he would go with the mission
to the Persian camp. Khatun-jan was overcome with grief and
said bitterly to her husband: "You have taken my son from me
and now you would leave me and your other children without
protection. How can you trust to one who has already over and
over again foresworn himself? Remain here and fight like a
brave man, and there is not a woman who will not be by your
side." All pleaded with him not to go, but they could not stop
him and he stepped into the boat with the waiting Persians. He
was paddled slowly towards the Persian camp, while the men
and women of the Bakhtiari followed along the bank weeping;
even Suleiman Khan wept, as did some of the Persian
soldiers.

It is difficult to assess from Layard's story what prompted
Mohamed Taki Khan to give himself up. By going he was likely
to destroy the rest of his family, as Khatun-jan had said, and he
would endanger the unity of the Chehar Lang tribe of which he
was so proud. Had the spirit of this proud warrior been broken?
Was he more afraid of the influence of the Shah than he allowed
in his boastings? Was there some weakness in his character

which made him unable to support adversity? He had complained of feeling a prisoner surrounded by reeds and water. He may, perhaps, have hoped that he might save his son Hussein Kuli. But Khatun-jan had not given up. When Layard told the story to Mitford in India the latter replied: "I cannot imagine what could have induced Mohamed Taki Khan to have put himself into his enemy's power, feigned friendship being such a stale Persian ruse." Layard gave no explanation; he never admitted that there was any fundamental weakness in this man, whom he loved and admired, and Layard was not one to condone cowardice or a weak acceptance of defeat.

Layard accompanied the party to the Persian camp with a sad heart. He had expected foul play but he had never supposed that Manuchar Khan, after all his promises, would at once put Mohamed Taki Khan in chains. When Layard returned to Fellahia that evening the Bakhtiari chiefs were wild with anger at the treatment meted out to their leader and at the perfidy of the Persians. They decided to attack the Persian camp that same night to attempt the rescue of Mohamed Taki Khan. Layard went with them. It was dark and there were no outposts, so the raiders were in the camp before the Persians knew of the attack. There was tumult and confusion. The Bakhtiari and Arab horsemen galloped about shouting their war cries and those on foot slashed around with their swords. The Persian horses broke from their tethers and there was continuous firing. Layard was with Au Khan Baba, another of Mohamed Taki Khan's brothers.

> I kept close to Au Khan Baba, who made his way to the park of artillery near which, he had learnt, were the tents in which his brothers were confined. I was so near the guns that I could see and hear Suleiman Khan giving his orders, and was almost in front of them when the gunners were commanded to fire grape-shot into a seething crowd which appeared to be advancing on the Matamet's pavilion. It consisted mainly of a Persian regiment which, having failed to form, was falling back in disorder.

Before the Bakhtiari could reach Mohamed Taki Khan he had been taken, still chained, into the presence of Manuchar Khan, who threatened to put him to death if the rescue attempt should seem to be succeeding. Some of Manuchar Khan's attendants were killed at his side, so near did the attackers come to success; but once the Persians had recovered from their initial surprise it was useless to continue the attack. The Bakhtiari had, however, managed to rescue one of the Chief's brothers, Au Kerim, whom they dragged away in spite of his chains. Having secured Mohamed Taki Khan, Manuchar Khan had no further reason to remain in the swamp area, and retired with his army to Shuster.

Preparations were made for the departure of Khatun-jan Khanum and the other Bakhtiari families to the mountains and Layard accompanied the mounted escort guarding the caravan. On the journey reports reached them that Manuchar Khan had succeeded in winning over the allegiance of some of the Bakhtiari chiefs and that there was warfare in the mountains where they had planned to go. Khatun-jan and the others therefore decided to ask for asylum with the Kashga, a powerful tribe in the country near Shiraz, which was not under the jurisdiction of Manuchar Khan as Governor of Isfahan. Au Kerim Khan, who had been rescued from the Persian camp, was chosen to go as envoy and Layard offered to accompany him. That this offer was accepted shows the confidence of the Bakhtiari in Layard's horsemanship and powers of endurance; his loyalty had long been beyond dispute. Layard was prepared for any adventure to help his friends; he may also have considered that from Shiraz he would be able to reach Persepolis.

On the third day of the journey Layard and Au Kerim came to a castle on the spur of a mountain. It belonged to one of the principal chiefs of the Bahmei tribe who had had a feud against the Bakhtiari, but Au Kerim was sure that the feud had been ended when the Chief's sister had become one of Mohamed Taki Khan's wives. All seemed to be going well until the return at nightfall of the Chief, Khalyl Khan, 'a tall, rather handsome man, but with a savage, sinister expression, armed to the teeth, and shabbily dressed in the Lur cap and outer coat of felt'. The Chief at once started a quarrel with Au Kerim and the two travellers were seized and locked in a cell. They could hear the Chief and his companions shouting in the large hall and the sound of Lur music; Khalyl Khan was a heavy drinker and the party caroused until late into the night. Layard, generally

77

optimistic, was convinced that they were going to be killed, for he knew the savage character of the Bahmei.

It was sometime after midnight when we were disturbed by the withdrawal of the bolt of the door. Au Kerim sprang to his feet, and I followed his example, not knowing who was about to enter and with what intent. The Chief's wife, whom we had seen in the afternoon after our arrival, stepped stealthily into the room. She denounced her husband to Au Kerim in a whisper as a ruffian who had no respect for the ties of family or the duties of hospitality. . . .

Then addressing me she said: "What have we to do with you, a stranger, and what have you done to us that we should do you harm? Go with him, and let not your blood be also upon our heads."

They crept out, found their horses, and led them down the steep mountain-side. By midday they were some distance from the castle but were being pursued. At last they came to a narrow valley with a small stream where there was good cover and they would both have escaped but Au Kerim's mare fell heavily with him and bolted, leaving him injured on the ground. Layard was about to dismount to help him but Au Kerim begged him to ride on as the pursuers were by then very close. Among the Bakhtiari it was not considered heroic to be caught in such an emergency if it were possible to escape and if he had stayed he would have been killed with Au Kerim.

Layard galloped away giving his horse the rein. At length he came to a secluded oasis where he fell asleep by a stream under the shade of a tree, his horse grazing peacefully beside him. He awoke refreshed and considered what he was to do; he did not think he would be able to find the Kashga tribe if he pursued his journey alone, nor would he be able to find Khatun-jan's party if he returned. He decided to try to get to Shuster to learn the fate of Mohamed Taki Khan.

After a perilous journey of about ten days across the plains in the heat of summer, Layard finally reached Shuster and went to the castle where Manuchar Khan had his headquarters. The eunuch was angry and insisted on knowing all that he had been doing: "You Englishmen are always meddling in matters which do not concern you, and interfering in the affairs of other countries. You attempted to do it in Afghanistan, but all your countrymen there have been put to death; not one of them has escaped."* Manuchar Khan ordered Layard to live in the house of Suleiman Khan, the Commander-in-Chief, and not to leave Shuster without permission. Layard discovered that Mohamed Taki Khan and Hussein Kuli were still alive and in Shuster, but knew it would do more harm than good if he attempted to contact them. There was no information about Khatun-jan Khanum and her party. In order to escape he needed a horse but all his money had been spent or stolen. An appeal to his friend M. Boré in Isfahan furnished him with funds after a delay of many weeks.

In August he was able to escape from Shuster and ride the two hundred miles across the burning plains to Basra, where he presented himself to the Agent of the East India Company. He wanted to return to Bagdad for news of his family and to send them some information about himself; the only way to get there quickly was to accompany the Arab postman employed by the Government of India, which meant travelling day and night through hostile tribes. The saddle-bags were filled with barley for the horses and in them Layard concealed his compass, watch, and the few silver coins, all the money he had left. He wore Arab dress with the *keffieh* kept in place on his shaven head by a cord of twisted worsted, and in order to protect himself from the sun he wore a Turkish fez under the *keffieh*. Towards the end of the journey when they were not many miles from Bagdad, the travellers were suddenly surrounded by a raiding party of the Shammar tribe, then at war with the Turkish Pasha of Bagdad. Layard was thrown to the ground, and his *keffieh* fell off, exposing his red fez. The tribesmen shouted triumphantly that they had caught a Turk and one of them drew a knife on him as he lay on the ground. He cried out that he was English and a young sheikh, who seemed to have some authority, ordered him to be released saying "he is my friend and the English

* It was July 1841 when Manuchar Khan made this statement, which was four months before the massacre of the British had taken place. Sir Alexander Burnes was murdered in Kabul in November 1841, and the slaughter of several thousand British and Indians in the retreat came later. Layard wrote that the only way he could explain this was that Manuchar Khan, who was in the secrets of the Persian Government, might have known that there was an Afghan plan to exterminate the English in Kabul and believed that it had already been carried out.

are the friends of my tribe''. The lives of Layard and the post-man were spared but they were left in the desert without horses or shoes and with very little clothing. They made their way towards Bagdad as fast as they could during the night to avoid the intense heat but were again robbed by Arabs who stole the rest of their clothing except for their cloaks. At last, early in the morning, they reached the city walls and sat down in a garden near one of the gates amongst a large crowd of Arabs who were waiting to take in their fruit and vegetables when the gate was opened.

> At length the sun rose and the gate was thrown open. Two *cawasses* of the English Residency, in their gold-embroidered uniforms, came out driving before them with their *courbashes* the Arabs who were outside, to make way for a party of mounted European ladies and gentlemen. It was the same party that, on my previous visit to Bagdad, I had almost daily accompanied on their morning rides. They passed close to me, but did not recognise me in the dirty Arab in rags, crouched near the entrance, nor, clothed as I was, could I venture to make myself known to them. But at a little distance behind them came Dr. Ross. I called to him, and he turned towards me in the greatest surprise when he saw me without cover to my bare head, with naked feet and in my tattered *abba*.

Dr. Ross took Layard to his house and help was arranged for the postman. The doctor then sent an angry message to Sheikh Sofuk, the most important of the Shammar sheikhs and in a few days' time the two horses, Layard's watch and compass, and all that had been stolen, except a few silver coins, were returned. Sheikh Sofuk expressed his regret at what had happened and vowed that if Layard ever wished to pass through the desert again and put himself under the Sheikh's protection, he could travel from one end of Mesopotamia to the other with 'a tray of gold on his head'.

5

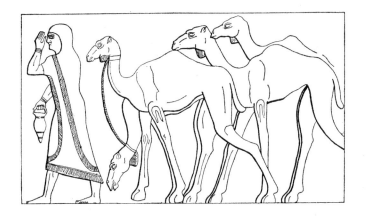

'I scarcely know which way to turn'

With his return to Bagdad Layard could once again correspond with his family after a gap of nine months. 'A correspondence most disheartening,' his mother described it, 'really I could mourn in sackcloth and ashes since your departure, so great and continual is my suspense and anxiety about you and the only certainty seems to be that you do not receive my letters.' The family had become so worried that they had asked the Foreign Office to make enquiries about Layard's whereabouts through the British Embassy in Teheran, diplomatic relations having been resumed.

The long letters Layard now wrote from Bagdad were full of much interesting material about the antiquities he had dis- covered and about his admiration for Mohamed Taki Khan, but they were of little comfort to his family; they did not reveal his plans, and gave cause for anxiety and annoyance. Layard was in a difficult position; he had to earn his living but he did not want

to go on to Ceylon. To return to London to his uncle's office
would be a confession of failure, nor did he want to be dependent
financially once more on Benjamin Austen. In this predicament
he put forward a number of contradictory arguments to justify
himself. He had learnt to sum up the reactions of wild Bakhtiari,
and even to have some insight into the subtle mind of a Georgian
eunuch, but he had not yet acquired the art of providing explanations satisfactory to his Uncle Benjamin and his Aunt Sara. His
boast that he had acquired a large fund of knowledge which
entitled him 'to a certain rank in society' weighed little with
the Austens; it seemed to them that he had merely been wasting
his patrimony and once more keeping very strange company. At
one moment Layard said that it was a good thing that he was
abroad and living so cheaply, at the next that he ought to return to
London and start again. 'Do not spare me if you think that I am
deserving of blame; I feel, however, confident that I have always
acted honourably.' Austen was a practical man with a great
many family worries; Marianne Layard also had her troubles as
she had had to buy commissions in the army for Frederick and
Arthur, while Edgar insisted on marrying before he had a job.
Neither Austen nor Marianne Layard were prepared to assure
Henry that everything he did was right—or to provide him with
any more money.

Layard wrote more frankly to Mitford: Telemachus when out
of the reach of Mentor got into precious scrapes, he admitted,
and that had happened to him when away from Mitford's 'more
sober judgment'. He said that he had had romantic ideas of
remaining two to three years with Mohamed Taki Khan to help
him civilise the Bakhtiari, establish commercial relations with
India, cultivate the land, export cotton, wool, and so on but these
plans had collapsed with Manuchar Khan's decision to break the
power of the Bakhtiari Chief. He hoped that Mitford had written
and sent his journal to the publishers, and said that he himself
had sufficient to fill a volume without touching on their mutual
experiences. 'My personal adventures have also been most extraordinary.'

Layard had, indeed, amassed a very great amount of interesting
material and during his stay in Bagdad he worked hard on a
long report for the Royal Geographical Society, making use once

more of Colonel Taylor's excellent library. With Lieutenant
Selby of the Indian Navy, who commanded the steamship
Assyria, he explored the mouths of the rivers Kerkhah, Karun,
and the Shatt el Arab, the combined waters of the Tigris and
Euphrates as they flowed into the Persian Gulf. Colonel Taylor
was much impressed by Layard's hard work and tremendous
interest in the history, people, languages, and archaeology of the
country. Layard had written a lengthy report on the possibilities
of trade which Colonel Taylor offered to send to Lord Aberdeen,
the Foreign Minister, with a suggestion that Layard should be
made British Vice-Consul in Shuster. There was also a plan to
send him on a mission to the Ameer Khalid of the Nejd and
Hejaz, but for various reasons these plans were not carried out.
While waiting for replies from his family he continued to study
and to travel.

In October 1841 Layard paid another visit to Shuster. From
there he travelled to the famous Jaffer Kuli Khan, Chief of the
Haft Lang Bakhtiari tribe, who had always been at enmity with
Mohamed Taki Khan. Even among the Bakhtiari he had an evil
reputation, having murdered fourteen of his relations, and was
known to be especially suspicious of strangers visiting his mountain stronghold. As Layard and his party approached, the fortress
could be seen in the distance, 'a huge mass of rock rising per-
pendicularly out of the valley'. At the foot was a cavern where
Layard was greeted by Jaffer Kuli Khan in a more friendly way
than he had expected. They were entertained with sweetmeats,
dried fruits, and sour Shiraz wine from an enormous bottle. The
Chief said that Mohamed Taki Khan should have taken refuge
in this fortress as Manuchar Khan would never have been able
to reach him there. Layard expressed astonishment, saying that
he had heard there was a blood feud between the families to
which the Chief replied:

> You were the friend of Mohamed Taki Khan and when he fled
> to the Cha'b, you buckled on your *kesh-kemer* [belt with powder
> flasks] and followed him, whilst we Bakhtiari went against him
> and aided his enemies. Those who ought to have helped him
> deserted him. I wish to be the friend of one who has thus shown
> himself to be a better man than us Musulmans. You are welcome
> to my *Diz* and you will always be so. This is a proof of my

confidence in you, for my own brothers are not permitted to ascend to it.

Layard remained for three days and then continued his explorations, returning to Shuster in December. He found that orders had been given for his arrest but Manuchar Khan was far away in Mohammerah which he had captured from Sheikh Thamer. Fortunately Layard was on good terms with the notables of Shuster and was unmolested. With the assistance of his friends he managed to visit the imprisoned Mohamed Taki Khan and was distressed to find him with iron fetters on his wrists and ankles attached to a heavy collar round his neck. Mohamed Taki Khan received him with his usual pleasant smile and showed the resignation of the good Mohammedan. He spoke of the plans they had made at Kala Tul for improvements, all of which had come to nothing. He begged Layard to visit his wife and family who had been captured and brought to Shuster, and Layard found them living in desperate poverty, so pale and emaciated that he scarcely recognised them. All crowded round and Khatun-jan expressed her relief and delight at seeing him, for she had thought that he had been killed after the capture and death of Au Kerim Khan. 'Their gratitude to me in return for my sympathy, which was all that I could offer them, was most affectionate. I found in these poor sufferers qualities and senti-ments which would have ennobled Christian women in a civilised country.' He was delighted to find that Hussein Kuli was well and receiving good treatment from the Shusteri notables.

Before returning to Bagdad Layard wished to visit the country of the Feili Lurs who lived in the mountains between Turkey and Persia in the Province of Pusht-i-Kuh. Layard knew that these dangerous people had murdered Grant and Fothering-ham, and that Rawlinson had advised any Europeans who wished to examine the remarkable antiquities in the province to travel in the meanest clothes and to live among the wandering local tribesmen, but he was confident that the well-known saintliness of his travelling companion, Seyyid Abou'l Hassan of Shuster, would protect him. In the foothills of the Zagros moun-tains they reached the encampment of the Feili Chief, known as the Wali of Luristan, and were conducted to the tent of one of the headmen who received Layard and Seyyid Abou'l Hassan courteously. The next day Layard was taken before the Wali, whose uncle had murdered the two Englishmen. It was not a friendly reception. "Why have the English placed ships on the Tigris and Euphrates?" said the Wali angrily. . . . "The English are about to take possession of our country, and they send this person to spy it out and to prepare for their arrival." Addressing Seyyid Abou'l Hassan, he said: "Why did you bring this man here to see me sitting on a carpet, when he should know that my forefathers were Kings of this country, and that they sat before the Shah on a throne and were his equals." Layard was then questioned in an insolent manner by one of the chiefs, who wanted to know why Layard had resided with Mohamed Taki Khan and argued that the presence of an infidel had brought bad luck to the Bakhtiari chief. It was a charge that might well have roused Layard's quick temper but he kept himself under control, knowing how dangerous the situation was. When Layard had returned to his tent his host apologised for the bad reception and advised him to treat the Wali as a royal personage since he was inordinately proud of his forebears. Layard was not sure that the plan would work and wondered whether he would suffer the same fate as the two officers. During a gloomy breakfast a Lur tribesman, who had been present at the murder of the two Englishmen, came to recount the details, which he thought would be of interest.

At the Wali's daily reception, held in a huge black tent, Layard managed to make a long harangue in praise of the Wali's ancient lineage, which was well received, and the Wali became much more friendly. While the morning meeting was proceeding, a Lur tribesman entered the tent and asked if it were true that a foreigner was in the neighbourhood; he looked hard at Layard, had a conversation with the Wali and departed. The Wali then explained that he had protected Layard from any questioning by describing him as a Georgian, on a special mission from Manuchar Khan, and had sent the man away. In fact the Lur tribesman had been looking for Layard as a result of the request from his family in London through the Foreign Office. When Sir John McNeill, the British Ambassador in Teheran, asked the Persian Government whether it had any information about Layard, the Vizier had said: 'That man! Why if I could catch him I'd hang him. He has been joining some rebel tribes and helping them.'

Layard returned to Bagdad at the beginning of 1842 and found a letter from his uncle which furnished him with matter 'for the most serious reflection' and filled his mind with 'very great uneasiness'. The various bills on Coutts's Bank had been refused and he begged his uncle to clear up the matter, 'as I fear thro' these unlucky mistakes I have acquired no very great name in the East'. Having suggested 'that he wished to return to London, he was most distressed to find in the letters from home that there was still gloom and disunity in the family; he could not bear family squabbles and it was one of the reasons why he had left London. 'I will candidly confess, my dear Uncle', he wrote now from Bagdad, 'that you very frequently caused me the most painful feelings from observations passed upon those who were the most nearly related to me. . . . I was too sensitive in those matters to allow your remarks to pass unheeded.' He did not see how his uncle could expect him to settle down to a profession like law 'without suffering both in body and mind'; nor, in view of the stories about his Uncle Charles's money difficulties, could he find pleasure in proceeding to Ceylon: 'The fact is that I scarcely know which way to turn, and I feel so miserable that I would willingly return and live among the wild tribes of the mountains, cursing the name of England.' They were strong sentiments to express to his Tory uncle.

Crabb Robinson, who continued to visit the Austens at Montague Place, commented in his diary at this time that Austen did not regard his nephew as a 'sober citizen' and did not want him to return to London; Robinson considered that Sara Austen was not at all friendlily disposed towards her nephew. Speaking of his aunt, Layard told his mother 'I have a powerful enemy to encounter; but as I have been accustomed these last three years to powder, shot, and furious noises, I may perhaps be able to withstand a few drawing-room skirmishes; at all events I must gird up my loins and make a stand.' He told his uncle that he would like to live in England if it could be with a moderate degree of comfort, 'professing my own opinions upon religion, morals and politics—nobody interfering with me, as long as I did not interfere with other persons'. He said he had no wish to make money or to live expensively: 'I only wish to be alone, with bread to eat, enjoying at least a quiet mind.' He wrote to his mother suggesting that they might set up house together in London; perhaps she could come with his brother Edgar to live with him abroad away from relations and 'colonize some un-inhabited island'.

Layard decided to remain until he received further news of the family situation. He still wanted to find out whether the steamers of the East India Company could trade direct between Shuster and the Persian Gulf. Colonel Taylor was well aware of the advantages if this could be accomplished and agreed that Lieutenant Selby should make the attempt in the steamer *Assyria*. Seyyid Abou'l Hassan, who had accompanied Layard to Bagdad and had been delighted by the reception he had received from Colonel Taylor, joined the party. They left Bagdad at the end of February 1842 and stopped at Mohammerah which was desolate after the Persian attack. (Sheikh Thamer had been driven to seek shelter with the Turkish authorities at Basra.) They managed to pass through the rapids at Ahwaz and reached Bendi-Kir where three rivers unite, flowing in three parallel streams of a different colour: 'The water of the Karun, which formed the centre band, was of a dull reddish hue; that of the Ab-Gargar, milk-white; and that of the Disful river, almost black, from the rich alluvial mould which it brought down.' They navigated to within seven miles of Shuster and then the ship went aground. Layard and Dr. Ross, who was with the party, strongly advised that they should do everything to get the steamer afloat immediately since in the spring floods the waters rose and fell very abruptly, but Selby waited until the next morning by which time the river had retreated and the *Assyria* was high and dry. It was not certain that the party would be well received at Shuster so Layard and Seyyid Abou'l Hassan galloped to the town and invited the Governor and notables to pay a visit telling them that the ship had come to improve trade and restore their ancient prosperity. This brought a large cavalcade of Shusteri who were received with full honours; Lieutenant Selby and Dr. Ross were in their dress uniforms and the crew drawn up as on parade. Friendship was established and during the next few days there was feasting on the ship and in Shuster. The ship was refloated

and managed to reach within a mile of the town. 'The fact that
vessels of the size of the *Assyria*', wrote Layard, 'could
reach . . . the foot of the mountains over which tracks
lead to Isfahan and into the very heart of Persia was thus
satisfactorily established.'

Mohamed Taki Khan was still in chains in Shuster and Layard
took Selby and Ross to see him. 'They were both', said Layard,
'struck by the nobleness of his character, his enlightened views
for the improvement of his people, and the resignation with
which he bore his misfortunes.' Khatun-jan, her children, and
the women of the family were still there and Dr. Ross did his
best to cure some of their ailments. Layard took leave with a
heavy heart of Mohamed Taki Khan and of Khatun-jan Khanum,
for both of whom he had a real affection.

> I had received from them during their prosperity a kindness
> and hospitality which, as a European and a Christian, I could not
> have expected in a tribe reputed to be one of the most fanatical,
> savage and cruel in Asia. I had shared with them their dangers
> and privations. I could not forget that even in moments of the
> greatest peril and of the greatest suffering, almost their first
> thought was for the safety of me—a stranger. I believed that we
> should never meet again. That thought, and the uncertainty of
> the fate which awaited them from those who delighted in cruelty
> and were at that time ingenious beyond most other Easterns in
> inventing new tortures, weighed upon me.

When the *Assyria* returned to Bagdad in May after being
away for three months, news had been received that the Sultan
was about to declare war on Persia; the Porte intended to try to
recapture Mohammerah which was regarded as part of Turkey.
The British Resident in Bagdad was very anxious that Sir
Stratford Canning, the British Ambassador at Constantinople,
should be fully informed of the situation as hostilities would be
harmful to British interests. Colonel Taylor urged Layard to
take despatches to the Ambassador and to hold himself in readiness to supply any information Canning might require. Layard
accepted very willingly and arranged to accompany a *tatar*
(postman) being sent by the Turkish Pasha of Bagdad to Constantinople with reports of the situation. Despite the heat of
June the two of them rode day and night, covering the two

hundred and fifty miles to Mosul in fifty hours. They remained there three days to rest and to wait for the reports being prepared by the Turkish Governor.

Layard had often thought about the Assyrian mounds at Mosul and Nimrud. Through Alexander Hector, a merchant friend in Bagdad, he had tried to interest a businessman in Sheffield to advance money for excavations, but without success. In Mosul he found that there was a new French Vice-Consul, Paul Botta, son of the historian of Italy, who had been sent out to see if there were any truth in the stories of Assyrian antiquities recounted by Claudius Rich. Botta was charming, generous, and intelligent; he had served in the French Consular Service in Egypt and China, but his health had been affected by opium-smoking. He persuaded his new friend to try a Chinese pipe but Layard was so sick he did not persevere. Together they visited the huge mounds on the other side of the Tigris from Mosul and discussed far into the night the great question as to what might be found beneath. They went over the accounts of the ancient Greek and Latin authors on the history of the area; but it was Rich who had aroused Layard's interest and also the interest of Julius Mohl of the French Asiatic Society. Rich had reported that a little time before he had arrived in Mosul in 1820 a sculpture, representing men and animals, had been dug out of one of the mounds. The Arabs from Mosul flocked to gaze at it, he had been told, but the Cadi of Mosul had ordered its destruction since the figures were regarded as idols of the infidels. Layard and Botta visited the mounds each day to explore; the latter had opened a few trenches in the central mound of Kuyunjik, but had only discovered a few bricks and fragments of limestone inscribed with cuneiform characters. Layard told him about the mounds at Nimrud and suggested that he might try excavating there, but Botta preferred to remain at Mosul. Ten months later he made his great discovery at Khorsabad.

6

Constantinople and Sir Stratford Canning

Layard rode on to Samsun with the *tatar*. In Trebizond he borrowed European clothes from the British Vice-Consul and in July 1842 took a steamer for Constantinople. Directly he arrived at the Golden Horn he hired a caique for the two-hour journey along the European shore of the Bosphorus to Buyukdere, where the British Ambassador had his summer residence. Layard knew that his mission was important and he expected to be received by Sir Stratford Canning as soon as he presented himself. He was kept waiting in an ante-room for a long time: 'At length a fashionably dressed young gentleman appeared, asked me roughly for the despatches of which I was the bearer, informed me that the Ambassador was too much occupied to see anyone, and, turning on his heel left the room without deigning to listen to what I had to say.' In those days the junior members of Embassy staffs were nearly all the younger sons of noblemen and Layard must certainly have looked unprepossessing; he was unkempt, burnt by the sun, in ill-fitting clothes and his face swollen by tooth-ache. 'I have applied a few leeches to my face and hope to be well in a day or two', he told his mother. He returned to his hotel, sent an angry letter to the Ambassador about the insulting manner in which he had been treated, and booked a passage on a homeward-bound ship. He had been accustomed to be received by the highest in the land during his travels, and did not take kindly to being considered as someone of no importance but he was mollified by a friendly note from Sir Stratford Canning, apologising for his reception and asking him to come to the Embassy to see him. Canning was then fifty-six years of age, his hair was white, and he stooped a little. Layard thought he was the handsomest man he had ever seen:

90

His earnest grey eyes seemed to penetrate into one's very thoughts. His thin, compressed lips denoted a violent and passionate temper. His complexion was so transparent that the least emotion, whether of pleasure or anger, was at once shown by its varying tints. A broad and massive overhanging brow gave an air of profound wisdom and sagacity. He was altogether a very formidable looking personage, and he made upon me the impression which he, no doubt, intended to produce.

The Ambassador asked many searching questions about recent events on the Turco-Persian frontier, and was impressed by Layard's knowledge and enthusiasm. He liked the dark, sturdy young man, who had taken so much trouble to map his routes, to learn Persian and Arabic and to discover the main centres of grazing and the movements of tribes, which were very numerous in Mesopotamia and Persia. Canning was attempting to persuade the British Government to act as mediator between Turkey and Persia in their quarrels over the frontier, and he realised that Layard's special knowledge would be of considerable use. He said that he wished to have further talks on the frontier situation.

Layard spent the next few days touring the wonderful city, but soon found that he had only just enough money left for the journey home, and he wrote to tell Canning that he would soon have to leave. Hearing nothing further he was on the way to the harbour to embark on a ship for England when he was overtaken by a *cawass* with a note from Canning: 'Instead of going away come and dine with me tomorrow, and I will try to arrange a plan with you.'

Layard let the ship sail and returned to his hotel. He had no misgivings about taking this important decision for he was confident that he would be of use to the Ambassador, and that the Ambassador would be of use to him. He wrote a long letter to his uncle explaining his change of plan:

I was induced to take the course I have decided upon for these reasons: first, I feel that my prospects in England are far from satisfactory, in every respect, both with regard to pecuniary advancement and happiness in my family; . . . secondly, I find that my mind is too active to admit of my returning cheerfully to any sedentary employment unaccompanied with an extraordinary degree of excitement and I fear that I should be unable to settle down to the Law; and, thirdly, I see in the East a vast field for the display of energy and abilities and the certainty of there being ere long a great political movement in which an enterprising and ambitious man will probably be able to take an active and elevated part.

Political interests and contentions appear to be daily moving from the West to the East and all things are ripe for a great outbreak in which probably there will be, altho' accompanied with great risk, great prizes. Such anticipations better suit my character than the anticipation of a quiet laborious life.

I have at the same time considerable advantages. The three years that I have spent in the East have been spent with the people. I have acquired a perfect knowledge, such as few Englishmen I believe possess, of the character of the Orientals, their manners, and their customs. I am also in some way acquainted with the language of Persia and Arabia. . . . Such is my case. I have only to hope that you will be kind eno' to write to me as soon as possible and give me your opinion upon the line of conduct I have adopted.

Benjamin Austen knew that his nephew would do exactly what he wished to do, and was relieved that he had decided not to return. His reply was sensible and sympathetic; he told Henry that he had never promised him a partnership and that if he came back now he would have to begin again; nor did he think the plan of living with his mother was a good one: 'She is of so unhappy a temperament that she damps the spirit of others by her own nervous feelings.' He had not been surprised at his nephew leaving England in 1839:

> I saw you were ambitious of distinguishing yourself and that you panted for new scenes which would give more scope to your active energies of mind and body. I saw this in you from a boy. . . . A little spice of vanity also, with much confidence in your own powers, and self-conceit in your own position (you will excuse my being frank with you), all tended to generate in you a strong desire to become more known, and a more public man than a seat in Gray's Inn could make you.

Austen pointed out that, although Henry might think that money was 'filthy lucre', he would need a salary and he should certainly follow up his chances with Sir Stratford Canning:

> You have a strong and active mind; add to it, if possible, a *cool* judgement; this is *most* necessary and what you *most want*. . . .

92

Without this much evil may arise and diplomacy is nothing without it. The Government may seize with avidity on all you say and
make use of you in every way when mere zeal and activity are
required, but beware of too much haste and want of caution, as
your former friends soon forget your late usefulness, and turn
around upon your *first error*.

Austen considered that the Ambassador was a man of great
talents and judgement but, 'the highest functionaries make use
of their subordinates in throwing upon their shoulders all the
mischances of their policy'. That might be, said Layard in reply,
'but do you not think it possible for the subordinate to make
the employer dependent on him?'

Canning certainly made full use of Layard's knowledge, but
did not forget his usefulness. It was Layard's good fortune that
the information he had acquired through the vagaries of travel
had become of great value; it was the Ambassador's good fortune
that Layard was never tired of observing and noting facts and
that he had done this throughout his travels. Layard was set to
work by the Ambassador to write a long report on the tribes and
geography of the Turco-Persian frontier area. 'Here I am then
turned profound politician,' Layard wrote cheerfully to Mitford,
'brooding over the interests of Great Britain, head full of Russian
intrigues.' He thought that great changes were taking place in
Turkey and the Eastern States of Europe which would be 'the
scene of European warfare and contention', the Ottoman Empire
was weakening daily and its Christian subjects were endeavouring to throw off the Turkish yoke; England, France, and
Russia were competing for the adherence of the Christian tribes
of Kurdistan, as allies in the approaching struggle. Layard considered Canning a man of firm and decided character, well able
to play a decisive part.

The Ambassador decided in August 1842 to send Layard on
a mission to the western part of Turkey in Europe to investigate
reported unrest in Bosnia and Serbia; he thought that it would
make a very interesting addition to his travels: 'I hope your
curiosity and enterprise will not expose you to unnecessary
danger.' Layard left by boat for Salonika where he met Blunt,
the British Consul, and Osman Pasha, the Turkish Governor;
he went on horseback through Janina, Monastir, and Semlin in

Austria, reaching Belgrade on 8 October. Here he had expected to find the British Consul, Thomas de Fonblanque, but there had been a national revolution and the Russian-sponsored ruler, Prince Milosh, had been expelled. De Fonblanque, who was pro-Russian, had closed the Consulate as a protest and left for Constantinople to report to the Ambassador.

Canning had instructed Layard to act as though he were nothing but a private traveller and on no account to give any indication that he was collecting information for the Embassy. Layard might, perhaps, have been able to maintain this fiction if the British Consul had been at his post, although it was known that he carried letters from the Ambassador. As it was, the Turkish Governor of Belgrade and the members of the newly formed provisional government considered Layard as an emissary who could be of use to them. Layard should have left Belgrade at once and carried out his investigations in Bosnia but he could not resist embroiling himself in an intricate political situation, and seizing the chance of playing a 'high game'. As a Radical he sympathised with the nationalists; he had often talked over similar situations with his Polish revolutionary friends intriguing to counter Russian influence. He considered de Fonblanque had favoured Russian interests in Serbia and was almost certainly giving the Ambassador a false view of the situation. It was his business, Layard thought, to investigate personally and to report to the Ambassador in Constantinople as soon as possible. Members of the new Serbian Government put their case to him and handed over documents, confident that these would be seen by Sir Stratford Canning. Layard made use of a 'richly caparisoned horse' with an escort sent by the Turkish Governor, and was ushered into the Pasha's presence 'with great ceremony'. The Pasha made all arrangements to help him return to Constantinople and he rode back at the remarkable speed of a hundred miles a day.

I reached Constantinople before dawn on the sixth day after leaving Belgrade. I had performed this journey of some six hundred miles in less time by some hours than Colonel Townley,[1] Queen's Messenger, whose *tatar* ride over the same ground had been mentioned by Lord Palmerston in the House of Commons as the fastest on record. I was consequently very proud of my feat.

In writing of this to his uncle he pointed out that it was his life among the hardy Bakhtiari which had enabled him to do it.

Layard returned to Constantinople well satisfied with what he had done, but in fact he had not completed his mission and his sudden return was tactless and unnecessary, for Stratford Canning understood the situation perfectly well and had ordered de Fonblanque back to his post with a reprimand. Layard commented almost with surprise: 'I found that he had already come to the same conclusion as I had as to the revolution in Serbia, and as to the policy which it behoved the British Government to pursue.' De Fonblanque was furious; firstly at being reprimanded for leaving his post and secondly, to find on his return to Belgrade, that Layard had been there apparently as the Ambassador's envoy, and had been on friendly terms with the revolutionaries. The Consul began a vigorous campaign against Layard; he had the right to send his despatches direct to the Foreign Office, with copies to Canning. These despatches raised many points which required explanation and the Ambassador wrote Layard a formal and severe letter in his own hand, over which he must have taken some trouble, for it is more legible than most of his communications. The Ambassador reminded Layard of his instructions to travel as a private citizen, and asked whether any of his actions warranted de Fonblanque's allegation that he had represented himself as an envoy of the Ambassador? Did he 'pay court' to the leaders of the Insurgent Party, had he been 'promenaded' in the Pasha's State carriage, and had he discredited Her Majesty's Consul-General in Serbia? These were difficult questions to answer. Although Canning himself agreed with Layard's liberal views on the Serbian question, there was doubt in his mind as to Layard's discretion.

De Fonblanque also made the charge that Layard had 'induced' the Queen's Messenger to advance him money against the Consul-General's account. Stories of Layard's dishonoured bills to Baron de Bode and to the British Resident in the Persian Gulf had already reached Canning through some of the British residents in Constantinople, who were jealous of the Ambassador's partiality for him. Layard, however, was able to explain that there had been money in the bank and that before leaving Serbia he had arranged for his uncle in London to pay back the money he had borrowed in Belgrade but he found that the Ambassador was not an easy person to convince and told his uncle: 'He sifts evidence more minutely than an Old Bailey lawyer and it would be difficult for anyone to deceive him; he is a man of great penetration and judgement and very candid.' After a series of gruelling interviews Layard stated in his diary: 'It is evident that I have acted rightly, altho' His Excellency may not at this moment be inclined to admit it.'

Layard had great self-confidence and resilience. Only two days after receiving the Ambassador's formal and severe letter he was writing to his Aunt Louisa: 'I see a brilliant career open to me in the East and I will sacrifice to it every consideration.' To his uncle he was more cautious, admitting that de Fonblanque was a powerful enemy and that past events were not going to help the Ambassador to persuade the Foreign Office to employ him: 'I believe that Sir Stratford Canning is *secretly* my friend but it is a delicate matter and I do not believe that he would take any step in it to save me.' The Ambassador had, in fact, written de Fonblanque on 26 November, the day after he had had his final interview with Layard: 'I do not hesitate to say that I am completely satisfied with Mr. Layard's explanation.' He also wrote to the Foreign Office supporting Layard in his defence against the charges. Nothing daunted, de Fonblanque put forward a fresh series of charges with the aim of discrediting the Ambassador's pro-Turkish policy and these received a sympathetic hearing from Aberdeen, who was pro-Russian in his views and suspicious of Stratford Canning's pro-Turkish sentiments. Support for de Fonblanque's views was given by *The Times'* correspondent in Constantinople, Mr. Hunter. Layard tried in vain to provoke Hunter to a duel by telling him that he was 'a scoundrel and a mercenary scribbler'. Layard became a centre of controversy and aroused considerable jealousy because he had become a protégé of the Ambassador; he was never very good at dealing with personal attacks. 'I have hydras to deal with', he told his Aunt Sara; 'one head is no sooner cut off than twenty spring up in its place.'

Layard temporarily forgot his troubles since he had a great deal of work to do for the Ambassador. Turkey and Persia had accepted the mediation of England and Russia in the boundary dispute and Layard had to draw up a series of reports on the country and the tribes; he also had to sort out a mass of evidence put forward by the Turkish and Persian Governments. The most important areas under discussion were those through which the navigable rivers flowed into the Persian Gulf and Layard had made them his special study. After many weeks of hard work he decided that the Turkish Government's claim to the left bank of the Shatt el Arab and to Mohammerah was justified, as Persia had never exercised more than a nominal jurisdiction over this territory at certain periods. He drew up a well-reasoned plan of boundary settlement which he submitted to the Ambassador, who endorsed it as a fair compromise and sent it forward to Aberdeen. Stratford Canning fully expected that Britain and Russia would recommend Turkey and Persia to adopt the plan. Russia, however, had proposed that Mohammerah should be given to Persia, and Aberdeen administered another snub to Canning by approving the Russian proposal. After the arrival of Lord Aberdeen's despatch to that effect Canning sent for Layard who recorded:

> I found him walking up and down his study like a lion in his cage—his brows knit, his lips compressed, and his delicate complexion flushed. . . . He broke into a violent tirade against Lord Aberdeen, whom he accused of being subservient to Russia, and of considering her interests more than those of his own country, and of being hostile to him personally, because he had considered it his duty to oppose her ambitious designs in the East.

Layard also was very bitter against Aberdeen. He had been greatly impressed by the importance of the position of Mohammerah, commanding as it did the river link from the Persian Gulf to the heart of Mesopotamia. 'These rivers were consequently destined, in my belief, to become great military and trading highways. It was to the interest of England that their mouths should not be in the possession of a Power which might be hostile to her.'

The Porte protested strongly against the arbitration but had to accept. The next step was to appoint a commission composed of representatives from Turkey, Persia, and the two mediating

Powers. Sir Stratford Canning proposed that Layard should be appointed as the British Commissioner, but the Foreign Office did not look with favour on his views with regard to Serbia or with regard to the Turco-Persian boundary, nor was it considered in London (though it was a point that Layard seemed to have forgotten), that he would be acceptable to the Persian Government in view of the part he had played on behalf of Mohamed Taki Khan. Instead, Colonel Fenwick Williams was appointed, with Mr. Robert Curzon as his assistant.

Layard was sunk in gloom for he did not see what other post he was likely to obtain. All his hopes and expectations were at an end, he said, after being kept six months in suspense: 'six of the most wretched months that I have ever spent—continually subjected to suspicions that I never invited and exposed to traps which I could not avoid'. On his twenty-sixth birthday in March 1843 he was able to make a more hopeful entry in his diary, and a little later he told his uncle that the Foreign Office had rejected de Fonblanque's charges.

When Zuban, the Minister of Justice in the new Serbian Government, arrived in Constantinople and renewed his friendship with Layard, which had begun in Belgrade, he was able to obtain useful information for the Ambassador, as Zuban entrusted him with secret information about the negotiations between Turks, Russians, and Serbians. In the meantime in London Lord Aberdeen expressed disapproval of de Fonblanque's decision to leave his post, but at the same time the Foreign Minister argued against Canning's thesis that the revolt in Serbia was an attempt on the part of a free people to elect their own chiefs. It was, said Aberdeen in the House of Lords, the result of a corrupt bargain between the Turkish Pasha of Belgrade and two or three ambitious Serbian chiefs. 'An utterly false statement', wrote Layard to his uncle; 'Mr. Fonblanque has deceived his Government in a most wicked manner.' There was dissatisfaction in the House of Commons with Aberdeen's explanation and Lord Palmerston asked that Sir Stratford Canning's despatches should be tabled so that the House could make up its own mind about the Serbian affair. Sir Robert Peel, the Prime Minister, stated that Mr. de Fonblanque's despatches would be made available, but not the Ambassador's as the facts were not so well known to him. Layard was much distressed:

> Sir Stratford Canning was deeply mortified and angered by being thus 'thrown over'; but with his usual independence and energy he held to the policy which he had adopted, upon what he considered just grounds, and continued to give all the support in his power to the popular party in Serbia, which was seeking to establish free institutions in the Principality. It was, of course, soon known to the English Foreign Office that it was partly in consequence of my reports that Sir Stratford Canning had adopted this policy, and that he was employing me unofficially and privately as the medium of communication with the Serbian leaders.

Layard expressed no surprise that an ambassador should pursue a policy which was directly opposed to that of his Foreign Minister. He began to regard Lord Aberdeen as an enemy to himself and to his chief in Constantinople. Through Canning's influence, he said, progressive and liberal-minded Turks had been brought into the Government to carry out the various reforms which had been decreed, but no sooner had Russia succeeded in the Serbian affair than these men were ejected, 'to the rage and despair of all those in Constantinople who wanted a strong Turkey'.[2]

*   *   *

Layard was leading a gay and busy life in Constantinople and was not as gloomy as might appear from his letters home and some of his diary entries. He lived at first in Pera with an Armenian family consisting of a mother and three lovely daughters, and then set up house with two newspaper correspondents, Mr. J. A. Longworth and Colonel Charles White. The latter had been aide-de-camp to the Duke of Cambridge, had married a niece of Beau Brummel and knew many of the leading figures in Europe; he was *The Morning Chronicle* correspondent in Constantinople, and Layard was helping him collect information for a book on the manners and customs of the Turks.[3] Longworth, correspondent of *The Morning Post*, had helped to nurse Layard back to health when he and Mitford had been in Constantinople four years earlier. He was a romantic traveller, said Layard, and had fought for the Circassians against the Russians in the cause of liberty. *

White retired to Brussels to write his book, and Layard and Longworth then moved to a small cottage in the charming village of Candili, which remains today one of the most beautiful places on the Asiatic side of the Bosphorus. He looked out from his window on the waters lapping the shore, as did Pierre Loti fifty years later. A little distance away was the famous 'Sweet Waters of Asia', a stream which used to flow clear and fast through lovely wooded country. Today, owing to the building of a dam, the water is so dark and sluggish that it is difficult to see even the large turtles swimming just beneath the green surface but there are still grassy banks and spreading trees, which help one to picture the gay, pastoral scene when the beauty and fashion of Constantinople used to picnic there. The Turkish ladies came on Fridays, and on Sundays the Greeks and Armenians. Layard would settle under a shady tree with cushions, his book, and a hookah. It was his favourite place for study—he also found it easier to enter into conversations with the women: 'As the vices of Europe have not yet penetrated to this secluded spot, the inhabitants have not acquired an indiscriminate dread of all men wearing hats and coats.'

Except for these holiday excursions he spent as much of the day as possible with his books, and repeatedly asked his mother to find him works on the antiquities, geography, and people of Mesopotamia. He wrote to his mother's friend Cecilia Berkeley:

> When I wander to the hills which overhang my village, I have at my feet a thousand spots rendered sacred by the most remarkable events of two empires. On these hills the young Armenian ladies (for my village is inhabited by Armenians) are wont to throw off their veils and sport with unconcealed charms. . . .
>
> I can gaze upon the city of Constantinople and can trace the windings of the Straits from their birth in the Black Sea to their junction with the Marmora. From my windows the view is more

* Longworth went into Circassia as correspondent of *The Times* to investigate the war waged by Shamyl of Daghestan against the Russians. He and David Urquhart were among the first Europeans, other than Russians, to visit the area in the nineteenth century. *A Year Among the Circassians*, by J. A. Longworth (Colburn, 1840).

limited. . . . In front of them stands the Castle of Europe, where the Ottoman conquerors first trod on European ground and laid the foundations of an empire which at one time promised to be one of the most extensive in the history of the world.

Friends used to come from Constantinople for dinner and to stay; his closest friend was Charles Alison with whom he used to go in search of various amorous adventures. Alison was chief interpreter and later Oriental Secretary at the Embassy and had, said Layard, 'real genius'; he was largely responsible for many of Canning's successes, though he worked much in the background. It was one of Alison's tasks to calm the Ambassador when he became excited and he performed it very well. 'Although Sir Stratford was little accustomed to tolerate opposition, which usually only further excited his quick temper, he could not but respect and admire Alison's perfect truthfulness, loyalty, and independence.'

At first Layard had worked for the Ambassador in return for board and lodging, but later he became Canning's secretary and was paid two hundred pounds a year out of the Ambassador's own pocket. He was also earning money as the Constantinople correspondent of various newspapers, writing strongly against Lord Aberdeen's pro-Russian policy and in favour of the Ambassador's anti-Russian policy. Layard, with his capacity for ignoring inconvenient facts, told his family that no one in Constantinople, except the Ambassador, knew that he was author of the articles, and that they must keep it to themselves. Charles White from Brussels warned Layard that it was impossible for such matters to remain secret—'seeing you on excellent terms with Sir S. C. is sufficient to excite the bile of some and the envy of others'. Fonblanque for one made it his business to find out and to inform the Foreign Office. The Ambassador was gratified to have the support in the Press but advised caution.

Now that Layard was earning a living and was on good terms with the Ambassador it might have been expected that relations with the Austens would have been satisfactory, but they were, in fact, nearly broken off altogether owing to a revival of the quarrel over Louisa, who still wished to marry Mr. Linton in spite of Sara's opposition. Sara believed that her nephew had been writing to Louisa from Constantinople encouraging her to marry Mr. Linton. Layard denied that he had had anything to do with the matter. The quarrel developed to a point where Austen told his nephew that his correspondence either with Louisa, or with his uncle and aunt, must cease. Layard was angry that he should have been faced with such an alternative: 'I can never be so base as to act in a dishonourable manner, even to retain your affection.' After nearly a year of acrimonious discussion the quarrel was settled by an agreement that he should not mention Louisa's name in his letters to the Austens. He was very devoted to his uncle and aunt and they to him, so that both sides were touchy and upset when there were differences. Layard, in spite of his many references to personal independence, felt the need for affection, which was furnished by his mother, and for a stable background, which was furnished by the Austens. When he was under the fire of Austen criticism it made him feel unhappy and deserted. He told his uncle that his temperament was 'particularly sensitive and easily subject to irritation'. 'It is really too bad', he wrote to his mother, 'that I should have been drawn into this family quarrel when a whole continent is between us.' He said that he had often been on the point of leaving for the Bakhtiari and getting away from all intercourse with Europe: 'How I long for a black tent, a horse, a flock of sheep, and a wife in the solitary mountains of Luristan, where I may do as I like and say what I like. This is the only life worthy of an independent man who does not wish to be the slave of a few shillings or a few guineas—hundreds or thousands—according to his means.'

At the age of twenty-six, Layard was still making rhetorical bids for freedom, but he knew very well that he could not escape by galloping off to the Bakhtiari mountains; he resented the fact that he was too tied by affection to his family, and by necessity to Stratford Canning, to allow him to become a wanderer again. Sara Austen pulled hard on the snaffle every now and again—and her nephew replied to one unkind missive: 'I trust that that letter gave you as much pain to write as it did me to read'. Layard wrote to Mitford at this time expressing his thankfulness that he was living far from his family, and in a happy state of independence: 'I am still the miserable being you remember, without any immediate chance of amelioration of fortune. As for marriage—the Lord have mercy upon me! I am destined to skip that great event in man's life.' Mitford had told Layard about his own marriage in Ceylon; he added that Layard would have been badly off if he had come there, for there was little patronage and the only means to advancement was through the deaths of senior officials—'and this place is so very healthy'.

Layard had developed and matured considerably in the three years that had passed since he parted from Mitford; he had thrown off much of his wildness and braggadocio. He was even shocked when there arrived in Constantinople in November 1843 a stranger and even more irresponsible character than he had ever been. This was Dr. Joseph Wolff, on his way from London to the Emir of Bokhara in an attempt to ascertain the fate of the two British officers, Stoddart and Conolly. It was feared that they had been put to death and their relations wanted to know what had happened. Layard was amazed that the doctor, instead of proceeding quietly and secretly about his business, had lectured upon his plans in the chapel of the Russian Embassy in Constantinople, and had published proclamations in the Moslem newspapers that he intended to enter Bokhara in the robes of an English priest to demand the prisoners in the name of God. 'All this is very admirable for a romance', Layard wrote to his uncle, 'but I am too well acquainted with the habits of wandering tribes and of fanatical eastern populations to have very sanguine hopes of his success. . . . Wolff is so obstinate and wild there is no talking sense to him.' Layard was not critical because Wolff was going to Bokhara; both he and Longworth had volunteered to go there, but the British Government, convinced that both officers were dead, was not prepared to subscribe any funds. Layard thought this was the height of meanness and little encouragement to others engaged in dangerous undertakings in Government service. Layard believed, incorrectly, that the two men were still alive and after collecting as much information as possible from travellers coming to Constantinople he had made a plan. He was critical of Wolff because he would not follow the plan to make Meshed his headquarters. Wolff wrote from Pera in November to thank Layard for his 'important intelligence, but nothing will bring this matter to a complete certainty than my going straight to the very gates of Bokhara, without stopping one single moment at Meshed, for I consider Meshed a very unsafe place'. This remarkable man did, in fact, reach Bokhara, helped perhaps by the fact that the tribesmen thought he was mad and therefore holy, but found that Stoddart and Conolly had been put to death.*

Layard was seeking a more settled life and was most anxious to be acknowledged as a member of the regular Diplomatic Service. He was carrying out various missions for Canning in Constantinople and had a great deal of responsibility without any assurance of support in the event of failure; he felt his position insecure, too, because his own quick temper might lead any day to a clash with the fiery Ambassador. Despite Canning's irritability, Layard enjoyed working for him and was in complete sympathy with his policy of supporting the Ottoman Reform Party; both considered that unless the corrupt administration of the Porte were reformed the Ottoman Empire would collapse. There was a bitter and ruthless struggle for power between Reshid Pasha, author of the new Constitution, and Riza Pasha, who was against all progress, except that which might increase the strength of the army, and he exercised considerable influence over Sultan Abdul Mejid. The Russian Ambassador's policy was to support Riza Pasha and prevent reform. He used gentle and persuasive methods to attain his ends, while Canning tried to enforce reforms by imposing his will upon the Turks, who resented both his haughty manner and the humiliations to which he exposed them. Layard wrote later in his *Autobiography* :

> I am convinced that, had Sir Stratford Canning shown a more conciliatory and appreciative disposition in his dealings with Turkish statesmen, he would have accomplished more, and might have saved the Empire from some of the disasters which subsequently befell it. The system he adopted was calculated to destroy the little prestige and authority which remained to the Porte, and it gradually undermined its independence, till each foreign

---

* On his return to London, Joseph Wolff wrote *Narrative of a Mission to Bokhara to ascertain the fate of Colonel Stoddart and Captain Conolly*, 1845. Wolff's bizarre and heroic adventures have been admirably retold in *A Person from England* by Sir Fitzroy Maclean (Cape, 1958).

Representative was endeavouring to outdo his colleagues in worrying the unfortunate Turks who were charged with the administration of public affairs.

Layard was used by the Ambassador as an agent to keep in touch with Reshid Pasha and the members of the Reform Party when they were in disgrace. His assignments were always secret and sometimes dangerous. Layard enjoyed this work as it suited his 'somewhat romantic disposition', and the Ambassador was fond of mystery and took pleasure in intrigue. Layard had many secret midnight meetings in the squalid quarters of Constantinople, or was introduced surreptitiously into harems where there was less risk of interruption. He made his way sometimes by boat at night across the fast current of the Bosphorus to a dark, secluded rendezvous upon the Asiatic shore; there were sufficient stories current in Constantinople of political intriguers disappearing without trace to satisfy his passion for adventure.

Layard also met many Turks at Ahmed Vefyk Effendi's home, where he and Longworth used to sleep two nights every week, although no Europeans were supposed to be in this Mohammedan quarter after dark. Ahmed Vefyk at seventeen was already an excellent scholar of Greek, Persian, Turkish, French, and English and the three of them would settle down in the evening after dinner to read Gibbon, Hume, Adam Smith, Shakespeare, and Dickens. At about two in the morning Ahmed Vefyk would retire to his room and the servants made up beds on the floor for Layard and Longworth. At sunrise the whole household was astir and the Englishmen had to leave. There Layard met officials from the Turkish Foreign Department, where Ahmed Vefyk and his father worked; Turks came from the provinces and sometimes a Circassian chief arrived to report on the war against Russia waged by Shamyl, the hero of the Caucasus.

Throughout the day he acted as secretary to the Ambassador, who shaved by candlelight and was at his office soon after six o'clock and was often still working at midnight. Canning wrote at the beginning of 1843 to his brother William, a canon at Windsor:

The business of the Embassy is certainly immense, and what is worse, it grows with success, and, what is still worse, buried affairs *walk.* . . . But you need not be told it is uphill work. Such roguery, corruption, and falsehood and deep anti-social selfishness. Still, my influence strikes a deep root, and I hope against hope. . . . Here, as elsewhere, a great man is wanted—the master-mind, the gigantic hands, that grasp and press and mould at will the scattered elements of empire. . . . We have boats, and carriages, and saddle-horses in abundance; but the difficulty is how to use them. When we do use our four greys and English postilions, half the town assembles to stare, though our Excellencies may go out on foot without drawing a look.[4]

He preferred going by water in his caique 'with its three pairs of oars, and the men—a Greek and two Turks—dressed in full white, Dutchman-like drawers, with gauzy shirts and naked breasts and arms, and red waistcoats picked out with delicate black embroidery'. In February Layard helped Lady Canning give a children's ball and he went dressed as a Bakhtiari. (It was the first time that Turkish boys and girls of good family danced with Christian children.)

The Embassy quarters were temporary and uncomfortable as the new 'palace' had not yet been built, so that the Cannings spent as much time as possible in a house they had hired at Buyukdere. Whereas the Russian, French, and Austrian Governments paid for their ambassadors' summer residences at Therapia and Buyukdere, Canning had to cover the cost himself, which he estimated at six or seven hundred pounds a year. It was a large wooden house on the water's edge with a large marble hall and a room to match it overhead. Layard was given a little house in the grounds and he wrote in August 1844 to Cecilia Berkeley:

I am now living in a very pretty kiosk upon the Bosphorus, in a village some miles from Constantinople. The water washes the walls of my room. . . . The windows, sixteen in number, are on a level with the sea consequently I have a continual circulation of cool air. These are at present my apartments and they are the resort of most people who admire *keff* and idleness. There is a constant succession of pipes and *hookahs*, and the atmosphere is enriched with the delightful fragrance of tobacco.

I have lately taken to the flute and play more out of tune than ever. . . . You are probably aware that in the winter and spring we have an Italian opera at which Donizetti and Co. are heard in high perfection. In the summer and autumn the orchestra wanders

along the shores of the Bosphorus, picking up the contributions of
the generous and the musical.

He was busy working on his notes of the Bakhtiari adventure
and doing research for an article on the Nestorians.* He often had
meals with the Canning family, helped organise musical evenings
when he sometimes played his flute, converted them to Wordsworth, listened to Canning read his own poems, and told stories
to the daughters at bedtime. Although he had no living expenses
he was obliged to keep up 'a genteel appearance and to keep a
servant, so that money is wanted'. The Ambassador's house was
like a home to him and Lady Canning was, he said, a really
delightful person—'he is the essence of acerbity, she of good
nature and gentleness'. Canning was also very kind to him,
encouraging him to be patient when he was on the point of
giving up and seeking his fortunes elsewhere. Layard had even
written to his uncle again suggesting that he might come back
to England to start work in Gray's Inn. The uncertainty 'weighed
considerably upon my spirits', he said, 'and was only alleviated
by the extreme kindness of the Ambassador and Lady Canning'.

Canning was fond of Layard and impressed by his high ability
and hard work. A few years later when Layard was excavating
at Nimrud, the Ambassador called at Montague Place where he
found Sara Austen alone. She told him of the happiness which
the Ambassador and Lady Canning had given Layard by their
kindness and that he had often written of this. Canning, she
said, had '*beamed* with pleasure' and had said: 'You make me
really happy in telling me all this. I could not know exactly what
he felt. I am so glad I came to talk to you. I have the greatest
. regard for him and interest in him, and am only sorry that Lord
Aberdeen baffled my views for him. Layard was often a great
comfort to me. You cannot think how hard he worked—nor

* Layard's work on the Nestorians was included in *Nineveh and Its
Remains*. He wrote his Bakhtiari adventures but did not consider that
he could send them for publication since Mohamed Taki Khan was still
a prisoner and might have been harmed, nor would it have done
Layard any good at a moment when he still hoped for employment in
the area. Major Rawlinson wrote: 'I regret exceedingly that you were
prevented from publishing your Bakhtiari travels—they would have
been infinitely more satisfactory than Bode's superficial notices.'
Mohamed Taki Kahn died in 1851 and Hussein Kuli in 1855.

how well. He had as much application as talent and energy—a rare combination. He *must* do well, if he will only have *patience.*'

It is doubtful whether Stratford Canning was the best master to teach Layard patience, or even tact and discretion. Master and pupil were too much alike; able, hard-working, intelligent, imperious, and high-handed. Layard was, however, very much more easy-going and companionable than Canning; it was his nature to encourage others and he did not suffer from Canning's besetting sin of jealousy. When Mr. Wellesley arrived as Secretary of the Embassy in 1844, Layard was shocked at the way the Ambassador treated him. It was rumoured that Aberdeen had sent Wellesley to keep an eye on Canning and make sure that he did not get into trouble with the Russians. Instead of trying to win him over, the Ambassador, said Layard, 'declined to communicate with him on public affairs, and almost went so far as to forbid him access to the Chancery, where he might see the despatches that passed between the Foreign Office and the Ambassador, and other documents relating to public affairs'.

In May of 1844 the Ambassador sent Layard on a journey of three months to the Turkish territory of Albania to report on an insurrection against the Porte and to investigate Russian activities in the area.[5] When he returned, after successfully carrying out his mission, he had expected to find news of his appointment, but there was nothing. He told his family that it could not be the Serbian affair that stood in the way, for the British Government must realise the true nature of the case, 'Lord Aberdeen must admit that I was right in my conjectures and predictions as to Serbia'. Layard never understood that being right was not always an advantage. It seemed, however, in this case that the Government had revised its opinion, for at the end of 1844 Canning received private information from the Foreign Office that Lord Aberdeen had finally agreed to appoint Layard as a paid attaché. The Ambassador was so pleased that he could not resist telling Layard, who at once wrote to Sara Austen. He said that he could not help feeling a little vain at having overcome all the difficulties despite his powerful enemies: 'I see much before me, and abound more in day-dreams and *chateaux-d'Espagne* than most people.' Formal confirmation of the appointment never came and there was no explanation. It may have been the publication of one of his despatches from Constantinople in *The Morning Herald* making a personal attack on Lord Aberdeen, though Layard himself never thought that this could have been the reason.

Layard again thought of leaving Turkey but he found, as he had following previous disappointments, that he could not abandon a country which was so full of fascination to him. 'It is difficult to understand a nation', he wrote to his family, 'which unites two characters and is merging from one into the other and is yet in the transmigration. It is thus with the Turks; they are scarcely Asiatics and have just acquired enough of the European character to destroy many of their virtues and to remove many of their vices. It is this change which is taking place and the uncertainty of its result which renders this country really interesting.'

PART TWO

Archaeology

1845–1851

1

'Visions of palaces underground'

'Come, I pray you, and let us have a little archaeological fun at Khorsabad', wrote Paul Botta to Layard in the spring of 1843 after his sensational discoveries north-east of Mosul. This was the Assyrian palace-city of Dur-Sharrukin (Khorsabad), founded by Sargon (722–705 B.C.). It was argued at first that Botta's discovery was not Assyrian but of a much later period, probably Sassanian. Layard assured him that the monuments were Assyrian and Botta repeatedly urged him to come to his help, as his knowledge of the subject would be of the greatest value, but Layard could not persuade the Ambassador to let him go. He aroused his interest, however, by letting him see Botta's exciting reports and drawings. These were eagerly awaited in Paris, but Botta generously allowed Layard to see them on their way through Constantinople, saying that he could copy what he wished and write about the discoveries; but he advised caution, 'for one more stroke of the spade' might completely change an opinion: 'You complain of the want of sacred symbols, and just

now I send you a bull with a human head, and winged figure with
a bird's head and a figure with the lotus. Do not be too hasty.'

Botta had urged the French Government to send him an
artist as he could not deal with everything single-handed and in
May 1844 Eugène Flandin arrived at Khorsabad where he worked
for eight months. At the beginning of 1845 Flandin broke his
return journey to Paris at Constantinople bringing the drawings
he had made. Layard was amazed at the beauty of the detail and
asserted that the discoveries were 'by far the most interesting
and valuable of the century'. He wrote a series of articles for
The Malta Times which were immediately reprinted in English
newspapers and periodicals.* He described vases, drinking cups,
sword scabbards adorned with lions' heads, shields engraved
with animals and flowers, chairs, tables, head ornaments, brace-
lets, and earrings; they were all, he wrote, designed with great
taste and rivalled objects from the most cultivated period of
Greek art. Fifteen chambers had been opened in a magnificent
palace; the walls were covered with inscriptions and sculptures
which illustrated sieges, naval manoeuvres, single combats, and
so on.

Rawlinson in Bagdad read Layard's articles with great
interest, but said that he was not in agreement with his classi-
fication of cuneiform writing: 'There is but one character
employed at Khorsabad and not two as you suppose', he wrote
in April 1845. 'The tablets look different it must be allowed but
the varieties are probably merely those of alphabetic modification
and dialectic change. My own idea is that one general semitic
alphabet prevailed from Ararat to the Persian Gulf.' In June
Rawlinson said that he was about to send to London, through
Constantinople, a translation of the Persian cuneiform in the trilingual inscription at Bisutun.

Layard was delighted with this arrangement and also with the
reports he was receiving from Botta which made him all the
more eager to go to Mosul. Botta said that the monuments
stretched for half a mile and were probably not a tenth part of

* Layard's first articles were published in *The Malta Times* in
January 1845. *Lettres de M. Botta sur ses découvertes à Khorsabad*
were published by M. J. Mohl later in 1845 after being first published
in the *Journal Asiatique*.

what still remained to be excavated. Rawlinson was also anxious for Layard to go. 'It pains me grievously', he wrote, 'to see the French monopolize the field, for the fruits of Botta's labours . . . will constitute a national glory in future ages, when perhaps the Turkish Empire, that we are now struggling so hard to preserve, shall be but a matter of history.'

Stratford Canning, however, was then interested in an idea suggested by Layard and which had been taken up by Charles Somers (Lord Eastnor), while on a visit he paid to the Embassy at Therapia. It had long been known that there were some beautiful sculptures from the tomb of Mausolus, known as the Halicarnassus marbles, which were built into the fortress of Budrum, occupied by the Turks. Lord Eastnor obtained permission to visit the fortress and reported that there were forty-two sculptures equal in execution and elegance to the Elgin marbles, but at first Canning failed, as his predecessors had failed, to obtain permission to remove the sculptures. He began to think seriously of letting his secretary, Layard, go to Mosul to make a preliminary report, for the Khorsabad sculptures had aroused great interest in Paris and London and there had been a visit to the Embassy in the summer of the previous year of the Rev. Percy Badger, who made a report suggesting that Layard might be right in thinking that there were antiquities to be found at Nimrud. Badger had been sent from England on a mission to the Nestorian Christians in Mesopotamia and had visited the mounds of Nimrud in March 1844 where he had found a stone slab covered in cuneiform which he had copied and sent to Major Rawlinson in Bagdad; the recent rains had also revealed blocks of cut stone and bricks with cuneiform inscriptions. Canning asked him to make a report which Badger did on his way to London in October suggesting that the Ambassador might like to put his name forward to the Earl of Aberdeen as willing to go to excavate Nimrud, if the Government were interested. * In that same month, however, Layard was already preparing to go to Mosul.

* The text of the report made to the Ambassador by the Rev. George Percy Badger is given in the latter's book *The Nestorians and their Rituals, with the narrative of a mission to Mesopotamia and Coordistan in 1842–1844* (Joseph Masters, 1852).

The Ambassador had asked him for an estimate of the cost for a preliminary survey and Layard had reported that Botta had paid his workmen three to five piastres a day—'for an experiment ten men a day at 4 piastres would I presume be sufficient'. The plan was to carry out the experiment at Nimrud even though the mounds opposite Mosul were regarded as the site of Nineveh, but these mounds would be closely watched by the inhabitants of Mosul whereas Nimrud was in the desert nearly twenty miles to the south. Layard reported that he would need a small tent, a horse and a guard and the total cost would be about sixty pounds for the journey and two thousand five hundred piastres a month (twenty pounds) in expenses. The Ambassador agreed to advance the money for an investigation lasting for two months. He issued very careful instructions, as he had done with the earlier missions. Layard was to be 'a traveller fond of antiquities and of picturesque scenery', avoiding politics and religious questions and, to prevent a repetition of the Belgrade incident, he was not to return without the Ambassador's agreement. Layard accepted this position of 'agent' to the Ambassador and was, indeed, most grateful to Canning for letting him go on this adventure.

When Layard left Constantinople in October 1845 he did not tell anyone outside the Embassy about the object of his journey and when he reached the house of Mr. Christian Rassam, the British Vice-Consul in Mosul, he informed him of the Ambassador's instructions. He told his mother and said that he hoped for success 'but Mr. Botta's great discovery makes one despair a little'. The Frenchman had completed his excavations some months previously and was already in Paris. Layard called on the Turkish Governor, the notorious Mohamed Pasha, whose cruelty and rapacity made the people despair. He had on several occasions interfered with the Khorsabad excavations, 'a little Nero' was Botta's description of him. 'The appearance of His Excellency', wrote Layard, 'was not prepossessing, but it matched his temper and his conduct. Nature had placed hypocrisy beyond his reach. He had one eye and one ear; he was short and fat, deeply marked by the small-pox, uncouth in gesture and harsh in voice.' The Governor was extremely curious to know the object of his visit, as was Botta's successor as Vice-Consul,

Ch. 1   'Visions of palaces underground'

M. Rouet, who had discovered the Assyrian rock sculptures at Maltayah and wished to maintain a monopoly of all the likely Assyrian sites. There were many ways in which the Frenchman could make difficulties for a rival, both with the Governor and with the fanatical Cadi of Mosul. Layard considered that it had been a very wise decision to leave until a later date a further inspection of Kuyunjik, the mound opposite Mosul which was believed to cover the remains of Nineveh.[1] Mr. Rassam managed a building business and was able to arrange for excavating tools to be made secretly in his workshops, while Layard spread the story that he was travelling south along the Tigris to hunt wild boar and he had the good fortune to find a friend and companion in Henry Ross, who was Rassam's partner.

They hired a raft and left Mosul on 8 November 1845, floating down the Tigris for seven hours until they reached the dam across the river opposite Nimrud. With them they had guns, spears, greyhounds, and excavating tools. Disembarking on the east bank they walked for some way before finding anyone, the villages were deserted, the inhabitants having left for the desert, afraid that Mohamed Pasha would take their flocks. Eventually they found a family in a tumble-down house and were invited in for the night. Their host was Awad, a sheikh of the Jehesh tribe, who was intelligent and anxious to earn money, so it was decided to tell him the object of the journey and to offer him a regular wage as superintendent if he could find men to dig. During the night Awad went to Salamiyah, a village three miles away, to look for helpers. Layard describes the beginning of his great adventure in his book *Nineveh and Its Remains*:

> I slept little during the night. The hovel in which we had taken shelter, and its inmates, did not invite slumber; but such scenes and companions were not new to me: they could have been forgotten had my brain been less excited. . . . Hopes, long cherished, were now to be realised, or were to end in disappointment. Visions of palaces underground, of gigantic monsters, of sculptured figures, and endless inscriptions floated before me. . . .
>
> After forming plan after plan for removing the earth, and extricating these treasures, I fancied myself wandering in a maze of chambers from which I could find no outlet. Then, again, all

117

was reburied, and I was standing on the grass-covered mound. Exhausted, I was at length sinking into sleep, when, hearing the voice of Awad, I rose from my carpet and joined him outside the hovel. The day already dawned; he had returned with six Arabs, who agreed for a small sum to work under my direction. The lofty cone and broad mound of Nimrud rose like a distant mountain in the morning sky.

As the party advanced towards the mounds the mists began to clear and Layard could see, as one can see today, 'a long line of consecutive narrow mounds, still retaining the appearance of walls or ramparts, stretched from its base and formed a vast quadrangle'. They walked towards the cone at the northern end of the mound which had for many years intrigued him. It is a *ziggurat* which originally had an Assyrian temple at the top but the main edifice has been worn by wind and rain resembling a tall smooth cone which is one hundred and forty feet high. Layard often calls it a pyramid and it did then look a little more like a pyramid than it does today. 'This was the pyramid', wrote Layard, 'which Xenophon had described, and near which the Ten Thousand had encamped: the ruins around it were those which the Greek general saw twenty-two centuries before, and which were even then the remains of an *ancient* city.' Xenophon called it Larissa and described it as 'a large uninhabited city'. This was Kalhu, called Calah in the Book of Genesis and Nimrud in later times. It followed Ashur (Kalah Shergat) as the capital of Assyria and preceded Nineveh and Khorsabad. Kalhu was founded as a capital city by Shalmaneser I (1272 to 1243 B.C.), and was the residence of several Assyrian kings, the most famous being Ashur-nasir-pal II (883 to 859 B.C.), who built the *ziggurat*, temples and a great palace, its entrances guarded by giant stone lions and bulls. This was the period when the Assyrians, as a result of the efficiency and ruthlessness of their government spread out from the small fertile area they inhabited in the northern region of the Tigris river near Mosal to found their Assyrian empire lasting three hundred years and extending from Persia to the Mediterranean and, for a period, into Egypt. Kalhu or Nimrud was a great city with many temples and palaces on the acropolis and the huge fort of Shalmaneser III on the eastern side of the plateau. The Tigris river skirted the western mound and its ancient river-bed can still be seen. It was dry even in Xenophon's day, the river having already retreated westwards towards its present bed which is nearly two miles west of the mounds. *

The visitor to Nimrud today will find the conical mound, or *ziggurat*, still the landmark that it was to Layard, and the surrounding desert has not changed. After the spring rains the landscape is covered with wild flowers and pasture for sheep and goats; in the summer it is parched desert again and the giant water-melons from the Tigris, which used to be brought on camel-back to the thirsty inhabitants of Mosul, are now taken by lorry in an hour along an asphalted road which runs almost to Nimrud. Layard used to ride to Mosul in three hours, and from the crest of a low hill half-way between Nimrud and Mosul it is possible, as he states, to see both the town and the ruins:

> On one side, in the distance, rises the pyramid, in the midst of the broad plain of the Jaif; and on the other may be faintly distinguished the great artificial mound of Kuyunjik, and the surrounding remains. The leaning minaret of the old mosque of

*Layard found parts of the quay-wall alongside the old bed of the Tigris and it was fully excavated over a century later by the British School of Archaeology in Iraq. Prof. Mallowan has described it in *Twenty-five years of Mesopotamian Discovery*: 'One of the most impressive monuments exposed in recent years has been the massive stone quay-wall which still stands twenty-six feet above the ancient bed of the Tigris. This in turn was surmounted by a lofty mud-brick wall which ran sheer down from the high-lying palaces whose floors towered more than forty feet above the river. . . . The southern side of the city was apparently flanked by a canal, the famous Patti canal built by Ashur-nasir-pal, which linked Nimrud with the river Zab seven miles to the south. In short the city was girt with water on two of its sides as well as being protected by massive walls on all four.' The building of the canal and the rebuilding of Kalhu during the first five years of his reign is recorded by Ashur-nasir-pal on a sandstone monument erected in 879 B.C. in the North-West Palace when he made it into the capital city of his empire. A list is given of the animals taken in the royal hunt—lion, wild bull, ostriches, apes and elephants—and there are details of the menu of the banquet given on the occasion to 69,574 guests: 'The people of Kalhu for ten days I feasted, wined, bathed and honoured them, and then sent them back to their homes in peace and joy', says Ashur-nasir-pal in the inscription. The monument was missed by Layard and later excavators, being discovered in 1951 by the British School of Archaeology in Iraq.

This contour map of Nimrud, drawn in 1956, shows the buildings excavated by Layard in the acropolis of Nimrud as well as the additions made about a century later. Layard's most famous discovery was the centre block of the North-West Palace — the royal and state apartments; the northern and southern wings, together with the quay-wall on the former bed of the river Tigris were excavated by the British School of Archaeology in Iraq. The palaces and temples on the western half of the mound were recovered mainly by Layard, and those in the eastern half mainly by the British School which also excavated several other large buildings in the outer town, including Fort Shalmaneser, the greatest military establishment of ancient Assyria.

MAGNETIC N

NABU TEMPLE — STREET — EZIDA — BURNT PALACE — GOVERNOR'S PALACE — DIG-HOUSE — TRACK — S.W. PALACE — CENTRAL PALACE — N.W. PALACE — DOMESTIC WING — WELL NN — WELL E — WELL B — Z.T. — GATE E — THRONE ROOM — GATE G — TOILET ROOM — ISHTAR TEMPLE — NINURTA TEMPLE — TOWN WALL FACE — HOUSES T.W. 53 — QUAY WALL — QUAY — ROCK SCARP

METRES
50 25 0 50 100 150 200 250 300
CONTOURS AT 2 METRE INTERVALS

A. B. C. OBELISKS

Mosul, may also be seen springing above the dark patch which
marks the site of the town. The river can be traced for many miles,
winding in the midst of the plain, suddenly losing itself among
low hills, and again emerging into the level country.

To the south of the *ziggurat* the Iraq Antiquities Department
have now erected an Assyrian gateway with two of the excavated
stone monsters, or *lamassu*, as guardians but having entered and
climbed up to the great plateau there is no sign of past grandeur.
It must have looked much the same in November 1845, though
to Layard it did not appear desolate, for he was buoyed up with
the hope that there were palaces beneath these man-made
mounds and that he would re-enact the adventures of Aladdin
from his favourite *Arabian Nights*.

Layard explained to the Arabs what he was looking for and
they brought him handfuls of rubbish among which he found,
to his joy, the fragment of a bas-relief, 'the material on which it
was carved had been exposed to fire and resembled, in every
respect, the burnt gypsum of Khorsabad'. Awad led him to a
piece of limestone which appeared above the soil and he told his
workmen to dig around it. In a letter from Nimrud to Sir Stratford Canning he described what happened on the day of his
arrival at the mound.

> I commenced excavating on the 9th [November]. Having opened
> a trench in a part of the mound in which a block of stone projected
> from the ground I came at once upon a chamber 25 feet long and
> 14 broad, formed of slabs of marble $8\frac{1}{2}$ feet in length, each slab
> containing an inscription in the cuneiform character! I opened one
> part of the chamber to the flooring, which I found to be of marble
> and covered with inscriptions.

He moved some of the men to the south corner of the long
mound, which ran from near the *ziggurat* along the west side of
the plateau, and found a wall of limestone and more cuneiform
inscriptions. It seemed at first to be one continuous mound
measuring roughly eighteen hundred feet in length and eight
hundred and eighty in breadth, but he had in fact on the first
day discovered a chamber in the famous North-West Palace
which was to yield so many treasures, and a wall in the South-
West Palace, the first built by Ashur-nasir-pal II and the second
by Esarhaddon (681–669 B.C.), though the names were not

known until some years later, when Assyrian cuneiform began to be deciphered. * In the rubbish near the bottom of the chamber of the North-West Palace he was overjoyed to find several beautiful ivory figures which still retained traces of gilding; there was the figure of a king, part of a crouching sphinx, and an ornamental border of flowers as well as other items which were to be the foundation of a remarkable collection.† He decided to concentrate his digging on the western side to begin with and to explore no farther, for the whole plateau was about 900 acres.

Henry Ross was caught up in Layard's enthusiasm, and described him as 'such a nice fellow—very clever and very amusing'. It was wonderful to think, Ross told his sister, how the Assyrians raised such immense mounds of earth upon which to build their palaces and to encircle their cities; three chariots could drive abreast on the walls. He estimated that it would cost about fifteen hundred pounds to excavate this site at Nimrud.[3]

A message came from Rawlinson in Bagdad to say how delighted he was that excavations had started, but he did not think that Layard would be as successful as Botta had been, since Nimrud was too far from the mountains where the limestone, or 'Mosul marble', was quarried; there would, however, be inscriptions. Rawlinson argued that these would be of infinitely greater value than bas-reliefs, for he was certain that

* The North-West Palace covered about six and a half acres but Layard did not excavate all of it, concentrating on the central block. The South-West Palace was in course of construction by Esarhaddon (681–669 B.C.), but was never finished. 'For its decoration', writes Dr. C. J. Gadd in *The Assyrian Sculptures*, 'he removed older slabs from the North-West and Central Palaces and, turning them with their face to the wall, intended to recarve them on their back. It is from the North-West Palace that by far the most numerous and best preserved of the sculptures are derived.'

The Central Palace which was discovered by Layard was built by Shalmaneser III (858–824 B.C.), son of Ashur-nasir-pal and rebuilt by Tiglath-pileser III (745–727 B.C.).[2]

† This was the first discovery of ivories and, with the later additions, the Nimrud collection is now the richest ever recovered from the ancient world. See *A Catalogue of the Nimrud Ivories in the British Museum* by R. D. Barnett, Keeper of Western Asiatic Antiquities.

very soon he would be able to decipher them completely but Layard realised that it had been the Khorsabad bas-reliefs which had aroused the interest of Europe and that urgently needed funds would not be raised for the finding of cuneiform inscriptions which might take many years to decipher. Stratford Canning agreed with this, for people, he said, resembled children in that 'they like to look at the pictures'.

On 28 November, in the S.W. Palace he made his exciting discovery of bas-reliefs taken, as he realised, from the N.W. Palace. [*Nineveh and Its Remains*, p. 35.] He wrote to Canning:

> Dear Sir, I am happy to inform Your Excellency that on Friday last I was sufficiently fortunate to find sculptures at Nimrud similar to those at Khorsabad. . . . After opening a tunnel about fifteen feet in length I found a wall with sculptures. I was proceeding to dig along this wall when a person from the Pasha requested me to stop the excavations. I had then only uncovered five tablets. One representing a combat with warriors in chariots, a second, the siege of a city, both designed and executed with considerable spirit; another slab, on which there are four sculptures, is only partly uncovered; it is *reversed* and contains, as far as I could see, a sea or river scene, a king or warrior on horseback, and several figures. Each tablet is divided by cuneiform inscriptions well preserved. The marble has been damaged by fire and is cracked in some places, but the sculptures could be removed with little care and are well worth sending to England.

To have the work stopped at such an exciting moment infuriated Layard. He jumped on his horse and rode quickly to Mosul to see the Governor, who said that there was no objection to his digging. It had become clear, however, that the one-eyed Pasha enjoyed playing pranks. He had recently had it announced that he was dead and, from within his harem, had watched the citizens of Mosul rejoicing at the news whereupon his men went round the town fining everyone who had expressed pleasure. Having encouraged Layard to think that all was well, the Pasha summoned him again to tell him that he had never been given permission to excavate and that the ban was for the Englishman's protection, since his life 'was more valuable than old stones'; the mound at Nimrud was a Moslem burial ground and the law forbade any disturbance of the tombs. In vain

Layard protested that not a single burial stone had been seen and that the story must have been invented by enemies in Mosul.

On his return to Nimrud he was amazed to see a number of Moslem grave stones on the mound. Eventually Captain Daoud, the Governor's representative, confessed that during the two nights Layard had been in Mosul, he had had to order his troops to bring burial stones from distant villages and set them up on the mound. 'We have destroyed', said Daoud, 'more real tombs of the true Believers in making sham ones than you could have defiled between the Zab and Salamiyah; we have killed our horses and ourselves in carrying these accursed stones.'

Layard told the Ambassador he suspected that the French Consul had been working against him since as soon as Rouet had become aware of the excavations, 'he sent agents all over the country to open mounds and to search for antiquities. I found myself compelled to follow his example.' The antiquities excavated by Botta were still at Bagdad waiting for a ship to transport them to France: 'I think we might manage to transmit some sculptures to Europe as soon, if not sooner than the French. This would be very important to our reputation . . . I trust you will now be induced to commence excavations on a large scale at Nimrud and to remove the sculptures which may be found there.' Layard made friends with Captain Daoud and a small gift enabled him to carry on excavating quietly. He continued to find beautifully designed bas-reliefs and wrote to his Uncle Benjamin on 15 December:

> The marbles which I have hitherto uncovered are beautiful, full of life and *mouvement*, and, in the opinion of those who have seen them, superior to those discovered by Botta. The inscriptions are exceedingly numerous and I have got work on hand for weeks to copy those already uncovered, a very, very small part of those still underground. You have no idea of the extreme tediousness of copying them; the patience of the most exemplary of the Patriarchs would be exhausted.

He had also found many bricks with ornamental painting and was amazed to see the colours still so well preserved, 'the blues and greens are particularly brilliant and laid on thickly with a glazing or varnish over'.

These discoveries made Layard insistent in his letters to the Ambassador throughout the early part of 1846 that a firman should be procured to allow him to dig and to remove sculptures so that the Governor of Mosul would not be able to interfere. He was nervous lest the French might try to lay hands on Nimrud since he lacked authority while he pretended to be a simple traveller. Rawlinson, he told Canning, was prepared to send up one of the steamers to take away the sculptures and she should arrive in March, so that the antiquities could be in England by next autumn, long before the French could get their antiquities to France: 'This would be highly creditable and give us the priority of European exhibition which in these things is almost as important as the priority of discovery.'

Eager as the Ambassador was to help he had begun to be worried about the expense. Layard had reported that the ground was so hard 'spades are utterly useless and even the steel points of the picks are soon turned'. The antiquities were so deeply embedded that ten men made little progress and the diggers had been increased to thirty. 'I cannot yet form an estimate of the probable amount of expenses attending the removal of sculptures', he had written on 1 December. 'The mound of Nimrud is probably the largest in Assyria, and should the whole contain sculptures, as is probable, the collection will be very great.' Canning realised that the enthusiastic Layard might run him into heavier costs than he was prepared to bear. He was also again hopeful of getting permission to remove the Hali-carnassus marbles from the fortress of Budrum and he could not ask the Porte immediately for permission to remove antiquities from Nimrud as well. He wrote a series of sympathetic and encouraging letters to try to keep Layard content: 'What would I not give to be with you when you succeed in working your way into the large edifice. . . . My curiosity is not only on tip-toe, but on stilts. . . . Take courage, however; be prudent as hitherto and civil, keeping your good humour, whether towards the Pasha or towards M. Rouet. If you can spy a favourable moment to get out of your present suspension, so much the better, if not be patient and I shall do my best to come to your aid.' Alison, too, sent encouragement, 'The Elchee is vastly pleased with you—you may be sure of his best exertions—and I have an idea that your labours, particularly in the deciphering line, may throw great light on what many people take such an interest in.'

The most cheering letter of all had been one from Rawlinson, though his reasoning, based on the faulty information of the ancient Greek and Roman writers, turned out to be inaccurate:

> I have lately examined with some attention the geographical and historical questions connected with Nimrud, and I can come to no other conclusion than that it is the original Nineveh which was destroyed under Sardanapalus, the ruins of Nebbi Yunis being those of the second Nineveh, that of the lower Assyrian dynasty. Khorsabad I consider to be the palace of Evorita, where Sarakos burnt himself in imitation of the example of Sardanapalus.

Rawlinson's letter was dated 10 December and five days later Layard wrote to his uncle to say he was very willing to rest satisfied with this result of his enquiries: 'There can be no doubt that Nimrud, whatever the city was, owes its destruction to fire.' In the second part of his letter Rawlinson shows his astuteness in recognising that there were non-Semitic elements in the writing, which he called Scythic but was Sumerian. The fact that no one yet knew of the existence of the earlier Sumerian civilisation, when cuneiform was invented, made deciphering all the more difficult; the Assyrians inherited many of the Sumerian traditions, so that the two elements—the non-Semitic Sumerian and the Semitic—occurred in the cuneiform writing. He wrote:

> I am delighted also to find that your figures at Nimrud wear high caps, for it confirms a theory I have long entertained, based originally upon one of the mutilated tablets of Bisutun that the Chaldeans inhabited Assyria in remote times and were Scythians and not of the semitic race. I doubt greatly if the Assyrian inscriptions are not throughout Scythic in their fundamentals of speech, but *Semitised* to a certain extent by the mingling of the two races. This is a very curious subject and promises to lead to the most important ethnographical discoveries.

These were some of the matters for discussion when Layard met Rawlinson for the first time that Christmas, staying with him as his guest at the Bagdad Residency; the former was twenty-eight and the latter thirty-five, both earnest and enthusiastic. The note on 'Rules of Conduct' Rawlinson had made in his diary

Ch. 1   'Visions of palaces underground'

as a young man might have been written by Layard: 'Create business for yourself. Lose no opportunity of making yourself useful. . . . Grasp at everything and never yield an inch.' There was another note which the younger man would have done well to follow: 'Above all, never stand upon trifles.'*

After the hardships of Nimrud it was very pleasant to be entertained in the luxury of the Residency where Rawlinson lived in as much state as had Colonel Taylor. Layard wrote to his mother that the two of them were deep in discussion and research on Assyrian, Babylonian, and Persian antiquities, languages and geography, on which subjects he considered his host to be the greatest authority. Perhaps within two or three years it would be possible to solve the mystery of Assyrian cuneiform and Nimrud would then give up its secrets. He said that he had not yet made up his mind about Rawlinson's theory that Nimrud was the true Nineveh. He did not spend all his time discussing antiquities. 'The morals of the ladies in this country are exceedingly lax', he wrote to the American painter, Miner Kellogg, whom he had known in Constantinople. . . . 'There is, however, little beauty in Mosul, but at Bagdad there are some remarkably pretty women. In Mosul, provided your dwelling is convenient, the ladies make no difficulty in walking in, not only when you want them, but uninvited, and at Bagdad the same good custom prevails.'(4) He told his mother that he had so many 'wives' that he would be glad to get rid of them. Alison, who was complaining of the difficulty of finding an inexpensive mistress in Constantinople, thought that the lax Mesopotamian morals described by Layard, 'must be a great resource on the whole to a youth of your complexion and beneficial to your health'.

* *A Memoir of Major-General Sir Henry Creswicke Rawlinson K.C.B., F.R.S., D.C.L., F.R.G.S.* by his brother George Rawlinson, Canon of Canterbury (Longmans 1898). The author describes the close co-operation between the two men, but under-estimates Layard in describing him as 'not a scholar, or a man of great culture, or of any wide reading'.

2

'They have found
Nimrod himself!'

When Layard returned to Mosul at the beginning of January 1846 he expected to find the firman from Constantinople giving him permission to dig and to remove antiquities, but nothing had arrived. Canning had obtained permission to remove the Halicarnassus marbles from Budrum and he could as yet do nothing for Layard but it was some time before he confessed the reason for the delay. He continued, however, to be excited

128

about the Assyrian discoveries and wrote to Lady Canning in London on 3 January 1846:

> Layard is making very important discoveries in Mesopotamia. . . . I am quite proud of my public spirit in the cause of antiquity and fine art. But I must not ruin either you or the children; and I intend to call in the aid of the Government—whether Whig or Tory—to accomplish what may easily prove beyond my reach. . . . Perhaps you think me crazy for caring about such trifles but they are trifles for which colleges, universities and nations would take each other by the ears, and, as Major Rawlinson tells me, the inscriptions are likely to throw much light upon Scripture history, particularly on our old friend Tiglath-pileser.

The need for a firman was not for the moment quite so urgent since the one-eyed Governor had at last been removed and replaced, temporarily, by a charming officer, Ismail Pasha, who authorised the excavations to continue at Nimrud. Layard returned there with Hormuzd Rassam, the seventeen-year-old brother of the British Vice-Consul, who was to act as his secretary and pay the workmen.

With the change of Governor there was much greater security and it was possible to move the headquarters to Nimrud from Salamiyah. Layard was delighted by the change in the countryside:

> From the summit of the pyramid my eye ranged, on one side, over a broad level enclosed by the Tigris and the Zab; on the other over a low undulating country bounded by the snow-capped mountains of Kurdistan; but it was no longer the dreary waste I had left a month before; the landscape was clothed in green, the black tents of the Arabs chequered the plains of Nimrud, and their numerous flocks pastured on the distant hills.

Everything seemed set fair for a good winter season of excavation and almost at once further important discoveries were made. He wrote to the Ambassador from Nimrud on 24 January:

> The most remarkable object which I have found is a magnificent Bull in the centre of the mound. Unfortunately the head and wings have been destroyed. . . . The splendid sculpture is fourteen feet in length and, when entire, must have been twelve to thirteen in height. It would be difficult to convey to your Excellency an idea

129

of the beauty of the design and workmanship and of the effect
produced. . . . All the walls hitherto opened have inscriptions
upon them. These I both copy and take off with wet paper—com-
paring the two carefully afterwards.

Botta had written to say that he was returning to Mosul and that
he intended to start excavations at Kuyunjik: 'I have long
wished', said Layard, 'to open the mound which is supposed to
mark the site of the real Nineveh, and have not hitherto done
so on account of its proximity to Mosul.' Botta, however, wrote
again to say that he was delayed as the French Parliament had
not, as yet, been able to vote the required sums of money; a
M. Guillois arrived to act temporarily as French Vice-Consul.
Layard was disturbed to hear that he was applying for a firman
to excavate Kuyunjik. He was worried also because the Cadi of
Mosul was trying to stir up the people against Layard and the
acting Governor had had to ask him to withdraw his workmen
from Nimrud until the trouble died down. 'I regret', said Layard
to the Ambassador, 'that this should have happened now that it
would be important to get as many sculptures uncovered as
possible to be ready for removal in case of the ascent of the
steamer.'

He left a few workmen on the mound to guard the excavations
and to do a little quiet digging, while he paid visits to sheikhs of
the local tribes. The Abou Salman Arabs were particularly
notorious as thieves and had already tried to raid the expedition's
headquarters at Nimrud; but he took presents of a silk gown,
coffee, and sugar to their principal sheikh, Abd-ur-rahman,
'one of the handsomest Arabs I ever saw', said Layard, 'tall,
robust, and well-made with a countenance in which intelligence
was no less marked than courage and resolution'. They became
friends and there were no more raids.

While riding back to the mound from this visit on 20 February,
two Arab horsemen approached him at full gallop from the
direction of Nimrud. They pulled up abruptly and shouted:
"Hasten, O Bey! for they have found Nimrod himself!" Layard
hurried to the mound; there the workmen were standing awe-
struck before a huge human head as tall as themselves. Layard,
too, stood gazing at it in wonder. 'I shall not myself easily forget
this enormous head appearing from the earth, at the bottom of a

deep trench, like some giant arising from the lower regions', he wrote to the Ambassador. 'News that old Nimrod had appeared spread among the Arabs who were completely lost in wonder. . . . The head is five foot high, and must form a part of a winged bull. . . . It is in perfect preservation and could be removed entire.' Layard was not surprised that the Arabs were amazed and terrified at this apparition for there were traditional stories about Nimrod and of fearful beings appearing to mortals slowly ascending from beneath the earth. When Abd-ur-rahman was told he and his other tribesmen mounted their horses and came galloping to see the marvel. The Sheikh of the tribe was eventually persuaded to descend into the pit. "This is not the work of men's hands", he exclaimed, "but of those infidel giants of whom the Prophet has said that they were higher than the tallest date tree; this is one of the idols which Noah cursed before the flood." The crowd agreed with him and there was great apprehension but Layard had sufficient control over his workmen to make them dig a trench in a direct line to find the other similar figure, since they were presumably guarding a gateway, and by nightfall it was found. A few workmen were told to sleep near the figures to prevent harm coming to them, while Layard returned to the village of Salamiyah, engaged some wandering musicians, gave a feast and the Arabs danced a great part of the night. The next day so many Arabs had arrived, including many from distant parts, that the *cawass* had to be stationed in the trench to prevent the crowds from coming too near. It was unfortunate that one of the workmen had been so terrified on catching sight of 'the monster' that he had run all the way to Mosul and had thrown the town into commotion. 'Entering breathless into the bazaars', Layard writes in *Nineveh and Its Remains*, 'he announced to everyone he met that Nimrod had appeared. The news soon got to the ears of the Cadi who, anxious for a fresh opportunity to annoy me, called the Mufti and the Ulema together, to consult upon this unexpected occurrence. Their deliberations ended in a procession to the Governor, and a formal protest, on the part of the Mussulmans of the town, against proceedings so directly contrary to the laws of the Koran. The Cadi had no distinct idea whether the bones of the mighty hunter had been uncovered, or only his image; nor did Ismail Pasha very clearly remember whether Nimrod was a true-believing prophet, or an infidel. I consequently received a somewhat unintelligible message from His Excellency, to the effect that the remains should be treated with respect and be by no means further disturbed; that he wished the excavations to be stopped at once, and desired to confer with me on the subject.' Layard went to Mosul to explain the situation to the acting-Governor and had to dismiss most of his workmen until the excitement had died down.

Layard had begun his excavations on 9 November and Canning had originally agreed to a survey of two months. By 20 February 1846, when the great head was discovered, the period had been exceeded by over a month and Layard wrote on 21 February: 'I have received no instructions from Your Excellency on the subject of expenses. I have ventured to draw for 2,500 piastres, as you appear to wish me to continue the excavations. I have also had recourse, as far as I am able, to my private resources and shall continue to do so until I hear from you—in the hopes that, should the Government carry on the excavations, I shall be refunded.' Besides the twenty pounds a month which had been spent on excavations, there had been other expenses such as presents amounting to 1,500 piastres (nearly £15), which included the gifts to Sheikh Abd-ur-rahman, paying a claim preferred by the owners of the land at Nimrud and an indemnity for the price of corn and barley which had been sown on the mound.

Layard still waited anxiously for the firman from Constantinople giving him permission to excavate; once that had arrived the acting Governor's hand would be strengthened against French intrigues and the machinations of the Cadi. He had not been told of the reason for the delay, but at last a letter arrived from the Ambassador to explain that the Porte had given permission for the Greek bas-reliefs to be removed from the walls of the fortress of Budrumand that Alison had been sent to extract them; he could not ask immediately for another firman for Layard. Although delighted that his friend Alison had been sent on the mission, Layard was bitterly disappointed at the delay, but he wrote very tactfully to Canning: 'With the Halicarnassus Marbles and (I hope) those of Nimrud, Your Excellency will indeed have made a most valuable addition to our National collection.'

Layard knew that the only way to get funds was to arouse interest through publicity in England, or by getting the bas-reliefs to London, but there was no money available to do this, and the steamer had failed to approach near enough to Nimrud to make loading possible. Alison received a disconsolate letter describing the discomfort of living at Nimrud; Layard said he did not think it would be easy to find another person to put up with it and who would 'sleep on the ground amidst all the vermin of an Arab establishment'. Indeed, wrote Alison in reply, it would not be easy to find another person who would be such a fool to live in such squalor: 'If you allow yourself to be put to any discomfort by a false delicacy in not providing yourself with what a gentleman's habits render absolutely necessary, I don't pity you a jot. . . . I see nothing, even in imagination, to encourage the gloomy forebodings which you are wont at times to indulge in; so fire away and never say die.' Alison was delighted at the success of his own mission to Budrum and proudly asserted, that it had only cost one hundred and fifty pounds to get the Halicarnassus marbles: 'The Elchee is in great glee and intends to present them to the British Museum' and they had been marked 'Canning Marbles'. Alison's cheerfulness was rather annoying for neither he nor the Ambassador began to understand the enormous task facing Layard. To remove vast mounds of earth, to pack up large monuments and to arrange for them to go by raft to Bagdad and Basra was not as simple an operation as the Budrum expedition had been. Besides that there were his living expenses; economical as he was Layard had to have a horse, a servant and pay postage which amounted to an average of £6 a month; above all, he had to entertain visitors. If he had not had considerable experience of orientals, Layard would have been involved in very much greater expense. The Arab compliment of 'My house is your house' was interpreted more literally than he desired. Sheikhs with dozens of mounted attendants used to journey many days to Nimrud to satisfy their curiosity and to settle down to be entertained by the English-man. It was essential to keep on good terms and to satisfy them with courteous words, killing as few sheep as possible for their entertainment. Returning from Mosul one day he found an important Kurdish chieftain with a numerous suite 'all dressed in the height of fashion'. Having heard of Layard's fame in the distant mountains the chieftain had come to see what was going on and what presents he could extract. Ingenuity was taxed to the utmost to avoid making gifts and yet maintaining oriental courtesy at an appropriate level. Eventually, after long negotiations, the chieftain left with his retainers, dissatisfied but not offended, and there were no more visits from Kurdish chieftains.

Encouraging letters received from various quarters made it all the more imperative that he should have funds to make the excavations a success. Botta, who was detained in Paris until the spring of the following year at least, had communicated Layard's notes and sketches to members of the *Académie des Belles Lettres* who had expressed great interest. Rawlinson wrote: 'Your discovery of an interior building at Nimrud in the sculptures of which the position of the high-capped warrior is revealed is most important. The inference is inevitable that you have distinct monuments of the first and second Assyrian dynasties.*

'I live among the ruins', Layard told his Aunt Sara in March, 'and dream of little else. For the time being, my hopes, fears, and joys centre in them. You may therefore conceive that it is not easy for me to separate myself from them, even for an hour when writing to you. Botta has just informed me that he gets 60,000 francs (£2,500)† from his Government for his Khorsabad discoveries. I have vague apparitions of 3,000 gold pieces fleeting before my eyes, and for the first time in my life have become intent on the prospect of accumulating riches. But these happy

* Dr. C. J. Gadd writes: 'Rawlinson evidently thought of the 1st dynasty as very early. Probably the best guide, however, is what Layard writes in *Nineveh and Its Remains*, vol ii, p. 217, where his general idea is correct enough that the Nimrud and Nineveh sculptures which he found were of two different periods and are now known to be not far apart, that is, 9th and 8–7 centuries B.C. The 1st and 2nd dynasties are now understood by scholars to be those of Babylon, the 1st being that of Hammurabi, about 1790–1750 B.C.'

† Flandin received a similar honorarium and the cost of the season's excavations was 140,000 francs (£5,840), so that the total spent by the French Government was about £10,840. (The franc was then worth about tenpence.)

visions are always backed by the hideous skeleton of Government generosity, and not much improved by the retrospection of time, health, and labour thrown away upon empty pockets. . . . I am still in ignorance of the intentions of the Government with regard to Nimrud, whether the excavations are to be carried on, or whether the field will be abandoned to the French.'

While waiting for the Ambassador to make up his mind Layard was busy copying cuneiform, drawing bas-reliefs, and making expeditions. 'I discovered on the banks of the Zab', he told Canning, 'a remarkable tunnel cut through the rock. The place is called by the Arabs, Negoub. There is a slab with two cuneiform inscriptions, evidently Assyrian. . . . The tunnelling is about one hundred and twenty paces in length and eighteen feet in height.' It is an impressive work—the water inlet for a large canal which had led the waters of the Zab river to Nimrud, but in Layard's time the tunnel was dry, as it is today. The Zab flows fast, deep, and clear, even in high summer, though it only enters the tunnel at spring flood so that it must have changed its course since Assyrian times.* After a visit to al Hatra where the great Shammar Chief, Sofuk, was encamped with his tribe, Layard returned to Nimrud in April. Even though only a few workmen were being discreetly employed they were able to show him a wonderful discovery at the entrance to a temple—two magnificent lions with human heads, each eleven feet long and eleven feet tall. They created a great impression on him and stood sentinel on the mound throughout his first expedition and were not removed to the British Museum until his second visit to Nimrud four years later.

If only he had money and permission to excavate he knew that he could amaze the world, but he had to wait patiently for Canning. The Ambassador had told Layard the reasons for the delay but even by the middle of March he was still unwilling to ask for another firman and was discussing with Rawlinson the propriety of removing antiquities to England before permission had been obtained. To Layard he continued to write encouraging letters. 'I quite agree with you that the Bull—the gigantic bull with a human head—is the very thing for a *British*

* This was the Patti canal (see note p. 119 and *Niniveh and Its Remains*, note p. 59, 1882 edition).

museum;—I presume you mean as a type of John Bull.' * 'The Ambassador', wrote Alison, 'is most zealous for your joint success' and was writing to persuade Sir Robert Peel to take an interest, but the letter that Canning wrote to the Prime Minister on 18 April, did not suggest that the matter was urgent. 'M. Botta's success at Nineveh has induced me to adventure in the same lottery, and my ticket has turned up a prize'; his 'agent' had succeeded in opening a gigantic mound at Nimrud and had discovered 'many interesting sculptures and a world of inscriptions'. There was reason to hope that 'Montague House [the British Museum] will beat the Louvre hollow,' and he concluded: 'Although the operations have hitherto proceeded at my personal expense, and without any formal permission from this Government, I look forward to the time when you will think it worth while to step in and carry off the prize on behalf of the Museum.' †

Layard worked hard copying and trying to decipher cuneiform; letters went backwards and forwards between Nimrud and Bagdad as Rawlinson and Layard discussed the subject. Rawlinson was still working on the Babylonian cuneiform alphabet; when he had completed that it would, he said, be a question of identifying 'the Babylonian characters with their Assyrian correspondents', but then came the most difficult task of all—to decide what the letters meant: 'Interpretation . . . will only yield to the most laborious analysis, for we have little or nothing to guide us in reconstructing the lost language.' These letters from Rawlinson are of great interest as showing the different stages in the search. He is still casting about for an explanation as to

---

* 'One cannot help thinking that these enormous Assyrian bulls had something very much in common with the ponderous, conservative philosophy of the mid-Victorian period, with its unshakeable faith in the best of all possible worlds, with its definite social castes duly prescribed by the Catechism.' *A Century of Exploration of Nineveh*, by R. Campbell Thompson and R. W. Hutchinson (London, 1929).

† Stanley Lane-Poole's *Life of Lord Stratford de Redcliffe*. Canning in his letter to the Prime Minister refers to Botta's success at Nineveh, presumably because of a report that Botta believed he had discovered Nineveh. It was said that his first message to Paris from Khorsabad had been '*Ninive était retrouvée*,' but there is no evidence that he said this and it is out of keeping with the modest tone of the letters he wrote at the time.

why the examples of cuneiform being sent to him by Layard should be made up of both non-semitic and semitic elements. Rawlinson wrote:

> I shall be particularly anxious to learn the results of your labours in comparing the two classes of inscriptions; must they, think you, be all referred to one language and one race, or is there sufficient variety to warrant our believing that the Semites merely adopted the writing of their Scythian predecessors [Sumerian] to express their own dialects? . . .
>
> It is very possible that the Semites may after their advent to power have retained the language and character of their Scythic-Chaldee predecessors for sacred and historical purposes independently of their own vernacular Aramaean.
>
> If the Jews indeed borrowed the squared Hebrew during the captivity, the cuneiform and Aramaean writing must have existed simultaneously, and so singularly adverse is the phonetic organisation of the two systems that it seems almost impossible to believe them to have been applicable to the same language or even to languages of the same family.

He said that he would rather work out 'a pretty extensive Babylonian alphabet', or he would place his 'imperfect materials in your hands and confide to you their completion'. Until the Babylonian and Assyrian characters were identified 'we have made no progress whatever'. Even when the alphabet was completed, 'we shall not be able to understand the inscriptions, unless an attentive analysis of the trilingual tablets obtain for us some insight into the language'. Rawlinson now thought it would take 'many years of intense labour before we arrive at satisfactory results'. Layard offered Rawlinson the results of the work he had so far done on cuneiform in the hope that the latter would concentrate on Assyrian cuneiform, instead of the Babylonian variety, since Botta and members of the *Académie* were working hard on the Assyrian language. On 6 April Layard wrote to the Ambassador:

> Instead of accepting my offer, he has kindly placed at my disposal the materials in his possession, which are very valuable, and has offered me every assistance. . . . I begin already to see some light. . . . By a comparison of inscriptions I have determined a large number of variants *i.e.* letters of the same value but differently

formed. This is highly important in the construction of an alphabet, as the various letters alone, unless such variants existed, would amount to several hundreds. . . . By a comparison of many similar inscriptions, I have determined most of the words in them. . . . We have good reason for believing that the names of cities are preceded by a particular sign and Major Rawlinson suspects that geographical names are similarly indicated. . . . The inscriptions hitherto uncovered are evidently religious from their endless repetition; but as we work into the building we must find an immense number of historical records.

So far Layard had been confident that Canning was doing his utmost to obtain the support of the British Government, but during April he received a letter from Rawlinson which quoted the Ambassador as saying: 'I am working on my own account though with a view to national benefit and Government support in due season.' They both interpreted this as meaning that Canning was loth to part with his control and that there would be further delays before funds could be obtained. Rawlinson wrote that he was prepared to give money for the excavations, provided he could get a share of the monuments, 'but Sir Stratford Canning would certainly think this an improper interference'.

Layard wrote the Ambassador a long letter, 21 April 1846, explaining why he thought that the excavations at Nimrud should be conducted by the Government rather than by individuals:

> The objects to be discovered cannot have any intrinsic value for their beauty, and altho' the sculptures of Assyria shew a wonderful *comparative* knowledge of the arts, when the time and country of their execution are taken into consideration, they are undoubtedly inferior to the most secondary works of Greece or Rome. But the field is full of interest to literature, philosophy and history. . . . The national honour is also concerned in competing with the French in deciphering the cuneiform inscriptions. To accomplish this task materials are necessary; the French have them in their Khorsabad inscriptions; we must seek for them at Nimrud.

He also pointed out how very economical he had been; after nearly six months of work, 'the entire excavating expenses amount to 8,644 piastres (£80); of this sum 2,254 piastres spent on experiments in various parts of the country and the rest at Nimrud'.

With the arrival in May of the new Governor of Mosul, Tahyar Pasha, Layard became more cheerful; the Governor was a cultivated Turk of the old school, who took an interest in the discoveries and encouraged the excavations. Layard was overjoyed and suddenly decided to break away from his severe regime of economy by giving an Arab party by the banks of the Tigris near Nimrud to show his appreciation of all the help and to create a friendly feeling with the tribes. He invited the British Vice-Consul and Mrs. Rassam, the French Vice-Consul and his attractive wife, a number of other Europeans from Mosul, and several hundreds of tribesmen. On a large meadow carpeted with flowers white tents were pitched for the ladies and distinguished guests and black tents for attendants and the kitchens. The sheikhs arrived in their best silks and the handsome Abd-ur-rahman came on a white mare, dressed in all his finery. At sight of the Frenchman's wife he was quite overcome and whispered to Layard: "What would you have more beautiful than that; her eyes are like the eyes of my mare, her hair is as bitumen, and her complexion resembles the finest Basra dates; anyone would die for a houri like that." Layard wrote to his mother:

> I collected all the drums and pipes in the country, and the neighbouring tribes came in by their hundreds to dance. We kept up the noise and festivities for five days and nights, the sheikhs bringing me presents of sheep, butter and milk and I feeding them and their attendants with enormous pillafs and sheep roasted whole. There was a general suspense of work in the neighbourhood. You would have been amused to see five hundred Arabs, men and women, dancing one great *dibke*, as their national dance is called, myself leading off with a sheikh of a neighbouring tribe. We had sword dances and other war-like exhibitions.

At the Embassy in Constantinople Layard's friends were rather shocked at the expenditure, especially after all his complaints about lack of money. 'You seem to me', wrote Alison, 'to conduct these things in a highly extravagant scale to say nothing of the highly immoral features of the entertainment.' But Layard knew how important it was to give hospitality. The festivities earned him much good will and for a long time they were talked about and when he needed help from the Arabs they were ready to give it. There was, he said a feeling of friendliness, 'which a little show of kindness to these ill-used people had served to produce'.

3

'A firman without funds!'

One night towards the middle of May 1846, Layard was sleeping
in the tent of Sheikh Abd-ur-rahman, who had invited him to
hunt gazelle at daybreak, when an Arab arrived with a letter. It
was the long-awaited authority from Constantinople giving him
permission to dig and to export antiquities to England. It was
sent by the Grand Vizier to the Governor of Mosul and was as
good as a firman from the Sultan: 'I read by the light of a small
camel-dung fire, the document which secured to the British
nation the records of Nineveh, and a collection of the earliest
monuments of Assyrian art.' He considered it gave him all rights
in the excavations, though his name was not mentioned

and he was referred to as an 'English gentleman'.* The Ambassador could have had the official letter drafted in such a way as to make himself the owner of any discoveries but he does not seem to have considered there was any necessity for that; he was instructing Layard as his agent, through the Grand Vizier, as to what was to be done. The Ambassador's directions were given in detail in an accompanying letter. He pointed out that Layard was not confined to any one spot and that it might be advisable to secure a prior right to any very probable place of discovery at once 'but not *too greedily* and with some respect, not only for the claims of others, but in some degree for their jealousy. I need not tell you that our Gallic neighbours are particularly in my thoughts.' He wanted specimens of sculptures sent to England as soon as possible. There was, however, 'the adverse consideration' of expense which would devolve on him personally

---

* The text of the Vizirial letter of 5 May 1846, translated into French and certified as a true copy by C. A. Rassam, Vice-Consul, is in the Layard Papers (38976). The important sentence is as follows: 'l'Ambassade Britannique a prié qu'il ne soit pas mis d'obstacles à ce que le gentilhomme susmentioné prenne des pierres qui peuvent lui servir, ainsi que celles qu'il pourra découvrir au moyen de fouilles qu'il fera dans les endroits que l'on croit renfermer des pierres de ce genre, et à ce qu'il les embarque pour les faire transporter en Angleterre.'

The Nimrud antiquities were not, therefore, a special gift to Canning by the Sultan as stated by Stanley Lane-Poole in his article on Lord Stratford de Redcliffe in the Dictionary of National Biography. They were, however, at first regarded as Canning property which he handed over to the nation, but owing to Layard's talent as a pioneer archaeologist and his vivid descriptions of what had been achieved, the antiquities became identified in the public mind as belonging to Layard, and he himself, not unnaturally, came to feel very possessive towards them. At the end of his life he reacted to some of the statements in Stanley Lane-Poole's *Life of Lord Stratford de Redcliffe* by stating in his *Autobiography*: 'The firman . . . was in my name. Consequently I might have claimed all that I found in the ruins as my own property. I made over my claims to the British Museum and the nation. In justice to myself these facts should be placed on record.' Funds, however, were required to excavate and transport to England and Layard was not in a position to meet all the expenses though he paid some of them. Honour is perhaps satisfied in that the Halicarnassus marbles are shown in the British Museum as presented by Canning, while the Nimrud and Nineveh monuments excavated between 1845 and 1851 are shown as presented by Layard.

until the matter could be taken up at home. When that happened he wanted Layard to be the Government agent, 'as for the present you are mine'. When he reached England in June, the Ambassador thought that he could accomplish their object, 'which unites in a great degree public usefulness and national glory'.

Layard was very relieved and wrote to the Ambassador on 18 May: 'I need scarcely tell Your Excellency how much gratified I felt by the receipt of the Vizirial letter, which is certainly as full and explicit as could be desired.' He said the French Vice-Consul had heard about the letter, was insisting on seeing it and claimed the whole of the great mound of Kuyunjik as French property. Layard had pointed out that the mound was nearly a mile in circumference, and replied in conformity with the Ambassador's instructions 'with every civility' suggesting that they should unite in their efforts. He told Canning:

> Their claims to Kuyunjik are groundless. This is an immense mound, which has been known to contain antiquities and has been dug into for generations. . . . I am inclined to make an attempt as the mound is usually believed to mark the site of Nineveh, and one could scarcely leave it untouched when expressly in search of Assyrian antiquities. I have employed ten men in digging there for a few days and am encouraged to proceed by the discovery of several fragments of sculptures. Previously to setting to work I examined the mound with great care, and I think I have commenced in the best place. If M. Guillois continues his trenches, where he has begun them, I have not much to fear.

'I wish you to be as modest and circumspect in your proceedings, as you are strong in your authority. . . . Exercise your own judgment with due reflection and sobriety,' Canning had written; but it was not many days after receiving those words of advice that Layard had a serious quarrel with the Cadi which might have brought to an end his career in search of Assyrian antiquities. Returning to Mosul in the ferry from Kuyunjik, Layard was insulted by his old enemy and hit him with a stick rather harder than he had intended. Although protected by an enormous turban, the Cadi's head was cut open and, covered in blood, he ran through the streets of Mosul calling on the populace to take vengeance on the infidels. Knowing how easily the Cadi could rouse the fanaticism of the Moslems in a town like

Mosul, Layard went straight to the Governor to ask that protection should at once be given to the Europeans and Christians. The Governor took immediate action and begged Layard to remain with him in his palace until the excitement died down, but Layard had decided not to alter his routine as he wished to show the people of Mosul that the Cadi had no power over him.

The story quickly reached Bagdad. Rawlinson, who was responsible for British interests in Mosul, was very critical of Layard's actions and did not consider that the provocation by the Cadi had justified personal violence. He said that a report would go to Constantinople and if Layard were not supported by the Embassy he would have to leave Mosul; while the trouble continued Layard should come to stay at the Residency in Bagdad. But Layard's experience had shown that it was a great mistake to withdraw in the face of trouble. Each day he rode through the streets as usual, crossed the Tigris to the mound of Kuyunjik, and returned through the narrow streets in the evening and, although the people continued in a state of unrest for several days, they were impressed by his indifference and no one attacked him. After a week Rawlinson admitted that the situation was calming down more quickly than he had expected. He was thankful, for he liked Layard and the close relations they maintained by post was most profitable to both.

The French Khorsabad marbles had been shipped from Basra in May 1846, and it was essential that the excavations should be continued energetically; but, said Rawlinson, 'what is the use of a firman without funds? Stratford's parsimony is to me quite inexplicable.' He suggested that permission should be obtained to send home a prospectus for voluntary contributions and he himself would subscribe a hundred pounds. Layard, however, thought that this would confuse matters and delay a Government decision to vote money. By the end of June 1846 all the money advanced by Canning had been spent, although work had been carried on with remarkable economy; Layard said he had learnt 'to struggle with every piastre before parting'. The best of the antiquities had to be sent to England, otherwise they would be broken to pieces by the Arabs, or the French would take over Nimrud. He decided to draw further sums on his mother in order to prepare some of the sculptures for despatch to Bagdad and Basra, where they could be put on a ship for England. He wrote to his Aunt Sara:

> The discovery is already beginning to make a noise in Europe [July 1846], and every post brings me letters from people wanting information and offering (scientific) assistance. I only hope that as much interest will be excited in England as on the Continent, and that the Government will not be able to back out of the matter. Mr. Power, * the sculptor, has been kind enough to send me the fullest instructions for taking moulds and then casting. . . .
>
> As I advance further into the mound, the sculptures become more perfect in preservation and superior in execution. . . . God knows when the ramifications of rooms and passages will stop.

By this time the workmen had tunnelled many feet under-ground and a steep descent of steps led into the rooms of the North-West Palace the walls of which were decorated with large bas-reliefs of kings, warriors, attendants, horses, and strange animals. The sculptured figures looked alive at the end of long passages in the twilit palace but the workmen were no longer frightened:

> The Arabs marvelled at these strange figures. As each head was uncovered they showed their amazement by extravagant gestures or exclamations of surprise. If it was a bearded man, they concluded that it was an idol or a Jin, and cursed or spat upon it. If an eunuch, they declared that it was the likeness of a beautiful female, and kissed or patted the cheek. They soon felt as much interest as I did in the objects discovered, and worked with renewed ardour when their curiosity was excited by the appearance of a fresh sculpture. On such occasions they would strip themselves almost naked, throw their kerchiefs from their heads, and, letting their matted hair stream in the wind, rush like madmen into the trenches, to carry off the baskets of earth, shouting, at the same time, the war-cry of the tribe.

As usual Layard was overworking himself. 'The stupidity of the men drives me wild', he told his mother, 'and I fear that I

---

* Hiram Power, the American sculptor, was working in Florence on a marble figure of a Greek slave girl which drew large crowds at the Great Exhibition of 1851, described as 'a young and beautiful Greek girl deprived of her clothing and exposed for sale to some wealthy eastern barbarian'.

have lost much of my good temper.' He hoped that, as his oaths were in Turkish and Arabic, the Recording Angel would not be able to book them. In the summer of 1846 the temperature often rose to 117° F. in the shade and the ground was parched, while locusts swarmed to eat the little vegetation that remained. Layard had a room cut out of a mud-bank at the edge of the Tigris, but he was much troubled by scorpions which came out of the earth walls as he worked on cuneiform; a little air could be obtained at night by putting the iron bedstead into the shallows of the river. Work on the mound was started at first light and towards ten o'clock in the morning there was often a hurricane, like the blast from an oven, so powerful that work had to be suspended while everyone hid below ground and sometimes it was almost dark for about three hours. In this heat it was a severe task to transport huge bas-reliefs, some of which were about nine feet square and a foot thick, of the most fragile material and covered with delicate sculptures. Twelve cases had been packed by July; they were placed on huge rafts made of poplar beams, supported in the water by inflated skins. It had been arranged that when the cases of antiquities from Nimrud reached Bagdad they were to be opened by Rawlinson who was eager to see them.

Layard had revised his earlier opinion about the sculptures; the ones found in the interior of the mound were, he considered, superior to the secondary works of Greece or Rome. He waited anxiously for Rawlinson's opinion, certain that he would be equally enthusiastic about them as works of art. The bas-relief of a lion hunt (see Layard's drawing opposite p. 151) was especially remarkable and he told his Aunt Sara:

> It proves that the Assyrians, even at this remote period, had acquired sufficient knowledge of, and taste for, the fine arts to make them no longer subservient to the mere representation of events, but to aim at *composition*. Of this essential feature in what may properly be termed the fine arts, the Egyptians appear to have been entirely ignorant. The Greeks were acquainted with it only at a comparatively recent period. . . . I compare the Assyrian sculptures with painting, as they comprised both branches, and it appears highly probable that the sculptured reliefs were merely subservient to the colours laid upon them. I think the Nimrud

bas-reliefs will furnish new ideas on the history of the arts, and throw a great light upon that interesting subject.

Rawlinson had a different view of Assyrian art and when his comments reached Nimrud, Layard was thrown into one of his emotional tantrums. Rawlinson wrote that the dying lion and the two gods (winged and eagle-headed) were his favourites and the battle-pieces were 'curious' but did not rank high as works of art. Dr. Ross, he said, had been altogether disappointed with the specimens, 'and I must confess I think the general style crude and cramped, but still the curiosity of the thing is a very great, if not a full compensation'.

Layard was so distressed by this lack of enthusiasm that he wrote immediately to Sir Stratford Canning in London to say that Rawlinson thought little of the sculptures and that it was useless to continue the excavations. Layard prided himself on his taste and knowledge of art forms; he knew that the Khorsabad bas-reliefs had caused a sensation, that the Nimrud material was older and better and that Rawlinson's interest was in inscriptions but he sent off the letter before he had allowed himself time to think. Canning took no notice for he was accustomed to these moods but Rawlinson was startled that Layard should take 'such desperate alarm' at his criticisms. He told him that he had written immediately to Canning in London to disabuse him of any idea that he was unfavourable to the continuance of the excavations. 'For God's sake', he told Layard, 'go on and prosper—and remember that every slab and every fresh bit of writing you gain, is so much new land rescued from the ocean of time'; the Nimrud finds were 'invaluable', unfolding the history, theology, language, arts, manners, military skill, and political relations 'of one of the most illustrious nations of antiquity'. They filled, he said, an enormous blank in knowledge of the early history of the world.

Layard had asked what was Rawlinson's standard of beauty when he criticised the Assyrian bas-reliefs and Rawlinson had replied that it was the Elgin Marbles:

> Now, I still think the Nineveh marbles are not valuable as works of art. The test is—can modern science learn anything from them? Can a mere admirer of the beautiful view them with pleasure?

Certainly not, and in this respect they are in the same category with the paintings and sculptures of Egypt and India. . . . I admit a certain degree of excellence in the conception and execution of some of the sculptures, but when we come to value, *a certain degree* won't do. We have specimens of the very highest art—and anything short of that is, as a work of art . . . valueless, for it can neither instruct nor enrapture us. I hope you understand this distinction and when I criticise design and execution, will understand I do so merely because your winged God is not the Apollo Belvedere.*

Greek art in the days of Pericles was Rawlinson's standard, as it was for others in Victorian England. In the art of Egypt, Assyria, and India they looked for qualities which did not exist and the absence of which prevented them from seeing anything else of value. Mitford told Layard that he found India 'quite barren in historical reminiscences and classical associations'; Hindu worship consisted of 'a disgusting adoration of the emblems

* Rawlinson's letter from Bagdad, 5 August 1846, Layard Papers (38977). Rawlinson was interested in discovering history through the decipherment of cuneiform and did not realise, as Layard did, that the art forms were another important source of information. Rawlinson was even then a little old-fashioned in his acceptance of Greek art as the only standard. James Fergusson, the architect, who became a great friend of Layard, had already published some of his studies of the beautiful rock-cut temples of India and had begun to question whether Greek art was the only criterion of beauty. In 1852, after publishing *Palaces of Nineveh*, he issued an essay on *An Historical Enquiry into the True Principles of Beauty in Art* in which he argued that Greece owed much to Assyria. He wrote that when the drawings of Flandin and Layard were published 'they will throw a stronger and clearer light, not only on the ancient history of Greece and Italy, but also on that of India, than any other discovery that has yet been made; and even if we should not be able to decipher the inscriptions the details of the art will suffice to point out the affiliation of almost all the primitive nations of Asia and Europe'.

'The ivories and metalwork from Nimrud', writes Professor Mallowan in *Twenty-five Years of Mesopotamian Discovery*, 'have proved beyond question that Oriental art directly influenced the Aegean and Etruria which, as early as 700 B.C., was probably importing bronzes from Urartu (Ancient Armenia). It is no doubt also true that the early character of Greek sculpture, which had so decisive an effect on its subsequent development, owed much to the older Oriental collections so highly prized by the Kings of Assyria.'

of generation'. Layard found much to instruct in the fact that the Assyrian winged god was created long before the Apollo Belvedere. He was delighted not only by the freedom in design shown by many of the sculptures, but also because the Assyrian artists had been using their imagination to create a new magic in the monsters guarding the temples and palaces, which aroused awe because they were not an imitation of man or nature, and he wrote in *Nineveh and Its Remains*:

> I used to contemplate for hours these mysterious emblems, and muse over their intent and history. What more noble forms could have ushered the people into the temple of their gods? What more sublime images could have been borrowed from nature by men who sought, unaided by the light of revealed religion, to embody their conception of the wisdom, power and ubiquity of a Supreme Being? They could find no better type of intellect and knowledge than the head of the man; of strength, than the body of the lion; of ubiquity, than the wings of the bird.
>
> These winged human-headed lions were not idle creations, the offspring of mere fancy; their meaning was written upon them. They had awed and instructed races which flourished 3,000 years ago. Through the portals, which they guarded, kings, priests and warriors had borne sacrifices to their altars, long before the wisdom of the East had penetrated to Greece, and had furnished its mythology with symbols long recognised by the Assyrian votaries. . . . For twenty-five centuries they had been hidden from the eye of man, and they now stood forth once more in their ancient majesty.
>
> But how changed was the scene around them. The luxury and civilisation of a mighty nation had given place to the wretchedness and ignorance of a few half-barbarous tribes. The wealth of temples, and the riches of great cities, had been succeeded by ruins and shapeless heaps of earth. Above the spacious hall in which they stood the plough had passed and the corn now waved . . . 'for now is Nineveh a desolation and dry like a wilderness, and flocks lie down in the midst of her: all the beasts of the nations, both the cormorant and the bittern, lodge in the upper lintels of it; their voice sings in the windows, and desolation is in the thresholds.' (Zephaniah ch. 2, 13 to 15; also quoted is the dramatic account of the rise and fall of Assyria in Ezekiel ch. 31.)

4

The Nestorians and
Yezidis

A visit to the Nestorian Christians, or Chaldeans,* in the Tiyari
Mountains was planned at the end of August for Layard wished
to leave the heat of the plains to visit an interesting people who
were, he considered, the descendants of the Assyrians, and he
also wanted to search for Assyrian monuments. With him went
Hormuzd Rassam, Ibrahim Agha, his Turkish escort, a servant,
and a groom. The mountains lay in a north-easterly direction
from Mosul and on the way they visited Khorsabad, about fifteen
miles distant. The chambers that Botta had excavated were
partly filled with earth, the sculptures were perishing 'and
shortly little will remain of this remarkable monument'. After

* Layard uses both terms to describe this Christian sect. The father
of Christian and Hormuzd Rassam was a Nestorian with the title of
Archdeacon in the Chaldean Christian community, and the then Patriarch, Mar Shimoon, described himself as Patriarch of the Chaldeans.
The Rev. George Percy Badger in *The Nestorians and Their Ritual*
published in 1852, argues that Layard and others were incorrect in
describing the Nestorians as Chaldeans.

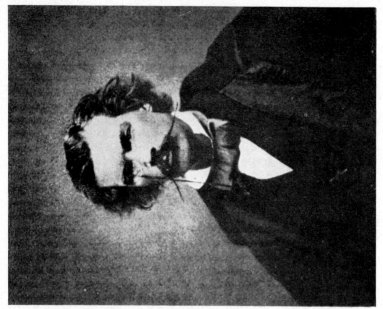

Henry James Ross

Hormuzd Rassam

King hunting lion, bas-relief from Nimrud

Warriors before a besieged city

Original pencil drawings by Layard at
Nimrud before the bas-reliefs were despatched to Bagdad and London

travelling some days they arrived at Mia, north of Amadiyah, in Kurdish country where the chiefs considered themselves independent of the Ottoman Government. A message came from the Kurdish chief that he could not receive the party until the morning. This was lacking in courtesy and Layard returned a rude answer through the messenger, declaiming it in a loud voice so that all could hear. The villagers, many of them Nestorians, lived in dread of the chieftain and were delighted by the message but trembled at the thought of what might be its result. It was not long before the chieftain himself arrived to make his apologies. 'In dealing with a Kurd', said Layard, 'you are generally safe as long as you can make him believe that you are his superior, or his equal.' Layard's reputation for courage, horsemanship, and pugnacity had penetrated to these mountains.

Arrived in the Nestorian villages of the Tiyari Mountains, the party was among friends and was given an enthusiastic welcome. There had been few visitors since the massacre three years previously when the notorious Bedr Khan Bey had invaded the Nestorian strongholds and killed many thousands. Layard was well known as a friend of the Nestorians and as a student of their history; workmen from Nimrud had returned to their villages and spread stories of his prowess as a horseman, a boar-hunter, and of his chastisement of the Cadi of Mosul. As the party approached the village of Asheetha, the cry was raised: 'The Bey is come!' and all hurried to welcome Layard and to kiss his hand. Girls, many of them fair and attractive, came in procession bearing fruits. They surrounded their fellow Nestorian, Hormuzd Rassam, and smothered him with kisses in appreciation of the kindness they had received from the Rassam family in Mosul—many of them had been sold into slavery by the Kurds and rescued by the British Vice-Consul. At Lizan on the Zab river, Layard came upon terrible evidence of the 1843 massacre, when the party could not avoid treading on whitened bones or dislodging the skulls which rolled down the mountainside. On his return to Mosul Layard urged the Governor to send an expedition to save the Nestorians from another threatened attack, but it was too late. Bedr Khan had already carried out a second massacre, killing the women this time as well as the men.

The mountain air had done Layard so much good that he decided to leave Mosul again and to accept an invitation from Sheikh Nasr, the Yezidi religious chief, to attend their religious festival at the tomb of Sheikh Adi. Layard stopped the night at the village of Baadri where he was received by Hussein Bey, the handsome eighteen-year-old chief of the Yezidis, who considered that Layard's arrival had brought the family food fortune as his wife had that day given birth to a son. "The child is yours", said Hussein Bey, "and he will grow up under your shadow; let him receive his name from you, and be hereafter under your protection." Layard wished to know what responsibilities he would assume by becoming godfather to 'a devil-worshipping baby' but reassured there were none, he gave the child the name of his grandfather, Ali Bey, the last independent chief of the Yezidis, who had been defeated by the Kurds and put to death.

At dawn the next day Layard accompanied Hussein Bey to the wooded valley sacred to their Sheikh Adi. 'As we descended through the thick wood of oaks, we passed many pilgrims on their way, like ourselves, to the tomb. . . . As each new body of travellers caught sight of the object of their journey, they fired their guns, and shouted the war-cry of the tribe to those below. . . . At some distance from the tomb we were met by Sheikh Nasr and a crowd of priests and armed men. The Sheikh was dressed in the purest white linen as were the principal members of the priesthood.'

This sacred place is today unchanged and retains all the peaceful, wooded charm that Layard found so attractive. Water runs clear from the fountains, the spreading trees give shade over the low stone buildings, and the courtyard outside the primitive church with its pool of spring water is still secluded. The walls of the fortress-like church are darker than ever with the smoke from the open oil lamps and the figure of the *Melek Taos*, the King Peacock, the symbol of worship is still shut away from strangers within a canopy in a dark inner room. It is through the King Peacock, or Fallen Angel, that the Yezidis propitiate the Devil for they believe he will be restored to the celestial hierarchy and no one must speak the name or any other word that even resembles 'devil'. Layard was not one to choose his words carefully and by using the ill-fated word he angered his hosts and the surrounding crowd and it was some time before they recovered their good spirits.

By nightfall about five thousand Yezidis had arrived on the pilgrimage and were wandering among the oak trees with lighted torches. 'The effect was magical', wrote Layard; 'the varied groups could be faintly distinguished through the darkness. . . . Thousands of lights were reflected in the fountains and streams, glimmered amongst the foliage of the trees, and danced in the distance. As I was gazing on this extraordinary scene, the hum of human voices was suddenly hushed, and a strain, solemn and melancholy, arose from the valley. It resembled some majestic chant which years before I had listened to in the cathedral of a distant land.' The chant changed to a more lively measure, tambourines were beaten furiously, flutes poured forth their notes, musicians threw their instruments in the air and contorted themselves on the ground. The crowd raised a great cry. 'It was midnight. The time and place were well suited to the occasion; and I gazed with wonder upon the extraordinary scenes around me. Thus were probably celebrated ages ago the mysterious rites of the Corybantes, when they met in some consecrated grove. I did not marvel that such wild ceremonies had given rise to those stories of unhallowed rites and obscene mysteries, which have rendered the name of Yezidi an abomination in the East.'

When Layard returned to Mosul at the beginning of October 1846 he found the Governor, Tahyar Pasha, was about to leave on an expedition into the Sinjar Mountains, where many of the inhabitants were Yezidis. Layard wished to visit them and to see an area which had once been an extremely fertile district of ancient Assyria. The Governor gave Layard permission to accompany him on the expedition which was not intended to be hostile to the Yezidis and the local people. Layard watched the preparations to get the Governor's household and the army on the move.

> The Divan Effendesi, although a man of the pen, strutted about with sword and spurs, followed by clerks and inkstand bearers. At the door of the harem waited a bevy of Aghas; amongst them the lord of the towel, the lord of the wash-basin, the lord of the cloak, the chief of the coffee-makers, and the chief of the pipe-bearers,

the treasurer and the seal-bearer. At length the Pasha approached; the *cawasses* forced the crowd out of the way; and as His Excellency placed his foot in the stirrup, the trumpets sounded as a signal for the procession to move onwards.

They remained two days at Tel Afer with its imposing castle which had been subdued by the one-eyed Mohamed Pasha, who had killed two-thirds of the population. The Turcoman people of Tel Afer had previously been semi-independent with their own hereditary chief and became wealthy by plundering caravans and raiding the Mosul districts in league with the Beduins of the desert and the Yezidis of the Sinjar Mountains. The Yezidis of the Sinjar, thirty miles away, had been watching the movements of Tahyar Pasha's army and when it began moving in their direction decided that they were once more to be attacked. Tahyar Pasha had sent messages to say that he was coming in peace, but as Layard with an advance-guard entered the village of Mirkan, the Yezidis opened fire, killing two men in front of him and wounding several beside him. This unprovoked attack exasperated the normally peaceful old Pasha and he ordered his troops to attack the village and to burn it down. 'Blazing fires were made in the neat dwellings,' wrote Layard 'and the whole village was delivered to the flames. Even the old Pasha, with his grey hair and tottering step, hurried to and fro amongst the smoking ruins, and helped to add the torch where the fire was not doing its work. The old Turkish spirit of murder and plunder was roused.' But the Yezidis had taken refuge in caverns in a nearby gorge leaving only some old men and women in the village who were beheaded, the heads afterwards being paraded about the camp and rewards for them claimed from the Pasha. For two days the Turkish soldiers marched boldly into the gorge to capture the Yezidis, but each time they were repulsed by well-directed fire from their unseen enemies. On the morning of the third day the Governor ordered a fresh attack.

To encourage his men he advanced himself into the gorge, and directed his carpet to be spread on a rock. Here he sat, with the greatest apathy, smoking his pipe, and carrying on a frivolous conversation with me, although he was the object of the aim of the Yezidis; several persons within a few feet of us falling dead, and the balls frequently throwing up the dirt into our faces. Coffee was brought to him occasionally as usual, and his pipe was filled when the tobacco was exhausted; yet he was not a soldier, but what is termed 'a man of the pen'. I have frequently seen similar instances of calm indifference in the midst of danger amongst Turks, when such displays were scarcely called for, and would be very unwillingly made by an European.

Layard, also, was not a soldier but he was a guest of the Governor and felt under an obligation to accompany him. It is even possible that Layard enjoyed himself sitting by the Pasha in the line of fire. He required from time to time, as he had told his uncle, 'an extraordinary degree of excitement'. He also considered that he might alleviate the sufferings of the Yezidis should they be captured, and counter the pernicious doctrines of the Cadi who lectured the Governor that it was his duty as a Mohammedan to slaughter the infidel Yezidis.

5

'Treated as a
master-bricklayer'

In Mosul Layard found letters from Sir Stratford Canning written from London in August and September 1846 saying that he had succeeded in obtaining all that was desirable: 'The British Museum undertakes Nimrud in my stead. The Treasury allows £2,000. You are the agent. You will have £500 for yourself, besides £100 for your expenses home. My outlay will be repaid. A sum between £1,000 and £1,100 will be applicable to the continuation of your works including the embarkation of the spoils. You are to finish all by the end of next June. . . .' It had been an effort for Canning to hand over to the British Museum, but he made sure that his part in the undertaking should be properly recorded, and he believed that the total of one thousand pounds would be sufficient for Layard to accomplish what he wanted. He must, however, have had misgivings for two weeks later Canning wrote again to say that Layard should write to him privately if there should be anything not quite to his taste: 'You will not, I am sure, think it worth while to object to a detail'; the next day he wrote again: 'I shall be disappointed if you are not satisfied.'

Layard was certainly not satisfied. He considered the sum of money ridiculously small and he was even more annoyed when he received from the Trustees of the British Museum a formal document, dated 21 September, setting out the terms of the contract, [1] he complained to his uncle of its 'littleness and meanness', treating him as if he were 'a master-bricklayer'. It was an annoying document for anyone to receive, but especially someone of Layard's temperament. Seven pages long and signed by the Rev. J. Forshall, the Secretary, the contract was a pompous Canning lecture with the addition of some trite remarks: 'The first object of the Museum is the preservation of monuments of antiquity. Mr. Layard will therefore be extremely careful not to injure any sculptures, inscriptions, or other objects.' Copies of inscriptions and impressions etc. were to be 'made in duplicate' and would be the property of the Museum. The last paragraph must have been prompted by the incident with the Cadi:

> The Trustees wish that every cause of offence should be avoided as well to the authorities as to the population, and particularly that proper respect should be paid to the religious feeling and habitual prejudices of all, whether Mohammedans or Christians. It will be very gratifying to the Trustees to find, when the operations on which Mr. Layard is engaged are concluded, that his prudence and good feeling have enabled him to leave Kurdistan an impression entirely favourable to the British character.

He might have found this document less offensive if it had not been for the heat and worry over a cholera epidemic which was ravaging Bagdad and other places in Mesopotamia. It was, however, the lack of funds which was really disappointing. With the very small means at his disposal, as much was expected of him, he said, as if he had a fortune to deal with: 'I have been so long unfortunate that I begin to despair.' He took satisfaction in the fact that he had, at any rate, acted 'more honourably than others', referring to the fact that Canning was being repaid his advances and he was not. Rawlinson wrote, 'the news is indeed glorious', for he understood that the grant was three thousand pounds and when he learned that it was only a third of that amount, he said that Layard had been 'holding himself too cheap throughout in this Assyrian business'; and as to the letter from the Rev. Josiah Forshall, it was 'thoroughly disgusting'.

The original sum of two thousand was cut by half because of the repayment of Canning's advances, the cost of Layard's return and his remuneration. He was now planning to use one hundred and thirty workmen at Nimrud which at the minimum wage of four piastres a day—and some were paid more—would come to about five pounds daily. * He was to finish in June, which meant about two hundred and sixty days work or a total of about thirteen hundred pounds for labour alone and besides that, there was the cost of material for packing, for making the rafts and for his own living expenses. In lengthy letters to the Trustees he complained that the amount of money would not be sufficient for the proper examination of even half the mound of Nimrud, considering 'the magnitude of the work contemplated'. He refused the five hundred pounds remuneration since, he said, he was conducting a scientific and national labour and he wished to use the money for the expenses of excavation. Alison was 'shocked beyond measure at the niggardliness of the terms made having always understood that £500 had been awarded independent of expenses', but tried to give Layard encouragement: 'You may depend upon it that there is more formality than real occasion for offence in the instructions. To begin with Sir Stratford Canning is jealous and suspicious as you know, fearful, above all things, that his part in the concern should be lost in yours; he therefore gives it as his discovery, mentions you as superintending the excavations, and the clerk draws out the instructions, as if he were addressing them to a log of wood.' Layard had also been upset by a statement by the Trustees that, at the conclusion of the excavations, it would be 'impossible for them to provide in any way for Mr. Layard's further employment, or to assist him in any objects he may have in view'. Alison pointed out that there was always a clause in Foreign Office instructions to persons first employed on special service to prevent them considering that they were permanently employed: 'you have no right to take umbrage. I think you have looked upon this subject

* Layard estimated 108 piastres to the pound sterling.

in its most disagreeable point of view and hope you have written a temperate letter to Sir S.C.'

Layard had not written very temperately, but Canning seems to have expected this and, on the whole, showed remarkable patience and understanding. He said that he was glad that Layard had spoken his mind freely: 'I could not but grieve at your dissatisfaction, even when I found it difficult to comprehend the cause of it.' Layard, very naturally, was worried about his future and in May, three months earlier, he had written to Canning: 'If we decide upon excavating as the French did at Khorsabad, two years at least would elapse before the whole would be completed. At the end of that time I should find myself again thrown upon the world at an age when I could no longer enter into a profession or hope for honourable occupation. These considerations depress me greatly.' The letter he had received from the British Museum had certainly not reassured him. Alison wrote to remind him of the importance of a post with the Foreign Office: 'This Nimrud thing is only a means to procure something else. In what can the stones themselves, and all the reputation connected with such things, avail a man who has to make his way in the world?' Alison had also pleaded Layard's cause with Stratford Canning, who had replied from London: 'Layard is making excellent progress and you may depend upon it that I am fully alive to his merits. His fiery temper and his eagerness for distinction will not, I trust, make him so impatient as to lose the goodwill of his friends. For one, I have every wish to serve him in things more important than archaeology.'

Canning told Benjamin Austen, who went to see the Ambassador at his house in Grosvenor Square, that Lord Aberdeen had been 'most unjustly prejudiced against Layard' owing to the proceedings with the Bakhtiari chieftain, but there was a much better chance with Lord Palmerston, who was now Foreign Minister. Austen said that he was prepared to help his nephew financially but he did not want him 'to spend the prime years of his life upon *uncertain* prospects which might end in smoke'. He wrote to his nephew: 'The mere excavating ruins will not advance your diplomatic interests and I am anxious to see you placed. . . . As I have often said to you, all great men use their subordinates for their own ends. Governments never do generous

159

or liberal acts.' Austen felt strongly about the niggardliness of
the Government and of the Museum Trustees and almost felt
like advising his nephew to denounce the Museum's offer and
present his discoveries to the French—'it would serve the
Museum right!' At the same time Austen said that it was difficult
to give advice, for his nephew had never explained what his
arrangements had been with Sir Stratford Canning. Indeed, if
Austen had realised that Layard in his letters from Nimrud to the
Ambassador had accepted the description of himself as Canning's
agent, he would have advised caution. Sara Austen was more
circumspect, being nervous lest Layard might throw up the
whole enterprise. In a letter of eight pages she said : 'The Museum
never thanks, it is not the custom. . . . This is the crisis of your
career and all that you do is so important that I feel quite ill with
anxiety lest any false step should mar all.' The letter was full of
good sense and had one admirable sentence, which summed up
both his strength and his weakness: 'The freedom of thought
and action which your strong intellect and bold heart require,
are really incompatible with the conditions of human existence.'
The Austens were delighted with the success of their 'vagabond'
nephew, 'All talk to us now about your researches.' Their local
clergyman, the brother of Lord Clarendon, called on Sara and
talked for two hours on the theme that the holy prophecies were
being fulfilled by the Nimrud excavations. In November 1846
Austen had attended a meeting of the Royal Institute of British
Architects and heard high praise of his nephew for his paper on
'important discoveries at Nineveh' and for his detailed drawings
of the palace of al Hatra. Living as they did near the British
Museum and within two doors of their friend Sir Charles
Fellows, the Austens knew what was going on and wrote long
letters to inform their nephew and to give advice.

'It pleases Providence at this time to afflict you with a preaching Aunt', wrote Sara again on 17 February 1847. She had much
to tell him about a visit paid to Montague Place by Sir Stratford
Canning who had spent the afternoon gossiping tête-à-tête
about him, wanting to know about his boyhood, youth, family
means, prospects, relations—he had met Lady Charlotte Guest
at Bowood—he said that he intended to recommend Layard to
Lord Palmerston 'as being most highly qualified for service in

the East—more so, indeed, than anyone I know'. She was delighted: 'What a fascinating man he is! The Canning curious eye was never off me, but I felt no nervousness.' In her letter she quoted much of his conversation: 'Only let Layard finish his work and we will stand together upon the highest ground and crow the *loudest* crow that ever was heard in this country. The Queen upon her throne shall hear us—and Layard's voice shall be the highest.'

Canning was prepared to be helpful, but not to be pushed into the background. 'I am anxious that you and Rawlinson also', he wrote to Layard, 'should have your respective shares of *honour* and *immortality* on account of the enterprise, and I cannot for an instant doubt that you will be careful to give me mine.' Canning had told Longworth in Constantinople that if he were to be remembered at all by future generations it would be for the bas-reliefs from the tomb of Mausolus. Now he realised that the Assyrian discoveries would be even more important and he was suspicious that Layard was intending to claim the discoveries as entirely his own. There had been an article in *The Bombay Times* which he had not liked, for it stated that Layard was presenting the antiquities to the British Museum and made no mention of Stratford Canning. Forshall told Austen that Layard appeared to be throwing off his allegiance to the Ambassador which was a mistake; the Trustees had been dealing with Canning, who had originated the scheme, obtained the permission to excavate and had directed Layard as his agent. Austen reported this conversation to his nephew and said that he had been cross with Forshall and had pointed out that his nephew was not the servant of Sir Stratford Canning or of the Museum, nor could they find anyone to replace him. 'You know well you could not', he had told Forshall, 'for no one would be found capable of doing it.' Layard was grateful to his uncle for standing up for him in this way, for of course he objected strongly to Forshall's remarks. 'I contemplated the excavations', he wrote in reply to Austen, 'whenever it might be in my power to undertake them, even before Botta made his discoveries. And altho' I was enabled by the liberality of Sir S.C. to carry out the plan, yet it can scarcely be said that he made the discovery and only employed me to look after the diggers.'

161

The Austens were doing their utmost to help their nephew's advancement. Sara had congratulated herself on the way that she had handled Sir Stratford Canning and was delighted by the fact that he had given Layard 'universal and unlimited praise'. She was, therefore, startled and annoyed to receive an unfriendly letter in reply to her long account of the interview. She asked Layard to read her letters again because he had quite misinterpreted them, and there was absolutely no need for his 'self-vindication'; if he were going to be on the defensive she would fear to write in future 'with abandon'. She reiterated that Canning had been full of approbation, except with regard to the incident of hitting the Cadi over the head for although he had admired Layard's 'spirit and courage' he had added: 'Diplomatists must learn to restrain even honourable impulses'. He had urged her to make the theme of her letter to her nephew '*self-control*', saying that Layard was 'too *impetuous*; too rash at present for the Statesman', and did not sufficiently recognise the necessity of obedience to higher powers—'obedience, or the submission of your own judgement and will, being the primary element of diplomacy'.

Layard did not care for these conversations between his aunt and his 'patron' for he was embarrassed and irritated when he was reminded of the relationship in which he stood to Canning and he was beginning to resent control now that he was in a stronger position. It was, indeed, Layard and not Canning who had earned European fame. He had discovered an 'Eastern Mystery' which was more fantastic than even Disraeli's imaginings. Living with these kings, warriors, priests, and strange protective monsters he had become possessive about them but his main concern was that the excavation of so rich a treasure should be well carried out. He was angry with the Trustees of the British Museum and with Canning for not realising the significance of the discoveries and the great expense entailed. They were more important than the Khorsabad discoveries but the funds were very meagre as compared with those furnished by the French Government. He saw around him a newly discovered civilisation, the remains of which could not be valued in tens of thousands of pounds, and only a small proportion of what he had found could be sent to England; the rest would be broken up by Arabs as infidel monuments or burned as lime for building. Detailed drawings were needed of all the bas-reliefs which could not be moved, but he could not persuade the Trustees to send him an artist, even though the great value of Flandin's drawings of Khorsabad must have been realised. His own drawings were accurate but it took him a long time to make them; there were the rooms of the palaces which had to be measured and set down to scale and he had to note what objects he found and where he found them. There were bronze ornaments, glass and tiles, lion pedestals, and the exquisite ivories; separating the fragments of ivory from the surrounding rubble took hours of delicate work with a small pen-knife. He nearly cried with misery when some of the unique and beautiful objects, brought too suddenly into the air and light, disintegrated while he was admiring them. Every day something of interest was discovered. In an area of about fifty square feet of the Central Palace there were one hundred bas-reliefs, all sculptured and packed against one another 'as slabs in a stone-cutter's yard, or as the leaves of a gigantic book'. Endlessly he copied cuneiform inscriptions trying to make as complete a record as possible since Rawlinson was desperately anxious for new material to work on in his race against the French, Germans, Danes, Swiss, and others to decipher cuneiform. 'I felt that I was far from qualified to undertake these multifarious occupations', Layard said. At the same time he knew that even if the Museum could find suitable people to send out who could speak the languages of Arabs, Kurds, Turks, and Chaldeans, and who could deal with the Turkish authorities, 'the whole sum granted would be expended before the excavations could be commenced'. He decided to make every sacrifice to ensure success, but he feared that there might be failure; he was not sure that his health would be equal to the strain, for he was suffering from a severe form of colic which was extremely weakening.

The Trustees of the British Museum certainly did not realise at first how fortunate they were to have Layard. Having decided that one man was to do everything, they could not have found another Englishman as capable. His early adventures, which had appeared so wasteful at the time to Benjamin Austen, were as good a training for archaeology in those days as it would have been possible to find—art in Florence, knowledge of the desert tribes of Mesopotamia, horsemanship, languages, diplomacy, the study of inscriptions and sculptures in various parts of Persia and Turkey. Indeed, the only period which does not seem to have been of any use to him was the six years spent in Austen's office, though it probably helped to train his mind so that he made good use of his extensive reading.

The man who now, as England's champion, stepped forth into the international contest for great archaeological discoveries [states H. V. Hilprecht in *The Excavations in Assyria and Babylonia*] was so exceptionally qualified and prepared for his task by his natural gifts and experience of his past life, and, at the same time, so eminently successful in the choice of his methods and men, in the overcoming of extraordinary obstacles and difficulties . . . that he at once became, and during the whole nineteenth century remained, the central figure of Assyrian exploration. . . . In the interests of science it remains a cause of deep regret that after his great discoveries, Layard did not at once find the same hearty support in England as his more fortunate French colleague so speedily obtained in Paris. Not even an artist was despatched to draw the sculptures and copy the inscriptions, though many of the monuments 'were in too dilapidated a condition to be moved'. . . . He was thus practically prevented by his own government from making a methodical exploration of Nimrud.

6

The Bull is taken
to the Tigris

With the cooler weather of the autumn of 1846, when matters
had been settled with the Trustees of the British Museum,
Layard had set to work to organise a proper encampment for his
workmen now increased to one hundred and thirty. A plan had
been marked out on the ground for a house for himself and
his servants near the village of Nimrud and in a few days it
was completed with mud-bricks he had had dried during the
summer ready for such development. On the mound itself a
large house was built in the same way for fifty Nestorian workmen and their families, above the great winged lions; near
them was a hut to which any small object found could be removed
for safety. The Arabs were divided into three parties; about
forty tents were pitched on different parts of the mound, at the
entrances to the principal trenches; there were forty more
round Layard's own house and others on the banks of the Tigris
to guard the sculptures prepared for embarkation on the rafts.
Layard had his servant, a groom, and two stalwart, loyal Turks
—the *cawass* Ibrahim Agha, and a standard-bearer, known as
the *bairakdar*, whose bravery Layard had noted during the
Sinjar operation and who had been allowed to join the Englishman's service. Hormuzd Rassam lived with Layard in the house;
he had obtained, said Layard, 'an extraordinary influence amongst
the Arabs and his fame spread throughout the desert'. Two
carpenters had been brought from Mosul and an intelligent and
skilful stone-cutter, Behnan, who was a Jacobite, or Syrian
Christian. Awad was still there as a superintendent and others
were appointed for different parts of the excavations, so that
Layard could be called as soon as a discovery was made.

Layard enjoyed life with his workmen. 'The Arabs were
naturally hospitable and generous', he said, and if one of them

from time to time was rich enough to buy some dates, raisins, or a piece of camel meat they would call together their friends:

> I was frequently invited to such entertainments; the whole dinner, perhaps, consisting of half-a-dozen dates or raisins spread out wide, to make the best show, upon a corn-sack; a pat of butter upon a corner of a flat loaf; and a few cakes of dough baked in the ashes. And yet the repast was ushered in with every solemnity; the host turned his dirty *keffiah*, or head kerchief, and his cloak, in order to look clean and smart; appearing both proud of the honour conferred upon him, and of his means to meet it in a proper fashion.
>
> I frequently feasted the workmen, and sometimes their wives and daughters were invited to separate entertainments, as they would not eat in public with the men. Generally of an evening, after the labours of the day were finished, some Kurdish musicians would stroll the village with their instruments, and a dance would be commenced, which lasted through the greater part of the night. . . . I endeavoured, as far as it was in my power, to create a good feeling amongst all, and to obtain their willing co-operation in my work.

They were all armed in case of raiders from the desert and looked to Layard to protect them and to dispense justice when there were disputes. On these occasions Rassam used to collect the evidence, the tribal Elders would be assembled and Layard would decided the case. 'I have a kind of Cadi's power', Layard wrote to Sara Austen, 'my judgements are never appealed against, and are generally executed with great promptitude and alacrity. . . . It is curious to see a Christian thus appealed to; however, they find it cheaper, as they have neither to give a bribe nor pay fees, which they would have to do, did they go to their own authorities.' The Chaldeans were toughened fighters from the Tiyari Mountains and there were many quarrels with the Moslems which led to 'the drawing of sabres and priming of match-locks'. The Moslems were outraged because the Chaldean women washed naked, as was their custom in the Tiyari Mountains; the women saw no reason why habits should be changed because Moslems were shocked. The Arabs were mostly from the desert and accustomed to a life of excitement with occasional inter-tribal fighting or plundering of caravans, so that sometimes

Lowering the great winged bull: Layard superintending from above

Progress to the river, with the mounds of Nimrud in the background

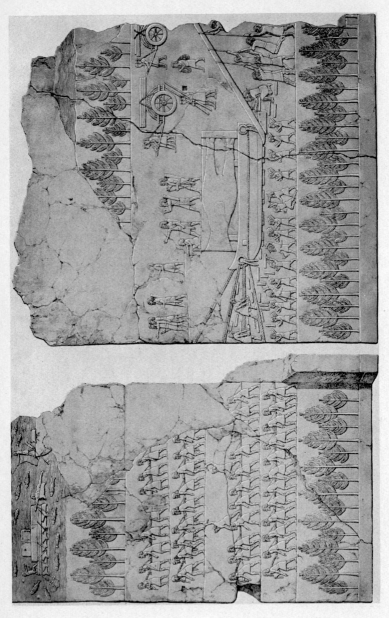

Bas-relief from Kuyunjik showing Assyrians moving a stone bull

the routine and hard work of the encampment proved irksome.
One evening Layard was surprised to see a large party of his men
returning home from the mound driving before them a large
flock of sheep which he knew belonged to the village of Nimrud.

Ashur-nasir-pal II

The men were 'shouting their war-cry, flourishing their swords,
and indulging in the most extravagant gesticulations'. When he
asked one of them what it was about, the man replied:

'O Bey! God be praised, we have eaten butter and wheaten bread
under your shadow, and are content—but an Arab is an Arab. It
is not for a man to carry about dirt in baskets, and to use a spade
all his life; he should be with his sword and his mare in the desert.
We are sad as we think of the days when we plundered the Anayza,
and we must have excitement or our hearts would break. Let us
then believe that these are the sheep we have taken from the
enemy, and that we are driving them to our tents!'

Layard had restarted excavations at the beginning of November, and came upon an amazingly rich harvest of finds. He wrote to his Aunt Sara during that month:

> I have now two places of different epochs, one contemporary with the building discovered by the French at Khorsabad, the other prior to it; marbles from the latter have been used in the construction of the former. . . . I have already uncovered thirteen pairs of the gigantic winged, human-headed lions and bulls, of one of which you have had the sketch. But the most remarkable discovery is perhaps that of the black obelisk about seven feet high, which I believe to be one of the most interesting and unique monuments of antiquity known! There are in all about 80 figures, all in the finest preservation and capitally drawn. You may conceive with what delight I dug out this splendid monument, and the satisfaction with which I saw it on Christmas Day fairly embarked on the Tigris for Bagdad.

Layard copied its two hundred and ten lines of cuneiform and the panels showing the king followed by his attendants, men bearing tribute and leading animals such as the elephant, camel, wild bull, lion, stag, and various kinds of monkeys. When it reached Bagdad Rawlinson was delighted with it, especially the long cuneiform inscription and considered it 'the most notable trophy in the world and would alone have been well worth the whole expense of excavating Nimrud'.[1] After a hazardous journey via Bombay it reached London and is today one of the principal Assyrian treasures of the British Museum.*

Before sending off this second load of antiquities, five months after the first load had gone, there had been tiresome delays, for the precious packing materials which were hard to obtain, such as mats, felts and ropes, had been stolen on their way to Nimrud from Mosul. A complaint was made to the Turkish authorities, who said that they could do nothing to punish the thieves as they

* The black obelisk of Shalmaneser III, son of Ashur-nasir-pal II. The whole of the inscription was roughly translated by Rawlinson just before the publication of Layard's *Nineveh* in 1849 and it was the first translation to be made of the purely Assyrian cuneiform. 'The achievement cannot fail to elicit unqualified admiration', states A. J. Booth in *The Discovery and Decipherment of the Trilingual Cuneiform Inscriptions* (Longmans, 1902).

were certainly desert Arabs and were beyond reach. 'If this robbery passed unnoticed', said Layard, 'the remainder of my property, and even my person, might run some risk.' He decided to deal with the matter himself and after four days the tribe responsible for the theft was known. Leaving at dawn, accompanied by the *cawass* and the *bairakdar*, he rode some hours into the desert and came upon the tribe which was more numerous than had been expected. Layard entered the sheikh's tent and sat down. A large crowd of armed tribesmen collected and he opened the conversation with the usual Arab courtesies:

'We have long been friends although it has never yet been my good fortune to see you. I know the laws of friendship; that which is my property is your property and the contrary. But there are a few things, such as mats, felts and ropes which come from afar and are very necessary to me, whilst they can be of little use to you; otherwise God forbid that I should ask for them.'

The stolen articles were clearly visible, but the sheikh replied:

'As I am your sacrifice, O Bey, no such things as mats, felts and ropes were ever in my tents. Search and if such things be found we give them to you willingly.'

The tribesmen all exclaimed that the sheikh had spoken the truth and that there were no such things. Layard rose saying that as there was doubt on the question, the Governor of Mosul would have to decide between them. He made a sign to the *bairakdar*, who handcuffed the sheikh, pulled him outside and was away on his horse dragging the sheikh behind him before the tribesmen had recovered from their astonishment. One tried to seize the bridle of Layard's horse as he mounted, but the *cawass* used his rhinoceros-hide whip and they got away. By the time they reached Nimrud, the sheikh was prepared to do anything to avoid being put in a Mosul prison. He sent a message to his tribe and the next day a donkey appeared loaded with all the missing property and with a peace offering of a lamb. The sheikh was sent back to his tribe and the story soon spread through the Mesopotamian desert with the addition of many horrifying details with the result that there was no more trouble from plunderers.

169

In January 1847 Layard wrote to his mother:

> I am now opening a series of painted rooms, but the ornaments and figures, which must have been very elegant, are almost entirely obliterated. I only manage to get sketches of a few of them, the moment they come out. Unfortunately the Assyrians appear to have had no material on which they could paint so as to ensure preservation of their colours, as in Egypt. They appear, however, to have been as much in advance of the Egyptians in taste and the disposal of their colours, as they were in sculpture. In the working of metals, in the carving of ivory and in all the minor details of art, they appear to have made very great progress and show a taste which argues a remarkable advance in civilisation.

He pointed out that the Assyrians occupied a country which was short of wood and of hard stone; had they possessed the granite rocks of Egypt they would have left much greater works while the Babylonians did not even have the fragile limestone or gypsum—'Mosul marble' as it was called—which the Assyrians used in their palaces. The lives of this newly discovered people were all around him pictured in their bas-reliefs so that he felt that he knew them. Longworth, who came to visit Nimrud, and descended into the N.W. Palace towards evening, was 'overpowered' by the contemplation of so many strange objects:

> The portly forms of kings and Viziers, were so life-like, and carved in such fine relief, that they might almost be imagined to be stepping from the walls to question the rash intruder on their privacy. Then, mingled with them were other monstrous shapes— the old Assyrian deities, with human bodies, long drooping wings, and the heads and beaks of eagles; or, still faithfully guarding the portals of the deserted halls, the colossal forms of winged lions and bulls, with gigantic human faces. All these figures, the idols of a religion long since dead and buried like themselves, seemed actually in the twilight to be raising their desecrated heads from the sleep of centuries: certainly the feeling of awe which they inspired me with, must have been something akin to that experienced by their heathen votaries of old (*The Morning Post*, 3 March 1847).

It may have been Longworth's visit which encouraged Layard to consider writing about the discoveries. Sara Austen had for some time been urging that he should, for his letters from Nimrud were, she said, 'so spirited and interesting; it requires a high degree of principle on my part not to publish some of them; I wonder if it would make you very angry if I did'. Layard was nervous that publication would arouse jealousy, for there had been trouble with the Trustees of the British Museum about articles written by visitors to Nimrud. At first Layard replied to his aunt rather haughtily: 'I question whether book-making be in these days a good recommendation for public employment, but I suppose, when there is nothing else to be done and a prospect of coin, one must turn jew in the matter.' Sara Austen, who had seen the success that Disraeli had made with his books, did not think that her nephew's reluctance was sensible: 'for in this reading age a good book makes a man's fortune here more certainly than by any other rapid means'. 'Write a whopper with lots of plates', said Alison; 'fish up old legends and anecdotes, and if you can by any means humbug people into the belief that you have established any points in the Bible, you are a made man.' 'A spice of the Bible and the old chroniclers would render the dish very palatable', said Rawlinson. Layard was considering writing a book which would be accessible to the general public and not, as Botta's book 'beyond the reach of all except crowned heads or public libraries'. A letter from Rawlinson of 20 January 1847 showed that there had been discussion on the subject and reveals some of the difficulties of decipherment:

> With regard to publication all that I should wish to do at present would be simply to announce the identification of the kings of Assyria and Babylon and to supply the elements for alphabetical analysis— as to giving critical translations of the inscriptions to accompany your descriptive work, I look upon that as almost impossible. There is a far better groundwork for reading Egyptian in the aid afforded by the modern Coptic, yet, after thirty years study, how few will venture to read a papyrus?
>
> I think the announcement of the names would rather stimulate than satisfy the interest excited in your work, but still, as I am mainly indebted to your kindness and to the accident of the marbles passing through my hands for the means of identifying the names, I should wish their announcement to depend on your approval. If you consented I would send my letter to the Royal Asiatic Society on the subject through you and you would thus be in full possession of my knowledge before its publication. Let me hear from you on this subject as, with all France and Germany alive about the matter,

I am fearful of being forestalled in the little I have hitherto in the way of discovery.

At that time the Trustees were against any publication, but they sent another five hundred pounds and wrote friendly letters. Canning had been most helpful in his communications with Mr. Forshall and wrote to Layard on 21 January 1847:

> No point of any importance mentioned in your correspondence is, I think, omitted, and you can hardly fail to perceive how sincerely anxious the Museum is to do justice to your disinterestedness as well as to your zeal and ability. The remuneration [the £500] you cannot, with any degree of propriety, refuse and I hope that you will excuse me for having continued the quarterly remittance of £50 on your account to the end of last year.

A letter of 22 January from Forshall reassured and pleased Layard so that he was able to write to his mother: 'You need not be vexed about my affairs with people at home. I think I shall be able to do as much as I wish, and fully as much, if not more than the Trustees of the British Museum can reasonably expect.'

Forshall had stated that the Trustees did not wish to discourage Layard's proposal to try to move one of the bulls or lions to the river for transport to Basra, but they would be 'reluctant to have any of the sculptures cut in pieces'. Botta had only succeeded in getting the Khorsabad bulls to the Tigris by cutting them up since the one he tried to transport intact with the aid of three hundred workmen had remained stuck on the way. Layard had been rather contemptuous of Botta's refusal to use mechanical contrivances, but when he was unable to obtain any lifting apparatus he realised that man-power would have to be used. In March 1847 he decided to try to move one of the bulls, a block of marble about ten feet square and two feet in depth, weighing more than ten tons. The method he employed resembled very closely that used by the Assyrians in bringing these huge monuments from the river to their palaces, as shown in bas-reliefs which Layard was to discover later at Kuyunjik.

When all was ready Layard climbed to the mound above the bull to direct proceedings. Below him Rassam, his workmen and many tribesmen were in position, waiting for his signal to start lowering the bull on to wooden rollers. Layard was very anxious,

for the ropes round the monster were not strong and the Mosul
limestone was fragile.

He gave the signal for the wedges to be knocked away and
the great bull began to tilt sideways. The Arabs were half-frantic
with excitement shouting their war-cries, while the Kurdish
musicians beat their drums and blew their shrill pipes. Once the
bull was in motion there was no holding him. Water was thrown
on the ropes but they stretched and broke when the monument
was four or five feet from the ground. The huge block of limestone fell with a crash and those who had been holding the ropes
went rolling over one another. There was a sudden silence and
the dust that rose in the air made it impossible for Layard to see
what had happened. He rushed down, expecting to find the bull
broken in pieces, but there it lay intact, precisely where he had
wished it to be placed. The Arabs, seeing that all was well, seized
the hands of the women, who were looking on, and danced in a
circle round the monster now lying on its side.

It was an evening of great festivity. Sheep were killed and
roasted whole and no sooner had the Arabs eaten than they started
to dance, continuing until dawn. Layard tried to persuade them
to rest after their labours especially as the next day they had to
get the bull to the river. 'Advice and remonstrances were received with deafening shouts of the war-cry, and outrageous
antics as proofs of gratitude for the entertainment and of ability
to resist fatigue. After passing the night in this fashion, these
extraordinary beings, still singing and capering, started for the
mound.' Layard had given a dinner to some of the chiefs. Sheikh
Abd-ur-rahman had watched the excavations from the day that
they had started and many things had puzzled him; having
eaten, he began to moralise:

> 'In the name of the Most High, tell me, O Bey, what are you
> going to do with those stones? So many thousands of purses spent
> upon such things! Can it be, as you say, that your people learn
> wisdom from them; or is it, as his reverence the Cadi declares,
> that they are to go to the palace of your Queen, who, with the
> rest of the unbelievers, worship these idols? As for wisdom, these
> figures will not teach you to make any better knives, or scissors, or
> chintzes; and it is in the making of those things that the English
> show their wisdom.

But God is great! God is great! Here are stones which have been
buried ever since the time of the Holy Noah—peace be with him!
Perhaps they were underground before the deluge. I have lived
on these lands for years. My father, and the father of my father,
pitched their tents here before me; but they never heard of these
figures. For twelve hundred years have the true believers (and,
praise be to God! all true wisdom is with them alone) been settled
in this country, and none of them ever heard of a palace under-
ground. Neither did they who went before them. But lo! here
comes a Frank from many days' journey off, and he walks up to
the very place. Here, says he, is the palace; there, says he, is the
gate; and he shows us what has been all our lives beneath our feet,
without our having known anything about it.'

The next day the workmen and tribesmen began to move the
bull, hauling on ropes which pulled it along wooden rollers.
There were many adventures before the bull, followed by one
of the giant stone lions, reached the river. The Mosul raft-
builders had said that it was impossible to make anything strong
enough to float these masses of stone, and raft-builders had had
to be brought from Bagdad, but even they were at first uncertain
as to whether it could be accomplished. Then there was trouble
with the workmen who had become dispirited at the immensity
of the undertaking and, believing that Layard was entirely
dependent upon them for success, they struck for more pay. All
the tribesmen had already left the district because of the drought
and it indeed seemed as if the workmen could dictate terms but
Layard was determined to break the strike. He sent a horseman
after Abd-ur-rahman asking him to return with some of his
tribesmen to help. This he did, so that the bull and the lion
were launched on their long journey without the help of the
regular workmen who afterwards begged to be taken back into
employment but were refused.[2]

It was decided to finish work at Nimrud by the middle of
May 1847 which left one month before the conclusion of the
expedition to set about finding the secret of Kuyunjik. The
French Consul's workmen were still digging pits haphazardly a
few feet deep and had been doing so for some months without
finding anything. Layard, having acquired experience of how
the Assyrians built their palaces, made another careful examination of the huge mound and decided to resume excavations near

the south-west corner, where he had begun the previous summer. After several days of digging the workmen found a bas-relief while Layard was in Mosul and two Kurdish girls, wives of workmen at the mound, were determined to be the first to give the good news and claim the reward expected on such occasions. On reaching the Tigris they blew up their goat-skins and swam across just as the Assyrians are depicted on the bas-reliefs. Layard gave them their reward and hurried to Kuyunjik. A palace had been discovered with winged bulls at the entrance and within a month nine chambers had been excavated. Layard wrote:

> In its architecture, the newly discovered edifice resembled the palaces of Nimrud and Khorsabad. The chambers were long and narrow. The walls were of unbaked bricks, with a panelling of sculptured slabs. The bas-reliefs were, however, much larger in their dimensions than those generally found at Nimrud, being about ten feet high, and from eight to nine feet wide. The winged human-headed bulls, forming the entrances, were from fourteen to sixteen feet square. . . . The bas-reliefs were greatly inferior in general design and in the beauty of the details, to those of the earliest palace of Nimrud; but in many parts they were very carefully and minutely finished; in this respect Kuyunjik yields to no other known monument in Assyria.

When Layard discovered the palace at Kuyunjik within a few days of starting excavations, it seemed like a miracle to the French Consul, but Layard considered that the Frenchman could have done as well if he had studied the matter:

> The Assyrians, when about to build a palace or public edifice, appear to have constructed a platform, or solid compact mass of sun-dried bricks, about thirty or forty feet above the level of the plain. Upon it they raised the monument. . . . Consequently, in digging for remains, the first step is to reach the platform of sun-dried bricks. When this is discovered, the trenches must be opened to the level of it, and not deeper.

Before completing the season of excavating and returning to Constantinople it was important to obtain an assurance from the Porte that the right to excavate should continue but the Turkish Government was now planning to have a national museum of its own in Constantinople, since foreigners seemed to consider these antiquities of importance and even of value in money. Wellesley, now Lord Cowley,[3] who was in charge of the Embassy while Canning was in London, succeeded only with great difficulty in obtaining this permission: 'It seems that very harming reports have been made here of the beauty of your discoveries and the Sultan himself repents of the permission he had given you', he told Layard. 'They [the authorities] do not, therefore, like to grant anything that will imply a permanent right of the British to continue later their researches.'

Layard was by now convinced that he had discovered Nineveh in Nimrud although he knew that everyone had always considered that the mound of Kuyunjik was Nineveh. Both he and Rawlinson were led to this conclusion for various reasons. Rawlinson believed that he had identified the name of Ninus in the cuneiform inscriptions from Nimrud; Ninus, according to the early Greek and Armenian historians was the first King of Assyria and was sometimes called Nimrod; the palaces discovered at Nimrud were earlier than those discovered at Kuyunjik.[4] One of the last letters that Layard wrote from Mosul was on 14 June 1847 to Cecilia Berkeley:

> If you refer to Lemprière's classical dictionary (the great authority on all such questions) you will find that there was a king called Ninus—whether he was Nimrod himself or his son, I will not pretend to determine. This Ninus we believe to have built the earliest palace at Nimrud, where I have been digging, and we think we have found his name in all the inscriptions. He appears to have been a mighty hunter for he loves to represent himself slaying the lion and wild bull with his arrows, or struggling at close quarters with similar monsters. . . . Besides the palaces at Nimrud I have lately discovered a building on the left bank of the Tigris opposite to Mosul. This may have been the palace of one of the Assyrian kings mentioned in the Old Testament—Sennacherib, Esarhaddon or Tiglath-pileser. It is of more recent epoch than those first discovered at Nimrud which appears to be the true site of Nineveh.

Layard, however, was always careful about his speculations and the suggestions that he and Rawlinson had already made that Nineveh was not, after all, on its traditional site of Kuyunjik had already aroused some comment. He was quite correct when he wrote to his family in June, 'no one, I suppose, will now be inclined to dispute that I have got hold of the true site of Nineveh between Kuyunjik and Nimrud'.[5]

Layard paid his respects to the dignitaries of Mosul and gave a farewell party to his friends and to his workmen, who were sad to see him go, especially the women, for he had insisted that they should be better treated. 'What shall we do when you leave us', they said, 'there will be nobody to help us.' Many of the workmen followed as far as the village of Tel Kef, where a large supper was prepared. The journey was then continued with Hormuzd Rassam, who was to go to Oxford, and a party of about fifty armed men. The country was overrun with plundering Beduin and for the first time Layard expressed apprehension lest they should be attacked, for he had nearly three hundred valuable drawings, the only proof in many cases of the existence of the treasures of Nimrud and Kuyunjik. Moreover he was exhausted and ill for the heat, dust, and flies had nearly driven him out of his senses. He wrote to his mother: 'I felt very much like old Job did when his friends gave him that comforting advice!'

There could be no doubt [writes Mr. Seton Lloyd in *Foundations in the Dust*] that his two years' work among the Assyrian ruins had produced results of which he could be proud. He had identified the sites of the Biblical Calah (Nimrud) and of Nineveh itself, and discovered the remains of no less than eight Assyrian palaces connected, as was subsequently proved, with such illustrious names as Ashur-nasir-pal, Sargon, Shalmaneser, Tiglath-pileser, Adad-nirari, Esarhaddon and Sennacherib. He had completed his own part in the transporting to England of some hundreds of tons of Assyrian sculpture.

Triumphal return
to England

Layard reached the Embassy at Therapia to stay with Lord
Cowley on 31 July 1847 after an absence of nearly two years.
Great interest was shown in the excavations and so many people
wanted to see his drawings that he feared the pencil marks were
fading, 'people use their hands rather than their eyes'. On 23
June, the day before he had left Mosul, the first consignment of
bas-reliefs from Nimrud was placed in the British Museum and
had aroused very great interest. 'I felt myself as a *little* bit of a
lion as belonging to you!' wrote his mother who had travelled
to London to see the antiquities. Kellogg wrote from New York
that the Ethnological Society there had elected Layard a member

for there was 'a deep interest in your discoveries and your letters to me have been read before it'.

Canning in London had been talking to Lord Palmerston, the Foreign Minister, and was able to write to Layard on 20 July that agreement had been given to his being attached to the Embassy in Constantinople where he was to be employed in establishing the line of the Turco-Persian boundary under the provisions of a treaty concluded at Erzerum. It was not yet official, said Canning, 'as some enquiry must be made as to the Shah's recollection of your *belligerent adventures*'. Having received friendly letters from the Trustees of the British Museum and from Canning, Layard considered that he could return to England 'without the anticipation of a fight in any quarter'. Canning had hoped that Layard would await his return to Constantinople, but the doctor stated that hard work and bouts of malaria had impaired his health and that he should return to England immediately.

Leaving Constantinople by ship in October, Layard stopped in Italy where he showed his drawings to Visconti and others interested, then he went on to Paris where he had a most friendly reception from Botta who introduced him to other *savants*, such as Burnouf, Lajard, Mohl, and Humboldt. Botta's Khorsabad antiquities had reached Paris the previous December, the French Government having sent a naval vessel to collect them from Basra, and they had been placed in the Louvre where they were attracting large crowds. Botta was working on his book and there was still no prospect of funds for further excavations at Mosul because of the unsettled state of France. It was arranged that Layard should speak before a distinguished body of the *Académie des Inscriptions et Belles Lettres*. Even he was a little intimidated and he described the scene to his Aunt Sara:

> I was still suffering from my attack of fever and one of the results of fever is a considerable excitement of the brain, consequent audacity, and no small additional loquacity, only controlled by physical debility. Consequently when placed in the middle of this rather formidable assembly, I contrived to make them, without nervousness, a moderately lengthy speech. . . . From all sides poured questions and compliments, from Messieurs Letronne, Mohl, Lenormant, etc. From opposite, old Humboldt, with all the

quiet blandness of a German philosopher, endeavoured, but in vain, to put a question. What German could be heard amongst fifty Frenchmen? It was equally in vain that I endeavoured to isolate myself in imagination from the mass to catch the words, real golden words, of M. Burnouf, who never says anything not worth hearing. Equally in vain the President agitated himself and his small bell to restore order. . . . People here were very much inclined to dispute the superior antiquity of Nimrud, and advanced many arguments in proof of that of Khorsabad; but I showed the *Académie*, or rather made them prove themselves, that they were greatly in error on the subject.

Layard felt overwhelmed by the kindness of Botta and the French *savants*, who displayed no particle of nationalistic jealousy. They wanted the drawings and inscriptions published as soon as possible and Burnouf offered to lend the excellent type which had been especially cut for the publication of Botta's cuneiform inscriptions.* Burnouf also wanted to arrange for Layard to see Louis-Philippe, but the King was out of Paris until 20 December and Layard wanted to have his Christmas dinner in England after an absence of eight and a half years. (Within two months Louis-Philippe was an exile at Claremont having fled to England as a result of the revolution in France.)

When Layard reached London the Austens gave dinner parties in his honour at Montague Place and he was invited to meet distinguished people at various houses. The Trustees of the British Museum were delighted with the work that he had done and were anxious that the drawings and copies of inscriptions should be published. They asked the Government for four thousand pounds—more than was spent on the excavations. Mr. Samuel Birch of the British Museum warned Layard not to count on such promises and advised him to obtain as much public support as possible, for 'English authorities are influenced more from without than from within'. At the end of 1847 Layard received from the Foreign Office a formal appointment, jointly with Lt. Colonel Fenwick Williams, to the Turco-Persian Boundary

* These were contained in the third and fifth volumes of the beautifully produced *Monument de Ninive*, the other three volumes containing text by Paul Botta and drawings by Eugene Flandin. It was published at French Government expense in 1849.

Commission. He wrote to thank Lord Palmerston, and asked for leave of absence on health reasons until he was required to proceed to the Persian frontier and this was granted. He also received a friendly letter from Sir Stratford Canning: 'You must make the most of the Assyrian antiquities. Do them justice and do yourself credit, and make the public understand that they have got a prize. But you must not expect as much pecuniary help as Botta has got. The times are bad and we have not the motives to that kind of expense which inspire the French Government. Could a subscription be got up?'

Layard decided that it was time that the British Museum made a thorough investigation of the whole of Mesopotamia and wrote a long letter in the New Year of 1848. He urged the Trustees: 'To effect for the antiquities of Assyria and Babylonia, that which the expedition of Lepsius, for instance, has done for those of the Valley of the Nile.' He proposed a series of expeditions to cover the area from the Taurus Mountains to the Persian Gulf, excavating the ruins in the neighbourhood of Orfa, 'supposed to be the ancient Ur', the ruins on the banks of the Khabour river, on the upper Euphrates, in ancient Assyria, Babylonia, and Susiana. The time was 'peculiarly favourable'; public interest had been aroused and the Turks themselves were beginning to realise the importance of the antiquities. Quick action was necessary:

> Orders have already been given to the Governors of the European, and some of the most western provinces of the Empire, to collect antiquities for a projected museum at Constantinople. The consequences have been that, as the Governors compel the inhabitants to excavate and transport objects of antiquity without remuneration, they (the inhabitants) destroy all remains that come within their reach to evade the forced labour. The work of destruction has already commenced.

He suggested that the expeditions should be planned for a period of at least three years and four to five thousand pounds should be voted for the first year: 'The casual discovery of the great edifices in the mounds of Nimrud, Khorsabad, and Kuyunjik show how little the contents of those apparent mere heaps of earth could have been foreseen.' The French and Prussian

181

Governments in sending expeditions to Egypt had earned well-deserved glory and the British Government could be the first to earn merit by carrying out thorough excavations over a wide area.[1] The reaction, however, was not favourable, but permission was given him to write a book on his own initiative. 'It will contain an account of the works carried on', Layard wrote to Kellogg on 16 January 1848, 'a slight sketch of the history of Nineveh, a short enquiry into the manners, customs, and religion of the Assyrians, my own adventures in Assyria, and a little information on the languages and character with an account of the progress made in deciphering. . . . I think the book will be attractive particularly in America where there are so many scripture readers.'

Layard felt very gloomy in spite of the Foreign Office appointment and the great interest aroused in his Assyrian discoveries. He was suffering from a serious liver complaint and felt unable to do any work or to write his book, and he fretted that he was not achieving anything. Alison asked what he was expecting to be—some sort of Nimrod or Metternich? 'Be satisfied with something less and be content in the meanwhile.' Layard spent some days with his mother at Cheltenham, but she was in her usual emotional state and frayed his nerves, while Benjamin and Sara were preoccupied because Austen's partner had absconded with a large sum of money; he went on to stay with friends and relations at their country houses and his health improved. 'These comfortable places, and the pleasures of English life, spoil one for the adventures and privations of the East', he wrote to Henry Ross, who was looking after the excavations at Kuyunjik. 'I find a great improvement in the upper classes; much more information, liberality of opinion, and kindness towards those beneath them. I think that, on the whole, things in England are much better than could be expected.' He had been staying with Danby Seymour, who had visited him at Mosul, with Lord Eastnor, soon to become Viscount Somers, who had married the beautiful Virginia Pattle, and with Sir John Guest who was responsible for seven thousand workmen and their families employed in his great ironworks at Dowlais, near Cardiff. Layard's cousin, Lady Charlotte, whose acquaintance his father had wished him to cultivate more than ten years earlier, had at the age of twenty-one married Sir John Guest, a widower of forty-nine, part-owner with Wyndham Lewis of the ironworks. Lewis had died in 1838 and Guest bought his share of the business; Lewis's widow married Benjamin Disraeli who was then able to pay off his debts to Benjamin Austen and others. Lady Charlotte by marrying 'into trade' earned the disapproval of the social world, but this did not bother her. She was a remarkable and talented woman with many interests including Greek, Arabic, Persian, and Welsh, and she translated *The Mabinogion*, which was an inspiration to Tennyson. She also helped her husband run the business, looked after six schools at Dowlais, and brought up a large family. Lady Charlotte liked her ambitious young cousin, Henry Layard, and he was a frequent guest at Canford and Dowlais. In March 1848 she noted in her diary 'In the evening Henry Layard showed us some of his drawings, but he seemed so ill he could hardly give any explanation of them.' She often played the piano—usually Mozart—while Layard accompanied her on his flute. With the Guest children he was a great favourite, acting with them in charades and telling them stories about his travels when they went to bed. He preferred being with them to going out hunting with the gentry. The Welsh workmen at the Dowlais iron-foundry gave him an enthusiastic reception when he spoke to them of the evidence for the truth of many stories in the Bible revealed by the excavations at Nimrud and Nineveh. He made friends with George Clark, one of the managers and trustees of the iron business, and with Henry Bruce,* who has given an account of Layard at that time: 'His face was singularly attractive and impressive; his figure suggested strength and power of endurance, rather than exceptional activity.' He had, said Bruce, tenacity, energy, and enthusiasm in all he undertook, warmth of affection and a horror of cruelty, 'which made him the champion of the oppressed'.

The drawing of him as a young man by G. F. Watts shows him as determined, self-confident with a hint of ruthlessness in

* Henry Austin Bruce, P.C., G.C.B., D.C.L., was M.P. for Merthyr Tydfil 1852 to 1868, Secretary of State for the Home Department 1868 to 1873, and created Baron Aberdare in 1873. He gave a description of Layard in the introduction to the 1894 summarised edition of *Early Adventures*.

the eyes, which is at variance with a full and sensitive mouth. It is more in character than the portrait of him in Albanian dress by Phillips who made Layard look romantic but rather weak and lackadaisical. Even though he was short and did not have much of a figure, Henry Layard was attractive to women, and he was attracted by the intelligent and talented ones such as Elizabeth Rigby who married Charles Eastlake in April 1849, Lucie Austin who married Sir Alexander Duff Gordon, his cousin Mary Pegus who married in 1844 Lord Aboyne, heir to the Marquess of Huntly, and it was rumoured that he was in love with his other cousin, Lady Charlotte, but there is no evidence for this, though it is clear that he had a great admiration for her. Later in his life he wrote of her: 'She is an extraordinary woman and her character a remarkable one, in some respects resembling that of Madame de Staël in the union of the feminine and masculine qualities.' Layard was at Canford and Dowlais throughout April 1848 when she was greatly distressed over the fate of the thousands of work people since the lease of the ironworks was due to end the next month and the terms for renewal demanded by Lord Bute, the landowner, were too high. 'What then is to become of the population', she wrote at Dowlais in her diary. 'I ran to my room to the window and sat there gazing for the last time on the bright fires in an agony of tears. Oh! how I wept and prayed that night.' Her prayers were answered. Lord Bute died and the lease was renewed in April. She was then thirty-six and had been married to Sir John Guest for fifteen years during which time she had given birth to ten children—five boys and five girls. Layard was thirty-one and she was anxious to help him in every way possible, giving parties in London and at Canford for her 'Ninevite'. John Murray had visited Canford and discussed the terms for publishing the book *Nineveh and Its Remains*. The Treasury had refused to grant funds for publishing the drawings and Layard told Ross: 'The state of finances and the events occurring on the Continent, have driven Nineveh and all other antiquities out of peoples' heads.' Lady Charlotte stated in her diary on 14 April 1848, that she had persuaded Murray to publish the drawings and there was to be a public subscription to cover the expense. She was also busy with plans for changes at Canford Manor, at a cost of fourteen thousand pounds, which was more than she had expected. It was being done by Charles Barry, who had designed the new House of Commons. Layard enjoyed his company at Canford for he had visited Jerash, various ancient cities in the Ottoman Empire, and shared a love for Italian architecture. Barry had built the Travellers Club and the Reform Club in an Italian style which he had also adopted in the modifications he made in 1847 on Smith's designs for the new British Embassy in Constantinople. One of the improvements at Canford was to be a 'Nineveh Porch' to contain Assyrian antiquities and Layard wrote to Henry Ross in Mosul to send certain bas-reliefs and figures which he specified.[2]

Layard worked on his book at Canford but paid occasional visits to London to keep in touch with the Foreign Office; on one occasion he had a private interview with Lord Palmerston, who was Foreign Minister. His health was improving slowly but the doctor did not consider him well enough to go to Erzerum to join the Boundary Commission and an extension of leave was granted. This enabled him to devote more time to putting his notes in order and to writing. He was particularly anxious to obtain the latest information on cuneiform research, as a great deal was being published. He was receiving letters from Rawlinson telling him that in the previous summer he had almost given up in despair trying to decipher the Babylonian writing but had made a quick visit to Hamadan to make a further copy of the Bisutun inscriptions: 'I got hoisted up on the opposite precipice and from a little nook in the scarp set to work with my big telescope. The letters are only distinguishable for a couple of hours during the day. . . . However, the results have exceeded my most sanguine expectations, for I have actually recovered almost one half of the entire inscriptions.' He said that he was still concentrating on the Babylonian cuneiform and had not yet had time to apply his discoveries to the Assyrian 'but I have recognised, as I have been copying, scores of the Nimrud words with the forms of which I was already familiar, and I am pretty sure that the languages are so nearly allied, the same key will answer for both.' He wanted more material from Nimrud: 'All I beg of you is not to supply Dr. Hincks with materials before I can also have access to them, otherwise I fear he might give me the go-by.' Rawlinson had written a long and rather agitated letter to Layard at the beginning of 1848 saying that he did not believe Burnouf's statement that he could understand the Khorsabad inscriptions; 'where the deuce did he get the language from?'; he did not think that there was anything in the Semitic family of languages which could furnish a key. Botta in the meantime had been working hard on Assyrian cuneiform and publishing in the *Journal Asiatique*, issuing in 1848 a separate *Mémoire sur l'Ecriture cunéiforme*. The revolution in France had interfered with his studies and delayed publication of the great work *Monument de Ninive*. He wrote to Layard in great distress in March 1848: 'Were we tattooed we would be exactly like New Zealanders [Maoris]; everybody must be ready to fight for his life and property and we think of nothing else but guns, cartridges, swords etc. That is what they call fraternity and if it lasts a little longer we shall be perfect barbarians.' * The troubles in France were a great hindrance to those interested in Assyriology and the French did not succeed in catching up the lead that had now been established by Layard.

There were a great many facts to collect for the book and not much time to do it in. It was an ambitious task for someone who had not previously written anything except newspaper articles. He had to try to sort out Assyrian history from the ambiguities and inaccuracies of the Hebrew, Greek, and Roman writers, those working on cuneiform decipherment were all the time throwing up different names and theories and Layard himself was exploring new ground with theories he wished to propound. He was also preparing for the press, drawings for the first series of *Monuments of Nineveh* and superintending publication of the copies of the cuneiform inscriptions he had made for the Trustees of the British Museum. Considering his literary inexperience, his ill-health,

---

* Paul Emile Botta, after being praised and rewarded for his wonderful work at Khorsabad and later on cuneiform, fell into disgrace for political reasons and was never sent back to Mosul. If he could have been there with Layard on his second expedition much of the unfortunate Anglo-French rivalry, which developed later over Assyrian antiquities, might have been avoided. Instead the French Government wasted a good man by sending him as Consul to Tripoli in Syria, where he died in 1872. It is extraordinary that in the 1960 *Larousse du XX Siècle* this pioneer of Assyrian archaeology is not mentioned.

and lack of time it is amazing what he achieved. It was a great pity that he had to work at such speed and could not have been given the time and money to make fuller use of his notebooks; the result might not have been such an entertaining book but it would probably have been even more useful to archaeologists. The work left him completely exhausted and he had to rely on the faithful Sara Austen to go through the proofs. He apologised to her for having looked through them in a slovenly manner: 'It is now a month since I have been able to put two ideas together and I begin to feel uncomfortable for the future.'

Even before publication of *Nineveh and Its Remains*, Layard's fame was increasing. In July 1848 his pioneer work was recognised by the distinguished degree of D.C.L. at Oxford. To Layard, who had always longed to go to a university, this was a greatly coveted honour; to some of his friends it came as a surprise. Crabb Robinson, who had remembered Layard as a brash and enthusiastic young man, considered it an abuse of academic rank, but after reading his book he expressed amazement at the amount of knowledge that Layard had acquired and the originality of many of his theories. In the same month of July, the Trustees of the British Museum wrote to Palmerston asking for permission to employ Layard on a second expedition to Mosul, but they had little to offer in the way of pay, only twenty pounds a month. Layard had no intention of accepting under such conditions and considered it a most disappointing reaction to his plan for excavating Mesopotamia. A little digging continued at Kuyunjik under Henry Ross, who had been asked by the British Museum to supervise, but he had to leave in July to deal with his business as a merchant. He wrote a series of letters to Layard from Mosul describing the excavations and the intrigues there. After a visit to Bavian on the Gomel river he gave Layard a detailed account of the Assyrian sculptures on the cliff-face, some of which Layard included in his book.[3] Ross said that he had not seen any of Layard's lady friends but he himself was having a great deal of trouble: 'Not another women shall put her foot within my door; for I know that fatality attends everything I have to do with women.'

Layard was beginning to wonder whether he wanted to be a member of the Boundary Commission even if the doctor passed him as fit. Alison advised strongly against 'this trumpery frontier work' in which he might become involved for years 'in endless squabbles about tribal pretensions'. There was also uncertainty as to what would be his position in relation to Colonel Fenwick Williams. It had at first been understood that Layard would be 'jointly' in charge, but there were reports later that he might find himself subordinate. In September he wrote to Lord Palmerston and to Sir Stratford Canning asking if he could be excused from the Commission. His release was agreed, but he was annoyed to be told that he would have received a salary of two hundred and fifty pounds a year as a member of the Boundary Commission, but that working in Constantinople he would only be an unpaid Attaché. Lord Cowley considered it 'unworthy treatment' and Rawlinson described it as 'a positive disgrace'.

In October fifty cases sent from Nimrud arrived in London after an eventful journey from Bombay, having been nearly sunk in a great storm off Ceylon. Layard was present when the cases were opened at the British Museum and was upset to find that the objects were not in the order he had placed them in the cases, broken pieces originally put together had been scattered while some objects had even been removed. A letter was written to the Government of Bombay and it was discovered that the cases, while lying on the wharf at Bombay, had been opened by members of the British community.

In November the Trustees wrote to Lord Palmerston acknowledging the services rendered by Layard and Canning: 'The entire collection will undoubtedly be regarded as one of the most important contributions to the materials of archaeological science which has been made in recent times.' But there was no offer of funds to continue excavations, nor had any efforts been made by the end of the year to collect from Basra the lion and the bull, which had been dragged to the Tigris with such difficulty eighteen months previously. There was nothing for Layard to do but return to the Embassy at Constantinople as an unpaid Attaché and he arrived there at the end of December 1848 in time to witness the departure of his friends Colonel Fenwick Williams and young Almeric Wood as members of the Boundary Commission. If he had gone with them he would at least have had an official post and a salary; he would also have been able to spend some time on archaeology, for William Kennet Loftus, the geologist to the Commission, was able to excavate at Warka (the biblical Erech), and later carry out extensive operations elsewhere in Mesopotamia.[4]

8

'The greatest achievement
of our time'

Layard's fortunes changed after the publication of *Nineveh and Its Remains* at the beginning of 1849, after he had arrived in Constantinople. It took the reading public by storm. 'Nobody asks: "Have you read it?" That is taken for granted', wrote a Foreign Office friend. Henry Ross was in London and described 'the perfect fever of attention' so that the book could not come fast enough from the press to meet the ever-increasing demand and people referred to Layard as 'the most extraordinary man of the day'.

The book was, indeed, a very considerable achievement. It shows unusual talent and industry that he was able to write in less than a year a scholarly work in two volumes of nearly nine hundred pages with carefully drawn diagrams and illustrations. No one had realised how fully he had made use of the many hours spent in Colonel Taylor's library in Bagdad, his studies in Constantinople, his conversations and correspondence with Rawlinson and his musings on the mounds of Nineveh and Nimrud. There is great detail, but the whole is enlivened by his enthusiasm, sense of adventure, power of observation, and his wonderful

190

talent for description. The second part of the book dealt with Assyrian art, architecture, furniture, language, methods of warfare, religion, and history. 'This part', states Dr. Gadd in *The Stones of Assyria*, 'faded as much of it is by lapse of time, contains much good observation, good sense, and good learning.' His drawings had also been published in two large folios by public subscription.

Edward Hawkins had been appointed Secretary to the British Museum and Austen reported that he had been indefatigable. When Prince Albert and all the Ministers had visited the Assyrian antiquities he had told them: 'These things are without price; no thousands could buy them and they have cost the country nothing.' Lord John Russell, Lord Lansdowne, and others had been so impressed that they had arranged immediately with the First Lord of the Admiralty to send a ship to collect the bull and the lion from Basra. Hawkins had also made sure that each Trustee had a copy of Layard's plan for excavating Assyria, Babylonia, and Susiana. Sara Austen's letters are as lyrical as those she wrote as a young woman to Benjamin Disraeli. 'I cannot', she told her nephew, 'even think of you, most glancingly, without more emotion than is at all good for me! Shame upon my years! What a fortune your brains will be to you.' She referred repeatedly to the astonishment and admiration aroused by the book: 'It is not only considered perfect in style, astonishing in knowledge, but a *marvel* in its interest and completeness. . . . It has achieved all that the highest ambition could desire.' Even the staid Austen wrote with emotion:

No one speaks of any other book but *Nineveh* & of its modesty. They abuse the Government & the Museum & praise your lenient treatment of them. Your course, my dear Henry, is now clear. *Nothing can stop you.* Not even a niggardly Whig radical Government. . . . Till your book was read no one knew how much the Government was indebted to you & I have taken good care to say that you did not take a pound of their money but spent part of your own patrimony. Lord Ellesmere said it ought to be alluded to in Parliament; his name is a tower of strength with the world of Fine Arts. . . .

I strongly recommend you not to put Ross forward but go yourself to Nimrud. The country will now see Justice done you and will not leave it to Lord Palmerston. I think he has behaved shamefully —and this affair of the Persian Commission shows it. . . . Surely they never could have expected you to go as private secretary to Williams. It is so contrary to what Sir Stratford said to your Aunt that I should like to know a little more about it. I have always felt, & do not hesitate to say, that your position at Nimrud was not put forward properly by Sir S.C. & no one at the Museum thought more about you than as a clerk or assistant, but thanks to your own plain, modest statement all now know better; but I cannot help expressing my opinion that Sir S.C. showed no particular kindness about it. It comes late but not the worse for that as it shows your moderation & all wonder how you could have gained such influence over a race of wild Arabs. Were you here now I fear your head would be turned, & it is well, therefore, you escape the intoxication. . . . Now is the time to strike. The iron is hot. Half the noblemen in the country are calling on Murray.

There was scarcely a newspaper which did not have a lengthy review and one of the most striking was in *The Times* of 9 February. *Nineveh* was described as 'the most extraordinary work of the present age', and the reviewer questioned whether a more enlightened or more enterprising traveller than Mr. Layard was to be met with 'in the annals of our modern history'. Reference was made to the author's strong mind, indomitable will, and desire to acquire knowledge, which had carried him into many lands and through a series of remarkable adventures, an account of which, it was hoped, he would sometime give to the world: 'Certainly no man has had greater experience of life, had more difficulties to contend with, or a nobler aim.' He told his uncle that he was embarrassed by all these newspaper articles: 'I am inclined to feel ashamed of myself, as if I were humbugging the public, when I read the flattering notices in the Press.' It was unfortunate that out of all the many articles to which he might have referred, he chose to single out the article in *The Times* of 9 February: 'I blushed on reading it and have been ashamed to show it here.' This remark upset Sara Austen a great deal, for she herself had written it. 'I wish you had expressed yourself differently,' wrote Austen, 'I much fear that her health has seriously suffered. You have no idea of her anxiety about your works and your prospects generally.' Murray had shown Sara the proof of a 'monstrous article' about *Nineveh* which was about to be published in *The Times* and she was told that it might be possible to stop it if she could supply an alternative, giving new information which other reviewers had not got. In a few hours she had written the review and it had been accepted. 'It was in everyone's mouth immediately', Austen wrote to Layard, 'and did more good than *all* the reviews put together.' He told his nephew that he was not in favour of his coming to London, as had been proposed, and considered that he should stay with Sir Stratford Canning, who might be hurt at all the praise he was receiving.

The book was dedicated to Benjamin Austen, though there had been the intention at first to dedicate it to Canning. No mention was made in the introduction of the part played by the Ambassador, though a tribute was included in the first chapter; more might have been said. The book was not discussed by Canning and was, Layard considered, a source of embarrassment. In talking to the Ambassador, Layard so far forgot himself on one or two occasions as to refer to 'my marbles'. He told his Aunt Sara that the Ambassador had not read any of the book and turned away from the reviews which created 'an uncomfortable feeling', though Canning was probably amused at the announcement by the reviewer in *Fraser's Magazine* that the Ambassador had advanced three thousand pounds from his own pocket for the excavations. Sara thought that Layard was imagining all this, since she knew that Canning had ordered four copies of *Nineveh*: 'He has been only *trying* you a bit by his seeming indifference, as he told me he sometimes did!' She was probably right and Layard admitted that the Ambassador was kind to him, and that as he was with Canning for ten to twelve hours a day, 'it would be very uncomfortable did anything but a good understanding exist between us'. On receipt of a copy of the book from Layard Canning had thanked him for the 'splendid memorial of Nimrud' and added a charming note: 'It reminds me most agreeably of my good fortune in having been the occasion of starting one so highly gifted on a long course, as I trust it will prove, of eminent service to the public and of brilliant distinction to yourself. Such occasions are the oases—few and far between—of diplomatic life.' Canning realised that Layard, by his talented book, had made the Assyrian discoveries his own, and does not

seem to have borne any grudge, contenting himself with the
fact that he discovered Layard. Ever since the latter had arrived
in Constantinople seven years earlier he had been trying to help
him obtain a diplomatic post and he was still trying to do this.
He was now helped by Lord Ellesmere, who had considerable
influence in the world of Fine Arts and had been quite carried
away by *Nineveh* which he considered 'the greatest achievement
of our time'. He wrote to John Murray 'no man living has done
so much or told it so well', and he sent a long letter to Charles
Arbuthnot, a close friend of the Duke of Wellington, saying that
the Assyrian monuments at the British Museum had been estimated to be worth about forty thousand pounds and Layard had
obtained them at a cost to the country of about three thousand
pounds:

> The man who has done all this and who has told the story of his
> achievements with singular modesty and simplicity, has damaged
> his health, spent his money, and is now an unpaid Attaché at Con-
> stantinople. . . . Sir Stratford Canning, a man sagacious enough
> and not easy to please, says he thinks Macaulay and Layard the
> two cleverest men he has ever met with. . . . I really think that
> Lord Palmerston who, I understand, showed him personal kind-
> ness and consideration lately in England, would do himself much
> honour on the Continent as well as here by bringing forward such
> a man. . . . He is one of those men of whom England seems to
> have a monopoly, who go anywhere, surmount anything and
> achieve everything without assistance, patronage or fuss of any
> kind.[1]

Arbuthnot sent the letter to Palmerston, who had seen Layard
when he was in London, and replied that he shared the interest
felt about Layard: 'He is certainly a very extraordinary man
and his enterprising exertions have accomplished very remarkable and important results.' He would keep him in view and avail
himself of any opportunity to turn his good qualities to account.

In the early spring of 1849 there were several deaths from
cholera among the British Embassy staff in Constantinople and
another paid Attaché was required. Layard was at last appointed.
Sara Austen was among the first to offer congratulations in a
letter of twenty-four pages in which she said rather wildly:
'Visions of stars, garters, and coronets flit before my aching eyes.'

Layard's cousin, Lady Aboyne, wrote to congratulate him and also to say that it was not the right moment for him to marry 'Miss A' who was not at all suitable. He had apparently become entangled when he was in England and had written to Lady Aboyne from Constantinople saying that he felt he was under an obligation to marry the lady. She replied tartly: 'Forget all that nonsense about *sacrificing*. It is quite clear that your own good and your own happiness ought to be your first concern.' That was the end of 'Miss A', and Layard became far too busy to think about young women and marriage.

The Government had at last agreed to take up Layard's suggestions to carry on excavations but not to the extent that he had proposed, though the reports he received from London suggested that his plan had been accepted. Mr. Hawkins had dined at Montague Place and had told the Austens that Lord John Russell and Lord Palmerston had agreed to a grant for excavations amounting to a total of twenty thousand pounds, that a commission was to be formed with Layard at the head and that the proposal for extensive excavations of Mesopotamia would be fully carried out; there would also be a doctor and an artist. Layard was delighted to hear all this. Austen told him that he was 'a prodigious favourite' at the British Museum where it was stated that he had brought more of the public 'than any ten previous contributors'. The Nineveh Room was full of people whenever Sara went there from her house almost next door. Henry Ross visited the room and described how members of the public crowded round him when they heard that he had exca-vated at Nimrud. Hormuzd Rassam was asked to many houses as a result of his connection with Nimrud and Kuyunjik. He was doing propaganda for the Nestorians and being attacked by the Puseyites. He wrote to Layard from Oxford:

> I do not suppose Mr. Palmer, Pusey and their friends will be pleased at all to see the letter which I wrote the Archbishop of Canterbury, as they say that the English Church has no right to protect the Heretical one [the Nestorian], and they think the sooner our Church will go to decay the better. But I am happy to say that our Bishop and the Archbishop of Canterbury are against the views of the Puseyites and they will do all they can to help the distressed and unoffending Tiyaris.

Rassam congratulated Layard on receiving the Gold Medal from
the Royal Geographical Society, and Layard was pleased that his
uncle had received it on his behalf. Following an address by the
President of the Royal Geographical Society, Mr. W. J.
Hamilton, on 28 May 1849, Austen had spoken enthusiastically
of his young nephew: a little speech which showed that he had
reconsidered his views about his early travels:

> When he left England, he had no letters of introduction, and
> no patronage or assistance of any sort; but, though young, his
> character was formed. Firm and energetic, with courage which
> nothing could daunt, he combined an indomitable and enterprising
> spirit with the most amiable disposition.

The Austens were much occupied in finding an artist for the
newly formed archaeological mission, buying guns and saddles,
and arranging Hormuzd Rassam's journey to Constantinople.
Austen's partner had been declared a bankrupt and he was 'overwhelmed with business', so that Sara had to make many of the
arrangements: 'She worries herself in such a manner that it
leads to words.' Austen said they had found an artist of twenty-
eight, a Mr. F. C. Cooper who was leaving behind a young wife
just confined 'and it was a sad parting'. He was to have £200 as
salary for the year and £30 for the journey; another £30 was
to be paid to Rassam and there was £200 for Layard's outfit;
there was also £200 salary to be paid to Dr. Humphry Sandwith
who was to join the expedition from Constantinople to watch
over Layard's health. Austen was distressed to find that the first
£1,500 was to last for eight months, until April 1850, and that
the various expenses were to come out of it. Layard was to be
granted leave from his post in Constantinople to lead the expedition, but he was horrified when he realised from his uncle's
letter how little money would be left for the excavations and
transport of the antiquities, after paying for the party's journey
from Constantinople to Mosul, for the workmen and the living
expenses. Hawkins was worried that Layard might not accept
and warned him that there were so many projects the Trustees
wished to carry out that the £3,000 would be lost for Assyrian
excavation if it were not accepted immediately.

Layard complained in a letter to Sir Henry Ellis, the Principal

Ch. 8 'The greatest achievement of our time'

Librarian at the British Museum, that there would only be three to four hundred pounds left 'for the excavations & transport of the sculptures to Basra', less than the amount he had received during the previous expedition. It is clear from his letter that he thought the Museum authorities had agreed to his plan:

> I need scarcely say that it would be utterly impossible with it alone to attempt the execution of the plan submitted to the Trustees during the winter, which comprised Babylonia and even Susiana. Indeed, after what has already been accomplished, it is hardly prudent on my part to embark on a second expedition with such very limited means at my disposal, but as the Trustees have reckoned on my services I will not raise difficulties at the last moment. . . .
>
> My private resources are far from considerable, but, such as they are, they shall be devoted to the undertaking.

To his uncle he wrote gloomily that it was 'utterly impossible' to do anything with the sum granted. The British Museum had paid Rawlinson two or three hundred pounds for a pair of bulls from Khorsabad,* 'and they expect me to excavate and remain and send to Basra whole collections for little more'. At the same time Rawlinson was furious with the Trustees because they had tried to bargain over the price and he considered them 'a pig-headed overbearing set'. Layard told his old friend Cecilia Berkeley that he was going on another expedition: 'I am not quite sure that my health will stand it; however, one cannot do better than wind up on the field of one's success and it would be a great thing to be buried in Nimrod's palace.'

Young Hormuzd Rassam was summoned to Constantinople but did not wish to leave:

> I will sacrifice myself for England and worship for ever the pure religion of Great Britain. . . . I cannot bear to leave, but still a man must do what he can in this miserable world and run from the east to the west and from the west to the east to find himself employment. I know you will laugh at my little sense if I say that

---

* These are the two bulls in the transept of the British Museum (excavated by Botta) described as 'Winged and human-headed bull with a winged attendant in human form which stood as guardian for a gateway leading to the palace of Sargon II.'

I would rather be a chimney-sweeper in England than become a Pasha in Turkey.

He had been expecting Layard to come to England and to travel out with him: 'rather awkward for me to leave England alone as I shall be like a body without a head', but he arrived safely in Constantinople and the expedition was ready to leave the Bosphorus by steamer for Trebizond on 28 August 1849. With them were Cawal Yusuf and other Yezidi notables, who had come to ask Layard's help because Yezidis had been included with the Moslems as conscripts for the army, which meant that certain rites and observances of their faith were violated. Stratford Canning brought their case to the notice of the Porte and an imperial order was issued which gave them some protection.

Dr. Humphry Sandwith, who had arrived in Constantinople from England six months before, found the party most interesting. Rassam, he said, was regarded by Layard with considerable affection: 'Chaldaean by birth, but English in tastes and education. . . . His duties are multifarious. He acts as interpreter and secretary. He marshals the servants, keeps the money-bags, speaks all the unknown languages, and keeps us all amused by his gaiety, varied by occasional sulks.' He was homesick for England and did not like wearing eastern costume which he declared was only fit for servants. Sandwith was impressed by Cawal Yusuf: 'His eyes were of brilliant black, his beard jet-black, and his large features were set in the regular antique model of the old Assyrian monarchs.' Another member of the party was Ahmed Agha, 'the travelling policeman'.[2]

From Trebizond the caravan travelled to Erzerum and then crossed eastern Armenia and Kurdistan into Mesopotamia. Layard wrote to Canning: 'We found nothing but alarm and disorder in all directions. The villages are being deserted and the Beduin are left masters of the country and of the property of its inhabitants. . . . Unbounded gratitude is displayed by the poor Yezidis at the exertions of Your Excellency on their behalf.' A large party of Yezidis led by Hussein Bey and Sheikh Nasr rode forty miles through the night to greet them, and act as escort against Arab marauders. Layard gives in *Nineveh and Babylon* a moving description of the welcome from his workmen:

Ch. 8 'The greatest achievement of our time'

As we neared Tel Kef we found groups of my old superintendents and workmen by the road-side. There were fat Toma, Mansour, Behnan and Hannah joyful at meeting me once more, and at the prospect of fresh service. In the village we found Mr. Rassam (the Vice-Consul) and Khodja Toma, his dragoman, who had made ready the feast for us at the house of the Chaldaean bishop. Next morning as we rode the three last hours of our journey, we met fresh groups of familiar faces:—Merjan, with my old groom holding the stirrup ready for me to mount, the noble animal looking as beautiful, as fresh and as sleek as when I last saw him, although two long years had passed; former servants, Awad and the Sheikhs of the Jebours, even the greyhounds who had been brought up under my roof.

Then as we ascend an eminence midway, walls, towers, minarets and domes rise boldly from the margin of the broad river, cheating us into the belief, too soon to be dispelled, that Mosul is still a not unworthy representative of the great Nineveh. As we draw near, the long line of lofty mounds, the only remains of mighty bulwarks and spacious gates, detach themselves from the low undulating hills: now the vast mound of Kuyunjik over-tops the surrounding heaps; then above it peers the white cone of the tomb of the prophet Jonah. . . . Hastening over the creaking bridge of boats, we force our way through the crowded bazaars, and alight at the house I had left two years ago. Old servants take their places as a matter of course, and, uninvited, pursue their regular occupations as if they had never been interrupted. Indeed, it seemed as if we had but returned from a summer's ride; two years had passed away like a dream.

On the following morning at sunrise Layard rode out to Kuyunjik. Henry Ross, much to Layard's regret, had left Mosul but had uncovered several interesting bas-reliefs during the time he had carried on the excavations. Since his departure the excavations had been placed under the charge of the British Vice-Consul, who had been asked by the Trustees of the British Museum to employ a few men to prevent any interference. Toma, 'the Fat', remained the overseer of the workmen. With him Layard descended into the subterranean passages excavated into the mound, lit only by holes pierced to the daylight through thirty or forty feet of hard soil.

These long galleries, dimly lighted, lined with the remains of ancient art, broken urns projecting from the crumbling sides, and the wild Arab and hardy Nestorian wandering through their intricacies, or working in their dark recesses, were singularly picturesque. . . . The sculptures, faintly seen through the gloom, were still well enough preserved to give a complete history of the subject represented, although, with the rest of the bas-reliefs of Kujunjik, the fire had nearly turned them into lime, and had cracked them into a thousand pieces. The faces of the slabs had been entirely covered with figures, varying from three inches to one foot in height, carefully finished, and designed with great spirit. In this series of bas-reliefs the history of an Assyrian conquest was more fully portrayed than in any other yet discovered, from the going out of the monarch to battle, to his triumphal return after a complete victory.

About a hundred workmen were employed on the mound of Kuyunjik, divided into twelve parties. Ali Rahal, a sheikh of the Jebours, had come to find Layard and was appointed 'Sheikh of the Mound' at Nimrud, being given his 'robe of honour'. He then left to collect men from his tribe to await Layard's arrival. Before going to Nimrud Layard accepted an invitation to attend the annual Yezidi festival at Sheikh Adi and at Redwan and was allowed to attend their rites in a way that, he believed, no other European had done. On returning to Mosul he wrote to his mother on 15 October: 'At Redwan I saw the celebrated Melek Taos, a bronze bird of the Yezidis, the existence of which has so often been disputed, and a very curious thing it is.' At the Sheikh Adi festival, he said 'I was allowed to be present at all the ceremonies, made a public profession of faith and was received into the bosom of the Yezidi Church. There is nothing in our solemnities to warrant the charge brought against the Yezidis by the Mussulmans—on the contrary everything is conducted with great decorum and reverence.'

Layard rode to Nimrud on 18 October and pitched a tent in the courtyard of his house to avoid the vermin swarming in the rooms. With Hormuzd Rassam the next day he made a tour of the neighbourhood and on 20 October he rode to the Nimrud mound and found a group of travellers on the summit. 'Beneath in an excavated chamber, wrapped in his travelling cloak, was Rawlinson, deep in sleep, wearied by a long and harassing night's ride. For the first time we met in the Assyrian

ruins, and besides the greetings of old friendship there was much
to be seen together, and much to be talked over.' One of the
things to be talked over was the date of Nimrud which Rawlinson had insisted was about 2,500 B.C. and was the original
Nineveh, and on this authority Layard had committed himself to this early date in his *Nineveh and Its Remains*. Five
months after its publication, however, Rawlinson had written
to Layard to say that he had previously given much too
early a date for Nimrud: 'I think that I can prove every portion
of the old Assyrian history to be mythical and the mere fact of
Ninus and Semiramis being myths necessarily limits very essentially the antiquity of the Empire. The 22nd Egyptian Dynasty
will, I expect, prove to be synchronous with the foundation of
Nimrud and Khorsabad followed, I am confident, after a very
short interval.' Layard had given the date as equivalent to the
nineteenth Egyptian Dynasty (though as a result of a printer's
error it had been given as 'fourteenth dynasty' in the early
editions).

In Mosul Rawlinson stayed in bed for two days with fever and
was unable to see much of the excavations but he managed to
make a hasty survey and then went on to Constantinople. From
there Rawlinson wrote Layard a friendly letter: 'I answered to
the best of my powers the thousand and one questions that were
put to me about "The Lion", as you are technically called here.
Your previous letter and explanations had prepared me for Sir
Stratford Canning's sly remarks—but I am, I confess, astonished
to find feelings and jealousy in such a man as the Ambassador.'
Canning wrote: 'I know not how to console you for the loss
of those fifteen centuries of which Major Rawlinson is determined to curtail you.' In England Rawlinson lectured to
the Royal Asiatic Society and stated that he thought that the
dynasty of Nimrud, which he now identified, correctly with
the Biblical Calah, flourished from 1300 to 1200 B.C. and the
later dynasty of Khorsabad 1100 to 1000 B.C.[3] Rawlinson dined
with the Austens and Layard received plenty of news, much of
which annoyed him. He wrote to his aunt reminding her that
it was Rawlinson who had insisted on the earlier date before
he had published his book. 'Rawlinson exaggerates everything I
have told him, and quietly sets me up to knock me down

again. . . . I have no doubt that he will ere long change most
of his readings. He is much too eager at snatching at a theory,
propounding a paradox and poohpoohing at once anyone who
does not agree with him. This is a great pity as his analysis is
generally excellent and his ingenuity in following out the connection of signs and passages very remarkable. He is a most able
and industrious man and has done more for cuneiform than
anyone living.'

Rawlinson, however, had not yet made any pronouncement
as to the site of Nineveh, though a little later he was to make
the surprising and inaccurate suggestion that it was the mound
of Nebbi Yunis opposite Mosul where there is the mosque to the
Prophet Jonah.[4] By the time Layard came to publish his second
book in 1853, *Nineveh and Babylon*, he had agreed that Kuyunjik
was the true Nineveh but he makes no reference to the fact that
the earlier book, *Nineveh and Its Remains*, had been mainly
about Nimrud. In fact it is sometimes only from the heading on
the top of the page that one realises that Layard on his second
expedition is thinking of Kuyunjik when he mentions Nineveh
and is no longer thinking of Nimrud.

9

The Winged Lions
leave Nimrud

At the beginning of 1850 in a room of the North-West Palace at
Nimrud, which Layard describes as 'the Treasure Chamber', a
series of interesting objects were discovered, 'which are', writes
Dr. Gadd, 'by far the most important collection yet discovered of
Assyrian metal-work'. Many of the objects were in a series of
copper cauldrons and are described in Layard's diary:

> January 4: To Nimrud by raft with Lynch; reached in 6 hours.
>
> January 5: Coursing with Lynch in the morning—caught four
> hares. The earth having been cleared away from the upper part of
> the chamber in which the cauldrons had been discovered we
> resumed our researches there. Near the cauldrons we discovered
> a nest of plates and dishes—one placed above the others—above
> one hundred must have been together. With great care—removing
> the earth with pen-knives—we detached the greater part of them
> unbroken tho' in the most fragile state. I found the greater part
> most beautifully embossed and engraved, and many in the finest
> preservation. We had great difficulty in removing the precious
> relics to the house.
>
> January 6: Returned to Treasure Chamber and emptied fourth
> cauldron. In it were several dishes, bowls and a copper ornament

203

. . . a cullender of metal for straining wine & other liquor; near the cauldron was a mass of ivory and iron and copper remains—two small glass bowls entire. . . . There were also sword handles, remains of tripods & vessels supported on the feet of animals. . . . all of which were in a most dilapidated condition.

January 7: Returned to Treasure Chamber; emptied a fifth cauldron in which were many interesting remains—amongst them several handsome ornaments resembling sword handles, a grotesque head in massive copper . . . near the cauldron two or three elephant tusks.

One tusk measured two feet and five inches; there were various human bones with cowrie shells and small beads and the remains of a throne.[1] These were important discoveries and he had them very carefully packed, helped by Mrs. Rolland, an attractive woman whose presence led to some trouble later.

Mr. and Mrs. Rolland were travelling in the East on their way to visit Colonel Fenwick Williams with the Boundary Commission. They arrived at Mosul at the end of the year and became very intrigued by the excavations, having seen a pavement uncovered at Kuyunjik, marked with ruts made by chariot wheels, and two bulls excavated. At the beginning of the year they came to stay in Layard's house at Nimrud. 'It is little more than a mud-hut', said Rolland, 'but he has put in glass windows, a table, and some sofas and made it as comfortable as circumstances will permit.' Layard's house built of mud was not very commodious. It was one thing to entertain an Arab girl for the night, but it was not entirely suitable for an European woman, and in January it was very cold with falls of snow. None of them, however, seem to have objected to the close quarters. Layard liked Charlotte Rolland and she worked hard dealing with the delicate objects from the Treasure Chamber, while Stewart Rolland was helpful in looking after the workmen. The latter wrote to his uncle, Mr. E. E. Justin, a friend of Benjamin Austen:

Layard is the most delightful companion I have ever met. He is exactly the same age as myself, born on the same day of the same year. I never in my life was so well or so happy as I am at present. My wife, too, thoroughly enjoys the wild life. . . .

You can have no idea of the difficulties Layard has to contend with, or the energy, talent, perseverance and shrewdness with which he surmounts them; or the exquisite tact and good humour with which he manages the different people he has to deal with . . . I do not believe any other man living could do it so well or at one tithe of the expense; an influence can only be acquired amongst Arabs by feasting them and making them small presents, as there is nothing they hold in such an estimation as generosity. Such, however, is the respect they hold him in, that one of his friends might travel Mesopotamia unhurt and untouched, though in the midst of tribes at war with each other. It is melancholy to see such a man so crippled for want of resources; while for his own re-muneration he receives literally nothing but his personal expenses, and his salary as Attaché to the Embassy at Constantinople.

Mr. Stewart Rolland, late of the 69th Regiment, was delighted to find that he could keep four horses, giving each of them nine pounds of barley a day at a cost of about sevenpence. He paid thirty-six pounds for an Arab horse, for which he would have paid more than three hundred guineas in England and he bought a little pony for seventeen shillings. Layard liked the Rollands and their enthusiasm for the archaeological life and found them a great deal more helpful than Dr. Humphry Sandwith, who was not interested in the excavations, spent most of his time in Mosul or in shooting and lost one of Layard's best guns on a hunting expedition.

The main work in January was clearing the Treasure Chamber and preparing to get the two great winged lions to the river for transport to Basra and London. The Museum said that he could have them sawn in half to make the journey easier but he was determined to try to send them whole for he had a romantic affection for the two lions as is shown in his diary entries:

January 28: Before visiting the Lions we rode to the bitumen springs. The flames and smoke rolling upwards in a thousand involved circles produced an effect difficult to be described. Abd-ur-rahman dined with us and rode to the mound but struck off to his tents little appreciating the object of our night expedition. In the evening rode with the Rollands and all our party to the mounds to see the Lions for the last time by moonlight. The night was cloudless and the moon at her full. The deep shadows cast by the side of the trenches on the lower part of the gigantic sculptures with a dim light; the heads fully lighted up by the moon. After centuries of repose this was the last night the pair would pass together standing in their old haunts.

In his book, *Nineveh and Babylon*, he developed the theme: 'It seemed almost sacrilege to tear them from their old haunts to make them a mere wonder-stock to the busy crowd of a new world. They were better suited to the desolation around them; for they had guarded the palace in its glory, and it was for them to watch over it in its ruin.' They were each heavier than either the bull or the lion removed during the first expedition. Instead of using ropes it was found more effective to tilt the first lion gradually upon mounds of loose earth and as the earth was removed it slowly descended upon a cart with enormous wheels. The manoeuvre was accomplished on 29 January, but unfortunately it rained heavily for several days and the cart was bogged in mud to the axles. Every device was used to keep up the spirit of the three hundred Arabs who were trying to pull the cart out of the mud. Layard and Rolland pulled with them while Mrs. Rolland rode on the lion. Cooper was appointed sheikh of the operation and music played continuously till, after a week of effort, the lion was pulled on to a hard surface.

The rest of the journey to the Tigris could be accomplished easily enough by the Arab workmen and Layard decided to pay a visit to Bavian. Henry Ross had given an interesting description of the Assyrian sculptures there three years before, but Layard had not had time during his first expedition to go there. Bavian lies north-east of Mosul and it is possible by car today to visit it in a morning from Mosul. It is near the village of Khinnis where the Kurds grow tobacco by the river Gomel. A little north of the village is a high cliff with sculptures of Sennacherib where the stream emerges. It is possible to lie in the water and study the Assyrian sculptures high on the cliff-face or to dive in to inspect huge Assyrian stone bulls lying in the water which is deep even in late summer. It was the beginning of February and too cold to bathe when Layard and his party arrived there after several days' ride from Nimrud.

Layard had brought ropes and was lowered down the face of the cliff to study the inscriptions: 'Standing on a ledge scarcely six inches wide, overlooking a giddy depth, and in a constrained

and painful position, I had some difficulty in copying them.'
The Assyrian fountain with lions on either side, which was there
in Layard's day, has disappeared and the sculptures continue to
be damaged by Kurds practising marksmanship on Sennacherib
and his attendants. Until the cuneiform inscriptions he had
copied were deciphered on return to London Layard did not
know that he was looking at the great empire-builder Sennacherib (702–681 B.C.). He believed that the water of the Gomel
was taken off by a canal similar to the system used to bring the
water from the Zab river at the Negoub to Nimrud. Indeed,
traces of a raised causeway of stone can still be seen today which
carried the water the fifty miles to Nineveh and some of the
blocks of stone are to be seen at Jerwan, where the canal was
carried across a broad valley by an aqueduct about forty feet
wide.[2]

When the party returned to Nimrud in the middle of February
preparations were made to move the second lion. Layard wrote
to Canning on the 28th: 'Three hundred men dragged the
monster in three days through every obstacle of mud and sand.
The two are now ready for embarkation.' He said that he was
hoping to find interesting remains in the pyramid at Nimrud
where he was digging: 'Unfortunately I am terribly crippled in
my means & cannot dig away as I could wish.' He had tried to
take a party of workmen to dig at Kalah Shergat but they refused
to go because of the unsettled state of the country. His thoughts
then turned to the Khabour river farther north which he had
often wished to visit because he believed that there were Assyrian
remains there. In the middle of February, Abdul Aziz, one of the
three chiefs of the Jebour, came to Nimrud from Khabour and
described how two bulls, similar to those of Khorsabad, had been
uncovered by the recent rains at Arban. The son of another chief,
Mohamed Emin, also arrived and confirmed the story of the
bulls.

Layard made up his mind to prepare an expedition and wrote
to Sir Henry Ellis to say that during the next three months the
expenses would be considerably increased as it was the only
season in which he could explore the mounds on the Khabour
and in northern Mesopotamia. The excavations at Kuyunjik and
Nimrud would be carried on 'by trustworthy superintendents

during his absence'. Ten days later he sent Sir Henry Ellis the accounts, making his usual wry remarks:

> I have omitted all my private expenses as well as those of the members of the expedition which have, of course, been borne by me as well as the expenses of outfit; no sum having been paid, as far as I can understand, for that object to my agents in England. . . . I have considered it my duty to adopt this plan rather than run the risk of a complete failure by applying only the *very small* sum which would have been left after deducting the outlay mentioned in the instructions.

He told Birch of the British Museum about his plans and said that after the Khabour he hoped to visit Carchemish, 'where there are ruins'. He had succeeded in securing the friendship of most of the Arab chiefs on the Khabour, 'after a vast deal of trouble, inconvenience, and personal expense'. A letter to Mr. Clutterbuck of Exeter College gave information about a present Layard was making to Oxford University: 'Two cases containing two colossal figures; one an eagle-headed god, the other a winged figure bearing a goat, the duplicate of which is now in the British Museum'. On 18 March, two days before the expedition left Mosul, he wrote again to Sir Henry Ellis saying that he hoped the Trustees would not consider the expedition to so interesting a place as the Khabour as money mis-spent:

> At Kuyunjik we have now explored 18 chambers. . . . The royal founder of this palace appears not only to have celebrated his conquests on its walls, but the building of the various cities and temples which took place during his reign. Many of the large chambers appear to have been entirely occupied by series of bas-reliefs representing the removal of great human-headed bulls, obelisks and stones, and the raising of large mounds on which palaces were built. . . . As most of these subjects are accompanied by short inscriptions recording the event, the names of cities and temples built by the king may eventually be recovered and will furnish highly interesting results. In the bas-reliefs recording the triumphs of the king are represented many nations which I have not found previously represented in the Assyrian ruins. Mr. Cooper has made about sixty drawings at Kuyunjik and Nimrud many of which are very elaborate and full of subject, containing as many as two hundred figures.

On 20 March the party, which consisted of the Rollands, Sandwith, Cooper, Rassam, and various grooms and servants, was
ready to leave. 'All our preparations were complete this morning.
The camels were collected in the graveyard behind the Consulate
and the loads brought out to be divided and apportioned.' They
left by the Sinjar Gate and two days later Layard notes in his
diary: 'We passed a sleepless night. The storm burst in great
fury upon us. The wind swept in hurricanes across the plain and
it required the united efforts of all our people to prevent the
large tent from being carried away. Mrs. Rolland was somewhat
alarmed but their English tent withstood the storm admirably.'
During the nine days that the caravan travelled to the Khabour
river Layard collected notes for a report on the state of the
country for Canning. He pointed out that whereas there were
now warring Beduin and Yezidis there must have been a vast
settled population in Assyrian times: 'From one spot in the centre
of Mesopotamia, to the west of the Sinjar, the traveller may
count no less than two hundred and ninety mounds scattered
over the vast plain—all the remains of ancient towns and villages.'
In his book, *Nineveh and Babylon*, he added:

> The great tide of civilisation has long since ebbed, leaving these
> scattered wrecks on the solitary shore. Are those waters to flow
> again, bearing back the seeds of knowledge and of wealth that they
> have wafted to the West? We wanderers were seeking what they
> had left behind, as children gather up the coloured shells on the
> deserted sands.

They camped by the Khabour river which flowed through rice
pastures and meadows: 'Its banks were now covered with flowers
of every hue, and its windings through the green plain were like
the coils of a mighty serpent.' On Sunday 31 March he explored
Arban and noted in his diary:

> We had to reach the Assyrian sculptures by a very narrow path-
> way carved under the precipitous wall of earth which had been
> left after part of the mound had been washed away. I found two
> human-headed, winged bulls, carved in limestone, about five feet
> high and much injured. They were evidently Assyrian but differed
> considerably in style from those previously discovered near the
> Tigris. There was a line of cuneiform inscription on each but it is
> doubtful whether it contains the name of a king.

Later a lion was found 'of very fine character', a bas-relief of a
human figure, and a second pair of bulls. The excavations were
carried on during April and Layard held receptions in his large
tent for Sheikh Mohamed Emin and other powerful local leaders.
A great deal of interesting information about Beduin customs
was collected and recounted in his book. Visits were paid to
various tribes and villages, including Mirkan, which had been
destroyed on his visit there with Tahyar Pasha, the Governor of
Mosul; it had been rebuilt, but the Yezidis were again in open
rebellion and at war with the Beduin tribes. After long discussions
he persuaded them to make peace with the Beduin and with the
Turkish authorities.

Layard was very happy in these beautiful surroundings and
the impression given by his letters and diaries is that he was
sufficiently attracted by Charlotte Rolland to arouse the jealousy
of her husband. He describes in his diary going off for a long
ride to visit a neighbouring tribe with Charlotte mounted behind
him on a *dheloul*, a fast riding-camel: 'We crossed a perfect
carpet of flowers and I never saw anything more beautiful than
the desert today', he wrote on 18 April. When they reached the
tribe after a ride of an hour and a half they were well received
for Charlotte's 'good nature and kind manner had made a great
impression on the Arabs'. Some days later he refers to 'a painful
scene' and in his letters home there is an account of Stewart
Rolland beating his wife and of Layard intervening. Whether
the beating was prompted by jealousy is not clear. Layard's
account to the Austens suggests that Rolland went a little mad
and had to be put under restraint and that afterwards he apologised for all the trouble he had caused. It seems that Rolland
returned to Mosul from the Khabour leaving Layard to look
after Charlotte. When they were together again in Mosul there
was further trouble and Layard insisted that the Rollands
should leave for England.[3]

Nineveh and Babylon

Layard was delighted to find that during his absence, as he told
Sir Henry Ellis in a letter of 13 May from Mosul, some remarkable bas-reliefs had been discovered at Kuyunjik, 'a long line of
figures bearing animals, trays of fruit, and vases filled with
flowers, which appear to form the sides of a passage . . . leading
to lower chambers'. At the same time he was much distressed to
find that 'two serious accidents' had happened to his beloved
lions—the nose of one had been injured and the other had been
divided into two. He vented his anger on poor Sir Henry Ellis,
who probably wished that Layard had remained at Nimrud to
supervise the packing instead of going to Khabour for nearly
two months:

> My regret is not diminished when I reflect that these accidents
> are mainly to be attributed to a parsimony truly unworthy of an
> undertaking, which has excited so much interest in England, and
> the results of which had proved, before the second expedition, so
> important in an archaeological point of view. Had proper means

been placed at my command, the Lions would have been embarked under my own superintendence. . . .

You are aware that the Bulls procured by Major Rawlinson from Khorsabad cost about £350 in removal to Bagdad, and they were sawn in many pieces. How could I then expend at one time out of the small grant allotted to the ends of the expedition a sum required for the transport of two Lions from this place to Basra! I was compelled to divide over a space of four or five months that which ought to have been done in one.

He was pleased, however, to receive the information that the Trustees had granted another five hundred pounds, which was additional to the fifteen hundred pounds due to be drawn as from April. One of the lions had a further adventure between Bagdad and Basra. The Tigris was in flood and the raft carrying it was swept through a gap in the bank of the river and carried over the flooded fields. 'It is very doubtful whether it can be recovered', Layard told Canning, but the gallant Captain Felix Jones[1] took one of the Euphrates' steamers through the gap and rescued the lion. He was able to tell the Ambassador in May that at Kuyunjik they had found 'an immense collection of inscribed terra cotta tablets which appear to be the archives of some of the Nineveh kings. I have already six cases full and the room is not half emptied. This is a highly valuable addition to our collection of Assyrian antiquities.' It was in fact the king's library and when he returned to England and wrote his book he enlarged on their importance:

> We cannot overrate their value. They furnish us with materials for the complete decipherment of the cuneiform character, for restoring the language and history of Assyria, and for inquiring into the customs, sciences, and, we may even add, literature, of its people. The documents that have thus been discovered at Nineveh probably exceed all that have yet been afforded by the monuments of Egypt. But years must elapse before the innumerable fragments can be put together, and the inscriptions transcribed.

In a temple near the *ziggurat* at Nimrud some interesting sculptures had been found, 'amongst them the figure of the early Nimrud King in an arched recess, sculptured in very high relief and covered with inscriptions on all sides, is perhaps the most remarkable and will form a most valuable addition to our national collection'. In a letter to Sir Henry Ellis in June he gives a description of bas-reliefs found in this temple (that of Ninurta) 'representing a winged figure driving out an extra-ordinary mythic figure—a dragon with a kind of trident, and by a human figure wearing a head-dress formed by a fish, the tail of which descends to his loins'.

The excavations were very successful both at Kuyunjik and at Nimrud but the members of the team were not happy together. Layard was good at getting on with his colleagues and subordi-nates, but he found his companions on this occasion exasperating. Cooper had become so ill that he could not draw accurately and Layard had to check the details. He was permanently home-sick and had made a drawing of his wife from memory: 'Every now and again he takes it out and looks at it', Rassam wrote to Marianne Layard, 'I only hope that I shall love my wife as much as he does.' Dr. Sandwith was amiable and clever but 'completely idle and careless', finding antiquities excessively boring. Sand-with realised that he was not of much help and some years later wrote to Layard a charming letter from the fortress of Kars beleaguered by the Russian armies: 'For the last five years I have laboured under a feeling of penitence and humiliation in my eyes for my laziness in Mesopotamia, but the fact is that cuneiform and winged bulls are not my fate, and I preferred shooting.' Then there was the Rev. Percy Badger, who was staying with his brother-in-law, Christian Rassam, and exasper-ated Layard for a number of reasons. Badger was writing a book about the Nestorians in which he was arguing that he had 'discovered' Nineveh; but the main reason for the quarrel was that Layard considered that this man, and other missionaries, had by their intolerance and quarrels among themselves been indirectly responsible for some of the Nestorian massacres. This Layard had said in articles to London newspapers which he had written from Constantinople in the 1840's soon after he had first arrived there, and according to Layard, Badger had threatened revenge. Cooper and Sandwith were warned about him, but they took his side against Layard. Nor had his relation-ship with the Rollands helped to calm his nerves. 'I try not to feel anxious', his mother wrote, 'knowing how well and prudently you have hitherto managed, but you seem to be surrounded by unquiet spirits. While all the world are talking of you in wonder and praise—I alone seem dull and inanimate, and yet I would wish you to think of me as I really am, proud and thankful and having you constantly in my thoughts.'

Layard was planning to travel to Van in the north and then to explore Babylon and the neighbourhood, but Canning was finding difficulty in obtaining permission for excavations in southern Mesopotamia because of articles published in the London Press which made the Porte realise that exciting discoveries were being made. The letter already referred to from Rolland to his uncle had been published in *The Times* in March 1850, stating that the Treasure Chamber at Nimrud was by far the most important discovery yet made. Having described many of the articles, which suggested to the Turks that gold had been found, he said that there were innumerable other articles which he could not mention as he had promised to observe secrecy. Layard was annoyed, too, with his Aunt Sara for sending some of his letters to be published: 'It is a pity people in England are so fond of putting everything into print', he wrote to her rather unkindly; 'the habit destroys all confidence of private correspondence and I shall drop letter-writing altogether if I find every epistle before the public in the *Literary Gazette* and in *The Athenaeum*.' Layard worked off some of his spleen in his letters home.

With the great heat of July, Cooper and Sandwith had to be sent away into the mountains while Hormuzd Rassam and Layard struggled on; 'fortunately our ague attacks did not coincide' and they were able to supervise alternately the packing of the antiquities. They then joined the others in the Kurdish mountains and made a long journey to Lake Van where Layard remained for a week with Rassam copying cuneiform inscriptions and examining 'its remarkable monuments of antiquity'. Dr. Sandwith and Cooper were from there sent back to Constantinople. In a letter from Van to Sir Henry Ellis on 12 August, Layard pointed out how heavy the work would be: 'From the beginning I have had but very little assistance and am now without any.' He returned with Rassam to Mosul where they arrived on 30 August 1850, relieved to be on his own again with his faithful friend Hormuzd. 'The whole party put together have

Layard being lowered to copy the Sennacherib inscriptions at Bavian

Layard copying bas-reliefs at Kuyunjik

Sketched by S. C. Malan

done less than I did when by myself during six months of the former expedition and everything seems to have gone wrong', he told
his Aunt Sara. 'In fact I cannot but look upon this expedition as
a complete failure as far as we have hitherto gone. I shall have
to pay Dr. Sandwith £100 or £150 for his year's attendance and
I calculate that the expedition will cost me at least £1,500 as I
have borne all the private expenses, those of outfit etc.' He was
annoyed to hear from his uncle that the Museum authorities
had grumbled at the expenses of the Khabour expedition, which
Layard considered had been 'highly important in an archaeological point of view', and had, he thought, been agreed by the
Museum. He wrote to Sir Henry Ellis on 2 September to say
that he would pay all expenses of the Khabour expedition except
for those of the workmen carrying out the actual digging. To his
uncle he protested:

> I think they might have had the generosity not to object to the
> Khabour expenses. What could I expect, however, when I am
> reminded in my instructions that my pay as an Attaché is continued!
> That, too, they shall have and I shall pass it to their account. I
> began with nothing and I end with nothing. I wish for no other
> reward than the knowledge that I have been of some use. As long
> as I have hands, unless crippled by disease, I can gain my bread.
> Every day's experience shows me more and more how little the
> world is to be depended upon. I despise the mere flattery, and
> lionising which follows the kind of success I have had and I do not
> think I shall be deceived by them.

It should be remembered that Layard had no one to talk to
except Rassam and the Arab workmen and that he was, as
usual, working too hard. 'He used to get up every morning
about 6 o'clock', Hormuzd wrote to Marianne Layard, 'and very
rarely went to bed before 12 or 1 and during the whole 17 or
18 hours he used to draw, copy inscriptions, and attend the
packing of the sculptures.'

A second attempt was made to excavate Kalah Shergat and a
large group of his workmen was sent there, but it was attacked
by a party of Beduin and had to return after losing everything.
Two large caravans from Bagdad were attacked within a short
distance of Mosul and the road between Mosul and Bagdad was
almost closed.

All these anxieties made him irascible and full of complaints but above all he was throughout the expedition suffering from a very great disappointment. Some of Benjamin Austen's letters from London had been unwisely optimistic and had given the impression that the Museum authorities had at last understood what was required and the money would be forthcoming, so that Layard believed that Hawkins, the Museum's energetic Secretary, had been successful in persuading the Trustees that Layard's great plan for excavating the whole of Assyria, Babylonia, and Susiana should be carried out. After the departure of Sandwith and Cooper, Layard had written to Benjamin Austen: 'Thus ends all hopes of the Nineveh expedition, which, on leaving Constantinople, was to have distinguished itself in the arts, sciences, and in archaeology; the result has been nil. I am now once more alone with Hormuzd and must again brace myself up to hard work. I only wish we had started alone; ten times more would have been done.' Austen was sympathetic: 'I should advise you to speak out most boldly about your limited means to carry out what is required. I am sure they only want to have it pressed upon them in the strongest manner, that they may go to the Treasury. . . . All the world are looking to your proceedings and you need not fear any laxity of interest and there will be plenty of money forthcoming, rely on it.' Austen was right to encourage Layard to continue to press his claims for it was the Treasury which decided the matter, but the Board of Trustees had to initiate the demands and it was a large amorphous body, not well-fitted to direct large-scale expeditions, and many of them were more interested in Grecian remains than in Assyrian. The complaining letters to Sir Henry Ellis and to his uncle were partly serious and partly an act. Layard was not as miserable as he made out, nor did he think that the expedition was a complete failure. He wrote, for instance, to his friend Cecilia Berkeley in September, after he had returned from Van and was alone with Rassam:

> The second expedition has, on the whole, been successful and much has been added to the knowledge acquired by the first, as well as to the collection of antiquities. I am now going to start for Babylon to begin excavations in that part of the world and hope during the winter to make interesting discoveries. My health has

been, hitherto, very good and will, I hope, continue so to enable me to complete my work by the spring of next year to return again to civilised life.

Layard, in fact, continued to be fascinated by the finds and wrote enthusiastically in his second book of the bas-reliefs found at Kuyunjik. *Nineveh and Babylon* is in many ways a better guide to his state of mind at the time than are his letters and the excitement he felt about his discoveries is vividly expressed throughout, as, for instance, in his account from Kuyunjik under the heading 'A Gateway of Nineveh':

> This gateway, facing the open country, was formed by a pair of majestic human-headed bulls, fourteen feet in length, still entire, though cracked and injured by fire. . . . Behind them were colossal winged figures of the same height bearing the pine-cone and basket. . . . Their faces were in full, and the relief was high and bold. . . . The naked leg and foot were designed with a spirit and truthfulness worthy of a Greek artist. It is, however, remarkable that the four figures were unfinished, none of the details having been put in, and parts being but roughly outlined.
>
> They stood as if the sculptors had been interrupted by some public calamity, and had left their work incomplete. Perhaps the murder of Sennacherib by his sons, as he worshipped in the house of Nisroch his god, put a sudden stop to the great undertakings he had commenced at the beginning of his reign. . . . The entrance formed by these colossal bulls was fourteen feet and a quarter wide. It was paved with large slabs of limestone still bearing the marks of chariot wheels. The sculptures were buried in a mass of brick and earth, mingled with charcoal and charred wood; for 'the gates of the land had been set wide open unto the enemy, and the fire had devoured the bars'. [Nahum, iii, 13.]
>
> They were lighted from above by a deep shaft sunk from the top of the mound. It would be difficult to describe the effect produced, or the reflections suggested, by these solemn and majestic figures, dimly visible amidst the gloom, when, after winding through the dark, underground passages, you suddenly came into their presence. Between them, Sennacherib and his hosts had gone forth in all their might and glory to the conquest of distant lands, and had returned rich with spoil and captives, amongst whom may have been the handmaidens and wealth of Israel. Through them, too, the Assyrian monarch had entered his capital in shame, after his last and fatal defeat.

Excavations on the south-east side of the palace revealed another grand entrance with ten huge bulls and six gigantic human figures. On four of the bulls were inscriptions containing 'the annals of six years of the reign of Sennacherib, besides numerous particulars connected with the religion of the Assyrians, their gods, their temples, and the erection of their palaces, all of the highest interest and importance'. There were also thirteen beautifully carved bas-reliefs depicting Sennacherib's siege of Lachish. 'Here, therefore', wrote Layard, 'was the actual picture of the taking of Lachish, the city, as we know from the Bible, besieged by Sennacherib, when he sent his generals to demand tribute of Hezekiah, and which he had captured before their return.' Layard was also particularly interested in a bas-relief which showed the warfare carried on by the grandson of Sennacherib, the conquerer of Susiana.

> It is highly probable that we have, in the bas-relief, a representation of the city [Susa]. Its position between two rivers well agrees with that of existing ruins generally believed to mark its site. The smaller stream would be the Sharpour, and the larger the Euloeus or river of Disful. The city was surrounded by a wall, with equidistant towers and gateways. The houses were flat roofed, and some had one tower or upper chamber, and others two. . . . Nor were they unlike the meaner houses of the modern town of Shuster, the representatives of ancient Susa.

It gave Layard satisfaction to be able to link this interesting discovery with 'the full account of these rivers, and a description of the ruins upon them', which was to be found in his memoir on the Province of Khuzistan, written while he was leading a 'vagabond' life.

*   *   *

Layard reached Bagdad on 16 October 1850 having accompanied several rafts laden with sculptures, one of which was attacked but his men put up a strong defence and killed a number of the attackers who retreated. He wrote to Sir Stratford Canning:

> The Arabs on every side are in open rebellion. It is now two months since any communication has been received from Basra. . . .

The result has been that during several months of the year Bagdad stands, like an island, in the midst of a vast pestilent marsh.

During the last three months—during my visit to the Hakkiari districts and my residence in Mosul and Bagdad, I have seen as deplorable a picture of misgovernment as could well be produced in the most barbarous states of the world.

Whatever may be the faults of the Arabs they have undoubtedly suffered enormous wrongs from the Government. There is scarcely a tribe which has not lost its chief and its principal members by some foul act of treachery on the part of the Turkish authorities. The very name of a Turk in this country is synonymous with treachery, tyranny and infidelity.

He developed this in *Nineveh and Babylon* in a passage which was much quoted against him in Parliament later when he became the defender of the Turk:

Wherever the Osmanli has placed his foot, he has bred fear and distrust. His visit has ever been one of oppression and rapine. The scarlet cap, and the well-known garb of a Turkish irregular, are the signals for a general panic. The women hide themselves in the innermost recesses to save themselves from insult; the men slink into their houses, and offer a vain protest against the seizure of their property.

The Pasha of Bagdad was out with his army to the east of Bagdad to try to deal with the Arab rebellion. Layard visited the Pasha and proceeded to Babylon with his workmen while Rassam had to remain in Bagdad as he was ill. The Governor of Hillah, near Babylon, was prepared to let him excavate at Babylon although the imperial permission had not arrived from Constantinople. Little was achieved with the excavations and he wrote to Sir Stratford Canning from Hillah on 13 January 1851:

The remains of Babylon are principally vast masses of brickwork without sculptures, ornaments or inscribed records as at Nimrud, and altho', were extensive excavations carried on, small objects of interest, detached sculptures and inscriptions, might be discovered, yet I question whether these would be considered worth the expense incurred. If, as Strabo tells us, Alexander the Great after employing 10,000 men for ten months to clear away the rubbish from the ruin, was obliged to give up the attempt, the Trustees of the British Museum may readily be persuaded that a couple of hundred pounds will not get far in exploring all the mounds which are to be found in the vicinity of Hillah.

Two days later he wrote to Sir Henry Ellis to say that the chief of the powerful tribe of Afaij Arabs, who lived in the Euphrates' swamps fifty miles south of Hillah, had sent horsemen to accompany him to their encampment which was close to Niffer (ancient Nippur), which he intended to excavate. Layard was well received by the Afaij Arabs and impressed them by predicting, from his almanack, a partial eclipse of the moon. From there he wrote to Sir Stratford Canning on 29 January to say that Rassam had arrived from Bagdad with the Vizirial letters giving permission to excavate:

> The ruins of Niffer are about six miles distant from the village in which I am residing but I can get no one to remain on the spot during the night & we are obliged to make daily voyages to and fro. The Afaij tribes occupy small islands in the centre of vast marshes formed by the Euphrates; Niffer is on the eastern edge of these marshes. I convey my workmen there in light boats of reeds & bitumen. . . . My principal enemy is the fever & I have suffered severely from his attacks during the last six months. . . .
>
> Major Rawlinson's exaggerated accounts of Mr. Loftus's discoveries have given rise to expectations which cannot, I think, be realised. I have been excavating for some days in the ruins of Niffer, probably the most important in southern Mesopotamia after those in the vicinity of Hillah, and I find nothing in them to induce me to recommend the Trustees to undertake more extended operations.
>
> Since my arrival the roads have been completely closed on every side and the most complete disorder prevails in this part of Mesopotamia.

In his book Layard gives an interesting account of the life of the marsh Arabs propelling their wicker boats (*tiradas*) through the channels cut in the high reeds which were crowded with little boats near the settlements.

> This singular scene recalled vividly to my mind the sculptures at Kuyunjik representing the Assyrian wars in marshes of the same nature, and probably formed by waters of the same river. The streets through the reeds, and the *tiradas* or boats of rushes

smeared with bitumen, are faithfully delineated in the bas-reliefs, showing how little the barbarous inhabitants of these great swamps have changed.[2]

He hoped to proceed farther south to excavate Warka where Kennet Loftus had worked for three weeks while with the Turco-Persian Boundary Commission, but the country was too unsettled. Layard fell very seriously ill with pleurisy and fever as a result of the unwholesome marsh air, so that he was unable to get up from his bed, but he managed to cure himself sufficiently to move about by applying a blistering fluid prescribed for a sick horse. In spite of his illness he forced himself to mount his horse for there was danger that the whole party might be cut off from Bagdad by the Arab revolt and he rode for fourteen hours although he had eaten nothing for a fortnight. Another forced march the next day brought the party to Bagdad. The doctor made Layard stay in Bagdad some days to recover and he wrote to his uncle: 'My nerves are regularly shattered; your letters do not add much to my spirit.' He said that he had been reading the well-known book by the Austens' old friend, Samuel Warren—*Diary of a Physician*—'I have been in a regular mess ever since and can scarcely get a wink of sleep at night.'

Layard and his Jebour workmen were relieved to get back to Nimrud, where the men felt at home. Indeed, it was remarkable that they had been prepared to accompany Layard to what was to them a strange country, which they knew to be in a very disturbed state and where lions and other wild animals abounded in the marshes of the Euphrates. Thomas Septimus Bell had arrived at Nimrud, sent out by the British Museum to take the place of Cooper. 'He draws nicely and carefully', wrote Layard to Sir Henry Ellis, 'and will, I have no doubt, make good copies of the bas-reliefs', but he was very young and inexperienced.

In the meantime, Layard's friends in London had become worried by his complaints about lack of funds. Lady Charlotte Guest wrote in her diary on 14 December 1850: 'They are making a private subscription to enable Henry Layard to complete his researches at Nineveh, his government funds being exhausted. Major Rawlinson called to ask Merthyr, who has given £100, to be on the committee. Prince Albert has promised to join.'[3] Layard did not approve of the idea and was right in thinking that it was likely to lead to confusion. He did not hear about the plan until April, in Mosul, when he wrote to Canning:

> The plan appears to me objectionable in many respects and I have declined availing myself of funds so collected. If Your Excellency knew how very inadequately I have been supported throughout and how many difficulties I have had to contend with, I do not think you would concur with the Trustees in the belief that I am very easily disheartened.
>
> The artist who has now been sent out here is a mere boy, very willing and industrious, but not the person any enlightened government would dream of sending out on such an expedition. . . . It is to me, of course, a matter of deep regret that such an opportunity has been lost of carrying thro' an undertaking of so much interest in a manner worthy of the British Government. I feel heartily ashamed when I compare my published drawings with those of the French. With the subjects, we had enough to have produced a ten times' finer work than our neighbours.

He told Canning in an earlier letter that he did not know whether the Museum was intending to continue the excavations but he was not prepared to carry on the work under the existing arrangements: 'The pecuniary loss to me is very great and, altho' the success of my work has fortunately hitherto enabled me to bear it, I could not do so much longer.' Canning had asked him to send some monuments which the Ambassador could present to Eton College, and in April arrangements were made to send 'two fine colossal figures—one of the king and the other of a winged priest' for which expenses amounted to twenty or thirty pounds at most.

Towards the end of April he informed Sir Henry Ellis that he was preparing to leave for Alexandretta taking a number of precious small objects with him together with the drawings and copies of the inscriptions. Bell, who was then in Mosul, was told that the excavations and the property of the Trustees were put into his charge. When Layard arrived at Alexandretta at the end of May he received a letter from Christian Rassam, the Vice-Consul, to say that Bell had been drowned while bathing in the pool at Bavian. Layard was distressed and in a letter to Canning again blamed the Trustees for sending so inexperienced a young man: 'A false economy has in his case, as well as in Mr.

Cooper's, led to the usual results.' In a letter to Sir Henry Ellis he said that the four servants who had accompanied him to Alexandretta would return on the horses belonging to the Trustees and they would be handed over to Christian Rassam on arrival at Mosul. The drawings which Bell had made at Bavian and at Maltayah were being sent from Mosul to London. Layard left Beirut in June by ship for England feeling disconsolate. He told Canning that there had been a great deterioration in the country since he had travelled through that area eleven years previously and he had found the people insolent; for example in a large village near Alexandretta, 'a young man threw a bucket of water over me in the market-place in the most wanton and insolent manner', and Layard had obtained no proper redress from the Government as the young man was one of the *mufti* and could not be punished.

In the excavations at Nimrud and Kuyunjik Layard had achieved a great deal, but he was a perfectionist and nothing ever came up to his expectations. His summing up of what had been done in the one palace of Sennacherib at Kuyunjik was impressive enough:

> I had opened no less than seventy-one halls, chambers and passages whose walls, almost without exception, had been panelled with slabs of sculptured alabaster recording the wars, the triumphs and the great deeds of the Assyrian king. By a rough calculation, about 9880 feet, or nearly two miles, of bas-reliefs, with twenty-seven portals formed by colossal winged bulls and lion-sphinxes, were uncovered in that part alone of the building explored during my researches.

Besides the antiquities sent to London there were valuable drawings, the copies of cuneiform inscriptions, the *papier-mâché* impressions of bas-reliefs, the plans of the palaces, and various other important documentary details. The most important discovery of all, as Layard fully realised, was the great 'library' at Nineveh consisting of inscribed tablets and cylinders which had filled many rooms to the height of a foot or more from the floor. It was natural that he should be distressed that so many things were left behind, valuable both for their beauty and for their historical record, and he was bitter at the thought that they could have been saved if the British Government had been prepared to spend more money and carry out excavations on a proper scale.

Dr. C. J. Gadd wrote of the work Layard accomplished between the end of 1845 and April, 1852:

> For what he did during those years eulogy would be impertinent; the walls not merely of the British Museum, but of a host of smaller establishments and collections in many lands, are eloquent enough. And the science of Assyriology has been founded and nourished upon the clay tablets which he chiefly recovered.[4]

PART THREE

Politics

1852–1869

1

'Visions of ambition'

Layard arrived in London in July, two months after the opening of the Great Exhibition of 1851, and went straight from the train to stay with Lady Charlotte Guest at her London house. 'Poor fellow, he is sadly altered', she wrote in her diary. Parties were given in honour of 'her Ninevite' and he was much in demand; luncheon with the Marquis of Westminster, dinner at Baroness Burdett-Coutts, evenings at the Duchess of Inverness, talks about Nineveh to the Duke of Wellington, breakfasts with Lord Cowley etc. 'I am heartily sick of London and its great people; it is perhaps as well to see as much of the world as possible and [make use] of an opportunity which may never occur again', he wrote to Lady Aboyne; 'I have sometimes visions of ambition—a little crazy I have no doubt you have often thought them.' He had hopes of obtaining a post in the Government, but it was not clear what kind of post he could expect, or, indeed, why he should have any post, considering that he had no knowledge of home politics and no backing. He was regarded by London society as a young phenomenon, but that did not necessarily give him a place in politics.

Long hours were spent at the British Museum superintending the unpacking and arranging of the antiquities from Nimrud and Nineveh. Layard was annoyed that no adequate arrangements were made for carrying on the excavations except to send another young and inexperienced artist, Mr. Hodder, to replace Mr. Bell, and he wrote to Sir Henry Ellis: 'The French have sent out an expedition comprised of four first-rate men. How Mr. Hodder—ignorant of the country, its languages, and its customs—can compete with them I am at a loss to conceive, if the Trustees wish to continue the researches creditably to the country. . . . Since my return to England I have not received one word officially from the Trustees implying their satisfaction at the result of my last labours on their behalf.'* Layard settled down to write another book; the first one was still selling well and giving him an income of £1,500 a year; he had edited *A Popular Account of Discoveries at Nineveh* published at five shillings for the railway bookstalls and very soon fourteen thousand had been sold.

At the end of December 1851 Lord Palmerston had to resign as Foreign Minister because Queen Victoria and the Cabinet disapproved of his favourable comments on Louis Napoleon's *coup d'état*, and he was succeeded by Lord Granville. High praise of Layard's industry and intelligence was given to the new Foreign Minister by Lord Cowley who had arrived in London from Constantinople. At the beginning of the year 1852 Layard's fortunes suddenly changed for the better. On 2 January he had an interview with Lord John Russell, the Prime Minister; on the 7th he visited Lord Lansdowne at Bowood; in February he saw Lord Cowley, who had been appointed Ambassador in Paris, and who offered him the post of Secretary of the Embassy at £500 a year. Granville, however, had failed to find an efficient Under-Secretary for the Foreign Office and decided that Layard was the man.

The appointment caused considerable surprise, since at that time nearly all Government patronage was given to a closed circle of big families, but it was well received by the Press. *The Daily News* complimented Granville for his high courage in calling a man of the people to his aid; *The Examiner* considered that it was a homage to letters and talent which was seldom paid, and *The Times* wrote that the Government could not in the case of this appointment be charged with excessive nepotism. There were many other young men who might have been chosen, and

* The French expedition consisted of Victor Place, who was sent to Mosul to carry on where Botta had left off, while Fresnel, Oppert, and the artist, Felix Thomas, were sent to excavate in Babylonia but with no better success than Layard had had.

The British Museum eventually wrote to express satisfaction with Layard's labours. They repaid the sums of money he had borrowed from his mother and that he himself had advanced from the royalties of his book towards meeting the expenses of the excavations. It is not clear how much money was advanced but he states in his *Autobiography* that he received no remuneration for his labours.

it is a measure of the extraordinary impression Layard had created that he should have been given this important Government post. He owed it to Nineveh. Not everyone was pleased, for his radicalism had been noted. Emily Eden, the Whig traveller and novelist, had written to Lord Ellesmere chiding him for his enthusiasm over Layard's book on Nineveh—she could forgive Layard for discovering Nineveh, though she was quite satisfied to take it as Jonah had left it, but she could not forgive Nineveh for having discovered Layard. In the family there was great rejoicing. 'I need not say how many years I have anxiously watched your progress,' said Uncle Benjamin, 'but little dreaming of so sudden an accomplishment of all my hopes' and Sara Austen was greatly excited. 'Few people', wrote Lady Charlotte Guest, 'have had so many momentous events crowded into so short a space of time.' Canning wrote a friendly letter of congratulation but was glad that Layard was dealing with European affairs 'as it would not be decorous for you to write instructions to your *recent* chief; you do well to keep the hemisphere to which we do *not* belong'.

Layard seemed set for an important career in the Government, whereas eight months previously he had been alone on the burning plains of Mesopotamia and frustrated by his difficulties with the British Museum authorities. Now he was a man of influence closeted all day in the Foreign Office with Permanent Officials, including the Chief of the Clerks, Mr. Edmund Hammond whom Alison had described as 'rather formal on first acquaintance but the best creature in the world'. Layard had met him three years before when he was trying to persuade the Foreign Office to give him a paid Attachéship in Constantinople and he had been helpful. Hammond had an admiration for Sir Stratford Canning and had accompanied him in 1851 to Constantinople to help fix the boundaries of the newly independent Greece and to arrange the accession of Otho of Bavaria as king. The rest of the day Layard led a busy social life—breakfast with Sidney Herbert, Thiers, and Lord Carlisle; dinner with Lord Granville; at a party with Lord Lansdowne, Macaulay, Senior, and George Grote with whom he discussed the famous retreat of the Ten Thousand Greeks described in Xenophon's *Anabasis*. Layard told the pundit on Greek history that he had made a mistake in a passage from Xenophon. Grote was a little taken aback but, after studying the matter, wrote to him a day or so later, 'I have overlooked one line in the text, which mentions three additional days' march to the Telebaos river. . . . Pray accept my thanks for pointing out the error.'

On 20 February Palmerston defeated the Government on their Militia Bill (a defence against a possible invasion of England by Louis Napoleon), and had his 'tit-for-tat' with Russell who resigned. The Tories came to power with Lord Derby as Prime Minister. Lord Malmesbury, the Foreign Minister, asked Layard to remain until his successor, Lord Stanley of Alderley, arrived from India; even though Layard had been at the Foreign Office for only eleven days he had created a good impression as an able man and a hard worker. Layard dined with Lord Granville and Lord Carlisle who considered that he should agree to Lord Malmesbury's request since he did not connect himself with the Tory Ministry by remaining temporarily. Two days later, however, he was told that Lord John Russell thought that he should resign, though Granville still advised him to continue in office, especially as Lord Malmesbury was prepared to give Layard a diplomatic appointment after the return of Lord Stanley.

To be plunged suddenly into the political and social life of London was not easy for the dogmatic, high-principled, and impetuous Layard. He took Lord John Russell's advice and resigned but he was soon to regret the decision for Russell was not helpful and it was nearly ten years before he was again given office. It is probable that Layard would have agreed to remain if Stratford Canning had been made Foreign Minister instead of Malmesbury—as many had expected he would be—but it was decided that there would be no peace with Russia, or in the Cabinet, with Canning in the Government. In his annoyance Canning nearly refused the peerage he was offered but his brother persuaded him to accept it and he became Lord Stratford de Redcliffe.

Layard expected that the Tory Government would soon be overthrown and expressed contempt for some of its members: Lord Lonsdale, 'notorious as one of the most unscrupulous men about town', placed in charge of education, and Disraeli 'a man

Lady Charlotte Guest by G. F. Watts

Henry Layard by G. F. Watts

formerly connected with half the disreputable bill transactions
in London' in charge of finance, 'all this is degrading to an
Englishman'.* Granville urged Layard to stand for Parliament
for the elections due to be held in the summer and Lord Carring-
ton arranged for him to be put forward as a Liberal candidate
for Aylesbury which he had not visited since his father's death.
Layard's brother Arthur and Hormuzd Rassam came to hear
him speak which he did well enough to be elected on 7 July
1852. Benjamin Austen was delighted and so far forgot his
Toryism as to give a large dinner-party in his nephew's honour.
'Don't you feel some twinges of compunction for converting
poor Mr. Austen?' wrote Frederick Layard who was a captain
in the army in India. At Canford Manor Layard was given a
tremendous reception. 'Nothing can have been more triumphant
and satisfactory than Henry Layard's election', wrote Lady
Charlotte. The elections did not change the balance of parties
and the Tory Government had much the same majority as
before.

Layard was everywhere a fashionable and popular figure
except with the Trustees of the British Museum, who did not
like the tone of his letters. It was unfortunate that nine cases
intended for himself and three cases intended for Lord Stratford
de Redcliffe had been sent by mistake to the Museum and could
not be removed without the sanction of the Trustees. 'The bas-
reliefs', he told them, 'were obtained from Nimrud and have been
given by me to the University of Oxford. They are mere duplicates of others already in the British Museum. The others are
likewise duplicates or mere fragments of little value which I

---

* 'The Earl of Malmesbury, Sir John Pakington, Mr. Walpole, Mr.
Henley, and the rest, were men whose antecedents scarcely gave them
warrant for any higher claim in public life than the position of chairman
of quarter sessions. . . . The head of the Government was remarkable
for his dashing blunders as a politician, quite as much as for his dashing
eloquence. His new lieutenant, Mr. Disraeli, had in former days
christened him very happily, "the Rupert of Debate", after that fiery
and gallant prince whose blunders generally lost the battles which his
headlong courage had nearly won. Concerning Mr. Disraeli himself it
is not too much to say that many of his own party were rather more
afraid of his genius than of the dullness of any of his colleagues.'
A History of Our Own Times by Justin McCarthy, M.P. (Chatto, 1880).

have collected for myself.' The Trustees released the cases, but began to question Layard's right to give away what they regarded as Museum property. In a letter of 25 March 1852 to Sir Henry Ellis he argued that he had been instructed not to send 'duplicates of sculptures and inscriptions already in possession of the British Museum' so that he had the right to give away replicas. 'Had they remained, they would probably have been all destroyed by the Arabs. . . . I cannot refrain from adding that it was only by actual want of means that I was prevented from sending more sculptures to the Museum and that, whilst the Trustees seem to be suspicious about a few insignificant specimens sent by me to Europe, a large number of highly interesting bas-reliefs . . . still remain at Kuyunjik.' This roused their interest and they wanted to know more. He told them that at Kuyunjik there was 'a highly curious series of bas-reliefs which appear to represent the siege of the city of Lachish' and they could be brought to London. At Nimrud some very important inscriptions had been made ready for transport, but there were so many of them that it would require 'some discrimination and acquaintance' with the nature of the cuneiform inscriptions to point out those not worthy of transport; impressions should also be taken 'of the inscriptions on the Bulls recording the wars of Sennacherib'.* He added that Rawlinson was chiefly occupied with the investigation of the inscriptions 'and has little time to devote to monuments'. The Trustees realised that it was important to send someone who knew about the excavations. As Layard would not go, and Rawlinson was too busy except to exercise general supervision, they selected Hormuzd Rassam, who left London in August 1852 and started his career as an archaeologist in his own right.

Layard continued to work on his second Nineveh book and spent some time with the Rev. Edward Hincks at his remote parsonage, at Killyeagh in Ireland, examining the cuneiform inscriptions brought from Assyria and Armenia. The trans-

---

* The name of Sennacherib had only recently been deciphered by the Rev. Edward Hincks and Major Rawlinson. On 23 August 1851, Rawlinson had given an account in *The Athenaeum* of the principal events recorded on the monuments of Sennacherib at Kuyunjik including the war with Hezekiah and the siege and capture of Lachish.

lations were used by Layard for his forthcoming book. 'To profound scholarship in the Semitic tongues,' wrote Layard, 'and
to the most extensive literary and scientific acquirements, he
added a wonderful ingenuity, acuteness, and sagacity, and a
singularly retentive memory, which peculiarly fitted him for a
decipherer. . . . Dr. Hincks had already deciphered the names
of Sargon, Sennacherib, and Esarhaddon, and had thus proved
that which I had been led to conjecture from a comparison of
the monuments and from other evidence, that the palaces at
Kuyunjik and Khorsabad, and in the south-west corner of the
mound of Nimrud, owed their foundation to these kings. . . .
Constant additions were made to our knowledge of the contents
of the cuneiform inscriptions . . . but scholars in this country,
whose learning was limited to the classics, were little inclined to
accept these interpretations, and were rather inclined to reject
them altogether as ingenious fictions.'[1] Layard himself had been
too busy to pursue his first attempts at decipherment, but whilst
copying them he was able 'to compare them and to classify to a
certain extent the various signs and letters which they contain'.
It is not surprising that he did not get very far. 'For the true
genius of a decipherer is a rare gift, and no amount of industry
or learning can compensate for its absence. Hincks and Rawlinson possessed it with exceptional intensity.'[2]

When the Derby Government fell in December 1852, over
Disraeli's budget, Layard understood that he would again be
given a post in the Liberal Government and this seemed to be
confirmed when, on 28 December, *The Times* published the
news of his appointment to the important post of one of the
Secretaries of the Board of Control. It was a coalition Government
of Whigs and Peelites under Lord Aberdeen with Lord John
Russell as Foreign Minister, Palmerston at the Home Office,
and Gladstone as Chancellor of the Exchequer. Everyone had
friends they wanted to include and Layard was bitterly disappointed to receive a letter from Lord John Russell informing
him that he had not been selected as a member of the Government, but it was hoped that an opportunity might occur before
very long of recommending him to Lord Aberdeen on account
of his 'distinguished merits' and his 'very handsome' conduct in
the previous year. Layard did not see how he could maintain

himself in Parliament without a Government salary and he believed that having once been shelved he would not receive another offer. 'You are not a man to give way to disappointment', wrote Lord Cowley from Paris, 'and you will see that with your character and energy you have a brilliant career before you', but he must beware of being too radical, 'we are living in an age when the too great power of the people must be kept in check'. Lord John Russell also tried to console him by offering the post of Consul-General in Egypt at a salary of seventeen hundred pounds a year, but Layard declined.

He was still hoping to make his mark in politics and he was perhaps a little over-elated by the adulation he received. *Nineveh and Babylon* was published in March 1853 and was in one volume of nearly seven hundred pages with illustrations and maps. The full title is, *Discoveries in the ruins of Nineveh and Babylon with travels in Armenia, Kurdistan and the Desert, Being the result of a Second Expedition undertaken for the Trustees of the British Museum.* The larger and more elaborate drawings of the bas-reliefs were published in a second series of the *Monuments of Nineveh.* The book was dedicated to Lord Granville who wrote that he hoped a slight official connection would lead to a long and cordial friendship. *Nineveh and Babylon* was well received by the Press and as widely read as the first book. Layard received numerous letters of congratulation including one from an earlier traveller to Nineveh, James Silk Buckingham, and one from Disraeli. 'Never have such important discoveries', he wrote, 'been narrated in so animated and picturesque a style since the days of Bruce.'* The book added to Layard's fame and in March he was made an Honorary Citizen of London.

While Layard was wondering what he should do, apart from sitting in Parliament as Member for Aylesbury, Lord Stratford de Redcliffe asked him to return for a short time to help him in Constantinople. He had retired as Ambassador in January, but

---

* J. S. Buckingham published his entertaining *Travels in Mesopotamia* in 1827.

James Bruce's *Travels to Discover the Source of the Nile* in the years 1768 to 1773, after being regarded at first as a work of romantic fantasy, had been accepted by African explorers as a remarkable early book on that part of unknown Africa.

had been persuaded by Lord Aberdeen, the Prime Minister, to return to exert his influence over Sultan Abdul Mejid in order to counter the intrigues of Prince Menshikoff who had been sent with a large Russian mission to intimidate the Sultan. Layard was not eager to go but considered that he was under an obligation to Lord Stratford for all his help in the past, and when Lord John Russell gave his approval, Layard decided to be away from London during the Easter recess. Rawlinson wrote from Bagdad to say that he was not surprised to hear that Layard had refused the post of Consul-General in Egypt, 'but to throw up £1,700 a year and at the same time to come to Constantinople on nothing, does, I confess, pass my comprehension'.

It was, indeed, a mistake, for Lord Stratford was in a bad temper at not having been made Foreign Minister or even given the post of Ambassador in Paris, while Layard was less willing to obey orders than before. The party stayed some time in Paris and Layard enjoyed dining with Louis Napoleon and the Empress who was, he said, 'decidedly pretty'. He did not think that Napoleon was likely to attack England, as many thought, but that sooner or later he would be forced into a war somewhere. Layard wrote a series of letters to Lord Granville in which he said that Napoleon seemed ready to act with England in helping Turkey against Russia, but he was very ignorant and shocked Layard by referring to Odessa as at the mouth of the Danube.

The Ambassador's party arrived in Constantinople at the beginning of April 1853 when the dispute between France and Russia over the Holy Places had become even more acrimonious than it had been at the time of Layard's visit to Jerusalem in 1839. The rivalry between the Latin Church backed by France, and the Greek Orthodox Church backed by Russia had become a struggle for power between the two governments. The French Ambassador, M. de la Valette, had told the Porte that a refusal of French demands by Turkey would mean war. Layard wrote to Granville that the Russians were taking the struggle very seriously and had collected a large force on the frontiers of Rumania (the Danubian Principalities of Wallachia and Moldavia) and that Prince Menshikoff was exerting great pressure on the Turkish Government; he said that it would be suicide for Turkey to concede all that Menshikoff demanded. To give

Russia the control of the Greek Church and the right to interfere with the affairs of the Greek community would mean that the Turkish Government would have renounced sovereignty over a great part of the population of Turkey in Europe. The more intelligent Greeks, he said, viewed the prospects of such concessions with alarm, for under the Turks they had the opportunity of developing their enterprise which they would not have been able to do under the Russians: 'The policy of England is to maintain the Turkish Empire in its present state until the Christian population may be ready to succeed the Mussulman. My conviction is that it is possible to do so, and that this policy is the only hope of a favourable solution to the Eastern Question.'[3] Towards the end of April Layard was planning to return home, for relations with the Ambassador were very difficult; 'to be of any use', he said, 'one must be at the head of the Embassy, not at the beck and call of a man who suspects everything and everyone and only has one end—his own selfish views'.

2

'Where are you to stop Russia?'

Layard left Constantinople at the beginning of May and very soon afterwards Prince Menshikoff issued what amounted to an ultimatum to the Turkish Government, which the latter rejected. As soon as Parliament assembled in London, Layard did his utmost to bring the Eastern Question before the House, for he was now convinced that there was danger of a war in which England might be involved but he repeatedly failed to bring forward his motion. The Aberdeen Government was uncertain as to what policy it should pursue and had no desire to have a debate in Parliament brought forward by one of its own back-benchers, regarded as an expert on Turkey. There was great division in the Cabinet, in Parliament, and in the country as to whether Russia was a friend or an enemy. If she were an enemy, could Turkey be made a bastion against her or was she already in dissolution; or again, whether it was right to support a Moslem country against a Christian one? Layard, of course, distrusted Aberdeen, and considered that he was allowing Russia to bully the Turkish Government. It was difficult for the general public to understand why the dispute, which started in Jerusalem over the Holy Places, had become so important, or why it might lead England into war. He tried to explain the situation in speeches and articles. It was not, he wrote, a question of religious privileges only, or of freedom of worship, but much more than that: 'The Greek clergy, in fact, are almost the political, as well as spiritual, heads of their flocks'; the object of the Menshikoff mission had been to try to force the Turks to recognise these special privileges in a formal treaty. The Earl of Clarendon, who had succeeded Lord John Russell as Foreign Minister, wrote to Lord Stratford de Redcliffe that Turkey had been right to reject

Menshikoff's proposals, for no sovereign could admit proposals which conferred upon another, and more powerful sovereign, a right of protection over his subjects; this would have meant that fourteen million Greeks in the Ottoman Empire would have regarded Czar Nicholas of Russia as their supreme protector and their allegiance to the Sultan would have been little more than nominal. There were, however, other members of the Government who did not understand the situation as clearly.

On 6 June Layard wrote to Lord John Russell again to say that he must call the attention of the House of Commons to affairs in the East; he did not wish to embarrass the Government, but rather to strengthen it and to show how important it was to support Turkey in her resistance to Russia. Russell, who was Leader of the House of Commons, referred the proposal to the Cabinet. It was decided that Layard's motion would be injurious to the progress of negotiations for peace which were being conducted in Vienna with France, Prussia, Russia, and Turkey. It was not easy for Layard, new to the House of Commons, to act contrary to this admonition, even though he felt extremely strongly on the subject. Lord Stratford de Redcliffe, Alison, and Humphry Sandwith continued to send him information from Constantinople showing how increasingly serious was the situation. They said they were relying on Layard and could not understand why he had not made his maiden speech: 'We are all very anxious to hear the voice of your first-born', wrote Alison.[1] It was impossible, however, to break through the net that was cast over him.

Palmerston, Clarendon, and Russell realised that Aberdeen's pacifism was encouraging Russian aggressiveness, but they believed that from within the Cabinet they could win over the majority against the 'Peace Party' consisting of Aberdeen, Gladstone, Sir James Graham, and Sidney Herbert. On 2 July the Russian army crossed the Pruth river, which meant that they had entered the Danubian Principalities of Wallachia and Moldavia, which were nominally, at least, under Turkish suzerainty. Layard put down a motion without referring to Russell but Palmerston made a strong appeal to him in the House of Commons to postpone it which he agreed to do. Meanwhile urgent letters continued to reach Layard from Constantinople:

'If the Turks do get licked they will die game', wrote Alison, 'Why didn't you make a speech—you are really too bad.'

On 22 July Layard found an opportunity to make a short statement, arguing that Russia's act of invasion was calculated, 'to put an end to all those treaties on which the system of Europe is founded. . . . Any powerful state may, on the same terms, annex any neighbouring state weaker than itself.' Those members of the House who thought as he did should have the opportunity of registering a solemn protest against a policy which was inconsistent with the dignity, honour, and interests of England and dangerous to the existence of not only Turkey but of every weak state in Europe. Every hour's delay increased Russia's opportunity, he said; if the negotiations were prolonged for a few months the weather would make it necessary for the British fleet to return to Malta from the Eastern Mediterranean, or Britain would have to violate the Treaty of 1841, which forbade the entry of warships into the Bosphorus. Members of the Government were annoyed that he should be so critical. *The Times*, prompted by Lord Aberdeen, published a leading article admonishing Layard for being so persistent in trying to bring on a debate when difficult and delicate negotiations were in progress. Layard was not sure what action he should take. The public was in a state of emotion and everyone was talking about the imminence of war. (Charlotte Guest, who was helping George Clark manage the huge Dowlais ironworks after the death of her husband, was worried that the Russian Consul would not pay for the railway lines sold to St. Petersburg before war broke out.) Layard's knowledge, authority, and determination made him a rallying point for back-benchers on both sides of the House, who disagreed with the Government's foreign policy. He began to dream of leading a party of his own and told George Clark that he had the strings of a great movement in his hands and found the responsibility of it very great; success, he said, would place him in a very good position and failure would do him immense harm. He believed that England would lose her good name if Aberdeen remained Prime Minister.

By 16 August 1853 the Cabinet believed that an agreement had been reached between Russia and the European Powers and that there was no longer danger in having a debate. Layard made his first major speech. England and the other Powers, he said, should compel Russia to evacuate the Principalities of Wallachia and Moldavia, otherwise the world would see that there was one measure for the weak and another for the strong: 'We forfeit our character and prestige in the East, rendering the position of our Ambassador in Constantinople utterly untenable.' The Government believed that disagreements with Russia could be patched up without material injury, but he believed that the conduct of Russia was part of a great scheme and her object was to encourage subversion in the Ottoman Empire so as to weaken Turkish power and to threaten those who opposed her—to render any other government but her own impossible in Turkey, at the same time she wished to prevent independent nations growing up within the Ottoman Empire. There were those who argued, he said, that it would not matter if the Turks were driven out of Europe and the Russians captured Constantinople, but if they humiliated the Sultan and destroyed his prestige, the wild tribes of Asia would be let loose. He pointed out that the Turks were merely a dominant tribe and that the far greater part of the population of Turkey in Asia was made up of Syrians, Arabs, Jews, Armenians, Kurds, and a variety of other races held together only by the moral and political prestige of the Turkish Government. There was, he considered, no alternative to Turkey, except Russia: 'Are we prepared to take possession of Asia Minor, Mesopotamia, Syria, and Egypt, or can we allow them to pass into the hands of Russia and France? For we must do one or the other, as there is no dominant family in any of those countries, except Egypt.' Karl Marx, who was then London correspondent for *The New York Tribune* and followed parliamentary debates closely, described the speech, in a despatch published on 2 September, as by far the best and most powerful that had been delivered, 'proving the illustrious scholar to be as intimately acquainted with Nicholas as Sardanapalus, and with the actual intrigues of the Orient as with the mysterious traditions of its past'. It was a good speech except that Layard had ignored Granville's excellent advice: 'Never, however tempting the occasion may be, condescend to personalities.' Layard had made a personal attack on Aberdeen which Charles Greville described as needlessly offensive and hostile.

Layard realised that he had taken a decisive step in showing that he was in opposition to the Government. 'The split between myself and the Ministers is now complete', he wrote to Lady Aboyne, 'and I suppose all chance of employment out of the question. I do not mind. I have done what I believe to be my duty, and I trust I shall always be able to refer back to what has occurred with conscientious satisfaction.' He considered that his speech had been well received in the Commons and in the country. 'I was well cheered throughout by a very large House for this time of the session. . . . If Ministers continue long in this unsatisfactory state, and refuse to give information to the public as to the real position of Turkey and Russia, there will be a very loud and very general expression of disapprobation.' He found it difficult to keep calm, for there seemed to him so much 'misunderstanding' on the Russo-Turkish question, and the arch-villain was, he considered, the Prime Minister. There was division as to whether England should support Turkey or Russia. As the likelihood of war drew nearer, bitterness increased and even families and friends were sometimes estranged over the Eastern Question. 'Surely', said Bulwer-Lytton, 'if there ever was a war waged on behalf of posterity, it is the war which would check the ambitions of Russia', while Carlyle, busy writing the *History of Frederick the Great*, considered it was all a mad business: 'A lazy, ugly, sensual, dark fanatic that Turk whom we have had for 400 years. I, for my part, would not buy the continuance of him there at the rate of sixpence a century.' A revealing letter was sent to Layard by Humphry Sandwith, who had become correspondent for *The Times* in Constantinople. It was from Delane, Editor of *The Times*, which was very influential and was supporting Lord Aberdeen in his pro-Russian sympathies. This is how he wrote to his correspondent in Turkey:

> You seem to think that England can desire nothing better than to sacrifice all its greatest interests and its most cherished objects to support barbarism against civilisation, the Moslem against the Christian, slavery against liberty, to exchange peace for war—all to oblige the Turk. Pray undeceive yourself. . . . We were slow to fight for him when he had more vitality, we are less than ever inclined to do so when he is visibly fading away and when no amount of protection can preserve his boasted 'independence and

integrity' . . . I trust, therefore, that in future you will have the modesty to forbear from off-hand censures upon English policy, to devote your whole attention to collecting and truly describing facts, and, if you must give opinions, to take care that they are not Turkish but English.[2]

Sandwith told Layard that he was not prepared to write in the 'unprincipled Russian style' in which *The Times* wrote about Turkey, and he soon ceased to be its correspondent.

Layard felt that he would have a nervous break-down if he remained in England; during the Parliamentary recess in September he went to Italy to soothe his nerves by looking at pictures. Lady Charlotte and Sara Austen also had plans to try to calm him down; they wanted to distract him from his self-imposed mission to get rid of Aberdeen by persuading him to marry an attractive young woman referred to as Miss L. But Layard was more interested in his mission, arguing that the Government's conduct was so utterly discreditable that he would have to expose it in the next session which meant that he would not get any Government employment and would have to consider how to earn his living. Miss L, he said, had been accustomed to a mode of life which would be unattainable with his means and his opinion of young ladies in general did not encourage him to believe that they were much inclined to sacrifice society and comforts for a sentiment 'which in these days is not very deep or of a very enduring nature'.

* * *

'Things get worser and worser, the beastly Turks have actually declared war', wrote Clarendon from the Foreign Office on 3 October 1853. Many in England believed that it would not be long before the Russians captured Constantinople and public sympathy for the Turks increased. Gladstone was severely criticised by the anti-Russians for a speech in Manchester in which he referred to 'the political solecism of Mohammedans exercising despotic rule over twenty million of our fellow Christians'. Gladstone stated later that he had made the speech during that critical October because he considered that the public was in need of more accurate information; he wanted to counter-balance the arguments of Layard and others who appeared to him to be propagating most dangerous delusions with regard to Turkey. He considered Layard perfectly sincere in his 'fanaticism,' but a powerful witness on account of his knowledge of Turkey filling the minds of the people with false ideas and with expectations which would be bitterly disappointed.

Layard's sense of mission increased as the situation became more critical, and he saw himself as a knight-errant defending Turkey against such men as Aberdeen, Gladstone, and Admiral Dundas, Commander-in-Chief of the British Fleet in the Mediterranean. Layard despised the latter for his failure to prevent the Russians from sinking seven Turkish frigates in the harbour of Sinope in the Black Sea when four thousand Turkish sailors were killed, many of them shot while trying to swim ashore. The Turks had shown great stubbornness and the British public was angered by the unnecessary butchery. A great welcome was given to the Turkish Ambassador, Musurus Pasha, when he drove to the opening of Parliament on 31 January 1854. Lord Derby made an eloquent speech for the Opposition, with which Layard was in entire agreement. The Tory leader argued that Aberdeen had misled the Emperor of Russia into thinking that England would leave Russia to do what it wished with Turkey; but it was essential in our relations with Russia, more than with any other country, to make it absolutely clear what could be allowed and what could not be allowed. During the last one hundred and fifty years, said Derby, Russia's policy had always been to advance gradually:

> It has never proceeded by storm but by sap and mine. The first process has been invariably that of fomenting discontent and dissatisfaction amongst the subjects of subordinate States—then proffering mediation—then offering assistance to the weaker party—then declaring the independence of that party—then placing that independence under the protection of Russia; and finally, from protection, proceeding to absorption, one by one of those States into the gigantic body of the Russian Empire.*

* Sir John McNeill, the former British Ambassador in Persia, published *The Progress and Present Position of Russia in the East*, which

Aberdeen made a poor defence in the Lords on 14 February, but was supported by Earl Grey who said it was not England's duty to act like knight-errants of old and protect every weak State which might be oppressed by a powerful neighbour. It was a mockery to talk of the independence of the Ottoman Empire, and impossible for the Turks to change their character while they remained Mahommedans. He drew evidence for his case against the Turk from the books of Mr. Layard who had shown 'by his clear and simple narrative' how every attempt at improvement was checked by the utter corruption, extreme tyranny, and total want of faith with which the tribes were treated by the Turkish authorities.

Three days later, on 17 February 1854, Layard was enabled to open a debate on Russia and Turkey. He countered the quotations from his books by saying that vast changes had taken place in Turkey recently and that she was ahead of Russia in many respects; she allowed more freedom for trade and for religion than did Russia which was a complete despotism. It had been argued, he said, that a despotic country had within itself the seeds of decay and would fall to pieces of its own accord—a most dangerous doctrine for the system could produce much evil before it perished. If he had lived at the time of the invasion of the Roman Empire by the Goths, Vandals, and Huns he might have foretold that those tribes would be either destroyed or absorbed but before that took place they deluged Europe with blood:

> How many centuries did they not throw back the civilisation of mankind! So it may be with Russia. She may eventually fall to pieces. I am convinced she will, but in the meanwhile she . . . may inflict a blow upon the liberties and civilisation of Europe from which it may take centuries to recover. . . . Where are you to stop Russia? Is she to go on taking the whole world?

was much read and information in it was drawn on by Derby, Lyndhurst, and others for their speeches. Layard made use of it, as did Karl Marx who wrote in a despatch to *The New York Tribune*: 'Mankind will not forget that Russia was the Protector of Poland, the Protector of the Crimea, the Protector of Courland, the Protector of Georgia, Mingrelia, the Circassian and Caucasian tribes; and now Russia, the Protector of Turkey!'

With regard to the Sinope 'massacre', he asked whether the
Government was so intent on preserving peace that it would
not allow the fleet to go out to prevent that terrible catastrophe,
or even to go out afterwards to see what had been done? Was
that an honourable way to preserve peace? Sir James Graham,
speaking for the Government as First Lord of the Admiralty,
considered Layard's speech able, but he resented its tone of
accusation. Disraeli, as Leader of the Opposition in the House
of Commons, said that the speech justly commanded the attention of his hearers. Alison asked from Constantinople the same
question as everyone was asking in London: 'Are we at war or
peace?' He said that Omar Pasha was at Shumla on the Danube
with a good army but no cavalry, and that if he were beaten
there would be little for the Turks to fall back on: 'Here we
have nothing for it but to look to Europe to know what is to be
done. When will you be able to tell us that?'

On a dull morning in February 1854 the Guards marched
through London, resplendent in their red uniforms and busbies,
and embarked in three large transports at Southampton. It was
thought by some that this demonstration would be enough to
make the Czar withdraw from Turkish territory and that the
troops would go no farther than Malta. Gladstone, as Chancellor
of the Exchequer, had only ear-marked funds to send them to
Malta but on 28 March Britain and France declared war on
Russia. Parliament was summoned for 31 March. Indecision
continued and there was still widespread distrust of Government
policy. Derby argued that if Aberdeen had not been Prime
Minister there would have been no war. In the Commons Lord
John Russell gave an excellent statement on the reasons for
declaring war. It delighted Layard who praised it highly but he
said he felt bound to ask whether Lord Aberdeen might not be
expressing in the other House opinions which were diametrically
opposed to Lord John's; the divergence of opinion in the Cabinet,
he said, had led to great dangers. He knew that neither in
Constantinople, nor in any other part of Turkey had adequate
preparations been made for provisioning or transporting troops.
This was not a moment for half convictions or shams:

It is not easy to meet the Russians in Turkey. You do not know
what Turkey is, or what are the resources of the country for the

maintenance of an army. The troops may become infected with the worst of fevers, and then how many of those men who are going to Turkey will return, unless you make some preparations more worthy of the occasion than you have done?

Layard spoke for about an hour and was followed by Bright who said that people talked a great deal about 'the balance of power'; if that was really worth a sanguinary war, why had not England gone to war with France when she had seized Algiers? If that phrase was always to be an argument for war, the pretext for war would never be wanting and peace could never be secure. England would have to pay for the war and Bright warned them that every man of them had a Turk upon his shoulders. Turning towards Layard, he said that the Honourable Member for Ayles-bury might content himself with the dream that they were supporting the independence and integrity of Turkey, but he doubted whether bringing three foreign armies on her soil, raising insurrections in her provinces and hopelessly exhausting her finances was a rational mode of maintaining her as an in-dependent power.

Palmerston, replying to Bright, said that he agreed with the Member for Aylesbury : while people might wish to see Christians governing the vast and fertile regions of the Ottoman Empire in Europe, the Turkish race was the only one that could keep the country together as an Empire and govern it as such. Disraeli again praised Layard for a speech of 'eminent ability' which he did not think had been properly answered by the Government. Able no doubt, said Lord John Russell in irritation, but why should he be so bitter? Why should the Member for Aylesbury, who took more interest in the welfare of Turkey than any other member, fill his speech with 'flimsy personal attacks' on the administration? The zealous Layard had, indeed, again been unnecessarily wounding in his personal attacks on the Prime Minister. Just before the debate Tom Taylor, of *Punch*, had written Layard an urgent letter imploring him not to attack the Prime Minister, saying it would be unpatriotic and suicidal; war had been declared and England's prestige rested mainly on belief in her good faith: 'I *know* you are not acting for personal motives. . . . I *know* you feel strongly on this question and that your course is dictated by motives worthy of respect. But! But!'

Layard had paid no attention. Turning to the Treasury Benches he asked: 'Is there some person among you who has mistaken his mission, or who is treacherous to the cause? I say then, throw your Jonah overboard; if you do not, your vessel will be wrecked.'

Layard had a single-mindedness, perhaps inherited from his Huguenot ancestors, which was admirable in certain circumstances but at others he obstinately pursued his course whatever the consequences, as if he took a pleasure in the prospect of martyrdom. The personal attacks on Aberdeen gave him satisfaction but were of no avail in achieving his object. The Cabinet could not throw their 'Jonah' overboard, for there was no successor; after their quarrel Palmerston would not serve again under Lord John Russell, nor the latter under Palmerston. Layard told Henry Ross that he had done himself harm but he believed he had done the State some service by helping 'a vacillating and undecided Ministry to a somewhat more definite line'. He had quarrelled with those in power: 'But I have been right and that is a great thing.'

It was not a great thing in the House of Commons. If Layard could have been more urbane and less aggressive; if he could have worn his virtue less conspicuously, he would have won greater support in the Commons and he would have been in the Government. His considerable talent and super-abundant energy could then have been put to good use. Lady Charlotte regretted that he was thrown into 'a fruitless opposition'. She thought he had been unnecessarily violent in his attacks on Aberdeen and she knew that Lord John Russell found it difficult to give Layard a post because he had made enemies of Aberdeen and of Gladstone. At the same time she liked her cousin's fearlessness and his refusal to compromise. 'I only wish that a magician's wand could temper your ardour now and then', wrote Lady Eastnor.

Layard's ardour had nearly brought an end to his Assyrian expedition when he knocked the Cadi on the head, and it now looked as if his promising political career might be brought to an early close. In a remarkably short space of time his energy and initiative had earned him world-wide fame for his excavations, but he was wrong to think that success would be achieved in the House of Commons by hustling. When Benjamin Disraeli had been hooted down during his disastrous maiden speech in 1837 a parliamentary friend had warned him not to try to take the House of Commons by storm but to get rid of his 'genius' for a session and to be dull. Disraeli learned the lesson and became a great and popular speaker in spite of his bizarre manner and the distrust he aroused. Layard who was sincere, patriotic, knowledgeable, and right in his views, had not yet learned how to win the House of Commons. 'If you will only learn that speaking *in* the House of Commons', wrote his friend Lord Goderich, 'it will never do to forget that you are speaking *to* the House of Commons.' To prove a point on one occasion, he read out long extracts from *The Times* which had written a series of pro-Russian articles and when Members made it clear that they were bored he threatened to read every one of the articles, 'for the more I read', he said, 'the more I shall strengthen my case'. It was his manner which annoyed the House. Justin McCarthy M.P. refers to his 'immense self-sufficiency and indomitable egotism. . . . He was fluent, he was vociferous, he never seemed to have a moment's doubt on any conceivable question.'[3] Arthur Otway M.P. gives a more sympathetic account: 'He was not an orator, nor could he be considered to be even a powerful speaker in an assembly which contained at the same time such men as Bright, Gladstone, Macaulay, Disraeli, Lowe, and Cowen (of Newcastle). Yet his speeches were always able, earnest, and straightforward. They were well delivered, and one could not but admire his leonine head and manly presence. He was fearless in denunciation of abuses, and his sympathy was always with the oppressed.'[4]

Layard came to be regarded as having a personal animosity against Lord Aberdeen and it is not surprising that he was horrified and distressed at some of the Prime Minister's statements. In June 1854 the former Lord Chancellor Lyndhurst made, at the age of eighty-two, a stirring and eloquent anti-Russian speech; Lord Aberdeen replied in terms which appeared to be a defence of Russia. Layard at once gave notice that he would move a critical resolution. There was a strong belief, wrote Karl Marx, that Layard's motion would unseat Aberdeen, and *The Morning Advertiser* published the list of the ministry which was to succeed him. Pressure was brought to bear on Aberdeen to make another speech and Queen Victoria on 26 June sent the Prime Minister one of her well-timed rebukes: 'The Queen hopes that in the vindication of his own conduct today . . . he will not undertake the ungrateful and injurious task of vindicating the Emperor of Russia from any of the exaggerated charges brought against him and his policy, when there is enough in it to make us fight with all might against it.'

Aberdeen made his speech of explanation and Layard withdrew his motion. In the debate of 24 July 1854 Layard attacked the commissariat. Being of a practical turn of mind he asked: 'Why does not the Government allow some great firm to contract for carrying on the war?' There was a startled silence and laughter, for to most members of the House it seemed a most extraordinary question—everyone knew that war was the concern of the military and of the Government. To Layard it seemed idiotic not to make use of the men of the Industrial Revolution, who were carrying out great projects in different parts of the world.

The British and French had so far taken no part in the war beside their Turkish allies. They had established themselves most uncomfortably at Gallipoli and then moved north to Varna, Bulgaria's Black Sea port, and to Devnor, where there was terrible mismanagement and hundreds were dying daily of fever and cholera. William Russell, *The Times* correspondent with the British army, asked the Editor if he were to describe the horrors or to hold his tongue. Delane, who was no longer a supporter of Aberdeen, said that he must tell all; he, himself, wrote powerful leading articles underlining Russell's despatches in an attempt to force reform of military administration. The British army under Lord Raglan, and the French army under Marshal St. Arnaud, were not yet in a position to bring help to General Omar Pasha, the Turkish Commander who was obstinately defending Silistria, with the gallant Lieutenants Nasmyth and Butler helping to stiffen resistance. By May the stubborn Turkish defence had forced the Russians to withdraw and they were in retreat across the Danube towards Odessa. In July 1854 the Anglo-French decision was taken to attack the Crimea.

PALMERSTON'S NIGHTMARE.

'Into the cannon's mouth'

After the parliamentary recess of August 1854 Layard left
England to visit the Crimea with Delane, Editor of *The Times*,
and Kinglake, author of *Eothen* who was to write the first history
of the Crimean War. Delane found them both excellent travelling
companions and listened to more good stories on the journey
than he had heard in the whole of the previous twelve months.
As they crossed to the Mediterranean they were infuriated to
hear Greeks and Italians sneering at the British army and saying
that the Turks were winning their battles without any help;
when a British transport passed their ship, the Greeks remarked

250

that she was taking parasols and veils, or perhaps rose-water, or to report who had won the last match of 'creket'. At Constantinople the British and French fleets were much criticised for not carrying out an effective bombardment of Odessa since the huge Russian army of about 40,000 men, which had been on the Danube, passed through Odessa unmolested to reinforce the Crimea. Layard wrote home that there was the greatest indignation and disgust at the 'utter incapacity' of our Admiral Dundas: 'On the whole the mismanagement on our part far exceeds anything I could have anticipated. Every word I said in the House was perfectly true.' Delane remained antagonistic to the Ambassador, criticising the Embassy staff for allowing the army to commit most cruel blunders, which had cost a thousand lives, and then making jokes at the expense of the generals, officers, and commissariat.[1] Layard wrote to John Murray from Therapia that everyone, except Marshal St. Arnaud, spoke of the expedition as hopeless and expressed opinions that it would be a complete failure. If he were in command, he said, he would send home anyone who dared to express such opinions.

News came to Constantinople that the fleet had left Varna on 5 September and three days later Layard with Kinglake and Delane entered the Black Sea in a small river steamer. It was three days before they came up with the armada of seven hundred ships carrying the British and French armies to the shores of Russia. Kinglake and Delane went on board *Britannia*, the flagship commanded by Admiral Dundas, while Layard was invited by Admiral Lyons on board *Agamemnon*. Delane was sorry that he was not also with Lyons, who was 'another Nelson', whereas Dundas, he wrote, was dilatory and accused throughout both fleet and army of having thwarted the expedition in every possible way. Layard wrote to the Austens on 13 September, the day before the landing in the Crimea:

> It is difficult to conceive anything more beautiful than the sight before the cabin window as I write. Twenty-three magnificent ships in line of battle enclosing to the southward several hundred transports. . . . Lyons with the French Admirals and Generals and our own, are now in conference upon the plan of proceedings. You may easily conceive how exciting the scene is . . . I intend to see as much as I can of the land operations. It is as well to have

some experience of these matters when one talks about them in the House of Commons, and I wish some of my friends were here.*

He wrote to Lord John Russell describing the landing of the troops, their high morale and the good feelings of the Tartar population towards them. He said that the only check to the prospect of capturing Sebastopol was the 'apparent complete incompetence and culpable negligence of Admiral Dundas: it is demoralising the army and navy and leading us into some great calamity'. After Delane had returned to London Layard wrote him a private letter criticising Dundas which was published in *The Times*. Layard told Austen that he had not intended it to be printed and it was all the more embarrassing that it was anonymous. He at once informed Admiral Lyons that he was the author of the letter so that he should inform Dundas. Layard was worried about the letter but did not realise how much trouble it was to cause, nor that he was to lose a Government post through Delane's indiscretion.

Layard was on board *Agamemnon* for the Battle of the Alma on 20 September and had the best view possible from the maintop of the battleship. Afterwards he went ashore with Admiral Lyons and visited the field of battle.

I could see every movement of the Allies' Armies and of the Russians as on a map. . . . The battle was won by downright British pluck and, as usual, at a great sacrifice of life. We have an unfortunate mania for going right into the cannon's mouth, instead of taking the side road. The French would have been an hour or two longer about it, but would have had half the loss. . . .

The scene after the retreat of the Russians was too terrible for description. . . . For about a square mile there was almost one continuous heap of the dead and wounded. . . . Only those who have seen a field of battle can know what such a scene is—and can understand the feelings which it excites. The amount of suffering is so great, the mutilations are so awful, and death is seen under so

* (L.P. 38982 September 16 1854). Layard kept a diary while he was in the Crimea with almost daily entries from 13 September to 8 November, covering the landing, the Battle of the Alma, the Charge of Balaclava, Battle of Inkerman and the siege of Sebastopol. Most of this is published as an annexe to his *Autobiography*, vol. ii. In this short account, some new material is drawn on from his letters to the Austens, Mr. John Murray and Lady Huntly.

many forms, that there is too much for sympathy, and almost complete indifference succeeds to the first feeling of consternation; . . . . you aid a wounded man without scarcely remembering the intensity of his sufferings. One friend suffering under ordinary circumstances would cause you infinitely more pain.

The Battle of the Alma had so demoralised the Russians that Layard anticipated, as did many others, that Sebastopol was as good as captured but the Russians rallied and received reinforcements, while cholera attacked the French and English. Winter closed in on them on the open plateau before Sebastopol. Among the sufferers from exposure for lack of a tent and warm clothing was Layard's brother Arthur, a captain in the Third Division. They were delighted to see each other, though Layard was distressed at Arthur's illness and arranged with the Commanding Officer that he should have a staff post, his knowledge of Italian and French being useful with French and Sardinian troops.

During the first weeks of the siege of Sebastopol Layard shared a tent with an old friend from Constantinople, Colonel Dickson, who commanded a battery on the right flank. On 25 October he witnessed the Battle of Balaclava and the disastrous charge of the Light Brigade. 'Who gave this frantic order no one seems to know—as usual there seems to have been no command', he wrote home. 'It was a frightful sight to see the poor fellows led into almost inevitable destruction for no earthly object, and reflects great discredit upon our military authorities.' He said that the men displayed the highest courage but the valuable cavalry had been disabled and both Lucan and Cadogan were quite incompetent. On 8 November he wrote about the Battle of Inkerman: 'Another such victory would be almost fatal to us.' More officers had been lost than at Alma and he attended the funeral of three generals, all of whom he had known. He told John Murray that when he returned home he intended to urge the need for younger and more efficient men in command, even though he would be disliked for doing it, and he complained that there was no 'master mind'. 'There are a number of red-waistcoated gentlemen, with their hands in their pockets, idling about—men of undoubted gallantry, but without a spark of enthusiasm or energy—all voting the thing a great bore and longing for Pall Mall.' He referred throughout his

letters to the excellent spirit of the navy because of the leadership of Admiral Lyons: 'The contrast with the army is the more
regrettable, as the materials in both are the same, and all that
is wanted is someone to make use of them. The fault lies at
home—Dundas will probably be made a peer and Lyons not
noticed. . . . Being at Headquarters I have an admirable opportunity of seeing everything. I wish Sidney Herbert could have
some such experience.'

Layard decided that the siege of Sebastopol would last a long
time and he had better return home: 'The heights of Sebastopol
will probably be turned into a kind of Torres Vedras for the
winter. The conduct of Austria has exposed us to most of our
difficulties, by allowing the Russians to send their army from
the Principalities to the Crimea. . . . I have no doubt that, as
usual, we shall succeed but our losses will, I fear, be very great.'

*   *   *

'Ever since the days of the Duke', wrote Richard Ford to John
Murray in October 'the sins of ministerial mediocrities have had
to be washed out by the blood of brave men. . . . I hope that
"Eothen" [Kinglake] and "Nineveh" [Layard], now that they
have exchanged the pen for the sword will, on their return, add
thoughts that breathe to words that burn.'[2] Several Ministers
wanted to see Layard on his return and many waited to hear
what he had to say when a special session of Parliament was
called on 12 December 1854.

Lord Derby in a vigorous speech for the Tories argued that
the theme of 'too late' was applicable to the whole conduct of
Her Majesty's Government in the course of the war and he was
followed by other critics of Aberdeen in the Lords and Commons.
When Layard rose he had the attention of the House for he was
the only member who had witnessed the great battles of Alma,
Balaclava, and Inkerman and had seen the situation in front of
Sebastopol. He made his usual mistake at the beginning of
emphasising how right he had been: 'Would that I had been
able to avert those calamities which I then foresaw', but he went
on to deliver a powerful speech. The naval operations in the
Baltic, the policy with regard to Greece and Asia came under

attack; he emphasised how important it was that the Circassian and Georgian tribes fighting Russia should be aided to prevent the reinforcement of Sebastopol, but the Government had done nothing and opened no communication with Shamyl.* 'Had it not been for the diversion made in the rear of the Russian army by the indomitable Shamyl, the whole of Asia Minor might even now have been in the power of Russia.' Layard concluded a long speech by saying that they must 'cut to the root of the evil', 'service in the Peninsular [War] must no longer be the qualification for high and responsible posts in the Crimea'. To place men of seventy years of age in such positions of hardship was, he said, unfair to them and to the public; at least one-third of the lives lost in battle and by disease might have been spared if the Government had done its duty.

It was an effective speech and the Government benches sat glum for they were under heavy fire throughout the country for the mismanagement.† As usual praise for Layard came from the Opposition. Disraeli said that he had made charges against the Government expressed with knowledge, spirit, and ability and he considered Layard to be a man of genius who would be remembered when the great portion of the existing Cabinet would be forgotten.

There was little doubt in everyone's mind that Layard would have to be given a Government post at the first opportunity for he was too good a man to omit and too powerful a critic to leave in opposition. On 12 December 1854, however, the story of *The Times*' letter about Dundas was brought up in the House of Commons by Henry Drummond, a close friend of the Admiral.

* Shamyl, 1797 to 1871, the great leader of the tribesmen in the Caucasus in the Murad Wars against Russia which lasted twenty-five years, from 1834 to 1859. See *The Sabres of Paradise* by Lesley Blanch (John Murray, 1960). The Soviet Government in recent years has found it difficult to make up its mind whether Shamyl was to be praised as a hero for resisting Czarist Russia or execrated as a nationalist.

† A leading article in *The Times* of 23 December made a deep impression: 'The noblest army ever sent from our shores has been sacrificed to the greatest mismanagement . . . . incompetency, lethargy, aristocratic hauteur, official indifference, favour routine, perverseness, and stupidity, reign, revel, and riot in the camp before Sebastopol, in the harbour of Balaclava, in the hospitals of Scutari, and how much nearer home we do not venture to say.'

Layard explained his action but confused the story with a great deal of unnecessary information. Some did not understand why the letter had been published anonymously, others thought that he had been a guest of Admiral Dundas on his flagship. Tempers rose at the suggestion that the Admiral was being accused of cowardice. Layard said he realised that the character of an English admiral was at stake, 'yet the character of England and of the English fleet is at stake likewise'. 'Good God!' exclaimed Admiral Walcot M.P., 'I am wounded to the quick at having lived to hear such a charge against a gallant member of my profession.' Sir James Graham said that he would be in his place as First Lord of the Admiralty when the charges were brought so that he could vindicate the character 'of that gallant officer'. There were many though who considered that Dundas should have been removed from the command and at the beginning of the following year he was retired while Sir Edmund Lyons took command. Layard, however, had handled his case badly in the House and had aroused unnecessary animosity against himself. The Dundas case dragged on for months and there was talk of a libel action against Layard which made it difficult to give him a post in the Government.[3]

Before Parliament reassembled in January 1855 John Roebuck representing Sheffield gave notice of his famous motion, which brought down the Government after a debate of four days. He moved for a Select Committee to enquire into the condition of the army before Sebastopol and to enquire into the conduct of the Government departments concerned. As a result of the motion Lord John Russell resigned on 25 January and on that day gave his reasons in a speech in the House of Commons which was as gloomy an account of the situation before Sebastopol as any of Layard's descriptions; troops on the plain before Sebastopol were short of food, clothing, and shelter, so that they perished at the rate of nearly a hundred a day, when the port of Balaclava was only seven miles away. He said that the Member for Aylesbury had pointed out the danger that might be incurred if the Russian army were allowed to reinforce Sebastopol from the Caucasus, which was an important question, but Lord John Russell had not received from Lord Aberdeen the support he had expected when the subject was under consideration of the

Cabinet. During the debate Layard made the mistake of revealing that he was against having a Commission of Enquiry since it would not be effective, but that he would vote for the motion in order to try to bring down the Government. Gladstone was quick to seize on this inconsistency. The Member for Aylesbury must be very short of means for attaining his ends if, in order to despatch the Government he disliked, he was obliged to vote for a motion he could not defend: 'He is not nice in the choice of his instruments. The Priest of old, when he was about to sacrifice, washed his hands and put on sacrificial garments before he plunged the knife into the heart of his victim; but it seems to me that the Hon. Member for Aylesbury does not much care in what condition his hands are.'

At the conclusion of this remarkable debate there was a majority of one hundred and fifty-seven against the Government. It was such an overwhelming defeat that the House did not at first believe the figures and then tension was relieved by roars of laughter. Lord Derby tried to form a Ministry but, to the annoyance of Disraeli and other Tories, he did not try very hard. In February Palmerston took over with the same Ministers as before, except for Aberdeen, the Duke of Newcastle, and Lord John Russell. On 8 February *The Times* announced that Henry Layard was to be made Under-Secretary for War and that it was a post for which he was well qualified. *The Morning Chronicle,* which had supported the Aberdeen Government, stated that no one else would be found more efficient. It seemed to nearly everyone that it was the right moment to bring in Layard to straighten out the muddle at the War Office.* If he had been given the post he would almost certainly have had from then on a successful and effective political career. He was not emotionally fitted to remain long in opposition without a proper job to do, and from this moment there is a deterioration in his grip over himself and in his capacity to deal with developments. There were, unfortunately, two powerful forces against him, the Queen and

* Sir Arthur Otway wrote that if Layard had been appointed to the War Office, ' in all probability many of the disasters and miscarriages which occurred (during the war in South Africa) owing greatly to the inefficiency and want of organisation in that office, would have been averted'. (*Sir Henry Layard, Autobiography and Letters.*)

Gladstone. Lord Palmerston went to see the Queen on 5 February with the proposal that Lord Panmure should be in charge of the War Department with Layard as Under-Secretary. 'We remonstrated against Mr. Layard's appointment as Under-Secretary for War', she noted in her diary, 'on account of his ill-conditioned abuse of Lord Raglan and Admiral Dundas—though not against his employment. Lord Palmerston was not averse to reconsidering this.'(4) The 'Peelites' who had throughout been the 'Peace Party' were against him and Gladstone wrote to Palmerston to say that he thought the question of Layard's appointment should be referred to the Cabinet in view of his hostility to Aberdeen.

If Layard had known of these forces working against him, perhaps he would not have made so many conditions before agreeing to join the Government but he insisted, among other things, that his friends Edward Horsman, Lord Goderich, and Danby Seymour should be given posts. The day that *The Times* had announced his appointment he believed that it was almost settled. He wrote to his cousin Mary, who was now Marchioness of Huntly, that he was to be Under-Secretary for War, which was a fine position as the conduct of all matters connected with the war in the House of Commons would devolve on him, 'but I will not accept unless I have my own way'. Considering that these negotiations for a post in the Government were proceeding, it was unnecessarily provocative of Layard to attack the Government violently in a debate on 19 February. He said that there was no reason to trust the new Government under Palmerston any more than the last; the only promise made was that commissions would go out to enquire into the conduct of persons implicated in mismanagement:

> Do you want a commission to enquire how old Captain Christie* is, or what is the state of Balaclava? . . . What we want are men, and not commissions. Make up your mind to put an end to this system at once, and to cut at the real root of the evil. Depend upon it you will be obliged to do it at last, for the country will ere long compel you.
> When at the time of the French Revolution, the French army

* Principal Agent of Transports, and responsible for the administration of Balaclava harbour.

was reduced to that state to which our army is reduced, what did the French Assembly do? They sent out their own members, men who had no party considerations, who cared not for aristocratic influence, who went out determined to sacrifice those who were guilty, regardless of persons. They did so. The result was that in a few months that army achieved deeds which were unparalleled in the history of the world.

It was an insult to say that they could not find a man. . . . If your man, however, must be seventy years old, a member of Brooks's, and one who has always voted with the Government, I grant that you may not find one of that class and stamp fitted for the duties which are required of him. But, when I see upon all sides of this great country works unequalled in magnitude since the beginning of the world; when I see men who from small means have risen to the positions which they now enjoy; when I see around me an amount of money and internal resources which are unequalled in the history of the world—why to tell me that you cannot find a man to put in order the harbour of Balaclava, or to bring it into a state of efficiency, is a positive insult to the common sense of this country.

He had no doubt that a Cavendish in the Cabinet was a very important thing, but the public thought more of 20,000 lives than they did of a Cavendish. It was not true, he said, that he was trying to pull down the aristocracy; he was trying to save them. The country had come to the conclusion that the rulers had sacrificed its dearest interests because they would not allow men of talent to come between them and the nobility: 'You have raised a voice that will take more trouble to allay than you may think.'

Palmerston was roused and replied heatedly that the Member for Aylesbury thought he had a public duty to point out what he considered to be defects in the management of the army, to argue that the country had been disgraced, and to mingle with his recommendations 'vulgar declamations' against the aristocracy:

Talk to me of the aristocracy of England! Why, look to that glorious charge of the cavalry at Balaclava—look to that charge where the noblest and the wealthiest of the land rode foremost, followed by heroic men from the lowest classes of the community, each rivalling the other in bravery, neither the peer who led nor the trooper who followed being distinguished the one from the other.

It was a moving speech and pleased many in the House of Commons and in the country, but to others it was poppycock. No one had criticised the bravery of the officers; it was the mismanagement and useless slaughter which was criticised.

Layard received many congratulations for his speech. Delane thought it was admirable and would tend to raise his reputation in the House and in the country and was glad that he was not 'muzzled by some paltry office'. Layard's Radical friend, Harriet Grote, thought the speech powerful and that it would have a most useful effect: 'I *will* have the blame fixed upon those who have failed in their duty towards the country and nothing irritates me more than to be put off with the vague term of the "authorities". If the "authorities" sent the green coffee, and did not send drugs, *who* are they, *name* them! . . . I am deeply mortified to think upon the sacrifice of life which mismanagement has brought about.'(5) 'His speech', wrote *Lloyds Weekly* 'made him truly the War Minister—without the appointment.'

Layard was himself over-elated. He told Lady Huntly that 'everyone' said that it was the best speech that had been heard for many years in the House of Commons. It was not a particularly good speech from a parliamentary point of view since there was no object in attacking Palmerston, who was the one man among the Liberals who was likely to prosecute the war with energy, as Layard had argued previously. 'I am perfectly indifferent', he told her, 'as to whether the new Government will offer me anything or not—my position in the country is now made.' He described his speech as a 'great experiment', and that it was, for he was challenging the whole organisation of Government. He knew that this was a dangerous thing to do, but he believed that it was his 'destiny' to do it.

John Murray warned Sara Austen that Layard was ruining himself by his imprudence, but she did not agree and wrote to Lady Eastlake 'He *must* be bold, or he would do no good, and I feel sure that if he saw himself likely to be fettered by the wretched routine & official twaddle which has hitherto prevailed, he will refuse office as untenable, because ineffectual to check the moral blight under which we languish.' Edward Horsman, M.P. for Stroud, who was hoping for a post with Layard if the latter had office, was watching his behaviour with considerable misgivings. He wrote to him on 24 February saying how he and Lord Goderich had been working for Layard and making his cause their own: 'You have inspired us with feelings of confidence and regard with which you will equally inspire others if they have faith in your judgment—but that you have got to establish.' He thought that nothing could prevent Layard's success except mistakes on his part and that he was now reaching a crisis in his fortunes. He should not overrate his position for he had no party combination, or political connections or family influence or proved business habit:

> You have won your position very rapidly by sheer force of talents and character, and the same fearless independence, which has made you warm friends, has also given you bitter enemies. These have therefore maligned you as a disappointed man; henceforth they will represent you, if they can, as an impractical one, and a false step on your part showing want of judgement, which is more valued than talent, will shake your supporters off from you and leave you isolated and fallen.

Horsman considered that Palmerston had made an immense concession in offering Layard office, for the Prime Minister knew that it would not be easy to control him:

> You have never found the necessity for that discipline and control which is essential to an official conducting a responsible department in the House. You have even thought more of truth than of its consequences, and one word or act, under the impulse of feeling in the House of Commons, may be seriously embarrassing to the Government.

He thought that Palmerston would be justified in imposing conditions on Layard, rather than the other way round: 'Do not mar all by asking for conditions.' Layard did overrate his position and did not modify his conditions. Disraeli was watching developments with interest and knew that the 'Peelites'—Gladstone, Sir James Graham, and Sidney Herbert—had made Layard's exclusion from office a condition for their joining the

Government. Clarendon, a power behind the scenes, was not much attracted by Layard: 'a mighty self-sufficient gent; nobody is right or knows anything but himself'.[6] The 'Peelites', however, resigned when they found that Palmerston felt obliged to let the Roebuck Committee proceed with its work; they had achieved nothing by joining the Government except to ensure that Layard could not be appointed Under-Secretary for War. Palmerston offered him the post of Under-Secretary for the Colonies. When he told Lady Duff Gordon in a letter* that he did not see how he could accept, she wrote with her usual good sense: 'I don't admire your second doubt at all. If the place is offered you, you must accept it', but Layard felt that it was against his principles to take an office for which he did not consider himself fitted, when he should have been given the job of helping to wage the war about which he knew a great deal. His slogan at that time was The Right Man in The Right Place. *The Times* criticised Palmerston for failing to appoint Layard to the post for which he was marked out 'by the almost unanimous opinion of the country'. Tom Taylor regretted that he had not accepted the Colonial Secretaryship and made a feature of a short article in *Punch*: 'Good Mr. Layard, be warned and instructed. Take any office; fitness comes after it. Even as the milk flows to the mouth of the baby, so does knowledge flow *from* office. Be assured of it; in this motherly way does the State suckle her youngest—and sometimes oldest Ministers.' Layard, however, had other ideas as is clear from a letter he wrote on 27 February to Lady Huntly, two days after Palmerston had withdrawn the offer of the Under-Secretaryship for War: 'I am now free again and am not sorry for it. The Brookite Whigs are determined to maintain their monopoly of Government, but it will not do.'[7]

*   *   *

'The breakdown of our aristocratic rulers, when their energies are put to the stress of a great emergency, is about the most consolatory incident of the war', wrote Cobden in January 1855.

* Lucie, daughter of John and Sarah Austin, married Sir Alexander Duff Gordon and was the mother-in-law of Henry Ross.

The Times on 14 February referred to 'the cold shade of aristocracy which seemed to be blighting the energies of the nation'.
Alison, writing from Constantinople, told Layard to make sure
that the officers were better educated : 'The young fellows sent
out are deplorably ignorant, and those highly connected, or with
any prospects at home, wish they were well out of it.' Layard
found more support for his campaign against aristocrats and
'the system' outside Parliament among industrialists and merchants than he did inside Parliament. He told Lady Huntly :
'There is a great spirit rising in the country which will be more
formidable than our good, easy aristocratic families, who look
upon ministries as their perquisites, can now comprehend' ; he
might be forced into the position of leading that great movement 'and an immense struggle will be the result'. The people of
Europe had had to resort to revolution to overthrow feudalism
and it seemed to him that perhaps England, too, could only
achieve good government through revolution. He considered that
it was his duty and destiny to try to direct this new spirit into
safe channels. Public opinion, he believed, was forcing him into
a position of leadership. Greville and some others, however,
argued that it was Layard and his like who were stirring up the
trouble. *The Times*, wrote Greville, was in the hands of Layard,
and one or two more men who were 'able, ambitious and
unscrupulous, and they will never rest till they have created
as much of a revolution as they can and it will be a good
deal'.(8)

The formation of the Sebastopol Committee * was one of the
effective ways of demonstrating to the public that Members of
Parliament were disturbed at the mismanagement, and therefore Layard accepted the invitation to join it. The Committee
met in a small room in the House of Commons and large crowds

* The Roebuck or Sebastopol Committee, composed of Liberals and
Tories, held meetings from 23 February to 1 August 1855. Useful
documents were collected and information obtained by cross-examination of Ministers, officials, and officers. Among those questioned were
the Earl of Aberdeen (by Layard), the Duke of Newcastle, Sidney
Herbert, Viscount Hardinge, Sir James Graham, and others. It was
shown that there was complete confusion as to whether the army or
navy were responsible for transport and Admiral Deans Dundas
revealed his incompetence under cross-examination.

gathered long before the proceedings began, but only a few could be admitted. Layard worked very hard, attending all except one of the meetings. He also travelled backwards and forwards between London and Aberdeen, as he was a candidate for the distinguished post of Lord Rector of Marischal College and University.[9] He was elected as Lord Rector and delighted the Scots with a gloomy inaugural speech about Nineveh, whose story, he said, had helped to form his character and had influenced his politics: 'The fate which befell Nineveh and Babylon may befall the mightiest of nations when public virtue is no longer held in honour, when great principles no longer guide its counsels and when the public weal is sacrificed and made subservient to private interests.'

These were not mere figures of speech but the expression of a deep-seated emotion. He was desperately unhappy at what he had seen in the Crimea, at the mismanagement revealed at the many meetings of the Sebastopol Committee (he had attended twelve sessions in the previous month of March) and at his failure, unlike the Prophet Jonah, to achieve any change. Working too hard, travelling too much, sickening for another bout of malaria, he was in an emotional state. In Aberdeen there had been the long ceremony of his installation as Rector, a formal luncheon, three dinners, and four long speeches to be made. He returned to London for meetings of the Committee on 17, 18, and 20 April, travelling to Liverpool on 21 April as guest of honour at a banquet of nearly three hundred prominent men from shipping, industry, and commerce for the launching of a large clipper ship on the Australian run. The banquet was held on deck with a band playing, flags flying, and with little banners on the tables bearing Nineveh devices in honour of their hero Layard. It was a good meal with plenty of wine and spirits which made the words fall easily from the lips of speakers. The Chairman of the company said that it had been Mr. Layard's sterling honesty in not allowing himself to be muzzled which had rallied round him the whole of England—it was for Layard that the phrase had been coined: 'The Right Man in The Right Place.'

Layard was impressed by the occasion. Around him on the great ship, which was to sail back and forth across the world, were the worthy and stalwart industrial and merchant warriors of this great Nineveh of England, but at the top was a ruling clique which was, he considered, ruining the country. It seemed to him that the occasion was right for a declaration of war against the ruling hierarchy beginning with Lord Hardinge, the Commander-in-Chief. This man had, he said, served in the Peninsular War, was long past the age for service and was 'utterly unable to discharge the duties imposed upon him'. In the whole of England's diplomatic service there was hardly a man who did not owe his position either to rank or to family and political influence; he went on to make sweeping denunciations of aristocrats, diplomats, soldiers, and politicians; he had expected that Palmerston would make changes in the Government but there was 'all the old Whig scum again to the top of the pot'. He went into detail about abuses of promotions in the army, which were, unfortunately, not always accurate, and he was so offensive that he must have known that he would be in great trouble later. While he had criticised military strategy in the Crimea which sent men into the cannon's mouth, instead of taking the side road, he did not see that this also applied to politics. He had condemned Cadogan as a madman, but was himself now in another Balaclava charge. All was well while he had men around him who had dined well and sympathised with his point of view, but how would he do in the House of Commons when he was up against the big guns?

Layard was right in thinking that the Government in London should have paid more attention to the views of the men in the provinces, who were building up a new England. If Lord John Russell's Reform Bill had been passed during the Crimean War they would have had more influence. He had to deal, however, with the existing House of Commons and it was there that the power lay. His friends were worried by the prominence given in the Press to Layard's wild words at Liverpool. Mary Huntly wrote him a long letter full of wholesome advice. He replied that he was fully alive to the 'very critical nature of the movement now commencing and to the enormous evils to which it might lead'. He had considered, however, that the safest course was to encourage it and to endeavour to direct it. But revolutions are slow in the making and Layard was too far in advance of this

BAITING THE NINEVEH BULL.

THE DEN DOWN UPON LAYARD

What may that frantic uproar mean; groans, hootings, shrieks, and howls,
The snarl and bark of angry curs, the screams of carrion fowls?
What makes St. Stephen's walls resound with cries more dire and dread,
Than you ever hear in the Regent's Park when the animals are fed?

LAYARD in eager zeal the mask from jobbery to strip,
Mistaken on a point of fact, has chanced to make a slip,
So down the vultures swoop on him, the ravens and the crows,
The wolves, jackals, and poodle dogs of state that are his foes.

The little foxes snap at him for showing up the Whigs;
In angry chorus round him grunt and squeak official pigs:
With threatening horns and bullying roar the stalled placeman-ox
Assails him; BERKELEY groans at him, and bellows COLONEL KNOX.

"He's down; and now set on him; at him LINDSAY, at him BYNG;
Before the public teach him names of gentlemen to bring;
Give it him well; pitch into him; to lesson other snobs
In caution how they venture on exposing army-jobs.

"Down, down upon him, PALMERSTON, with final crushing stroke!
His is a mouth that must be stopped; a voice that you must choke,
Take we the opportunity that Fortune kindly sends,
Kick him, and kick him hard; he has among ourselves no friends!"

"Friends!" to the yell within the House an echo from without
Repeats, and thrice ten millions "Friends" unanimously shout;
"Hit LAYARD? hit him if ye dare! avast, dishonest crew,
Humbugs, get out and make room for a better man than you!"

Punch, 12 May 1855

one.* He had made a serious error in over-estimating the significance of the Liverpool meeting, and he believed in the effective-
ness of a new organisation which he was helping to found called

THE MEMBER FOR NINEVEH DIGS OUT THE BRITISH BULL.

APRIL 7, 1855.]   [PUNCH, No. 717.

'The Administrative Reform Association'. Again malaria fever
made him a little light-headed: 'I think the time is now come
to strike', he told Lady Huntly. 'It is an arduous task and Providence seems to have destined that it should be undertaken now—

* Describing the rise of the new plutocracy headed by the Brasseys
and the Guests in his book, *Helen's Tower*, Sir Harold Nicolson writes:
'To us, who from the perspective of another century look back upon
that period, it seems as if those years between 1853 and 1856 marked
the moment when the industrial revolution first drove home its wedges
into the fabric of society. It needed a war and the passage almost of a
generation before the Reform Bills shifted the incidence of power from
the territorial aristocracy to the rising middle class.'

and as a variety of circumstances have placed me in my present position, I am determined not to shrink from it.'

It was unfortunate that Layard should have been in such a weak state of health when he had to meet violent attacks in the House of Commons. On 26 April *The Times* published a series of extremely offensive letters exchanged between Lord Hardinge, the Commander-in-Chief, and Layard following the latter's Liverpool speech. It was known that these would be read out in the House of Commons the next day, which was a Friday; usually members dispersed early for the week-end, but the House remained crowded with no less than three hundred members present. The military and naval members had made a point of being in their places to crush the presumptuous Layard who had insulted the Commander-in-Chief and who apparently wanted to organise a revolution to overthrow the Government. In reply to the many attacks on him Layard delivered a confused speech and lost his temper, which made his opponents believe that they had defeated him, and the House got out of control. Catcalls, whistlings, and yellings interrupted his explanations: 'They bayed at him', wrote a parliamentary correspondent, 'in a strain sufficient to affright the ghost of Nebuchadnezzar.' Another correspondent reported that Layard made the great mistake of not remaining cool and quiet: 'He argued, he got into new blunders, he expostulated with the uproar—catching at and replying to passing phrases. The House was very full and very excited and very brutal, as the House always is at such times, and a man of veritable intellect would not have made such a shocking mistake as to fight with such an audience—more especially when in the wrong.' Bluff old Tories such as Colonels Knox and North, were very contemptuous of Layard, who was, they considered, no gentleman, and they rejoiced in their belief that he had brought his political career to an end. The Prime Minister expressed deep regret that the Member for Aylesbury should have placed himself in such a position that evening. He again condemned Layard for his criticisms of the aristocracy and concluded with a moving tribute to 'the public spirit and manly feeling' which characterised the gentlemen of England, but he was blamed by some for helping to work up feeling against Layard, instead of trying to calm the House.

269

John Ruskin was distressed that Layard had allowed himself to become involved in ridiculous arguments on detail:

Why do you not fix on the main facts of promotion by *purchase* in itself, as in its own essence, a Monstrosity and Horror and unendurable business. Let's dwell on the pure, brazen impudence of the whole thing, until it comes out on you like a Nineveh monster and then see what you can make of it. There's assuredly good butting in those brows of yours—if you once get the rags out of your way.[10]

Layard was blamed by a parliamentary correspondent, for his 'too-conceited obstinacy' in not admitting his mistakes for that would not have affected his general argument: 'that the system of the Horse Guards is an infamous system, degrading to the nation, disgraceful to individuals'. The correspondent said that if only Layard could subdue 'the presuming self' there was a fine and honourable parliamentary career before him. 'He has the earnestness and the honesty which claim respect; and his vast special knowledge of the whole question of the war already constitutes him a power which the public is eager to recognise,' but in the House he should not pretend to so prominent a part as impeaching a Ministry or 'starring' it in the provinces, for he was without company.

Layard was indeed without company in the House but there was a growing company outside. On the next day at a big double meeting in the London Tavern and the Guildhall to inaugurate the Administrative Reform Movement, Layard was enthusiastically cheered as one of the leaders. Both meetings were crowded and £20,000 was collected for the movement. *The Times* on 1 May 1855 gave full support and described its object as the foundation of a league, 'designed to upset the whole system of corruption and favouritism, and to introduce into public matters the energies and enterprise of private management'. Similar meetings on Administrative Reform were held by influential people throughout the country in places such as Birmingham, Derby, Sheffield, Liverpool, Aylesbury, Deptford, and Greenwich. The Government was disturbed at the strength of the movement. One newspaper pointed out that Members of Parliament realised that Layard stood for a policy which they could not denounce and they were forced to content themselves 'by trying to pick him to pieces among knots of sympathising back-biters and circles of congenial calumniators'. It was at this period that he was named by his enemies 'Mr. Lie-Hard'.

Layard was playing a lone hand, deferring to no one: 'He is the Beduin of Parliament, and finds a foe in nearly everyone who belongs to it.' His friends were increasingly worried for he was in a strange uplifted mood, unbalanced and feverish from his malaria. In a hand shaking with fever he expressed high-flown sentiments in a letter to Lady Huntly: 'Whether I perish or not in the attempt, it signifies little. I hope England is not so much in want of men as not to find plenty to fill my place. . . . Lord Palmerston is determined to rest his claims upon a class and he must make use of their sympathies and prejudices. He turns them to account in the most vulgar and discreditable manner. However, he will have his term.'

Lady Huntly was not reassured. She was a little sceptical, too, as to the significance that Henry attached to the avalanche of letters with which he was deluged from men of every class and from all over England. 'The country is heartily with me,' he told her, 'and such being the case I have no fear. If only I keep my health I shall be able to carry on the war.' A poor man offered Layard two hours a day of his labour, another wanted to form a nationwide association to advocate his principles; people dedicated books to him; a soldier wrote to say that he would need all the wisdom, prudence, and caution imaginable, otherwise he would be killed and several people wanted him to be Prime Minister. It is not surprising that Layard was moved and rather overwhelmed by these letters pouring in day after day. It seemed to him that the people of England were crying out to him for help. They were, indeed, unhappy and frustrated; they felt that Layard was fighting their battle and needed their sympathy.

'It is a good fight that you have begun', wrote Roebuck, 'and the people of England by their approbation will compensate for all the trouble and annoyance to which you will be subjected. . . . The very virulence [of the attacks] proves your importance and the efficacy of your blows at the system.' Alison wrote from Con-stantinople, 'you have got the right pig by the ear and don't let

271

him go. . . . Here are orders, counter-orders, disorders, and confusion.' Humphry Sandwith looking after the wounded in the fortress of Kars besieged by the Russians wrote, 'for God's sake don't give in and don't be muzzled by either threats or bribes'. John Forster wrote that he and Charles Dickens recommended drawing up a list of officers who were not willing to go to the Crimea: 'This would be the best answer conceivable to Palmerston's rubbish about the devotion of the aristocracy. I hope you survive this silly incivility of Palmerston's who is clearly falling into dotage.' 'We are with you sincerely in the good fight you are fighting as is everybody we most esteem', wrote Lady Eastlake. 'Rely upon it the country will stand by you', said Lord Londesborough. Others advised caution. Lady Eastnor could not help trembling since errors of judgement, slight as they were, 'might be attended with the gravest results', and Mary Huntly sent long letters of good advice. Lady Charlotte had earlier expressed admiration for Layard's boldness and countered criticisms of his indiscretions: 'one may weigh every word and every expression till one becomes a nonentity like the greater part of the rest of the world'. It was a pity that at this period she and Layard were not seeing each other for Layard disapproved of her plans to marry her son's tutor, Charles Schreiber, who was fourteen years younger than herself. It is easy to be critical of Layard for not playing his cards well but amid all the confusion and slaughter his aggressiveness and refusal to compromise was a guide and comfort to many. Sara Austen wrote to a friend: 'We have learnt both from his career to the present time & from the extreme rectitude of his character, that we must content ourselves with seconding his own views of life as far as we may be able, or of holding a light to the smaller dangers which, in his rapidity of thought and action he might overlook.' Benjamin Austen made the practical suggestion that, as Layard was clearly overworked, he should take on a secretary and named a young gentleman who was prepared to do the job, but Layard did not want to lead him into trouble, 'I am engaged in a desperate cause, the result of which is very doubtful'. He knew that others had failed who had embarked on such an enterprise—'defying the upper classes and the House of Commons, and relying entirely upon the people for support'. In spite of the warnings the gentleman was prepared to take on the job and came to live on the ground-floor of Layard's lodgings at No. 9 Ryder Street.

'The movement has now fairly commenced', Layard wrote on 3 May. *The Morning Advertiser* (which had the largest circulation after *The Times*), *The Daily News*, and the Sunday newspapers were giving him full support and every military man he spoke to admitted the facts. He decided to take an early opportunity of restating the case in the House of Commons but he wished he could see some men in whom he had perfect confidence joining him at the head of the movement.

On 18 May there was another attack on Layard but it misfired. Sir James Graham speaking from the Government benches used arguments which were so clearly untrue that Layard won sympathy in the House, as it was an obvious political manoeuvre to try to crush him. 'You may succeed in that,' said Layard, 'but you will not crush the cause with which I am identified. You shout me down because I attack a system by which you, Honourable and Gallant Members, rise in the ranks of the Army and sit in the House of Commons without encountering the dangers and fighting the battles of your country. (Cries of 'Oh! Oh!') You may hunt me down but the country will not stand it.' Sir John Pakington stated that if Layard were crushed he would have crushed himself, but Disraeli reminded the House that Layard's abilities were European in fame and that 'with his talents and excellent disposition' he would outlive the prejudices against him which, Disraeli must tell him frankly, had 'some fair foundation'. Layard was encouraged by the reception he received following the debate. Charles Dickens wrote on 20 May to say that he had been delighted to see Layard looking more cheerful, 'a young man, with the spirit of England at his back and its heartiest voice cheering him on, is bound to look his best'. He invited Layard to dinner to meet Lemon, the Editor of *Punch*, and either Leech or Tenniel, who had been drawing cartoons of Layard on such themes as the 'Nineveh Bull' being attacked by a pack of M.P.s shown as hounds. Dickens wanted the caricaturists to have an opportunity 'of making the Nineveh Bull a little more like'.[11] From Samsoun on the Black Sea Henry Ross wrote 'Your exposure of Sir James Graham's false statements, is the theme of conversation even here, and everyone is glad you defeated so well the attempt to cry you down in the House—all such attempts will harm the aristocracy and add to your strength. My prayers are with you and I have the conviction that you are destined to accomplish great changes; that in every great emergency of nations, the man necessary for the times and circumstances has been produced; that we are fast rushing to a new phase of our Constitution and that you are the crest of the popular wave, which is to sweep away the exclusiveness of privileged castes and abuses.'

Developments in England were being watched closely from the Continents of Europe and of America, for it was thought that England was working up to a revolution such as had occurred in France in 1830 and in 1848. *The New York Daily Times* wrote a leading article entitled 'The New English Reformer':

> Very many on this side of the Atlantic are watching with great anxiety the result of Mr. Layard's motion for administrative reform, to be brought before the House of Commons immediately after the May holidays. There are strong appearances of a profound political revolution in present progress through the English people. The miserable incapacity and blind stubbornness of the Aristocracy, bringing fruits of shame and disaster, have deeply aroused the public mind to the evils of the Administration. The great middle classes—the men professional, mercantile and practical—who, after all, there as everywhere else embody the real power, are rising up and in the steady moderate English way are considering turning out the nobility, as such, from office and putting, as the phrase is—'the right man in the right place'.

One of Layard's friends, Blackett, who was following the House of Commons scene from Paris and who had experience of Parliament, wrote him a long and sensible letter. He thought that the wording of the motion Layard was to bring forward on Administrative Reform was much too extensive in its range; it would gratify the vague spirit of discontent in the country, but to most in Parliament the wording would be repugnant and there was such a variety of matter that each separate set of 'time-servers' would have an excuse for deserting him and voting for the Government. Blackett hoped that Layard had secured the support of such men as Roebuck, Lowe, and Goderich; if not he advised him to reconsider his position. It was because he wanted to see Layard as Foreign Secretary that he had always been so anxious that he should keep right with the House of Commons. It was clear that he had made some very bitter personal enemies and since he did not have a large following it would be better to keep quiet for a time. Blackett agreed with Layard that while the motion might be a failure in the House it might be a success with the country:

> But that is the most dangerous ground that I could see you standing on. After all your profession is that of a Member of Parliament, by which you can rise after two or three tumbles, to a post of ministerial usefulness, and not to that of a mob agitator. Cobbett, O'Connell, Cobden have all tried to rule Parliament *out* of Parliament and have all failed. I wish for a much better career for you and therefore I have troubled you with this. In your place, I would confine myself at the present to debates on the war, diplomacy and the Crimea, on which your knowledge and power are unrivalled, and do not mix yourself up with these questions of patronage and promotion, on which the veriest blockhead, who happens to be in the Guards, is sent to floor you.[12]

On 13 June 1855, there was a second meeting of the Association for the Promotion of Administrative Reform in Drury Lane Theatre with Samuel Morley in the Chair, and he opened the meeting by explaining why the Association had been formed. He quoted the census return of 1851 showing that there were four and a half million men in England of twenty years and upwards, while at the same time there were less than a million men who had the power to vote. Such a state of things was not safe and the House of Commons was a mere sham. Layard was very well received at the beginning of his speech. He said that his experience had shown him that a speaker in the House of Commons could make wilful inaccuracies if he had a party behind him, but that a speaker who stood alone and made a blunder had to beware. He then proceeded to make a serious mistake—he accused Lord Palmerston of jesting at the sufferings of the country and of vilifying the people. He might have attacked Palmerston effectively as a Prime Minister who had shown himself opposed to enlarging the franchise, but, putting his criticism in the way he did, turned the audience against him, for Palmerston was extremely popular as a staunch patriot. When Layard brought forward his motion two days later he reminded the House of Commons that a large and powerful Association had been formed comprising men of wealth, talent, and enterprise to investigate why merit and efficiency should continue to be sacrificed to party and family influences and to a blind adherence to routine. Committees had been organised in the largest towns of the country and such an agitation might lead to great mischief, he said. If the House could remove the necessity for the agitation, it would be a service to the country. It was a long speech and many of the things he had said before, but he marshalled his arguments well and did his utmost to avoid hurting the feelings of individuals.

Sir Edward Bulwer-Lytton, M.P. for Hertfordshire, in moving an amendment considered that Layard had proved his case with regard to aristocratic privilege. Cabinets had always been drawn from a combination of families 'like a sacred caste' and they had contrived to alienate whole classes of the people and to mortify the pride of a numerous gentry, whose birth was as ancient, but who happened not to be allied to the ruling houses. At the same time he could not vote for the original motion since he considered that it was linked with the movement of Administrative Reform outside Parliament, in which he saw great danger to the fundamental principles of representative institutions. Lytton argued that the influences of party were the sinews of freedom and without these influences there might be able men in office but they would have exchanged 'the nerve and muscle of popular government for the clock-work machinery which belongs to despotism'. The outside agitation was dangerous because it was an attempt on the part of certain persons to disparage the character of the House of Commons and he regretted that a distinguished Member of Parliament and scholar should countenance it.

Near the end of the debate Palmerston rose to speak but was not prepared to discuss the subject before the House until he had expressed his anger at Layard's reference to him at the Drury Lane meeting. 'I never jested at the sufferings of the people', he shouted; 'I never made light of their unfortunate condition.' When Palmerston turned to discuss Administrative Reform he still kept to the personal note: 'When the Member for Aylesbury had charged Government with systematic disregard of talent, and a dry, dogged adherence to routine and favouritism, did he forget that he himself was a living proof of the falsehood of the charges?' He had not been made Under-Secretary of State for the Foreign Department in 1852 because of family connection or routine, said Palmerston. The then Secretary of State for Foreign Affairs, 'without any personal knowledge of the Honourable Member, acting entirely upon what he had heard of his talents and energy—which no man will dispute whatever he may think of the discretion of his conduct—brought him from being nothing but a paid Attaché at Constantinople to be Under-Secretary of State here, and proved, therefore, the recognition of merit by the Government'. It developed into an interesting debate and such enthusiasm for reform was shown on all sides of the House that Lord Malmesbury noted in his diary that while Layard's motion was defeated by a majority of three hundred and thirteen, he thought that Lord Palmerston, by adopting Sir Edward Bulwer-Lytton's amendment, had probably saved the Government from defeat.

4

'We looked to you as our champion'

The meetings of the Administrative Reformers and the debate in the Commons had influenced the Government to initiate some reforms and the movement lost much of its impetus. It no longer received the powerful support of *The Times* since Delane had decided that Layard was too emotional and aggressive to be the rising political figure that he had believed him to be.[1] Layard had also lost interest. He was working with friends in the City to organise a bank in Turkey. It absorbed a great deal of his time and energy, and for that reason, perhaps, he spoke less in debates. It is surprising, for instance, that he did not speak on the need to relieve the fortress of Kars besieged by the Russians, which was causing much concern in England. The long defence by Turkish troops virtually under the command of General Williams, against the Russian armies was being described to Layard in moving and dramatic detail by Dr. Humphry Sandwith who was in charge of the hospitals in that isolated fortress:

June 9, 1855, 11 p.m. Two Russian divisions are in full march upon us and we expect to be engaged tonight or tomorrow. . . . I hope you will make a noise about the matter. We have been shamefully treated and Lord Stratford de Redcliffe is a base traitor, who has sacrificed the honour of his country in order to indulge his own private feelings of personal animosity [against Fenwick Williams], and you may say this on my authority. He ought to be denounced. *Nothing* has been sent us, not even cavalry sabres but you know all this from my former letters.

August 5. I do hope that your thunder will be heard in the House of Commons, especially as Indian troops have not been used; they might just have turned the balance of the war.
August 21. We have now been beleaguered 65 days by a first-rate,

278

well appointed army. . . . Will you kindly let us know when our reinforcements are to arrive?

August 25. We are highly disappointed that you have not taken up our cause in Parliament. We had looked hopefully to you as our champion; no other M.P. knows anything at all about the Asia Minor question. We are forsaken now by all the world. It is true that you gave Ministers a prophetic warning of what might happen. Can you not remind them of it? But I forget at what season I am writing; it is now too late. I suppose you are all grouse-shooting now.[2]

Layard was certainly worried about the fate of his friends and he thought of trying to enter Kars, but he was afraid he would not arrive in time. During the summer of 1855 he was suffering from one of his nervous disturbances and he could not make up his mind what to do. The only certainty was that he wished to turn his back on England and have a complete change: 'It is only by the greatest exertions that I can make myself decently bearable in society.' He thought of going to Troy where he was tempted to buy a farm with the help of Calvert, the British Consul, but he finally decided to go to Italy and take comfort from pictures. He was hoping to meet his brother Arthur, who was due to return on leave from the Crimea, but Arthur had a fatal attack of dysentery on board the ship just before he was due to leave Balaclava harbour and died on 7 August. He was buried at a secluded spot near Balaclava.

Layard received this sad news in Italy. He wrote home that when he thought of the many gallant spirits who had fallen victim to the terrible war, he might have felt some consolation in the family's loss, but so many of the lives had been needlessly sacrificed. The death of Arthur and of the others had not advanced the character or honour of England: 'To me the prospect is so very hopeless and I look almost with despair upon the results of this war.' He did not think he could be any use at home and he took his Aunt Sara's advice to remain abroad. He had become interested in Italian fresco painting, 'by far the most interesting and most beautiful of the work of the great Italian painters'. They were slowly being destroyed through lack of care and in his usual methodical way he spent three months making tracings, especially in the Chapel of the Santa Maria Novella in Florence.

He returned to England at the end of the year with a good collection of copies of fresco paintings from Giotto to Fra Bartolomeo. He thought of publishing a selection as nobody knew anything about frescos; some were printed by the Arundel Society.

Layard was less interested in politics, disappointed that he had failed to win office and had not had more influence on events. The movement for Administrative Reform had petered out and, with the death of Czar Nicholas in March 1855 and the fall of Sebastopol in September, the war was soon to be concluded. 'Another year', he wrote to Kellogg in January 1856 'would have placed us in a position to have obtained some substantial concessions, which would have materially crippled Russia. As it is we leave her in a position to carry on her schemes in the East.'

He had begun to be interested in a number of enterprises. He was working hard at organising the union of the two colleges at Aberdeen and for this purpose corresponding with the Earl of Aberdeen and the Lord Advocate. In February he was re-elected Rector of Aberdeen University after the names of the Duke of Newcastle and the Lord Advocate had been withdrawn as candidates. In the same month the Ottoman Bank was founded with himself as Chairman and two of the principal private bankers in London, Messrs. Glyn and Hankey, as directors. Layard's versatility is surprising and it is impressive that, without any experience of banking, he should have been selected as head of this important new venture. Lord Stratford de Redcliffe was pleased that the Ottoman Bank had met with a most favourable reception in the City and told Layard that the field was 'spacious and full of promise'; Turkey was in need of the capital, the science and the industry of Europe 'to give her civilisation and wealth'. The Crimean War had given a great impetus to trade with the East and to investment there,* and there were many rival French

* British holdings abroad increased from about £284 million at the end of 1855 to £388 million at the end of 1860.

Praise is given for the way that the affairs of the Ottoman Bank were handled from the beginning in *Bankers and Pashas*, by David S. Landes (Heinemann, 1958) and a comment is made on the influence of Huguenots in the banking world: 'Like the Jews, they were, everywhere they went, a solvent, a force from without, intrusive, ambitious, free of the entanglements and commitments of vested interest.' An

concerns entering the market. The Sultan sanctioned the setting up of the Ottoman Bank in March but it was still necessary to obtain a charter from the British Government. At the beginning of April, Clarendon, the Foreign Secretary, congratulated Layard on the arrangements and said that he would try to accelerate the charter—'The scheme has in it the germ of great Turco-British political results.'

Layard went to Paris to carry out negotiations with French banking interests. Great efforts were being made by the giant *Crédit Mobilier* to establish a National Bank in Turkey with French influence and capital but he managed to avoid being engulfed by this very large concern and, at the same time, to obtain French backing which was of great value. Layard wrote to Mary Huntly at the beginning of April that he had been very successful in Paris and that those connected with the Ottoman Bank were highly delighted and gave him credit for being 'a great financier'—he would be pleased when the profits were such as to enable the Chairman to be paid, since so far he had been out of pocket.

Layard could not keep his thoughts entirely on banking for Humphry Sandwith's letters from Kars continued to reach him. On 1 September (1855) a wounded messenger, wrote Sandwith, had arrived from Erzerum pursued by a yelling pack of Cossacks and out of the post-bag had tumbled a letter from Layard, 'I need not say how glad I was to see your hand-writing'. On 29 September came a great battle outside the walls of the fortress and a few days later, on 4 October, he wrote to Layard:

> Our ragged, half-starved army fought splendidly and inflicted tremendous losses on the Russians; we have already buried 6,500 of the enemy. . . . We are still blockaded but we daily expect that General Mouravieff will raise the siege since his army must be ruined and demoralised. . . . You will be glad to hear of the glorious finale of our campaign which began so gloomily.

But they had to surrender at the end of November for no reinforcements came, the Russians did not withdraw, and provisions

account of the formation and rise of the Ottoman Bank and the part played by Layard is given in *Banking and Politics in the Near East*, by A. S. J. Baster (P. S. King, 1935).

were running short. The Russian Commander-in-Chief, General Mouravieff, praised the garrison for its gallantry and behaved generously. Fenwick Williams was taken to Moscow and Dr. Sandwith was allowed to go free. Arriving in London in January 1856 he went straight to Layard in Ryder Street. 'He was glad to see me, but when I told him that I had the best part of a book in MS. he became quite excited, jumped up and said: "Come along to Murray, he lives close by."' Within a few months the book was published, widely read, and well reviewed by *The Times*.[3]

Peace was signed in Paris on 30 March 1856 and General Fenwick Williams returned to England where he was given a hero's welcome. He was made a Knight Commander of the Order of the Bath, received the Freedom of the City of London, an Honorary D.C.L. Degree of Oxford, and voted one thousand pounds a year for life by Parliament. Layard considered the whole thing overdone; the British Government and the people were delighted to have a hero to fête after the disasters of the Crimean War and he referred to 'the disgraceful Williams' humbug, for which I blame the British public more than the hero'. Layard's friends wrote to say that he was the right person to bring forward a motion to express admiration for the gallantry of the defenders and criticism of the Government for allowing Kars to fall. They had not realised that he had other views. The motion was brought forward by Mr. Whiteside on 26 April and the debate lasted for three days. When Layard rose to speak, everyone expected him to support it, but he startled and shocked his radical friends by taking the side of the Government, even praising Lord Panmure, Minister for War, for having deceived the House of Commons the previous summer by saying that the Turkish position in Asia was perfectly secure. He added that if he had been in Lord Panmure's place he would have said the same: 'Why, if Lord Panmure had said that the garrison was starving, that it had no provisions, no artillery, no money, he would only have encouraged Mouravieff to persevere in the siege.' Bulwer-Lytton said sarcastically 'The Member for Aylesbury, who rarely speaks without some, doubtless, just but complimentary allusion to his own peculiar frankness and honesty . . . thinks a British Minister justified in deceiving Parliament!'

Layard then launched into the still more perilous sea of defending Lord Stratford de Redcliffe, who was generally considered to have been gravely at fault. 'The great offender in this matter was Lord Stratford de Redcliffe', said Mr. Maguire, 'and in attempting to justify his conduct, the Honourable Member for Aylesbury has inflicted a heavy blow upon his own public character—a character which he had made by courage and independence.' Whiteside concluded by attacking the Administrative Reformers as mock patriots saying he was surprised that they were not to have Layard's vote, for, 'if there was any member who was bound by his antecedent declarations to vote for such a motion, it was the Honourable Gentleman'.

Layard believed that once Aberdeen had decided not to help the Turks in Asia, as a diversion to the Sebastopol siege, it was too late to defend Kars and Fenwick Williams should have fallen back on Erzerum as he had been told to do. He knew that many British and Turks in Constantinople considered that Williams had shown, as Layard wrote to John Murray, 'the greatest incompetency and acted so diametrically against his orders that he ought to be tried by a court-martial'.[4] It is difficult, however, to give a satisfactory explanation of Layard's attitude to the debate, whatever he may have thought about the rights and wrongs of defending Kars. He had lost interest in attacking the Government once the war was over and he had begun to learn that it was a mistake to make enemies of the politically powerful but in adopting this entirely new approach he made no attempt to explain himself. He overdid support for the Government, just as previously he had been too bitter in his attacks. He lost his radical friends, who had admired his courage and had supported him as a leader, without gaining new ones. Some accused this 'Administrative Reformer' of wanting to keep on good terms with Clarendon and Stratford de Redcliffe in order to make money out of the Ottoman Bank, while others said that he had been jealous of General Sir Fenwick Williams ever since the days of the Turco-Persian Boundary Commission, but these are too simple and cynical as explanations.

There is much that is difficult to explain in Layard's character. He was consistent in his passion for individual liberty and in his desire to help the oppressed, but he had his own ideas of what

was meant. 'As a Liberal I am of the school of Mr. Grote, who
hated injustice and intolerance under whatever shape or colour.'
So vague a definition was suitable to a writer such as Grote, but
not for a politician. Layard's friend Sir Henry Bulwer, the elder
brother of Edward Bulwer-Lytton, the novelist, warned him:
'A man may be as Liberal as he pleases without injuring an
official career, if his Liberalism is of a kind that grooves in with
the Liberalism of others.' Layard, however, was not prepared to
follow the cynical Bulwer, who told him: 'I have always tried
to emulate Voltaire in my diplomacy who dedicated his plays to
a Pope whilst attacking the Church, and corresponded with
sovereigns whilst he waged war against absolute powers.'

Layard often appeared inconsistent, switching from one profession to another for what seemed to be motives of self-interest,
but he was not concerned so much with having a profession as
in having an interest. He was the true amateur, mastering many
different aspects of life, coming as near to the Greek ideal of the
complete man as any Victorian was able to do. After achieving
more in five years of archaeology than anyone before or since,
he ceased to take much interest in what others were doing in
the Assyrian field; having been passionately interested in politics,
he abruptly turned his mind to banking and found it equally
absorbing. He did not appear to realise that there were likely to
be inconsistencies, or, if he did, he saw no reason to give explanations. It seemed sometimes as if he changed his much talked of
principles with his job, and many of his political opponents
believed this to be the case. By temperament a creative artist, he
was more suited to saving Assyrian monuments and Italian
frescos than to the life of politics. He was ambitious, but not
prepared to compromise, and he was more interested in discovering and proclaiming 'Truth' than in achieving personal
success. 'You have even thought more of truth than of its consequences', complained Horsman. Of course that was so—had not
his Huguenot forebears on St. Bartholomew's Day been prepared
to think more of their Protestant faith than of saving their lives?
He was much influenced by his Huguenot background and in
his *Autobiography* he gives an account of the various members
of the Layard family who escaped from France and settled in
England. Writing of his school days in France, when he was

mercilessly bullied as a Protestant and a heretic, he said: 'I have
a better right and title than most people to the credit of having
been a martyr for my religion's sake.' He was not referring to
religious faith for he had little of that, but he was defending his
own idea of 'Truth', which was an individualistic interpretation
of the Huguenot tradition. When he said as a young man in
Constantinople that Aberdeen must come to realise that he,
Layard, had been right about Serbia, he meant that Aberdeen
would come to see the Truth. When he told Henry Ross 'I am
right and that is a great thing', it meant that he had kept to his
idea of Truth and had not compromised. But had he not compromised when he said, during the Kars debate, that a Minister was
justified in deceiving Parliament? Not according to his own
reckoning—he was expressing a common-sense point of view that
in war-time certain subterfuges were permissible. He had earlier
been in favour of the reports from the Crimea being published
in *The Times*, for it was only through pressure from the Press
and the public that he thought Ministers could be made to do
their duty; but at the same time he realised the dangers. A year
before the Kars debate he had said in the Commons: 'The public
demand to be told what the British generals look like in their
uniforms, so that in the next battle about eight generals are
killed; they want to be told what reliefs are being sent up and
in what strength and what are the positions of the guns before
Sebastopol and how many rounds they have to fire.' As a result
of the 'electric telegraph' the information contained in *The
Times* and other newspapers arrived in St. Petersburg the same
day and was immediately transmitted to the Russian Commander-
in-Chief in Sebastopol. No one had thought of censorship and
the only plan put forward was to try to prevent *The Times*'
correspondent, William Russell, from drawing rations on the
army! The same arguments applied to the siege of Kars.

Layard with his intelligence and experience was nearly always
right and he believed that all that was required was time for
others to come round to his point of view; but he was not very
persuasive. He did not speak in Parliament in a contemporary
idiom and his thinking was slightly foreign. No member of
Parliament, for instance, was prepared to approve his proposal,
borrowed from the French Revolution, that the Crimean military

confusion should be cleared up by the despatch of Commissars. Layard's very strong patriotism was sometimes in conflict with his high sense of moral purpose and he might not have accepted the distinction made by his friend Camille Cavour: 'If we did for ourselves what we do for our country what rascals we would be.' Layard wanted quick results and was bored with the game of manoeuvring people which was intensely interesting to some-one like Disraeli who remained a novelist, studying the vagaries of human character, even when he became a professional politician. Layard judged people by their actions, according to their patriotism, their views on Russia and Turkey, and their attitude to himself. If he had been interested to find out what prompted people to hold views contrary to his own, he would have been less aggressive and have discouraged them from coming to wrong conclusions as to the reasons for his own actions. 'I wish all the world knew you as well as we do', wrote Virginia Eastnor, 'and they would never mistrust your motives.'

5

India during the Mutiny

Frederick Layard, a captain in the Indian army, wrote to his brother from Berhampore in Bengal in June 1857 a month after the Mutiny had broken out saying that all was quiet there at the moment but no precautions had been taken in case of a rising: 'Just the way with English people; afraid of being thought to be afraid and so do nothing. . . . A fearful crisis has come upon us which will lead to great changes in the country and its constitution. We are but a handful at the mercy of armed and trained mercenaries.' Henry Layard abandoned the holiday he had planned in Italy and decided to go to India to judge for himself 'before forming any very decided opinions.' As usual, however, he had already formed some definite opinions.

The Liberal Government had been defeated because of its aggressive action in China and Persia and Layard, with many Liberals, had voted against what he described as the 'Palmerston doctrine'—'that in dealing with Eastern nations we are not bound by the same laws of right and wrong that govern the relations of Christian States'. The electorate, however, liked the 'doctrine'. Palmerston was returned and Layard, with many others, lost his seat. In his farewell speech to the Aylesbury constituency he argued vehemently against the hysterical demands for revenge in India which came from *The Times* and other newspapers. It was not vengeance that the British Government should look for, he said, but the reconstitution of an empire—'the bringing together of those who govern and those who are governed. Hitherto nothing has been done towards that.' He hoped that India, instead of being under the East India Company, would become an integral part of Her Majesty's dominions so that there could be good government. Mary Huntly wanted force used to suppress the religion of the country. 'Are we to hold the Bible in one hand and the sword in the other?' Layard replied. 'If so, what can we say to the Turks and other Eastern nations who would oppress Christians?'[1]

Delhi had been occupied by the rebels but recaptured in September 1857. Mutiny had broken out in Lucknow; Cawnpore had fallen and the wretched British men, women, and children, who had been given safe conduct by Nana Sahib and Azimollah Khan, had been massacred in their houses and in their boats on the Ganges. It was typical of Layard that he should decide to go at such a time, and that he should want to see India as an Indian and not as a European—'we never get the Indian story'. He thought, rather naïvely, that he was going to travel as he used to do in the East—'buy a pony, throw a pair of bags over the saddle and go straight on trusting Providence and my good management'. When he arrived in Bombay in November 1857 he was given the luxurious hospitality that Indians give to a distinguished visitor. He was met by a large crowd of eminent Bombay citizens, put in a fine house with several servants, and when he went out he was accompanied by sepoys and horsemen. After a fortnight in such luxury he went to Poona and from there to Hyderabad. Travelling was slow and expensive. He had to hire a palanquin with twelve bearers who carried him about twenty-four miles a day, while his servants came in bullock carts and on ponies. 'My plans for travelling as free from encumbrances and luggage as I used to do in Turkey were soon upset', he admitted and by the time he reached Moominabad, near Aurangabad, at the beginning of January 1858 he had acquired an enormous escort which he was forced to have by the Minister of the Nizam of Hyderabad and the British Resident. There was an elephant and a pony for his own use, a group of cavalry and a suite, members of which had their own retinue of servants and camels.

This leisurely way of travelling, however, enabled him to read books about India during the heat of the day and to make contact with the people in the country districts. A young Brahmin, a scholar of Elphinstone College in Bombay, had agreed to accompany him as guide and interpreter and proved very useful —'a kind of Rassam'. Layard found the country still in a very

disturbed state, but he considered that the really formidable part
of the rebellion was over by the autumn. The British had had
a narrow escape; in the part of India that he had visited, he
considered that the sympathy of the people had been with the
rebels. He wrote to the Austens at the beginning of 1858 that it
was not difficult to understand the causes of the general hatred
of British rule. It was partly deserved and partly undeserved and
would have existed in almost any circumstances.

> We differ from the people in everything which might form a
> bond of sympathy between a conquered people and their rulers;
> in language, religion, manners, habits and feelings. We have done
> nothing to form any other bond of sympathy, or to create mutual
> interests. The people we govern are treated like a distinct race,
> inferior to us—more, indeed, as if they were of a lower order of
> creatures. . . . They are excluded from all share of government,
> they can never rise to anything beyond the most inferior posts.
>
> We are endeavouring to force upon them our old worn-out
> judicial system, with all its technicalities and delays, which we are
> gradually ridding ourselves of at home, and which is infinitely
> more odious to them than it could ever be to us. We have Sanitary
> Commissioners and Boards interfering with all their private and
> domestic affairs; no doubt, all for their own good, although they
> won't so understand it. We are meddling with customs which are
> of no real importance and yet are clung to with extraordinary
> tenacity by the people. We are breaking faith in the most scandalous
> manner with native princes, and annexing their territories. We
> are suddenly demanding proof of title to lands one hundred years
> back, and seizing, in the most arbitrary manner, men's papers and
> title-deeds. . . .
>
> All we have really given them in return is perfect security, and
> this is certainly a great boon! Under it, money-lenders and fat
> Parsees and Baboos can make their fortunes and enjoy them; but
> the cultivators—and there is no one else in India, our rule having
> utterly destroyed the native gentry—are reduced to the utmost
> poverty. We have done nothing to bring the people to us.

Layard managed to find out a great deal about India during
the few months that he was there, having, as usual, built up an
excellent intelligence service. He had written to officials throughout the country to obtain information on specific subjects and
there were hundreds of letters in reply giving him the facts,

but many of the statements he made in his letters home about the general hatred of the British were too sweeping, nor did he allow sufficiently for the great difficulties with which British administrators were faced. 'Do not judge hastily of native feeling against the Government', wrote his brother Frederick, 'it is a difficult question to decide in a hurried visit.' After twenty years' service in India, and having had much intercourse with the villagers in out-of-the-way places, Frederick said he had not found that there was hatred of the Government. Edward Irving, working in education, wrote that he had come out to India with clear ideas on points that seemed very doubtful to him after some time in the country: 'I had a romantic faith in the native which has gone.'

One of the District Officers described in long and interesting letters the difficulties of eradicating the extraordinary beliefs and superstitions among the country people. He told Layard that the Indian women were for a long time in a panic because they believed that the European magistrates had ordered two silver bowls, the size of half a cocoa-nut, and with these the breasts of all the women in the district were to be measured.

> Any woman whose breasts could not be got within the bowls was to be fined and taken away to the Sahib—those 'too full in bud for puritannic stays' and nursing mothers left their homes and hid themselves for days before their fears could be removed. When any of your friends talk of Europeanising the native mind, tell them this story and add that this district has been for years under the most enlightened magistrates—Outram, French, Evans and Keatinge—all of whom were personally known to the greater portion of the people.

When Layard returned to London in May 1858 after six months in India he spoke to a crowded meeting in St. James's Hall, Piccadilly. He argued that the rebellion had been the act of the people of India; the story of the greased cartridges covered in pig's fat had been the excuse and the war with Persia the opportunity. At Benares he had seen a number of essays written by pupils in the schools on the origin of the mutiny, and all had given as the principal causes the annexations of territory and the treatment of natives. He pointed out that the Governor-General Lord Dalhousie had annexed a territory with fifteen million inhabitants—more than one-half the population of the British Isles—in violation of a treaty. Another cause of the rebellion, he argued, had been the interference by the British with the religion and customs of the natives, especially the abolition of the law of adoption, which had been the great complaint of Nana Sahib.

Charlotte Schreiber attended the meeting and considered Layard's speech 'eloquent and moderate', but that was not the opinion of the British in India. His brother Frederick wrote that reports of the speech had raised a cry of indignation throughout India and the English Press there had taken it up most violently. Frederick found that the people he knew in Berhampore could not bring themselves to discuss the speech with him. He made the same complaint as others had—that before reaching his admirable conclusions his brother exaggerated so much and out-raged the feelings of so many people that he spoilt the effect. Frederick said that Henry was wrong in stating that no Euro-peans were kind to natives in the Provinces; it was untrue that there had been no mutilations of Europeans, nor should he have said that the way in which the Europeans had treated the natives justified the atrocious treachery and brutal massacre at Cawnpore—a statement that had caused 'a great sensation!' Frederick thought that there were many things that Henry could have said in criticism of the British in India without turning 'the whole European community of this country against you, as you have done, by publishing reports and statements furnished by others and unauthenticated'. In the main Frederick agreed with him and was not surprised that the British were hated and detested: 'the only wonder is that the whole nation does not rise and exterminate us. We are as oil to water out here; luckily we are the oil and remain at the top.' Frederick was as eager as his brother to help the country people and he described what great improvements could be carried out by making use of the enormous water power of the country, but the East India Com-pany's policy was then to be interested only in immediate returns.

Layard was attacked by the English Press in India but was deluged with letters from Indians who were delighted that some-one 'spoke the truth'. It was a melancholy fact of human weak-ness, he wrote to the Marquis of Huntly, that power made even the civilised Englishman 'cruel, overbearing, and indifferent to the sufferings of others'. In July 1858 he published an article in *The Quarterly Review* which Frederick thought excellent. In it he emphasised the aloofness of British rule in India and how different it was from the rule of other invaders. The Moslems had looked upon the country as their future home and adopted the manners, prejudices, and laws of the country; but the English had formed cantonments, sometimes three or four miles from the native city, and these had become little colonies in which 'the fashions and manners of London and Paris are aped with a punctiliousness unknown even in the most formal capital of Europe'. When they first arrived it was true that the British had adopted in many respects the habits of the country, marrying Indian women and participating in Indian festivals and sport: 'Then it would have been impossible for a whole army to mutiny without some information having been conveyed to its officers, nor would those officers have been butchered without pity or mercy.'

Layard found it difficult to stand again for Parliament because of the expense; the constituency of Chester wanted him to put down five hundred pounds, and he stood for York but just failed to be returned. For some time to come, wrote Harriet Grote, he would have to be John the Baptist, 'content to bawl in the wilderness'. At the end of 1860, however, he achieved a great success in being returned to Parliament for the large working-class district of the important Borough of Southwark. Elizabeth Eastlake wrote to Sara Austen to say how glad she was and that her husband had rushed up the stairs 'hurrahing' and could not have been more glad if it had been his own nephew; 'and now, dear Mrs. Austen, let us hope that with no less independence of feeling he may exercise a little more discretion, & find that more is to be done by gentle means than by violence'.

Layard was delighted to be back in the fray and it was not long before his abusiveness angered both the Liberal Lord John Russell and the Tory Lord Derby. On practical matters, such as the reorganisation of the British Museum, which suffered from being administered by a Board of forty-eight Trustees, he was admirable, and was working with his friend William Gregory to try to introduce order. The South Kensington Museum, which was intended for science, had the cartoons of Raphael and a number of pictures by Reynolds; there were pictures in the British Museum and Turner drawings in a damp shed. There was, wrote Layard, an incongruous herd of sphinxes, Assyrian bulls and bearded men in the cellars, while other groups 'shivered beneath the damp and chilly classic portico'. In an article in *The Quarterly Review* in April 1859 he wrote: 'We obstinately continue to think only of the outside of our public edifices; we persist in raising Greek temples, Palladian Palaces and Mediaeval townhalls for museums, institutions, and public offices, without reference to what they are to contain, to the purposes for which they may be required, or to the comfort and convenience of those who are to use them.'

Palmerston's Government in 1860 appointed a Committee to enquire into the arrangements of the British Museum; William Gregory, M.P. for County Galway, was Chairman and recommended the adoption of Mr. Layard's 'grand idea to have one great Central Hall of Antiquities', which would enable the visitor to see history develop through Ancient Egypt, Assyria, Greece, and Rome. But none of their fine schemes succeeded because Gladstone, as Chancellor of the Exchequer, wanted rigid economy. The Ottoman Bank was progressing well under Layard's practical and efficient control, and he had begun to make money as Chairman. He studied the political developments on the Continent and was regarded in the House of Commons as an expert on Italy as well as on Turkey. It was a new experience for Layard to find himself in agreement with Palmerston, the Prime Minister, and Lord John Russell, the Foreign Minister, who were pursuing a liberal policy in Europe, and they were pleased that Layard should be giving the Government his able support. While his old companion Bright was describing British foreign policy as nothing but 'a gigantic system of relief for the aristocracy', Layard kept silent. He had become an orthodox and effective parliamentarian and his speeches on Italy and Turkey were, said *The Morning Post*, the best in the House.

In July 1861 Lord John Russell was made an Earl and went to the House of Lords, so that Palmerston needed a strong spokesman for the Foreign Office in the Commons. He chose Layard. The Queen, however, could not forgive his radicalism; she considered that he was passionate and inaccurate and she must have heard that his enemies called him Mr. Lie-Hard. In a letter of 22 July, she told Palmerston that she did not want Layard: 'In the contact with foreign countries we should be represented by a thorough gentleman' and she thought that on further reflection, Lord Palmerston would agree that the appointment 'would not be conducive to the public good'. In a letter the following day Palmerston pressed the case hard: 'He is a very able and active-minded man, has shown himself when Under-Secretary to Lord Granville at the Foreign Office to be a very good man of departmental business, is very efficient as a speaker and debater in the House of Commons, and is very conversant with all the affairs of Europe of late years'. As to communication with Foreign Ministers, 'his manners in personal intercourse are conciliatory and agreeable', he therefore hoped the appointment could be agreed. Her Majesty was not to be moved and replied at once that she recognised the importance of parliamentary exigencies, 'but the Queen cannot sacrifice to them the higher interests of the country'. Palmerston argued further and took the matter up with the Prince Consort but the Queen still held out and went so far as to say that the appointment 'would be a serious evil'. She did, however, give Palmerston an opening, though she did not expect him to take it:

> If Lord Palmerston, on sincere self-examination, should consider that without it [the appointment] the difficulties of carrying on his Government are such as to endanger the continuance of its success, the Queen will, of course, have to admit one evil for the country in order to avert a greater. She still trusts, however, that, knowing the nature of the Queen's objections, he will not place her in this dilemma.

Palmerston was not prepared to let the Queen interfere for a second time over Layard's appointment. He thanked her for her 'gracious and condescending acquiescence', which made the Queen and Prince Albert very annoyed.[2] Layard was made Under-Secretary for Foreign Affairs at the end of July 1861. Prince Albert died in December and Queen Victoria started her long period of mourning.

THE SOUTHWARK RACE ᴏʀ WHO'S TO WIN?

'Collared and harnessed'

Harriet Grote approved of the appointment. She told Layard
that there was still 'too much of the Beduin' left in him, and that
the best thing for him was 'to be collared and harnessed and
regularly set to work'. Sara Austen was very excited and talked
about the day when he would become Prime Minister. Benjamin
Austen, who had been ill, died a month after his nephew's
appointment, leaving twenty to thirty thousand pounds to Sara
and £500 to his nephew. Layard had remained convinced that
he would be his uncle's heir, and was much disappointed. Sara
at the age of seventy was still a very formidable woman and
would not have allowed her husband to make her dependent on
her nephew, devoted as she was to him.

Layard was too busy to worry about personal matters; there

was important work to do and he developed in stature and assurance. Palmerston and Russell trusted his judgement and during the late summer, when Ministers went to their country estates, he was often left on his own at the Foreign Office to deal with the many problems. 'I shall never get through this mass of papers', wrote Russell, 'I leave it entirely to your discretion.' That was a situation Layard enjoyed. Italy was moving towards independence, there was trouble between France and Prussia, the Schleswig-Holstein affair, the American Civil War, and an awkward situation in Abyssinia.* After policy had been decided Layard had to write to the diplomatic representatives abroad—to Lord Cowley in Paris, Sir Charles Elliot in Vienna, Sir Henry Bulwer who had succeeded Lord Stratford de Redcliffe in Constantinople, and to the representatives in America and elsewhere. All the outgoing and incoming despatches from Embassies, Legations, and Consulates were written by hand. Lord Cowley's writing must have been a trial to all of them and Russell's spidery hand was not always easy to read. It is not surprising that Palmerston, who wrote boldly and clearly, should have burst out occasionally in despair—'more a foot than a hand!' Layard's writing, which was generally very clear, became almost illegible as he tried to keep up with the correspondence. 'Yours is the most illegible writing I know', said Richard Cobden; 'I suppose you learned it among the cuneiform inscriptions.' They were all overwhelmed at times and even Palmerston, who retained his jauntiness at the age of seventy-eight, sometimes lost patience, complaining that it was impossible for him to deal with despatches just as he was stepping into his carriage to go to the House of Commons: 'Whatever hour at which I go, the Foreign Office continues to send me such a box, just at that time, and to mark it *immediate*.' Working close to Palmerston, Layard had learned to appreciate 'his great powers of mind and had found him the kindest and most considerate of chiefs in the House of Commons'.

Considering the amount of work that Layard had to do it is

* When Layard left his post of Under-Secretary after five years, he took away many official documents and memoranda with comments by Palmerston, Russell, Gladstone, and others which fill many large volumes in the Layard Papers.

remarkable that he still managed to write an occasional article. One on Pompeii in *The Quarterly* pleased Odo Russell, British Agent at the Vatican: 'What a wonderful man you are to find time for everything, and how I envy you that great and rare faculty.' Layard helped people whenever he could; his efforts to improve the pay and conditions of British Consuls in the Middle East and elsewhere earned him many letters of thanks. David Livingstone wanted him to make sure that the British Navy should issue to the sailors of ships off the East coast of Africa a medicine of his own concoction against African fever, * and also wanted a document from the Sultan of Zanzibar; Kinglake asked him to help a friend become 'Paper stainer and Decorator to the King of Italy'; Leighton, travelling to the East, required letters of introduction; Ruskin wanted to know where to find a particular fresco; and Lady Eastlake asked his advice about purchasing pictures for the National Gallery as her husband was ill. Sarah Austin, the wife of John Austin, asked him to arrange for the proofs of her daughter's book (Lady Duff Gordon's *Letters from Egypt*) to be sent to her in Cairo. Lady Duff Gordon's daughter, Janet, who had married Henry Ross, suddenly appeared at the Foreign Office to ask for Layard's help; the bank in Egypt of which Ross was a director had run into difficulties as a result of the extravagances of the Khedive Ismail, and Ross himself was seriously ill.

Although Layard had resigned from the chairmanship of the Ottoman Bank when he had been made Under-Secretary, he was attacked by his political opponents on the charge of using his official position to help the bank. He was also accused of supporting liberty in Italy, while encouraging the Turks to suppress it in the Ottoman Empire. Edward Freeman said contemptuously that Layard's liberalism was 'geographical'. William Gregory attacked Layard in the House of Commons on the same grounds:

> The assailant of Italian priests, the advocate of Italian independence, the denouncer of those who oppressed the ryots of Bengal,

* Palmerston was angry because the prescription was turned down by the reports of 'prejudiced and jealous medical men' overruling Dr. Livingstone's practical experience—'If this is not red-tapeism, I know not what it is', said the Prime Minister.

was the same man who now cast scorn and contumely on these unfortunate Christians [of the Ottoman Empire] who wished to do no more than the Italians were doing. He would fain have England believe that the Turkish Government was mild and beneficent, and that Turkey was a capital field for the profitable investment of capital.

Gregory and Layard, however, remained close friends, 'there never arose a cloud over our intimate and friendly relations', said Gregory.[1] But there was a cloud over.Layard's relations with Humphry Sandwith who had disliked his attitude in the Kars debate and agreed with Gregory and others who were against the Turks. He sent Gregory a quotation from a recently published book on Turkish law showing how bitterly non-Moslems were regarded by the Turks, which was used in a speech in the House. Sandwith had anticipated 'that Layard would sneer at it and say that the passage was as misleading as a similar one would be from the laws of Queen Elizabeth against the Catholics, and that in these modern times all was changed and that any sort of persecution was obsolete', and therefore he wrote a letter to Cobden stating that the principles of the book were in full vigour in all the remote parts of the Ottoman Empire. After Layard had spoken on the lines that Sandwith had envisaged, Cobden made an effective reply quoting from the letter amid laughter. 'I fancy Layard never forgave this', said Sandwith.

Layard dealt with such attacks much more calmly than he had in the past, but every now and again he could not help revealing his dislike for politics. In one speech he attacked a member of the Opposition for entering 'the dirty arena of politics'. Earl Russell did not care for the expression at all. 'What is this "dirty arena"?' he asked. 'Is it the arena in which all our great men have fought? . . . I do not like to have my profession and years depreciated. It is one of the noblest in the whole circle of human employments and arts.'[2] 'Politics', Layard considered, 'is a fight between parties without principles and ready to sacrifice anything for power.'

It was, however, a new Layard who faced the House of Commons almost every evening to deal with some point of foreign policy. *The Times* in a leading article on Layard quoted the poet: 'That men may rise on stepping-stones of their dead

selves to higher things. . . . The most merciless of critics has
become the most versatile of apologists; the most dashing of
assailants has shown himself a master in the tamer arts of
defence. . . . Though we cannot help smiling at his altered tone
and official complacency, we should be the last to reproach him
with it as a fault.' At the beginning of 1864 Layard wrote a letter
to Sir Augustus Paget, the British Representative in Copenhagen,
which he certainly would not have written ten years earlier.
Emotion had been increasing in England and the Continent over
the dispute concerning Schleswig-Holstein, which the King of
Denmark wished to incorporate into his territory and which
Bismarck intended to make part of Germany. Paget expressed
himself very violently in a despatch to the Foreign Office in
defence of Denmark and in abuse of Prussia. Layard explained
to Paget that he had edited the despatch in order to avoid trouble
with Germany:

> We think that strong expressions, such as 'common sewer',
> 'perfidy' etc. etc. applied to Germany could only weaken the cause
> of Denmark. When a man or a country is in the right, the more
> calmly his case is stated the better. We have therefore struck out
> those expressions. . . . I can easily understand that amidst the very
> natural excitement and irritation, which prevail at Copenhagen,
> you may forget for a moment that the first duty of a Minister of
> the Queen is to consider what is necessary for the great and para-
> mount interests of her Realm.

It was an interesting letter for the emotional Layard to write and
an annoying one for a diplomat to receive.

The Danes counted on the help of England and went to war
with Prussia. Public opinion was on the side of the Danes and
Palmerston had made a speech (23 July 1863) in which he seemed
to imply that if anyone interfered with Denmark's rights
England would come to her aid. England, however, did nothing
and Denmark had to give up the Duchies and pay an indemnity.
On 4 July 1864 Disraeli moved a resolution condemning the
Government for having failed to maintain their avowed object
of upholding the integrity and independence of Denmark. The
Government's case was weak and Disraeli had no difficulty in
making a most effective speech. Layard spoke on the third night
and Lord Palmerston, at the age of seventy-nine, made his last

great speech. The Government was just saved by a majority of eighteen. Layard wrote to Sara Austen on 8 July:

> We had a great triumph last night. The scene was indescribable, and such as the House of Commons has not seen since the excitement of the Reform Bill. Men waved their hats and handkerchiefs, cheered, rushed round Lord Palmerston to shake his hand and a great crowd waited in Westminster Hall and in Palace Yard to greet the old gentleman as he came out. It is most gratifying to me to find that both sides of the House declared that my speech was the best and most telling delivered during the debate. . . . Dizzy was very angry and had nothing to say in answer but a foolish joke about Nineveh bulls.

Layard often rated his own abilities highly, but it was indeed a very good speech and it was thought that it had saved the Government. Earl Russell was so delighted he sent two letters of congratulation. Lord Napier, the Ambassador at St. Petersburg, wrote 'to deliver such a speech to such an audience on such an occasion must really be a triumph of intellectual satisfaction, such a triumph as we poor votaries of the silent craft can never know'. Bulwer, who read the speech in Constantinople, was not quite so enthusiastic; though he praised Layard for his ease and copiousness in speaking, he told him that he sometimes diverged from his good humour 'into using a much stronger expression than the case justified; what I will call impertinences. Sharp things which don't crush, or inflict a deep or dangerous wound, but which sting and create a bad feeling towards you.' He thought that Layard should consider more carefully what he should leave out—'It is not necessary to say everything.'[3]

'There is always a great deal of talent in Bulwer's letters', wrote Earl Russell, 'but a great deal of sensitive jealousy also.' Bulwer was under criticism for encouraging a project for a loan by a British group of financiers instead of persuading the Turkish Government to make use of their own bank—the Ottoman Bank which Layard had helped to start and was now called the Imperial Ottoman Bank. Bulwer denied helping the rival project and considered that Layard had been much too warm in defending his old protégé, thus exposing himself to attack: 'Had I been disposed to treat you as an enemy, I believe I could have done you considerable harm.' Layard also criticised

Bulwer because he had bought the island of Plati (Yassiada), which he eventually sold to the Viceroy Ismail of Egypt for nearly forty thousand pounds. 'He ought never to have had the island at all', wrote Earl Russell to Layard; nor did Russell think that he should have sold it to the Viceroy 'and thus mixed public with private interests. . . . Bulwer has been a very clever and sagacious ambassador. He will now quietly retire.' Layard had to write to tell him and Bulwer replied in a twenty-five page letter which was passed to Russell and Palmerston but there was no change in the decision. Bulwer retired to Hyères in France feeling that he had been treated badly by the Government and by Layard. He amused himself by reading biography, 'the more entertaining and instructive part of history', by looking through his memoirs, which 'astonished him for their interest', and by commenting shrewdly and sometimes maliciously on Layard's progress in public life. Bulwer watched with interest how Layard and Russell would deal with the problem of the European subjects in Abyssinia who had been imprisoned and chained by the leg on the orders of the Emperor Theodore. At one time there were as many as fifteen Europeans imprisoned. Among these were Captain Duncan Cameron, the British Consul in Abyssinia, and the Reverend Henry Stern, agent of the London Society for Promoting Christianity among the Jews, and a number of German Protestants. At first there was confidence that Palmerston, who had made Europe resound with his defence of Don Pacifico, and Layard, who so often talked of prestige, would deal firmly with the Emperor but it was not easy to deal with Theodore for he was far away and a little mad. One explorer after another offered advice or his services—Samuel Baker, Dr. Charles Beke, Gifford Palgrave, and others. Layard, who in his young days had railed at the British Government for their 'infamous' conduct in not sending to rescue Stoddart and Conolly from the Emir of Bokhara, now used that as a precedent for not sending an army to rescue the prisoners in Abyssinia. It was a very difficult situation for the Government. Sir Hugh Cairns, Lord Chelmsford and others urged that more decisive action should be taken. Bulwer wrote to Layard:

> How miserable, shabby, paltry our whole conduct. A housemaid of the defunct Britannia would have been ashamed of it. If I was

but well I would engage to hang Theodore—nothing less would
satisfy me—and nothing less will render our travellers safe and
our name respected in those parts.

The Government had sent a one-man mission with a letter
from Queen Victoria to the Emperor of Abyssinia—a very belated
reply to a letter from Theodore which got mislaid between the
Foreign Office and the India Office. Layard was personally
involved in the mission for the man chosen was his old friend
Hormuzd Rassam, now assistant to the British Political Officer
in Aden. Rassam had been chosen as he had shown his competence
on missions from Aden to Zanzibar. There was, however, much
criticism of the choice because he had been born a subject of
the Ottoman Empire and the Emperor Theodore considered the
Turk as his principal enemy, for he was cut off from the sea by
the Turkish occupation of Massowah and Zeilah, while to the
west and north Egyptian forces seemed to threaten him from
the Sudan.

Rassam had been sent by ship from Aden to Massowah whence
he was due to go into the interior as soon as an invitation came
from the Emperor of Abyssinia, but the months passed and there
was no invitation. Layard received frequent letters from Rassam
complaining of the harm done by the British Press in its criticisms of Theodore. None of the reasons put forward in London
for the failure to obtain the invitation was correct, said Rassam ;
no one, in fact, could account 'for the foolish actions of a mad
man, except that Providence did not bless him with a right
mind'. Layard tried to encourage Rassam by telling him that
he must not mind what the newspapers said, 'The more honest
a man is and the better he does his duty, the more they abuse
him.' A series of letters from Henry Stern to his wife in England
describing the terrible sufferings they were undergoing was
published in the Press, and caused an outcry. Layard, as spokesman for the Government, was accused of showing indifference
to the sufferings of Christians. There was resentment that Russell
and Layard should put the blame for what had happened on the
shoulders of Captain Cameron, a prisoner. It was argued that
Cameron should have gone direct to Massowah as ordered,
instead of going for several months into Egyptian territory in
the north which made Theodore suspicious that he was intriguing

with his enemies. There had been a change in Government policy and it is doubtful if Cameron realised it. When first appointed Consul in Abyssinia in 1860, after serving in Turkey under Sir Fenwick Williams, he had been encouraged to make a treaty with Theodore, as an independent sovereign. When, however, the French began to be active on the Red Sea Coast and in Abyssinia, Palmerston decided to counter French influence by encouraging the Turks and Egyptians to become more firmly established along the Somali coast at places such as Massowah and Zeila. As the Sultan of Turkey considered Abyssinia a part of his territory it became more difficult for the British Government to pursue an outright policy of support for an independent Abyssinia. A change was seen in the attitude of the British Consul in Jerusalem, who before 1862 had been active in helping the Abyssinians retain their buildings in the Holy City, but after that date it was argued that the Abyssinians were Turkish subjects and must appeal to the Porte. All this seemed quite logical to Layard, but it angered the Emperor Theodore who came to regard the English as his enemies rather than his friends. This endangered the lives of the prisoners and Rassam was kept in Massowah. Russell became impatient and wanted to accept Gifford Palgrave's offer to go to Abyssinia in the place of Rassam and Layard had great difficulty in persuading the Government that Rassam should be allowed to continue his mission. Palgrave was sent as far as Cairo.[4]

For a time Layard was too busy to write encouraging letters to Rassam. In July 1865 Palmerston was defeated over a Parliamentary Reform Bill, a section of the Liberal Party led by Robert Lowe and Edward Horsman (the 'Adullamites') having gone over to the Opposition. In the elections, however, Palmerston strengthened his Government's position and Layard was returned unopposed for Southwark. Three months later Palmerston died at the age of eighty-one and Earl Russell became Prime Minister with Gladstone as Leader of the House of Commons. Lord Clarendon, Foreign Minister, asked that Layard should remain as his Under-Secretary.

Layard went to Italy to look at pictures and to carry out commissions for Sir Charles Eastlake, Director of the National Gallery, who was so ill at Milan that his wife, Elizabeth, had to write all his letters. Layard was asked to advise as to whether certain Italian Renaissance paintings were worth the price asked and were suitable for the National Gallery. Layard himself had been buying pictures when he could get them cheap and Eastlake congratulated him on obtaining a Madonna and Child by Giovanni Bellini and the portrait of the Sultan Mahmud II by Gentile Bellini.* Layard carried out the commissions and wrote that he was showing John Millais round the Uffizi and Pitti galleries and that Millais preferred Sandro Botticelli to all other painters. There were four for sale which Layard urged Eastlake to buy for the National Gallery.

Sir Charles Eastlake was dying and by the time that Layard returned to London at the end of 1865, Earl Russell was looking for a successor as President of the National Gallery. His choice fell on Layard who, he thought, could keep his post as Under-Secretary and have additional 'influence', but then he had misgivings and decided that artists, who were jealous people, might object to being supplanted by a politician. Russell accepted Layard's suggestion that he should take the post of Director without pay, but then changed his mind again and appointed Layard a Trustee which enabled him to keep his post as Under-Secretary, while Henry Boxall, an artist, was appointed Director. Russell then had another idea which caused confusion—to appoint George Joachim Goschen, who had only entered Parliament as a Liberal in 1863, to be Chancellor of the Duchy of

* The first painting Layard acquired was a fragment of the fresco representing the fall of Lucifer by Spinello Aretino from Arezzo which he sent to the Art Treasures Exhibition in Manchester in 1857. In October 1860 he wrote to Janet Ross that he had been 'rummaging about in various holes and corners in search of something to throw away my money upon' and had only succeeded in finding one picture within his means—St. George and the Dragon which he thought might be by Palma Vecchio. The next year he went to Holland and the Low Countries in order 'to examine the Dutch and Flemish Schools of painting of which I know so little'.

The portrait of the Sultan Mahmud II had been sold to Layard in Venice by an old man who particularly wanted him to have the picture and it cost five pounds. Layard wrote to Morelli to say how delighted he was with it and that he was sure it was genuine. It had the name of the painter and the date—1480. '*Les détails sont d'une finesse merveilleuse. Mantegna n'y a pas même arrivé.*' (See p. 390.)

Lancaster with a seat in the Cabinet. Layard wrote Russell an angry letter arguing that he had more right to a seat in the Cabinet since he had first held office under Russell in 1852. Clarendon and others were strongly against this promotion over the heads of more senior politicians such as Layard. 'The minor gods', said Clarendon, 'who had toiled through the heat of the day . . . were rabid at the new man coming in at the eleventh hour and receiving his penny.'(5) Layard threatened to resign, but Clarendon told him that the Queen had been most kind in her expressions about him and entirely agreed that his resignation would cause embarrassments. The Queen had changed her opinion of Layard and she decided that his knowledge of art would be of great use if he would agree to take Eastlake's place as a member of the Committee for the Memorial to the late Prince Consort. Layard was flattered and agreed to continue to work for Clarendon as Under-Secretary for Foreign Affairs. Layard liked working for Clarendon and there was plenty to do. During 1866 there was war between Prussia and Austria, and the latter evacuated the Venetian Province of Italy. France was apprehensive of the growing power of Prussia. He was busy as Trustee of the National Gallery, as Member of the Albert Memorial Committee, helping to organise working men's clubs, and speaking on political reform. His thoughts were often with Rassam who had, at last, at the beginning of 1866, begun to make his dangerous journey from Massowah to the Emperor Theodore at Magdala.

Rassam wrote to Layard on 7 February 1866 stating that he had arrived in Abyssinia and that the Emperor had given him a most magnificent reception; at Debra Tabor, a message had been sent to have the prisoners unfettered and they were all to be handed over to him. Rassam planned to leave with them at the end of March: 'The Emperor has written a most *polite* letter to the Queen which I am sure will please Her Majesty and the British Nation.' Russell was delighted at the news of Rassam's success and congratulated Layard on his good judgement in defending Rassam 'against torrents of abuse'. The information was received in London on 23 May and was published in the Press with large headlines; it was expected that the prisoners would arrive in London within a few months.

Once more, however, the prisoners were thrown into chains—
and Rassam as well. Rassam wrote that the Emperor's change of
attitude was due to the arrival in Abyssinia of Dr. Beke, who
came with petitions from the prisoners' relations, so that there
was uncertainty as to who was the Queen's envoy. Dr. Beke
considered that it was because Rassam did not know the customs
of the country and had angered the Emperor by not following
the proper etiquette.* 'The Emperor's behaviour', Rassam wrote
to Layard, 'is most extraordinary and cannot be fathomed. There
is no doubt he entertains great liking for me and why he puts
me and my companions in chains is quite a mystery.' Rassam
continued patient and uncomplaining, as stoic as Henry Stern
the missionary though he never suffered as much. Ever since he
had stayed with Layard's mother when he went to Oxford as a
young man he had corresponded with her and now he sent her
his journal: 'You will be glad to know', he said, 'that I am treated
kindly though I am in chains.' He had obtained tomato seeds
from Aden and amazed the Abyssinians by obtaining several
hundred tomatoes to each plant. Rassam was still very hurt at
all the unkind things said about him in the British Press: 'If I
am to see England no more I hope you will make it known', he
wrote to Layard, 'that your unworthy friend was never ashamed
of his descent.' He asked that Mrs. Layard might remember him
in her prayers. Finally a military expedition had to be sent from
India under Sir Robert Napier, who arrived in front of the
great rock fortress of Magdala in the spring of 1868 and defeated
the Abyssinians. Theodore sent Rassam, Cameron, Stern, and
the other prisoners to the British lines and then committed suicide.
Rassam returned to England in July and went to stay with
Layard.

*   *   *

* According to Beke, Layard made such a violent attack on him in
the House of Commons that the *Hansard* report had to be bowdlerised.
Layard was angry at the attacks on his protégé Rassam and because
Beke, according to Layard, had said that Rassam had acted as Layard's
pimp in Mesopotamia. *The British Captives in Abyssinia*, by Charles
Tilstone Beke (London 1865). Hormuzd Rassam published in 1869,
Narrative of the British Mission to Theodore, King of Abyssinia.

Throughout England there was demand for a reform of the franchise and Layard made a good speech in favour of the Liberal Government's Electoral Bill. He attacked the Opposition for mistrusting the working classes: 'You have no right to throw it in the teeth of the working classes that they are unfit to exercise the franchise because they are corrupt, while you are their corrupters.' He was surprised that there was an uproar and that exception was taken to the remark. In June 1866 Earl Russell's Government was defeated.

Layard rightly considered that there would be a great deal of trouble as a result of this failure to meet the demands for extending the franchise. There were meetings throughout the country and the League for Reform planned a large meeting in July in Hyde Park which the Conservative Government, led by Lord Derby and Disraeli, were unwise enough to ban. The railings were torn down and crowds poured into the park, many hundreds spending the night there. Emily Eden drove round in her carriage afterwards to see what damage had been done and felt 'boiling and bloodthirsty' against all demagogues. 'When we are hanging demagogues', she wrote to Lord Clarendon, 'would you mind a small, inexpensive gibbet for Layard? Did you like the man when he was your Under-Secretary or did you only put up with him?' She still could not forgive Nineveh for discovering Layard.[6] Clarendon, however, had come to like him. 'Our official relations together', he wrote to Layard, 'have ripened into sincere friendship on my part.'

In the autumn of 1866 there was a general exodus of Liberals to Italy. Gladstone went to Rome and every morning at eight o'clock, said Clarendon, lectured his wife and daughter on Dante requiring them to parse and give the root of every word. 'If he were soaked in boiling water and rinsed till he was twisted into a rope', said Emily Eden, 'I do not suppose a drop of fun would ooze out of him.' Russell and Layard had gone to Venice to see the Austrians hand over the province. 'The entry of the King of Italy', said Layard, 'was a magnificent pageant with barges and gondolas decked with silk hangings and rich stuffs, rowed by gondoliers dressed in the costumes of the fifteenth and sixteenth centuries.' He was delighted to see the last Austrian depart and the raising of the Italian standard in St. Mark's Square.

Layard was busy with the Imperial Ottoman Bank and with his big Southwark constituency. In the early summer of 1867 he took a party of two thousand workmen from his constituency to see the great Paris Exhibition. The French Government had persuaded Abdul Aziz of Turkey to visit the Paris Exhibition, a unique journey for a Sultan. He was accompanied by his two nephews Murad and Abdul Hamid and the party proceeded to England to be received by Queen Victoria, who showed them the strength of the British Navy in a review at Spithead in stormy weather—it did not bother Queen Victoria but the Ottoman party spent much of their time below.

Layard paid many visits to Italy at this time studying pictures and he was in Venice again at the beginning of 1868 when he founded the Venice and Murano Glass and Mosaic Work Company with Signor Salviati as manager. A contract was obtained for fifteen years to repair the Mosaics of St. Mark's and to maintain them. He and Salviati had formed a school of young mosaicists and a department for painting on glass: 'I am convinced', he wrote to Sara Austen, 'that mosaic is the only external and internal decoration on a great scale which will suit our climate. It resists all the effects of our atmosphere, and is so brilliant that even our dark days would scarcely interfere with it. Fresco painting has so completely failed that I have given it up.'

At home the demand for reform of the franchise had been so strong that the Conservatives, having refused the moderate measure of the previous Government, were obliged to pass a more radical one. Lord Derby had taken his 'leap in the dark' and retired, leaving Disraeli to succeed him. Layard must have expected that sooner or later Disraeli would become Prime Minister but he wrote to George Clark: 'What an astounding fact—Dizzy Premier. The triumph of jugglery and political immorality. A man whose name is not connected with one political measure either good, bad or indifferent—whose career has been one continuous, cynical contempt of everything honest, upright and true.' It was a short premiership and the new electorate returned the Liberals to power and Gladstone, the Prime Minister, appointed Layard to be Commissioner of Works and Buildings, making him a Privy Councillor.

*   *   *

'This is a sad solitary life—this hanging on without an interest or affection' Layard had written to William Gregory on the latter's marriage in December 1867, 'and altho' I can never hope to change my lot, I am not so selfish as not to rejoice sincerely when I see one of my friends taking a step which will lead to his happiness.' A year later, however, at the age of fifty-two, Layard proposed to Enid Guest, who was Lady Charlotte Schreiber's eighth child and was aged twenty-five. At least one of Layard's friends thought he intended to marry Enid's younger and more attractive sister, Blanche, who had been in frequent correspondence with him, and it is not clear from Enid's very reserved account in her diary that even she expected him to propose. A few days after she had accepted his proposal in January 1869 Layard wrote to Blanche:

> You know how fond I have always been of you—from your babyhood upwards—and my happiness in having gained the affection of your darling Enid has not been a little increased by the reflection that I do not come among strangers, but among those whom I have so long known and loved. Depend upon it that nothing shall be wanting on my part to render your sister happy. I know full well her worth and how deserving she is of all that I can do for her and of my entire devotion.

Marianne Layard, who wrote with emotion about so many things, was surprisingly unenthusiastic in the letter she wrote to her old friend Lady Charlotte. 'I hope that she will never regret the change! Rather a novel way of wishing happiness, but the *romance of life* is rather over!' Lady Charlotte was pleased[7] and Harriet Grote thought that marriage would help to get him into the 'orbit of English existence' after his 'vagabond life'.

'None of us had a happy home and were all glad to get away', wrote Enid, referring to all the 'fighting' there had been after her mother had married Schreiber; until then she had had quite a happy time at home in a large family. [8] She rode, read, improved her mind, helped to print with the Canford Press,* watched

* The printing Press was at Canford Manor and the family published some poems of Tennyson, one of which he wrote especially for them. They printed *Canfordians*, the *Self-Help Society*, and *The Portland Times*. Viscount Wimborne possesses a number of these books and occasionally others appear for sale on the book market.

cricket at Canford Park, played near the house, and went to the Church on the estate. It was a self-contained family unit, and they often corresponded with one another in a secret writing they had invented. Visitors came from London, and there were dances and charades in which Henry Layard liked to take part. He had always been a romantic figure to them, arriving suddenly for the week-end from the East, from Italy or his Government office in London. With three of her sisters married, Enid was beginning to feel restless. By 1868 Lady Charlotte had taken a house in London so that her eldest son Ivor, on marrying Lady Cornelia Churchill, could install himself at Canford, and when Lady Cornelia became Lady of the Manor, Enid found everything altered, 'no longer a welcome and a feeling of going home'. In spite of the difference in age Henry and Enid were well suited and grew very fond of one another.

Enid was a tall rather stately woman, taller than the burly Layard; she was determined, practical, and industrious. Brought up in wealth, she was a little patronising, and held all the correct views, 'a woman should stick to the man she loves through thick and thin'. She believed in the virtues of good breeding and George Clark made her very angry when he recalled that her father, Sir John, had not been either well educated or of good family. Enid did not bother much about fashion, but she had good taste and a liking for diamonds. Layard was never very enthusiastic about spending money on jewellery and gave her various antiques he had picked up at Nimrud and Nineveh. On their engagement he asked Phillips of Bond Street to make up a bracelet for her out of Esarhaddon's signet. Then there was an elaborate necklace for special evening dress occasions made out of cuneiform cylinders which covered her white bosom in a heavy row of dull, unsparkling browns.

The marriage was celebrated on 9 March 1869 at St. George's, Hanover Square, with William Gregory as best man. 'I felt very proud of her and more in love with her than ever', wrote Layard to Lady Charlotte from the Elizabethan manor of Milton Court, near Dorking, where they were spending their honeymoon. Layard showed himself to be a considerate husband concerned about her health, while Enid, who had always had a great admiration for him, seems to have been happy from the first. She reveals little of her thoughts in her diary and carried on a correspondence with her sister Blanche in the Guest secret writing which Layard was annoyed to find he could not decipher.(9) When they returned to London they set up house at 21 Grafton Street and Enid was 'astonished' at the happiness of her life and the peace of her small home. She had many friends and relatives in London so that she did not feel too lonely while her husband was kept busy at his office and in the House of Commons. There was reorganisation of the National Gallery in Trafalgar Square, committee meetings on the sculptures for the Albert Memorial, what to do with the many statues of famous people which were in government store, decorating the hall of the House of Commons with mosaic, dealing with a petition from Robert Lowe, Chancellor of the Exchequer and a fervent cyclist, on behalf of the 'Honourable Society of Bicycle Riders' protesting against the difficulty of riding in London because of the traffic. Layard's main concern was the improvement of London. Almost the whole area along the Embankment between Charing Cross Station and the Houses of Parliament belonged to the Crown and was to be rebuilt. Layard hoped to place, 'on that wonderful site', the new Law Courts, the Museum of Natural History, the Admiralty, War Office, National Gallery, and several other buildings, making good architectural use of the river Thames in the same way as other cities—Paris, Rome, Florence—made good use of their rivers. 'Here then', he said, 'was an opportunity which had never occurred before and can never occur again, of placing on the Embankment a continuous line of great public buildings from the Temple to the Houses of Parliament, and thus opening one great highway through the Metropolis, unequalled for its magnificence in any capital of the world.'

Layard introduced his Bill on 10 May for acquiring a site on the Embankment for the new Law Courts buildings, instead of using the cramped area of Carey Street. There were vested interests in the latter site and the lawyers so powerful and 'unscrupulous' that the Carey Street site was chosen. Layard complained bitterly that nearly every question connected with the improvement and embellishment of London had been made political and that Gladstone had shown weakness. During the ten months that he was Commissioner of Works there was another incident, which did as much as the battle of the site for the Law Courts to disgust him with political life. Mr. Raikes argued in the House of Commons that Layard had behaved incorrectly in engaging Signor Salviati of the Murano firm to decorate with mosaic the central hall in the Houses of Parliament, since it was known that Layard had been closely connected with the firm. Layard explained that he was not making money out of this but that he had always had two passions in his life— Italy and Art—and that mosaics were a worthy cause for which funds had been collected, subscribed to by distinguished men in Parliament. Raikes withdrew his request for a committee of enquiry and that should have closed the matter but it took many years for Layard to get over Raikes' 'gross and unwarrantable personal attack'. He considered that he been abandoned by Gladstone and had been left to defend himself as best he could. He was angered also by the repeated interference by the Treasury in all matters connected with his department for which he blamed Acton Ayrton, a parsimonious friend of Mr. Gladstone. While Layard and Enid were on holiday in Europe in August and September, various intrigues were going on in London which affected him but of which he was ignorant. Owing to a quarrel between Ayrton and Robert Lowe, the Chancellor of the Exchequer, Gladstone decided to separate them by appointing Ayrton as Commissioner of Works and sending Layard, who was considered to be extravagant with his plans to embellish London, as Minister to Madrid. The Foreign Minister, Clarendon, considered that it was 'very unjust to stop promotion in the stagnant diplomatic profession, merely because Lowe and Ayrton can't control their tempers'. He asked Granville to give him some good reasons for Layard's appointment since he could discover none and 'would never be able to explain matters to his flock'.

On 10 October Layard, then in Naples, received a telegram from Lord Clarendon offering him the Madrid Mission and, after talking it over with Enid, he accepted, and returned immediately to London. He was pleased to receive a friendly letter from Gladstone about the changes, but infuriated to learn from others that the object had been to find a post to separate Ayrton from Lowe and to achieve greater economy in

Public Works. 'The only consideration is to be', wrote Layard, 'not how well but how cheaply can a thing be done and this will not do for the Arts.' William Gregory thought that Layard had resigned and was much disappointed, chiding him for not biding his time. 'It would have been impossible', said Layard, 'I am much more sensitive than either you or the world supposes. I cannot tell you what I suffered from that unmanly and ungenerous attack of Mr. Raikes. I would not go through it again for anything in the world. I never could stand the misrepresentations and calumnies to which I was exposed in the House, and a man who is sensitive and cannot accept such things calmly is scarcely fit to hold office.' Sir Henry Bulwer wrote that he was glad that a man he knew and liked was going to Spain, but it had been unsatisfactory that there had been no 'eminent diplomatist' willing to take on the job and he was not sure that Layard had acted wisely in accepting the post, but perhaps he would be able to shake off his 'bitter enemies' in the new career. Sir James Hudson begged him not to import the noxious plant 'zeal' into his diplomatic garden—'*surtout point de zèle*'. *The Times* thought Layard would be a loss to London and wrote on 27 October: 'We were encouraged to think this much-neglected city would be in capable hands. We had a man at the head of the Department of Works who had received a long and practical art education, who had seen all forms of architecture, who had made it the business of his life to understand them, and who must be in a position to know that from the time of Nineveh no city of similar importance has been so ugly and has boasted so few fine buildings as London.'

PART FOUR

Diplomacy: Spain

1869–1877

1

Bismarck and the
Spanish King

One of Layard's first successes in diplomacy was to dissuade his determined mother-in-law from coming immediately to Spain. He had always been very fond of her and did not want to hurt her feelings, so it was arranged that she should visit them later. The Minister and his bride left London in November 1869 arriving in Madrid at the beginning of December. He presented his credentials as the first British Minister to be accredited since the revolution of 1868, when the Bourbon Queen Isabella II had been banished with her infant son, Alfonso, and the Constituent Cortes had adopted a monarchical form of Government, against the protests of a vociferous minority which wanted a republic. The handsome Marshal Francisco Serrano (Duke de la Torre), one of the ex-Queen's former lovers, was Regent of Spain and General Juan Prim (Count Reus) was Prime Minister. The Layards were living in an hotel as the Legation was not ready. Sir John Crampton, the previous Minister, had understated the case when he had told them that they would not at first perhaps be struck by the beauty or comfort of the Legation. It was infested with bugs so that the wallpaper and much of the woodwork had to be burned; there was only one lavatory, in a box in a cupboard of the dining-room and the stables below were full of filth from the horses. Enid set to work and in a few weeks the rooms on the first floor were habitable, decorated with silks, Kurdish carpets, embroideries, and tapestries which they had brought with them. Layard told his mother-in-law that Enid had shown great taste and ability, had the most perfect temper imaginable, and showed great tact with everyone. She kept all the accounts and was an excellent hostess, which meant a great deal of work as they held

DON LAYARDOS IN MADRID.

DON LAYARDOS IN MADRID

(A Spanish Ballad)

"We had thought, if any office could have kept thee from unrest,
'Twas the Aedileship of London, arbiter of art confest:
That if e'er peg fitted socket—round to round and square to square—
DON LAYARDOS and the Board of Works that peg and socket were!"

Sternly spake out DON LAYARDOS, from beneath his bended brow,
With a frown like the Olympian's when the Giants he would cow: . . .
"'Tis not Serpentine that stinketh; Law-court scheme accepted not;
Not abuse for a queen in the Abbey scoured as bright as pewter-pot;
Not our statues—e'en the latest, worst that decorate thy ridge—
Art and Science, Trade and Commerce—ill-used new Blackfriars bridge!

"'Tis that my strong soul sniffs battle in the Spanish realms afar,
Royalists, Republicanos ranged with PRIM and CASTELAR!
Ministerial muzzle irks me! midst the fighting fain I'd be,
Where the 'bravo Toro's shouted and the crowd roars like a sea.

"Now the Dons are up in quarrel, I would be amidst the fray,
Backing one side or the other, in a diplomatic way.
'Twill be hard, when blows are flying, if my share thereof I lack;
Never yet hard knocks were round me, but I gave and took my whack! . . .

"Estimates I'm tired of fighting against Philistine M.P.'s,
Of not pitching into humbugs, and not saying what I please . . .
Quite enough of Spain hath CRAMPTON; Spain hath had enough of him.
Ministers in troubled waters should be people who can swim;
Give the works to whom it likes thee; and let me have CRAMPTON's berth—
In Madrid they say the Raffaeles are the finest upon earth."

"Now, nay, answered EL CID GLADSTONE, "twere a parlous choice, I trow,
Of all men to make an envoy the unlikeliest art thou,
With the habit hot upon thee still of speaking out thy mind,
And of punching heads whenever heads for punching thou canst find.

"Tweaking we shall have of noses, treading we shall have on toes;
For Diplomacy's mild zephyrs, breezes that may come to blows:
Stiff-necked ever were the Spaniards, and high-stomached among men;
One *Tornado* case was plenty: DON LAYARDOS will make ten."

Straightway answered DON LAYARDOS: "Nay, my Cid, so mote it be!
For Tornados—let these Spaniards a Tornado try on me!
Well, I ween, it were for England, and for Europe Spain should know
That when courteous words are idle, there is such thing as a blow!

"Saddle and from the Museum lead my Babylonian Bull,
On his back, of Madrilenos I will face the *plaza*-full.
Though in choosing of a Sovereign Spaniards cannot yet agree,
When I come to them thus riding it may chance they will have *me*!"

Punch, 6 November 1869

dances in the Legation every Monday and gave dinner parties for twelve to twenty people.

Madrid society was very divided; the grandees would have nothing to do with such 'revolutionary' Liberals as Serrano and Prim. Nearly all Layard's staff of young aristocratic gentlemen preferred the receptions given by the grandees and therefore did not meet the Layards, who went to those given by Serrano, Prim, and other Liberal politicians. The Spanish Roman Catholics were in a state of fanatical excitement over the discussion about the infallibity of the Pope which was made dogma at a Vatican Council in July 1870, and they bitterly hated the Spanish revolutionaries who were despoiling churches and monasteries. The British Legation, however, gradually came to be considered as neutral ground and politicians of different parties were encouraged to meet there—even some of the grandees decided to come when they heard that the food was good and there was dancing. Enid had a good staff to help her organise her receptions. From England had come an excellent Italian butler, Giovanni Morlini, and Miss Hill, who had been a lady's maid at Canford Manor, also Mr. and Mrs. Beale who looked after the household. M. Joubert, the best cook in Madrid, had been handed on by the retiring French Ambassador, and the Spanish servants consisted of a coachman, who drove a pair of horses purchased in Madrid, a *valet-de-pied*, a housemaid, and a watchman, who filled an important role in view of the many revolutions. Layard had been accustomed to a grand style of living in other people's country-houses in England and Italy, but not at his own expense and the cost seemed excessive.

In society and politics the Spaniards kept rigidly to their own groups, but everyone went to the bullfights—except Enid. When there were visitors she was prepared to go with them to see the picturesque concourse of people in the arena, but she would push her way out when preparations were made to release the bull. Layard took visitors such as Lady Charlotte and Charles Schreiber, Sir Charles Dilke, and Dean Stanley, but he made it a rule never to accept an invitation from members of the Government for he did not wish it to be said that the British Representative showed that he approved officially of bullfights. He considered that the sport was a blot on the Spanish character, encouraging treachery and cruelty rather than courage, and the number of women who attended shocked him. Serrano's wife, the Duchess de la Torre, seldom missed a fight, taking her three daughters with her, the youngest of whom used to cover her face during the bloody episodes and was jeered at by the others. The Duchess de la Torre was one of Enid's close friends: 'she is still a very beautiful woman', said Enid, 'very much painted but most successfully for though nearly forty she looks twenty-five' and Lady Charlotte described her as 'a pretty little soubrette'. She was a rich Cuban whom Serrano had married when he was Spanish Governor-General of Cuba, and when he became Ambassador at the Court of Napoleon III she learned to dress fashionably, receiving in Madrid the latest Worth models from Paris. Enid often went to breakfast with her and was able sometimes to give Layard important news to pass on to the Foreign Office. In the view of Percy ffrench, First Secretary at the Legation, the member of staff who worked the hardest was Mrs. Layard. Besides her household duties, she played the harmonium in the English church, learned Spanish, and was repeatedly copying long despatches for London, because the Legation staff of young gentlemen were not always there when required. They had adapted themselves to the grandee social habits of going to bed at five o'clock in the morning, breakfasting at midday and arriving in the office not much before three o'clock when the mails left. Layard complained to Edmund Hammond, the Permanent Under-Secretary at the Foreign Office, but failed to break them of the habit.

Spain was an intensive training ground for a diplomat and Layard made a great success of his mission, partly because he disliked the Spaniards so much that he did not get involved in their politics; but he considered that it was a total banishment from things, persons, and places in which for so many years he had taken an interest: 'It is the end of me and of any usefulness that might have been in me.' In Italy he would have been happy for he loved the country and he was known there, whereas in Spain, as he told Gregory, scarcely twelve people had ever heard of him. One of the Spanish Ministers told Enid that when Layard had been appointed to Spain they had had no idea that he was interested in art and was famous for having discovered Assyrian monuments; they had been worried because all they could learn about him was that he was '*un homme féroce*'. Layard was suffering from violent indigestion most of the time in Spain and he suffered from periods of great depression as a result. It was discovered eventually that this was due to a form of lead poisoning from the pipes carrying the drinking water: 'It is a nuisance to one who did not know that he possessed a stomach.'

Layard had great intellectual curiosity but he needed a foil and an audience and after visits paid by Henry Cole* of the South Kensington Museum and Giovanni Morelli he was much more cheerful. Pictures were always a pleasure and he spent many happy days in the galleries, studying the Spanish School of painting and becoming a great admirer of Velasquez. He was interested in the differences between Spanish and Italian painting:

> The all-powerful and ever-meddling Inquisition had forbidden the representation of the nude, and especially of the female form. . . . The sprawling Venuses and Cupids of the Italian Schools are replaced by well-clothed saints and monks. The Virgin, like the queens and great ladies of Spain, may not even show her feet, and the Infant Jesus is usually swaddled up to the chin with the utmost care. Except in the 'supreme' moment of being skinned or boiled, a martyr cannot be seen without his clothes.†

It was a real delight to him when Giovanni Morelli came to stay and they visited the churches and galleries of Madrid, Seville, Granada, and other Spanish cities. In the Prado museum Morelli made several interesting discoveries, including a fine picture by Giorgione, which had been assigned to Pordenone, and one by Lorenzo Lotto, which had been thought to be a Titian. He was, said Layard, the greatest expert on Italian

---

* Sir Henry Cole, who was nine years older than Layard, was a man of remarkable energy who had launched the scheme for building the Royal Albert Hall opened in March 1871. He had been an active organiser of the Great Exhibition of 1851 and had arranged that the funds should be invested to purchase a large estate at South Kensington for buildings to house a department of science and art.

† Article on Velasquez in *The Quarterly Review*, October 1872 in which he corrected some of the statements made by Mr. Stirling in his *Velasquez and his Works*. Layard was also revising for John Murray the art section of Richard Ford's famous *Handbook on Spain*, 1847 edition.

pictures; instead of relying on Vasari, who sometimes included gossip and unreliable reports in his biographies of painters, he sought to identify pictures by internal evidence. He would study, when possible from the original drawings, how any particular painter drew an ear, eye, or foot and also his general composition; in this he was helped by his knowledge of anatomy acquired during six years as a medical student in Germany. By studying the detail and the general composition of the painting he strove to see beneath the work of successive restorers. 'To visit with him a picture gallery', said Layard, 'or to examine a collection of the drawings of the old masters, was an intellectual treat, which those who have enjoyed it are not likely to forget.' He often expressed his regret that Morelli was not there: 'How many times passing through the magnificent galleries of Madrid have I not thought of you', he told him. Layard persuaded the Spaniards to start a Fine Arts Club, which he hoped might lead to the discovery and preservation of many treasures hidden in private houses.

In his long *Memoir* on his seven years in Spain, Layard gave a detailed and interesting account of the period and of the extraordinary characters who ranted on the political stage speaking in the grandiloquent terms of Don Quixote. There were great orators such as Castelar, who knew very little of the outside world and had some strange ideals, and there were the Communists, Internationalists, and very extreme Republicans, who were so determined to be free in every way that they brought chaos to the country when they came to power. On the extreme Right were the grandees, who believed they were still living in the heroic days of Charles V, there were fanatic Roman Catholic Dignitaries who hated all Protestants and would have liked to reintroduce the Inquisition, and from the north-east of Spain the Carlists, with their dreams of a former Austrian Empire, waged war against all Liberal governments.

Juan Prim was convinced that there would be serious trouble in Spain if he did not succeed quickly in finding a king in accordance with the new Constitution but he searched the *Almanac de Gotha* in vain for a suitable candidate. No one seemed to want to be king of so turbulent a country. The Prime Minister had even considered as candidate the Duke of Genoa, nephew to King Victor Emmanuel of Italy, who was a boy of fifteen studying at Harrow. The story told in Madrid was that the Duc de Montpensier had bribed the Headmaster of Harrow to dissuade him, for Montpensier wanted his wife, sister of the banished Isabella, to have the throne, while ex-Queen Isabella wanted her small son Alfonso to be king, but there was no enthusiasm for a return of the Bourbons. In the autumn of 1869 Prim had sent his emissary, Don Eusebio de Salazar y Mazarredo, on a secret mission to find out whether Prince Karl Anton of Hohenzollern Sigmaringen, head of the Roman Catholic branch of the Prussian Royal family, would agree to let his married son, Prince Leopold, be put forward as a candidate, but the proposal was declined. These intrigues were described by Layard in his despatches which Clarendon enjoyed, finding it a novelty to be kept well-informed. He said that Crampton had never found anything to relate 'in that strange country where one can only reckon surely upon that which was not foreseen'; indeed, the terrible climax of Prim's search for a king had not been foreseen when Clarendon wrote thus to Layard in May 1870.

In every country Layard visited he set up his own efficient intelligence service by writing and receiving numerous letters and in Spain, too, he kept himself well informed. There were certain important intrigues, however, which only Prim and the Prussian Minister knew about and even they did not know everything. Bismarck knew more than anyone, since he was the prime mover in trying to get Prince Leopold of Hohenzollern made King of Spain. His object was to have Spain as an ally and to weaken France in the event of war, since she would have to defend two frontiers. In his struggle with Austria Bismarck had found it very useful to have Prince Leopold's younger brother on the throne of Rumania. He was secretly putting pressure on Prince Karl Anton of Hohenzollern to reconsider his refusal to let his son Leopold be a candidate and while he was sending secret agents to Prim to keep him interested, Prim was sending Salazar to negotiate with Bismarck. On 1 June, Bismarck sent Prim an optimistic letter and Prim sent back messages urging speed. The latter wished to have the candidature of Prince Leopold decided by the Cortes before it adjourned for the summer at the end of June for he regarded further delays as most dangerous.

Ch. 1   Bismarck and the Spanish King

Layard and other diplomats, except the Prussian Minister, did not realise that there was any question of trying to revive the Hohenzollern candidature. There had been a sigh of relief in England and throughout Europe when Prince Leopold had declined to be a candidate. It was realised that France would probably go to war with Spain rather than allow a near relation of King William of Prussia to take the Spanish throne. To Layard and others it seemed that the country was more than usually tranquil. Madrid had become almost unbearably hot; in the British Legation the windows were kept tightly shut and the curtains drawn to keep out the hot winds. Layard amused himself by reading Bulwer's despatches of over twenty years earlier describing the complicated intrigues of the Spanish marriages when he was British Minister, and had been given twenty-four hours notice to leave Spain. Immersed in that extraordinary story which nearly led to war, Layard was oblivious of the intrigue being carried on between Berlin and Madrid, which was as dangerous for the peace of Europe as had been the earlier intrigue. If there had not been a mistake in the decoding of a telegram from Salazar to Zorilla, President of the Cortes, Prince Leopold of Hohenzollern would almost certainly have been elected King of Spain before the Cortes adjourned.* Lord Granville announced in the House of Lords on 27 June that the world had never been so profoundly at peace.

Layard went happily on holiday with Enid to La Granja which, as San Idelfonso, had been the royal residence of Charles V and Philip II. They were the guests of Marshal Serrano and were delighted by the extensive gardens, the shady groves on the northern slopes of the Guadarrama Mountains, and the wonderful fountains which were almost as fine as those of Versailles but in a more striking setting of lofty mountains and dark forests.

* The full story of this fascinating and complicated intrigue was not told until after the defeat of Germany in the Second World War and it was possible to study the German Foreign Office archives. A summary relating to this question was published in 1957 in *Bismarck and the Hohenzollern Candidature for the Spanish Throne*, edited by Georges Bonnin (Chatto). In 1962 Harvard published *Bismarck, the Hohenzollern Candidacy, and the Origins of the War of 1870* by Lawrence D. Steefel.

There was, however, to be no question of a holiday. On 28 June a telegram announced the death of Lord Clarendon, the Foreign Secretary, whose knowledge of Spain would have been most useful at this critical moment. His successor was Lord Granville. On 4 July Enid went as usual to sew with the Duchess de la Torre and was given the startling news that Prince Leopold of Hohenzollern had after all agreed to be put forward as a candidate for the throne of Spain. She hurried home to tell Layard who was horrified. The Ministers drove from Madrid to La Granja that same evening to hold a Cabinet Council with the Regent which continued until five o'clock in the morning. Afterwards Layard had an appointment with Prim, who was unusually agitated. He had at last found his king who was in many ways most suitable, but it had not turned out as planned. He told Layard that the announcement had been made in the worst way possible. His emissary Salazar had returned from Sigmaringen Castle with the agreement of Prince Karl for the candidature of Leopold but, instead of reporting to Prim, Salazar had told Zorilla, President of the Cortes, who went from one government office to another shouting triumphantly 'at last we have found a king!' Within a few hours the news was known in Madrid and Paris. The French Government was furious. Prim had hoped, he said, that he would have had time to persuade the Emperor Louis Napoleon that there would be no danger in this arrangement or of Spain allying herself with Germany. The last thing that Prim wanted was war with France, but now he did not consider that there was any way of avoiding it. The Cortes was to be recalled for 20 July and it was expected to accept Leopold.

The British Government received the first news of this decision from Layard and there was consternation in London. Granville telegraphed one of those ambivalent instructions which governments sometimes give their representatives in times of crisis— he did not want Layard to interfere in Spanish affairs, but he was to do his utmost to bring about the abandonment of the project which might bring on 'great European calamities'. The British Government did not then realise the sinister part played throughout by Bismarck and considered that it was up to the Spanish Government, encouraged by Layard, to prevent war.

'The removal of the cause of dissension rests primarily with Spain', telegraphed Granville.*

Layard remained a few days at La Granja to write despatches; Prim and the Ministers returned to Madrid. While the capitals of Europe were filled with rumours of war, San Idelfonso was reminiscent of Versailles at the end of the eighteenth century with the Duchess playing the role of Marie Antoinette. During this period of crisis, the Regent and the Duchess organised one of their magnificent picnics at a lovely place in the hills called Boca del Asino, by the river Balsain. A large table was spread for lunch under the trees. While the gentlemen fished, the ladies gossipped in the shade and Enid made tea in her samovar. The elegant young Spaniards paid court to the Duchess, who was the belle of the picnic, catching beautiful butterflies which they stuck with pins into her hat; 'the poor things were alive', commented Enid.

Layard returned to Madrid on 9 July and hastened to call on the Prime Minister. He found General Prim at his private apartment in the Ministry of War pacing up and down in a state of fury at a speech delivered by the French Foreign Minister, the Duc de Grammont, which was insulting to Spain and to himself personally. His eyes flashed as he denounced the arrogance of France in thinking she could dictate to Spain. War was inevitable, he said, and it only remained for him to prepare for it. His voice became so loud and passionate that his wife, who was in her bedroom next door, rushed into the room half-dressed thinking that something terrible had happened. When at last Layard had Prim's attention he argued that Prince Leopold had not yet been proposed as a candidate to the Cortes; the communications which had taken place could be regarded as private and there was still time to induce Leopold to withdraw. Prim was prepared to act on that suggestion provided the British Government would help in obtaining a suitable candidate for the throne, for without a king to hold Spain together there would be chaos; the Carlists would conquer or the Bourbons would return. Layard's instructions from Granville were such that he could offer no help, but he continued to press the case.

* Parliamentary Papers LXX, 1870, 'Correspondence respecting the Negotiations Preliminary to the War between France and Prussia'.

Worn down by Layard's persistence and being himself opposed to war with France, Prim finally agreed to send a telegram to Prince Karl of Hohenzollern representing the dangers menacing Spain unless Prince Leopold withdrew. Layard waited until he saw the telegram handed to one of Prim's secretaries for despatch to Sigmaringen Castle; Prim also sent General Lopez Dominguez to Sigmaringen as an emissary.

Four days later, on the morning of 13 July, Layard received a private note from Prim to say that Prince Karl, in order to save Spain from war, had withdrawn his son's candidature. Layard immediately telegraphed the welcome news to London. By persuading Prim to send the telegram he considered that he had saved Spain from war with France, and this view was shared by the British Government.* Lord Cowley wrote that Layard had created for himself a position in Madrid which no other English Minister had ever possessed and he looked forward to the time when Layard would be Foreign Minister. On this same day, 13 July, there took place the famous meeting at Ems between King William of Prussia and the French Ambassador followed by Bismarck's announcement giving his interpretation of the meeting, which made war between Prussia and France inevitable, just as the Chancellor had intended. On the evening of 15 July Layard went to take leave of Prim before resuming his holiday, when the telegram arrived announcing France's declaration of war against Prussia and all was turmoil once more. Layard referred to the 'morbid suspicion' entertained by the French of Count Bismarck's designs but Hammond told Layard that the guilt of the French consisted in their not sufficiently appreciating Bismarck's character and the war was the result of 'the intrigues and machinations' of Bismarck during the previous three years.

During July and August, Layard scarcely had a full night's rest owing to the number of telegrams exchanged between

---

* In *The Origins of the War of 1870* Mr. Robert Lord argues that other emissaries had arrived at Sigmaringen and that General Dominguez was 'sent too late to have any influence on the course of events' but there is every reason to think from Layard's account that Prim sent the telegram which must have arrived some time before Dominguez.

Ch. 1   Bismarck and the Spanish King

London, Madrid, Paris, Berlin, and Vienna. At eight o'clock on Sunday morning, 4 September, when he was trying to gain a little sleep, Giovanni knocked at the bedroom door saying there was a telegram with important news. MacMahon had surrendered with his whole army, Louis Napoleon had been taken prisoner, and a Republic had been proclaimed in Paris. Layard was amazed. The punishment for France had been, he said, as swift and terrible as in a Greek tragedy and he did not think that a parallel could be found in history for such an event. The Spanish Republicans thought that their opportunity had come and nearly every town had its Republican Junta, while the priests were rousing the Carlists and in some places distributing arms outside the churches.

If Layard had known more of Bismarck's intrigues he would not have been as hostile to the French and as sympathetic to the Germans, 'who were struggling', he said, 'to effect their unity and to occupy the place which they feel they ought to occupy in the world and which the French are determined to prevent their attaining'. He liked the vigour of the German race and, after being in Spain, he appreciated their discipline—Spaniards were 'about as fit for universal suffrage and constitutional government as Fiji Islanders'. At the same time he wanted the British Government to help Spain in her distress and he thought that it was very faint-hearted of Granville not to try to persuade the Italian royal family to produce a candidate—'our modern theories of non-intervention, of thinking but of the ledgers of the mercantile community . . . will be fatal to the honour of England'. The horizon was black in Europe and he thought that this was due to the position England had taken of late under the influence of 'a few narrow-minded radicals'.

2

'They will kill
him too'

The Cortes was due to meet and General Prim was growing
more and more desperate to complete the Constitution by finding
a king. 'Tell Lord Granville', he said, 'that this is the supreme
moment if anything is to be done to save my country.' There
was serious unrest in Spain and Bismarck was trying once again
to revive the Hohenzollern candidature. At last the Italian royal
family allowed Prince Amadeo of Savoy, Duke of Aosta, second
son of King Victor Emmanuel, to be put forward as a candidate.
The Republicans were furious and their newspapers published
fantastic stories ridiculing Aosta and inciting his assassination.
On 16 November 1870 the Cortes voted that he should be invited
to be King, and Zorilla, as President of the Cortes, went with a
deputation to Turin to inform the Duke of Aosta of the decision.
The Duke was due to arrive in Spain at the end of December.
On 27 December Prim was attacked by six men as he returned
from the Cortes; a blunderbuss fired at point-blank range
lodged six balls in his shoulder and elbow. The carriage took
him to the Ministry of War where his wife was waiting for him
and, in order not to alarm her too much, he walked up the
staircase although in great pain. As he entered her room with
his face covered in blood and gunpowder he said 'I have been
shot at but it is not much to matter'. He was then carried to a
bedroom where only the surgeons and Marshal Serrano were
allowed to see him. There was fear of a revolution and Serrano
remained four days and nights in uniform, his horse saddled,
ready to lead his troops. Juan Prim died after three days of great
agony and Layard went sorrowfully to the funeral with the other
diplomats. There was a delay in the procession because the dis-
traught widow insisted on having the coffin opened so that she

could see him again, but when the bearers put it down to carry out her wish she fainted and had to be taken away. Layard had lost a friend and considered that without the firm hand of Juan Prim as Prime Minister the life of the new King was endangered. Prince Amadeo of Savoy only learnt of Prim's death when he arrived by ship at Carthagena. It was a tragic moment for the young Italian when he went to the Church of the Atocha in Madrid to pay his respects at the bier of the man who had brought him to Spain and was no longer there as a protector.

On 2 January 1871 Layard in his uniform and Enid in full court dress wearing her diamond and emerald tiara went to the Cortes to witness Aosta swear to the Constitution, becoming Amadeo the First. The King rode back to the Palace on a beautiful bay horse, brought from Italy, taking off his hat to the people in a martial and precise way which was peculiar to the House of Savoy. He had refused the carriage, which had had the Bourbon fleur-de-lis changed to the cross of Savoy, and rode through the streets ahead of the main crowd of courtiers. 'This proof of his chivalric courage,' wrote Layard, 'his tall and martial figure and the firm and graceful manner in which he sat and managed his high-mettled steed, increased the general admiration.' The British Government was the first to recognise the new King and Layard went, on 10 January, to present his credentials. He wrote to Granville: 'A King who gets up at 7 o'clock in the morning, visits the barracks and hospitals, and curtails his own expense in order that the public schoolmasters may receive their miserable stipends, now some months in arrears, is quite a phenomenon.' But it was his courage and trust in the people, which gained their hearts, and indeed probably saved his life. Serrano considered that King Amadeo was the bravest man he had ever known.

The new Queen of Spain, who was pregnant, was delayed in Italy by illness, suffering, said the British Consul, from 'politico nervoso'. Both she and her husband were being threatened in the Spanish Press and through anonymous letters with the same fate as befell the Emperor Maximilian, executed in Mexico three years before, while his Empress went mad. The Queen arrived in Madrid on a lovely day in March. The streets were crowded with people and the windows of the houses dressed with gay hangings; the only exception was the Veloz Club where young aristocrats stood ostentatiously on the balconies with their hats on and refusing to bow. This insult to the King and Queen caused a great deal of trouble in Madrid and in the British Legation, for Layard insisted that ffrench should resign from the club. (The women demonstrated their Spanishness and their objection to foreign royalty by appearing in public, as in the old days, with high combs in their hair and wearing mantillas.) Enid paid visits to Prim's widow whom she scarcely recognised, so old, shrunken, and dishevelled was she; a little toy terrier rested in her lap under her twitching fingers. 'I had followed Prim everywhere in his exile and his political conspiracies', she told Enid, 'and now I must follow him to the tomb.' She had been pleased that the King had paid her a visit but she said bitterly: 'He has cost us very dear. He had better look out or they will kill him too.'

With the revival of Court life there were many receptions and Enid looked very handsome in her white satin, which was not very fashionable; but, as she told Layard's mother, all the handsomer for not having any flounces—'now that Paris is closed there are no fashions just now. What a blessing!' Enid was a little annoyed that the Duchess de la Torre had managed to obtain the latest and last Worth model out of Paris.

In June 1871 Henry and Enid managed to take their holiday which had been postponed from the previous year. In Paris they were distressed to see the damage caused by the German occupation in March, and by the fighting in May between the French Government forces and the Communists, who had set fire to the Tuileries, the Louvre, the Palais Royal, and the Hôtel de Ville. The Rue de Rivoli was still impassable and many of the public buildings were blackened by fires: 'Paris', said Layard, 'was like a dead city and the tinkling of the small bells attached to the harness of the horses was the only noise which broke the awful silence.' After seeing their friends in England, Henry and Enid visited the Italian Tyrol, Florence, Genoa, and Venice. They were considering buying a house in Venice, and asked Rawdon Brown to look out for one. In Florence Henry saw the Italian Foreign Minister, who said that the King of Italy was advising his son to resign in view of the hostility of the Spaniards.

The Layards returned to a life of continual crisis in Spain; it was 'pandemonium run loose'. Mails did not arrive because the Carlists were controlling the railway lines to the north; Foreign Office telegrams were sometimes indecipherable; the Legation was short of staff and Enid continued to work hard copying despatches as well as painting, singing, playing the guitar after dinner, and the harmonium in church.

The Republicans in the previous year had been encouraged by the events in France and now they thought they would be helped to power by events in England. There had been many references in the Spanish and Continental Press to the Republican movement in England and, owing to Queen Victoria's unpopularity, it was expected that 'Don Carlos Dilkey' would be President of England. In spite of all the confusion the Layards gave their first ball of the winter in December and it was a great success. It was not easy for Enid to arrange these entertainments, for partisanship had entered the Legation and the pro-King Giovanni was having a great deal of trouble with the anti-King Spanish servants. By the end of the year the royal family was in great danger; both Serrano and Zorilla, the Prime Minister, had turned against him; the King's secretary, Marchese Dragonetti, came to ask Layard whether, in the event of an attack on the Palace, the Queen and her two sons might seek safety at the Legation. The King was determined to defend himself in the Palace relying upon a small body of picked troops but the crisis was averted when Serrano refused to place himself at the head of the movement against the King.

In the middle of the trouble Layard fell seriously ill with erysipelas in the head and was not allowed to go out or to read or write, so that Enid had to take despatches at dictation. In January Enid went to visit the Queen who had just given birth to a son. On Sunday, 9 February, Enid was told in confidence by Marchesa Dragonetti that the King had decided to abdicate. Layard was ill but so worried by the news that he left his bed to go to the Palace. The Ministers had been taken by surprise at the King's decision. Zorilla came to see Layard; kneeling and in tears he begged him to dissuade the King from abdicating otherwise all the progress and advantages of the 1868 revolution would be lost. Layard was disgusted and refused to take any action since Zorilla had been one of the principal intriguers against the King. A message was sent to Marchese Dragonetti to come to the Legation and to bring the Queen if necessary. The Duchess de la Torre, in view of the threat of trouble, made sure of reserving beds at the British Legation and arrived there early with her five children to stay the night. Enid proceeded calmly with her plans for a ball on the Monday, and was surprised when only six people arrived—she lamented that the musicians were brought and the supper prepared in vain.

The next day Marshal Serrano came to the Legation to see his wife, the Duchess de la Torre, and his family, but his main purpose was to ask Layard to persuade the King to remain. He had at last realised how disastrous abdication would be, and was prepared to form a coalition Government to try to maintain the policy for which Prim had worked so many years and for which he had lost his life. It was too late. The King had sent his message to the Cortes and nothing would alter his decision. The Queen, who was still weak after the birth of her son, insisted on going with him and they were to leave at five o'clock the next morning, Wednesday, 12 February 1873. At dawn the Queen was taken from her bed in a litter and at the station the King carried her in his arms to the compartment. The doctor said that she was so weak that she must immediately have some food but owing to malice or incompetence there were no supplies on the train for the thirty-six hour journey to Portugal. She never recovered from that arduous journey and died four years later.

3

'Revolutions give one
a deal of work'

The situation deteriorated rapidly. Communist and Inter-
nationalist agents hurried to Spain; the army was demoralised,
the men refusing to obey their officers, prisons were opened,
gunsmiths were raided and the mob controlled Madrid. House-
holders were 'like rabbits in a warren, popping in and out of
their holes at the slightest alarm', and they organised their own
groups to reconnoitre the streets at night to protect property.
Trains were crowded with families leaving for France since the
Carlists were only a short distance from Madrid. The Square by
the Senate House and the British Legation was filled with
ragged *descamisados*, 'shirtless ones', most of them wearing the
red Phrygian caps of Liberty. The Layards and their servants
watched them warily from the windows for occasionally shots
were fired. The 'shirtless ones' were fairly orderly and remained
bivouacked in the Square without entering private houses.
Layard had received a number of threats that the Legation had
been marked for destruction, and he borrowed a Union Jack
from the Consul in Cadiz which made him feel safer. 'The worst
of these revolutions', he wrote to Sara Austen, 'is that they give
one such a deal of work and writing.'

Castelar and the other Ministers declared themselves Dictators.
They called themselves Federalists because they intended to
divide Spain into fifteen States, each of which would be to a
great extent independent, raising its own taxes and having its
own armed forces. This extraordinary policy of the idealist
Castelar was prompted by a theory that the increasing power of
the United States was due to her Federal system. The Government was in a very weak position having to depend for security
on the Federalist volunteers and the *descamisados*, as the army

was disorganised. There was no control exercised over the crowds who were hunting down the moderate Liberals such as Serrano, intent on killing them. Rumours reached the British Legation that Serrano had been captured and the Layards drove boldly into the city to try to obtain information. There were no carriages to be seen and the streets were silent except for the hum of voices, but the people made way for the Legation carriage and frequently saluted. 'Probably few mobs,' said Layard, 'even in the most civilised States of Europe, which had complete power in their hands, would have behaved so well', but they returned to the Legation without any news. The Square outside was crowded with 'Volunteers of Liberty', who told the British Minister that they wanted to save him inconvenience by preventing Spaniards, such as Serrano, taking refuge in the Legation. He arranged for distribution of cigars, bread, and wine, and the 'Volunteers' behaved quietly and respectfully, retiring to their houses at nightfall.

On 24 April a prominent Radical, Albareda, walked into the British Legation escaping from the mob who were determined to shoot him. He managed to get through because a lady friend had brought him in her carriage, concealing him under her voluminous skirts. The same day the Layards were startled to receive a message from the Dictator, Castelar, asking whether they would receive Serrano under their protection as the Government was unable to control the people and he had no wish to allow prominent Spaniards to be killed even though they were in opposition. Layard agreed and sat up waiting with Albareda late into the night. There was a knock at the door and they went downstairs to receive Serrano but it was a telegram from Queen Victoria asking if they were safe. At one o'clock in the morning Castelar himself arrived with Estevanez, Governor of Madrid, in a Government carriage, bringing Serrano disguised in a wig. Castelar and Estevanez then went to the prison and managed to bring out Senor Becorra, another prominent opposition member belonging to the Democratic Party. They returned with him to the Legation on foot, muffled in capes but the Legation porter suspected a trick and would not let them in. Fearing they would be murdered by the mob if the porter did not let them in quickly they were forced to reveal their identities.

The Layards were delighted that these men had been saved but found their visit exhausting and worrying. It was a relief, at any rate, when the Duchess de la Torre and her children left for France. Albareda, Serrano, and Becorra each belonged to a different political party and throughout the four days they spent in the Legation they had political discussions from morning to night; Layard warned Albareda that his powerful and sonorous Andalusian voice, which was very effective in the Cortes, could be disastrous if heard by the mob in the Square outside the Legation. They were all, however, quite indifferent to the danger either to themselves or to their hosts, and would sometimes continue their discussions at the windows of the house. Becorra suddenly left without any word of thanks—Enid did not like him and made the strange comment: 'If he had not white hands one would think he was a game-keeper.' Layard reminded her that political leaders considered that they had a right to asylum; whenever there was a serious disturbance, they went to the diplomatic missions, and it would have been considered a breach of the laws of hospitality to have closed the doors against them.

How to remove Serrano from the Legation was a serious problem. Throughout Madrid the walls of houses were plastered with a proclamation denouncing him as an enemy of Liberty and of his country and stating that every means was being employed to discover his hiding place and to bring him to justice. The proclamation was signed by Senor Estevanez, Governor of Madrid! Layard wrote to Hammond that he thought he would be amused at the 'truly Spanish idea' that Castelar and Estevanez should denounce the men, whom they themselves had saved. It soon became generally believed that Serrano was in the British Legation. The Liberation guards in the Square outside were doubled in the determination to prevent his escape and while the Layards became more and more anxious, Serrano remained entirely indifferent as to what might happen. On 30 April, Castelar told Layard that an attack on the Legation had been planned and that the Government was not strong enough to protect it; he did not wish to endanger the good relations with England or the lives of the inmates. Castelar said that the only way to get Serrano out of the country was for the Layards themselves to take him to a seaport, pretending that he was an English friend of theirs and as the northern railway was in the hands of the Carlists they would have to go to Santander. It was an extraordinary demand to be made by the Dictator of Spain and Castelar knew that it would put the Layards into a situation of considerable danger; he had by then realised that his ultra-liberal policy had created such chaos that Serrano might still be needed to save Spain. Layard consulted Enid, who would have to play an important part in such an adventure. 'She was', he said admiringly, 'very calm and resolute in her determination to assist in the Marshal's escape, notwithstanding the danger it involved.' Layard reported that they were ready to leave that same evening and a plan of campaign was worked out. The most dangerous part of the journey was the departure from Madrid, as the Federalists occupied the station and searched the trains. Serrano shaved off his moustache and beard, dyed his hair a light colour and put on false sandy-coloured whiskers and dressed in one of Layard's light travelling suits with a white, broad-brimmed felt hat. Giovanni and Miss Hill were informed and told to accompany the party. They left in the Legation carriage for the station. With Hill taking one of the Marshal's arms and Enid the other they walked through a side-gate to the train, which had been stopped for them outside the station. At Avilla an armed mob searched the train. Enid, tall and formidable, took up her position in the corridor to protect one side of the compartment and the burly Layard stood at the other. The mob hesitated in front of two such very determined figures, perplexed by the unusual sight of an angry English woman. Mobs were kept at bay in the same way at Valladolid, where they waited twenty minutes, and at Valencia. Serrano himself took no part but remained in a corner with his arms folded, most of the time asleep.

When they arrived at Santander the station was again controlled by the Federalist mob, but here the Layard party were met by the British Consul, Mr. St. Martin, who had been warned and hurried them out to a waiting carriage. A crowd soon collected and Enid became exasperated when Serrano stood aside, bowed, and insisted that she should get in first—etiquette, she thought, might be dispensed with at such moments. They drove to the St. Martins' house near the quay where a little Belgian steamer had been commissioned to take a passenger to St. Jean de Luz in France and at dusk Serrano was put on board. While the Captain was getting up steam, a patrol of five Civil Guards walked up to ask what was going on. This was too much for Enid. 'Come away, my legs shake', she said to Hill, 'and I cannot stay here to see him taken at the last moment.' The Guards wanted to board the steamer but Layard took up position on the gang-plank and told them that he was an English diplomat and that they could only pass if they used force. He shouted to the Captain to get under way, the engines throbbed and Layard jumped for the shore. The Guards fortunately did not open fire, and the little steamer moved out of the harbour.

Layard reported their success in a telegram to Castelar. The Marshal's escape and the way it had been achieved was soon known. The Federalists were infuriated for they feared that Serrano might return to establish a dictatorship, but the Layards were not molested. Layard realised what a risk he had taken and was worried as to how the 'correct' Gladstone and the 'timid' Granville would react. Hammond wrote suggesting that he should look at the archives and refer to May 1848 when Bulwer had to leave Spain because he had allowed himself to become too identified with the opposition to Queen Isabella. Layard replied that the situation was very different, for he had acted at the request of the Spanish Government. At last there was a reassuring despatch from Granville, asking the Minister to convey to Mrs. Layard his admiration 'for the courage with which she associated herself with an undertaking of so perilous a nature.' Lytton,* who was Chargé d'Affaires, in Paris wrote that Layard had been 'the hero of the day for a whole week'. When the Layards went to London on leave that summer they had luncheon with Gladstone and everyone wanted to hear the story including the Prince of Wales and Queen Victoria, who invited the Layards to stay at Osborne.

* Edward Robert (1831–1891), son of Baron Bulwer-Lytton, the novelist, and nephew of Sir Henry Bulwer (Lord Dalling) became Baron Lytton in 1873 and Minister in Lisbon, 1874–6.

4

'Presumptuous Dons'

Layard complained that his friends had forgotten him and that Granville did not keep him informed as to what was happening in the world outside. As to Spain, he said, nothing occurred as it should logically occur and the most important events were often brought about by some sudden passion or some miserable private ambition. It was difficult to penetrate the minds of men, 'who are more like Easterns than Europeans in their skill and deceit and intrigue, and more like children than men in their fickleness of character and their passionate impulses.' More and more he disliked 'this stiff-necked and ill-conditioned people'. Nothing stable or serious could be expected when those who governed thought that statesmanship consisted 'in words and well-turned phrases', and who wasted their time in speculations about political organisms and the dignity of human nature, looking upon themselves as 'the guides and teachers of the whole civilised world'—yet they maintained slavery in the Spanish colonies of Cuba and Porto Rico.

The United States and England had been protesting against the slavery, and towards the end of 1871 war nearly broke out between Spain and the United States Government which was supporting the Cuban revolution against imperialist Spain. Graham Dunlop, the British Consul-General in Havana, sent Layard a graphic account of the terrible incident when young Spanish students were shot by Crespo, the Spanish Governor-General. When Crespo arrived in Madrid and was fêted as a hero by the grandees, Layard refused to meet him, which made the British Minister still more unpopular with the Right Wing faction.

When Layard returned to Madrid in October 1873 there was again danger of war between Spain and the United States because of a new incident. The American ship *Virginius*, which had been gun-running to the rebels in Cuba, had been captured by the Spaniards on the high seas. Fifty of the crew, of whom sixteen were British, had been executed 'in circumstances', said Layard, 'of the most horrible and revolting brutality'. General Sickles, the United States representative, was outraged and announced his intention of leaving Madrid with all his staff. Granville had telegraphed that Layard should do his utmost to settle the matter and agreed not to press for redress with regard to the British subjects executed until the United States' demands had been satisfied.

Layard decided that the first thing to be done was to persuade Castelar to communicate direct with the United States Secretary of State, Mr. Fish, through the Spanish Minister in Washington. In that way he would avoid General Sickles, who wanted war, and his own Foreign Minister, Senor Carjaval, who also did everything to encourage it. Carjaval was a rude and uncouth character who liked to draw up grandiloquent and war-like statements in reply to General Sickles and before despatch he would read them in a loud voice to his Republican cronies sitting in his favourite Madrid café. Layard considered that they contained 'expressions so unusual in diplomatic correspondence and so offensive' that a rupture appeared inevitable, especially as Sickles wanted an excuse for the United States to annex Cuba.

Layard had acquired considerable influence with Castelar, who was grateful for the rescue of Serrano *; he also realised that the Spanish parties had been wrong not to encourage King Amadeo to remain. In the middle of a cold November night in 1873, Castelar asked Layard to come to him at the Ministry, as he feared war was imminent between Spain and the United States and he wanted advice as to how to avert it. Layard told him that the only way was for him to make much greater concessions than he had done. They argued through the night and finally agreed proposals which Layard thought might be accepted and he remained until Castelar sent them direct to the United States Government. They were accepted. Sickles was furious that the affair had been negotiated direct with Washington and that he had been outflanked but the family remained packed in the

* Castelar was still writing to thank him five years later when Layard was Ambassador in Constantinople.

hope that there might after all be a rupture in relations. Lord Granville sent Layard a telegram: 'I selfishly congratulate myself every day that you are in Madrid.'

Granville, however, was soon to go. The Gladstone Government fell in January 1874 and Disraeli became Prime Minister for the second time; Lord Derby, son of the former Prime Minister, was Secretary of State for Foreign Affairs. In Spain General Pavia, Governor of Madrid, turned out the Cortes by force and Serrano returned to power as President of the Executive. Layard was violently attacked in the Spanish and British Press as it was believed that he had arranged the whole thing and he was accused of using his position to further the policies of Serrano. The British Government recognised the Serrano regime, but it did not last long. Serrano, said Layard, was ambitious for power, but having obtained it he made no exertion to retain it. Although he knew of the powerful elements in the army who wanted the young Prince Alfonso, son of ex-Queen Isabella, as king, he took no measures to counter them.

On 28 December 1874 the army made a *pronunciamento* in favour of the seventeen-year-old Alfonso, who was being trained at Sandhurst. Serrano's wife and five children came as usual to seek refuge in the British Legation, and Enid brought out the children's picture books which she had ready 'against a revolution'. This visitation was worse than usual, for the Duchess insisted on receiving all her friends, while the Ministers came to see Layard. In the afternoon he and Enid went for a drive in order to find peace away from the Legation. The young King landed at Valencia on Tuesday, 11 January 1875, and on Thursday he made his entry into Madrid riding a fine white Spanish horse.

The return to power of the Bourbons meant that the political and religious reactionaries once more dominated Spain. Protestant places of worship were closed, the sale of Protestant books forbidden, and antiquated Roman Catholic and Court customs revived. Layard made it clear that there were many things that he disliked under the new regime both as a Protestant and as the representative of a free country. Because of this and the fact that he had been the first Minister to be accredited to the progressive Government after the revolution of 1868, there were

The Duke of Aosta, King Amadeo of Spain

General Juan Prim, Count Reus   Marshal Francisco Serrano, Duke de
la Torre

Mr and Mrs Layard in the drawing-room at the British Legation in Madrid

further attacks on him in the Spanish newspapers which were repeated in the British Press. Members of the Alfonsist Women's Club passed a resolution that they would not invite the Layards to any social function nor would they go to the British Legation. They hoped to be able in this way to force the Layards to leave. Stories were being circulated in London that the British Legation had become a rendezvous for those who opposed the Government and it was suggested that the Minister should be recalled. Layard's old friend Delane was distressed at all the talk and asked Layard for information which he could use to put matters right.

Lord Derby did his utmost to stop the attacks by a speech in the Lords on 26 January 1875, and Granville also praised Layard from the Opposition benches. 'You have done more than anyone to keep the peace', Derby wrote to Layard, adding a reminder: 'Spain may or may not be a free country, but it will be expected to be treated as such.' Derby was fighting a battle in London to retain Layard in Spain against the wishes of Queen Victoria, who was attracted by the romance of a youth of seventeen from Sandhurst suddenly becoming King. She wished him to have every support possible, and did not think that Layard was the right person to give it. Disraeli agreed with the Queen and told Derby: 'It is unfortunate, at this crisis, we have such a man as Layard there. Though of unquestionable talents, he is prejudiced and passionate, and always—I will not say misleads—but certainly misinforms us.' Derby, however, strongly defended Layard against both the Queen and the Prime Minister. He told Layard that he did not know of any despatches he had received at the Foreign Office which he read with so much interest:

I had difficulty in inducing the Queen to believe that they were not over-coloured. She takes a strong personal interest in the young King and naturally wishes to see things that concern him in the most favourable light. But the concurrence of testimony from other and independent sources has had its effect, and your accuracy is not now disputed.

One of Layard's reports concerned a chapel in a private house belonging to a British subject which had been closed and members of the congregation arrested because their prayers and singing might have been heard in the street outside. Gladstone wrote to Layard that if he succeeded in having the chapel re-opened, Alfonso ought to make him a grandee of Spain for the service he would have rendered. Layard knew that unless Alfonso could restrain the violence of the clerics and the right-wing politicians he would lose his throne and there would be a further period of chaos. Derby wrote to Layard on 12 April that whereas opinion had been at first universally in favour of the young King there had been a complete change: 'Your predictions as to the true character of the restoration have been fully realised, and those who thought them unduly gloomy have nothing more to say in their defence.'

Queen Victoria, however, continued to press for Layard's removal and Disraeli was still inclined to support her. He did not agree with all the fuss about Protestants, who 'really are nothing', he told Derby and referred to 'the exaggerated view' Mr. Layard took of Protestant interests in Spain. Derby wrote to Disraeli on 22 April:

> The question really is whether our representatives abroad are to send statements of fact which seem to them true, or to colour them and dress them up to suit what they suppose to be the prevailing ideas at home . . . I cannot agree to any proposal for [Layard's] removal, unless it were to give him a better post; and even then I do not think that this would be a convenient time.

Disraeli let Derby have his way and wrote to 'the great lady' to say that in the opinion of the Government Layard was substantially correct in his views and that he could not be removed for it would be a triumph for the *'parti prêtre'*.

Layard, as a Huguenot, certainly felt more strongly about the Protestant religion than did Disraeli, who had become an indifferent member of the Church of England at the age of thirteen, after his father had quarrelled with the rabbis. Certainly Layard was passionate on the subject of Roman Catholicism, especially when he saw its excesses in Spain under Alfonso—'That vile and detestable superstition which would crush all freedom of thought and all that is most precious in modern civilisation.' When the ancient custom of the *Lavatorio* was revived and the King ceremonially washed the feet of twelve old men in the presence of the Diplomatic Corps Layard excused himself from attending. It was against such men as Layard that the Archbishop of Valencia issued a pastoral letter saying that Spain would repel any foreign influence which was in favour 'of the exotic and wretched thing styled religious liberty'. A bishop declared that religious toleration was founded on the doctrine of the sovereignty of the people, which was a new doctrine accepted by England where there were four million human beings who did not believe in God.

'The only way of dealing with Spaniards', said Layard, 'is to treat them as Palmerston did and let them know that we have a fleet of which we can make use if necessary. France and Germany threatened them and had their way, but England was kind and obtained no redress.' He was not always kind himself. There was a Court ceremony revived from ancient days called the *Besamanos*. In a letter to William Gregory, who had been appointed Governor in Ceylon, he described the ceremony: about two thousand people passed before the King making a low bow, while the King 'looked awfully bored with his eyes on the gods and goddesses on the ceiling—like the idol worship in a Buddhist temple'. At one of these *Besamanos* Layard quarrelled with the Master of Ceremonies, a grandee 'blown out with pride and conceit'. In front of the Diplomatic Corps, who were in full dress at the Palace reception, Layard seized and shook him so hard that his uniform buttons nearly flew off; it was, he said, the only way to deal with 'presumptuous dons' and it helped him to work off his bile. Layard had been brought up in the diplomacy of Stratford Canning and Spain was as exasperating a country as was Turkey. Being proud and high-handed themselves the Spaniards appreciated Layard's determined and forceful character. On a visit to Bilbao he refused to receive the Commander of the Government troops there, General Barriel, because as Governor of Santiago in Cuba he had been responsible for the execution of the crew of the *Virginius*. Barriel complained of this 'outrageous' behaviour and when the Spanish Foreign Minister asked Layard for an explanation, he said he had no intention of meeting an 'assassin' who had not been brought to trial. That did not improve relations with the Spanish Government but it started good relations with Mr. Caleb Cushing, the new United States Minister. Derby supported Layard in this as in other cases—'You know my views on Spanish matters and you know also that I have entire confidence in your judgement.' With their tradition of vendettas, the Spaniards could not help admiring his persistence (his family motto was *Perseverando*). When Frederick Roberts, an English engineer, had been murdered in Seville, Layard pursued the murderer for five years until he was brought to justice. Frederick Roberts had given a ball to which he had not invited the son of the local mayor and this was regarded as a terrible insult to the family. The next day in the street Roberts was held by the mayor while the son stabbed him to death and the mayor's wife danced on his body. The Superior Court of Seville acquitted the three of them on the argument that Roberts had insulted 'the world-renowned noble and chivalrous character of the Spaniard'. Layard insisted that the case should be carried through one court after another until eventually the murderer was condemned to thirteen years penal servitude.

Layard behaved as he considered an Englishman ought to behave and showed his contempt for the corrupt high society of Madrid and its 'utter unblushing immorality' which exposed himself and Mrs. Layard 'to the insolent rudeness and discourtesy of the ignorant, bigoted, and priest-ridden fine ladies of Madrid'. He was even more contemptuous when, on the visit of the Prince of Wales, all the grandees suddenly became friendly because they wanted to meet His Royal Highness at a ball at the British Legation. It was remarkable that Layard had managed to survive seventeen administrations alternating often from one political extreme to another while all other countries had changed their diplomatic representation at least once during that period. He told Hammond that he was on good terms with men of all parties, scrupulously abstaining from giving advice or interfering. When Spaniards asked his opinions he replied that he considered all of them 'a parcel of fools, if not something worse, for sacrificing their country and themselves to trumpery personal squabbles and petty ambitions!' 'Political life here is not unlike dram-drinking in other countries,' he wrote to Elizabeth Eastlake. 'One gets a kind of political D.T. and nothing but war, revolution, murder and sudden death satisfies the appetite'.

Layard's views were much influenced by events in Spain and in France. Having seen the attempts to set up extreme democratic institutions abroad he realised 'how dangerous and fatal to civilisation and order and peace' they were, and he hoped that in England the working classes would have sufficient good sense to be suspicious of those who wished to foist a republic upon them. He had, indeed, moved some way away from Liberalism and a long way from Gladstonian Liberalism. Layard argued very sensibly that he was a diplomat serving whatever government was in power in England. Though he knew he should be discreet, it was his nature to express himself strongly and, since he wrote so many letters, his views were fairly widely known.

PART FIVE

Diplomacy: Turkey

1877 –1884

1

'Gladstone a mere vulgar pamphleteer'

Unrest in European Turkey, which had started in Herzegovina and Bosnia, had spread to Bulgaria where Turkish officials were massacred in April and May 1876. The Turks reacted violently and took their revenge by killing many thousands of Bulgarians in villages of the Rhodope Mountains. Edwin Pears, a lawyer in Constantinople, sent reports to *The Daily News* and anti-Turk feeling ran very strong in England. Layard who was on leave in London during the summer of 1876 thought that everyone was mad on the subject of Turkey. 'The English have these periodical lunacies particularly when religion is involved', he told Morelli. Disraeli was very flippant in his speeches and thought at first that there was much exaggeration, saying that the consular reports did not support such figures as twenty-three thousand deaths given in stories from newspaper correspondents. Gallenga, correspondent of *The Times* in Constantinople, wrote 'diplomacy did thus throw a gauntlet to journalism

which the Press was in duty bound to take up and a conflict
arose'. In speeches in and out of Parliament bitter things
were said and 'the Jew' was accused of being indifferent to the
sufferings of Christians. Gladstone had retired from the leadership of the Liberal Party, to the relief of many in the party
including Layard, and was writing on religious subjects at
Hawarden, but the atrocities committed against Christian Bulgarians roused him and he poured out his emotion in his pamphlet
Bulgarian Horrors. Layard read the proofs of it in John
Murray's office with disgust and said it would lead to war. Forty
thousand copies were sold in a few days and two hundred thousand in all. Disraeli considered it passionate, vindictive, and not
strong, but it created a powerful body of opinion in the country
against Disraeli's support for the Turk as a bastion to Russia.
Carried away by Gladstone's rhetoric—talk of 'fell satanic
orgies' and of Turks as 'the great anti-human specimen of
humanity'—many believed that true religion was in danger.
Gladstone dedicated the pamphlet to Stratford Canning and
borrowed his Shakespearian phrase that the Sultan should be
cleared 'bag and baggage' out of Europe. In a letter to *The
Times* he explained that he was referring to the Turkish officials
and not to the people as a whole, though Disraeli, Layard, and
others argued that he was demanding the expulsion of the
Turkish race from Europe. 'You cannot drive three millions of
Turks out of Europe into starvation and hopeless misery',
Layard wrote to Gregory. 'The wild humanitarian cry about
Turkey will lead to serious mischief. It is grievous to see a man
like Gladstone turned into a mere vulgar pamphleteer.' Layard
was a humane man and condemned the Turks for the atrocities,
but he had been close to massacres and knew that in the state of
semi-barbarism and fanaticism which existed among both
Christians and Moslems of the Ottoman Empire, they could
hardly be avoided every now and again. When Nestorians and
Yezidis had been butchered hardly anyone in England had
objected; this was the first massacre the British public had been
moved to notice. Layard considered that Gladstone was entirely
ignorant of the East and he disliked moral fervour worked up in
the Hawarden study. He argued, as Sir Henry Elliot had argued
in a famous despatch, that the emotional outcry was leading

people to forget England's interests—to prevent Turkey being
engulfed by Russia. It was for that reason he considered
Gladstone's pamphlet had struck the heaviest of blows 'to the
influence, interests and Empire of England'. He was thankful
that Disraeli was Prime Minister and that, being 'a great
political gladiator' in debate, he could counter Gladstone's
pernicious views. It was, therefore, with dismay that he heard
that Disraeli had allowed himself to be removed from the
House of Commons by accepting a peerage to become Earl of
Beaconsfield.

In Madrid Layard read the heated debates in the House of
Commons throughout the summer of 1876 and the violent anti-
Turk and pro-Russian articles written by Edward Freeman, who
considered that 'the names of Alma, of Balaclava and of Inkerman are names of national humiliation'. Some had known in
1854, said Freeman, and all knew in 1876, 'except professed
diplomatists,' that Turkish promises of reform were valueless
and that the Turk must be got rid of.[1] This point of view was
anathema to Layard. He considered that affairs had gone wrong
in Turkey because British influence had not been properly
maintained. 'We want another Lord Stratford if we could find
him', he wrote to a friend. 'To break up the Turkish Empire in
its present state would be to run the risk of forming two great
European Powers—Russia and Germany—the most serious
danger to England, to say nothing of Austria which would be
completely extinguished.'

When Layard heard that Murray was having an article
written for *The Quarterly Review* on Turkey, he wanted to
state his views, but as a diplomat he was not allowed to. He was
tempted, however, to send from Madrid some 'rough notes' to
William Smith, the Editor, who was going to write the article.
When published it aroused a great deal of interest and Layard
was glad 'for Smith's sake', but the views and the style are
clearly Layard's. Dr. R. W. Seton-Watson in his book *Disraeli,
Gladstone and the Eastern Question* accepted the article as
Layard's[2] and argued that it deserved special attention 'not
merely as the considered view of Disraeli's chief exponent in
the East, but also as the ablest and most reasoned contemporary
statement of the Turcophil position'. Layard was, he said, 'one

of the most original and arresting figures of the period and no other Englishman could have been found who possessed the same intimate knowledge of Turkish affairs'.

British policy in the past, Layard argued in the article, had been to maintain Constantinople and the Dardanelles in the hands of a power which was not to be feared for its hostility or ambition; the Turks were supported because there was no one to put in their place except Russia. 'Every true Englishman, until lately, felt instinctively that Russia in possession of that post would be the greatest danger and menace to England. It is now a fashion to put these opinions on one side as something almost too ridiculous to deserve serious consideration.' He considered that the Bulgarian massacres had been an exceptional occurrence, 'a brutal and horrible revenge for acts committed by Christians'. He was in favour of allowing the Ottoman rule to expire of itself, inducing the Turkish Government to administer justly and impartially, and giving the Christians time to educate themselves. Russia, however, did not want a strong and independent power to be established to the south of the Danube, whether Turkish, Slav, or Greek, and therefore discouraged all education and liberal institutions. She wished to bring about the break-up of the Ottoman Empire in Europe as soon as possible, so that she could keep the peoples of the Balkans weak and divided. Russia, argued Layard, believed it was her destiny to occupy Bulgaria, Constantinople, and the Dardanelles. In that position she would be able to concentrate her naval strength in the Black Sea and from there issue forth to attack the Suez Canal and by sinking a few vessels in it she could cut off British communications with India—'Are we to occupy Besika Bay for ever, or to take possession of Cyprus, or Crete, or of Egypt itself?' Russia, in possession of Constantinople, would in course of time inherit the Turkish Empire, for lawlessness would furnish constant pretexts for further extension of territory.

The way to deal with the problem was to bring diplomatic pressure to bear from without upon the Porte. Under the governments in which Mr. Gladstone had been one of the leading members, however, the policy of non-intervention had been extended to Turkey, and the Ambassadors were discouraged from interfering in the affairs of the country. Economy was the order

of the day and British Consuls were removed: 'To this policy and
state of things may be traced much of what has recently occurred,
and we therefore charge upon Mr. Gladstone much of the
responsibility for recent events. . . . It is difficult to understand
how men, calling themselves Liberals, should advocate injustice
or persecution against a whole race, merely because that race
is not Christian.' Layard wrote that encouraging Christian
minorities would result in an internecine war which would be
more horrible than anything that had happened so far; it would
eventually lead to the organised tyranny of Russia instead of
the irregular tyranny of Turkey. That would be the result of
the policy advocated in Mr. Gladstone's 'untoward pamphlet'
which was re-echoed by men 'happily of little consideration'. If
diplomatic pressure could be exercised by the representatives of
all the Powers, instead of by one, so much the better, 'provided
that it can be exercised honestly and disinterestedly'. The next
step was to ensure something like permanent Government in
the provinces and, far more important than decrees, was to find
the right men for the posts. There should be civil and religious
equality, a code of civil and criminal law and of commercial law,
a cadastral survey, a proper system of taxation, and colleges for
training men of all creeds to be judges.

That was Layard's brief for an ambassador to Turkey and he
hoped that he might be the one to carry it out. General Ignatieff,
the Russian Ambassador in Constantinople, knew very well that
Layard as ambassador would be a formidable opponent and he
took advantage of his friendship with Lord Salisbury during the
conference in Constantinople in December 1876 'to warn him
against the candidature of Mr. Layard'. He reminded Lord
Salisbury that Layard had close connections with Turkey and
was mixed up in its financial affairs so that he did not offer 'the
necessary guarantees of impartiality'.[3]

When Sir Henry Elliot, the British Ambassador, was recalled
after the abortive Constantinople Conference, Layard's hopes
rose, but he knew that there would be great opposition to his
appointment as for some reason, he said, he was regarded as
pro-Turk and that Gladstone would be 'frantic'. It was the most
important diplomatic post to fill at that time and there were a
number of diplomats eager for it. Beaconsfield wrote to Lady

Bradford: 'What we want is a man of the necessary experience and commanding mind at this moment in Constantinople—and one not too scrupulous. But such men are rare everywhere.' He decided that Layard was the best man, having revised his first view of him as a diplomat.

The Layards left Madrid on 12 March 1877 very thankfully. Layard had the satisfaction of considering that he had saved Spain from two wars, one against France and the other against the United States.

2

Disraeli makes Layard Ambassador

Queen Victoria, who had not liked Layard when he was Minister in Madrid, was won over by his charm when she received him as the new Ambassador to Constantinople. They also had a bond in their dislike of Gladstone and she told Lord Beaconsfield, the Prime Minister, that she was much pleased with Layard's 'tone', adding, 'he is very strong upon the vital interests of this country, which Mr. Gladstone and some of his followers have entirely forgotten'. Layard received many letters of congratulation; 'more charming than words can describe that you should now be the great Elchi', wrote Odo Russell; 'What a time and a place for your energies', said Dean Stanley; 'Don't get us into another Crimean War', wrote Lord Granville. Gladstone was not pleased at the appointment and Granville tried to reassure him about Layard, 'he is a very strong man with orientals and I think he will be faithful to instructions, if the latter are of the right sort'. Gladstone, however, was convinced that Layard would encourage the Turks to resist reform and, being headstrong and forceful, would carry out his own policy in Constantinople, putting British interests above morality, as Gladstone considered Sir Henry Elliot had done in his reaction to the Bulgarian atrocities. *

* Sir Henry Elliot's despatch of 4 September 1876, expressed views very similar to Layard's and caused an uproar. He said that he was not a blind partisan of Turkey and that he had been guided by a firm determination to uphold the interests of England : 'That those interests are deeply engaged in preventing the disruption of the Turkish Empire is a conviction which I share in common with the most eminent states-men who have directed our foreign policy, but which appears now to be abandoned by shallow politicians or persons who have allowed their feelings of revolted humanity to make them forget the capital interests involved in the question.' Lord Derby, the Foreign Minister, reacted strongly and cabled the next day that any sympathy England had felt

357

'What is to be the consequence to civilisation and humanity', said Gladstone in the House of Commons, 'if British interests are to be the rule for British agents all over the world, and are to be for them the measure of right or wrong?' He praised Layard for his 'able and zealous work' in Madrid but in the House of Commons, said Gladstone, Mr. Layard had been 'by far the most effective, and by far the furthest-going advocate of the Government of Turkey'; the appointment had been the special subject of thanks by the Turkish Government which considered it a 'delicate attention'. *'A delicate attention!'* exclaimed Gladstone, 'to that Government which has made itself responsible for the massacres of Bulgaria!' He said that if Russia failed in dealing with Turkey it would be a disaster for mankind 'and the condition of the suffering races, for whom we are supposed to have laboured, will be worse than it was before'; if Russia succeeded in helping them she would secure for herself 'undying fame'.[1] Sir John Drummond-Hay, who was Minister at the Court of Morocco and had served with Layard in Constantinople under Lord Stratford de Redcliffe, wrote to say that he agreed that it would be a very difficult post: 'An ambassador cannot look alone, as in the days of Ponsonby and Redcliffe, to the course he deems would best serve the interests of his country —and I may add of Turkey—but he must seek to satisfy lynx-eyed humanitarians and others, even though he may know that the real cause of humanity will not be benefited.'[2]

*   *   *

The Layards left London in April 1877 for Brindisi where they embarked in the Royal Yacht *Osborne,* which had been lent by Queen Victoria and they arrived off the Dardanelles at daybreak on Friday, 20 April. The new Ambassador was sailing into the most exciting, stormy, and important period of his political life. For the next three years he was to be one of the

for Turkey had been completely destroyed by the Turkish atrocities in Bulgaria and that if Russia declared war against Turkey the British Government 'would find it practically impossible to interfere in defence of the Ottoman Empire'. (*Parliamentary Despatches Turkey No. 1,* 1877.)

View of Therapia (Tarabya)

The British Embassy Summer Residence

Sultan Abdul Hamid riding to the Mosque

key figures in the climax of the nineteenth-century battle by
Russia to control Constantinople and the vast disintegrating body
of the Ottoman Empire. No more would he be subject to the
will of the haughty and irascible Lord Stratford de Redcliffe:
'To be of any use one must be at the head of the Embassy',
Layard had once said. From the deck of the yacht Layard pointed
out to Enid the landmarks of the romantic city of Constantinople
of which she had heard so much. As the sun rose and slowly
dispersed the mists she found the scene extraordinarily beautiful: the wooded shores of the Asiatic side, Princes' islands, and
the hump of Plati, Bulwer's island. As they sailed out of the Sea
of Marmara into the narrow neck of the Bosphorus she saw, rising
above them, the mosque of St. Sophia, the Sultan Ahmed, with
its six minarets, and the great mosque of Sultan Suleiman and
to port above the sea-wall was the huge Palace of the Seraglio.
Sailing boats and caiques crowded the waters and over the
waves dashed restlessly hither and thither flocks of shear-waters
—condemned human souls according to the Turks.

The Royal Yacht rounded Seraglio Point and made fast to a
buoy in the entrance to the Golden Horn below the famous
tower of Galata and the Embassy caique came alongside to take
them ashore. The Ambassador was received by Turkish Government officials and a guard of honour drawn up in their bright
ceremonial uniforms. Layard and his party stepped into open
carriages and drove in procession up the steep hill to Pera
through the Galata quarter and passed the great Galatasaray
Lycée. Enid was delighted by the variety of the Constantinople
crowds, porters with huge loads, women and children in bright
costumes, old wooden houses, the horses and the donkeys.
Everywhere was noise and confusion. Then at the top of the hill
the carriages turned into the gateway of the British Embassy, a
haven with large trees, grass lawns, and flower-beds, with only
the noise of the horses' hooves and the jangle of harness; it was
almost like an arrival at Canford Manor. They alighted at the
imposing entrance and Layard greeted many old friends among
the English and Turkish staff.

The British Embassy in Pera is a fine, solid building of three
storeys but the rooms are so high that it is the equivalent of
about four storeys of a normal house. Layard was surprisingly

harsh in his comment 'a monument of lavish expenditure of
public money, combined with false economy, ignorance and bad
taste'. Its thirteen large windows on the south look out over the
Embassy gardens to the Golden Horn and to the many famous
mosques on the high ground on the other side; its site is one
of the most beautiful in Istanbul. Following a great fire in
1831 the new building was designed by Mr. W. J. Smith and
Sir Charles Barry made some modifications and gave it the
magnificence of an Italian palace with a huge glass-covered
courtyard from the ground to the roof and a broad white marble
staircase leading up to the first floor.* Enid found it 'very cold
and dull and grand'. It had not been too grand for Lady Stratford
de Redcliffe who enjoyed giving fancy-dress balls in the magnificent ballroom with its glittering chandeliers. The Embassy
had been gutted in the great Pera fire of 1870, when Sir Henry
and Lady Elliot had had to run from the building; it had been
refurnished and newly decorated but had not been quite completed for Layard's arrival.

Enid Layard enjoyed giving balls† but she never grew to like
the British palace at Pera, preferring the summer residence of
the Embassy at Therapia. This was Layard's favourite too, and
on the first Sunday he was free they went there in the Embassy
caique with ten rowers in white shirts and frilled trousers tied
under the knee, white stockings, no shoes, and red jackets
embroidered in gold. The waters of the Bosphorus raced strongly
against them like a vast river flowing between the Black Sea
and the Mediterranean, but there was calmer water in the little
bays fringed by charming old wooden houses; sometimes they
had to be pulled along by men on shore and every now and again

---

* *The Builder* in February 1847 stated that Mr. W. J. Smith was
the architect, whereas on a picture of Sir Charles Barry in the
Embassy the building is ascribed to him. There is also some dis-
crepancy with regard to the date. In the Latin inscription on the
facade of the Embassy it is given as 1844; according to Ministry of
Works' records it was not completed until 1851.(3)

† Today only very occasionally does an enterprising Ambassadress
give a ball during the summer when the Ambassador moves from
Ankara and takes up residence for a few months at Istanbul; otherwise
part of the building is the house and offices of the Consul-General.

one of the rowers recited a verse from the Koran as encouragement. They passed near the long front of the baroque white marble palace of Dolmabache, where Sultan Abdul Aziz had been seized and imprisoned by Midhat Pasha and where his nephew Murad had lived during the brief period that he was Sultan. Layard pointed out the Cheragan Palace, where Murad was then kept a prisoner by Sultan Abdul Hamid, while on the hill above could be seen the trees of the huge Yildiz Park where Abdul Hamid had taken up his residence behind high walls. It had seemed safer than the Dolmabache Palace, exposed to gun-fire from the sea, and haunted with evil memories of deposed Sultans. It was exhilarating to be travelling again along the Bosphorus and Enid was an enthusiastic companion; it was nearly thirty years since he had first travelled that way by caique to deliver Colonel Taylor's despatches and had been ill-received at the Embassy at Therapia, or Tarabya as it is now called. They passed the elegant mosque of Ortakoy, the fishing village of Arnaut Koy, the village of Bebek, and then the towering walls of the four-hundred-year-old castle of Rumeli Hisar. Boats were repaired in the creeks and after rounding the promontory of Yenikoy they met the usual strong current and had to be towed the last part of the journey to Therapia. There were few roads in those days and the Bosphorus was the main channel of communication. In the summer most of the Embassies moved towards the Black Sea, the British, French, and Italian Embassies to Therapia, and the Russian, German, and Greek to the next bay of Buyukdere. 'It is just at this time of the year [May to November], when the capital of the Ottoman Empire stretches throughout the whole twenty miles' length of the Bosphorus, that the unmatched loveliness of this channel is seen to the greatest advantage.'[4]

When the Layards disembarked at Therapia there was no main road to separate them from the steep path, which led them up to their summer Embassy standing on a rocky platform with the Bosphorus below and a sheer cliff rising in wooded terraces behind. Enid liked the large wooden house which was to be their home during a greater part of their time in Constantinople, and she described it as roomy with two wooden turrets and a delightful garden full of lilac, roses, and laburnum

in full flower with 'the nightingales singing lustily'. The house
that Layard had known had been burned down but he shared
Enid's pleasure in the new one.* Even the careful and timid
young prince Abdul Hamid had been moved to have a romantic
affair at Therapia in the spring of the previous year with Flora
Cordier, the fair young Belgian who kept a milliner's shop
there in the summer. The shop was much frequented by the
members of Embassies and in the evening she was able to tell
Abdul Hamid some of the gossip which he was always avid to
hear. Regretfully the Layards embarked in the evening to
return to the Embassy at Pera. The current was so strong that
they were rowed the ten miles from Therapia to Galata in one
hour, half the time taken for the outward journey. As in Venice,
water was the main means of communication and it was one of
the reasons why they loved both cities. 'You are accustomed to
the gondolas that glide among the palaces of St. Mark, but here
at Stamboul it is a 120-gun ship that meets you in the street.
Venice strains out from the steadfast land, and in old times would
send forth the chief of State to woo and wed the reluctant sea;
but the stormy bride of the Doge is the bowing slave of the
Sultan. She comes to his feet with the treasures of the world—
she bears him from palace to palace—by some unfailing witch-
craft she entices the breezes to follow her and fan the pale
cheeks of her lord—she lifts his armed navies to the very gates
of his garden—she watches the walls of his *serai*—she stifles the
intrigues of his ministers—she quiets the scandals of his courts
—she extinguishes his rivals, and hushes his naughty wives all
one by one. So vast are the wonders of the deep!' Layard would
have been quick to comment that what Kinglake wrote in
Eothen over thirty years before as to the ruthlessness of Sultans
was no longer true, and that Ministers were banished to Europe
instead of being drowned in the Bosphorus.

*   *   *

* This house was also burned down in 1911, but the wooded hill and
gardens remain an attractive site and travellers from England are
sometimes given permission by the British Consul-General to camp
beside the Bosphorus where the Embassy summer residence used to
stand.

Ch. 2   Disraeli makes Layard Ambassador

Before leaving London Layard had had long talks with Beaconsfield, Salisbury, and Derby. The Sultan and the Sublime Porte
were to be told that they had forfeited England's sympathy
owing to the massacres of Bulgarian Christians and because those
responsible had not even been punished. Layard was to make it
clear that if there were to be war between Russia and Turkey
the British Government would not give any help and the Porte
was to be advised to do its utmost to avoid war.

The Turkish Ministers were extremely anxious to know what
the British Ambassador had to say. They knew him well as a
friend of Turkey and there had been messages from Musurus
Pasha, the Turkish Ambassador in London, suggesting that
Beaconsfield and Queen Victoria were well disposed, but they
knew that Gladstone and others had worked up strong feeling in
England against them. The Porte was apprehensive, for the
country had no money nor any prospect of obtaining any following
the suspension in 1875 of interest payment on the debt. Both
Austria and Germany were working with Russia, and France
was still recovering from the Franco-Prussian war, so that England was their only hope. Edhem Pasha, the Grand Vizier,
was irritable with anxiety and Safvet Pasha, the Foreign
Minister, suffered more than usual from a nervous twitch in his
face. When Layard had given his message they left in deep
gloom to report to the Sultan who was eagerly awaiting them at
the Yildiz Palace.

On 24 April 1877 Layard presented his credentials. Accompanied by sixteen members of the Embassy staff he drove in
the State carriages sent by the Sultan. After proceeding to the
Bosphorus through the narrow Pera streets, the five carriages
continued along the water's edge until they reached the Cheragan Palace, where they turned up the hill into the large Yildiz
Park and stopped before the modest 'Star' Kiosk, which was
Abdul Hamid's Palace. It was more like an exotic country-
house, and the marble steps were less impressive than the staircase at the British Embassy. The Ambassador and his party
were received by the Sultan in the main reception room on the
first floor. After the formal ceremony Abdul Hamid said he
wished to talk to the Ambassador privately and accompanied by
Safvet Pasha they went to a small room opening from the hall

Layard observed closely this reserved young man of thirty-four, who had been Sultan for less than a year. Little was known of him for he had always been secretive. On his visit to Paris with his uncle, Abdul Aziz, in 1867 he had not revealed that he knew French so that he might learn the more, and in London he had kept silent while his brother Murad angered the Sultan by stealing the limelight with his vivacity and intelligence. Layard noted Abdul Hamid's profound melancholy and the pallor of his skin:

> The Sultan was somewhat below middle height. His figure was slight and lithe. His beard and hair jet black. His features showed no trace of Tartar origin, nor did he appear to resemble any of his predecessors—except perhaps Sultan Mohamet, the Conquerer, whose portrait by Gentile Bellini, taken from life, is in my possession. The type was rather that of the Armenian or Jewish race; which seemed to give some countenance to the scandal current in the gossipping circles of Pera and Galata that he was not the son of Abdul Mejid, but had Armenian blood in his veins. . . . He was very simple in his dress wearing a frock-coat and nothing to distinguish him from an European gentleman except the red Turkish fez on his head.

The Ambassador repeated the message that he had brought from the British Government; the Minister of Foreign Affairs acted as interpreter and Layard was able to follow the Turkish well enough to judge if his important statement was properly translated. The Sultan listened in silence and then said:

> I am sure that the Queen of England will feel for me. I came to the throne very young and without experience, at a time of unexampled difficulty, and under circumstances with which the world is acquainted. I cannot be held responsible for the state in which I found my Empire. I am willing, ready and desirous, to do all in my power to ameliorate its condition. I know that war can only make that condition worse. . . . I would not intentionally crush an ant under my foot. How then could I be capable of wishing to sacrifice the life of a single man? But a great Power is determined to force me into war.

Layard continued to emphasise the need for concessions as he had argued in Spain with Prim and Castelar. It seemed to him that he would be successful but while he was still talking with the

Sultan a telegram arrived from the Turkish Ambassador in Moscow announcing Russia's declaration of war against Turkey.

If there had been more time Layard believed that he might have succeeded in preventing war. He reported to Lord Derby that the Sultan had 'insisted upon his desire for peace in a very touching way, and with tears in his eyes. There could be no doubt as to his perfect sincerity'. Hammond, who had retired from the Foreign Office and had been made a peer, told Layard that Russia's sudden resolve to go to war might be due to her apprehension lest Layard's influence at the Porte should lead to reforms, 'and so cut from under the Moscovite feet all pretext for hostilities'. Harriet Grote wrote from England:

> Society is very much distracted between its two aversions—the Merciless Turk and the Barbarian Russ but I am inclined to think that the Turk is the least liked of the two. . . . You are now the principal figure, as it were, in Eastern Europe and I doubt not exercise a prodigious influence there. Your Predilection for the Turk is so generally recognised that I need not comment upon your partiality. I suspect, however, that you have plenty of sympathisers here—in high places at least.[5]

There were divisions in the Cabinet. Salisbury and Carnarvon were suspicious that the Prime Minister wanted war with Russia; Derby was very friendly with the Russian Ambassador, Shuvaloff, and did his utmost to discourage an anti-Russian policy; the Queen, who had become very anti-Russian, was worried 'day and night' lest Britain should act too late and lose her prestige. With Beaconsfield and Layard she believed that Russia intended to try to take Constantinople, in order to control Eastern Europe, the Eastern Mediterranean and the Persian Gulf. Gladstone considered that Beaconsfield and Layard were indifferent to the sufferings of the Christians of the Ottoman Empire; Edward Freeman assured Mme. Novikoff* 'there are numbers of

* Olga Novikoff, daughter of a Russian Officer, was known in London for her charm, intelligence, and vivacity and had as friends such men as Gladstone, Edward Freeman, Froude, Carlyle, and Kinglake. She took up writing and politics after her brother, Nicholas Kireyev, one of the first of the Russian volunteers in the Serbian war against Turkey, was killed in 1876. Mme. Novikoff had considerable influence in the pro-Russian set in England and Beaconsfield called her 'Member of

English-men who thank God for the success of Russian arms, who rejoice at the deliverance of Armenians and Bulgarian Christians'. Layard regarded such talk as treachery and considered that it was wicked to make it a religious question—to be concerned about the fate of Christians and not about the fate of Moslems. He had a very vivid memory of the gory Turkish heads laid at the feet of the Prince of Montenegro, who had become such a hero to Freeman and others. Layard reported to Derby in June: 'The Montenegrins appear to have been indulging in their old habits of horribly mutilating the Mussulmans who had fallen into their hands.' It seemed to Layard that the gigantic sacrifices of the Crimean War, and all that he had so vehemently fought for over twenty years before, had been in vain. Russia was advancing to engulf the Ottoman Empire; after that it would be the turn of India, and the British Empire itself might be doomed. Layard saw the future in dramatic starkness, and felt himself to be alone in this battle. None of his diplomatic colleagues were prepared to support Turkey against Russia, and in London there was as much confusion and division as at the time of the Crimean War. *

On the day that Russia had declared war, 24 April 1877, she had sent an army corps across the Pruth river and had advanced upon Jassy, while the Rumanian troops retired. A Russian army had entered Asiatic Turkey and was advancing on Batum. Hobart Pasha, who was serving in the Sultan's navy, arrived at Constantinople in a gunboat from the Danube where he had run the gauntlet of the Russian shore batteries. Layard had to tell him that, as England was neutral, he would be struck from

Parliament for Russia'. W. T. Stead, the well-known journalist, was in close touch with her during the Russo-Turkish War of 1877–78 and wrote *The M.P. for Russia: Reminiscences of Olga Novikoff* (Andrew Melrose, 1909).

    * Professor J. A. R. Marriott writes in *The Eastern Question*: 'With the break up of so extensive an empire as the Ottoman and with the fear of Russian intentions it was natural that there should be a cleavage in opinion as to what should be done. The difference was very often between those who argued that the Ottoman Empire should be left to destroy itself forthwith, and those who, like Layard, argued that its collapse should be delayed until other nations of the Balkans were ready.'

the British Navy List if he remained in the service of the Sultan.
Hobart decided to stay with the Turkish navy for which he
was violently attacked by sections of the Press in England.

Gladstone, presumably to annoy Layard, sent him another
pamphlet, in which he said he had lodged 'a fearful accusation
against the Ottoman Government'. He wrote that for the last
eight months he had given the whole of his time and thoughts
to the Eastern Question: 'It is a matter of honour and duty that
I should continue to do so; I hope that it will be the last of my
political anxieties. My first desire is the liberation of the disturbed
provinces.' Layard considered that Gladstone knew nothing
about the Eastern Question and was continuing to do infinite
harm. 'The agitation in England', he replied, 'has caused the
unhappy war which will certainly lead to incalculable misery
to Christians and Mohammedans alike.' He added that the
numbers of killed in the Bulgarian atrocities had been much
exaggerated, that he had a high opinion of Sultan Abdul Hamid's
character and that the new Turkish Parliament had so far
worked well. Gladstone was not convinced.

The Porte was in a panic and Layard received almost daily
communications from the Sultan asking for advice. These came
through General Said Pasha, head of the Sultan's military household who had trained for several years at Woolwich, spoke
excellent English, and had a liking for tea. The other messenger
was the Greek, Zarifi, who was the Sultan's private banker and
had been his close companion when as a young prince he had
shown a great interest in figures and accounts. There was hardly
any money in the Treasury so that the troops were without pay
and some nearly starved; Layard showed the Sultan a sample
of the bad bread that the troops were expected to eat.

While insisting to the Sultan that no help would be forthcoming from England, Layard in his telegrams to London urged
that the Russian advance must be stopped. He prophesied disaster
from Constantinople and the Queen was doing the same from
Windsor, sometimes using Layard's phrases. Referring to the
reports from Layard she wrote to Beaconsfield to say that warning
after warning had arrived and Lord Derby did not say a word—
'Such a Foreign Minister the Queen really never remembers!'
Two days later, on 27 June, she wrote that the Russians would

be before Constantinople 'in no time'; the Government would then be fearfully blamed and the Queen so humiliated that she thought she would abdicate at once. She wanted her Prime Minister to be bold and to rally his followers and to tell them that the interests of Britain were at stake. It was for conquest that Russia was waging the cruel, wicked war and not for the Christians, who were 'quite as cruel as the Turks. . . . Only say Russia *shall not* go farther and she will stop but if this be not done and done quickly it will soon be too late; and we shall then have to do much more than we shall have to do now.' That was Layard's repeated argument.

The Prime Minister was distressed at Derby's dilatoriness and took the unusual step of by-passing his Foreign Minister and writing to Layard directly, in secret. 'Understand', he said, 'that this is not an official communication, but one strictly personal and of the utmost confidence.' He wanted Layard to consider whether there were not ways of placing England in a commanding position when the conditions of peace were discussed 'notwithstanding the paralysing neutrality in vogue'. He praised Layard for his skill and energy. Layard knew that the Sultan would not agree to any of the proposals that Beaconsfield had put forward in his letter, unless England were prepared to declare herself as Turkey's ally. He told Beaconsfield that his position was a most difficult one 'with much to ask and nothing to give, and what has passed has given the Porte great suspicion and distrust of us'. He argued that in order to check Russia, England would have to abandon her position of neutrality; but that was a policy that the Government could not pursue, as Beaconsfield kept on trying to explain both to Layard and to the Queen. Layard did not realise how divided the Cabinet was until he received his first letter from Lord Derby at the end of June. It seemed to him to have been written by a man who did not realise the consequences of the Russo-Turkish war or the interests of England and it was at variance with the theme of the Prime Minister's secret letters. Derby said he could well understand Layard being disappointed at the abandonment of the Turkish cause and he realised why it should have given rise to such bitterness, but opinion in England had been practically unanimous. There had been apprehension that England might be involved in another Crimean struggle, and 'dislike of war is just now the strongest feeling'. Germany, he said, was wholly with Russia, France kept to herself, while Austria held different language to different Powers. With regard to Layard's strong reaction to the peace proposals which had been put forward by the Russians, all Derby had to say was 'Your opinion is just what I believed it would be.' Layard considered that it was the duty of a great statesman to guide and not to bend to public opinion. He could only hope that Beaconsfield would succeed in dominating the Cabinet.

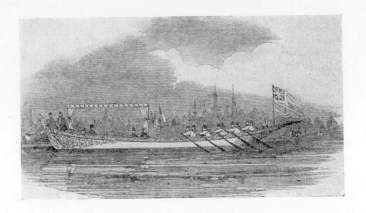

'The amiable
Sultan Abdul Hamid'

On 15 May Layard and Enid had been invited to visit the Sultan
but when they arrived at the Yildiz Kiosk they were told by
Said Pasha that His Majesty was indisposed and could not see
them. Layard learned that Rediff Pasha and Mahmoud Pasha,
the Sultan's brother-in-law, were with Abdul Hamid. Both
Pashas were hostile to England so that Layard guessed that they
had arranged that he should be refused an audience, but he
made it clear that he did not intend to be put off in this way.
General Said Pasha took them round the gardens and gave them
luncheon in the Malta Kiosk which Enid considered was well
served—cutlets and cold meat with dolmas of rice in vine leaves,
good cheese of the country and 'splendid' strawberries while
decoration of diamonds on the coffee-cups fascinated her. She
found the gardens lovely, full of trees and flowers; there were
miniature lakes with waterfalls crossed by little bridges, aviaries

of birds, many varieties of duck, swan, geese, and gazelle. This huge park was a pleasure-ground in which Abdul Hamid took great pride; he used to wander through it admiring the flowers and birds, visiting one little summer-house after another, often stopping to take coffee.[1]

After luncheon they were told that Abdul Hamid would after all receive them. The Sultan, said Enid, 'bowed and then put out his hand and shook hands' asking her to sit in an arm-chair near him. The four of them sat together with Said Pasha acting as interpreter. It was a pleasant room with good carpets and fairly comfortable chairs instead of divans, and there were one or two little tables which had been made by Abdul Hamid with delicate mother-of-pearl inlay. Layard was delighted by the view from the window: 'It overlooked Stamboul with its innumerable domes and minarets, Seraglio Point, the Golden Horn, the Bosphorus for nearly half its course, and the sea of Marmara with the Princes' islands, backed by Mount Olympus, still covered with snow and the distant mountains of Bithynia.' For two hours they sat and talked, most of the time rather gloomily. 'We are accused by Europe of being savages and fanatics,' said the Sultan, 'but we are not the savages who have brought on an unjust and horrible war, which will lead to the sacrifice of innumerable human lives; nor are we the fanatics who have incited the Greeks, Bulgarians, and Armenians to exterminate those who differ from their religion.' Layard emphasised the need of an amnesty for captured Bulgarians which had been promised, but the reply was that it would be dangerous to release men who would incite the Bulgarian population to rebellion and bring about further massacres, 'thus furnishing,' said the Sultan, 'fresh material to Mr. Gladstone for denouncing me and my government and thus again arousing the indignation of England.' Layard continued to urge the need for the amnesty and for punishing the Turks responsible for the massacres; at the same time he was impressed by the Sultan's good sense and intelligence: 'He was calm and logical and listened to me with patience and kindness, although I ventured to address him with complete frankness and without reserve.'

There is a reliable witness to the work that Layard did on behalf of the Bulgarians in Mr. George Washburn of the

American Robert College, who stated that Layard's relations with
the Sultan 'were more intimate than those of any other Ambassador before or since. He was consequently in a position to mitigate,
in some measure, the severity of the treatment of the Bulgarians
by the Turkish authorities. We were able, through his influence,
to save some lives in Bulgaria of old students and others.' Mr.
Washburn also revealed the difficulties facing the Sultan, whose
orders were not always obeyed, and this led him eventually
to try to take all power into his own hands. There were fifty
Bulgarians, mostly former students of Robert College, who had
been imprisoned by the Turks, and Layard was, said Washburn,
given details of each case:

> He saw the point and took our paper to the Sultan, who also
> saw the point and in Mr. Layard's presence ordered the immediate
> release of these men. Nothing was done and Mr. Layard again
> spoke to the Sultan. He immediately summoned the official to
> whom he had given orders and asked why his orders had not been
> carried out. It was said that they had not yet verified the statements
> in our paper. Again he gave orders and again nothing was done.
> A third time Mr. Layard called the Sultan's attention to the matter.
> He gave this answer: 'Have I not given my word?' Nothing was
> ever done until the Russians at San Stefano secured their release.[2]

Enid liked the Sultan but found him very nervous: 'His nails
were bitten to the quick, but he seemed full of intelligence
and the desire to do right, and every now and then his eyes
flashed with merriment when anything amused him—a dear
little man.' Layard told Derby that the Sultan had more decision
of character and more firmness than he had expected, but that
he was timid and alarmed. Men such as Rediff Pasha and Mahmoud Pasha worked on the Sultan's fears so that he had, said
Layard, 'mental hallucinations and a terror of assassination'.

Abdul Hamid had long known that there was a ferment
beneath the surface in Turkey, for he had attended some of the
meetings of the 'Young Ottoman' reformers with his brother
Murad when they were princes. In the spring of 1876 Sir Henry
Elliot, then the Ambassador, had reported that even the porters
in the street and the boatmen on the Bosphorus were openly
demanding a constitution and should Sultan Abdul Aziz refuse
to grant one he would be deposed. Elliot had been eager for a

constitution and worked closely with Midhat Pasha, the Grand
Vizier, to that end. Abdul Aziz had wished to make his country
flourishing and powerful, but had no idea how to set about it,
preferring to watch cock-fights in his palace. 'What is the use of
a blockhead of a Finance Minister if he knows not where to
find money?' he had said. Sir Henry Bulwer, when Ambassador,
had described him to Layard:

> The secret springs, which set the resources of a country in move-
> ment and produces wealth out of which armies and navies are
> maintained, are unknown to him. They strike him as mere
> details. . . . Tho' in nowise cracky, he is certainly over-excited and
> does not show that straightforward simplicity in his character and
> conversation that there was formerly. Too much, in fact, has been
> put on his mind and the constant suspicion and doubt under which
> he lives has produced a sort of nervous anxiety.

'There was no thing so deeply seated in his brain as the con-
sciousness that the whole world was made for himself alone.'[4]
Yet Sultan Abdul Aziz was so afraid of poison that he endangered his health by a diet of hard-boiled eggs, since he believed
that they could not be tampered with, and when he was deposed
at the end of May 1876 by Midhat Pasha, there was nothing
left to him and he committed suicide with a pair of scissors
borrowed from his mother to trim his beard.[3] Murad had been
taken from prison in the Cheragan Palace, and placed on the
throne, but Midhat Pasha soon found that he was unable to
assume the responsibility, as his mind had been softened by
excessive alcohol. Midhat needed the support of Hussein Avni,
the strong man of the Cabinet, at such a period of near revolution. Gallenga, who had been in Spain when Layard had first
arrived there, regarded him 'as the Prim of the May revolution',
but Hussein Avni was assassinated, as well as another Minister,
by a disappointed Circassian fanatic:

> By that tragedy of the 16th of June, Turkey was placed in the
> same position in which Spain was left when deprived of Prim's
> master-mind by a band of cowardly assassins, and Murad's sur-
> viving Ministers must have realised the feeling of King Amadeo,
> when he alighted, a lonely stranger at the Atocha in Madrid, and
> saw lying in his bier, bathed in blood, the man who had been the
> builder and who alone could be the supporter of his throne.[4]

These assassinations drove Sultan Muzad out of his mind. He too, had to be deposed by Midhat Pasha and Abdul Hamid was made Sultan on 31 August 1876. Even from the beginning of his reign divergent views were held about the new Sultan, Abdul Hamid the Second. Gallenga attended the 'Ceremony of the Sabre' on 7 September, when a procession of six caiques rowed by white-clad Albanians took the Sultan along the Golden Horn to the mosque of Eyub. Abdul Hamid passed within two yards of Gallenga: 'It seemed to me the countenance of a ruler capable of good or evil, but knowing his own mind and determined to have his way, a man conscious of himself and bent on exacting his due.' To Salisbury, who saw him at the time of the Conference of Powers in 1876, the Sultan had seemed 'too helpless and nervous, too hopelessly a prey to a variety of fears, to be capable of independent thought and action'.

Abdul Hamid had been eager to be Sultan, but that did not mean that he was grateful to Midhat Pasha. He considered that the dethronement of two Sultans in three months was too much responsibility for one man, and feared that it might develop into a habit. He could exile Midhat, but he could not get rid of the Constitution and the Parliament, not immediately at any rate. The Turkish Parliament showed itself surprisingly useful, kept in order firmly by Layard's old friend Ahmed Vefyk Pasha, the President of the Chamber. It was attended by Arabs from Syria, Mesopotamia, and Arabia, by Christians, Armenians, Albanians, and others, 'a respectable, intelligent, and dignified body of men,' Layard said. 'I believe that the Turkish Parliament was the most hopeful and most important reform that could have been introduced into the Turkish Empire.' He gave proof of his approval by giving a large party at the Embassy in Therapia for a number of the delegates. The Sultan often praised the Parliament for he realised that it impressed England and Europe. He told Layard that, although Midhat had obtained the credit for the Turkish Constitution and Parliament, it was he, Abdul Hamid, who had suggested them: 'Do you think that I should wish to destroy my own handiwork?' Layard realised the Sultan was more truthful on another occasion when he said angrily that the Parliament was run by a few men who had been to Paris and 'dressed in the French fashion with bright

The Golden Horn

The Bosphorus

Abdul Hamid II

neckties and polished boots, who had brought back revolutionary
ideas about equality'; they were scamps, without religion or
morality, who had used the name of Murad and Midhat to
undermine his authority and to upset his Ministers.

In order to achieve anything in Turkey the ambassadors had
to frighten the Sultan or gain his confidence and it was better
to do the second. In the first year or so Layard kept ahead in this
competition. He and the Sultan liked each other; the Sultan was
touched by Layard's enthusiasm for the people and regions he
had visited in the Ottoman Empire and reassured by the sense
of confidence he inspired, representing qualities which the Sultan
had come to associate with England. Abdul Hamid's father had
instructed him to count on England as Turkey's best friend and
Stratford Canning had made a deep impression on the youthful
prince by patting his head in a kindly way. Ever since his
beautiful Circassian mother had died of consumption at the age
of twenty-six, when he was seven, he had wanted kindness but
had generally rejected it in mistrust; his foster-mother, Peresto,
had watched over him but he gave little indication that he realised
her kind nature. In Mrs. Layard, a year older than himself, he
found both the kindness and assurance which he appreciated
and admired. The Sultan wanted friendship from England, but
his overtures were rejected. The Queen of England and the
great Prime Minister, Lord Beaconsfield, seemed friendly yet
at times they appeared to be less powerful than Mr. Gladstone
and what was called 'public opinion'. This seemed to Abdul
Hamid a sign of weakness.

Layard was reassured by what he had seen of the Sultan.
'He is just the man who, under guidance and control, could and
would do much for the happiness of his subjects', he wrote to
Lady Eastlake. To the Prime Minister he said that the Sultan
had given 'a very significant proof of his friendly feeling', that
the Ministers were well disposed, and those who had been hostile
to the employment of Englishmen in the Turkish forces had
been removed. 'I heard from Mr. Layard today', wrote Beaconsfield to Lady Bradford on 6 September 1877. 'He seems to have
completely re-established our influence at Constantinople, and
to have entirely gained the Sultan's confidence, whom he continually represents to me as one of the most amiable men he

ever knew; with nothing but good impulses. . . . Do not mention this letter of Mr. Layard, as ours is a "secret" correspondence.'

The Layards were frequently invited to visit the Sultan at Yildiz, and it was regarded as a special mark of favour when Mrs. Layard was invited to dinner, as it was the first time that the wife of an ambassador had been entertained in this way. Abdul Hamid was anxious that everything should go well and before dinner on the first occasion walked round the dining-room with his secretary, to make sure that everything was in order. The party consisted of the Sultan, the Grand Vizier, the Foreign Minister, Mahmoud Pasha, the Sultan's brother-in-law, and Said Bey, the private secretary who acted as interpreter.*

> The dining-room opened upon the conservatory, which was lighted up with coloured lamps. The splash of the fountain added to the charm of the place and gave a sensation of coolness, which was exceedingly agreeable. The dishes served to us were French, with the exception of an excellent Turkish pilaff, and not good. Wine was handed to us, but not to the Sultan or his Mohammedan guests. His Majesty drank a kind of sherbet of which he partook with Mrs. Layard, who, like himself, was an abstainer from wine, helping her himself out of his own bottle. The dinner was not ill-served, but the attendants were slovenly in dress and had no livery or uniform.

The Sultan spoke about his visit to England with his uncle, Sultan Abdul Aziz. He had especially admired the gardens in England and he pointed with pride to the flowers on the table. Enid was delighted when he spoke of his fondness for birds and how their songs cheered him when he was feeling anxious and melancholy. He questioned Layard about Spanish bullfights, expressing his abhorrence of them and saying that he did not believe the story that they were introduced into Spain by the Arabs, since cruelty to animals was absolutely forbidden by the Moslem religion. He talked, said Layard, unaffectedly, agreeably, and sensibly and 'few crowned heads could have shown to

* He was usually known as 'Little Said' and later became Grand Vizier, responsible for many of the Sultan's reforms. Layard distrusted him but considered him very able. The Ambassador's friend was another Said, General Said Pasha, known as 'English Said'

better advantage'. They were kept until late in the evening, the Sultan smoking one cigarette after another and talking on all manner of subjects. Afterwards they were conducted back to the Embassy at Therapia by an escort of cavalry, each horseman carrying a paper lantern.

*   *   *

Dr. Seton-Watson has argued that in dealing with the Turkish question, 'the initial blunder was Layard's profoundly mistaken estimate of Abdul Hamid, readily endorsed by Beaconsfield and for a time accepted by Salisbury'. He was writing after Abdul Hamid became known as 'The Red Sultan' because of his responsibility for the terrible Armenian massacres. Most of those who have written of Abdul Hamid have regarded him as sinister, deceitful, and intent on being an autocrat from the first moment he came to power. Today, however, there is a reassessment, concentrating more on the many educational and other reforms he introduced than on the massacres and it is possible that the final estimate may be nearer to Layard's picture of him.[5]

Layard had had a great deal of experience in judging the character of orientals and had learned to expect deceit. He realised that Sultan Abdul Hamid was impressionable but believed he could be guided on the right lines if his entourage were well chosen. In the very full and interesting accounts of Abdul Hamid in his long *Memoir*, Layard describes him as a man genuinely anxious to help his people—certainly in the first two years or so—but he was overwhelmed by events and too much was put on his mind. He had, Layard considered, inherited the taint of insanity from his ancestor, Sultan Ibrahim—'his father, Sultan Abdul Mejid, and his Uncle Abdul Aziz, and his grandfather, the celebrated Mahmud, showed in different ways and degrees the symptoms'. Although brought up in ignorance among eunuchs and concubines, Abdul Hamid had by his intelligence and shrewd observation in France, England, and Constantinople learned a great deal of 'the secret springs which set the resources of a country in movement'. There are many witnesses to attest his charm and intelligence, but few have written as favourable an account of him as Layard. Certainly

377

his opinion of the Sultan changed, but it is possible that he is right in arguing that circumstances, and they were terrible enough, changed the character of the Sultan. To Layard he was a figure of high tragedy—he became a plotting Iago, but he was driven to it by fear and as a means to maintain the independence of his country.

The internal unrest brought about by the war made the Sultan terrified of intrigues to reinstate his elder brother Murad on the throne and Murad's mother was active in trying to prove that her son had recovered from his insanity and should there-fore again be Sultan. She sent agents to the British Embassy pleading that the Ambassador should visit Murad to see for him-self, but Layard naturally refused; information he received showed that Murad was still insane. The daily reports from his many spies, often invented, filled Abdul Hamid with such panic that he suffered periodic fits of madness. He could have been rid of the fear that Murad might return to the throne by having him murdered, as most of the preceding Sultans would have done. The existence of this unhappy prisoner in the Cheragan Palace frequently drove Abdul Hamid to frenzy. He would wander from one room to another at night in Yildiz, fearful of sleeping and expecting an assassin behind every door. He became suspicious of his courtiers, his Ministers, and of his generals and a small telegraphic apparatus was fitted up in one of his rooms at Yildiz to enable him to keep in direct contact with the Commander-in-Chief in Bulgaria and to give him orders which did not help the progress of the campaign. He never, however, took any steps to have Murad murdered.

4

'Turkey is fighting
our battle'

Layard wrote to his friend Lord Lytton, Viceroy of India, that
the Turkish Ministers were in a panic and were turning to
England for advice and help but 'we can give neither'.[1] The
Porte became suspicious of British intentions, encouraged by the
many Russian agents and by the German Ambassador, Prince
Reuss, who was advising the Sultan to make a secret agreement
with the Russians, since England and Layard were working
against Turkey's interest. Layard told Beaconsfield that the
Turks could not understand English policy; they were made to
believe that, 'although we will not help them, we are disposed
to help ourselves and are looking out for our share of the spoils'.
He argued that it was very important to fortify the Gallipoli
Peninsula and perhaps occupy it with British forces. The
Ambassador's position was made more difficult by the visits to
Constantinople of Mr. Butler Johnson, M.P. for Canterbury,
who had considerable influence with the Sultan and who said
that the English people would compel the Government to help
Turkey and that it was a mistake to listen to the Ambassador's
advice to the contrary.

Layard's first year in Constantinople was one of great labour
and anxiety. Sometimes he wondered whether he had acted
wisely in accepting the difficult mission. When the Turkish
town of Ardahan fell to the Russians in May 1877 theological
students from Asia Minor tried to break into the Turkish Parliament to protest against the Turkish defeat. By the end of June
the Russians had crossed the Danube and by July had captured
the principal towns in northern Bulgaria. General Gurko struck
south with his light cavalry raiding as far as the Thracian valley
of the Maritza river. Behind his forces came large groups of

Bulgarians, who had taken refuge in Rumania following the Turkish massacres of 1876 and who now returned as 'The Avengers' and were as ruthless as the Turks had been. There were disturbances in Constantinople as each day brought ever worse news of the massacres of the Turkish population in the Balkans. The Sultan directed his Ministers to call the attention of the European Powers to these outrages which he considered far exceeded the atrocities of the previous year in Bulgaria by the Turks. It would be for Europe to judge, he said to Layard, who were the real 'barbarians'. Layard wrote to Derby on 11 July that the Sultan's mind and health might give way altogether, faced as he was by disaster for Turkey and failure to prevent the massacre of Moslems. Thousands of refugees took ship from Varna to Constantinople and distressing reports from the British Consuls in Bulgaria and Eastern Rumelia were published as Parliamentary Papers (Blue Books) and made a considerable impression in England, though Gladstone attacked Layard for sending what he considered to be false reports. It was a new doctrine, said Lord Elcho, 'that Consuls and Ambassadors were not to be trusted or believed, when they do not act and report in the same sense he would like'.

The Sultan appealed to Queen Victoria to use her influence with the Czar to put an end to the atrocities : 'His Majesty can scarcely believe that the Czar desires that this war should become one of extermination, and one waged rather by brigands than by a civilised nation'. The Queen was very distressed by the message, and Layard's telegrams continued to add fuel to her indignation. She considered that Mr. Layard's arguments could no longer be disregarded and that Gallipoli must be occupied. The language of the Russians against England was so insulting —'it makes the Queen's blood boil! What has become of the feeling of many in this country?' On 20 July Layard was able to telegraph to Lord Derby that the Turks had at last begun to build fortifications in Gallipoli. He had had to make an appeal direct to the Sultan which had infuriated the Grand Vizier, Edhem Pasha. In a rage he told Layard that the orders had been given to please the Ambassador and in the interests of England, who had betrayed and deserted the Turks: 'What does it signify whether the Dardanelles are in the possession of Russia or not?

We can make better terms with her ourselves than through the interference of England.'

In August 1877 news was announced of Osman Pasha's important victory at Plevna. Beaconsfield was delighted; he told Layard that, if the Turks could hold their positions through the summer, the Russians would have to mount a second campaign in the winter if they wished to carry on the war. The Prime Minister in his secret letter of 6 August allowed his imagination to have free play and it has been argued, not at all conclusively, that Beaconsfield wanted war in the summer of 1877.* He was not confident, however, that the Turks would be able to hold out and thought that the Russians might rally and reach Adrianople in the autumn. 'What then is to be done?' he asked Layard. 'With her suspicions of England, Turkey would be ruined.'

Layard found relief in pouring out his distress to Lytton, emphasising that his letters must be considered as strictly private. He spoke freely, but at the same time he was bound, he said, to carry out Government policy. He considered that Lord Beaconsfield in the Indian, as in the Turkish Question, held to the opinions of those great statesmen 'who made the British Empire what it is', but he had to contend with men who would reverse 'our ancient and wise policy'. He thought they would ruin the Turkish Empire, which would sow the seeds of the ruin of the British Empire.

The British had placed themselves in the undignified and fatal position of leaving Turkey to her fate, although she was 'fighting our battle'. There was rejoicing when she won a victory because England profited, though she said no word in Turkey's defence and allowed Russia to undermine Turkish influence and interests: 'all this is because some passionate and irregular minds discovered a year ago that a semi-barbarous government permits semi-barbarous things'. Layard could not stem the torrent and he could only prepare for the time when the English

---

* Dr. Seton-Watson in *Disraeli, Gladstone & the Eastern Question*, pp. 218, 219, states: 'There can be little doubt that Beaconsfield was very materially influenced by Layard's alarmist and inflammatory letters, and that the two encouraged each other in a fantastic forward policy, which fortunately did not appeal to the Cabinet as a whole.'

people were ready to resist Russia: 'We are essentially a great Mohammedan Power and I cannot conceive anything more likely to strike a blow at our dominion and prestige in India than if we were to allow Russia to conquer Constantinople, and to drive out the Sultan.'

Salisbury did not at first agree with the Layard-Lytton view that Turkey could be supported or that Russia was a real danger. He was an aristocrat, who prided himself on his common sense which he administered in frequent doses. If the noble Lord would use a larger map, wrote Salisbury to Lytton, he would not be so worried about the likelihood of Russia invading India; if Lytton listened less to the advice of soldiers he would not be so gloomy, and anyway it was a mistake to trust to experts. Layard found his aloof aristocratic attitude tedious and rather dangerous. He regretted that Salisbury had not been more expert as a diplomat when he represented Britain at the Constantinople Conference of 1876; alternatively he should have acknowledged his ignorance and trusted his diplomatic expert, Ambassador Elliot. 'He set at nought the most elementary rules of diplomacy by showing his hand at starting' wrote Layard, for both he and Lady Salisbury had sided with the Russians 'and declared themselves in open enmity to Elliot and the policy he pursued'.

Salisbury was against the Crimean policy and in favour of partition of the Ottoman Empire. He summed it up in his phrase: 'The commonest error in politics is sticking to the carcasses of dead policies.' As a Radical Layard would have agreed, but in reference to Turkey and Russia he preferred the traditional policy nor did he think that Salisbury was the best judge to decide when any policy had become a carcass. He told Lord Lytton that Salisbury was 'a fatal influence' over the Cabinet, he was a strong man with a decided will but no knowledge of Turkey, or of India or Russia. Layard considered that at the Constantinople Conference 'we recklessly threw away all our power for good to obtain absolutely nothing in return, except the cynical contempt of Russia and of other Powers. What Turkey has been able to do [the victory at Plevna] shows how completely ignorant Lord Salisbury, and others of his school, were of her resources and of the vitality which still existed in her people.' This ignorance was to be regretted, but it was the 'treasonable' statements of some of the members of the Opposition which made Layard almost sick with anger. If it were true, Edward Freeman had said, in a speech which received considerable publicity, that British power in India would be imperilled and the civilised world would crumble should a Russian ship appear in the Mediterranean 'then, I say, perish the interests of England, perish our dominion in India, rather than that we should strike a blow or speak a word on behalf of the wrong [Turkey] against the right [Russia]'.(2) Layard could not forget that speech and he believed that Gladstone and others were behaving in a manner which he considered to be treacherous. Out of these divisions of opinion and high emotion there developed the 'Negroponte Affair' which did more to damage Layard's career than any other single incident. If he had paid attention to some of Henry Bulwer's advice he might have avoided getting himself into such trouble.

Negroponte was a Greek resident of Constantinople, described by Layard as 'President of a Secret Committee' actively engaged in promoting insurrection among the Greek population in the Turkish provinces bordering on Greece. He had asked Gladstone for his opinion as to the best course for the Greek subjects of the Sultan to pursue to obtain their independence and, unwisely, Gladstone replied to him in two letters. It was not clear what Gladstone intended, but Layard took it for granted that he wished to encourage Negroponte to stir up insurrection and wrote to Beaconsfield on 22 August 1877, 'Mr. Gladstone is doing his best to incite the Greeks to rise. His letters to a Mr. Negroponte, a well-known Greek intriguer and conspirator here, are shown about. . . . One could have believed that the course taken by Mr. Gladstone last year [over Bulgaria] had cost carnage and misery enough without adding a Greek rebellion to it.' Layard had been shown one of Gladstone's letters in the middle of an Embassy garden party and had remarked that there was a good story there for Mr. Gay, the correspondent of *The Daily Telegraph*. Layard's views on Gladstone were well known in Constantinople as well as in London and *The Daily Telegraph* was pro-Turk. On 27 August, a few days after the Embassy party, a slashing attack was published by its Constantinople correspondent accusing Mr. Gladstone of fomenting the Greeks to insurrection and it was not surprising that Layard was suspected of having had something to do with it. Gladstone protested in a letter to *The Daily Telegraph* against what he considered to be a dastardly attack made anonymously, 'there is some Polonius behind the curtain and I call upon him to come out'.[3] Layard did not come out because he had gone with Enid to visit the British fleet and make an excursion to Troy. Gladstone also had difficulty in clearing up the matter with *The Daily Telegraph* as Mr. Gay had gone to report the siege of Plevna.

When Layard returned to Therapia he found copies of *The Daily Telegraph* and sent a despatch on 29 October stating that the correspondent's report from Constantinople was nothing to do with him and he added some criticisms of Gladstone. Lord Tenterden, Permanent Under-Secretary at the Foreign Office in succession to Hammond, sent the despatch to Gladstone, who wanted certain questions to be asked of the Ambassador. Layard did not answer any of the communications he received as he had, he considered, more important matters to deal with. Finally Lord Derby telegraphed to ask if the Ambassador was preparing a despatch, to which Layard replied, 'I have not thought it necessary to continue controversy with Mr. Gladstone'. When the latter received that answer he was so infuriated that he decided to bring the dispute to an issue, but it was some time before the matter was brought up in the House of Commons. Layard's Liberal friends considered that he had got himself into unnecessary trouble by refusing to reply—'We all feel that your case would have been saved by a final letter', wrote Hugh Childers.

What Gladstone thought did not worry Layard. He was much more concerned with his failure to obtain any clear instructions from London as to the policy to be pursued. Lord Derby was full of praise of Layard's despatches and wondered how he managed to find time to write them and thought it 'impossible to have dealt more prudently with a delicate situation'. That was little comfort. Derby, in November 1877 when it looked as if Plevna would fall and Adrianople be at the mercy of the Russians, was still saying that he did not want the Ambassador to try to obtain terms or to suggest mediation, until it was decided who would be the winner in the campaign. Layard commented bitterly in his *Memoir*:

> In the face of such grave events as the dismemberment of the Ottoman Empire, and of the reversal of the traditional and secular policy of England with respect to Eastern Europe, Her Majesty's Government were still in doubt as to the course they should pursue. The weakness of a divided Cabinet had its natural consequences in weakness and indecision in action.

All he could do was to try to maintain a personal influence over the Sultan and to prevent the Porte from abandoning herself to Russia in some secret agreement, while at the same time he had to avoid saying anything which would compromise the British Government. He wrote to Beaconsfield on 28 November stating that if Plevna and Adrianople fell the lines of Gallipoli and of Bouyuk Tchkmedji would be the only protection to Constantinople.

> In the present state of things, in our own interests as well as those of Turkey, I am bound to be exceedingly prudent and cautious. But hesitation and over-caution are not the best helps to diplomatic action in a great crisis. . . . Although I stand alone here and can neither expect sympathy or support from any of my colleagues who have a voice in the fate of Turkey, I do not despair of holding my own, and of maintaining the honour and interests of England, if I could only know what the intentions and objects of my Government really are, so that I could act with confidence and resolution.

The Porte was urging Layard to obtain funds to enable them to carry on the war. Beaconsfield was anxious to help, but his hands were tied by the Turkish decision two years earlier to suspend payment of interest on the Ottoman debt, a decision which was said to have been encouraged by the Russian Ambassador, General Ignatieff; nor in the circumstances was it possible for the Imperial Ottoman Bank to raise money on the London market. Beaconsfield was appealed to by the Turkish Ambassador in London, Musurus, and wrote to Layard on 22 November —'Most Secret—It has occurred to me, that some substantial assistance might be afforded to the Porte, if we could contrive to purchase some territorial station conducive to British interests.

Anything in the Mediterranean might excite general jealousy.'
He suggested various places, such as Batum or a commanding
position in the Persian Gulf, if Armenia were lost to Turkey: 'I
wish you would consider this matter and advise me thereon'. In
his reply Layard allowed himself to be carried away into memories
of his youth. He said that there was one important place at the
head of the Persian Gulf—Mohammerah—and he recounted
how he had examined the country with great care and was the
first to prove the navigability of the Karun; how a railway
would probably be built in the course of time through the
provinces of Khuzistan and Fars to Baluchistan and Sinde. The
idea of such a railway was no doubt gigantic, he said, but things
apparently equally impossible had been accomplished. He added
—to Beaconsfield of all people!—'If there be one quality
greater than another which is required in a Statesman it is the
power of seeing into the future. Now Mohammerah would give
us the command of the low country between the great and
difficult range of Zagros.' But Layard's advice that Mohammerah
should be given to Turkey had not been accepted in 1841 and
it belonged to Persia, so that the suggestion was not very helpful.[4]

After the fall of Kars in November 1877 Layard considered
that Russia would soon be mistress of Armenia and that they
were witnessing 'the end of the Byzantine Empire over again;
but the Turks are a far nobler race than the Greeks, and history
will perhaps do them more justice than we have'. He had a
heart-rending interview with Edhem Pasha who said that he could
not begin to understand how the nations of Europe could allow
all the bloodshed to continue. The Pasha estimated that one and
a half million Turks had died in battle, or had been massacred
or died from wounds, want, and exposure, and that half a
million Moslems, mostly women and children, had been driven
from their homes in Bulgaria and Eastern Rumelia. He argued
that with the advance of the Russians into Asia Minor, British
interests were seriously threatened but Layard could give no
hope and reminded the Grand Vizier that the British Government from the outset had made it clear that it had no intention
of taking any part in the war.

In December Layard wrote to Lytton that the end was

approaching for Turkey unless England went to her help. Russia had at first made the mistake of underrating Turkey's strength and resources but was now exerting her strength. She had Rumania with her, Serbia was preparing to go to war against Turkey, Greece was threatening invasion and Montenegro, said Layard, 'was already sending her barbarous warriors to burn and devastate the adjoining territory of Turkey'. England, he said, looked on 'hopeless and helpless' and it was all due to the 'unpatriotic and insensate' conduct of Gladstone. 'I write to you', he told Lytton, 'from the fullness of my heart and with something like feelings of despair.'

The news that Plevna, after a stubborn resistance of five months, had at last fallen on 10 December came to Layard from Lord Derby in London, for communications in the Ottoman Empire from the battle-front were exceedingly slow. Layard commented in his *Memoir* that the moment was opportune for peace terms to be drawn up, for the Czar had achieved an important victory: 'It was in the power of England to bring about peace, if her Government had chosen to act at this critical moment with energy and decision—and incalculable suffering and misery and complications and troubles and injury to our interests, prestige, and influence might have been avoided.'

Three days after the fall of Plevna, the Sultan decided to open the second Ottoman Parliament. It was an imposing ceremony attended by members of the Diplomatic Corps; the Sheikh el Islam, the Judges, Ulema, the Ministers, heads of the various religious communities—Moslem, Christian, Armenian, and Jew —the Senators, and the newly elected Deputies were collected to receive the Emperor of the Ottomans and their Caliph. With a plain uniform underneath the regulation military cloak His Imperial Majesty entered, accompanied by his two young brothers and other members of his family, and stood before a magnificent golden throne, part of the spoils of a campaign in Ancient Egypt. A secretary read Sultan Abdul Hamid's speech in Turkish. After referring to Russia's responsibility for the war and to the high proofs of patriotism shown by his people, he talked of the Constitution which conferred equal rights upon all the populations of his Empire and declared his intention of maintaining it in all respects; the war had prevented him putting

387

into force the many reforms he had intended. Afterwards Layard was summoned to a private meeting with the Sultan who dictated an appeal to Queen Victoria. He sent his deep sympathy for Osman Pasha in his misfortune and his high appreciation of the devotion he had shown in the defence of Plevna; he asked if the British Government would ascertain without delay if the Czar would agree to an armistice of three months, during which the terms of peace could be discussed; he added that, relieved of the anxieties of war, he would be able to introduce some measures for the improvement of the condition of his Christian subjects as would satisfy Europe of his firm intention to carry out the reforms he had promised.

In London on 17 December there was a stormy Cabinet meeting of two and a half hours and Beaconsfield threatened to resign in view of the hostile attitude of Derby and Carnarvon, but found unexpected and powerful support from Salisbury. It was finally decided that Parliament should be summoned for 17 January, that there should be a vote on an increase of the armed forces and that England should negotiate between the belligerents. Beaconsfield wrote after the meeting to Layard: 'If the Russians find a Plevna in Constantinople, or anything like it, the Ottoman Empire may yet be saved.' At the same time he considered that the Turkish Government should accept peace terms 'consistent with their existence as an independent Power of some importance. I have confidence in you at this trying moment, the most searching occasion since 1815.'

5

'It is Poland over again'

The year 1878 was one of continuous crisis. The Russian army advanced to within a few miles of Constantinople and it was thought that they would occupy it—a Christian power in the capital of the former Byzantine Empire after more than four hundred years. Layard kept much calmer in a crisis than might have been expected and displayed his abilities to the full, but he gave free expression to his misery in letters to Lord Lytton:

> It is Poland over again—and again Europe stands by indifferent, whilst the crime is committed. . . . If we lived in the days of Chatham or Pitt, I should say, if Russia attempts to annex Batum or any part of Armenia, let England at once take possession of that port and of the Dardanelles and of the mouth of the Bosphorus, and hold them until Russia is driven back over the Caucasus and

an independent state is formed between her and Persia. But in these days I fear that such heroic measures will not suit the spirit of Birmingham and Manchester.

The Government was, he said, paralysed by the Gladstone agitation and the opposition of the Liberal minority, but he hoped that the Prime Minister might find himself more free to act:

> He recognises and understands the extreme gravity of the situation, and the danger that the occupation of Constantinople by the Russians would be to our Imperial prestige and interests. . . . If public opinion renders it necessary that we should throw over Turkey, look to our share in the spoils, and think no more of our imperial interests, I am convinced that the part we shall play in this Turkish question will be the first step in the decline of the British Empire.

He had, he said, been telling the British Government so strongly and repeatedly what the dangers would be if Eastern Armenia fell to Russia that he expected to be in disgrace:

> Do not think that I am in favour of war; on the contrary I am doing my utmost here in favour of peace. I am persuaded that the best way to obtain it is by holding firm and unequivocal language to Russia and her confederates who think they can treat England as an effete nation.

At the beginning of January the Russian armies began to break through the Balkan mountains which were Turkey's main protection. On 7 January General Said Pasha, in charge of the Imperial household, came to the British Embassy with a moving message from the Sultan urging that the British Government should obtain the requested armistice without delay. He was being pressed by prominent Turks, supported by the German and Austrian Representatives, to separate himself altogether from England and to come to a direct understanding with Russia as the only means of saving his Empire. That course was repugnant to him but it would be an immense responsibility for him to carry on the war unless there were some promise of aid from England. Could Layard give him some assurance speaking either in his capacity as Ambassador or as friend? Layard had to reply that he could not give any assurance or advice in any

Mahmoud II by Gentile Bellini

Opening of the Turkish Parliament

capacity. The same evening Layard had another long and unhappy interview with Edhem Pasha, and with Server Pasha, the Foreign Minister. The Grand Vizier spoke with great bitterness against England for having put Turkey in such a perilous position. On 10 January came news of the overwhelming defeat of the Turkish army at the Shipka Pass, when forty battalions were surrounded. The Sultan sent another appeal to the Queen of England and Empress of India.

Queen Victoria wrote to the Prime Minister that she could not remain sovereign of a country 'that is letting itself down to kiss the feet of the great barbarians, the retarders of all liberty and civilisation that exists. . . . Oh! if the Queen were a man, she would like to go and give those Russians, whose word one cannot believe, such a beating!' Beaconsfield was ill and had failed to win over the Cabinet to more positive action to stop Russia's advance. On the same day as he received the Queen's emotional letter he had to see the Turkish Ambassador and he may have expressed his own sympathies with Turkey in a more decided manner than was wise, as he apparently had already done on a previous occasion. The telegram from the Turkish Ambassador gave the Sultan and the Porte the impression that England was taking up Turkey's cause with Russia; in fact the Czar had snubbed and angered Queen Victoria by replying to her appeal that his Commanders-in-Chief in Europe and Asia knew the conditions on which a suspension of hostilities could be granted. The Sultan, believing that discussions had already started between England and Russia, ordered his troops to cease fire but the Russians continued to advance to the confusion of the Turks. When a telegram came from Derby stating that the only way for the Porte to learn the terms was by making direct contact with the Russian Commanders at their headquarters in Europe and Asia, the Sultan and the Porte considered that England had betrayed them.

The Grand Duke Nicholas, who commanded the forces advancing on Constantinople, informed the Porte that there could be no armistice until the bases of peace were determined. As it would take some time to conclude peace terms, it meant that the Russians intended to advance as far as possible in the meantime. The Turks had at the same time to deal with the

Montenegrins and Serbians who had entered Turkish territory
and with the Greeks who were preparing to cross the frontier.
The Turkish Press, controlled by the Palace, published carica-
tures illustrating Britain's 'cowardice'. Derby was still in the
Cabinet and as indecisive as ever so that it was difficult to reach
a clear-cut policy. Layard was outraged by an 'insolent' remark
made to him by Prince Reuss, the German Ambassador, who had
said that Lord Derby would no doubt find a way to reconcile
with British interests anything that the Russians might do,
including the occupation of Constantinople and the Dardanelles.
Layard had warned Beaconsfield in December 'the new element,
the German, in Eastern politics deserves our grave consideration'.
Prince Reuss was, he said, altogether favourable to Russia and
was working against mediation and to exclude England from
all share in the Eastern Question. On 12 January Layard's
despatches were discussed at a stormy Cabinet meeting which
lasted three hours. There was also a memorandum from Queen
Victoria in which she reminded the Cabinet that it had already
on a previous occasion decided that a threat to Constantinople
would free England of any obligation of neutrality. If those were
merely empty words, she said, England would sink to a third-
rate Power.

Layard was fighting on two fronts, against Gladstone who
was following up the Negroponte Affair, and against the German
Ambassador in Constantinople. Prince Reuss reported to Berlin
that Layard was more unreliable and mendacious than Ignatieff,
who 'at least deceives his fellow-men with ingratiating elegance. . . . The Turks cannot bear him and he abuses them, so
that they will no longer do what he advises.'[1] Bismarck was at
that time working very closely with the Russians and the German
Embassy in Constantinople had taken over the protection of
Russian subjects in the Ottoman Empire, refusing the Porte's
request that some, who were acting as agents for Russia, should
be removed. Layard told Beaconsfield that Prince Reuss openly
declared that Russia must dictate terms of peace in Constantinople. It was natural that he should dislike Layard who was
doing his best to maintain Turkish morale.

On Thursday 24 January the Layards were giving a dinner-
party to Prince Reuss and the Greek diplomatic representative,

Condouriotis, when an important telegram arrived from the Foreign Office. Layard left the dinner-table and went to his study to help in deciphering. It stated that orders had been sent direct to Admiral Hornby, Commander-in-Chief in the Mediterranean, to enter the Dardanelles and to proceed to Constantinople. Layard was to inform the Sultan and he sent the Oriental Secretary, Alfred Sandison, to the Yildiz Kiosk, where the Ministers remained in almost permanent session with the Sultan, so fearful were they that the Russians might capture the city by a *coup de main*. The German Ambassador had told the Porte that the British Government would never send the fleet, so that Layard was delighted to be able to snub him. He returned to his guests and said 'You will hear some news tomorrow but I cannot tell you what it is now', which intrigued Prince Reuss but he could get no more information. When the guests had left Henry told Enid and the staff that the fleet would arrive the next morning.

By the time that full daylight had come the news of the impending arrival of the fleet had quickly spread throughout the Moslem and Christian quarters. The Turks looked upon it as a heaven-sent intervention in their favour. Some Europeans welcomed it as a protection to themselves; others hoped for the entry of the Russians. The Diplomatic Corps was divided. So tense was the situation in Constantinople, owing to the proximity of the Russian armies, that thousands of people of all classes, races, and creeds had gathered upon every available spot overlooking the sea of Marmara and the Golden Horn to await the fleet. Henry, Enid, and the staff watched from the upper storeys of the British Embassy at Pera—but the fleet never came.

At breakfast Layard received a telegram from Lord Derby to say that instructions had been sent to Admiral Hornby not to enter the Straits. They ate in silence. 'We felt awfully low and disgusted', wrote Enid. 'Of course, we are the laughing stock of the place, especially of the Germans.' The newspapers of all languages in Constantinople poured ridicule on England and one caricature showed the inhabitants of Constantinople looking through telescopes for the fleet, which was being towed away by a small Russian boat.

The German Crown Princess wrote to Queen Victoria on
30 January: 'My Beloved Mama, . . . As to politics . . . I am in
horror and despair! The counter-order to the fleet has had a
deplorable effect; and all the *enemies* of England laugh and rub
their hands.' This time the vacillation had been due, not so
much to indecision in London, but to an unfortunate ciphering
mistake made in the British Embassy in Constantinople.[2]
While the Foreign Office was trying to decide what the telegram
meant the Russian Ambassador handed Lord Derby the text of
the terms which had been telegraphed from St. Petersburg 'in
case', said Shuvaloff, 'they should be distorted by Layard'. It
was finally decided in London that the despatch of the fleet was
not justified. Derby, who had sent in his resignation, now withdrew it as the order to the fleet had been cancelled. Layard considered that the Government had used the mistake in one
ciphered word in his telegram as an excuse and gave vent to his
feelings in a telegram to Lord Derby on 26 January. The counter-
order to the fleet, he said, had been attributed by the Turks to
fear and to the decay of that spirit which once characterised the
English people: 'England can no doubt afford to treat with
indifference or contempt these natural consequences of disappointed hopes and of international jealousies, although it
cannot be otherwise than painful to an Englishman to hear the
terms in which his country is now spoken of.' Layard was sure
that Shuvaloff had not communicated to Derby the full terms,
some of which were wholly unacceptable to the Turks. The
Grand Duke Nicholas and General Ignatieff, were delaying
negotiations as long as possible to enable the Russian troops to
advance on Constantinople.

The hourly reports about the Russian advance caused a ferment in the City of London and in Constantinople there
was panic and danger of serious disorders. Abdul Hamid,
convinced that his life was in danger, sent to Layard secretly
asking for asylum for himself and his family in case of emergency.
The Embassy gunboat *Antelope* was made ready. It was said
the Russians intended to make the seizure of the British Embassy
one of their first objectives and it was arranged that Enid and
the archives should go on board the gunboat *Flamingo* if the
Russian troops entered the city. The thousands of destitute and

desperate refugees pouring into the city from the west could have led to a very serious situation, but they were so starved and frozen when they arrived that they docilely accepted any relief that could be given. Enid was president of a committee of English women working for the refugees and the wounded Turkish soldiers. 'The Embassy is turned into a vast workshop', said Layard, 'and even the guards at the door, to say nothing of secretaries and attachés are set to roll bandages. . . . The distress among these poor refugees is quite dreadful.' The streets of Constantinople were encumbered by hundreds of thousands of them trying to keep warm in the heavy snow which fell at the beginning of 1878. George Washburn of Robert College, said that three hundred thousand refugees entered the city, and many died from typhus, smallpox, and starvation, 'altogether the most terrible experience that Constantinople had witnessed since the Turkish Conquest'.

Enid Layard went with the wife of one of the military attachés, Major de Winton, to see the trains full of refugees arrive from the west. The women and children were in trucks, the men on the roof. Some had fallen off numb with cold, others were frozen to death on the trains and stories were told of mothers in despair throwing their dead or dying children out of the windows. In the mosque of St. Sophia alone there were five thousand refugees. Layard and Enid paid a visit to the gallery and looked down on an extraordinary scene. The pavements of the vast building were covered by a mass of human beings crouched together in the utmost squalor, the sick and the dying together. Every now and again the dead were carried out. Major de Winton, and Mr. Bartlett, who had brought supplies in a ship chartered from England, distributed bread, soup, and charcoal. 'It was a curious contrast', said Enid, 'looking down on this misery and then looking up at the glorious building—the finest temple in the world—with its gold mosaics and fine marbles.' She took Henry to see the house taken over by the 'Compassionate Fund' which she controlled and a new smallpox hospital her organisation had started in school buildings handed over by Ahmed Vefyk Pasha. The latter had been named 'Prime Minister' for the Sultan considered this a more modern title than Grand Vizier. Enid Layard's committee was able to draw on generous helpers in England. Baroness Burdett-Coutts sent Layard twelve thousand pounds for the refugees, the administration of which added to his work; Mr. Young and Dr. Leslie came with a second ship chartered from England with seven thousand pounds' worth of commodities for the wounded and Queen Victoria sent two cases of bandages. 'Mr. Layard's account of the sufferings and misery of the poor Turks', she wrote to Lord Derby, 'makes one's heart bleed, and makes one also blush to think we have allowed this.' Those who came to help were not all as efficient as Mr. Bartlett and Mr. Young. Lady Strangford was setting up a hospital and causing a lot of trouble, according to Enid, who considered that she was mainly interested in publicity about her own heroic conduct. 'Just now', wrote Enid to her mother, 'we see rather too much of these philanthropists and their squabbles.' There were also pro-Russian philanthropists collecting money in England for the Russian wounded and some of them were at the front, including Layard's former friend Dr. Sandwith. He had been on a mission supplied with large sums of money from English sympathisers to help the Serbian refugees, had congratulated the Russian Chancellor on the capture of Plevna, and at the end of 1877 went to Bucharest as a delegate of the Russian Sick and Wounded Association.

With Greece's invasion of Turkey there was still more suffering. A 'wanton, wicked and cowardly' act, Layard described it for Greece had given assurances to the Porte and to the Western Powers that she had no intention of attacking Turkey. He relieved his feelings in a sarcastic despatch to Derby:

> Upon the recognised principle of international law, that in order to establish a legitimate claim to a neighbour's territory one has only to cause a disturbance in it, Greece has invaded Turkey. Prudently following the example set by Serbia, she has waited until the Turks are down, and can offer little resistance to a wanton aggression. Blood will flow afresh, fields and villages will be desecrated, and thousands of old men, women and children will be driven from their homes to die of want or to live in hopeless misery. But all this is done 'in the purest spirit of philanthropy' and religion; the invaders will probably be wished God-speed in their holy mission.

It would not have mattered if such despatches had been read only in official quarters, but then even confidential despatches were communicated to the House of Commons or published remarkably quickly as Parliamentary Papers (Blue Books). Layard warned Derby of the mischief which could be caused by publishing information secretly obtained. The Porte was very nervous as to what might appear in the dreaded Blue Books, but Derby wrote 'I have always been anxious that the public as well as the Cabinet should have them [the despatches] in order that the whole case should be as fully as possible before the nation.'[(3)]

At this period of high emotion, when the citizens of Constantinople were expecting the arrival of the Russians, Layard received letters from Schliemann at Troy and from Rassam at Mosul; they wrote from within the Ottoman Empire, but were entirely concerned with their own affairs and oblivious of the war. Schliemann invited him to Hissarlik to prove that he had discovered Troy and announced the happy news that Mrs. Schliemann expected 'a little Priam or Hecuba'. Rassam wanted Layard to obtain a more comprehensive firman as he believed he had discovered an Assyrian city fifteen miles east of Mosul. This was the discovery of the famous bronze gates at Balawat over which there was much controversy. Birch of the British Museum wrote asking Layard to encourage Rassam, for he thought it would be the last chance for the British Museum to carry on excavations as Russian influence would paralyse all future operations in Mesopotamia. He also received a letter from de Cesnola, who had been excavating in Cyprus, stating that he owed his successful discoveries to Layard. 'Many a time I felt despondent and tired', he said, 'but by the perusal of your books and letters I found new strength and courage.'[(4)] A letter came from George Dennis, whom Layard had first met in Venice in 1839, asking if he might dedicate his book *The Cities and Cemeteries of Etruria* to 'the patriarch of British explorers, by whose example in resolutely overcoming difficulties all subsequent excavations have greatly profited'. It was good for Layard to have his thoughts deflected to archaeology.

Layard found strength and encouragement in Enid with whom he discussed his troubles. She followed events closely, copied telegrams, acted as hostess, visited Turkish ladies and organised relief for the refugees. Apart from the war Layard and Enid could not imagine a better place to live than on the Bosphorus, especially during the spring and summer when they were in the lovely Embassy summer headquarters at Therapia. They were good hosts and gave excellent parties at the Pera Embassy and at Therapia. When the staff of the Embassy came to dinner Enid sang Spanish songs playing her guitar and she held dances weekly, as at Madrid. During the year the staff was increased by the arrival of more military attachés including Layard's nephew, Julian, son of General Frederick Layard. They rode through the lovely countryside, gardened, played croquet, badminton, and tennis, in which Layard joined when he could spare the time. Admiral Hornby, the Commander-in-Chief of the Mediterranean Fleet, used to arrive in his launch with parties of officers to dinner-parties and dances. There were receptions at the German, Austrian, Italian, and French Embassies and visits to Layard's Turkish friends. Enid paid visits by caique along the Bosphorus, or by carriage and sometimes by sedan chair because of the narrowness of the Pera streets.

The Russians threaten Constantinople

On 31 January 1878 an armistice was signed and the Turks laid down their arms but the Russian advance still continued. Sympathy for Turkey was growing in England owing to the severity of the Russian terms. The Cabinet was preparing for the eventuality of war but the Opposition was unwilling to agree to a credit of six million pounds. While this was being debated on 8 February, a telegram from Layard sent on 5 February was read out in the House of Commons. It was a dramatic announcement that the Russians were very near to Constantinople and continuing to advance, intending to occupy the lines of Tchataldje on that day. This had a great effect on the House. The Russian Ambassador followed up immediately with a note from the Russian Chancellor, which was also read to the House before the debate was concluded, denying rumours of an advance on Constantinople. A friend in the Foreign Office told Layard that he believed the Russian Ambassador had a drawer full of such official *dementis* which he produced at appropriate moments. The credit, however, was agreed. The Foreign Office tried in vain to get confirmation from other Governments of Layard's despatch which had been sent via Bombay as there were serious delays by the normal route, but none of the other Ambassadors had used this quicker means of communications.

The Opposition had tried to throw doubts on Layard's trust-worthiness by giving prominence to interviews published in *The Daily News* on 7 February that their correspondent had had with members of the Turkish Delegation at the Russian head-quarters. These Turkish officials argued that the British Ambassador in Constantinople had throughout been encouraging the Porte to resist the Russian demands. The correspondent said

PUNCH, OR THE LONDON CHARIVARI.   [MARCH 2, 1878

PUNCH'S ESSENCE OF PARLIAMENT.

Punch quoted Layard's telegram stating that he had never encouraged the Turks to go to war: " 'If sympathy for human suffering, a desire to uphold the interests and dignity of my country, and efforts to promote the cause of civil and religious liberty are considered offences', concludes Layard, 'I confess to having been guilty of them.' But as nobody has accused Mr. Layard of these 'offences', his denial is superfluous . . . what he is accused of — viz playing the Nineveh Bull in the Stambul China-shop"

that one Turkish official quoted Layard as having said: 'Do you think I, as a friend of Turkey, was sent here for nothing? Do you not see that it was to encourage you and offend Russia? Believe me; have courage. Make no peace. Fight to the end.' That was exactly what Gladstone, Edward Freeman and others had expected of Layard, and it was good ammunition with which to attack the Government. Beaconsfield described the interview as a fabrication and the Cabinet were 'convinced of the truth of Layard's news'.[1] Layard was wise enough on this occasion to take quick action. Lord Derby stated in the House of Lords that he had received a telegram from the Ambassador in Turkey which contained a vindication of his personal character from attacks publicly made 'which have obtained much notoriety in this country' and he thought it should be made known. 'I deny', said the telegram from the Ambassador, 'that I ever encouraged the Turks to go to war or to continue the war, or ever promised or encouraged them to expect material aid from England.'

Layard was very hurt that he continued to be attacked by members of his own party with a 'rancour and vindictiveness' that had rarely been shown to an Ambassador who had to carry out instructions. If his wish had been to bring about war, he said in his *Memoir*, he could easily have done so—'During those anxious and critical moments when the Russians, flushed with victory, were advancing upon the capital—an ill-considered step or even implied encouragement to continue the struggle, might have led to war.'

In February Layard was told from London that the Prime Minister had things his way and would be able to do what he liked until opinion veered again. Rôles were now reversed; London began to press for action and Layard advised caution from Constantinople. On 9 February Admiral Hornby, Commander-in-Chief in the Mediterranean, received orders to proceed to Constantinople to protect the lives and property of British subjects with warships *Alexandria, Temeraire, Swiftsure, Ruby* and *Salamis* and the Ambassador was told to arrange for the necessary orders to be sent to the Turkish forts to prevent them opening fire.

Layard was not pleased with the decision because he had throughout argued that the Gallipoli Peninsula should first be made secure against its capture by the Russians, otherwise the fleet might be caught in a trap; he thought that the excuse of protecting the lives of British subjects was a bad one since it gave the Russians also the excuse to advance into Constantinople to protect the Christians. There was, too, the danger that there might be another fiasco over the fleet, since the British Government took it for granted that the permission for the fleet to move into the Bosphorus, which had been granted several weeks previously in entirely different circumstances, was still in force but, with the armistice signed, the Sultan and the Porte were frightened to renew the permission.

Layard hoped that his friend Ahmed Vefyk Pasha might be persuaded to agree. Server Pasha, the Foreign Minister, bluntly refused and there was no help from Ahmed Vefyk Pasha who wrote: 'We cannot commit suicide; we seriously want peace. . . . Who could have spoken of danger to foreigners? What an example to give to each country which has a fleet and wished to force the Dardanelles! *La Guerre de Troie et ses dix années de lutte reviendraient donc dans notre siècle!*' The refusal was cabled to London and Layard went for a walk in the garden with Enid to tell her all the troubles and to try to calm down. Early next morning Vefyk Pasha informed Layard that the British fleet had not attempted to enter the Dardanelles when it was found that no permission had been given, and had returned to anchorage at Besika Bay—'so a second time now we have cut a foolish figure', wrote Enid in her diary. Layard telegraphed Derby for instructions, adding that he had 'no reasons to apprehend at present any danger to English subjects or property'.

Lord Salisbury, who now agreed with Beaconsfield that a more determined policy was necessary, considered that the fleet should be ordered to force its way through. In a letter to Beaconsfield on 10 February he showed that he was prepared to support the Prime Minister against any weakness in the Cabinet 'Yet if, after all that has been said, the fleet once more returns to Besika Bay, our position will be utterly ridiculous. We shall disgust our friends in the country and lose all weight in Europe. . . . You will see in Layard's letter circulated today that its recall a fortnight back was ascribed by the Porte merely to timidity.'[2] At least one member of the Cabinet was very agitated. Gathorne-Hardy wrote in his diary: 'Very critical is our position. Too

late—too late! sings in my ears, what can we do? We came to
an unanimous conclusion that the fleet must go up, although
the firman were refused, but what can be its action? What may
be its risk! If the Russians occupy Constantinople, danger there
—and if the Dardanelles, more there . . . God give us wisdom
for our work.' The telegram from the British Government
reached Layard on 11 February stating that the fleet was to
leave at daybreak on Wednesday, 13 February, without waiting
for the firman. It is not clear why nearly three days were
allowed between the order being given and the actual departure
of the fleet. It meant that the unfortunate Sultan, his Ministers,
and the Ambassador were subjected to a war of nerves which
nearly ended in disaster. On 11 February, when they had
learned of the order to the fleet, the Czar and the Grand Duke
Nicholas sent telegrams to the Sultan stating that they were
considering sending part of the Russian forces into Constantinople to protect the lives and property of Christians. There were
repeated visits of Turkish Ministers to the British Embassy to
persuade Layard to stop the fleet coming. The Foreign Minister argued vehemently that even a temporary occupation would
have a terrible effect on the whole Moslem world. What would
the Moslems of India say when they learned that the Russians
had entered the capital of Islam in the very presence of the
English fleet? Britain was pretending to act as a friend but in
fact she was proving herself Turkey's greatest enemy.

At one o'clock in the morning the five warships passed through
the Straits in a heavy snow-storm—the flagship *Alexandria*
grounded, but was refloated without damage—and the ships
anchored off Princes' islands in the Sea of Marmara. Admiral
Hornby came to the Embassy at Pera in his launch and there was
a conference. The Grand Duke sent a peremptory demand that
unless the Turkish fleet were handed over, thirty thousand
troops would occupy Constantinople. The Prime Minister was
prepared to give way, but the Sultan stood firm and, rather than
surrender the ships, ordered preparations to be made to scuttle
them, which were so thorough that the largest ironclad, the
Mahmoudiyeh, was nearly sunk by mistake.

Layard had not seen the Sultan for many weeks, as there
was nothing he could do to help him; an interview in such

circumstances would have been embarrassing. After the arrival of the fleet, however, he went to Yildiz Kiosk. The Sultan was in his dressing-gown, full of fight but rather hysterical. 'The sight of one Russian soldier in my capital would humiliate me', he said, 'and I would never recover. I would rather die first and my children perish with me.' He told Layard that he would place himself at the head of his troops and, followed by a few horsemen, throw himself upon the enemy: 'Before the Russians enter the city they will pass over my dead body.' Layard knew that the Sultan had little physical courage, and that at the next moment he might be begging for asylum in a British warship.

The presence of the British fleet gave courage to the Sultan and new life to the Beaconsfield Cabinet, even though Lord Derby was still a member. Preparations were made to be ready in the event of war between England and Russia. The Government was not prepared to stop the Russians openly by force, but the Ambassador was instructed to acquire secretly by purchase four of the best Turkish ships of war and to tell the Sultan that the British Government would do its utmost to prevent Russia from occupying Constantinople. Admiral Hornby informed Layard he had orders 'to take part by force in efforts to prevent Russians entering Constantinople and Commerell [the Vice-Admiral] is to flank the Boulair lines if they are attacked.' He wanted from Layard the earliest information possible of the Turks' determination to resist any attempted entry, for it would take two hours for warships to reach San Stefano (Yesilköy), now the Russian headquarters, which was only eight miles from Constantinople.

Here was a changed situation; in such circumstances Layard was delighted to have the fleet near by. He received an encouraging letter from his friend Hugh Childers saying that the majority of Liberals did not agree with Mr. Gladstone and disliked 'neutrality'. He said that England should never have lost the initiative and that the fleet should have been at Constantinople in October 1876. The Liberals also feared hostile influences in Egypt now that Turkey was Russia's vassal. This change of opinion was good news to Layard who had been endeavouring to keep up Turkish morale for that very eventuality. It was now all the more important that he should be watchful and prevent the Porte from giving in at the last moment. Opinion was moving against Russia in Austria and Layard found that the Austrian Ambassador was eager to co-operate with him, whereas before he had been under the influence of the German Ambassador. It was believed in London that Bismarck had changed his policy and was encouraging Austria to join England in resisting Russia. Layard was told by London that it was considered important to have the fleet in position so that it could, if necessary, interfere with the return by sea of the Russian army, which would help Austria, reported to be mobilising against Russia. Layard had a plan of his own and let it be known that he would call up the fleet if the Russians crossed a small stream which divided them from the Turkish forces. The Russians continued to press the Sultan to hand over the fleet and Layard told London that if a crisis should arise he would take upon himself the responsibility of requesting Admiral Hornby to seize the Turkish ships. He wrote in his *Memoir* 'To have allowed the Russians, in the very sight of our ships, to possess themselves by force of the Turkish fleet would have been an insult to the dignity and honour of England and a danger to her influence and interests to which, I felt convinced, my countrymen would never quietly submit.' He was encouraged by letters from Beaconsfield who wrote on 21 February: 'Amid the torrents of disasters which nearly overwhelm us, I write this line that you should at least know that your Sovereign and Her Ministers entirely approve of your conduct and fully appreciate the energy and resource which have distinguished your management of affairs.' The Prime Minister referred to a plan to hold a conference to discuss the terms that Russia was demanding from Turkey, but it was doubtful if it would be held and he feared that 'the incoherency' of the situation might produce war. That was the danger the Opposition also feared. If there were war they believed that Layard would bear a heavy responsibility for enabling the Turks to resist some of the Russian demands. Gladstone accused him of 'holding a diplomatic war, while the Government at home have been neutral'. Layard had certainly played an important part in keeping the Russians out of Constantinople. On 19 February the Sultan received a telegram from the Czar stating that he had abandoned, for the present, his intention of occupying

Constantinople, taking into consideration the crowded state of the capital.

On 3 March 1878 the Preliminaries of Peace were signed at the village of San Stefano a few miles from Constantinople. It was a severe disappointment to the Russians that they had not signed the treaty in Constantinople itself. General Skoboleff said that every Russian was born with the belief that it was the destiny of his country to take possession of Constantinople and that the Czar was 'the legitimate successor of those who had reigned on the Bosphorus'. There was great hatred against England and Mr. Layard for having prevented them from fulfilling their destiny. Mme. Novikoff told General Grant, who was doing a world tour after his second term as President of the United States, 'it is difficult to give you an idea of the disappointment throughout all Russia when it was found that Constantinople, after all, was not to be the place where we were to dictate peace. Our troops are deeply humiliated for not having been allowed to cross Constantinople—to please Mr. Lie-Hard.'(3)

Layard had helped to win the first battle, but he knew that there was still great danger of war between England and Russia and that he would have to exert his diplomacy to the full to avert it. During this critical period he was the subject of a severe attack in the House of Commons as a result of the revival of the Negroponte story. Learning that Mr. Evelyn Ashley was to bring forward a motion on the subject, he sent a despatch to the Foreign Office to try, rather belatedly, to help meet criticism. He denied that he had been party to any attack on Gladstone's character, but admitted that he might have behaved 'indiscreetly' in having called the attention of a newspaper correspondent to a letter which was 'already public property'. He concluded with the provocative remark that his view of the duty of an ambassador was that he should faithfully serve the interests of his sovereign and his country, 'and not those of a faction or of an individual. I do not know whether this is the view of Mr. Gladstone.'

The debate in the House of Commons on 12 March was reminiscent of the bitter attacks against Layard in the Commons nearly twenty years earlier. The Opposition almost gained their vote of censure, failing largely because they attacked with exaggerated violence. If the motion had been more successful,

The Mosque of St Sophia

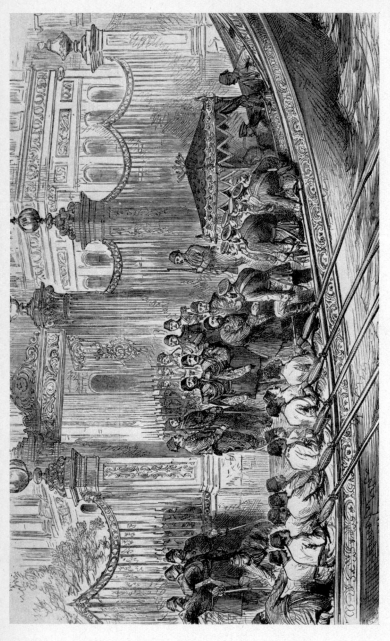

The Grand Duke Nicholas being received at the Dolmabache Palace by Ahmed Vefyk Pasha and Raouf Pasha on the occasion of a visit to the Sultan

said *The Times*, the Ambassador would have had to resign, for Layard was revealed in the debate 'as a more thorough-going partisan than any of his predecessors in an office which seems to have carried the taint of partisanship with it'. He could be acquitted, said *The Times*, of deliberately setting on foot a calumny but he could not be acquitted of 'the most indecorous readiness to believe disparaging stories against him [Gladstone] and to assist in their further dispersion'; at the same time Mr. Gladstone ought to take warning of the danger of corresponding 'as freely as he is wont with persons in whose discretion, or even in whose good faith, he can place no reliance'.

The Opposition continued their attacks on the Government throughout March. Some of the M.P.s said that there was no reason why the Turks should not be left to carry out the terms of the Treaty of San Stefano, severe as they were. In a private letter to Lord Beaconsfield on 20 March, Layard argued that the Treaty of San Stefano, unless greatly modified, would not only destroy the Turkish Empire in Europe but that it threatened to undermine it in Asia: 'There is now an attempt, promoted by Russian intrigues, to put forward the claims of a fantastical "Armenia", to be considered an autonomous province, and placed under Christian government; in fact, another Bulgaria to be dependent upon Russia and to be annexed when convenient.' The Grand Duke Nicholas was endeavouring to obtain permission to occupy a position on the upper Bosphorus, such as Buyukdere or Kavak, with the object, he said, of embarking Russian troops for Odessa. The Sultan had consulted Layard secretly on the subject and had refused to give permission. They both believed that the Russian object was not to embark troops, but to be in a position to control the water supply of the city which came from the huge artificial reservoirs in the forest of Belgrade near Buyukdere. Layard protested to London about the Russian demands and there was considerable discussion on the question in England and in Europe. Emperor William of Germany enquired how Britain could object to Russia sending her troops home in unarmed transports, while at the same time the British fleet adopted a threatening attitude. There was a powerful group of English businessmen in Constantinople who wanted life in the city to return to normal so that they could trade and they were very critical of the Ambassador, since they believed that his hostility to Russia might lead to war. On 22 March *The Times* published a despatch from their correspondent in Constantinople who described the British Ambassador as leading a war party:

> He is sincerely convinced that England ought to go to war with Russia to avert what he regards as the grave danger of Russian aggrandisement, and that if she does not go to war now, she will be throwing away a favourable opportunity of doing what she will otherwise have to do later at still greater cost; but he is so carried away by his dread and hatred of Russians and a life-long sympathy with his friends the Turks . . . that he is in constant danger of deceiving first himself and then his Government.

Such an article in *The Times* was a delight to Layard's enemies in England and to those who were opposed to Beaconsfield's policy. Layard in his early days in Constantinople had realised how important it was for the Ambassador to have a good Press. 'Although I had early obtained this experience, I did not in after life profit by it', he wrote in his *Autobiography*. 'I have always had a dislike to newspaper publicity, and have never taken the slightest pains to conciliate newspaper writers and correspondents. . . . The race may improve in the course of time . . . but I could never bring myself to take them into my confidence.' He considered that most of them were anti-English and pro-Russian and therefore not fit to be spoken to. 'It is a strange and bad sign of the times', he told Lytton, 'that public opinion and consequently England's policy is to be directed by newspaper correspondents.' He never tried to make use of them to put over his own views and, as he treated them with contempt, they retaliated.

The Russian Government continued to insist that the Treaty of San Stefano was a matter arranged between themselves and Turkey and refused to have the terms discussed by an European conference. The British Government therefore decided on 27 March to call out the Reserve and to bring a force of Indian troops to Malta.

7

Negotiations for Cyprus

Lord Derby did not agree with the new policy and resigned, sending Layard a friendly letter saying that he would always hear with real pleasure of Layard's personal success, 'you have passed through an anxious time but probably the worst is over'. Layard thought that was optimistic and was very apprehensive when he heard that Lord Salisbury was to be Foreign Minister. He had not realised that Salisbury had been making a reassessment of the Eastern Question and drawing nearer to the view held by Beaconsfield and Layard. This period had been for Salisbury a 'nightmare oppression' in which his spirits sank to the lowest ebb and he exclaimed, as Layard might have done, 'we shall be handed down in history as the Government which, through sheer incompetence, plunged Europe into the greatest war of the century.'[1] The result of his reassessment was his famous 'Circular to the Powers' of 1 April 1878. In that he criticised the terms of the Treaty of San Stefano and demanded that it should be submitted to the judgement of the Powers of Europe—'No Power can liberate itself from the terms of a Treaty [Treaty of Paris of 1856] without the consent of the other contracting Powers.' He simplified the issue to be resolved by concentrating criticism upon a single point, 'the covert appropriation by Russia of the influence inherent in Turkish sovereignty'. Crown Princess Frederick of Germany wrote to Queen Victoria: 'Now we know that England *has* a policy, and that it is a clear and right one, and this has already changed the aspect of the whole question.'

The first expeditionary force (consisting of seven thousand men) ever to sail from India were on their way to Malta and there was much discussion in London as to how they might be used. It was considered that Malta was too far from Constantinople and that a *place d'armes* was needed in the eastern Mediterranean. Salisbury told Layard that he had observed 'how utterly impossible efficient and prompt military action is from a port [Malta] which is four days sail from the scene of action'. As England, he said, was a democratic country it could not be counted on to act in any uniform way or follow any consistent policy; it would probably abandon the task of resisting any further Russian advance to the southward in Asia, 'if no other but speculative arguments can be advanced in favour of action. But it will cling to any military post occupied by England as tenaciously as it has clung to Gibraltar; and if any movement were made which would threaten it, while assaulting the Ottoman Dominions, its action might be counted on.' Salisbury wanted to find some strong place on the Persian Gulf or the Aegean coast and told the Ambassador that he had not invariably agreed in all the views he had expressed but he admired 'the skill and unsparing energy' with which his functions had been performed: 'You have hitherto laboured to prevent Russian preponderance by sustaining the Turkish break-water. But the breakwater is now shattered, I fear, beyond repair and the flood is pouring over it. Another dyke may have to be established behind it.' Layard did not believe that the breakwater was shattered beyond repair and had written to that effect to Beaconsfield on 3 April: 'People in England are too much inclined to underrate the strength still left to the Sultan.' Beaconsfield and Salisbury were now working closely together and the latter was determined to conduct his own foreign policy so that there was an end to the secret letters between Beaconsfield and Layard. But Salisbury kept Layard fully informed of the way he was thinking. He wrote on 2 May:

> The time is passed for talking about 'independence and integrity'. It was something of a sham in 1856, as events have proved. But it would be a pure mockery now. The Porte must recognise that it needs protection. . . . In Asia, it is otherwise. Its Government there has been as good as that of any other Power except England's, and from Asia it will continue to draw that which is its real strength; the magnificent Mussulman material of its armies. How is the Asiatic Empire to be saved from disintegration?

Layard certainly did not agree with all this, but he was relieved that Salisbury saw the danger of Russia spreading south and east from Armenia. Some of the arguments were similar to those Layard had used in *The Quarterly Review* article written before he became Ambassador. Salisbury said that the mere presence of the Russians at Kars would cause Persia, Mesopotamia, and Syria to turn northwards; a Russian party would arise in each country, creating disorders of which the Russians would take advantage and the provinces would be turned into Russian 'satrapies'. Turkey's disintegration could only be avoided if England were present at some port in the Levant. He had for some time been thinking of Cyprus. It would be Turkey's last chance: 'If our proposals are rejected this time, we must turn our thoughts to other means of security and the Ottoman Empire will enter upon the last stage of decay—Russification.' Salisbury realised that there was danger for India and no longer argued that those who were afraid of Russia invading India must be looking at small-scale maps.

Layard wished that the new policy could have been decided upon at least a year earlier for many tragedies could have been averted, and there would, he considered, have been less danger of war with Russia which was now a real threat. The Russians were now so deeply committed that it might be difficult for them to withdraw, even faced with the danger of a war with England. He told Salisbury that he believed he could obtain agreement for a *place d'armes* provided the Porte considered that a real community of interests was being established between the two countries. So far England had expected everything from Turkey and given little in return—'I have to hold out no hopes, and yet not leave the Porte hopeless.'

On 18 May the Russians, without warning, moved their front line forward from San Stefano towards the capital and there was general alarm. Valentine Baker Pasha, who was in command of the Turkish lines to the south of Constantinople, said that the Russians had advanced right up to the Turkish outposts and he thought that an attack was imminent. Layard was summoned to the Sultan, who was inspecting maps of the country round Constantinople and wanted the Ambassador to ask Salisbury what course England would take should Russia attempt to occupy

Constantinople and the Bosphorus; would she make an alliance with Turkey? 'Never was the danger of war between Russia and Turkey so great as during that time. If it had broken out again there can be no doubt that England would have been involved in it', commented the Ambassador.

On 20 May there was a revolt which had a serious effect on the Sultan's character and on the destinies of the Ottoman Empire. The rumours about conspiracies to dethrone Abdul Hamid and to replace his brother Murad on the throne had continued and Murad's mother was in touch with Ali Souavi Effendi, one of the teachers who had been exiled for his liberal views. Ali Souavi had visited England and on his return had been recommended to Midhat Pasha when he was Vizier, and had been appointed director of the large Government College of Galatasaray. On the afternoon of 20 May 1878 Ali Souavi arrived at one of the gates of the Palace of Cheragan, where Murad was a prisoner, and with two or three hundred armed refugees obtained admission. Murad's mother brought her son out of the harem and they tried to persuade him to put on his sword and to place himself at the head of the movement but Murad was terrified and wished to return to the harem. As a result of this delay the guards had time to assemble and Ali Souavi was killed with most of his followers.

At the time Layard did not think a great deal of the affair as he was extremely busy dealing with the stream of telegrams and despatches from Salisbury on plans for the future, which entailed a great deal of work, for Salisbury had instituted a 'secret department' at the Foreign Office consisting of the Foreign Minister's private secretary, Philip Currie, and a select few. There were certain telegrams that only this 'secret department' were allowed to cipher and decipher, and in Constantinople only Layard, Enid, and Alfred Sandison, the Oriental Secretary, were in the secret. On the night of 24/25 May Layard received one of these telegrams from Salisbury telling him to propose secretly to the Sultan a defensive alliance for the purpose of securing his territories in Asia. If any of these, such as Batum, Ardahan, or Kars should be retained by Russia, or any attempt were made to take further territory, England engaged herself to join the Sultan in defending them by force of arms and in return the Sultan was to promise to introduce necessary reforms. In order to enable England to carry out her undertakings, the Sultan was to agree to hand over the Island of Cyprus to be occupied and administered by England, while payment would be made to Turkey. It was impossible for England, wrote Salisbury, to exercise the necessary vigilance in Syria and Asia Minor, unless she possessed a stronghold near the coast. Another telegram was received early on Saturday, 25 May, followed immediately by a third, marked Personal and Most Secret:

> Press on immediate acceptance of the terms in my telegram of to-day with all the energy in your power. Point out that the arrangement makes safe Asiatic Turkey, the field from which the Sultan's army is supplied with men and that it must be accepted at once if the Sultan wishes to retain the goodwill of England. The opportunity, if neglected, will never recur.
>
> We are on the point of an arrangement by which the Russian army will be withdrawn from Constantinople and the autonomous Bulgarian Principality will be limited to the north of the Balkans. If the Sultan does not consent to the above engagement, it will not be in the power of England to pursue the pending negotiations any further, and the capture of Constantinople and the partition of his Empire will be the immediate result. . . . Make the Sultan understand that you must have a written engagement as above not later than Sunday evening and that the most absolute secrecy must be observed.

In the meantime in his palace at Yildiz the Sultan could think of nothing but the Ali Souavi plot, which his spies had encouraged him to believe was a widespread conspiracy and for three nights he had had no sleep. He was temporarily insane and prepared to believe any story including one, believed to have been circulated by the German Ambassador, that Layard was coming to carry him off to a British warship where he would be assassinated and Murad placed again on the throne. When the Sultan was told that the British Ambassador wanted to see him in private audience, he thought that the plot was being put into effect. Elaborate precautions were taken and his armed Circassian guards were summoned to be near at hand. Layard knew nothing of the Sultan's suspicions when he arrived at the

palace with only two days to carry out his instructions and he
described a most extraordinary scene:

> Instead of receiving me, as was his usual habit, in his small
> private room, he was standing on a raised place in one of the
> corners or recesses of the large hall on the ground floor, where he
> could be seen, although not heard by his attendants. I observed
> Osman Pasha and a number of Circassians in one of the chambers
> opening into the hall. He drew back when I approached him and
> his frightened look surprised me. . . . As I spoke in a very low voice,
> so as not to be heard by persons who were in the hall and might
> have been listening, this added to his alarm and made him draw
> back from me with an expression of terror, when I approached him.

Layard asked the Sultan to receive him in a private room so that
they should not be overheard, but that only increased his fears
and he excused himself by saying that it was cooler where they
were. Layard had to make the best of the situation and began the
preamble to his important statement but he had not advanced
very far when the Sultan said that he was too ill to continue the
conversation and retired. Layard made a full report to Sadyk,
who had replaced Ahmed Vefyk as Prime Minister or Grand
Vizier and to Safvet Pasha, the Foreign Minister. They were
both in agreement with the proposals and said that they would
discuss them with the Sultan later. In the meantime Abdul
Hamid had recovered his composure sufficiently to send a message
excusing the abruptness of his withdrawal but, in view of what
had happened, Layard was doubtful if he would be able to carry
out his important mission in the very short time allotted. Throughout Saturday Layard worked out the text of the agreement with
the two Ministers and by eight o'clock in the evening it had been
agreed with the Sultan and the copy of the completed document
brought to Therapia. Layard, Sandison, and Enid then spent
several hours enciphering the document which was sent off late
on Saturday evening—Enid was so busy that she could not
attend the dinner she had arranged to celebrate the Queen's
birthday for thirty of the British community.

Salisbury, in London, was attending a big reception at the
Foreign Office in honour of the Queen's birthday and throughout that Saturday evening he expected some news from Constantinople but nothing came. If the Sultan refused Salisbury had

pledged himself 'to such a sudden and complete reversal of policy as would have produced a convulsion of agitation throughout Europe'.[2] He was relieved when the agreement of the Porte reached the Foreign Office on Sunday morning and the Ministers were quickly informed of Layard's success.

For Layard it was not a restful Sunday. In the afternoon he received a note from General Said Pasha begging him to come to the palace at Yildiz immediately. Layard was apprehensive lest the Sultan had had second thoughts about the agreement. He drove from Therapia in one and a half hours and reached the palace at eight o'clock in the evening, but the Sultan was not worrying about the Cyprus Convention, and Layard described what happened in his *Memoir*:

> When a chamberlain announced, after I had eaten, that His Majesty was ready to see me, Said Pasha led me to the gates in the high wall surrounding the detached building occupied by the 'Princess', the children and the ladies and female slaves who form part of the Imperial household of the Harem. Said Pasha knocked at the gates and, on making himself known, they were thrown open by a portly black eunuch who said that His Majesty desired to be alone. Said accordingly retired and I was led through the garden into the house and shown into a chamber on the ground floor where I found the Sultan stretched on a sofa. By his side stood Dr. Mavroyeni, a Greek physician who had attended him for some years before he came to the throne, and in whom he placed great confidence. He directed this gentleman to act as interpreter. At the end of the room hung a large curtain. From behind it came the stifled sound of women's voices and the noise of the rustle of women's dresses. . . .
>
> I found the Sultan in a state of great mental excitement. He assured me that he possessed positive information of a plot against his life which was to be put into execution the following morning. He had consequently but a few hours to live. He had sent for me, he said, to implore me to protect his wife and children. He had heard that when I was the Queen's Minister in Spain I had, with Mrs. Layard, saved the lives of Marshal Serrano and his family. He entreated me to render him the same service. . . . He did not fear death, but he could not bear the thought of being immured for the rest of his life in the gloomy buildings on Seraglio Point, deprived of his liberty and separated from his wife and children.
>
> Whilst he was talking in this strain, the sound of a trumpet in a

distant camp and of the tramp of feet were heard. He started from his couch with a look of terror, exclaiming that the trumpet was the signal agreed upon by the conspirators and that they were approaching to assassinate him. He walked rapidly up and down the room in great agitation, talking of his children.

Towards dawn the Sultan grew calmer and at four o'clock in the morning Layard managed to return to the Embassy, 'from one of the most painful and distressing scenes' that he had ever witnessed. But he had hardly got into bed when an aide-de-camp, who had galloped all the way from Yildiz, arrived with an urgent message from the Sultan that he wished to see Mrs. Layard and the Ambassador without a moment's delay. There was also a pathetic note written in French in the Sultan's own hand saying that there would be an attempt on his life the next day and that Layard must arrange for him to leave the country: 'If you do not come in time everything is lost. I hope that Mrs. Layard will do for me what she did in a similar case in Spain. Do not forget that my wife and children must be saved.' Layard did not consider that any good would be achieved by returning and he went to bed after writing a note for the aide-de-camp to take back to the palace. The next morning, however, he arranged for the *Helicon* to anchor off the Cheragan Palace so that she might be in full view from the Yildiz Kiosk and reassure the Sultan. Abdul Hamid, however, had forgotten about his appeal to Layard for asylum and sent a peremptory message to demand that the ship should at once be removed.

When Layard informed the Turkish Prime Minister of what had passed it was agreed that it was absolutely essential to keep the Sultan's madness secret. But Abdul Hamid, perhaps disappointed at only receiving a note from Layard in reply to his appeal, had summoned the German Ambassador and had also appealed to him to protect him in case of danger to his life which meant that the Sultan's condition would be reported to St. Petersburg. Layard told Salisbury that, according to Mohammedan law, a Sultan could not continue on the throne if insane or otherwise incapacitated from discharging his religious and political duties as Caliph of Islam and Sovereign: 'I grieve most sincerely for the poor Sultan, for whom I cannot but feel pity and even affection. If, however, the safety of the

State, and our paramount interests require that he should be put aside, he must be sacrificed.'

It had been a strenuous week-end but Layard had achieved a difficult task and on Monday, 27 May 1878, he heard that the Queen had been pleased to bestow on him the Grand Cross of the Order of the Bath. The Cyprus Convention was signed on 4 June, the day after the Russian Government had finally agreed that a congress of European Powers should consider the Treaty of San Stefano at Berlin. The Sultan expressed to Layard 'in very warm and suitable terms his gratitude to the Queen, Lord Beaconsfield, and Lord Salisbury for the Convention and his sense of its importance to himself and his Empire'.

The Sultan's health was improving but he continued to suffer from fear of conspiracies and assassination and these had 'a most unfortunate influence upon his character and his actions'. He told Layard that the Prime Minister himself had been implicated in the Ali Souavi conspiracy and had appeared at the Yildiz Palace with two revolvers, which made it clear to the Sultan that he intended to murder him. 'The Sultan declared solemnly to me,' said Layard, 'that he had seen the butt ends of the pistols protruding from Sadyk's waistcoat, and had it not been for his notorious cowardice he would have committed the act he had contemplated.' Lord Salisbury agreed that the Sultan's state was really pitiable 'and unless we can restore him to some strength, we shall have no fulcrum on which to rest measures either of defence or reform'.

From the time of the Ali Souavi plot there was, said Layard, a complete change in the Sultan's character and disposition. Whereas Abdul Hamid had shown clear intelligence, Layard was now the unhappy witness on several occasions of his mental derangement: 'The Sultan believed that he was surrounded by conspirators who were plotting to dethrone and murder him. He suspected his most honest, faithful and loyal advisers and attendants, whom he unjustly and cruelly treated, sending them into exile.'[3] He became, said Layard, even more timid and further precautions were taken at Yildiz. Guard-houses were built round his palace and the Sultan never left the grounds, except on Friday when he went to the mosque through a hedge of soldiers: 'Like most weak men labouring under this terrible infirmity, he sought by duplicity and cunning to escape from difficult questions. Full reliance could no longer be placed on his words. . . . His mistrust of everyone meant that he took everything into his own hands. He undertook what he could not accomplish and the business of the state fell into complete disorder.'

Layard was worried lest the Sultan might again have the illusion that Britain was working against him and inform the German or French Ambassadors about the Cyprus Convention. Lord Salisbury had emphasised how essential it was that it should not be announced prematurely since there would certainly be an outcry from the French as well as from the Russian Governments, and probably considerable opposition in the House of Commons. The Turkish Delegates to the Berlin Congress were told to keep silent. As so much secret information in the past had been made public both in London and Constantinople, Layard watched anxiously but, miraculously, nothing was revealed.

There was at the beginning of June an unfortunate breach in Foreign Office security, but not with regard to Cyprus. Salisbury had been proud of his security arrangements with his inner 'secret department'. This had dealt with a very important document entitled, 'Heads of Agreement', carefully worked out between Lord Salisbury and Count Shuvaloff, the Russian Ambassador, so that time could be saved at the Congress. In spite of all the precautions this document, which had not been intended for publication at any time, had been given by mistake for copying to a Mr. Charles Marvin, a poorly paid temporary clerk, who sold it to *The Globe* newspaper. As the Official Secrets Act was only introduced following this embarrassing incident Mr. Marvin had contravened no law. When the details published in *The Globe* were telegraphed to Constantinople the Sultan and his Ministers considered that such bargaining with Russia over important areas of the Ottoman Empire was proof positive that England had betrayed Turkey. Layard wrote to Sir Henry Elliot, Ambassador in Vienna: 'The consequence here is most serious and there is not a Turk or a Christian who is not now convinced that we have been playing Turkey and Europe false; that . . . we have been all along in secret agreement with

Russia and Austria to dismember the Turkish Empire and take our share of the spoils.' The result was that when the time came at the Congress of Berlin for Salisbury to announce the news of the Cyprus Convention, the Sultan refused to ratify it. Salisbury was furious and instructed Layard to say that if the Convention were not ratified at once, England would offer no further opposition to proposals made at the Congress for detaching certain parts of Turkey. The Sultan signed but the threats confirmed his view that England was working against Turkey. The publication of the secret Anglo-Russian Protocol in *The Globe*, wrote Layard to Salisbury, 'has toppled at a blow the edifice which it has taken me months of labour to raise'.

The first official announcement about the Cyprus Convention was made on 8 July in Parliament and at the Berlin Congress. Layard gave the news at a dinner at the Embassy on 9 July and Lady Charlotte Schreiber, who was present, noted in her diary: 'History is being enacted all around us, but we know nothing of it until it is a *fait accompli*.' She and Charles Schreiber had arrived at Constantinople direct from the Berlin Congress where she had talked with her old friend Beaconsfield: 'It was very pleasant', she wrote, 'more especially when he spoke of Henry Layard, which he did in the warmest manner, praising his great ability and assiduity and, above all, his untiring energy.'(4)

In Berlin there was consternation and anger at the agreement. England, it was said, was getting her picking in spite of all her protestations of friendship for Turkey; if she did not consider it necessary to consult Europe on such matters, why should not Russia deal direct with Turkey? The only person who seemed pleased was Condouriotis, the Greek representative in Constantinople, who thought it was an excellent idea. Layard made the comment in his *Memoir*: 'Perhaps he foresaw that if England acquired it from the Porte, she would end by handing it over to Greece, as she had surrendered to her the Ionian Islands. This might soon be accomplished, Condouriotis probably thought, through Greek intrigues amongst the Christian population of the Island, and a well-directed Hellenic propaganda.' Indeed, the propaganda started almost as soon as the Cyprus Convention was made public. By August Layard was receiving reports from the British Vice-Consul in Corfu, that Greek newspapers were publishing articles about the traditional claims of Greece to Cyprus. It was proposed in the Press that the 'patriotic Committees' in Greece and elsewhere should encourage the emigration of Greeks to Cyprus with the object of establishing and maintaining an effective majority. When that had been accomplished, the committees would set to work on the second part of the scheme—inculcating the idea of annexation to Greece 'by stirring up and keeping alive agitation and political intrigues.'

Layard was annoyed that he was scarcely consulted during the Berlin Congress. He considered that he did little more than act as postman, passing on appeals from Armenians, Lazes, Bulgarian Moslems (Pomaks) and others. Like the Greeks, Serbians, Bulgarians, and Montenegrins, they regarded the Berlin Congress as a place where the dismemberment of the Ottoman Empire was being decided and made extravagant claims and appeals. Layard was apprehensive that there would be a great deal of trouble in the future, especially with regard to Armenia. The Patriarch and the 'Council of the Armenian Nation' had sent delegates to the Berlin Congress who argued that Armenia was a state comprising the Turkish Pashalics of Sivas, Van, the greater part of Diabekir, and the ancient Kingdom of Cilicia extending south of the Taurus range to the sea. The Patriarch had said that unless their demands were satisfied the Armenians would rise and join with Russia.

Layard wrote to Elliot that the Congress, far from settling the Turkish or Eastern Question, would unsettle everything: 'We are calling into life new nationalities and dangerous ambitions, and affording fresh motives and fresh facilities for Russia to carry on her intrigues with the object of destroying the Empire and possessing herself of the heritage.' He received one letter from Salisbury in Berlin to say that as a result of the negotiations they hoped to draw a wall across the peninsula of the Balkans and across Armenia, which would give Turkey respite for twenty or thirty years; there would have to be Europeans to help carry out reforms in the Ottoman Empire:

> Signing constitutions is no great effort for a sovereign. Taking power out of your own hands and lodging it in the hands of men who, being your superiors in rule, are not likely to let it slip back —this is a greater sacrifice than most sovereigns are capable of

achieving. I should like to know whether you think the Sultan's good intentions will ever get so far as this, and whether it is worth our while looking out for men.

Layard considered that it was worth while, but he had not realised how stubborn the Sultan could be when he wished to retain power in his own hands.

Beaconsfield returned from Berlin in triumph and made his 'Peace with Honour' speech, which was referred to by the critics as 'the Peace that passeth all understanding and the Honour that is common among thieves'. There was a full-dress debate in Parliament on the results of the Congress and the Sultan noted that Gladstone considered the Cyprus Convention had been 'a mad undertaking', that Turkey in Asia was to be managed as 'an outpost of British power', that Turkey had been partitioned and her population reduced from seventeen to six million. Beaconsfield's mathematics were different: the Powers had 'restored' to the Sultan two-thirds of the territory which he had lost and a population of two and a half millions in Eastern Rumelia. The fact remained, however, that the Sultan's territory had been reduced as a result of the defeat by Russia though the Sultan put the blame on the Berlin Congress and on Britain.

8

Another quarrel with Gladstone

Lady Charlotte stayed at the Embassy at Therapia for a month and was charmed by the Turks and the scenery: 'I had no idea of anything so enchanting as the Bosphorus.' When she visited the British fleet at Princes' islands on American Independence Day, the town, the mosques, the Turkish ships and all the windows along the Bosphorus were lit up, 'the grandest sight I ever saw'. She watched a cricket match being played on the banks of the Sweet Waters of Asia and attended a *fête champêtre* given by Enid in the garden at Therapia; with a large sail from the *Antelope* spread over it the tennis court served as a ball-room, and there was a band from the British fleet. On other evenings after dinner the Embassy party used to sit in the round room in the centre of the house, while the gentlemen smoked their *narghilés*. Lady Charlotte generally sat next to Layard: 'he talks of old times and things that he remembers in a way that is most interesting. All day he is busy beyond belief, and we see but little of him, but he bears his work well.' She was very interested in all the political developments and described how, on returning from a walk with Enid on 15 July 1879, they found a meeting of 'The Powers' at the British Embassy at Therapia. The German Ambassador's steam launch was waiting at the landing-stage and the Russian Ambassador's horses were held by a smart Cossack. The Ambassadors, including the French and Austrian, were discussing sending a commission to investigate massacres in the Rhodope mountains. During May there had been an extensive rising against the Russians by the Moslem Bulgarians who had been driven to desperation by the treatment they had received. The rising worried the Russians for it seemed at one time as if the Greeks of Macedonia might join it. The

Lady Layard in Venice, wearing the Order given her by
Sultan Abdul Hamid

Sir Henry Layard in his study at Ca Capello,
painting by Ludwig Passini

Russians and Christian Bulgarians suppressed the rising with great brutality, so that still more refugees flooded into Constantinople.

Enid Layard continued to organise relief on a large scale. Fourteen of the English men and women who devoted most of their time to working with the refugees contracted typhoid and several died, while in the mosque of St. Sophia the death rate had increased to thirty a day. The Sultan was very touched by the amount of work done by Mrs. Layard and in the summer of 1878 announced that he had decided to found an 'Order for Ladies' and that she was to be the first to be honoured. When Enid had received permission from Queen Victoria, the Sultan gave a dinner-party and at a little ceremony afterwards pinned the new Order on her dress.

At such moments Abdul Hamid was charming, but most of the time the Ambassador had to try to force reforms on a reluctant and bitter Sultan, who had persuaded himself that Turkey's situation was even worse after the Berlin Treaty than before and considered England was responsible. Salisbury said he understood the Ambassador's difficult position; it would be a constant struggle, for he would be 'in the front of the battle for the interest of both England and humanity in the East'. There had to be such a battle for there were rival interests to satisfy and the Government had had to choose between 'an immediate appeal to arms', or, substituting for it, 'a protracted diplomatic struggle' in the hope that war with Russia might be avoided. The greatest difficulty, Salisbury said, would be with the Asiatic reforms, which would have to be far-reaching, 'but they must not withdraw any of the semblance of power from the Sultan, nor too much of the reality'. He summarised the main reforms as, choice of better governors, an adequate *gendarmerie*, free tribunals and no extortion in the raising of revenue.

A despatch of 8 August 1878 contained a scheme of reform, which was to be pressed on the Sultan. The Ambassador was urged to lose no time. Salisbury stated (18 September) that in the last year and a half since Layard's arrival there had been 'a very considerable increase in the authority and influence of Great Britain at Constantinople'; it had been achieved 'by constant labour and vigilance' on Layard's part and that would have to be maintained, but Salisbury considered 'the Sultan's inclination to come to an agreement and our power of insisting upon it will diminish with each succeeding month'. A number of able British officers were appointed as Consul-Generals in Armenia to advise and watch over reforms. There was little, however, that any of them could do except make reports, for control remained with Abdul Hamid in his palace at Yildiz.

The Sultan had a strong argument: there could be no reform without funds. Salisbury failed to persuade Parliament that England's responsibility for reform entailed the voting of credits. Layard's influence with the Sultan and the Porte, as he very well knew, lasted as long as it was thought that Britain would come to Turkey's aid. England had failed to give military aid and now was refusing to give financial aid; all she did was to lecture about the need for reform. There was little chance of success for the Ambassador in these circumstances.

The massacre in the Rhodope mountains roused bitter feelings in England against the Russians and those who sympathised with the Russians. The reports from the British Consuls near the area and Layard's despatches were published in Parliamentary Reports. The effect they had in England pleased Layard but he could not restrain himself from using in one of his despatches a remark which was quite clearly aimed at Gladstone. 'Those', said Layard, 'who denounced Bulgarian atrocities, and incited in the cause of humanity one of the most cruel and unrighteous wars, are now silent!' Gladstone was quick to notice this wounding statement, and told Layard that he believed the reproach was intended for him 'the more so, as I am aware that indirectness is a characteristic of your modes of accusation'. He required answers to three questions as quickly as possible, for he intended to make the matter public. Firstly, what grounds had Layard for thinking that Gladstone possessed evidence of outrages committed by the Bulgarians, 'in any way approaching that for which I waited in 1876 nearly four months before condemning the outrages committed by the Turks'? Secondly, on what declaration had Layard founded the assertion, 'that I incited the Russo-Turkish war'? Thirdly, on what authority had Layard reported officially to Lord Salisbury that Gladstone had been silent 'as to outrages committed by the Christians on the Mussulmans'?

Layard replied that there had been plenty of evidence. There had been the Blue Book presented to Parliament early in the year, which contained reports of atrocities against Moslems of the most terrible descriptions and during the whole of 1878 the Press of England and of Europe had published, almost daily, similar reports while the Russians themselves had admitted that General Gurko's raid to the south of the Balkans had led to brutal treatment of the Mohammedan population: 'The evidence at your disposal to prove the outrages committed by Bulgarians upon Turks must have far exceeded in amount and trustworthiness that which you possessed in 1876, as regards the outrages with which the Turks were charged.' He did not consider that he had accused Gladstone of inciting the Russo-Turkish war, though his answer made it clear that he had done so: 'What I believe, and my conviction is too deep to be shaken, is that the so-called "Bulgarian Atrocity Movement" in 1876 was the main cause of the terrible and cruel war that has devastated this country.' As to Gladstone's silence, he argued that there had been no large meetings and no pamphlets to denounce the massacres: 'Yet, I believe, if your powerful voice had been raised in behalf of a defenceless population; if you had denounced with your matchless eloquence, the conduct of those who were guilty . . . they would have been long ago stopped and an unparalleled amount of human suffering might have been prevented.'

Gladstone was not mollified. He replied by making a serious charge against Layard. He could not, he said, make an appeal on behalf of the Turks and Pomaks when the information published was not reliable: 'Information was forwarded from the East in certain cases to excite the public mind at home. Unauthenticated ex-parte statements did not become official or responsible by passing through the Embassy.' He asked Layard to deny publicly, as he had privately, that he was referring to him in the despatch under dispute. As it was clear that Layard had been aiming at Gladstone, there was little more that could be said and he broke off the correspondence in a final letter of 17 October. It was not final for Gladstone.

The dispute was the subject of debate in the House of Commons
on 16 December 1878. One speaker said that both Consul-
General Fawcett, the British Representative on the Rhodope
Commission, and Sir Henry Layard were known to be 'steeped
to the eyes in philo-Turkish prejudices' and that it was impossible
for them to give an unbiased report. Gladstone went over the
ground covered in his correspondence and said that the Ambassador had exhibited a portion of his fellow-countrymen to the
world 'in a most odious and offensive light' and he insisted that
there was no distinction drawn by him between Christian and
Moslem suffering.

Whereas Gladstone had disapproved of Sir Henry Elliot's pro-
Turk policy, he did not dislike him personally and argued that
Elliot discharged his duties 'in the spirit of an honourable and
enlightened Christian diplomat'. But between Layard and Gladstone there was a bitter personal element. Layard at times had
gone out of his way to be provocative and combined ambition
with a youthful and unthinking indiscretion. As an impetuous
young man of thirty he had attacked the Prime Minister, Lord
Aberdeen, with what was then an attractive fearlessness. He had
had a good cause to fight and had been prepared to suffer, though
with some complaints, his failure to obtain office. Now, over
sixty, he was still fighting with the same methods, making
remarks which, as Bulwer had said 'sting and create bad feeling'.
He often weakened his case by exaggerations. Hammond, who
was himself very anti-Gladstone, reminded Layard that when
the devil is painted blacker than he is, people will find him an
angel. Layard's missionary zeal and single-mindedness prevented
him from taking the trouble to understand Gladstone's point of
view or to appreciate that it was sincere and had some sense in
it. He told Hammond that he seldom read Gladstone's speeches
'as it is pure waste of time to do so, and, moreover, it is inexpres-
sibly painful to me'. At the same time he always knew what
Gladstone had said about him. Layard was of the opinion that
one of the objects of Gladstone's Midlothian speeches was to
diminish his influence at the Porte. Emotion was high in London
as well as in Constantinople. Angry crowds smashed the windows
of the Gladstones' house in Harley Street. When Layard charged
Gladstone with being indifferent to the fate of Turkish civilians,

he had to defend himself and, having no good defence, he attacked. They each thought that the other was responsible for terrible massacres, Gladstone because he defended Russia, and Layard because he defended Turkey. Layard believed passionately in furthering the interests of his country as did Gladstone, but Gladstone confused Layard and others by introducing appeals to a higher morality, which in practice (according to Layard), amounted to protecting Christians, destroying Moslems, and working against the interests of England.

Gladstone had confessed in a speech at Oxford in January 1878 that for eighteen months he had played the part of an 'agitator' and that his object had been 'to counterwork what he believed to be the purposes of Lord Beaconsfield'. W. T. Stead explained a little of what was meant by being an 'agitator'. When he was editor of *The Northern Echo* he acted as liaison between Gladstone and Mme. Novikoff in Russia, and referred to 'the invaluable services which Mme. Novikoff rendered in baffling the war policy of our jingoes'. Stead discussed the morality of this: 'The question whether, when the Government of your country is threatening to embark upon what you believe to be an unjust war, you are justified in entering into a close working alliance with a citizen of the possible enemy in order to avert war, is one that was settled in the affirmative in 1876–78.'[1] It was settled in the affirmative, he considered, by Gladstone's speech at Oxford. That was certainly not Layard's view of morality. He considered it treachery. Layard was writing home to his friends in what Harriet Grote described as 'his most lachrymose style'.

*   *   *

The heavy strain of the previous months had affected Layard's health and in February 1879 he was too ill to write so that Enid had to do his correspondence. One of their friends, Princess Nazli, sacrificed a lamb for his recovery. There were many callers; some came out of sympathy and others to try to discover the truth or falsehood of stories circulating in Constantinople that the British Ambassador had gone mad. The Sultan sent many messages and finally asked if his emissary, Hamdi Pasha, might

be allowed to see the Ambassador. Enid knew that the object was
to discover whether the stories were true. Layard had not gone
mad. He was reading in bed when Enid took Hamdi Pasha upstairs so that 'he might satisfy himself on the truth'. A telegram
was sent asking for leave of absence which was granted, and on
18 February the Layards took leave of the Sultan who was at
his most charming. He said that he knew that the Ambassador
always refused presents but he did not think that Layard could
refuse to accept his own watch as a specimen of Turkish workmanship. Layard was very touched when the Sultan drew it
from his pocket pointing out that it was engraved with an *A* on
one side and an *H* on the other—Layard's own initials. The
Sultan then took from behind a cushion on the sofa a long
envelope on which he had written *Je vous prie, Madame,
d'accepter ce petit objet comme un souvenir de mon estime et de
mon amitié*. When Enid reached the waiting-room downstairs,
she was able to open it. 'My present', she said delightedly, 'was
a lovely diamond bracelet with sixteen enormous diamonds in
it.' Layard was startled and said that she must return it at once,
but Enid was overcome at the thought of being parted from
such a lovely thing, 'there is really nothing to be done now', she
said. He accepted the situation for he knew how difficult it was
to separate Enid from jewellery, but nevertheless he went on
worrying. When they arrived in England and went to stay at
Windsor Castle he told Queen Victoria that the Sultan had displeased him by giving his wife a valuable bracelet. 'Quite right
of the Sultan', she said; 'he ought to give her anything he
pleases.' Enid entered that important royal pronouncement in
her diary.

The Layards dined out a great deal. The Duke of Cambridge
invited them to meet the King and Queen of the Belgians, the
Prince and Princess of Wales, the Crown Prince and Princess
of Germany, the Duke and Duchess of Teck with Princess Mary
and Lord Granville. There also was dinner with Lord Beaconsfield
and with the Salisburys, who were very welcoming. Layard
found that he was in complete agreement with the views of the
Prime Minister and of the Secretary of State for Foreign Affairs.
He was impressed by Beaconsfield's remarkable knowledge of
the most minute details relating to Eastern affairs. It is interesting

to find Layard writing 'he had none of that absurd and senti-
mental affection for the Turks and orientals in general or
sympathy for their misgovernment and misdeeds of which he
was accused by his political adversaries'. Layard dined out so
much with royalty that he did not apparently learn of the popular
music-hall song 'We don't want to fight but by jingo if we do',[2]
which he would have appreciated, for a year later he had to ask
Lord Granville the meaning of 'jingo'. Granville must have
smiled as he explained it to Layard, regarded by many as the
biggest 'jingo' of all.

They returned to Constantinople on 18 May, Layard feeling
very much refreshed. A week later, however, he nearly lost his
life when he went to see the Sultan. Before dinner Abdul Hamid
was discussing with Layard and Sir Alfred Sandison a new rifle
which he held in his hands. The two were standing in front of
the Sultan when the latter suddenly raised the rifle, cried '*Fuoco!*'
(Fire!) and pulled the trigger. It was loaded and the ball passed
very close to Layard's head. Ministers and attendants came
running to them thinking that there had been an attempt on
the life of His Majesty. The Sultan was horrified, and begged
everyone to keep the matter quiet. If Layard had been killed
he would have been accused, he said, of murdering the British
Ambassador and a grave international problem would have
arisen—perhaps war.

The Layards were settled at their lovely house at Therapia
and enjoyed themselves, especially as the situation was a little
less tense than it had been for the previous two years. 'It is very
fortunate that our life here is so pleasant', Henry wrote to Sara
Austen. They had a number of visitors. Blanche and Edward
Ponsonby, Laurence Oliphant, and Enid's eighteen-year-old
niece, Alice Du Cane. Alice thought her aunt strict for she disapproved very strongly of young girls using powder, and threw
one powder-puff into the Bosphorus. Alice found an unusual
excuse for writing briefly to her mother 'I should have written
a longer letter only Uncle Henry wanted me to copy his letter to
Lord Salisbury'. She enjoyed riding with her uncle; they would
stop to rest at a wayside coffee-house 'and Uncle Henry had the
inevitable *nargilieh*.' The only secretary who ever came with
them was Mr. Nicolson 'the nicest of all, a dear little man with

curly hair'.(3) They all played a great deal of tennis on a gravel court which every morning was covered with sea-water. Alice was a little taken aback when her Aunt Enid stated that they would go into mourning for two months on the death of Marianne Layard; 'Aunt Enid said that she would give me an old bonnet of hers, which did not suit her.' Marianne Layard had reached the age of nearly ninety, 'but it is always sad and always a shock', said Layard. 'It is one more tie removed, and one feels that it brings one nearer to the last.'

In the evenings Alice read aloud Mrs. Burton's book on Syria, as an expedition was being planned to Jerusalem and Damascus in the autumn. The suspicious Sultan believed it portended a conspiracy against him, especially as the British Ambassador had persuaded him to recall Midhat Pasha from exile and to appoint him as Governor in Syria. In the middle of September the Layards left on the Embassy gunboat *Antelope* with Alice, Sandison, Nicolson, Hill, and Jerry.* Except for bugs in the ambassadorial bed in their hotel in Jerusalem it was a very successful tour. Henry rode into the city on a fine horse beside Raouf Pasha, the Governor, bowing to right and left as he passed through crowds lining the route while behind came the rest of the party in a long procession of carriages. They went from Beirut to Damascus along an excellent road (the French *diligence* service took only twelve hours).

The sun was setting as they entered Damascus and there was a soft veil of evening mist; large crowds of people in pretty dresses lined the route. Enid was with Midhat Pasha in an open carriage at the head of a long procession with Layard in a carriage behind. They drove through the enthusiastic throng to a splendid house with elegant courtyards and fountains, where they were lodged at the town's expense. They visited Abdul Kader, the famous Moroccan chieftain, and the country of the Druzes, being received hospitably in the castle of the Jumblatt family. Layard was delighted by the good reception everywhere, 'My entry into Damascus was the most striking thing I ever saw—a city which twenty years ago was the most fanatical in the Empire.' It was

* Jerry was a negro boy who had been rescued by the British Navy from slavery in Madagascar and handed over to Enid to look after.

a very different entry from his previous one nearly forty years before. Then he had arrived in rags with no money, now he was resplendent in uniform and the representative of England— 'She is looked up to by all the populations as the country most disinterested in her policy and most desirous of their progress and welfare.'

Beirut, which Layard had known as a dirty, half-ruined village, had become a 'flourishing town full of handsome buildings and with a wealthy progressive appearance'. Arabic newspapers representing the views and opinions of Moslems and Christians, discussing local and European affairs, were eagerly read by all classes, and the policy of the Porte was criticised in the coffee-houses. He reported to Salisbury:

> This advance in public opinion is so marked and the determination to obtain from the Porte the reforms which the Syrian populations consider absolutely necessary, is apparently so strong that, unless the Turkish Government is prepared to yield, it will ere long have serious difficulties to contend with in Syria as well as in other parts of the Sultan's dominions.

The reports of British Consuls in Syria, Armenia and other parts of Asiatic Turkey showed that there was an extensive movement for independence and even for the deposition of the Sultan. That information was fully confirmed by Midhat Pasha, who was watching developments with some anxiety.

Layard was delighted with the success of his tour and wrote to George Clark on the return journey: 'I may say, without vain boasting or exaggeration, that no English ambassador, not even Lord Stratford, has held a higher or more influential position in Turkey.' There had been a time a little over twenty years earlier when Layard had been intoxicated by his political success in the provinces in England, but it did him no good because he had antagonised those in the seats of power in Westminster. He could make triumphal tours in the Turkish provinces but what was to be the effect on the Sultan sitting in his palace at Yildiz? Abdul Hamid had been kept fully informed of the unrest in Syria and Lebanon. Because he hated and distrusted Midhat, he believed that it was the Governor of Syria himself who was fomenting the trouble and that Layard was his accomplice. He was encouraged to think this by foreign diplomats in Constantinople who accused England of wanting Armenia as well as the coast of Asia Minor. The French Ambassador, Monsieur Fournier, was especially vocal and there were violent attacks on Layard and on England in the Paris Press.

9

'The very heart of chaos'

The Syrian tour was a turning point in Layard's relations with the Sultan, though he attributed the loss of influence to other causes. The situation became more critical with the appointment as Grand Vizier of Mahmoud Nedim Pasha, well known to be pro-Russian. It was believed in London that the Russians still intended to try to occupy Constantinople and that they might use the new Grand Vizier to obtain permission for their troops to enter the capital. Then the Sultan was thrown into one of his highly emotional states by what he believed to be another attempt on his life when a Greek named Kayenopoulo, armed with a dagger, tried to enter the Yildiz palace. The result was that when the Constantinople newspapers published a telegram from London stating that the British fleet had been ordered from Malta to Besika Bay, Abdul Hamid was convinced that the British were coming to invade Turkey. Unfortunately Salisbury had forgotten to inform Layard, so that the latter was not able to prepare the ground and allay the Sultan's suspicions.

There was great excitement in the city and panic at the palace. The Grand Vizier and other Ministers went backwards and forwards between Yildiz and the British Embassy begging the Ambassador to stop the fleet from coming. The Ministers believed that in his madness the Sultan might take some rash action and indeed he sent a peremptory message to Layard that unless Lord Salisbury stopped the fleet he would give orders to the Turkish navy to proceed to the Dardanelles to defend them against the British warships. England seemed to think, he said, that it could treat Turkey as a kind of Afghanistan! There was a report that Layard had himself summoned the fleet to Constantinople in order to have the Sultan dethroned, in a plot with

Midhat Pasha and other reformers. The Turkish Press, which was under rigorous palace control, said that England wished to employ Englishmen in every public post, and to give Baker Pasha the command of the Turkish army in Asia, so as to prepare for the annexation of the country.

When Layard told London of the Sultan's violent reactions, the order to the fleet was cancelled. Salisbury apologised for not having kept Layard informed but, he said, the fleet had been so much in the habit of wandering 'all over the Aegean' that he had not realised that the Sultan would look on it as a menace to himself. Layard always argued that it was Salisbury's failure to inform him about the fleet which had led to his loss of influence with the Sultan. 'I am really very sorry to learn that *you*, at last like others, are under suspicion', wrote Layard's old friend, General Said Pasha, who had fallen from favour and been sent as Governor to Ankara and then to Aleppo, where his health was much affected. He said that he had been counting up the number of Lady Layard's cups of tea which he would have received had he still been in Constantinople; one day he expected repayment. Said Pasha wrote that the Sultan would eventually ruin his empire because he had the great fault of distrusting his truest friends, adding boldly: 'To be faithful to the true interests of one's country is the same as to be faithful to its Padishah; but it does not follow from this, that to serve the interests of the sovereign of a country is to serve the interests of that country.'

A little time before Sir John Drummond-Hay had written to Layard 'no one has wielded such power at Constantinople as you since Lord Stratford was the terror of Constantinople'. Layard wondered why this was no longer the case and whether perhaps there was something to be said, after all, for Lord Stratford's forceful methods. The former Ambassador was still, at the age of ninety-three, concerning himself with the Turkish question and in July 1879 sent Layard a long memorandum about reform which he wished to be sent to the Sultan. 'The pump does not work, water is wanted. How is it to be obtained?' asked Lord Stratford in an eight-page letter to Layard. The confidence of capitalists had to be restored and the Capitulations modified 'so as to increase the duties and preclude the existing abuses' but, he said, anything that he had to suggest would have already occurred to Layard 'placed as you are now in the very heart of chaos'.[1] That was Layard's problem. What was he to do in the heart of chaos? How could he prime the pump when there was no money with which to do it? 'The notion of our being able to induce the Turks to establish decent government in any portion of their dominions is too preposterous. . . . I dare say that even you with all your energy and goodwill will have begun to despair of effecting anything', wrote Sir William Gregory, who had retired as Governor of Ceylon in 1877 and was planning to pay a visit to Layard in Constantinople.

Layard had, indeed, begun to despair. Long and frequent reports arrived from the newly appointed British Consuls in Asia, which warned of the danger of insurrection among Kurds, Arabs, and Armenians unless the Sultan could be made to carry out reforms. These reports, which the Sultan saw when published as Parliamentary Papers, made him dislike the presence of the Consuls all the more; he considered, accurately enough, that their presence was a focus for discontent, and a formerly submissive population was encouraged to hope for better times. The consular reports were being sent direct to Salisbury so that Layard had no chance of editing them before publication. He found also that the prompt publication of his own despatches without proper editing was often embarrassing and added to the Sultan's suspicions when he read these confidential reports some weeks later. Layard reminded the Foreign Office that his despatches from Spain had been very carefully edited by Hammond and had sometimes been suppressed in order not to hurt the feelings of the susceptible Spaniards. Salisbury, however, liked this strange form of open diplomacy, which would never be countenanced today, and he considered that the quick publication of despatches in Blue Books was a powerful influence for reform. In reply to Layard's plea for restraint Salisbury wrote 'I should be sorry to abandon the practise of printing your vigorous portraiture of the abuses you see before you. . . . We have a timid Sultan to deal with, and every roll of distant European censure that he hears, reminds him how the displeasure of Europe ended in the case of Ismail Pasha.' But to remind the Sultan that the Viceroy of Egypt, Ismail Pasha, had been deposed six months previously only made him more obdurate and autocratic. 'The prospect is not bright', wrote Salisbury on 6 November. 'The character of the Sultan appears likely to be the doom of his race. But there is no course left to us but "pegging away". Since the collapse of the Western Empire, I doubt whether history has presented any case of such complete confusion over so large a region of country.' Layard did not agree entirely with Salisbury's gloomy views; he knew that there was such fertility in the Ottoman Empire that, given some degree of stability and order, the Empire could become prosperous. Professor Medlicott has stated in *The Congress of Berlin and After*, that Salisbury never understood 'the mysterious recuperative powers of the Porte, and its capacity for existing indefinitely in conditions which would certainly have produced chaos in western countries. . . . In his private correspondence with Layard he did not appear to concern himself with commerce and trade in the Mesopotamian region, although Layard insisted that the route to India through northern Syria would some day become the great highway, and that Britain ought to secure the means of controlling it.'[2]

To the Sultan Layard used to describe the wonderful riches of the land he ruled, especially in Mesopotamia fertilised by the great Tigris and Euphrates rivers. He knew that beneath all the confusion there was great vitality and the capacity to survive. Abdul Hamid appeared to be, and probably was, most interested in Layard's stories of what he had himself seen in those regions and how trade could be developed. The Ambassador wrote long memoranda about development and the Sultan received them with apparent enthusiasm. All Layard's dreams as a young man to develop the area through Mohamed Taki Khan came flooding back. The Bakhtiari chief had been willing but not sufficiently powerful and now Layard was in a position to influence the Sultan himself, who could, by giving a few orders on the lines that Layard suggested, make himself and his Empire rich and his people contented. It seemed impossible to Layard that the Sultan should not see it as he did. Abdul Hamid was eager for reform and did much for education but he was caught up in his own web of suspicion and surrounded by sycophantic intriguers who opposed reform because it would lose them opportunities for growing rich on corruption. They played on his suspicions, reminding him that Mohamed Ali Pasha had made Egypt rich and had become too powerful, that Midhat Pasha as Governor of Bagdad had also started to make the area rich and had planned revolt. The story seemed to be repeating itself, now that Midhat was Governor in Syria, while the British Ambassador must have some sinister motive, so Abdul Hamid was repeatedly told, in praising the wealth of the area and talking about the danger of insurrection.

Salisbury was in a hurry to settle the Turkish Question and Layard made no headway. Difficulties increased when the Ambassador became involved in what Salisbury considered was an unnecessary quarrel with the Sultan. It concerned a Dr. Koelle, a clergyman of the Church of England employed in Constantinople by the Church Missionary Society, and his friend, a Turkish Mullah named Ahmed Tewfik. Both had been put into prison because they had translated into Turkish the Bible and other Christian books, which were considered to be offensive to the Moslem religion. Layard in his impetuosity had become involved before realising that Dr. Koelle was a German and that it would have been very much better to have left the matter to the German Ambassador to deal with. It is true, as Professor Medlicott has commented with regard to the Koelle affair, that the frustrations and continued crisis reacted unfortunately 'on the Ambassador's uncertain temper and easily distorted sense of proportion'; there was also Layard's Huguenot background which made him eager to protect Protestants. His argument to the Foreign Office was that two great principles were at stake, firstly religious liberty and secondly the rights of foreigners under the agreements known as the Capitulations. He recalled the strong action taken by Sir Stratford Canning in the case of an Armenian who was beheaded in 1843 for apostasy. Layard considered it very important to check the fanatical spirit growing up around the Palace and he did not think that Lord Salisbury took the matter up with sufficient warmth.

The affair had started before the Ambassador's Syrian tour and when he returned he had expected to find it settled; but Dr. Koelle was still in prison and the Mullah had been condemned to death. Layard resumed his campaign and argued the case for hours with the Sultan, but the latter was convinced

437

that the Mullah had been plotting against his life and would not give way. It was not easy for him to make concessions on a religious question, for he was anxious to try to extend his influence throughout the Moslem world by emphasising his position as Caliph. Abdul Hamid wanted to establish his religious influence, especially in India, and was in secret communication with several Indian princes who were not favourably disposed to the British occupation. On one occasion he told Layard that he considered his inheritance as Caliph 'as even more sacred than that to which he had succeeded as Sovereign of the Ottoman Empire'. The Ambassador had always been impressed at the deference with which the Sultan was treated by visiting Moslem dignitaries from India, Afghanistan, Arabia, Tunis, and elsewhere. He was given a striking example of this when his friend, the Nawab of Oudh, had come from Bagdad to stay at the Embassy and had been presented to the Sultan. He was an exceptionally enlightened Moslem of independent character, belonging to the Shia faith which was bitterly opposed to the Sunni faith held by the Sultan and the majority of his subjects in the Ottoman Empire, so that Layard was amazed at the scene that he witnessed when he presented his friend. 'He threw himself at the Sultan's feet', said Layard, 'and sought to kiss the hem of his garment. His Majesty, who was simple in his manners and averse to such oriental demonstrations of reverence, endeavoured to raise the prostrate prince. He was no sooner on his legs than he again threw himself on the floor and a struggle took place between them before the Sultan could induce him to rise and sit on a chair.' Layard asked afterwards why a Shi'ite should behave in this manner to a Sunni. 'What could I do', the Nawab protested, 'after all, he is Caliph and the representative on earth of our Prophet.'

Layard in his letters to Lord Lytton had emphasised the importance to Britain of the Sultan's religious influence, provided it was possible to keep some control over him. From that point of view he believed that it was a mistake to humiliate the Sultan, but at the same time Abdul Hamid's passion for astrology, which he had studied as a boy with his strange foster-mother, had led him to be surrounded by fanatics and soothsayers who were not the best advisers for reform in the Ottoman Empire. This

was one of the many dilemmas Layard had to face and he understood the problems clearly enough; it was his tactics which were
sometimes at fault. The German Ambassador would certainly
have taken up the case of Dr. Koelle and Layard could have
given valuable support which would have improved relations
between the two Embassies but instead Layard had made it into
such a personal issue with the Sultan that the German Ambassador was only too pleased to stand aside and watch the British
representative make himself still more unpopular.

The affair aroused great interest in Europe and the papers
concerning the case were laid before the British Parliament.
Layard had the satisfaction of getting Dr. Koelle out of prison
and saving the life of the Mullah, but only by threatening to
ask London for his recall. Salisbury did not approve but agreed
that they would have to push the matter through as Layard was
so much committed, but he feared it would have a bad effect in
India and Arabia where it would be interpreted that proselytism
was 'the secret spring of our policy'. 'I am afraid', he wrote of
Layard to Odo Russell, 'that he has lost his temper with the
Sultan, and like a Portuguese sailor in a storm is disposed to
beat the idols he worshipped.'[3] He thought Layard was adopting
Stratford Canning's out-of-date methods and that the old policy
of governing the Porte 'by diplomatic thunderstorms' could not
be relied on to arrest the Ottoman Empire 'in its haste to ruin'.
Yet only a few months before Salisbury had written to Layard,
in reference to the possible collapse of Turkey, 'It is worth while
exhausting every source of argument and menace to avert such
a catastrophe. . . . In the long run influence belongs to those
who can hurt most.' The reaction to the advance of the English
fleet made him think that threats would achieve what was
required and he had encouraged Layard to adopt a policy of
menace. Salisbury's sudden change in attitude was due to advice
from Bismarck. The latter was working for closer relations with
England because there had been increasing friction between
Germany and Russia ever since the Berlin Congress. Russia felt
isolated and the Russian Minister for War told the German
Emperor: 'England is organising and arming Asia Minor;
officials, generals, and officers disguised as Consuls flood that
country: that means hostile intentions against our possessions in

THE ENGLISH OF IT.

BRITISH AMBASSADOR. "YOUR MAJESTY *MUST* REFORM!"

SULTAN. "'MUST'!!!—IS THERE, THEN, A NEW GRAND VIZIER IN ENGLAND?"

BRITISH AMBASSADOR. "NO. BUT THERE'S GOING TO BE A *GENERAL ELECTION!*"

the Caucasus. The conflict in the East is at hand.' Bismarck did not want war and he was fearful lest Layard and Fournier should bring it about. He regarded them as 'vainglorious blunderers', and told Count Hatzfeldt, his new Ambassador in Constantinople, to avoid any kind of aggressive coalition 'in favour of the policy of Layard and other Hotspurs.' Bismarck's views on Layard were influenced by the hostile reports which had been sent by Prince Reuss but Layard was on much better terms with his successor, Hatzfeldt, whom he had known in Madrid. Impressed by Bismarck's arguments against threats and lectures Salisbury told Layard that British influence would suffer, 'if we make virtue so disagreeable, while vice [encouraged by Russia he means] is so very pleasant'. He wanted Layard to avoid 'absolute menace'; the time might come for it and any step we took would then be a serious one. The Government, he said, had to take account of the plot thickening at St. Petersburg and Paris. *

Layard softened his tone to the Porte and regained a little of his former friendly personal relations with the Sultan. By then Salisbury was saying that he did not think that a renewal of good relations would postpone the collapse of the Ottoman Empire, though he thought it would be an advantage if Layard could defer it until 'the revolution in Russia' had taken place. It was not only the Sultan who objected to the reforming Consuls. 'There are too many great Powers', wrote Salisbury in December, 1879, 'who have an interest in baulking any scheme of the employment of Englishmen in the administration to leave us the slightest hope . . . and a general employment of Europeans of all nations, would, I fear, mean one of those international governments which are worse than Turkish misrule.' Layard would have liked to have given the system a fair trial for five or

---

* Count Hatzfeldt echoed Bismark's view in a conversation with the British Foreign Secretary, who reported it in a letter to Sir William White, then Ambassador in Constantinople : 'Russia did not worry the Porte with questions of reform as we did. She went to war sometimes and took a morsel of land, but then left them to repose. England did not take the land, but she destroyed the repose.' (Letter from Lord Iddesleigh dated 27 August 1886, quoted in *Sir William White* by H. Sutherland Edwards, Murray, 1902).

six years, but in April Beaconsfield's Government resigned and
Salisbury wrote:

> I have tried to induce the Sultan to take the only course by which
> his Empire could be preserved and have to thank you most heartily
> for the unwearied assistance you have given to me, and the vigour
> with which you have discharged a thankless task during a time of
> great perplexity. What lies before us is hard to predict, but my
> impression is that the Sultan's day of grace is past, and that in
> every Court of Europe his Empire is looked upon as doomed.

It was a sad letter for Layard to receive, especially as he had
come to the same conclusion. Layard, in spite of all his great
energy, experience, and determination had failed to overcome
the obstinacy and suspicion of Abdul Hamid. 'The Empire'
said Layard, 'has been sacrificed to palace intrigues, corruption,
and incapacity.' He would have liked Turkish rule to disappear
'if it could be replaced by any other that would suit the interests
of peace, humanity, and civilisation' but there was no other
bastion against Russian expansion and so the battle for rehabilita-
tion of the Ottoman Empire had to be carried on. He felt frustrated
and bitter that he could not make the Sultan and the Porte understand what was required of them. Edwin Pears, who used to see
the Ambassador about once a week and discuss the Turkish
situation, gives an interesting account of his changed views about
the Turk. At first Layard was so strong an advocate of everything Turkish that Sir Edwin was constantly opposed to his
views, but as the weeks drew on he found himself, to his surprise, defending the Turks against Layard's charges.

10

Gladstone recalls
Layard

Layard was not only anxious about developments in Turkey but also about the coming elections in England, for it was expected that the Liberals would return to power and that Gladstone, who had continued to attack Layard, might be Prime Minister. In a speech in March 1879 he had said that throughout 1878

443

there had been the possibility of England being involved in war and that the part played by the Ambassador in Constantinople had been clearly set out in the Parliamentary Papers. 'The Ambassador at Constantinople', said Gladstone, 'was holding and declaring the opinion that it was necessary for this country to interfere in the struggle and to intervene with the purpose of supporting the Ottoman domination. That is recorded in his own words.'

Layard found it difficult to determine where his allegiance lay and he was not the only Liberal to be puzzled:

> The ancient Liberals, who had supported Poland in 1830 and Hungary in 1848 and were bitterly opposed to Russia at the time of the Crimean War, were for the most part thorough-going Turks, and Sir Henry Layard was one of them. . . . But the Liberals of the year 1877, the 'Gee-Gees', as Sir Robert Morier called them, —followers, that is to say, of Gladstone and Granville—could not abide the Turk; for which reason Sir Henry Layard, though like them he called himself a Liberal, was for Turkish affairs by no means their man. . . . He was quite as Turkish as Lord Beaconsfield himself. [1]

Sir Arthur Otway commented that Layard was 'as sturdy an upholder as Lord Palmerston of the right and duty of England to take a bold and active part in the politics of the world', but he was never thoroughly at home in the party system and should be described as the first 'Liberal Imperialist'.

When the Liberals were returned at the elections and Gladstone became Prime Minister in the spring of 1880, Layard's friends told him that he would not remain Ambassador in Constantinople. It was clear that Gladstone and Layard would never agree on the Eastern Question. The Queen fought hard for Layard's retention. Granville, who was Foreign Minister, told her that Layard had written to say that he was prepared to carry out any change of policy that might be decided upon: 'He is an honourable man who would obey his instructions, and a new Ambassador (besides the choice of one being difficult) would have difficulty in dealing with a state of things and a place, both of them new to him.' At the same time, he told the Queen, it had been pointed out in the Cabinet that Layard in the House of

Commons had been 'clever, but impulsive, not discreet, and seeing only one side of a question'. It had been thought that he had shown some of these defects at Constantinople in dealing with the Porte and with his diplomatic colleagues. The Cabinet had also discussed the Negroponte affair and there had been references, reported Granville, to the charges which Sir Henry Layard had suggested to the correspondent of *The Daily Telegraph* to make against Mr. Gladstone, 'for which he made a perfectly insufficient explanation'. Gladstone had wished that matter to be excluded in making their decision, but Granville believed that it had had weight with some, 'who thought there could be no reciprocal confidence between the Government and Sir Henry Layard'. His retention 'would cause great dissatisfaction in the Liberal Party', and it was decided that a new representative would have more influence with the Turkish Ministers than one whom they had looked upon to be 'as Turkish as themselves'. Lord Salisbury, said Granville, had made up his mind before leaving office to replace Layard as his influence at Constantinople was 'worn out'. There was little that Queen Victoria could say in further support of Layard, except that his removal should be postponed until Europe was reassured that the new Government did not intend to upset the foreign policy of the late Government 'and to act in accordance with Russia's views'.[2]

While Layard's future was being discussed in London, he and Enid were enjoying themselves on the Bosphorus. At tea the Sultan had helped Enid to two plates of strawberries to her satisfaction and he had given Alice Du Cane 'a lovely diamond tiara'. The Sultan told Enid that Alice reminded him of his mother, who had been very beautiful and to whom he had been devoted; she had died when not much older than Alice. The Layards went on a pleasant cruise on board H.M.S. *Antelope* to the island of Plati. It was, said Enid, a most romantic place, entered through a narrow creek between huge rocks and there was a miniature Gothic keep built down to the water's edge. They walked up a steep hill to the castle, which Bulwer had had built sixteen years before, the dream castle in the Bosphorus where he kept his mistress. It was now falling into ruins and in it was a solitary old man.

On 6 May when the Layards had moved to their house at Therapia and Enid was unpacking the things she had brought from the Embassy in Pera ready for the summer, Layard called to her to say that a telegram from Granville announced that the Government were sending out Mr. Goschen as Special Ambassador and that he was to return on leave to England. 'This is a great blow', wrote Enid in her diary, 'as I feel sure we shall never return here.' They sat at home that evening by themselves playing dominoes and thinking out their future. Layard was unhappy and angry at the abrupt manner in which he had been informed. The telegram had not been sent in cipher so that the news was common knowledge in the city. This was discourteous to the Sultan, who should have been asked for his agreement, and the next morning Abdul Hamid, who had been the first to be told about the telegram, sent a number of angry messages asking whether the omission was intentional. If it were, he would instruct his Ambassador in London to state that His Majesty refused to accept Mr. Goschen. He also wanted to know if Mr. Goschen were coming on a financial mission such as he had carried out some years earlier in Egypt. If Granville could have heard some of the things that Layard had to say, he would not have written rather blithely, 'I am not sure whether my telegram yesterday will have been a relief or a disappointment to you. Your heart and soul are in the work, but, on the other hand, it must be annoying to see how little effect you have been able to produce upon the Porte.' This was a reference to a long despatch Layard had sent to Granville on 27 April, informing him of the situation and explaining how difficult it was for him to do anything considering that there was an incompetent Porte and an obdurate Sultan. This despatch caused a great deal of trouble. Granville said that it had been decided 'to try a change in the character of the Representative for a time', so that Layard did not know whether it was intended that he should return to Constantinople.

Layard poured out his troubles to Sir William Gregory and his young wife Augusta* who arrived to stay, and he wrote for

* Sir William Gregory's first wife had died in 1873, a year after marriage and in March 1880 he married the talented Augusta Persse who lived near his house at Coole Park, County Galway. She was

advice to Hammond in London. The latter told him to state his views but not to assume they would be essentially different from those of the new Government: 'Do not impute blame to them, or advert to any ill-natured things any persons may have said of you. . . . Do not assume that any personal feeling would enter of necessity into the decision.' Hammond said that many of the attacks were due to the fact that Layard was considered as the whipping post on which to scourge his former employers; the Government was strong and broadly based and it was unrealistic of Layard to think that Gladstone should not have been Prime Minister. Layard did not take his removal from Constantinople as light-heartedly as had Bulwer, who had written to Layard at the time: 'One is constantly judged unjustly in details, but upon the whole one is judged justly in the gross: and nothing is so small or so foolish as to be fidgetty and querulous about one's reputation.'

Layard's old rival Joachim Goschen disembarked at Constantinople with his brother on 28 May. He brought with him the printed proof of Layard's gloomy despatch of 27 April as the Government wished to publish it. It was indeed excellent evidence as to the ineffectiveness of the Ambassador and the advisability of making a change. Layard edited the proof carefully, but he must have realised that what was left in the despatch would almost certainly end the friendly feelings the Sultan still had for him and be a barrier to his return. There seemed no reason why Layard should have agreed to publication but he argued afterwards that it would have been almost impossible to refuse owing to the pressure on the Government to publish despatches fully and quickly. At the time, however, he does not seem to have been worried about the prospect of publication and was pleased when Hammond (who had been made a peer) wrote to congratulate him on the despatch. Layard may have thought that

twenty-eight and he was sixty-three, the same age as Layard, but despite the differences in their ages she loved him deeply, according to Elizabeth Coxhead in *Lady Gregory* (Macmillan, 1961) 'because he was far and away the most vital and intelligent person who had come into her world'. When Sir William died in 1891, she edited, with Layard's help, his *Autobiography* (Murray, 1894) and then became famous as a playwright and in the creation of the Abbey Theatre. She died in 1932.

publication would show his enemies that he could be as critical as anyone and that it was nonsense to talk about him as a partisan of Turkey. His critics, however, interpreted it as a bid for popular favour following the change of Government and attacked him the more. It was an honest despatch expressing what he had felt for several months—that the Sultan was a hopeless case and that his Ministers were too frightened to act independently of him. Edwin Pears was indignant when he read the charges that Layard had altered his policy to keep his job and wrote to the Press stating that he had seen the change taking place gradually in the Ambassador's opinions and that 'he had been driven by the force of facts to recognise that no reforms could be extracted from Sultan Abdul Hamid'.* When Layard subsequently saw the effects of the publication of his despatch he came to the conclusion that it had been a plot engineered by Gladstone.

The despatch was still unpublished when the Layards went to say goodbye to the Sultan. Layard had seen him the day after Goschen's arrival, when Abdul Hamid had said with great emotion that it had been principally owing to Layard that he was still on the throne. If it had not been for the Ambassador, his fleet would have been given up to Russia and Buyukdere would have been occupied by Russian troops. It had only been with Layard's support, and acting on his advice, that he had been able to resist the demands of the Russians, for all his Ministers and advisers had urged him to yield. Had he done so, his capital would have fallen. After the farewell dinner Layard once more warned the Sultan of the dangers that threatened him and his Empire, because the Porte had allowed the countries of Europe to become so mistrustful of any promise made. Layard

* *Forty Years in Constantinople*, by Sir Edwin Pears (Jenkins, 1916). In *Turkey and its People* he wrote of Layard: 'No Ambassador ever worked harder in trying to show the Turks that what England advised through him was in their own interests. But he was compelled to admit that he had entirely failed, and those, who like myself, often saw him and observed how from month to month his illusions fell before the steady resistance of Abdul Hamid, were not in the least surprised when his famous despatch of April 1881 [correctly 1880], was published admitting his failure. It recorded an honest change of opinion arrived at by the irresistible force of evidence.'

said the Sultan listened, as he usually did, without any sign of displeasure. When they took leave Abdul Hamid was near tears and Enid almost broke down at all the kind things that he said about her. They returned to Therapia at midnight, having passed the whole day at Yildiz. Shortly afterwards Layard learned that Abdul Hamid was planning to give Enid a magnificent set of diamonds. He sent Sir Alfred Sandison to explain that it would not be possible to receive it, but it was a difficult mission; the Sultan's feelings were hurt and Enid was bitterly disappointed.

It had been arranged that Layard should present Goschen to the Sultan, but there were many delays. The Porte refused to accept the original address that Goschen had been instructed to deliver as it was full of advice and admonition. It was embarrassing for both Layard and Goschen to be together at the Embassy and finally on 1 June the Layards decided to leave the next day without carrying out the formal presentation.

On the afternoon of 2 June 1880, they embarked in H.M.S. *Helicon* and Goschen accompanied them half-way down the Bosphorus. They anchored for two hours in the Golden Horn to take leave of friends and to receive an emissary with kind messages from the Sultan. It was a beautiful summer evening with hardly a breath of wind and they all sat on deck to watch, said Enid, 'the fairy-like city fade away gradually into the evening mist'.

She was less optimistic than Layard about the likelihood of returning and had packed all her household things—two hundred and seventy cases in all. To her it was the last sight of a wonderful city where she had been able to entertain in surroundings worthy of the Arabian Nights. She liked the Sultan and he certainly took great trouble to try to please her—a little overwhelmingly at times. When, at her first dinner at Yildiz, Enid had complimented the Sultan on the bread baked in the palace, she received a daily supply from the royal kitchen brought by a man on horseback; when she admired the birds he had in the Yildiz Park he sent thirty cages full of exotic varieties. When she said she liked milk he sent her three cows and there was to have been a fourth but it was calving; the day before they sailed for England Abdul Hamid sent to say that the cow and calf were ready to go on board the ship for England. Enid preferred the jewellery.

Layard could not believe that he was parting for ever from a city which he had known for forty years and which he considered the most beautiful place in the world. He was a great ambassador in the tradition of Lord Stratford de Redcliffe. His failure, in spite of great zeal, to carry out the brief for an Ambassador which he outlined in the article he wrote before being appointed to Constantinople, became a personal tragedy. Layard may have been foolhardy in thinking that he could reform the Porte, but perhaps he would have succeeded if the other Powers, such as Prussia, Austria, and France, had worked with England. His fears of Russia were justified, and he did perhaps more than anyone to keep the Russians out of Constantinople and the Mediterranean. He had failed in a quarter he had not expected to fail—with the Turks themselves. That was due to Abdul Hamid, but Layard bore him no ill-will, considering him an intelligent and humane man, overwhelmed by events. In his *Memoir* he wrote of Abdul Hamid:

> Finding that he could no longer oppose the enemies of his country, and preserve any part of his Empire and his independence by force, he turned to hypocrisy, duplicity and cunning for the only arms of defence which remained to him. With his rare abilities and natural cleverness he became gradually an adept in these arts. He was soon an accomplished hypocrite; with his frank and plausible manner and address it was almost impossible to know whether he was playing false or not. . . . I was compelled to bear this in mind whenever I had to transact business with him in which he had reason for disagreeing with or opposing the views of my Government. In other matters he was exact and sincere. I rarely knew him forget a promise he had made to my wife or myself. . . . To express surprise at and to condemn him for his cunning, as it has been the habit in England, is like making it a sin in an animal to endeavour to escape from its mortal enemies by deceiving them. He was convinced that he had nothing to expect from other Powers but that, on the contrary, they were leagued against him and his Empire.

It was a hypocrisy which Layard understood and now he was journeying to England to deal with a man whom he considered

450

was as hypocritical as the Sultan, but without the excuse for it and with none of the charm—England's new Prime Minister.

*   *   *

In London the Layards were invited to No. 10 Downing Street. Lady Layard sat on the sofa with Mrs. Gladstone while Layard talked to the Prime Minister. 'They did all they could', said Enid, 'to wipe from our minds all Gladstone's former abuse of Henry.' At Blackheath they sorted out the family affairs after the death of Marianne Layard. 'A most painful thing', said Enid, 'to open all her private drawers and handle her keys which she was so particular not to let anyone touch.' Poor Sara Austen was nearly ninety and did not recognise Henry; pointing at a Nineveh bas-relief he had given her she said 'We dug that up at Herculaneum.' They stayed at Canford where Ivor Guest, who had become Lord Wimborne, was giving magnificent house-parties, cricket in the park, an Italian band on the bowling green, and dancing in the evening; in a quadrille Layard partnered Crown Princess Frederick of Prussia. He told Lady Charlotte that the rain was pouring down into the 'Nineveh Porch' and had 'deeply furrowed' a winged figure: 'It is heart-rending to see how these precious monuments and the pictures etc. are perishing from neglect. It would, perhaps, have been better had they never been brought here.' She asked him up to London to meet Lord Salisbury but he could not go as his old friend Mc-Lauchlan Rate, a director of the Ottoman Bank, had invited them to Milton Court to meet Matthew Arnold and Kinglake; in any case he did not consider that he could have met Salisbury, since everyone would say he was intriguing against the Government. Layard had suddenly become over-cautious for there was no reason why he should not meet Salisbury in a private house. He had not seen him since before the Cyprus Convention and the Berlin Congress and in conversation he might have been able to re-establish good relations. The former Foreign Minister considered that Layard had acted contrary to his instructions in getting involved over the Koelle dispute and this had an ill-effect on Layard's future.

After staying with the Rates at Milton Court the Layards returned to London and discussed plans. Layard was on full pay for four months and thought there was still a chance of returning to Constantinople but if that were not possible he wanted the Rome Embassy. They finally decided to go to their house in Venice and await developments. There Layard arranged his pictures, bathed at the Lido, and wandered about Venice with Morelli, Henry Cole, and Sir Frederick Burton who came to talk about purchases for the National Gallery.

Layard, however, was angered by some spiteful things said in the Commons. Henry du Pré Labouchere had argued that it was an anomaly that Layard should continue to be paid the large salary of £8,000 a year—more than the Prime Minister was paid. Lord Randolph Churchill suggested that he was being allowed to work out his time doing nothing, in order to earn his pension, and there was talk of cutting the Foreign Office vote in order to reduce his pay.[3] The debate was extremely unfair to Layard and he felt impelled to try to justify himself by collecting together his despatches with a view to publication. He was surprised, he told Lord Hammond, at what he had been able to do and how many nice things had been said to him by Derby, Beaconsfield, and Salisbury: 'I may say conscientiously, and without vanity, that until the unfortunate business of the fleet last autumn, no ambassador, not even Lord Stratford in his palmy days, held the position that I held at that time and was able to effect so much for British interests.' He listed what he had accomplished: The Cyprus Convention, the Constitution for Crete, the Slave Trade Convention, preventing the Russians from capturing Constantinople, and keeping England out of war. He wrote all that to Hammond, he said, not out of a feeling of vanity, but to express his conviction that it would be 'an act of injustice' if Gladstone and Granville removed him from the Diplomatic Service and would revive 'the calumnies' that were heaped upon him by his old radical friends and colleagues, who would 'triumph at his dismissal'. There was also the financial factor; another four years of service would give him a substantial pension.

Hammond was worried lest Layard should do something rash. He pointed out that warm approval of Layard's actions by the last Government was a good enough reason for the new Government to wish to employ someone else, and he should not on any account speak of himself as 'an ill-used man', nor should he 'rush into print', which might involve him in serious difficulties —'I strongly hold that no diplomatic servant is justified in making public the instructions under which he has been acting or the manner in which he has acted upon them.' Lord Tenterden, the Permanent Under-Secretary at the Foreign Office, reminded Layard that the despatches he had asked for were only supplied to him for his own private use and might be recalled at any moment.* Hammond begged him to accept any post he was offered abroad so as to work out his time until his pension was due but Layard had already written to Granville to say that he would not accept any post of a lower grade; his reputation was at stake for his dismissal had been a 'slur' on his character. 'I am so much disheartened at my position', he told Hammond, 'and feel so much as if I were under a cloud by my summary removal from Constantinople without receiving another appointment, that I feel no desire to return to England.' The cloud, said Hammond, was entirely of his own imagining; Lord Granville could not find him a job if there was not one available. Goschen was not doing well at Constantinople and Hammond warned Layard not to be critical for it would do no good and would not be creditable: 'It is not in mortals to command success, especially when dealing with such wretches as the Turks.' Layard replied that he entirely agreed that it would be a mistake to denigrate Goschen and added 'I believe your butler could have done just as much!' He had no wish to show himself as a martyr, or to give any chance to the Opposition to attack him, for he realised that 'a man who is believed to have a grievance is always a very objectionable person', yet he continued to write long, complaining letters to Granville.

Layard had had bad luck in politics and now he was to experience misfortune in diplomacy. He was excellent company because he was an enthusiast and interested in so many things. He had read widely, enjoyed music, was an expert on pictures,

---

* They were not recalled and remain among the Layard Papers. He instructed Enid that they were not to be given up even after his death as they were his property.

and loved beautiful things; he was kind, generous, loyal to
friends, and very helpful to people in distress, but the public
image of him was entirely different. The Spaniards had heard
that he was *un homme féroce*; Arthur Nicolson liked working
for Layard, but had very nearly refused to go to Constantinople as
an Attaché under him because he had heard he was 'violent and
inconsiderate' and St. Vallier, the French Ambassador in Berlin,
who had never met Layard, wrote of him '*Mauvais esprit,
haineux et jaloux, capacité surfaite, le tout dirigé par une vanité
sans limites; je le regarde comme un agent dangereux pour toute
l'Europe, à commencer par son gouvernement, à qui il se fait une
gloire de ne jamais obéir.*'(4) Bulwer had hoped that in Layard's
diplomatic career he would shake off the violent enemies he had
made in politics, but his part in the Russo-Turkish battle only
increased the hatred. He was accused of lying, treachery, money-
lending, vanity, disloyalty, and subordinating to self-interest his
principles, of which he spoke so frequently. The Eastern Question
continued to arouse wild emotions and the bitterest feelings. 'I
never remember a question', said Lord Salisbury, 'which has so
deeply excited the English people, moved their passions so
thoroughly, and produced such profound divisions and such
rancorous animosity.' Layard had been at the centre of the
whirlpool and, strong swimmer as he was, he was rather
exhausted by the time that he reached his native shores. But
there was still no peace for him there. A friend remarked that
Layard must have become so accustomed to abuse throughout
his life that he would have learned to be philosophical about it,
but that he never did, being always at a loss to know how to
behave when angry and frustrated—nor did he realise that it
was partly his own aggressive attitude in the past which had
created the hostility. Although passionately anxious to serve his
country, he knew that he was not entirely suited to public life
because he could not 'accept abuse calmly'. As a member of
the Diplomatic Service he had now to suffer in silence the rancorous attacks and was in no position to strike back. Like the
Assyrian lion struck with the spears of his enemies he turned
this way and that to find a way to take his revenge. An example
of the nonsense written was an article in *Truth* of 14 October
1880 by Labouchere:

A coarse man, without any feelings of his own or the smallest consideration for those of other people, is a sort of person who commonly succeeds in English public life, if he can once establish a footing there. . . . Whether Sir Henry (or Sir Austen, which is it?) belongs to this category of British worthies has often been discussed and sometimes decided. He is not an agreeable or a popular man, but he is fortunate—very fortunate. He seems to have set his own interest steadily before him, as the most desirable object to be obtained in this life; and he has really done well for himself.

Prince Albert, who was not precisely a good judge of character, first brought him into notice on account of his Nineveh book, which was generally understood by Oriental scholars to have been mainly the work of Sir Henry Rawlinson; that is to say, the facts, ideas, and whatsoever was valuable in it came from Rawlinson, who then resided in the remarkable retirement of Bagdad, and the handiwork was Layard's. So said men like the late Lord Strangford, Sir Charles Alison, and others, who were likely to be well informed. . . .

In office the new man was bumptious and inefficient. . . . Layard who had got his place by Court influence, and had profited by one of the plainest jobs on record, suddenly began to stump the country as an administrative reformer. He became a crony of the then editor of *The Times*, who was in want of sensational copy— for *The Times* was not always dull reading. Day after day, therefore, the clubs were amused by hearing a puppet whom the Court had set up, and a sworn henchman of 'finality John' (as it was the custom to call Lord Russell) storming against all the things that had made him, and enacting the burlesque part of a rough red Radical. Perhaps he was sincere: perhaps he wasn't. Who shall understand the secrets of the human heart? One thing only is now certain, and this is that the Layard rumpus soon ceased. With half England behind him, and cheering him on (for it came to that at last), Dr. Layard let go the subject of administrative reform like a hot coal. . . .

He has been made a Privy Councillor, a Commissioner of Public Works and Buildings, a Minister (very) Extraordinary at Madrid, where he converted the Legation into a receptacle for *bric-à-brac*, which was selling cheap, owing to a revolution; an Ambassador (more extraordinary still), at Constantinople, and he is now under-stood to be enjoying the desirable salary of eight thousand a year, which is earned by somebody else. Has not there also been some talk about fine presents of jewels from the bankrupt Sultan? Truly administrative reforming is a bad trade; and there are others far more prosperous.

*   *   *

Since it was widely known that Layard wanted the Rome Embassy, he wondered whether it would be correct for him to go on a visit to Rome. Many of his friends there had written that they were longing for the time when he and Enid were appointed to the Embassy instead of Sir Augustus and Lady Paget. Again he turned for advice to Hammond, who did not see any reason against his going 'but you would have to keep your feelings under, and not pose as an aggrieved person, or lay yourself open to criticism as forming a party adverse to the Embassy'. Hammond pointed out that the polite remarks made by his Italian friends were not necessarily prompted by their affection for Layard and he should be careful not to be led astray. Sir Augustus Paget also sent a warning letter which made the situation quite clear. He said that he was not surprised that Layard wished to come as Ambassador to Rome, but he was so attached to Rome himself that he was not in a position to help him—'nothing would induce me to leave it'.

The Layards spent the winters of 1880 and 1881 in Rome. The stately Enid and the handsome, swashbuckling Walburga, Lady Paget, formerly Countess Hohenthal of Saxony, did not get on together. Layard grumbled that Paget did not offer to present him to the King and to the Italian Ministers but he made his own arrangements through Marchese de la Stuffa, Master of Ceremonies at the Palace, who was anxious to be helpful to a friend of Janet and Henry Ross. The Marchese let his villa at Castagnolo near Florence to the Ross's, but lived there too when he could get away from Rome; he was reputed to be Janet's lover, and at the same time Ouida, the novelist, wanted him to marry her. When de la Stuffa came to arrange for Layard's visit to the palace, Enid was intrigued to see him 'after all the history about him and Ouida'. He was a big man with a black beard and she thought him 'capable of taking care of himself (I should say he thought himself a lady-killer)—and one cannot imagine it was necessary for Janet Ross to interfere to save him'. The Layards had been staying with the Ross's and it was probably Janet's story that she was protecting de la Stuffa from Ouida. Enid found that Florence and Rome were full of tales about the rivals and there had been added excitement when Ouida had published her novel *Friendship* as a means of venting her anger on Janet Ross. Layard's remarks about Ouida and her novel were unprintable, while Lady Paget on the other hand defended Ouida 'What must a woman suffer who, with such a thirst for beauty, has been treated thus by nature?' Lady Paget tried to persuade the beautiful Queen Margherita that her Master of Ceremonies was under an obligation to marry Ouida. The Queen complained to Enid that she found the whole business ridiculous and embarrassing and thought Lady Paget most tiresome. This quarrel over Ouida was a bond between Queen Margherita and Enid, making an endless source of conversation and Layard was looked on with favour by the King and the royal family for the help he had given to the Duke of Aosta in Spain. When the Pagets saw how well the Layards got on with the royal family they became very friendly, realising that Layard might be a more formidable rival than anticipated. In spite of Hammond's advice he had become involved in a party adverse to the Embassy.

In March 1881 the Layards returned to London, after Henry had received official notice that he was no longer Ambassador to Constantinople; leave on full pay had ended in the autumn. He had lost about £5,000 in the failure of his banker Willis Percival, a few years earlier, so that there was a problem of money, for the Layards had acquired a liking for good living with plenty of entertaining. Layard's friends rallied to try to get him a job. Lord Stratheden and Campbell argued in the House of Lords that the withdrawal of Sir Henry Layard from Constantinople had been an error as it had reduced British influence in the Ottoman Empire. Lord Granville in his reply brought up the fatal despatch of April 1880 pointing out that the Ambassador himself had described how ineffective had become his work in Constantinople. Lord Salisbury declared that the Ambassador had served his country with great energy, devotion, and ability and had claims on the public which he was sure that Lord

Granville would acknowledge. 'Your case is so utterly unique,' wrote Sir James Hudson, 'that Parliament ought to have passed a special law in your favour . . . who would devote his best years and long experience to the Public service if the end is to be shelved and left out in the cold ?'

Throughout April the story circulated in London that Layard was to be appointed to Rome after all. Lady Hammond said it was definite and Lord Cowley confirmed it; Paget was to be sent to St. Petersburg and if he refused he would be pensioned off. Layard was indeed being seriously considered for Rome, but Paget was a determined man, backed by a small but powerful clique in the House of Commons, and Walburga Lady Paget was a formidable woman. 'She gives herself such airs does Lady Paget', said Queen Victoria, 'she makes even *me* feel quite small.'(5) On 17 April Lord Granville wrote to Gladstone: 'If you remember on several occasions, we agreed it would be best to send Dufferin to Constantinople, Paget to St. Petersburg, Layard to Rome.' Paget had refused to go and sent a medical certificate to show that it would be dangerous for his wife and daughter to go to St. Petersburg. It was also discovered, said Granville, that Lady Paget had been very offensive in Rome to the Czar's two younger brothers; it was better, therefore, not to send Paget to St. Petersburg, but he had been in Rome for five years which was officially the period of a mission though most had been kept longer. Was Layard or Paget to have Rome ? Granville said Layard was much cleverer than Paget, but added (rather unfairly considering how much Granville had praised Layard when in Madrid), 'he made himself unpopular both at Madrid and Constantinople. He is looked upon by the Diplomatists as an intruder in the profession.' They would complain that Paget had been turned out 'in order to make a nest for the unpopular cuckoo, who has not been very careful in the language he has used about us'. Granville followed this up with a letter on 23 April to Gladstone: 'Paget arrives here on Monday, assuming a leave, which I did not give. It will not be a pleasant subject to discuss. I incline much for Layard—you did not give an opinion.' The next day he had 'a painful hour with Augustus Paget'. Gladstone replied to Granville's question on 26 April: 'I am given to understand you would do well to communicate with R. Grosvenor and possibly with Dilke as to the feeling of the party about Layard.'[6]

To shelve the decision to 'the feeling of the party' was not very honest. Granville had said that he wanted Layard and it was for the Prime Minister either to support his Foreign Minister's view, as Beaconsfield had supported Derby when Layard was under attack in Madrid, or to tell Granville that he did not want Layard. It was much the same method as Gladstone had employed in 1855 when he did not want Layard to have the Under-Secretaryship for War and asked that the matter be referred to the Cabinet. Gladstone's devious answer did not make it easy for Granville to come to a decision and Paget was sent back to Rome for the time being. Enid was sensible and urged her husband to lose no more time waiting but to settle down to write books and articles. They decided first of all to go salmon-fishing in Norway with Enid's brother, Lord Wimborne. It was a wonderful holiday and they returned refreshed. Layard had put all thought of Rome out of his head but unfortunately Granville raised his hopes again by suggesting that it was still possible that he might be appointed.

In the meantime Layard accepted the Government's invitation to be one of the honorary commissioners with Lord Aberdare to the International Geographical Congress held in Venice in September 1881. There were a number of visitors to their palazzo of Ca Capello, including Arminius Vambery who amused the Layards with stories about the Sultan and Sir Henry Bulwer,* Richard Burton, who dyed his moustaches so black that

---

* It is probable that he did not tell an interesting story which he recounts in his book, *The Story of My Struggle*; 'Once Lady Layard sent me for presentation to the Sultan, a picture of herself in a very valuable frame, and when I delivered it on the occasion of an evening audience, the Grand Seigneur, generally so completely master of himself, became quite excited, and pointing to the portrait he said to me: "For this lady, whom you see there, I have the very greatest respect, for during the war she has tended my wounded soldiers with great self-sacrifice, and I shall always feel grateful to her; but as for her husband, I have torn him out of my heart, for he has shamefully abused my confidence." Thereupon he tore at his breast as if he would pull something out, and slinging his empty hand to the ground, he tramped excitedly on the floor, as if he were demolishing the heart of the absent delinquent. . . . I tried to pacify the angry monarch by reminding him

the colour came off on the table napkins, and Mrs. Burton, who, said Enid, exaggerated things as she did in her books. Ismail Pasha, the deposed Khedive of Egypt, came to call with Wassif Effendi, who had helped to arrange Layard's Syrian tour as secretary to Midhat Pasha, who had since been arrested and tried on a trumped-up charge that he had taken part in the 'murder' of Sultan Abdul Aziz. * The King and Queen of Italy came to the Congress and were as kind to the Layards in Venice as they had been in Rome. Queen Margherita was still annoyed with Lady Paget because the latter had insisted on presenting Ouida at Court and had written Queen Margherita a long letter about Ouida's claims on Marchese de la Stuffa, which had not improved relations between the Palace and the Embassy. Sir William Gregory and his young wife, Augusta, came to stay at Ca Capello and tried to persuade the Layards to come on a voyage to Egypt and Ceylon, but Layard wished to remain within call of London in case his services were required.

He settled down again to write about his work in Constantinople and Madrid. By October 1881 the equivalent of one printed volume had been completed covering only one year of the Constantinople Embassy. The printed despatches alone filled five large folio volumes—neatly gummed in by Enid. Re-reading the despatches was not good for his peace of mind, rousing him to anger and self-pity. Once again he told Hammond that the more he read, the more 'astonished' he was at the subsequent treatment he had received: 'My own reputation requires that I should leave a record for those who come after me.' He worked every morning and by December he had finished the first draft of the three years at Constantinople. He wished to have on record material for a history of an important and critical period: 'I look

that Layard, as Ambassador, had done his duty in delivering the message, and that those gentleman alone were to blame who had allowed such confidential communications to become public property, but it was all in vain, the name of this deserving English diplomat had quite upset the Sultan.'

* Midhat Pasha was sentenced to death but the whole trial had so clearly been organised by the Sultan that strong pressure was brought to bear on Abdul Hamid by the Western Powers. Midhat Pasha was given life imprisonment and sent to Arabia where he met his death, believed to have been strangled.

on what happened during the time I was at Constantinople as the end of the Turkish rule in Europe and ultimately elsewhere. . . . I trust I have written impartially as a non-party man.' After a visit to England he continued to write through the winter of 1882. It gave him pleasure and amusement but every now and again it 'roused his bile'.

If only he had still been in Constantinople, he did not think that there would have been war with Egypt and the bombardment of Alexandria in September 1882. British policy, he told Hammond, used to be to conciliate the Sultan and to look to him for assistance in settling the many delicate questions which arose, but England had abandoned that policy and had decided to treat Mohammedans aggressively. Under the new policy England would have to be prepared to carry matters with a high-hand and to see other Powers doing the same thing. No doubt the British army would defeat Colonel Arabi, but it would be after that that England's troubles would begin. England would then have to deal with 'the real Egyptian Question'. He was in favour of indirect rule through the Sultan, who was accepted as sovereign of a large area and his influence as Caliph was very considerable. It would have been a wiser policy to have acted through the Sultan with regard to Egypt, for instance, but the Sultan himself had refused Lord Dufferin's repeated appeals to send Turkish troops there. Perhaps he would have done so, if he and his advisers had not become so resentful of British policy following the naval demonstration off Dulcigno in December, 1880; as a result he had been forced to surrender the port to Montenegro. Layard considered the whole business 'an outrage'.

At the beginning of 1883 Layard was told by friends that the Pagets were definitely leaving Rome and that he was to be appointed Ambassador. Arthur Otway, who was now Deputy Speaker, was doing his best to help Layard and was certain that he would go to Rome. Even Lady Paget admitted it, said Enid, 'but said that she would make the place too hot to hold us, and was going about telling all kinds of dreadful stories about us'. Once again, however, there was disappointment. Granville and Gladstone by their indecision about the appointment had allowed a group of M.P.s—Labouchere, Lord Randolph Churchill, and

Sir Drummond Wolff—who were opposed to Layard's appointment, to become powerful. Otway described it as 'a cabal' which had managed to secure 'the nominations to high offices of State, which should be made on the responsibility of the Secretary of State'. The troubles in Ireland, Afghanistan, South Africa, Egypt, and the Sudan made the Government sensitive to any opposition and Granville, who was not supported by the Prime Minister on the Layard issue, gave way. On 6 March, when Enid was dressing to go to a party with the Murrays at 50 Albemarle Street, Layard came in and showed her a confidential note he had received from Lord Granville. It stated that the Pagets were leaving Rome, but that it had been decided not to offer the post to Layard. 'This is very hard to bear after all that has gone before,' said Enid; Granville had so often hinted to Henry that he had only 'to bide his time'.

The next day Layard went to see Granville but the latter was not prepared to discuss Rome. Convinced that the Negroponte incident was still rankling with Gladstone, he asked to see the Prime Minister, but was put off. 'The meanness of both Granville and Gladstone, trying to avoid seeing their victim', wrote Enid, 'how truly despicable it is.' She was angry with her brother-in-law, Edward Ponsonby, who argued from a party point of view 'and did not seem to see that Henry was being ill-treated'. On 9 March, their fourteenth wedding-day anniversary, she recorded that she was much broken down by the worry, 'and could not keep from crying at breakfast, which I would have given my eyes not to have done'.

When Gladstone heard from Granville that Layard wished to see him about the Negroponte affair, he wrote to say that there was no reason for a meeting: 'Nothing that has passed between you and me remains on my mind as a cause in any degree for resentment, and my desire is that all such matters should be entirely excluded from the consideration of any question which may at any time arise with reference to your being employed in Her Majesty's service.' Layard then wrote a six-page letter to Gladstone pleading his case and saying that he would still like to have a personal interview to explain the 'unhappy misunderstanding'.[7] It was an undignified letter and Enid, instead of copying it, should have torn it up. Gladstone agreed to see him but it achieved nothing. 'I have seen Layard', he wrote to Granville, 'a mournful business. He says that the impression he has offended me has been his ruin. I told him that this was at variance with all such information as has reached me. Also that I was ready on any proper occasion to assure the House that there was no offence whatever on my part.' It sounded magnanimous but it was too late; it had the effect, however, of making Layard believe for a time that it was Granville, rather than Gladstone, who was making difficulties for him.(8) From then on he became very bitter against Granville, who was in a difficult position but continued to try to get a post for his old friend. When Odo Russell, who had become Lord Ampthill, died in August 1884 as Ambassador in Berlin, Granville put Layard's name forward to the Queen as a possible successor along with that of Sir James Hudson, but Gladstone was not satisfied, considering that Hudson was too old and suggesting that Layard had not the 'particular gifts'. The appointment was given to Sir Edward Mallet, who had been Layard's Secretary of Embassy in Constantinople— 'not suitable for Berlin where a strong man is needed', said Layard. Granville managed, after much difficulty, to get Layard his pension of £1,700 a year. With Enid's income, his own income from his mother's estate and from his Aunt Sara, who had died at the age of ninety, the Layards were sufficiently well off to be able to enjoy themselves.

PART SIX

Retirement

1884–1894

1

Art and Writing in Venice

Although the Layards could not go to Rome, they became the unofficial ambassadors in Venice. Everyone came to see them, either on visits to Venice or when passing through by ship to Egypt, India, or the Far East and the house 'seemed to be made of rubber it stretched so much'.[1] Henry liked it to be full of young people; Enid's nieces Ola and Nela Du Cane were frequent visitors, Aberdare's daughters and Janet Ross's niece, Lina Duff Gordon[2]—'his harem' they were called. The Crown Prince and Crown Princess Frederick of Germany often came to Venice and the Layards went to stay with them at Potsdam. Robert Browning was a neighbour and gave Enid verses written with a crow-quill in characters so small that she could hardly read them. Marzials, the composer, came to stay and Leopold Orsi made himself useful singing and cutting the claws of Enid's small birds. Charlotte Schreiber, by then a widow, stepped perilously in and out of gondolas at the age of nearly seventy in search of rare fans and playing cards. The Layards had had a reputation in Madrid and Constantinople for being excellent hosts and Sir Alfred Sandison had written Layard sad letters about how gloomy it was in the Embassy under Goschen after they had left, though it was gay again when Lord Dufferin became Ambassador. Turkish friends also wrote to recall their kindness and hospitality. General Said Pasha said that it was ten years since he had had his last cup of tea at the Embassy served by Lady Layard; as he used to have two cups of tea a week he had worked out that he was owed '520 × 2' cups of tea: 'I can never forget you', he wrote, 'I can never forget Sir Henry's hard work day and night to help Turkey during those troublesome times when the Empire was tottering on its foundations.'

In Venice the Layards entertained generously and kept up a large establishment. They still had their old retainers Hill, Giovanni, and Joubert, who continued to cook wonderful meals, besides a number of Italian servants and the two gondoliers, dressed in uniform, who served at table. Everything went smoothly under Enid's competent management and Layard remained in his study a great part of the day writing and reading. This happy and peaceful life was suddenly upset by a domestic upheaval in the smooth-running household. Hill gave notice and the stately Enid was reduced to tears. But worse was to follow, for Giovanni suddenly became abusive and said he was going to follow Hill and to marry her. Enid was astounded and cried again; then Giovanni started to cry because, according to Enid, he did not want to leave and dreaded marrying Hill. Enid considered that it was all Hill's fault; she was taking away the best butler and general factotum they had ever had—'When shall we be quiet and settled again?' Hill won and married Giovanni and some months later Enid saw the bride and bridegroom in the Army and Navy Stores and noted contemptuously 'he was meekly following her from counter to counter while she made her purchases'. Miss Felice Mason, who had been with Lina Duff Gordon in Florence, replaced Hill but it was not easy to find anyone who did as well as Giovanni.

Enid spent her time painting, playing the guitar, singing, entertaining and bathing at the Lido. It was then in its very early days as a resort and the Layards were pioneers as regular swimmers. There was a rather primitive restaurant built out over the sea on pillars and the men were supposed to keep to one side of the pillars while the women bathed on the other. Henry was very angry one day to hear from Enid that some young Italians had swum into the forbidden sea among the women; he considered complaining about it in a letter to *The Times*.

Layard amused himself writing, talking, and hunting for pictures for Lord Wimborne at Canford Manor and for the National Gallery and for his own collection. He continued to be interested in the Murano Glass Company and when the staircase at Canford had been destroyed by fire in 1884, Layard advised Lord Wimborne to have it replaced by a staircase carved by

Biraghi, a well known wood-carver in Venice. There was a plan to include carved portrait heads of Wimborne, his wife Cornelia, and of Biraghi but Layard's head is the only one which can be seen today on this heavily ornate and ugly staircase at Canford. Layard sat for his portrait to the Crown Princess Frederick and to Passini, a Viennese, who painted him writing in his library, looking, said Layard, 'very much like an old jew-dealer in his bric-a-brac shop'. Layard still had a magnificent head of hair and a large beard, both now white.

Layard was happy because he had been able to return to his interest in pictures, which had given him pleasure since he was a boy and to which he had always turned in moments of crisis and distress: 'I am leading the life which, from my earliest days, I aspired to lead—what more can I want?' His own pictures hung in the big hall of Ca Capello and was a distinguished collection, mentioned in Baedeker and in Murray's Guide to Venice.[3] Ruskin came to Venice and praised his Cima as the finest he had ever seen, and considered the Carpaccio, Luini, and Gentile Bellinis as (according to Layard) 'entirely lovely'. He had expected Ruskin to denounce the changes that had taken place in Venice, but he said that the penny steamers were in no way objectionable and that the restoration of St. Marks had been 'lovingly and carefully done'. Layard did useful work as a Trustee of the National Gallery, persuading Sir Frederick Burton, who had succeeded Boxall as Director, to make up his mind about buying pictures. His friendship with Morelli, then the greatest expert on Italian pictures, helped Layard to choose well. He had written to John Murray in November 1880:

> My friend Senator Morelli, who I believe to be the highest living authority upon pictures, has just published a book under an assumed name which deserves your attention. He calls himself Ivan Lermolieff (an anagram of his name). . . . The book is entitled *Die Werke Italienischer Meister*, is written in German (of which language he is a master) and is supposed to be the exposure by a barbarian Russian of the pretentious dogmatism of the German art critics. He 'walks' a little into Crowe and Cavalcaselle, especially the latter for whom he has no love.

Murray made the mistake of declining, but the work had such a tremendous influence that he decided to publish a translation twelve years later.[4] Layard himself began work, with the help of Morelli, on a new edition of Kugler's *Handbook of Painting*, which had first been published in 1837.[5] In the introduction of Layard's edition of Kugler published in 1887 he wrote of Morelli's book :

> In many respects, the most important contribution ever made to the study of Art, and may be said to have caused a revolution in the history of Italian painting, and to have been the first successful attempt to give a sound and scientific basis to investigations into the genuineness of pictures ascribed to the Italian Masters. . . . The novelty of his opinion, his method of analysis, and the unsparing way in which he destroyed the reputation of many famous pictures, and exposed the falsity of many time-honoured traditions in the history of painting, raised, at first, a storm of protest. But his views have now, for the most part been accepted ; . . . in England and elsewhere his method of investigation has been approved and adopted by the ablest writers on Art. . . .
>
> It must not be forgotten that there are but few pictures by the old Italian Masters, whether in private or public collections, which have not undergone the fatal process of 'restoration' . . . and the work of the painter is alone seen in the composition. It is therefore, as Signor Morelli has pointed out, only by recognising peculiar and characteristic forms, such as those of the hand and fingers, of the foot, of the ear etc., that a picture can be frequently ascribed to its true author. He consequently urges the study of the original drawings and sketches by the old Masters, which have not been tampered with, as affording the best materials for coming to a right judgement as to the genuineness of works attributed to them.

The art student is less often led astray today than he was thanks to the work of Kugler, the Eastlakes, Cavalcaselle, Crowe, Morelli, and of Bernard Berenson,* the 'pupil' of Morelli. Layard also played an important part with his two volumes of

---

* Hallam Murray wrote to Layard in June 1893 : 'A Mr. Berenson —a pupil of Morelli—has just been to see us with a letter of introduction from Lady Eastlake. He brings with him a monograph on Lorenzo Lotto which he wishes us to publish. We should consider it a great favour if you would be so good as to look at it and give us your advice.' The reply is not available but Murray at this period was not enthusiastic about art books and it was not published until two years later by Putnams as *Lorenzo Lotto, An Essay in Constructive Art Criticism.*

700 pages based on Kugler which he revised and partly rewrote. In order to make it as correct as possible, Layard visited most of the galleries and churches mentioned in it, which entailed a great deal of travelling. He had the advantage of being accompanied on many of these visits by Morelli 'and of learning from his own lips his views of pictures and their authors'.[6]

While working on Kugler, Layard was writing his autobiography and going through his diaries of the early 1840's describing his travels through Mesopotamia, Persia, and the Bakhtiari mountains. 'I have left the MS. just as it was written 35 years ago,' he told Murray, 'only omitting some passages and correcting palpable mistakes.' Murray had been annoyed that he should have allowed Mitford to publish before him.[7] This did not affect the sales of Layard's *Early Adventures* which was published three years later, in 1887, but there was one thing in Mitford's book which upset Layard very much. A reviewer had commented that Mitford had continued with his journey from Persia to Ceylon whereas his companion had been less determined and had turned back. Layard wrote rather crossly to Mitford, who was slightly puzzled and replied : 'I cannot recall your mentioning your intention of going on, and when you now look back on what you have achieved you must congratulate yourself on having escaped from the comparative obscurity of the career of a lawyer and Judge in Ceylon.' Layard was in such a fuss about the review that John Murray had difficulty in dissuading him from writing a letter of protest to *The Times*.

Layard seems to have been caught up again in the emotions he went through in 1840 when he had been uncertain whether to try later to cross the Seistan desert or to continue his wanderings in Mesopotamia and when his family had been very critical at his decision to turn back from his journey to Ceylon with Mitford. Layard considered that the publication of his *Early Adventures* 'answers a question constantly asked me—what led to my going to Nineveh ?' It does not, in fact, answer the question, for chance played an important part. The readers, however, were not so interested in this question as in discovering a delightful adventure story. John Murray was very pleased with the favourable notices received by *Early Adventures* published in two volumes. 'Best of all, however, is the effect the book will

have in displaying the true nature of your mind and character.
Some people ask if it is all true? As though it were too good to
be true.' One young woman, Miss Isabella Bird (Mrs. Bishop),
was 'so fired with enthusiasm' that she decided to visit the
Bakhtiari herself and, through Murray, asked Layard for letters
of introduction in Persia. Lord Aberdare wanted him to add
another volume for 'there never were two more successful
volumes' and he understood that there was ample material for
another in Layard's original journals. Aberdare was later to
write an introduction to an abridgement of *Early Adventures* in
which he echoed Murray's remark:

> Excellently as Layard was gifted as a traveller in his power of
> observation and description, I venture to think that, from the
> earliest to the latest of these recorded journeys, it is the *man* who
> constitutes the chief and central interest. . . . In the previous works
> as well as this last we are attracted by the same indignation at acts
> of cruelty and oppression, the same intense sympathy with
> suffering. . . . In all alike we find the same sense of humour,
> which was doubtless the secret of much of his popularity and
> influence among those wild children of nature, whether Arabs or
> Kurds, and was not without its effect upon the stately and reserved
> Turks; a natural gift, let me be permitted to add, which gave a
> peculiar charm and zest to his daily intercourse.

For the celebration of Queen Victoria's Jubilee in 1887, the
balconies of Layard's palazzo in Venice were gaily decorated with
huge silk and velvet hangings worked by Enid, with the arms
and devices of Layards, Berties, Guests, and Austens. Layard
went frequently to the exhibition of Italian National Art being
held in Venice, which was visited by the King and Queen of
Italy. 'One meets one's Venetian friends there', said Layard,
'attracted more by the music and the ices than the pictures.'
There were many fêtes and *serenatas* on the Grand Canal, dinner
by moonlight on one of the distant islands near Torcello and a
dinner at Ca Capello on 21 June for English residents to celebrate
the Jubilee.

Layard hoped that in the year of the Jubilee he would be
given a peerage, for it would have enabled him to speak on such
subjects as foreign affairs, the organisation of galleries and
museums. He knew that his name had been put forward for one

by Edward Ponsonby, who was Deputy Speaker in the House of Commons; a friend had written to say that he expected to see him soon as Baron Layard of Nineveh. But nothing happened. It seemed to him that only people who brewed beer were put into the House of Lords. When Salisbury proposed a Bill for life peers he thought he would be included and listed his claims to William Gregory:

> I am a Privy Councillor and G.C.B.; I have been an Ambassador and a Minister; twice Under-Secretary for Foreign Affairs and First Commissioner of Works; I obtained Cyprus for England; have made discoveries which distinguished the Victoria era, am a corresponding Member of the French Academy, an honorary D.C.L. and honorary member of I don't know how many learned societies, English and Foreign. I don't think I shall be charged with vanity or presumption if I venture to doubt whether there are many persons who have more qualifications and claims, if peerages are to be bestowed according to the terms of the Bill.

Salisbury, however, withdrew his Bill. Layard wrote to everyone he knew who was in a position to help him find an official job or a peerage, but could say unblushingly, to Gregory: 'I adhere to the rule I have made to myself never to ask for anything.' There is a letter to George Clark which is typical of his attitude: 'I had not the slightest wish to be made a peer—not having any claim to a peerage, never having brewed beer, good or bad, and altho' the Prince of Wales told me that I was to have one, I never took the slightest step to press such claims as I had, and which far exceeded those which Lord Salisbury in the Bill he introduced declared entitled a man to the honour.' In January 1888 the Empress Frederick wrote to Lady Ponsonby in the hope that Sir Henry Ponsonby, Secretary to the Queen, might speak to her about Layard:

> You know I have a great opinion of Sir H. Layard's talents and knowledge and experience! I know quite well all that is said against him, but also that his capacities could be turned to good account! A man who at his age can write two good books in one year has a good deal of energy left. I know the Queen has great prejudices against him; poor Odo [Russell] used to tell me to do what I could to smother these! Both parties, Tories and Liberals, had grievances against him—still there was an idea once of getting

him into the House of Lords. . . . Are no more peerages to be given on account of the Jubilee?[8]

Layard certainly deserved a peerage and he could have continued to do useful work in the House of Lords, but he had made too many enemies. Lord Salisbury should have put forward Layard's name when he left Constantinople, but apparently he considered that Layard had, at the end of his Embassy, acted contrary to his instructions in adopting too menacing a tone towards Abdul Hamid. Queen Victoria had objected very strongly to the despatch of April 1880 criticising the Sultan. With her strong trade-union sense she did not consider that another sovereign should be criticised in such terms by one of her servants. It was bad luck that Layard should continue to be bitterly attacked for his support of the Sultan, while he failed to get a peerage because he had criticised him. Sir William Gregory, who had been very active in trying to get Layard into the House of Lords wrote at the end of 1890 to tell him that the difficulty was the Queen's dislike of his despatch. Layard was astonished: 'All this about my unfortunate despatch is a complete mystery to me'; it was ten years since it had been published and he had been in good relations since then both with the Queen and the Prince of Wales. He suspected that there was 'an intriguer' at work, as had happened during the Crimean War when he was 'calumniated and misrepresented to the Queen and Prince Albert' so that they both had 'the falsest impression of his character and motives'. He suggested various ways in which the matter could be put right, but none of them seemed satisfactory. Layard was always trying to catch up on calumnies and it was generally too late.

When he realised that there was no more chance of being given any public employment, he settled happily to a life of retirement in Venice with his writing and his pictures but he still appreciated having political news from his friends in London 'like the old hunter turned out to grass he still wanted to look over the fence when the hounds were in cry'. Gladstone's policy continued to horrify him and certainly 'non-interference' had led the Prime Minister into strange adventures in Ireland, Egypt, the Sudan and in Afghanistan, over which there was nearly war with Russia.

In February 1885 Layard wrote a strongly worded letter to *The Times* on the 'wicked' bombardment of Alexandria, the 'shocking slaughter of Arabs' near Suakin, 'the hopeless mission of the heroic Gordon and his desertion and death', and the expedition up the Nile. 'Why are we going to Khartum? No one it seems can answer that question, and yet the soil of the Sudan is reeking with the blood of our soldiers and with that of the wretched Arabs we are pleased to call "rebels". Why "rebels"? They are not our subjects, and have done us no wrong. . . . Our only course is to allow the Sultan, who is the legitimate owner of the Sudan, to occupy it once we have retaken it.' England, having to rule over Moslem tribes, could, he said, have invoked the help of the Supreme Head of Islam; but that policy had been abandoned and there had been wholesale annexations of territory and there would be more. 'The Sultan, I understand, is desirous to re-establish the relations of amity which existed between England and Turkey before the advent to power of Mr. Gladstone's Ministry. It is to our interests to meet his overtures.'

When Gladstone went out of office in 1886, Layard was delighted, believing that the country was rid of him for ever, but he was not encouraged by what he knew of the younger generation. Lord Wimborne's brother-in-law, Lord Randolph Churchill, 'had no principles or political training'; he and Chamberlain, said Layard, were like mischievous schoolboys throwing squibs and crackers into a crowd without considering who they might injure or burn to death. In the 1889 elections he voted Conservative.

Layard would almost certainly have had a happier and more successful life if he had crossed the floor of the House during the war debates in the 1850's. If he had not had a contempt for Disraeli because of his rather wild early life he might have accepted Disraeli's offers, made when he had first entered Parliament. He now described Disraeli to Gregory as 'one of the most extraordinary geniuses that ever lived'. Gregory considered that Disraeli was a 'charlatan' and did not approve of the article that Layard wrote for *The Quarterly* on Disraeli's early life. Layard, however, still considered himself a Liberal. He told Clark that he could not be accused of having changed his opinions, 'it is the

Liberal party which has done so under the evil influence of Gladstone'.

In foreign affairs, which was his main interest, he was less of a Liberal than he had been in the 1850's. Spain and Turkey had cured him of radicalism, and in his old age he had become as respectable a Tory as ever Benjamin Austen had been. He found the world around him 'tending to the ridiculous'; schoolboys were striking against books and lessons; women thought they should take the place of men and administer the affairs of the country—'Where is all this to end?' Mrs. Bishop had travelled in the Bakhtiari country and Layard was sent her book. He was so shocked he refused to review it. He told Murray that he had no sympathy for 'these women who unsex themselves and do what no refined or modest woman would do. . . . Ladies ought not to take such adventurous journeys amongst Bakhtiari and Kurds and other wild peoples. It is bad eno' for young gentlemen to do so; they can only lose their property or their lives. Ladies may lose that which should be more precious to them than either!' He was shocked, too, when his mother-in-law insisted on buying for her collection some 'immoral' playing cards— 'Collectors seem insensible to all feelings of decency.'*

Layard's name was kept before the public through the numerous articles he wrote as well as his books.[9] He had been made in 1890 a *Membre de l'Institut* of the French Academy and Honorary Foreign Secretary of the Royal Academy on the death of Robert Browning: 'I thought that I was well forgotten by the world and practically amongst "the late"—and I have been somewhat surprised by these posthumous honours.' In his seventies he had taken a great interest in the Huguenot Society, wrote various articles and became their London President. In the summer of 1889 he represented the Huguenot Society of London at the bicentenary of the *Glorieuse Rentrée*[10] in the Vaudois Vallée when he made a speech in French to eight thousand Huguenots assembled at La Tour (Torre Pellice).

---

* Lady Charlotte Schreiber published *Playing Cards of Various Ages and Countries*, 3 vols., 1892 to 1895, and was given the Honorary Freedom of the Company of Makers of Playing Cards. After making her famous collection of china she had become interested in fans and published *Fans and Fan Leaves*. She died in January 1895.

Having failed to secure a peerage for Layard, Sir William Gregory wanted at least some permanent recognition of his work for the British Museum. Botta's portrait had been placed in the Assyrian Department of the Louvre and it was considered that Layard's services should be recognised in a similar way. It was decided that there should be a bust by the fashionable sculptor, Boehm, and many subscribed including the Empress Frederick, Lord Salisbury, Sir Henry Rawlinson, and even Gladstone. The ceremony of presenting the bust to the Museum authorities took place in the Museum board-room on 11 June 1891. Lord Arthur Russell made a flattering address and Layard replied. He was most touched at the honour and grateful to Gregory for his 'ever generous friendship'. Only a few months later Gregory wrote, 'I must tell you as my oldest friend, the whole truth—I am extremely ill.' He had very little care for life, but he would have liked a few years more to help Augusta and his young son Robert, who was Layard's godchild. He died in March 1892. Then came the death of John Murray III whom Layard had known since he was a boy: 'He has always been a most kind friend to me, and in business transactions a most generous one.'

In the previous year many of his other friends had died; Morelli, Ahmed Vefyk, Lord Lytton, and his brother General Frederick Layard. 'Were it not for others I would be glad to join the group', he said. 'I can no longer be of much use in this world, and the little work I could do has been done—and nothing remains to me.' New generations were growing up and he was pleased that his godchild, John Murray IV, had a reputation for intelligence, industry, and honesty—'qualities which seem hereditary in the race'.

2

'The Thieving of Assyrian Antiquities'

Layard had been delighted when the British Museum authorities had placed his bust in the building, but he was to pass the last few years of his life on very bad terms with them. He became annoyed first of all because they would not put Rassam's name 'to the splendid series of sculptures representing the lion-hunt', or to the bronze gates of Balawat, which were, he considered, Assyrian remains of the utmost importance. Layard began to take a dislike to Wallis Budge of the British Museum. 'I learnt', he wrote in 1888, 'that when Budge was at Bagdad he fell into the hands of some designing Jews who, to serve their own purposes, made disgraceful charges of theft against Rassam and one of his brothers.' Budge had brought these stories to the notice of the British Museum. 'This he appears to have done to supplant Rassam, one of the honestest and most straightforward fellows I ever knew, and one whose great services have never been acknowledged—because he is a "nigger" and because Rawlinson, as is his habit, appropriated to himself the credit of Rassam's discoveries.'[1]

In the early pioneering days of Assyrian archaeology Layard had had great difficulty in persuading the Museum authorities of the importance of the Assyrian discoveries, but since then world-wide interest had been growing and there was great competition to obtain Assyrian antiquities. Arab and Jewish dealers in Bagdad and Mosul were in contact with wealthy buyers in New York, London, Paris, Brussels, Berlin, and other capitals. The British Museum authorities considered that everything from the sites, for which at sometime or another they had obtained firmans, belonged to them. There were many sites and when in 1879 it had been thought that Russia would control the whole of Mesopotamia, Rassam had been instructed by the Museum to

open up as many mounds as possible and to get away all that he
could before it should be too late. Having done that, it was
impossible for Rassam, with the little funds at his disposal, to
leave proper guards on all the opened mounds. Valuable Assyrian
antiquities were being sold commercially in various capitals and
the British Museum regarded many of them as their property.
The Trustees sent Wallis Budge to Bagdad and Mosul to
investigate and report. For several years stories were being spread
in London that Rassam and his relations were implicated in these
sales of antiquities and Rassam, who was very hurt, made repeated
complaints to Layard. They suspected that the rumours sprang
from Budge's reports to the British Museum but as these were
confidential it was difficult to prove libel. Budge, however,
repeated his charges to Layard who informed Rassam, and
Rassam decided that he had grounds to bring a libel action.
Layard tried to reach a settlement and obtained an apology from
Budge, which should have been accepted but Layard considered
it 'mean, shuffling and untruthful'. Layard was warned that he
and Rassam would have against them the whole strength of the
Museum authorities, who would all support each other. That
made Layard all the more determined to support his old friend.
Rassam claimed one thousand pounds damages and won his case
to the extent of being granted fifty pounds.[2] It was a Pyrrhic
victory, for Budge's expenses were paid by the Museum authorities
and he was soon afterwards promoted to be Head of the Assyrio-
Egyptian Department of the Museum.

The case caused Layard many sleepless nights and may have
hastened his death. Despite the judgement of the Court the
magazine *Nature* published an attack entitled: 'The Thieving
of Assyrian Antiquities'. Budge's lawyers had argued that the
statements made to Layard had been privileged, as he was
connected with the British Museum, and that he should not have
passed the information on to Rassam. The magazine took this
up and said that officials would be chary of making honest
reports to their superiors if they were to be fined by the Law
Courts. *Nature* also argued that there should be an enquiry as
to how Assyrian antiquities came into private hands and quoted
the monuments at Canford Manor which had been sent there
by Sir Henry Layard.[3]

Layard wrote an angry letter to a friend saying that the monuments he had discovered had been his own property, that the Sultan's firman had been given to him personally, that he could have sold the whole of his discoveries and made a comfortable fortune thereby, but instead he had presented them voluntarily to the nation—'such is one's recompense for serving the public'.(4) There was some exaggeration in this but it must have been extremely galling to Layard to be accused in this way considering the efforts he had made at the time of his excavations to obtain adequate funds from Stratford Canning and from the Trustees of the British Museum. There had been so much more material available for transport to London than the Museum was then prepared to pay for; if Sir John Guest had not covered the expenses of the transport the Canford marbles, too, would have been lost, as would have been the monuments that Layard sent to Oxford.(5)

Layard's old, but not forgotten, emotions were revived when Lane-Poole's *Life of Stratford de Redcliffe* was published in which Layard was referred to as the Ambassador's 'agent' in the Nineveh excavations: 'As if', said Layard, 'Lord Stratford de Redcliffe had originated them and discovered the ruins . . . he was extremely jealous of anyone who, he thought, might in anyway interfere with the credit which he desired to reserve exclusively to himself, whether it were in matters political or archaeological.' Layard told Murray that the book was too long: 'It is a mere panegyric upon him and gives no idea of the man. . . . Lord Stratford had great failings which, with his want of temper, unfitted him for a diplomatist; altho' he believed that he had not his due, he was really a singularly fortunate man and has left a reputation far above its merits.' Layard talked over Stratford de Redcliffe's character with Enid who begged him to write down his views 'so that history might not be distorted' but he argued that it would probably be taken for ill-nature on his part.

3

'What many have attempted you have done'

Layard was displaying restraint in his old age. He was not bothering so much about justifying himself in the face of criticism but had become enthusiastic about the new idea of cremation advocated by the wellknown surgeon Sir Henry Thompson for Layard objected very strongly to the 'odious practice of interment'. He considered it a great triumph for Sir Henry Thompson that by 1891 three distinguished people had been cremated—the Duke of Bedford, Kinglake, and Huddleston—'there is every hope that this mode of disposing of our mortal remains will ere long be very generally adopted'. Sir Henry Thompson, who was a great enthusiast in anything he took up, had made designs for 'ash-urns' which Layard liked. The Venice and Murano Company had also made a beautiful vase of glass, onyx colour, to hold the ashes of Castellani, the celebrated jeweller. Layard said that their shop in St. James's Street had specimens of funeral glass urns based upon the Roman models. They were rather costly but he hoped that he would be given one free for his own ashes, considering how much he had done for the Murano Company; 'they would be very ornamental for a chimney-piece, for those who wished to keep the ashes of their friends and relations'.

Throughout his life Layard was attracted by the ghoulish. There had been the dress taken from the murdered Albanian girl and sent to a friend in England; the stories he told his mother about gory Turkish heads brought by Montenegrins and the description of tortures carried out by Persians. In 1885 he made a special journey with Enid to the little village of Gliss near Brieg which he visited as a boy with his parents. He showed her the charnel-house full of skeletons, and told her how his father had had a bet with their maid of sixteen from England that she would not fetch him a skull in the middle of the night, and how she had won the bet. Perhaps the visit was to prove to Enid that it was preferable to be cremated.

In spite of discussions about cremation, the Layards continued to live a very gay life in Venice, especially when the Empress Frederick came there. 'We have been living in a vortex of excitement and amusement,' Layard wrote to Sir Henry Thompson in November 1892; there were daily picnics, excursions, evening concerts, and *tableaux vivants*. 'I rejoice to hear that you feel hungry about tea-time, that is a very good sign', wrote Lady Eastlake. There was an interruption to entertainment when Enid caught typhoid fever in the spring of 1893.

At the beginning of 1894 Layard wrote to his brother-in-law, Edward Ponsonby, to order 'a fresh carriage' to be ready for the time that they returned to England about the beginning of May as he wished to attend the Royal Academy dinner. 'Venice as a residence', he said, 'has many attractions for me, but one misses the society of one's superiors.' In February the Layards went to stay with Sir James Lacaita at Taranto where they took part in olive-picking and watched the peasants' dancing. Enid danced a *tarantella* and Layard ate quantities of oysters.

In Venice in March 1894 they celebrated their silver wedding with their house full of guests. 'When I married', he wrote, 'I could not have believed that I should reach my silver wedding. Well, I have been very fortunate, and I can say, what few married men can say, that my wife and I have never been separated for one single day and that we have never had a quarrel.' They exchanged presents, there was a dinner and a dance at Ca Capello, which Enid and Henry opened with the 'Sir Roger de Coverley'. Enid also wrote that she was thankful to be spared to keep that day and to have so many kind friends 'to share our happiness with us'. On 3 April, while the guests were still in the house, Layard was told by his Italian doctor that he must leave for England immediately to consult Sir Henry Thompson. The doctor told Enid that he feared that Layard had a malignant tumour in the groin and that even a few days' delay might be fatal. 'I can hardly believe in this dreadful thing', wrote Enid in her diary that day, 'just as we were so happy with our silver wedding and having such nice friends and Henry seeming so well. I am bewildered. I begged them all not to pity me for I had to be brave.' They reached London with difficulty. Sir Henry Thompson and Sir James Paget came to see Layard. The malady increased during the following months and Henry told his nurse, 'I think this is going to finish me.' He had to be lifted up and down stairs and sometimes he was lifted into their new carriage for a drive.

Many old friends came to No. 1, Queen Anne Street and there were telegrams from the Prince of Wales, the Empress Frederick, and the Queen asked for a regular bulletin. 20 June was a bad day; a clot of blood had gone to his lung and gave him pain, but he was cheerful and 'chaffed' them all. Enid was in great distress and slept little. 'When I bid him goodnight I asked him to say "God bless you darling", and he did so.' By the 4th of July his brain was slightly affected. 'He knew me', she wrote, 'and liked to hold my hand and twice raised my hand to his lips and tried to kiss it. It was a terrible night.' One of his visitors at the beginning of July had been his old friend Henry Reeve, but Layard had to remain in bed and Reeve was too old to go upstairs. On returning home Reeve wrote him a charming letter which was one of the last Layard received:

> We are both of us on the shady side of the wall, and for myself I have almost entirely withdrawn from society. . . . But one lives in the recollections of a generation which I prefer to the present one. It is a dream-like society of the past, which has an infinite charm to me. Much more brilliant and various are the groups and scenes of an active and I may say glorious life, which surround your sofa. Few men have so much to look back upon with the satisfaction of fulfilment.
>
> What many have attempted you have done, and the past is sufficiently bright to colour the dusk of the present. These at least are my feelings. . . . The only malady for which there is no cure is old age.

Layard died on 5 July 1894 at the age of seventy-seven. The doctor assured Enid that he had not suffered. 'The suffering has passed to me', she wrote, 'and at 8.15 he left me for ever.'

A Hundred Years
Later

M. E. L. Mallowan C.B.E., Fellow of All Souls and Professor Emeritus of Western Asiatic Archaeology in the University of London, and Dr. R. D. Barnett, Keeper of Western Asiatic Antiquities at the British Museum, have written for this biography of Layard the following comments on his archaeological work.

Dr. Barnett writes:

A little over a hundred years have passed since, in those two brief campaigns at Nimrud and Kuyunjik, Layard, following in the steps of Botta but quickly overtaking him, suddenly opened men's eyes to a new age of historical and archaeological thinking, as much by what he revealed with the spade, as by what he provoked by the pen. The century which followed was one made brilliant by so many other great archaeological discoveries—those of Schliemann at Troy, Mycenae and Tiryns, of Furtwängler at Olympia, of Evans at Knossos, of Koldewey at Babylon, of Carnarvon and Carter in the Valley of the Kings, of Woolley at Ur, to name only the best-known of Mediterranean or Near Eastern expeditions—yet even when seen after all these, the sheer extent of Layard's achievement remains to me, and surely to others, truly astonishing. The age was in some ways favourable to the event. The romanticism of Byron and his death had turned Western eyes towards the East. (Layard was sculptured in marble by Park, in 1855, looking truly Byronic.) There was beginning to be an interest in art beyond that of classical Greece alone and men had for some time been finding merit in Gothic, Indian, and even Chinese art.

Not only did Layard's keen eye spot the richest site for productive excavation (how rich still, and how well chosen, the brilliantly renewed excavations of Professor Mallowan and his staff in our own time have shown) but his genius instinctively directed him towards getting the best results from the site. Indeed, Nineveh and Nimrud were not the only sites he noted; Carchemish and the Khabour region were also marked by him as full of promise—a promise realised in the case of the former, first in 1879, followed by excavations between 1911 and 1914 (the latter only in 1911), then in 1934-39.

A Hundred Years Later

I have often thought that there is a close analogy between a good general and a good excavator. The general has to fight an enemy whose strength may be partly concealed behind the hill. The excavator's unseen enemy is Time, which mocks his smallest mistake: his Intelligence Service is made up of clues from potsherds and scraps, surface indications and ancient reports. Both soldier and archaeologist have the same problem; once having joined forces with the enemy how are they to bring matters to victory in a swift campaign, with often desperately small resources, in a brief season, closely limited by climate and by cash—and how are they to avoid getting bogged down in a wrong ratio of men employed and money and equipment expended on skirmishes, which, though perhaps useful and even interesting, are not decisive, judged by the value of their results? Layard knew, yet he had no predecessors to train him, no professors to advise and no financial backers except the cautious and (seen in retrospect) somewhat niggardly Canning and British Museum Trustees. But what a general he proved himself! He worked practically alone for very long periods at two great sites, Nimrud and Kuyunjik, supported only by the young Hormuzd Rassam but, fired by the excitement of his discoveries, he evolved empirically his own techniques of observation and recording, by diary, letters, and drawings, long before the now classical exponent of archaeological method, General Pitt-Rivers (who owed much to Layard), had put pen to paper. It is true that Layard knew nothing about section drawings and nothing of stratification, though he grasped that there could be one habitation level above another in a site; nor did he greatly need to possess such knowledge, and who did, before the young Dörpfeld brought order into Schliemann's excavations? Nor did Layard know the mysteries of typology or excavating mud-brick walls, often difficult to distinguish from the surrounding earth. As he found himself looking mainly for sculptures which lined the palace rooms a few feet below the surface, he found it best frequently to follow their faces by means of tunnels. This method was cheap and cool for the workers in the heat. In his tunnel into the *ziggurat* at Nimrud and those at Arban, I myself scrambled and rested from the heat in 1935. Layard knew that every relief must be drawn in detail, especially those which had to be left behind because they were too bulky or too broken. The camera was not yet available to scholars, but no artist was sent out to help him until his second campaign. We have today in the British Museum many drawings of sculptures by Layard's own hand; most of these illustrate the reliefs of Ashur-nasir-pal from the North-West Palace or of Tiglath-pileser and Esarhaddon from the Central and South-West Palaces. Many of these

485

illustrate slabs now completely lost and still more were found but were never drawn. But it was too much for one man. In addition, he was occupied in the monotonous task of copying all the long cuneiform inscriptions in pencil and ink and of taking 'squeezes' or papier-mâché moulds. These texts were afterwards mostly published by himself and Rawlinson in a standardised cuneiform printed type, but scholars were referred for confirmation to Layard's 'squeezes' in the British Museum. Unfortunately these were destroyed after the last war though fortunately Layard's original pencil and ink copies still survive as the final evidences of an eye-witness. As to their accuracy, I can only say that I collated with otherwise authenticated versions, his copies of the Urartian inscriptions at Van copied from the almost inaccessible and dangerous cliff faces (a by-product of his work in Mesopotamia) and, although these copies were among the earliest to reach Europe, I found them correct in every sign; indeed in one place they preserved the correct reading of a passage, incorrectly recorded by others. This accuracy is all the more extraordinary in that neither Layard nor most of his contemporaries could yet decipher these signs.

In his second season, he found the Royal Library of Ashurbanipal, some 25,000 clay books, containing every aspect of ancient literature and science (hymns, dictionaries, medical, astronomical, historical, and administrative documents). The main groups were in the Palace of Sennacherib, abandoned in the sack of Nineveh in 612 B.C. This collection of tablets became the key to our knowledge of the lost Assyro-Babylonian world and the corner-stone of Assyriology, drawing many experts to the British Museum for study. It may also be said that, of the small objects he brought back from Nimrud and Kuyunjik, of the Phoenician ivories and bronze remains, the former were for one hundred years, and the latter still are virtually an unique collection.

There existed originally a plan to publish all the drawings Layard had made, but it was too costly. A selection only, therefore, appeared, paid for by public subscribers and published by John Murray in the form of *Monuments of Nineveh*, in two volumes. The unpublished drawings remained in the British Museum forgotten until brought into the light of day by Dr. C. J. Gadd in 1936. It accordingly remains the duty of the present generation to make them completely available as soon as possible, which we are attempting to do. The first volume, *The Sculptures of Tiglath-pileser III*, is already issued and Layard's drawings are placed opposite the original stones, where they survive, so that it is possible to judge the accuracy and vigour of his pencil.

But it is often the fate of the able to be disliked. Layard later seems to have kept aloof from both Museum and archaeology. Unfortunately, the record in Layard's later years of his work in archaeology was somewhat obscured by the jealousy and ill-will of Sir Wallis Budge—in other ways a great man and a great scholar—manifested through and after the latter's law-suit with Rassam. This is not the place to go over that ground again, except to say that Rassam, stung by Budge's unjust and repeated calumnies, sued Budge for slander and won his case. In effect the young Budge was really attacking the then ageing Layard, Rassam's life-long protector and friend, and knew what he was doing. Budge, though he had powerful supporters, lost the case, but won the field in other ways, and instituted a sort of *damnatio memoriae* of both Layard and Rassam. Time and death by now have largely purged away these bitternesses, but much knowledge and fruitful energy have been lost in the process. Both Budge and Layard were great men, in vastly different ways, and it was a tragedy, both unnecessary and inevitable, that they should clash.

Layard, and Botta to a less extent, paid the penalty of being many years before their time, of being praised and admired but isolated. Today, a Layard, on returning home, instead of being driven to give up 'antiquarian studies' and enter politics for a career, would have been offered a fellowship at a university in England or America, or appointed head of a British archaeological school, and expected to teach his doctrine to others. But, as it was, Layard left no pupils. To be sure, public opinion stung the Trustees into sending out Rassam again in 1852 for a couple of years to Kuyunjik but Rassam was not really Layard's true pupil in an intellectual sense, only rather his gifted and devoted major-domo. The same public opinion demanded the sending out of W. K. Loftus on behalf of the specially created Assyrian Trust Fund. Yet he, too, was hardly more than a half-instructed competitor, certainly no pupil, and the results were hardly all happy, as may be read in Dr. Gadd's *Stones of Assyria*. Layard's legacy as an excavator really lay dormant till Schliemann, another self-taught genius, picked on Hissarlik as the true site of Troy in 1868. Writing to the American Vice-Consul, Calvert, who owned part of the site, he revealed that he knew nothing about excavation, whereupon Calvert instructed him in the work of Layard, about which also he appears till then to have been unaware.

In England, subsequent excavations for the rest of the century depended either on the re-employment of Rassam or, in France, on such men as de Sarzec—men who had no specialist education at all, but knew the East. Alternatively, the authorities went to the opposite extreme and sent out, in 1876, George Smith, a brilliant decipherer of cuneiform who, though at first partly successful, knew nothing of

A Hundred Years Later

digging or of the East and who fell sick and died. The concept of an excavator as a specialist in his own right with knowledge both of the East and of antiquities, proclaimed in Egyptology by Petrie, was not established again in Mesopotamia until the turn of the century, when the German scholar Koldewey began his career at Babylon, and the modern age of Near Eastern archaeology may be said to have begun.

*   *   *

Professor Mallowan, who was Director of the British School of Archaeology in Iraq from 1947 to 1961, writes:

In March, 1949, ninety-nine years after Layard had left Nimrud for the last time, the mound, long deserted except for the presence of a shepherd and his flock, began to show signs of life, for the excavations were to be opened up once more. Once again the peasantry tramped in from their villages between the Tigris and the Zab, clambered up the acropolis, were given work, and broke the reluctant turf.

We were just in time to recapture a glimpse of the countryside in all its freshness before the pasture was to yield to the tractor, and the greensward was to be replaced by miles of dusty furrow. The shades of Layard still haunted the acropolis, and I used to imagine the place where he found Rawlinson asleep after an all-night ride. Perhaps in another world, as Socrates perpended of Minos, we may have the joy of speaking with these great ones of the past about their labours and ours; we may yet talk of that corporate tradition of long sustained scholarship in which they and many of us have shared.

It was indeed Layard himself, long dead, whose unforgotten words had invited us to return. Above all, the unfinished plan of the North-West Palace, the faithful architectural and artistic record of a monumental royal building made it clear to me, no less than the appearance of the site itself, and the man's own lament in *Nineveh and Babylon*, that a harvest no less rich than the one which had already been reaped, remained for other labourers.

A grant from the British School of Archaeology in Iraq enabled me to direct an expedition to the site. This time there was no opposition from the Government: on the contrary, the Iraq Antiquities Department gave us a cordial welcome and we were hospitably received by the Governor of Mosul. What a contrast to the conditions with which Layard had to contend!

Traces of the Ottoman Empire had long vanished, but a few old men remembered what it was to be persecuted, and that in the countryside it was every man for himself. Nor had the character of the simple folk who worked on the land changed since Layard's time.

A Hundred Years Later

Indeed without some measure of Layard's psychological under-standing every digger's efforts must be doomed to failure. Two things that he realised have long impressed me : that a Kurd will take a man at his own valuation, and that to an Arab the one unforgivable sin is meanness.

The other difficulties remain much the same : above all the struggle for money; to extract something from a reluctant Treasury. 'The times are bad', Stratford Canning wrote to Layard in 1847, 'and we have not the motives to that kind of expense which inspire the French Government. Could a subscription be got up?' When have things ever been different?

For Layard the lack of money meant lack of supervision, and when, inevitably, success brought with it financial support on a more generous, though still far from adequate, scale, the choice of staff was not entirely his own. He therefore failed to discover at Nimrud any inscribed clay tablets, for these, unlike the majority from the Royal Library at Nineveh, were of unbaked clay and therefore extremely difficult to recognise unless the soil was constantly watched by a keen and well-trained eye.

A belief that the Nimrud tablets were still to be found was to me one of the strongest inducements for returning, and there is in fact no single building in which we have not unearthed archives, some-times in hundreds, on subjects which include business, history, government administration, medicine, religion, and magic. A dis-taste for excavating mud-brick walls undecorated with stone reliefs sometimes prevented Layard from completing the excavation of buildings still rich in antiquities, for example the domestic and administrative wings of the North-West Palace where we found hundreds of texts, and the sandstone memorial of the Founder, inscribed with one hundred and fifty-three lines of cuneiform writing which was an inventory of the city's possessions and population. This was missed because neither Layard nor his immediate successors realised the significance of a mass of toppled mud-brick which had fallen against the throne-room façade and so concealed a niche con-trived for a special purpose.

Moreover, since we were able to spread our work over a period of fifteen years instead of compressing it into five, and in the course of time obtained the confidence of the local landowners, we eventually succeeded in excavating beyond the acropolis, in the outer town, on a scale beyond Layard's technical means. From these operations came the discovery of Fort Shalmaneser, the greatest military building known to Assyria, the plan of which is now virtually complete thanks largely to the labours of David Oates. A collection of ivories which is probably the richest as well as the finest in the world has been gathered together here, and in other buildings. In the Palace wells too, where Layard abandoned digging because he was deterred from going below water level, we also found treasure in abundance.

These criticisms, however, are no denigration of Layard to whom the world owes a greater debt than to any of his archaeological successors. He was possessed of a visionary genius; it was he who foresaw the desirability of making a series of controlled expeditions at sites widespread throughout Mesopotamia, and with an unerring eye probed ancient mounds which have subsequently become famous, or else remain a potential mine of discovery for archaeologists in time to come. It is a poor generation that cannot improve on its predecessor's technique, and is not conscious of its own defects. Whatever else has been done, or may yet be done for the archaeology of Assyria, Layard must take his stand among the immortals.

Notes

The Layard Papers Additional MSS, in the British Museum, which number about two hundred and forty volumes, are referred to as L.P.

INTRODUCTION

1. *Letters from the East, 1837 to 1857*, by Henry James Ross (Dent 1902); The Fourth Generation by Janet Ross (Constable). The painting of Layard is by Henry Phillips.
2. Letter to Lady Layard from R. J. Kennedy of the Foreign Office, 21 June 1900 (John Murray MSS).
3. 'Canford and Cuneiform: A Century of Assyriology', by Dr. R. D. Barnett in *The Museums Journal*, vol. 60, No. 8, November 1960.
4. *Stones of Assyria*, (Chatto, 1936) and *The Assyrian Sculptures*, (B.M. 1934) by C. J. Gadd, then Assistant Keeper in the Department of Egyptian and Assyrian Antiquities of the British Museum.

PART I. TRAVEL 1817–1845

Sources. 'Autobiography from my birth to my return to England in 1847', was begun 24 January 1882. This was published posthumously as *Sir Henry Layard, G.C.B., D.C.L., Autobiography and Letters*, edited by the Hon. William N. Bruce (Murray, 1903), and covers the period up to his appointment as Minister in Madrid in 1869. *Early Adventures in Persia, Susiana and Babylonia, including a residence among the Bakhtiyari and other wild tribes before the Discovery of Nineveh*, by Sir Henry Layard (Murray, 1887); his diary of his Bakhtiari Journey and other notebooks kept during his travels (L.P. 39092, 39083 to 39090). Miscellaneous letters 1838 to 1844 while working for Sir Stratford Canning (Lord Stratford de Redcliffe), British Ambassador in Constantinople (L.P. 38975; diary 39094/5). Letters exchanged between Benjamin Disraeli and Layard's uncle and aunt, Benjamin and Sara Austen (L.P. 45908). Layard obtained these letters on the death of Mrs. Austen in 1892 and copies were sent to W. F. Monypenny for *The Life of Disraeli*. As they dealt largely with Disraeli's financial difficulties he did not publish them, but Dr. B. R. Jerman made good use of the material in *The Young Disraeli* (Oxford, 1960). The quotes from Edward Ledwich Mitford, Layard's companion on his early travels, are from his book *A Land March from England to Ceylon Forty Years Ago* (W. H. Allen, 1884).

CHAPTER 3

1. *Narrative of a Residence in Koordistan and on the site of Ancient Nineveh*, by Claudius James Rich (London, 1936).
2. 'Notes on Two Journeys from Baghdad to the ruins of Al Hadra in Mesopotamia in 1836 and 1837', by John Ross, *Journal* of the R.G.S., vol. ix, 1839.

CHAPTER 4

1. Layard's copy was of great interest later to Rawlinson who described it as unique. It was published with other cuneiform inscriptions from Nimrud and Kuyunjik by the British Museum in 1851 — *Inscriptions in the Cuneiform Character from Assyrian Monuments discovered by A. H. Layard.*
2. Layard continued to work on a detailed account of the Province of Khuzistan which was published by the Royal Geographical Society in 1846 and, together with his Assyrian excavations, earned him the Society's Gold Medal. ('A Description of the Province of Khuzistan, Political conditions and divisions', by A. H. Layard, vol. xvi.)
3. *Travels in Luristan*, by C. A. de Bode (Madden, 1845). In an article in the Journal of the R.G.S., vol. xiii, 1843, he describes his meeting with Layard dressed as a Bakhtiari.

CHAPTER 6

1. This was published in Layard's *Early Adventures* in 1887 and refers to Colonel Townley's famous ride from Belgrade in 1849 to bring the important information that the British Government would support the Sultan in his refusal to hand over the national hero Kossuth and other Hungarian leaders to the Austrian Government. Colonel Townley, after reading Layard's book, wrote in January 1888: 'I left Belgrade on a Saturday at 4 p.m. and reached Constantinople the following Friday at 5 a.m.—and Therapia about 9 a.m.—and thoroughly knocked up I was. . . . You are quite right in saying that I could not have danced, as you did, after the ride from Belgrade.' Townley was not sure that Layard had beaten his time since they had both arrived on the sixth day.
2. Layard commented in his diary for 26 November 1842: 'Metternich [who was then Foreign Minister of Austria] is reported to have said that it was the conservative feeling existing in Europe

which alone preserved the integrity of the Ottoman Empire, and that the Porte, by encouraging a revolution in her own dominions, connived at her own ultimate destruction.' Layard analyses this and concludes: 'From the establishment of Turkish interests in the adjacent provinces, Austria has nothing to fear—from the establishment of Russian influence she has everything to fear, and by endeavouring to avoid the one, because it may be the effect of a revolutionary or anti-monarchical movement, she inevitably hastens the other' (L.P. 39095).

3. *Three Years in Constantinople or Domestic Manners of the Turks in 1844*, by Charles White (Colburn, 1845).
4. *The Life of Lord Stratford de Redcliffe*, by Stanley Lane-Poole (Longmans, 1888).
5. An account of the journey (L.P. 38940) and *Autobiography*, vol. ii, in which Layard reveals the ruthless treachery of the Turks.

PART II. ARCHAEOLOGY 1845–1851

Sources. The first expedition to Mosul, October 1845 to June 1847, is covered in Layard's *Nineveh and Its Remains* (Murray, 1849) but the material used is mainly from the Layard Papers, which were also drawn on by Dr. C. J. Gadd for his *Stones of Assyria* (Chatto, 1936). There are the letters from Paul Botta, from Charles Alison, and those exchanged between Sir Stratford Canning and Layard (L.P. 40637, 38976 to 38980). These volumes contain many interesting letters from Rawlinson in Bagdad revealing his difficulties in deciphering cuneiform and showing that he considered that Layard knew enough about cuneiform to be able to help him. Letters to Miss Cecilia Berkeley and others (L.P. 38978, 39076 to 39078 and 39056). There is also correspondence with the Austens and his mother (Murray MSS).

The second expedition from August 1849 to April 1851 is described by Layard in *Nineveh and Babylon* (Murray, 1853). The sources used, however, are mostly Layard's diary, his letters to Sir Henry Ellis, Librarian of the British Museum, to Sir Stratford Canning, and to Mr. Birch of the British Museum (L.P. 38942, 38943, and 39096 etc.).

CHAPTER 1

1. Sir Wallis Budge in his *Rise and Progress of Assyriology* (Hopkinson, 1925), pp. 69, 70, makes three mistakes: Layard did not arrive at Mosul with a firman (an authority from the Porte) to

excavate anywhere in the Pashalic of Mosul and it was seven months before Sir Stratford Canning obtained the permission; he did not begin by digging at Kuyunjik (Nineveh), nor did Layard go to Nimrud because he believed that it was the site of Nineveh. The same mistake is made about the firman in *The Antiquity of Iraq* by S. A. Pallis, Professor in the University of Copenhagen (Copenhagen, 1956).

2. These palaces are described in *The Stones of Assyria*, by C. J. Gadd (Chatto, 1936); in publications by Professor Mallowan and the reports of the British School of Archaeology in Iraq which is still excavating at Nimrud; *The Sculptures of Assur-nasir-apli II (883–859 B.C.), Tiglath-pileser III (745–727 B.C.), Esarhaddon 681–669 B.C.), from the Central and South-West Palaces at Nimrud*, by R. D. Barnett and M. Falkner (British Museum, 1962).

3. *Letters from the East, 1837–1857*, by Henry James Ross (Dent, 1902).

4. (L.P. 42711 P.) Layard to M. K. Kellogg, a portrait-painter born in Cincinnati, U.S.A., 1814–1889.

CHAPTER 5

1. L.P. (39077, 38977).

CHAPTER 6

1. Rawlinson wrote to Layard from Bagdad on 20 January 1847 that his curiosity had been so aroused by the obelisk that he had during the previous fortnight 'thrown aside all other cuneiforms and set to work tooth and nail at the Assyrian. Your comparative sheets [probably 'table of variants' showing the same word or sign in different ways] having been my chief guide' (L.P. 38977).

2. The lion and the bull took two years to reach the British Museum.

3. Henry Richard Charles Wellesley succeeded his father as Baron Cowley in 1847. He was Ambassador to France (1852–1867) and was created Earl Cowley in 1867.

4. Rawlinson had written to Layard from Bagdad on 31 March 1847: 'I have no doubt that ⟨cuneiform⟩ is the Ninus I of history and that he founded Nimrud, but I greatly doubt his being the founder also of the Assyrian dynasty.' On 14 April he wrote again asking if Layard had found Ninus's tomb: 'All things considered I do not think it by any means past hope that in digging pretty well down to the level of the plain at that part of the mound where the remains of the pyramid are to be

seen you may really light on some trace of the old gentleman's carcase' (L.P. 38977).

5. In Part II of vol. ii of *Nineveh and Its Remains* in which Layard discusses cuneiform writing and genealogies he wrote: 'An attempt to prove that the earliest palace of Nimroud was founded by Ninus who gave his name to the Assyrian capital, might not be altogether unsupported by plausible arguments. I hesitate at present to decide upon Major Rawlinson's identification of the name which occurs in the inscriptions, with that of the Ninus of history; although any suggestion coming from such authority must be entitled to the greatest respect. This name it will be remembered,

is ►►𝍦 ⪦ 𝍦 (It was deciphered later as the name of Ashur-nasir-pal).

CHAPTER 7

1. Layard's letter to the Trustees of the British Museum, 4 January 1848 (L.P. 38977).
2. Letter written at Canford to Henry Ross, 27 March 1848 (L.P. 38978) is of interest as showing the provenance of some of the antiquities obtained for Sir John Guest. Other letters from Layard to Ross at this time (L.P. 38941).
3. These letters are published in *Letters from the East*, by Henry Ross (Dent, 1902).
4. *Travels and Researches in Chaldea and Susiana*, by W. K. Loftus (London, 1857).

CHAPTER 8

1. Lord Ellesmere's letter of 8 February 1849 (L.P. 38977).
2. *Humphry Sandwith, A Memoir* compiled from autobiographical notes by his nephew, Thomas Humphry Ward (Cassell, 1884).
3. Published in the *Journal of the Royal Asiatic Society*, vol. xii. 1850. Nimrud was, indeed, founded by Shalmaneser I about 1300 B.C. but it was re-founded by Ashur-nasir-pal who made it his capital and lived there from 884 to 859 B.C. and the monuments that Layard discovered were nearly all from the later period which was the period of the Assyrian Empire.
4. 'We have historical proof', said Rawlinson, 'of this particular mound [of Nebbi Yunis] having been locally termed Nineveh . . . and I think, moreover, that we may gather from the inscriptions that the ruins a short distance to the northward, which are now termed Kuyunjik, were not the true Nineveh itself, but formed a

suburb of that capital. The proper name by which Kuyunjik was
known I have not yet been able to make out upon the bricks. . . .
Mr. Layard, however, will hardly leave Assyria without securing
some specimens from the site and these will be at any rate sufficient to decide the question of nomenclature' (*Journal of the
Royal Asiatic Society* vol. 12, article on the inscriptions of Assyria
and Babylonia, by Major H. C. Rawlinson; read at the Royal
Asiatic Society meetings, 19 January and 16 February 1850).

After some difficulties Layard obtained permission to dig for
antiquities near the Mosque of Nebbi Yunis and considered that
he was able to show that it was not the actual site of Nineveh.

CHAPTER 9

1. Rawlinson was delighted when he heard about the discovery of
   the throne and wrote to Layard from London on 27 March 1850:
   'Your proceedings at Nineveh still divide public attention with the
   Greek blockade, Madame Chusten's *poses plastiques* and Major
   Edwardes's beard. Considering the temper of the London public
   the discovery of the throne was a great hit. If you could now find
   Sardanapalus's toilet table or his *pot de chambre*, people would be
   in ecstasies' (L.P. 38979).
2. Sennacherib stated in the inscription he had cut in cuneiform on
   the rock face at Bavian: 'At that time I enlarged the area of
   Nineveh . . . its fields which were neglected and destroyed for lack
   of water, while its owners ignorant of artificial irrigation lifted
   their eyes to Heaven for showers—[these fields] I watered. . . .
   I dug 18 canals and turned their courses into the river Khosr
   (Hu-su-ur). From the boundary of the city of Kisiri to the interior
   of Nineveh I dug a canal. I led waters into this. I called it the
   Sennacherib canal.' It is described as 'one of the most impressive
   engineering feats of Oriental antiquity' (*Assyria, Nineveh and
   Babylon*, by André Parrot, Thames and Hudson, 1961).
3. 'Some days ago he [Rolland] beat his wife most cruelly', Layard
   wrote to Henry Ross from Mosul on 24 June 1850, 'I was alarmed
   by her screams and, seeing her struggle with him in an open
   tent, had him immediately seized. . . . When he recovered from
   his mad fit he apologised etc., but I refused to accept any apology
   or reparation unless he consented to return to England immediately. . . . I shall feel her loss much as she is the only person who
   has given me the slightest assistance—copying inscriptions, notes,
   M.S., and taking bearings. . . . I enclose a letter for her, and she
   will probably write a few *private* lines, to let me know how they

have got on, which she will entrust to you—pray take them and forward them to me . . . (L.P. 38979).

CHAPTER 10

1. Felix Jones of the Indian Navy stationed in Bagdad was very interested in Layard's excavations and Rawlinson's researches. He did careful surveys of Nimrud and Nineveh, which showed that the total circuit of the latter was seven and a half miles comprising 1,800 acres (*Notes on the Topography of Nineveh*, Records of Bombay Government XLIII).

2. Layard gives a fairly detailed account of his excavations in lower Mesopotamia and also of the art of hawking in which he was most interested. Sir Wallis Budge cannot have read *Nineveh and Babylon* very carefully for he asserts in *The Rise and Progress of Assyriology*: 'There is no record that he [Layard] ever visited the great mounds in Lower Mesopotamia, e.g. those of Nuffar.'

3. This was 'The Nineveh Fund' headed by the Prince Consort with £100 and subscribed to by the Earl of Ellesmere, Major Rawlinson, and many others.

4. *The Assyrian Sculptures*, by C. J. Gadd (B.M. 1934).

PART III. POLITICS 1852–1869

Sources. The principal volumes dealing with this period are L.P. 38981 to 38996 and 39101 to 39120, thirty-six in all. Many of these are official papers, Foreign Office minutes and correspondence with British envoys abroad during the six years from 1861 that Layard was Under-Secretary for Foreign Affairs. Another twenty-three volumes contain interesting correspondence with Sir Henry Bulwer, Ambassador in Constantinople, with Hormuzd Rassam in relation to his mission to the Emperor Theodore in Abyssinia (L.P. 38987 to 38993, 38944 to 38947, 39054, 38959/60, 38966/7, 39118 to 39120), and correspondence about building the Albert Memorial (L.P. 38993 to 38997); *Lady Charlotte Schreiber. Extracts from her Journal 1853–1891*, edited by the Earl of Bessborough, P.C. (Murray, 1952) in continuation of *The Diaries of Lady Charlotte Guest* (1950); *Letters of Queen Victoria*, edited by A. C. Benson and Viscount Esher (Murray, 1907), vol. iii, 1854–61 (second series).

CHAPTER 1

1. Preface to the abridged edition of *Nineveh and Babylon* (Murray, 1882).

2. *The Discovery and Decipherment of the Trilingual Cuneiform Inscriptions*, by A. J. Booth (Longmans, 1902).
3. From a series of letters to Lord Granville (Murray MSS).

CHAPTER 2

1. Series of letters from Charles Alison and Dr. Humphry Sandwith describing the situation in Constantinople under the Russian threat (L.P. 38981).
2. Letter of 5 September 1853, quoted in *John Thadeus Delane*, by A. I. Dasent (Murray, 1908).
3. Mr. Justin McCarthy, M.P. in *A History of Our Own Times* (Chatto, 1880).
4. 'The Parliamentary Life of Sir Henry Layard', by the Rt. Hon. Sir Arthur Otway in *Sir Henry Layard, Autobiography and Letters* (Murray, 1903).

CHAPTER 3

1. *John Thadeus Delane*, by A. I. Dasent (Murray, 1908).
2. *At John Murray's. Records of a Literary Circle, 1843–1892*, by George Paston (Murray, 1932).
3. In a review of A. W. Kinglake's *Invasion of the Crimea* Layard wrote of Admiral Dundas: 'By designed negligence he would seem almost to have set himself to frustrate all the operations of the Allied armies.' No one apparently raised any protest.
4. *Regina v. Palmerston*, by Brian Connell (Evans, 1962). The letter from Gladstone mentioned below is given in *Gladstone and Palmerston, 1851–1865*, by Philip Guedalla (Gollancz, 1928).
5. Harriet Grote's letter (L.P. 38983). This also contains the long letter from Edward Horsman quoted later.
6. The Earl of Clarendon to Lord John Russell, 4 October 1854 (Public Records Office, G & D, 22/11).
7. Letters to the Marchioness of Huntly during this period (L.P. 38944).
8. Charles Greville to Lord John Russell (Russell Papers, P.R.O., G & D, 22/10).
9. A union had at last been effected between Marischal College and the University which were within a mile of each other and each had exercised the powers of a University.
10. John Ruskin to Layard, 28 April 1955 (L.P. 38938).
11. Charles Dickens's letters to Layard (L.P. 38947).
12. J. B. Blackett, 1 May 1855 (L.P. 38983).

CHAPTER 4

1. *The History of The Times, 1841 to 1884*, p. 206 (Printing House Square, 1939).
2. Series of letters from Dr. Humphry Sandwith, besieged by the Russians in the fortress of Kars (L.P. 38983/4).
3. *A Narrative of the Siege of Kars and of the Six Months' Resistance of the Turkish garrison under General Williams to the Russian Army* (Murray, 1856).
4. Layard's letter of 29 May 1856 (Murray MSS). 'The whole story of Kars is a very curious one', writes Layard. There is another letter from Constantinople on the subject, 22 December 1856.

CHAPTER 5

1. Letters dealing with Layard's visit to India (L.P. 38944, 38985/6, 38948) and family letters; some letters are published in *The Autobiography and Letters*.
2. *Regina v. Palmerston*, by Brian Connell (Evans, 1962).

CHAPTER 6

1. *Sir William Gregory, Autobiography*, edited by Lady Gregory (Murray, 1894). The subsequent quote is from the *Memoir* on Dr. Humphry Sandwith.
2. Letter from Earl Russell, 12 December 1863 (L.P. 38989). Other correspondence (38987/38988).
3. Letters from Sir Henry Bulwer from Constantinople and from Egypt (L.P. 39102/3/4).
4. Correspondence regarding the imprisonment of Captain Cameron, the British Consul, by the Emperor Theodore, with a number of missionaries and the mission to Abyssinia of Hormuzd Rassam (L.P. 38989, 39157, 39111 to 391120, 38992/3).
5. *The Life and Letters of George William Frederick, 4th Earl of Clarendon*, by Sir Herbert Maxwell (Arnold, 1913).
6. *Ibid.*
7. There is unfortunately a gap for this period in Lady Charlotte Schreiber's valuable and detailed diary. The only entries she makes concern the prices for which she was buying and selling china, which had become her great hobby, and are valuable as references for collectors.
8. Enid Guest started her diary a little time before marriage and it became an almost regular daily diary after that; it is a most useful background document even though disappointingly factual. There

are thirteen volumes written in a clear hand from the date of her marriage on 6 March 1869 to Layard's death in 1894 (B.M. MSS 46153 to 46164 and 50182); there are six more volumes up to the time of her death in 1912.

9. Following is a replica of part of the letter written the day after her marriage to her younger sister, Blanche.

PART IV. DIPLOMACY: SPAIN 1869–1877

Sources. L.P. 38932 to 38934 is a rough MS. of the story of Layard's mission to Spain, but there is a fuller, typed version, arranged by Lady Layard (Murray MSS). This and Lady Layard's diary are the main documents for the period in Spain (B.M. MSS, 46153 to 46156 and 50182); there are also letters to Sir William Gregory (L.P. 38949) and to Lord Hammond (L.P. 38954/5 and 38960). Correspondence with Senator Giovanni Morelli (L.P. 38966, 38963); fifteen volumes of general correspondence (L.P. 38997 to 39011); letters to G. T. Clark of Dowlais and family letters. The published ducuments on Bismarck's intrigues to have Prince Leopold of Hohenzollern placed on the throne, the most recent of which is *Bismarck, the Hohenzollern Candidacy, and the Origins of the Franco-German War of 1870*, by Lawrence D. Steefel (Harvard, 1962).

PART V. DIPLOMACY: TURKEY 1877–1884:

Sources. The main documents are Layard's *Memoir* and Lady Layard's diary. The *Memoir* is made up as follows in the Layard

Papers: 38934, March to May, 1877; 38935, June to December, 1877; 38936, January to April, 1878; 38937, May to August, 1878; 38938, August 1878 to May 1880. The better copy is the typed one in the possession of John Murray. Lady Layard's diary of eighteen volumes (British Museum M.S. 46153–46170 and 50182); the letters from Layard to the 1st Earl of Lytton, Viceroy of India (L.P. 38971) and those from Lytton to Layard (L.P. 38969/70). There are twenty-five volumes of general correspondence (L.P. 39012 to 39036); letters from Lord Hammond to Layard (L.P. 38955 to 38958) and from Layard to Hammond (L.P. 38960 to 38962). There are also family letters. Some of the 'secret' correspondence between Layard and Disraeli is published in *The Life of Benjamin Disraeli*, by Monypenny and Buckle (Murray, 1929) and between Lord Salisbury and Layard in *Life of Robert, Marquis of Salisbury*, by Lady Gwendolen Cecil, vols. ii and iii (Hodder, 1921); *The Letters of Queen Victoria*, 2nd series, 1862 to 1885.

CHAPTER 1

1. 'The True Eastern Question', by E. A. Freeman, December 1875, in *The Fortnightly Review*; also 'The Turks in Europe', October 1876, in *The British Quarterly Review* and *The Ottoman Power in Europe* (Macmillan, 1877).
2. *Disraeli, Gladstone and the Eastern Question*, by R. W. Seton-Watson (Macmillan, 1935). In Layard's *Autobiography* the article 'The Eastern Question and the Conference' is listed as by Henry Layard and William Smith.
3. Quoted by Dr. R. W. Seton-Watson in *Disraeli, Gladstone and the Eastern Question* (R.B.D. iv No. 165; Ignatieff to Gorchakoff, the Russian Chancellor, 22 January 1877).

CHAPTER 2

1. At the end of April, 1877, a debate was continued for five nights on five resolutions moved by Gladstone, who attacked the Government for not forcing Turkey to punish those responsible for the Bulgarian atrocities and for not making the Porte carry out the necessary reforms.
2. *A Memoir of Sir John Drummond-Hay* (Murray, 1896).
3. *The Builder*, 27 February 1847, published an engraving of the Embassy building then only two storeys high. Mr. Gordon Whitteridge, while Consul-General in Istanbul, helped to try to sort out these discrepancies.

Notes

4. *Two Years of the Eastern Question*, by A. Gallenga, correspondent of *The Times* (Tinsley, 1877).
5. Harriet Grote, 14 October 1877 (L.P. 39016).

1. Sultan Abdul Hamid moved to the Yildiz or 'Star', Kiosk in the large Park soon after the opening of the Russo-Turkish War, adding each year a number of quickly constructed buildings. It became the seat of Government instead of the area known as the Porte. It was an armed camp, a town of twelve thousand people and Abdul Hamid's 'prison' which he hardly ever left. He had in the park a theatre, library, arsenal, museum of arms, porcelain works, furniture factory, museum of stuffed animals, saw-mill, foundry, kennels, hospital for dogs, birds in huge cages, five imperial stables, two mosques, and a number of charming kiosks and little gardens.

   The Yildiz Kiosk has been kept by the Turkish Government very much as it was in the days of Sultan Abdul Hamid and it is sometimes used for distinguished visitors. The rooms are well-proportioned, the furniture is comfortable, and the decoration attractive. The Yildiz Kiosk is not imposing and ornate as are the other palaces but is more homely and has great charm.

2. *Fifty Years in Constantinople and Recollections of Robert College*, by George Washburn (Houghton Mifflin, 1911).

3. The British Embassy physician, Dr. Dickson, was satisfied when he went to see the body of Abdul Aziz, that it was suicide. Later Sultan Abdul Hamid staged a trial with the object of convicting Midhat Pasha of the assassination of the former Sultan.

4. *Two Years of the Eastern Question*, by A. Gallenga (Tinsley, 1877).

5. 'Abdul Hamid was far from being the blind, uncompromising, complete reactionary of the historical legend; on the contrary, he was a willing and active modernizer . . . Politics apart, the first decades of Abdul Hamid's reign were as active a period of change and reform as any since the beginning of the century. . . .' *The Emergence of Modern Turkey*, by Bernard Lewis (Oxford University Press under the auspices of the Royal Institute of International Affairs, 1961).

CHAPTER 4

1. Lord Edward Robert Lytton went from Portugal to be Viceroy of India in 1876. (Queen Victoria had been proclaimed Empress of India on 1 January of that year.) (L.P. 38971.)

2. Speech at the 'National Convention on the Eastern Question' at St. James's Hall, Piccadilly, on 8 December 1876, attended by Gladstone, Canon Liddon, and many prominent people in Church and Politics.

3. Gladstone's letter published in *The Daily Telegraph* of 25 September 1877. *The Times* had on 15 September, published a letter from M. J. Negroponte in which he denied that Gladstone in his letter had encouraged the Greeks against the Turks.

4. In his *Memoir* Layard explained his ideas more clearly. He said that if it were not possible to have Mohammerah itself then the Sultan should be persuaded to concede 'some position on the right bank of the Shatt el Arab near its mouth, and at the same time to have opened the navigation of the Euphrates and Tigris to the commerce of all nations'. If Russia were to extend her conquests in Armenia and Asia Minor, 'England might in a very short space of time send troops up the two rivers in flat-bottomed boats, towed by steamboats, and, acting with the Turks, operate on the flank of the Russian advancing army'.

CHAPTER 5

1. Quoted in *Disraeli, Gladstone and the Eastern Question*, by R. W. Seton-Watson (Macmillan, 1935).

2. The telegram from Layard giving the terms of Bases of Peace issued by the Russians contained an important paragraph: 'The question of the Bosphorus and Dardanelles to be settled between the *Congress* and the Emperor of Russia.' The British Government had feared that a private arrangement would be made about the Straits between the Emperor of Russia and the Sultan without consulting England or the other Powers, but, according to Layard's first telegram received in London, everything was all right—the Russians would refer the matter to 'Congress', which meant the European Powers. Northcote rushed off to Beaconsfield, who was in bed at No. 10 Downing Street, and it was decided that in view of this information there was no justification for sending the fleet and so the order was cancelled. The next day Layard sent a correction stating that the question of the Straits would be settled 'between the Sultan and the Emperor of Russia'. 'How we gnashed our teeth!' exclaimed Northcote when the correction was received; he thought that subsequent events showed that it had been a very great mistake to counter-order the fleet, and Queen Victoria wanted to send the fleet after all, 'else we are sure to be duped,

which would be fatal'. But the Cabinet was not prepared to issue a third order within twenty-four hours.

On the original telegram in the Foreign Office archives there is a marginal note, presumably by the clerk who deciphered it, stating with regard to the word 'Congress' that 'alteration of one figure in the group makes Sultan'. Layard considered that the Foreign Office could have interpreted the telegram correctly in the first instance (Layard's telegram is F.O. 78/2809, No. 102, 24 January).

3. The publication of these despatches also did Layard personally a great deal of harm, partly because of the partisan way in which he wrote, but he did not seem to realise this.

In *A Century of Diplomatic Blue Books, 1814 to 1914* (Cambridge, 1938) the authors (Harold Temperley and Lillian M. Penson) point out in the Introduction how difficult it was for governments in the nineteenth century to withhold publication of documents, and even the powerful Palmerston could not refuse the demands of the Commons: 'In the Disraeli period public opinion forced the unwilling hands of Derby and Salisbury, and drove them to follow the lavish tradition of the Palmerston age. The curious fact emerges from this study that the advent of a more democratic era resulted in a restriction on the publication on foreign affairs in some important ways. . . . As Parliament became more democratic its control over foreign policy declined and, while Blue Books on domestic affairs expanded and multiplied at the end of the nineteenth century, those on foreign affairs lessened both in number and in interest.'

4. Luigi Palma di Cesnola was born in 1832, served in the Crimean War with the Sardinian forces and fought in the American Civil War; he was for eleven years United States Consul in Cyprus and worked on archaeology. His collection was purchased in 1873 by the Metropolitan Museum of New York and from 1879 until his death in 1904 he was Secretary and Director of the Institute (L.P. 39018, 39021).

CHAPTER 6

1. *Gathorne-Hardy, First Earl of Cranbrook*, edited by the Hon. Alfred E. Gathorne-Hardy; report of Cabinet meeting of 8 February 1878 (Longmans, 1910).

2. *Life of Robert, Marquis of Salisbury*, by Lady Gwendolen Cecil (Hodder & Stoughton, 1921).

3. *Russia und England* by Olga Novikoff; her reply to General Grant, President of the United States, who had asked her why the Russians had not occupied the Turkish capital when it was entirely in their hands; quoted in W. T. Stead's *The M.P. for Russia: Reminiscences of Mme. Olga Novikoff* (Melrose, 1909).

CHAPTER 7

1. *Life of Robert, Marquis of Salisbury*, by Lady Gwendolen Cecil, vol. ii (Hodder & Stoughton, 1921).
2. *Ibid.*
3. There were a number of conspiracies, including the Cleanthe Scalieri plot two months later. 'In the minds of the Turkish Liberals Murad lived on as a potential saviour of the Empire', states Professor Mardin in the *Middle East Journal*, Spring 1962.
4. *Lady Charlotte Schreiber's Diary, 1853–1891*, edited by the Earl of Bessborough (Murray, 1952) and from the original in the possession of Viscount Wimborne.

CHAPTER 8

1. *The M.P. for Russia: Reminiscences of Olga Novikoff.* Gladstone's speech was made at the Palmerston Club in Oxford on 30 January 1878.
2.
> We don't want to fight,
> But by jingo if we do,
> We've got the ships, we've got the men,
> We've got the money too.
> We've fought the Bear before,
> And if we're Britons true,
> The Russians shall not have Constantinople.
3. Arthur Nicolson, who became Lord Carnock, father of the Hon. Sir Harold Nicolson.

CHAPTER 9

1. Lord Stratford de Redcliffe's memorandum (L.P. 39143 f. 3).
2. *The Congress of Berlin and After. A Diplomatic History of the Near Eastern Settlement, 1878–1880*, by W. N. Medlicott (Methuen, 1938).
3. *Life of Robert, Marquis of Salisbury*, by Lady Gwendolen Cecil (Hodder & Stoughton, 1921).

CHAPTER 10

1. *Sir William White*, by H. Sutherland Edwards (Murray, 1902). He was for some years British Consul-General in Belgrade after de Fonblanque and was for six years Ambassador at Constantinople.
2. *The Letters of Queen Victoria*, 1879 to 1885, 2nd series, vol. iii, pp. 92 to 94 (Murray, 1928).
3. Debate on the Civil Estimates, 16 August 1880.
4. *Documents Diplomatiques Français*, 1871 to 1914, 14 November 1879.
5. Lady Layard's diary, 10 February 1882, quoting Lady Ely, one of Queen Victoria's ladies-in-waiting.
6. Quotes are from *The Political Correspondence of Mr. Gladstone and Lord Granville, 1876–1886*, edited by Agatha Ramm (Clarendon, 1962). Lord Granville referred to Layard's unpopularity in Madrid, but he had sent several very complimentary telegrams to Layard when he was Minister there.
7. Layard's letter to Gladstone (L.P. 39140).
8. Layard wrote a long memoir recounting how badly he considered he had been treated by Lord Granville (L.P. 38934).

PART VI. RETIREMENT 1884–1894

Sources. Letters from Lord Hammond to Layard (L.P. 38958) and from Layard to Hammond (L.P. 38962); letters to Senator Giovanni Morelli (L.P. 38967/8) and from Morelli to Layard (L.P. 38964/5); correspondence with Sir Henry Thompson, the surgeon (L.P. 38973/38974); general correspondence fifteen volumes, October, 1883–July, 1894 (L.P. 39037 to 39048, 39098 to 39100); letters to Edward Ponsonby, who married Blanche Guest, and became Viscount Duncannon, later 8th Earl of Bessborough (L.P. 39097).

CHAPTER 1

1. Ca (or Casa) Capello is a fourteenth century *palazzo* standing at the corner of the Rio di San Polo on the Grand Canal.
2. Lina Duff Gordon (Mrs. Aubrey Waterfield) has described staying with the Layards in Venice in *Castle in Italy* (Murray, 1962).
3. Sir Henry Layard bequeathed his Italian, Spanish, German and English paintings to the National Gallery where there are eighty of his pictures.

4. The full title is: *Die Werke Italienischer Meister in den Galerien von München, Dresden und Berlin; ein kritischer Versuch,* by Ivan Lermolieff. It was translated by Miss C. J. Foulkes with a preface by Sir Henry Layard—*Italian Painters* (Murray, 1892).
5. That part of Kugler's book dealing with the Italian Schools of painting had been edited by Sir Charles Eastlake and published in 1851; following the publication of Crowe and Cavalcaselle's *History of Painting in Italy from the Second to the Sixteenth Century,* Lady Eastlake revised it again in 1874. With the publication of Morelli's book, Layard considered that another edition was required and this was published as *The Italian Schools of Painting based on the Handbook of Kugler,* revised and in part rewritten by Austen Henry Layard (Murray, 1887).
6. Bernard Berenson told the author that he considered Layard's edition of Kugler most useful to the student and had himself found it valuable.
7. *A Land March from England to Ceylon Forty Years Ago,* by Edward Ledwich Mitford (W. H. Allen, 1884).
8. *Letters of the Empress Frederick,* edited by Sir Frederick Ponsonby, p. 273 (Macmillan, 1928).
9. Articles in *The Quarterly Review* were: 'The National Gallery', October, 1886; 'The National Portrait Gallery', April 1888; 'Early Life of Lord Beaconsfield', January 1889; 'The Italian *Condottiere*', January 1890. In 1891 there was a revised sixth edition of *Kugler's Handbook of Painting.*
10. The Waldenses, or inhabitants of the Vaudois valleys in Piedmont, were celebrating the return to their valleys of an heroic band of their forefathers, led by Henri Arnaud, which fought its way through mountain passes defended by the armies of Louis XIV and the Duke of Savoy. Sir Henry Layard described his visit in his presidential address in 1890 to the Huguenot Society of London (Huguenot Society Proceedings, vol. 3, xcviii).

CHAPTER 2

1. Layard to Gregory, Venice, 8 December 1888 (L.P. 38950).
2. The case lasted for five days in June and July 1893. It was reported in *The Times* and *The Daily News,* July 4, and Sir Wallis Budge devotes eighteen pages to it in *By Nile and Tigris* (Murray, 1920).
3. *Nature,* 10 August 1893.
4. Letter to Lord Duncannon, 11 October 1893 (L.P. 39097).

5.   Seven small Assyrian bas-reliefs given by Layard to Sir John
and Lady Charlotte Guest for the 'Nineveh Porch' at Canford
Manor were sold at Sotheby's on 16 November 1959 for £13,485.
They had been placed as a frieze high up along the walls of the
interior of the 'Nineveh Porch' and at some time were painted
over. When the 'Porch' was taken over as a tuck-shop for Canford
School, the frieze became further concealed behind tins of sweets
and packets of breakfast food. There they remained for many
years until the late Sir Leonard Woolley and Dr. Barnett of the
British Museum re-discovered them and they were dug out.
Layard, with his interest in education, would have been pleased
to think that indirectly he had made a handsome grant to a new
school. The larger monuments in the 'Nineveh Porch' presented
by Layard had previously been sold to the Metropolitan Museum
of New York.

Index

Index

Afghanistan, 48n, 53, 56, 65, 78–9, 474

Ahmed, Sheikh, 36–7

Ahmed Tewfik, Mullah, 437–8

Ahmed Vefyk Pasha, in youth, 105; President of Chamber of Turkish Parliament, 374; Prime Minister, 395, 402, 414; death of, 477

Ainsworth, William, 42, 44

Al Hatra, 43, 135; ruins of, 42–4, 48, 160

Albania, 16, 28, 108

Albareda, Señor, 336–7

Albert, Prince Consort, 191, 221, 294, 455

Albert Memorial, 305, 311

Aleppo, 32, 38–9

Alexander II, Czar of Russia, 391, 394, 403

Alexandria, bombardment of, 461, 475

Alfonso XII, King of Spain, 317, 324, 342–5

Ali Naghi Khan, 57, 67–70

Ali Pasha, Governor of Bagdad, 46–7

Ali Souavi Effendi, plot of, 412–13, 417

Alison, Sir Charles, 101; extracts from letters, 125–7, 133, 136, 139, 158–9, 171, 182, 188, 245, 263, 271; on Hammond, 229; presses Layard to speak on Eastern Question, 238–9; *Truth* quotes, 455

Alma, Battle of, 252–3

Amadeo I, King of Spain (Duke of Aosta), 330–4, 341, 373

American Civil War, 296

Ammon (Amman), 37–8

Antelope, British embassy gun-boat, 394, 430, 445

Antonio (guide), 35, 38

Arban, 207, 209, 485

Arbuthnot, Charles, 194

Ardahan, 379, 412

Armenia, massacres in, 2, 377; ancient Urartu, 148n; Russian threat to, 389–90, 411; Russian scheme for autonomy of, 407; appeals for independence, 420; British Consul-Generals in, 424, 435; near rebellion, 435

Arnold, Matthew, 451

Ashley, Evelyn, 406

Ashur (Kalah Shergat), 118

Ashurbanipal, Library of, 486

Ashur-nasir-pal II, 118, 119n, 135n, 168n; Palace of, 121–2, 177

Asia Minor, journey through, 29–32, 41, 198; Egypt's aims in, 33; advance of Russians through, 386; Britain engages to protect, 412–13

Assyria and Assyrians, destruction of Ammon by, 38; mounds of, 40–5, 89; Empire of, 41–2, 118; remains in Bakhtiari Mts., 57–58; discoveries at Khorsabad, 113; capitals, 118; canals, 119n, 135n, 207; dynasties, 134; art, 138, 146–9, 170; descendants, 150; lack of building materials, 170; method of building palaces, 175; Layard's plan for excavating, 216, 490; danger to antiquities, 181, 207; Anglo-French rivalry over, 186n; bas-reliefs depicting life in, 200, 208, 220–1; libraries, 212, 223–224, 486, 489; thieving of excavated remains, 478–9; great military building, 489

Assyria, SS., 83, 87–8

Assyrian cuneiform, 126–7, 126–8, 168n, 185–6

Assyrian Trust Fund, 487

Au Kerim Khan, 77–8, 84

Au Khan Baba, 76

Austen, Benjamin, his kindness to young Disraeli, 14, 16, 18–19, 21; offers to educate nephews,

Index

14; Layard in office of, 17, 29; in Montague Place, 21, 24; disappointed in Henry Layard, 22–3, 25, 82; consults Crabb Robinson, 23; letters to, 64, 66–7, 86, 91–2, 94–6, 98, 102–3, 107, 124, 126, 161, 197, 215–16, 221, 251, 289; does not want nephew home, 86, 92, 193; letters from, 92–3, 159–60, 192, 195, 216, 229; quarrels with nephew, 101–2; visits Canning, 159; stands up for nephew, 161; praises Layard's work, 191–2; accepts Gold Medal for Layard, 196; over-optimistic, 216; pleased at nephew's success, 229, 231; advises taking secretary, 272; death of, 295; mentioned, 58, 182–3

Austen, Sara, 16; and young Disraeli, 14, 16, 19, 20n; Crabb Robinson on, 23; and sister Louisa, 24–5, 101–2; displeased with nephew, 29, 82, 86, 101; letters to, 49, 64, 96, 102, 108, 134, 145–6, 166, 168, 170–1, 179–80, 193, 201–2, 214–15, 300, 335, 429; Canning visits, 107–8, 160–2; letters from, 160–1, 170–1, 191, 193–4; and *Nineveh and Its Remains*, 170–171, 187, 192–3; makes arrangements in London for second expedition, 196; Rawlinson visits, 201; publishes Layard's letters, 214; match-making plans of, 242; on Layard in Parliament, 260–1, 272; in old age, 295, 451; death of, 463; mentioned, 5, 195, 229, 279, 292

Austin, John and Sarah, 262n, 297

Austin, Lucie—*see* Lady Duff Gordon

Austria, helps Russia in Crimean War, 254; leaves Venetia, 305, 307; danger to, of Turkish

collapse, 353; works with Russia against Turkey, 263; turns against Russia, 405

Autobiography, quotations from, 11n, 13–15, 22n, 104, 228, 284–5, 408; annexe to, on Crimea, 252n; writing of, 471

Awad, Sheikh, 117, 121, 165, 199

Aylesbury, 21, 231

Ayrton, Acton, 312

Babylon, mounds of, 48, 220; excavations at, 219–20

Babylonia, dynasties of, 134n; lacked building stone, 170; Layard's plan for complete excavation of, 181, 191, 197, 214, 216; French excavations in, 228n

Babylonian cuneiform, 136–7, 185

Badger, Rev. George Percy, 115, 213; *The Nestorians and their Rituals* of, 115n, 150n

Bagdad, journey to, 38, 79–80; river trip to, 44–5, 218; Layard in, 45–9, 81–2, 86; Botta's antiquities wait transport at, 124; visits to Rawlinson in, 126–7; women of, 127; transport of antiquities to, 146, 168; raft-builders from, 174; isolated by Arab unrest, 215, 218–19; Layard ill in, 221; Budge in, 478–9

Baker, Samuel, 301

Baker Pasha, Valentine, 411, 434

Bakhtiari Mountains, 53, 57–62; antiquities in, 57–8, 60–2; Persian army in, 65, 67–8; Layard writes of stay in, 107, 471

Bakhtiari tribes, 56–7; Layard's adventures with, 1, 55 *et seq.*, 88; women of, 59, 63–4; hostility of, 60–1, 68, 83; descendants of Parthians, 64; collecting taxes from, 65, 67; assemble in Mal-Emir, 67–9;

Index

attitude of, to Layard, 68, 83; Manuchar Khan divides, 70, 72, 77; seek to rescue chieftan, 76–7; return to mountains, 77; Layard's plan to live with, 82, 102; Mrs. Bishop's journey among, 472, 476

Balaclava: Battle of, 253, 259; harbour at, 256, 258–9

Balawat, bronze gates of, 397, 478

Barnett, Dr. R. D., on Layard and Budge, 3–5, 487; assesses Layard's achievement, 484–8

Barriel, General, 345

Barry, Sir Charles, 185, 360

Basra, Layard escapes to, 79; antiquities shipped from, 144, 179; transport of antiquities to, 145, 172, 205–7, 211–12; bull and lion awaiting shipment at, 188, 191; mentioned, 74, 87

Batum, 366, 386, 389, 412

Bavian, 187, 206–7, 222–3

Beaconsfield, Benjamin Disraeli, 1st Earl of, Layard becomes disciple of, 2; and Eastern Question, 3, 351–3, 365, 367–8, 375, 381, 388, 390–1, 428–9; in youth, 13–14, 16–21; and Austens, 14, 16, 18–19, 21, 23, 183; books of, 14, 18, 34; travels in Eastern Europe, 16–17; debts of, 18–19, 21; poem of, 19, 20n; and Lady Charlotte Bertie, 20; stands for Parliament, 20–1; on illness of Henry's father and mother, 21; maiden speech, 23n, 247–8; on Beduin, 34; marriage, 183; Layard on, 230–1, 308, 475; looked at askance by own party, 231n; congratulates Layard on book, 234; praises Layard's speeches, 245–6, 255; learns political manners, 248; speaks for Layard, 273; contrasted to Layard, 286; on Schleswig-Holstein question, 299–300; Prime Minister, 308, 342, 353; supports Queen in asking for Layard's recall, 243–4; accepts peerage, 353; appoints Layard to Constantinople, 355–6, 363; his 'secret correspondence' with Layard, 368, 375–6, 379, 381, 383, 385–6, 392, 407, 410; raises question of buying *place d'armes* from Turkey, 385–6; and negotiation of peace terms, 388; realises danger of Russian occupation of Constantinople, 390, 400; Queen Victoria's letter to, on Russo-Turkish situation, 391; appears to have misled Turkish Ambassador, 391; praises Layard, 401, 405, 419; and sending of fleet to Constantinople, 401–2; and result of Berlin Congress, 421; Gladstone 'counterworks' purposes of, 427; resigns, 441

Becorra, Señor, 336–7

Bedr Khan Bey, 151

Beirut, 32, 223, 430–1

Beke, Dr. Charles, 301, 306

Belgrade, 94–6

Bell, Thomas Septimus, 221–3

Bellini, Gentili, 304, 390

Bellini, Giovanni, 304

Berenson, Bernard, 470

Berkeley, Cecilia, letters to, 100, 106, 176, 197, 216

Berlin Congress, 417–21

Bertie, Lady Charlotte—*see* Lady Charlotte Schreiber

Bewsher, Rev. James, 15

Besika Bay, fleet in, 402, 433

Bessborough, Earl of, 7

Bible, archaeological proof of truth of, 38, 118, 171, 177, 183, 218

Biraghi, Signor, 469

Birch, Samuel, 180, 208, 397

Bishop, Mrs. Isabella (née Bird), 472, 476

Index

Index

Index

Index

Index

382; despatch of, on Bulgarian massacres, 352, 357n; Layard's letter to, 420; Gladstone and, 426; mentioned, 360

Ellis, Sir Henry's letters to, 196–7, 207–8, 211–16, 220–3, 227, 232, 418

Esarhaddon, palace of, 121, 122n, 177, 485

Eugenie, Empress, 235

Euphrates River, transport of steamers to trade on, 42n, 85; surveys of, 48; ship from, reaches Shuster, 87–8; ruins on upper, 181; swamps of, 220–1

Federalists, 335, 338–9

Feili Lurs, 52, 84

Fellahia, 74–6

Fellows, Sir Charles, 26, 32, 160

Fergusson, James, 148n

ffrench, Percy, 321, 332

Flandin, Eugène, 50, 53, 134n; drawings of, 114, 163, 180n

Florence, 12–14, 16, 279, 332

Ford, Richard, 254, 322n

Forshall, Rev. Josiah, 157–8, 161, 172

Forster, John, 272

Fotheringham, Lieutenant, 52–3, 84–5

Fournier, M., French Ambassador in Constantinople, 432, 441

France, supports Egypt against Turkey, 29; opposes Russian aims in Jerusalem, 33, 235; sending antiquities to, 124–5, 179; finances archaeologists, 134, 162; claims Assyrian sites, 143; repercussions of revolution, 186; new excavating expedition sent by, 227–8; declares war on Russia, 245; quarrel of, with Prussia, 296, 324–5, 328–9; active on Red Sea coast, 303; and throne of Spain, 235–8; Republic declared in, 329; re-

covering from war, 263; attacks on Layard and England in, 432

Franco-Prussian War, 328–9

Fraser, Baillie, 26, 70n

Frederick, Crown Prince (later German Emperor), 428, 467

Frederick, Crown Princess (later German Empress), letters of, to Queen Victoria, 394, 409; visits Layards in Venice, 467, 482; Layard sits for, 468; seeks peerage for Layard, 473–4; mentioned, 428, 451, 477, 483

Freeman, Edward, 297, 353, 365–366, 383, 401

Gadd, Dr. C. J., 4, 191, 205, 224, 486

Galata, 359, 362

Gallenga, A. C. N., 351, 373–4

Gallipoli, 249, 401; fortifications of, 379–80, 385

Gathorne-Hardy, Gathorne (later Earl of Cranbrook), 402–3

Gay, M., *Daily Telegraph* correspondent, 383–4

Genoa, Duke of, 323–4

Germany, Layard's sympathy for, 329; danger of great, 353; works with Russia against Turkey, 363, 369, 392; new danger in Eastern politics, 392; seeks to come nearer to Britain, 439

Gladstone, William Ewart, at enmity with Layard, 2, 247, 257–258, 261, 384, 392, 405, 425–7, 443–4; and Eastern Question, 3, 238, 352–3, 357–8, 363, 365, 367; Chancellor of Exchequer, 233, 245, 293; anti-Turkish speeches, 242–3; Leader of House, 303; Clarendon and Emily Eden on, 307; Prime Minister, 308, 311–12, 342; letters to Layard, 344, 380; *Bulgarian Horrors* of, 352–3, 355; results of Turkish policy

Index

Index

Index

Index

Index

Gallery, 304–5, 311, 468; Commissioner of Works and Buildings and Privy Councillor, 308, 311–13; marriage of, 309–11, 482; dislikes Spain and Spaniards, 321–2, 329, 340, 345–6; pro-German, anti-French attitude, 328–9; gives sanctuary in Legation, 333–4, 336–7, 342; helps Serrano to escape, 337–9; prevents war between Spain and U.S., 342–3; Press attacks on, 342–3, 454–6; Queen Victoria seeks his recall, 343–4; his 'way of dealing with Spaniards', 345–6; changing political views, 347, 475–6; and anti-Turkish feelings aroused by massacres, 251–5; reactions to appointment of, to Porte, 357–358; presents credentials, 363; urges Government to stop Russian advance on Constantinople, 367–8, 381, 389–90, 399; his relations with Abdul Hamid, 367–8, 371–2, 375, 390, 413–414, 423–4, 430–1, 433–6, 448–449; on character of Sultan, 375–7, 450; German Ambassador and, 392–3; and fleet movements, 393–4, 401–3, 433–434; publication of Turkish despatches of, 397, 424–5, 435, 447–8; attacked in England for his encouragement to Porte, 399–401, 405; instructed to purchase Turkish ships, 404; plans seizure of Turkish fleet, 405; his part in keeping Russians out of Constantinople, 405–6; on terms of San Stefano Treaty, 407; accused of warmongering, 408; his attitude to Press, 408; Salisbury's communications with, 411–13; negotiates purchase of Cyprus when Sultan insane, 413–16;

awarded Order of Bath, 417; on leakage of Anglo-Russian protocol, 418–19; on Berlin Congress, 420; his efforts to get reforms in Turkey, 423–4, 434–7, 440, 442; rumour of madness of, 427–8; Sultan's present, 428; on leave in England, 428–9, 446, 451–2; nearly shot by Sultan, 429; visits Syria, 430–1; loses Sultan's confidence, 430–2, 433–7, 442; defends Dr. Koelle, 437–9; his change of attitude to Turks, 442, 448, 457; first 'Liberal Imperialist', 444; Gladstone recalls, 444–53; his despatch criticising Sultan, 446–8, 459n, 474; his farewell to Sultan, 448–9; a great Ambassador, 450; wishes to publish despatches, 452–3, 460; public and private images of, 453–4; cannot 'accept abuse calmly', 454; in Rome, 456–7; at International Geographical Congress, 459; Sultan's anger at, 459n; writes of his work in Constantinople and Madrid, 460–1; approaches Gladstone, 462–3; pension for, 463; in retirement in Venice, 467–74; translates Kugler's *Handbook of Painting*, 470–1; fails to get peerage, 472–4; in old age, 476–7, 481–483; 'posthumous' honours for, 476; bust of, in British Museum, 477, 478; supports Rassam against Budge, 478–9; on Lane-Poole's *Life* of Canning, 480; enthusiast for cremation, 481; attracted by ghoulish, 481–2; last illness and death, 482–3; assessment of archaeological achievement, 484–90

Layard, Julian, 398

Layard, Lady (née Enid Guest), 3, 310; diaries of, 5, 30n, 311, 402,

Index

Mallowan, Prof. M. E. L., 4, 5; *Twenty-five Years of Mesopotamian Discovery* of, 119*n*, 148*n*; assesses Layard's achievement, 484, 488-90

Malmesbury, 3rd Earl of, 230, 231*n*, 277

Malta, 16, 239, 245; Indian troops sent to, 408, 409-10

Maltayah rock sculptures, 117, 223

Manjanik ruins, 62

Manuchar Khan (the Matamet), 55-6; and Mohamed Taki Khan, 63, 65-9, 72-3, 75; hostages to, 67, 70; in Shuster, 70-3, 78-9; treachery of, 70-2, 75-6; on massacre of English in Afghanistan, 78-9; breaks power of Bakhtiari, 82; orders Layard's arrest, 84; captures Mohammerah, 84

Margueretta, Queen, of Italy, 457, 460, 472

Marmara, Sea of, fleet in, 403

Marx, Karl, 240, 244*n*, 248

Massowah, 302-3, 305

Mausolus, tomb of—*see* Halicarnassus marbles

Mavroyeni, Dr., 415

Menshikoff, Prince, 235, 237

Mesjid-i-Suleiman, 61

Mesopotamia, archaeological research in, 4-5, 181, 187, 191, 195, 478-9, 490; encouraging trade between India and, 42*n*, 64, 74; Persian army in, 49; importance of Mohammerah to, 97, 386; morals of women in, 127; present-day equivalents of Assyrian scenes, 175, 220-1; signs of great former population in, 209; railway through, 386; Russian threat to, 411, 478; potential wealth of, 436; thieving of remains found in, 478-9

Midhat Pasha, deposes Sultans, 361, 373-4; Governor of Syria,

430-1, 437; Abdul Hamid suspects, 434; trial of, 460; mentioned, 412

Millingen, Dr., 30

Mitford, Edward Ledwich, Layard accompanies on his travels, 1, 25, 26 *et seq.*; character of, 30; Layard temporarily separates from, 34, 38; his interest in birds, 42, 45; in Mosul, 42; in Bagdad, 46-9; joins caravan for Persia, 49-50; parts company with Layard, 53-4, 58; on Mohamed Taki Khan, 76; letters to, 82, 93, 102-3; Memoirs of, 82, 471; marriage of, 103; on Indian art, 148

Moab, 33, 36, 54, 58

Mohamed Ali Pasha, Viceroy of Egypt, 29, 32-3, 437

Mohamed Pasha, Governor of Mosul, 116-17, 154

Mohamed, Shah of Persia, 48, 50*n*, 52-3, 65

Mohamed Taki Khan, 56, 62, 81; family of, 59, 62-3, 67; and Manuchar Khan, 62, 65, 67-72; Layard's life with, 64-5, 82; sons of, 68-9; takes refuge in marshes, 73-5; gives himself up, 75-6; prisoner in chains, 76, 79, 84, 88, 107*n*; attempt to rescue, 76-7; Jaffer Kuli Khan and, 83-4

Mohammerah, 84, 87-8, 97, 386

Mohl, Julius, 50*n*, 89, 179

Montenegro, 27-8, 366, 387, 392

Montpensier, Duc de, 324

Monuments of Nineveh (Layard), 186, 234, 486

Morelli, Giovanni, letters to, 304*n*, 323, 351; visits Layard, 322-3, 452, 471; *Die Werke Italiensche Meister* of, 469-70; death of, 477

Morley, Samuel, 275

Morlini, Giovanni, 320, 333, 338, 468

525

Index

Mosul, Layard's journeys to, 1, 38–9, 53, 88–9; mounds across Tigris from, 40, 89, 116, 130, 199, 202; Layard in, 115–17, 128, 144; Pasha of, 116, 123–5, 129, 131–2; Cadi of, 117, 130–2; road between Nimrud and, 119; 'marble', 122, 170; excavations obstructed from, 123–4, 130–2; women of, 127; Layard's violence to Cadi in, 143–4, 151, 157, 162; Layard leaves, 177; second expedition to, 187, 199; Rawlinson in, 201; attacks on caravan to, 215

Mouravieff, General, 281–2

Murad, Sultan, 372–5; in France and England, 308, 364; imprisonment of, 361; intrigues to reinstate, 378, 412–13

Murad Wars, 255n

Murray, Hallam, 470n

Murray, John (III), *Handbooks* of, 24, 322n; publishes Layard's books, 184, 192, 194, 471–2, 486; letters to, 251, 252n, 253–4, 283; on Layard's imprudence, 260; publishes Sandwith's book, 282; offered art books, 469–70; death of, 477; mentioned, 352–353, 462

Murray, John (IV), 477

Musurus Pasha, Turkish Ambassador, 243, 363, 385, 391

Nana Sahib, 288, 291

Napier, Lord (later Lord Ettrick), 300

Napier, Sir Robert (later Lord Napier of Magdala), 306

National Gallery, 297, 303–5, 311, 452, 468

Nazli, Princess, 427

Nebbi Yunis, 43, 126, 202

Negoub, 135, 207

Negroponte Affair, 383–4, 392, 406, 445, 462

Nestorians (Chaldeans), 115, 150–151; Layard writes on, 170; Badger's book on, 115n, 150n, 213; massacres of, 151, 213; Rassam's propaganda for, 195

Nicholas, Grand Duke, 391, 394, 403, 407

Nicolson, Arthur, 429–30, 454

Nicolson, Sir Harold, 268n

Niffer, excavations at, 220

Nimrod (Ninus), King of Assyria, 44, 130–2, 176

Nimrud, Layard's excavations at, 1, 116, 119 *et seq.*, 168 *et seq.*, 191, 195 *et seq.*, 284–6; mistaken for Nineveh, 4, 126–7, 176, 201–2; first visit to, 43; mounds of, 43, 89, 115, 223; finds at, 115, 119n, 121–7, 129–32, 135, 145, 163, 168, 170, 177, 212–13; arrival at, 117–18; *ziggurat* of, 118–19, 485; history of, 118; quay-wall at, 119n; North-West Palace, 119n, 121–2, 145, 203, 485, 488–9; plan of, 120; evidence of burning of, 121, 123, 126; cuneiform inscriptions, 121–4, 185, 232, 489; South-West Palace, 121, 122n, 485; Central Palace, 122n, 485; ivories found, 122, 148n, 163, 486, 489–90; excavating held up, 123–4; 'Arab burial ground', 123–4; permission to dig, 125, 128–9, 132, 141–3, 175–6; transport of finds to Britain, 125, 133, 135, 142, 144–5, 168, 172–4, 178, 188, 191, 205–7; 'Nimrod' found, 130–2; paying expenses of excavations, 132–6, 138, 156–9, 191, 196–7, 211–12, 215–16, 480; discomforts of living, 133, 146; Arab visitors, 133–4; artistic value of finds, 138, 146–9; question of ownership of finds, 141–2, 161, 480;

Index

Index

Paris, Treaty of (1856), 282, 409

Patti Canal, Nimrud, 119*n*, 135*n*

Pears, Sir Edwin, 351, 442, 448

Peel, Sir Robert, 98, 136

'Peelites', the, 258, 261–2

Pegus, Mary—*see* Marchioness of Huntly

Pera, 99; British Embassy at, 359–360

Persepolis, 58, 77

Persia, strained relations between Britain and, 25, 50, 56, 65; ancient monuments of, 42; invades Mesopotamia, 49; Layard and Mitford in, 50–4; Layard's travels in, 55 *et seq.*; barbarities practised in, 56, 58, 88; encouraging trade between India and, 64, 74; tribal unrest in, 65; no war between England and, 66, 68; artillery of, 70; dervishes of, 73; Ambassador in, enquires for Layard, 85–6; Turkey at war with, 88; mediation between Turkey and, 91, 96–8; Russia and, 411

Persian Gulf, encouraging trade through, 42*n*, 64, 74, 83, 87; British need for strong place on, 386, 410

Petra, 33, 35–6

Phillips, Henry, portrait by, 184

Pisani, Countess, 30*n*

Plati (Yessiada), island of, 301, 359, 445

Plevna, 380, 384–5, 387–8

Ponsonby, Edward, 8th Earl of Bessborough (married Blanche Guest), 429, 462, 473, 482

Ponsonby, Sir Henry and Lady, 473

Prim, General Juan (Count Reus), 317, 320, 334; seeks for King for Spain, 323–8, 330; assassination of, 330–1, 373; widow of, 332

Prussia, trouble between France and, 296, 305, 328–9; and Schleswig-Holstein, 299; war between Austria and, 305, 324; and throne of Spain, 324–8

Pruth River, 238, 366

Punch, 246–7, 262, 267; cartoons, 250, 266, 268, 273, 318–19, 400, 440

Pusht-i-Kuh, 52, 84

Quarterly Review, Layard's articles in, 292–3, 297, 322*n*, 475; article on Turkey in, 353, 411

Raglan, Lord, 249, 258

Raikes, H. C., 312–13

Ramsgate, 12, 14, 17

Rassam, Christian, British Vice-Consul at Mosul, 42; 116–17; at Arab party, 139; father of, 150*n*; welcomes Layard back, 199; mentioned, 44, 142*n*, 151, 222–3

Rassam, Hormuzd, libel action of, 3, 479, 485, 487; helps at Nimrud, 129, 165–6, 214, 216; visits Nestorians with Layard, 150–1; father of, 150*n*; in Oxford, 177, 195–8; returns to Nimrud with Layard, 196–8, 200; Sandwith describes, 198; at Khabour, 209; letters to Marianne Layard, 213, 215; ill in Bagdad, 219–20; in England, 231; excavates on own account, 232, 487; his mission to Abyssinia, 302–3, 305–6; his discoveries at Balawat, 397, 478; British Museum and, 478–9, 487

Rate, McLauchlan, 451–2

Rawlinson, Rev. George, Canon of Canterbury, 127*n*

Rawlinson, Sir Henry Cheswicke, thinks Nimrud was Nineveh, 4,

Index

126–7, 176, 201–2; deciphers cuneiform, 47, 114, 136–8, 163, 168n, 171, 185–6, 237n; British agent at Kandahar, 47–8; copies Bisutun inscription, 50n, 185; on Susa, 57–8, 60–2; Layard anxious to meet, 58; on Feili Lurs, 84; on Khorsabad discoveries, 114–15; on Nimrud excavations, 122–3, 129, 134; prepared to transport sculptures from Nimrud, 125; Layard meets, 126–7; Rules of Conduct of, 126–7; his correspondence with Layard, 136–8, 144, 147–8, 171, 185–6, 201, 235; condemns Layard's violence to Cadi, 144; seeks to finance excavations by subscription, 144, 221; his reactions to Nimrud finds, 147–8, 168; his views on beauty in art, 147–8; on British Museum financial offers, 157–8; sends Khorsabad bulls to British Museum, 197, 212; decides Nimrud is not Nineveh and visits Nimrud, 200–1; Layard on, 201–2; given credit, by *Truth*, for Layard's books, 455; subscribes to bust of Layard, 477; mentioned, 55, 64, 107, 135, 188, 220, 232

Reeve, Sir Henry, 2, 483

Reform: Bills, 265, 268n, 303, 307–8; riots, 307—*see also* Administrative Reform Movement

Reshid Pasha, Grand Vizier, 16, 104–5

Reus, Countess, 330–2

Reuss, Prince, German Ambassador to Porte, 379, 392–3, 413, 416, 441

Rhodope Mts., massacres in, 422, 424

Rich, Claudius James, 42, 89

Rickett, Louisa, quarrel over proposed marriage of, 24–5, 101–2;

letters to, 27, 29, 96; letter from, 66

Robert College, Constantinople, 372, 395

Robinson, Henry Crabb, 22–3, 25–6, 58, 86, 187

Roebuck, John, 256, 271; Committee of, 262–4

Rolland, Charlotte, 204, 206, 209–210, 213

Rolland, Stewart, 204–6, 209–10, 213; letter of, on Layard at Nimrud, 204–5, 214

Rome, Layard considered for Embassy in, 452, 456, 458–9, 461–2; Layards in, 456–7

Ross, Henry, 297; helps in Nimrud excavations, 117, 122; letters to, 182, 184–5; at Kuyunjik, 187, 199; letters from, 87, 275–6; on publication of *Nineveh*, 190; on Nineveh Room of British Museum, 195; at Bavian, 206; illness of, 297; mentioned, 247, 262n, 456

Ross, Janet (née Duff Gordon), 1, 5, 297; letter to, 304n; and Marchese de la Stuffa, 456–7; niece of, 467

Ross, Dr. John, 43, 48, 80, 87–8, 147

Rouet, M., French Vice-Consul at Mosul, 117, 124–5, 139, 143

Royal Geographical Society, 26; Layard's reports of travels to, 30, 32, 34, 62, 82; Layard awarded Gold Medal of, 196

Royal Navy, and Russo-Turkish problem, 239; fails to attack Odessa, 251; lands troops on Crimea, 251; morale in, 254; ordered and counter-ordered to send fleet to Constantinople, 393–4, 401–3; ordered to prevent Russian occupation, 404–5

Rumania, 235, 238, 366, 387

Rumelia, Eastern, 380, 386, 421

Index

Ruskin, John, 270, 297, 469

Russell, 1st Earl (Lord John), and Assyrian antiquities, 191, 195; Prime Minister, 228, 230, 303, 307; recommends Layard's resignation, 230; Foreign Minister, 233, 237, 293; offers post to Layard, 234; Leader of House, 238; and Eastern Question, 238, 245; objects to Layard's abusiveness, 246, 292; Palmerston and, 247; resigns, 256–7; Reform Bill of, 265; Layard's chief in Foreign Affairs, 293, 296, 300–1; writing of, 296; on politics, 298; and Abyssinian Question, 302–3; appoints Director of National Gallery, 304; appoints Goschen over Layard's head, 304–5; in Venice, 307; mentioned, 2, 252, 293, 455

Russell, Odo (later Lord Ampthill), 297, 357, 439, 463, 473

Russell, William, *Times* correspondent, 249, 285

Russia, Layard visits, 24; and Montenegro, 28; intrigues in Jerusalem, 33, 235; and Afghanistan, 48n; Turco-Persian boundary, 93, 97; Serbian revolt, 94, 99; intrigues in Turkey, 104, 108, 235, 240; threatens Turkey, 235, 353–5, 410–11; invades Turkey, 238–9, 366, 379; at Sinope, 243, 245; Derby on, 243, 244, 354–5; Crimean War, 245; Shamyl, 255; gains by disruption of Turkey, 353–5, 442; declares war on Turkey (1877), 365; threat to Britain, 366, 368, 381–2, 390; peace proposals, 369; Turkey asks for peace terms, 388, 391; armistice, 391, 399; kept out of Constantinople, 403, 405–6; danger of war with Britain, 404–6, 408, 411–12, 474; demands on Bosphorus, 407; Salisbury's views, 410–11; Gladstone's and, 427; friction between Germany and, 439; British Consuls in Asia Minor, 439, 441

Russian army, invades Turkish territory, 238–9, 366, 379; driven back by Turks, 249; passes safely through Odessa, 251; defeated at Alma, 252–3; reinforcement from Caucasus, 255–6; before Kars, 278, 281–2; *Times* reports communicated to, 285; threatens Constantinople, 389, 391, 399–408

Russo-Turkish War, 365 *et seq.*; divided opinions on, in England, 365–9; Russian successes in, 379, 386–7; Turkish casualties in, 386; Gladstone and, 424–5

Sadyk, Turkish Prime Minister, 414, 416–17

Safvet Pasha, Turkish Foreign Minister, 363, 414

Said Bey, 376

Said Pasha, General, 367, 370–1, 376n, 390, 415; appreciative letters of, 434, 467

St. Arnaud, Marshal, 249, 251

St. Sophia Mosque, 359; refugees in, 395, 423

Salisbury, 3rd Marquis of, Ignatieff's warning about Layard, 355; Turkish policy of, 363, 365, 382, 409–11, 436–7, 454; on Abdul Hamid, 374, 377, 435–6; supports ordering of fleet to Constantinople, 402; Foreign Minister, 409–10, 428, 445; 'Circular to Powers' of, 409; 'secret department' to deal with Eastern matters, 412, 418; proposes purchase of Cyprus, 413–15, 418; told of Sultan's

Index

Index

Sinjar Mts., 153–4

Sinope, 243, 245

Skoboleff, General, 406

Smith, George, 487–8

Smith, W. J., 360

Smith, William, editor of *Quarterly*, 353

Sofuk, Sheikh, 80, 135

Somers, Charles (Viscount Eastnor and 3rd Earl Somers), 155, 182

South Kensington Museum, 292–293, 322n

Southwark, 292, 303, 308

Spain, Layard Minister to, 312–13, 317 *et seq.*; 1868 Revolution in, 317; bull-fights in, 320–1, 376; Layard's dislike of, 321–2, 329, 340; *Handbook* on, 322n; factions in, 323, 329; search for King for, 323–8, 330–1; Bismarck's intrigue with, 324–6; danger of war between France and, 325–8, 356; fear of revolution in, 329, 330, 333; abdication of King of, 333–4; revolution in, 335–9; danger of war between U.S. and, 340–1, 356; results of Bourbon restoration in, 342–6; ancient ceremonies revived in, 344–5; Layards leave, 356; editing of Layard's despatches from, 435

Stead, W. T., 427

Stern, Rev. Henry, 301–2, 306

Stoddart, Colonel Charles, 103–4, 301

Stratford de Redcliffe, Viscountess (Lady Canning), 106–7, 360; letter to, 129

Stratford de Redcliffe, Viscount (Sir Stratford Canning), 90–1; advances money for excavations, 1, 116, 125, 144, 161, 480; Ambassador in Constantinople, 88, 90 *et seq.*, 358–9; Layard carries despatches to, 88–9, 90–1; employs Layard,

93–9, 101, 104–8; pro-Turk, 90, 98, 101; angry with Aberdeen, 97–9; quick temper of, 101, 104, 480; his manner to Turks, 104–5; on work at Embassy, 105–6; kindness to Layard, 107, 159–60; Austens and, 107–8, 159–62; character of, 108, 480; interested in Assyrian archaeology, 113, 115, 129; and Halicarnassus marbles, 115, 125, 128, 132–3; letters to, from Mesopotamia, 121, 123–5, 129–30, 132, 135, 137–8, 143, 147, 159, 198, 207, 212, 218–220, 222; letters of, 125, 129, 135–6, 172, 179, 181, 201, 489; and public financing of excavations, 129, 132, 135–6, 138, 143–4, 156–9, 172; and ownership of Nimrud antiquities, 142, 161; Lane-Poole's *Life* of, 142n, 480; repayment of advances of, 156–8; seeks share of credit for excavations, 156, 158, 161, 480; and post for Layard, 179, 188, 192, 194; Austen criticises, 192; reactions of, to *Nineveh and Its Remains*, 193–4; and Yezidis, 198; seeks permission for excavations, 214; congratulates Layard on appointment, 229; 1931 mission of, to Constantinople, 229, 234–6; disappointed of Foreign Ministry, 230; peerage, 230; cases for, delivered to British Museum, 231; Layard finds he cannot work with, 236; presses Layard to speak on Eastern Question, 238; criticised by Delane, 251; criticised about siege of Kars, 278, 283; on Ottoman Bank, 280; Abdul Hamid's memory of, 375; letter of, in 1879, 434–5; mentioned, 237, 437

Stuffa, Marchese de la, 456–7, 460

Index

Index

219, 297–8, 435; war and Persia,
88; mediation, 91, 96–8; Christians try for freedom, 93, 351;
Russian intrigues in, 93, 104,
240; Layard's mission, 93–6;
Layard fascinated by, 109;
interest in antiquities, 181, 214;
Arab rebellion, 215, 218–21,
435; Russian threat, 235–6,
237, 353–5; Orthodox Greeks,
236, 238; wild tribes, 240;
declares war on Russia, 242;
changes in, 244; Ottoman Bank,
280–1; Abyssinian enmity to,
302–3; dangers of disruption of,
353, 357n, 366; Gladstone's
policy of non-intervention, 354–
355, 443–4; Layard appointed
Ambassador to, 355–6, 357–8;
British policy towards, 363,
379, 381–2, 384–8, 390–3, 461;
in financial difficulties, 363,
367, 385, 435; Russia declares
war, 365–6; ferment beneath
surface, 372–4, 431, 435;
Constitution for, 372, 374, 387;
Britain agrees to negotiate peace
terms for, 388; pressure on, to
separate from Britain, 390, 432;
feeling against Britain, 391–2,
418–19; German Embassy pro-
tects Russians in, 392; Russian
terms to, 394, 399; Greece
invades, 396; armistice, 399;
sympathy in England, 399,
404; refuses entry to British
fleet, 402–3; Britain decides to
support, 404; San Stefano
Treaty, 407–10; proposed alliance with Britain, 412; purchase of Cyprus from, 413–15,
417–21; effect of Berlin Congress
on, 420–1; seeks financial aid
from Britain, 424; British Consuls, 424, 435, 439, 441; potential wealth, 436–7; imminent
collapse of, 439, 441–2; British

influence lessened, 457—*see also*
Armenia; Constantinople
Turkish Navy, Russians sink ships
of, 243, 245; Hobart Pasha in,
366–7; Russia demands handing over of, 403–5; Layard
instructed to purchase ships of,
404; Layard plans seizure of,
405
Turkish Parliament, 374–5, 387
Turks, Layard's sympathies with,
2, 101, 109, 351–4, 365–6,
381–3; hospitality of, 31–2;
Canning's manner to, 104; and
permission to excavate, 141–3,
173–6, 214, 219–20; indifferent
to danger, 154–5; destroy antiquities, 181; cruel and treacherous, 219; massacres of, in
Bulgaria, 380, 386; Liberals and,
444

United States, 178–9, 274, 340–1
Urquhart, David, 100n

Vambery, Arminius, 459
Van, 214, 486
Varna, 249, 251
Venice, visits to, 26, 307–8;
Austrians leave, 305, 307; Lay-
ards' house in, 332, 452; com-
pared to Constantinople, 362;
International Geographical Con-
gress in, 459–60; Layards'
visitors in, 459–60, 467; Layard
in retirement, 467–74, 482;
exhibition of Italian National
Art, 472
Venice and Murano Glass and
Mosaic Work Company, 308,
312, 468, 481
Victor Emmanuel, King of Italy,
307, 456–7, 460, 472; nephew
of, 324; son becomes King of
Spain, 330, 332
Victoria, Queen, and Palmerston,
228; rebukes Aberdeen, 249;

47

B
Layard
Waterfield
Layard of Nineveh